ANCESTORS A
IRA JOHNSON AND AE

FROM 1990 to 2003

Edited by

WILLIAM A. BLANDIN

AND

GERALD GARTH JOHNSON

A REVISED AND EXPANDED SUPPLEMENT TO

THE GENEALOGY OF CAPTAIN JOHN JOHNSON OF ROXBURY, MASSACHUSETTS

BY

PAUL FRANKLIN JOHNSON, EDITOR
1945

AS CORRECTED AND ADDED TO
BY ADA JOHNSON MODERN, 1948

HERITAGE BOOKS
2004

HERITAGE BOOKS
AN IMPRINT OF HERITAGE BOOKS, INC.

Books, CDs, and more – Worldwide

For our listing of thousands of titles see our website
at
www.HeritageBooks.com

Published 2004 by
HERITAGE BOOKS, INC.
Publishing Division
1540 Pointer Ridge Place
Bowie, Maryland 20716

International Standard Book Number: **0-7884-2493-8**

For

The Preservation Of The

History and Genealogy Of

The Johnson And Allied Families

The Editors

William A. Blandin was a Transportation Design Engineer for the City of Seattle, Washington before his retirement. Bill and his wife Alice live on Camano Island, Washington. Mr. Blandin is a graduate in Civil Engineering from the University of Washington, Seattle, Washington and in 1997 completed study for a Certificate of Genealogy and Family History from the University of Washington extension program. Blandin has a strong interest in preserving family history and has pursued this within the Johnson and Allied families as well as families outside of this group. Mr. Blandin is a member of the New England Historic Genealogical Society in Boston, Massachusetts, and is a life member of the Seattle Genealogical Society in Seattle, Washington. He also is a member of the Harney County, Oregon Historical Society in Burns, Oregon, and has devoted more than thirty years to preserving family histories for his own family and those of others.

Gerald Garth Johnson, Ph.D., a cousin of William A. Blandin, is a retired educator and State of Oregon education and social service program administrator who lives in Salem, Oregon with his wife, Nancy Ticknor Johnson. He is the author of several education, law, and historical non-fiction books, many of which are reflective of his interest in family genealogy and in 17th Century early America. He holds Bachelors and Masters Degrees in Education from Willamette University and a Ph.D. in Public Administration from California Western University. Dr. Johnson has done post-graduate study and research at the University of Oregon, Eugene, Oregon, Yale University, New Haven, Connecticut, Willamette University and Lewis and Clark College, both in Oregon, as well as various genealogical societies and libraries in Boston, Massachusetts and in Oregon and Washington. Johnson's memberships include the American Historical Association, the Ancient and Honorable Artillery Company of Massachusetts, New York Biographical and Genealogical Society, New England Historic Genealogical Society, the Omohundro Institute of Early American History and Culture, and the Boston Athenaeum.

Also by Gerald Garth Johnson

Alan, Lord of Buckenhall

The Johnson papers, Volumes I and II

Ancestors and Descendants of Ira Johnson and Abigail (Furbush) Johnson, 1984 version

The Oregon Book of Juvenile Issues (Published by Portland State University Press, Portland, Oregon)

Post-High School Planning Book (Copyright transferred to Cascade High School, *Turner, Oregon)*

The Stage-Curtis Genealogy

Understanding the Alcoholism in Your Family and Its Effect on You (Copyright transferred to NW Kaiser-Permanente Health Plan, *Portland, Oregon)*

The Ticknor Family in America, Supplement

The following three books are companions to this revised and updated edition of the *Ancestors and Descendants of Ira Johnson and Abigail Furbush Johnson* and are available from Heritage Books, Inc., Bowie, MD:

*The Diaries of Nancy Johnson Brown and William H. Brown of Edwards, New York (editor) Heritage Books, Inc., Bowie, MD

*The Biography and Genealogy of Captain John Johnson from Roxbury, Massachusetts Heritage Books, Inc., Bowie, MD

*Puritan Children in Exile, Heritage Books, Inc., Bowie, MD

Textual Notes

In cases where quoted passages, especially from religious works, diaries, sermons, and poetry seemed ambiguous because of spelling and punctuation, these have been changed to modern spelling and punctuation. Further, in cases where the meaning of a word, or the relationship to an ancestor seems unclear, the meaning or the ancestor have been added within [brackets.]

Since 1984 many, many genealogy software programs have become available. Mr. William A. Blandin has chosen The Master Genealogist (TMG) V4.od for Windows, Gold Edition, distributed by Wholly Genes, Inc., Copyright 1992-2000 by Wholly Genes, Inc. All rights reserved. Information about the software can be found at www.whollygenes.com. It is our belief that this software program makes the data more understandable.

The manuscript was typed in Microsoft WORD, Professional 2000 version in Times New Roman font 11.

With the assistance of several family members, additional and in most cases, better quality pictures, were made available for inclusion in this book.

ANCESTORS AND DESCENDANTS OF

IRA JOHNSON AND ABIGAIL (FURBUSH) JOHNSON

CONTENTS

ACKNOWLEDGMENTS

No genealogy of any family is possible without the cooperation, information, and interest of its members. We have been warmly blessed by the help from various relatives including Karlene M. Messer, Salem, OR, Mary Buck Spadaro, Syracuse, NY, Kathy Buck Waits, Houston, TX, Harriet Johnson Jenne, Hermon, NY, David E. Johnson, Branford, FL, Richard Brown, Edwards, NY, Jim and Crystal Whitford, Edwards, NY, Jean Merithew, DeKalb Junction, NY, Debbie Johnson Mathews, Hermon, NY, Abel Johnson, Largo, FL, LaVerne H. Freeman, Edwards, NY, Connie Brown McElwain, Potsdam, NY, Gabrielle Johnson, Rainier, OR, Dr. Lloyd and Virginia Johnson, Everett, WA, Mrs. George (Jackie) Spencer, and, Joan Grappotte, Watertown, NY. Even with all the help, we know that some family members are not listed within this book. We deeply regret any omission of names. It was not intentional. Some family members chose not to forward corrections and additions for this book. However, future corrections or additions can be sent to William A. Blandin, 2307 Honeycomb Lane, Camano Island, WA 98282-6306.

We are greatly indebted also to the technical assistance we received from Darren Baze, Heritage Books, Inc., Bowie, MD. His helpfulness and professionalism regarding marketing, style, and other technical aspects were invaluable for the completion of this book.

An Index of top quality is essential to assure the value and usefulness of this book. We owe a great deal of gratitude to Mr. Daniel McNaughton of Paleograph Editing Services, Chicago, IL for the superb job of indexing. Thanks, Mr. McNaughton, for your understanding of our family, our hope for the book, and your perseverance to make this a meaningful family history to all.

Note: *Unless otherwise indicated, this genealogy of the Johnson and Allied Families* **includes** *natural born children, step-children, and adopted children of couples. There are some situations where step-children actually use the surname of the step-father; where marriage dates and birth dates seem chronologically incorrect. This happens when there is no distinction in the children's parentage.*

Children in such phrases like "Children of Capt. John Johnson and Mary Heath were as follows" (as the example on page 75) would include natural children, step-children, and adopted children.

INTRODUCTION

The original effort and subsequent book on the ancestors and descendants of Ira Johnson and Abigail Furbush Johnson was accomplished in 1984. The format used at that time to report the names and dates of family members was modeled after the *Genealogy of Captain John Johnson of Roxbury, Massachusetts by Paul Franklin Johnson (*1951) so that the two books could be used together by the thousands and thousands of descendants of Captain John Johnson.

The sources for most of this genealogy came from the *Captain John Johnson Genealogy* by Paul Franklin Johnson [1951] and *The Ancestors and Descendants of Ira Johnson and Abigail Furbush Johnson* [1983/4) by Gerald Garth Johnson. Additional information has been based upon marriage, birth, and death records compiled by Karlene M. Johnson Messer, Salem, Oregon as well as from personal information from many other relatives. William Blandin inserted census and other documented information when found.

Additionally, when we discovered double dates or triple dates for a birth, marriage, or death, the "primary dates," used in this book are considered to be the most accurate date when there was confusion caused by multiple dates. We have tried to copy all of the Vital Statistics as accurately as possible, but it must be said that some records are next to impossible to read. Further, even people from the same family had ancestors with different dates of birth, marriage, or death. The handwriting of the 17th and 18th Centuries was very difficult to decipher. We truly regret any errors and omissions.

Lastly, we eliminated **all** of the original ancestry beginning with Maurice Johnson and Jayne Lacey that had been suggested in the 1984 Edition of the *Ancestors and Descendants of Ira Johnson and Abigail Furbush Johnson* because there is no possible way to determine the accuracy of that connection. Unfortunately, the

1

Stamford, England Maurice Johnson – Jayne Lacey connection to John Johnson has been repeated over and over again on the Internet and has been used in other printed books.   We believe that this information **is in error** and should **NOT** be cited as the ancestry of Captain John Johnson, of Ware and Great Amwell, England, and later from Roxbury, Massachusetts.

William A. Blandin
Gerald Garth Johnson
August, 2003

AUTOBIOGRAPHICAL AND BIOGRAPHICAL SKETCHES

CAPTAIN JOHN JOHNSON

This Puritan immigrant ancestor from Ware, England and first member of the Johnson family in America arrived on April 8, 1630 in the harbor of Salem, Massachusetts with the Winthrop Fleet in the lead ship, *Arbella*, a ship mastered by Peter Milburn and named for Lady Arbella Johnson who was married to Sir Isaac Johnson. There is no known relationship between Isaac Johnson and John Johnson. The other ships in the Winthrop Fleet were the *Ambrose, Talbot* and the *Jewell*. Over 1000 immigrants arrived in 11 ships in a short period of time and settled in 7 different Massachusetts' towns.

After a month at Naumkeag (Salem Harbor) John Johnson and his family with others settled in an area they named Roxbury, which was about three miles from Boston. [note: Roxbury now has been incorporated into the City of Boston] While John Johnson was a fiercely religious man, he obviously came to Massachusetts Bay for commercial and political reasons in addition to his desire to avoid religious persecution in England.

The relationship between Isaac Johnson and John Johnson has not been determined. However, a genealogist at the Lincolnshire History Center, England, believes that they were not related.

John Johnson, later called Captain John Johnson, arrived with his second wife, Margery, and six children. His first wife was Mary Heath and they were married in 1613 in St. Mary-the-Virgin Church in Ware, Hertfordshire, England. He was chosen by the General Court as Constable of Roxbury on October 19, 1630 and was admitted as a freeman (a property holding voter) on May 18, 1631. John Johnson held many, many civic, military, and governmental responsibilities in Roxbury and the Massachusetts Bay Colony.

In addition to his many activities, he had a tavern in Roxbury that has been identified as being located on what is now the southwest corner of Washington Street [previously known as Roxbury Road] and Ball Street. This property is now owned by the Commonwealth of Massachusetts. His house, tavern, and all of his out-buildings were destroyed by fire August 2, 1645 following the explosion of 17 barrels of Massachusetts Bay Colony gun-powder. Unfortunately, most of the records of the beginning of Roxbury were destroyed in this fire since John Johnson was the town clerk. These records were later reconstructed, though incompletely, from memory and have now been published in a book.

John Johnson died on September 29, 1659 in Roxbury, Massachusetts. Johnson's second wife, Margery [whose last name is not known] died June 9, 1655 and following her death, he married 3rd, Grace Negus Fawer, a widow of Barnabus Fawer. When she died December 19, 1671, she left her estate to her two brothers, Jonathan and Benjamin Negus.

Of the ten children whose mother was Mary Heath Johnson, Johnson's first wife, those accompanying John Johnson and his second wife, Margery, to New England were:

Isaac, Mary, Humphrey, Elizabeth,
Sarah, and Hannah

[note: four Johnson children died before the migration to New England]

A complete genealogy of John Johnson's children is in the book, *The Biography and Genealogy of Captain John Johnson from Roxbury, Massachusetts* written by Gerald Garth Johnson and published by Heritage Books, Inc., Bowie, MD.

MEHITABLE JOHNSON

Written by Gerald Garth Johnson

Over the course of the last twenty years, it became evident that the 1984 version of the *Ancestors and Descendants of Ira Johnson and Abigail Furbush Johnson* did not provide equal recognition to female Johnsons and their ancestors and descendants. In this book, in addition to the biographical information regarding Nancy Johnson Brown, Lulu Belle Johnson McHargue, and the ancestry of Abigail Furbush Johnson, the story that follows provides readers a glimpse of Mehitable Johnson's tragic life as a result of the King Philip's War (1675-1675) in New England. (King Philip, so-called by the New Englanders, was actually Metacom, son of Massasoit.)

Mehitable Johnson was the first child of Humphrey Johnson and Elinor (Ellen) Cheney Johnson. She was a granddaughter of Captain Johnson, and was born in Roxbury, Massachusetts in April, 1643. (NEGHS, Vol. 6: 183) It is noted that other birth dates are cited for Mehitable by some genealogists. All genealogists, however, agree regarding her death date on August 4, 1689 in Weathersfield, Hartford County, CT, at the age of forty-six. (D. G. Weymouth Research)

Mehitable married first, Samuel Hinsdale, son of Deacon Robert Hinsdale and Ann Woodward Hinsdale, on October 31, 1660 in Medfield, Suffolk County, MA at the age of seventeen (Colehour & Kreger Ancestry).

Samuel Hinsdale, who was born prior to January 28, 1636 (Baptismal date) in Pulman, England, was killed along with his father Deacon Robert Hinsdale and his two brothers, Barnabus and John Hinsdale, on September 18, 1675 at what is now referred to as "Bloody Brook" near Deerfield, MA. (D. G. Weymouth Research)

Samuel and Mehitable Johnson Hinsdale had the following children:

1.   Mehitable, b. October 18, 1663; She died prior to 1702 in Weathersfield, CT.   Married to Obadiah Dickenson. Married 2nd, Joseph Hills.

2.   Mary, b. July 22, 1665; Married Thomas Sheldon.

3.   Ann (Anna), b. February 22, 1667; married Martin Kellogg. She died July 19, 1689.

4.   Sarah, b. 1669. Married Samuel Janes. Sarah and Samuel Janes were killed along with their children on May 13, 1704 by Native Americans during the French and Indian War of 1704.

5.   Samuel, b. in Deerfield, MA 1670; Married Susannah Rockwood. He died 1694.

6.   Mehuman, b. 1673, Deerfield, MA; Married Mary Rider. He died 1694.

7.   John, b. 1675.

(The Genealogy of Captain Johnson; Hinsdale Genealogy; Descendants of Governor Thomas Welles)

Following the death of Samuel Hinsdale, Mehitable Johnson Hinsdale married John Root.   John Root also was killed by the Native Americans in 1677.

Mehitable and John Root had one child:

1.   Thankful, b. 1677, Northampton, Hampshire County, MA.   Married, Thomas Welles, January 7, 1697 in Weathersfield, Hartford County, CT. (Descendants of Governor Thomas Welles)

After the death of John Root, Mehitable Johnson Hinsdale Root married Deacon John Coleman on March 11, 1679. John Coleman and Mehitable had the following children:

2.   Ebenezer, b. August 29, 1680; Married Ruth Niles March 11, 1705; He died 1741.

3.   Nathaniel, b. October 18, 1684; Married Mary Ely. He died in 1755. (Genealogy of Captain John Johnson,

Vital Records of Greenfield, MA, and History of Hadley, MA by L. M. Boltwood, reprinted, 1976.)

The King Philip's War, the first major Indian War in New England, is considered by historians as the bloodiest war in American history on a per capita basis. It was the joining together of the Nipmuck, Wampanoag, Pocumtuck, and Squaheag tribes in the Autumn of 1675 that was the downfall of the Deerfield, MA men. The thirty-nine adult Puritan men were greatly out-numbered by the combined tribes. The town was abandoned after the Indians burned most of the houses. Deerfield was not re-settled by the Puritans until 1782.

Deerfield residents endured *thirty* Native American attacks in the town's first fifty years. Two of these attacks, 1675 and 1704, had devastating results.

Deerfield had approximately 200 residents with only 39 adult men and 29 adult women. It was not only a "young man's" town but was considered a poor Massachusetts village because the struggle to survive in the hostile wilderness took away from the task of making a living. And in addition, the isolation of Deerfield in the 1670's made markets for trade next to impossible. The average married couple between the ages of 21 and 40 years of age had five children to support.

Mehitable's father, Humphrey Johnson (Sergeant) fought along side his brother, Captain Isaac Johnson, of the Roxbury Company in the Narragansett Expedition now called the "Great Swamp Massacre" that took place on December 19, 1675 near Four Corners, Sakonnet River, Rhode Island. Captain Isaac Johnson was killed in the Great Swamp Massacre. (Genealogy of Captain John Johnson)

Not only did Mehitable Johnson lose two husbands and an uncle to the King Philip's War, her daughter Sarah's entire family was killed by Native Americans in 1704.

7

Mehitable was only 46 years of age when she died leaving three children motherless: Thankful Root, age 12; Ebenezer Coleman, age 9, and, Nathaniel Coleman, age 5.

ABEL PRATT JOHNSON

Written by David E. Johnson and edited by
Gerald Garth Johnson for this publication

Abel Pratt Johnson, was the son of Charles Alvah Johnson and Rachel Pratt Viall, a widow of Samson Viall. Abel was born on June 7, 1821 at Russell, St. Lawrence County, New York. He was born fourth out of seven children born to the couple. The seven Johnson children joined four Viall sisters born earlier to Rachel Pratt and Samson Viall. One of Abel's sisters died in 1818 from being scalded by a tub of water that she pulled over onto herself. The genealogies of the eleven Viall and Johnson children are contained within this book.

At this writing, little is known about the specifics of Abel's youth except to say that he grew up in a large family of pioneering, religious, and hard working farmers. His was one of the first families to settle Northern New York in the early 1800s: indeed, even to settle in America, as the family does date back to pre-revolutionary times in America. His grandfather Ira Johnson fought in the war for independence from Great Britain as an American patriot. His father, Charles Alvah Johnson, helped to cut the military road from Russell to Edwards, New York to Sackets Harbor about 1812. Charles also served in the War of 1812. The family, who had already come to Massachusetts Bay in 1630, were in New York by the 1790s. Two of Abel's brothers settled farther west as early as 1838 with Charles Victor Johnson moving to Pittsfield, Illinois and later, Hiram Alvah Johnson, Sr. who joined him in 1839 and migrated to Oregon in 1847.

At the age of 25, Abel married Lucy E. Haile, daughter of John and Celia Haile, on September 15, 1846 at Edwards, St. Lawrence County, New York. Abel and Lucy had eight children.

It is presumed that Abel pursued the life of a carpenter in Edwards during the time his eight children were born. However, by about 1868, the family was in Pine Valley, Chemung County, New York. The author of this article speculates that their move to this area may have been prompted by relatives who already settled there. It is known that other Johnsons had settled the Catherine Valley area of New York as early as the 1790s. A Robert Charles Johnson owned the first sawmill at Odessa, New York in 1799; and also was a partner in the first gristmill of the area. This mill was known as the Johnson, Coe, and Beardsley Mill in 1801. Abel was a millwright for some twenty years and was the original patentee of the Waterwheel Double Turbine (a forerunner of the Double Steam Turbine.) Therefore, it seems reasonable to assume that he was associated with the Johnson mills of that area.

Abel and Lucy lived in the Pine Valley area for some fifty-two years and were considered a prominent and respected family. This period of history was a most marvelous time, with most of our modern inventions coming to fruition: the train, steamship, automobile, airplane, telegraph, telephone, and radio. There were wars aplenty including the Civil War, the Indian Wars, and World War I. In addition, there was the opening of the western territories to settlement with eventual statehood. What an exciting era in which to have lived. There must be hundreds of stories he could have told, but alas, we are left with so little. He lived to see the birth of thirteen grandsons which made him very proud. The family home was located one-half mile north of Clair Street on the right-hand side of what is now Route 14, Pine Valley, NY. Unfortunately, the house was taken down in early 1982 to make room for a parking lot.

Abel died of a cerebral hemorrhage at the age of 98 years on April 12, 1920 while visiting with his daughter at Southampton, Suffolk County, New York (Long Island). He was buried in the Johnson vault with his wife and children on April 16, 1920 at the Pine Valley

9

Cemetery, Pine Valley, New York. His wife, Lucy Haile Johnson, and two children had preceded him in death.

CHARLES VICTOR JOHNSON

Written by Garnie Thornton (now deceased)
and edited by Gerald Garth Johnson

When Charles V. Johnson was born May 11, 1815 in Russell, St. Lawrence County, New York, he was the first of a family of seven Johnson children. He was presented to four little half-sisters, Harriet, age 10, Susan, age 7, Levitia [Louisa], age 5, and Phila, age 2. The girls' father was Charles Victor Johnson's mother's first husband, Samson Viall.

The parents of Charles Victor Johnson were Charles Alvah Johnson, born February 26, 1785 in Brookfield, MA and Rachel Pratt Viall Johnson, born May 18, 1787 in Willsboro, New York. They were married on December 16, 1813 by Reuben Ashman, J.P. officiating in Russell, New York.

As he grew up in the pleasant valley with its dairying and cheese industries and big maple groves rivaling the Vermont hills to the east, he knew that Congress had awarded 160 acres of land to each war veteran, including his father, in a far off new state called Illinois. They were located in the Military Tract. Hoping to secure a quarter section either on his father's right or to pick up an unclaimed or abandoned farm, he worked his way west, arriving at Quincy and later at Pittsfield, Illinois in 1837.

The next year he married Emily Spann who had joined her relatives in Pittsfield, leaving her birthplace of Vernon, Indiana. She traveled down the Ohio River to Cairo, Illinois, up the Mississippi River to St. Louis, Missouri and on horseback 140 miles to Naples, Illinois where she was met by her relatives.

Emily Spann was born June 5, 1814 in Vernon, Indiana, the twelfth child of Mary Layton Spann, born 1769 and Jesse Spann, born October 17, 1766 in England. Jesse served in the Revolutionary War as a scout, in Spartanburg, South Carolina, the Battle of the Cowpens, and possibly with Marion's Men in the Swamp Fox. For his service he received a tract of land in Jefferson County, Indiana.

Mary and Jesse were married at Spartanburg, South Carolina, September 18, 1789. Mary Layton Spann died June 15, 1859 and Jesse Spann died 1848. Both are buried in Craig's Cemetery, Jefferson County, Indiana.

Charles Victor Johnson and Emily Spann Johnson bought a title to a soldier's patent in Section 21, Hardin Township, Pike County, Illinois. The 160 acres had some timberland and part of it was fertile Honey Creek bottom land. The deed was signed by President Van Buren. It is assumed that the land had at least one, if not two, owners. Here they had a fine spring and they built a log house and a log barn close to it. Eight children were born to this couple but only five attained the age of adulthood.

Charles Victor Johnson was a vigorous down East Yankee and as restless as any of the pioneers. In 1849, he caught the California gold fever and the next year joined a party of neighbors for the westward trip across the plains and over the mountains. He had traded a ten acre strip along the east side of his farm for a yoke of oxen but they died on the way to California.

The genealogies of the children of Charles Victor and Emily Spann Johnson are contained in this book.

BIOGRAPHY OF NANCY A. JOHNSON BROWN AND WILLIAM H. BROWN

Written in 1963 by Carson P. Buck, husband
of Martha Clark Buck, and edited by Mary Buck
Spadaro and Gerald Garth Johnson

William and Nancy lived first in Pitcairn, NY for about 2-3 years until about 1846-7. When they married, William said that he "had an axe, a wife, and a dollar." He paid the minister by borrowing a team of oxen and hauling a load of black salt to Odgensburg, NY and selling it for $1.00. [black salt, which was used for soap and glass manufacturing, was made from various ingredients, among them: burned wood, leeched ashes and lye.] Their first home was a shack built up by the rocks [perhaps the cliff known as "Bald Mountain"] in Pitcairn, NY and wolves howled outside their back door.

After moving from Pitcairn, NY they lived for a short time outside Edwards Village, NY on the road to Fine, NY, possibly where the Ingrehm place was located [on a map of 1865]. Here, Nancy had cupboards for the first time that had doors.

Next they moved to the Tannery house in the village of Edwards, NY while William worked for the Tannery for a time. The Browns' next move was to what was called the Brodie Farm where William became overseer for Mr. Brodie. The farm was about a mile Southwest of Edwards. This move must have occurred around 1848 because their son, Charles Hiram, was born in the overseer's house.

On April 10, 1865, a Monday, William moved into the Brodie House which lay across the road. Mr. Brown bought the house from Mr. Brodie. This house was a three-story mansion with a ballroom on the third floor. Practically the entire house was built from materials shipped from Scotland where it had been fashioned ready to erect, somewhat in the manner of pre-fab houses of today [1963]. They lived in the "Brodie" house until November 27, 1883.

12

Clara, the Brown's daughter, died of scarlet fever and other complications [whooping cough, measles and pneumonia] in 1868, and was laid to rest in the old cemetery in Edwards, NY. On the original tombstone was the following inscription:

"Her little heart is cold
Her pulse beat no more
Her little spirit saved
Upon the shining shore."

Nancy Brown brooded over Clara's death for years, particularly on anniversaries.

In the early days, William had oxen instead of horses. Occasionally he would walk to Ogdensburg, NY to get manufactured nails. He walked along trails [that were] along streams. He made furniture and did not want to use blacksmith nails.

The Browns had lots of food in their cellar: barrels of apples and potatoes. At that time people would come to the house selling berries at 10 cents per quart.

William was a very capable man. He could lay chimneys and brick walls, and he could make a wagon wheel. He was gifted with lots of common sense. At one time he was the head of the highway department and directed the men in his section. He paid his taxes in this way. He planted maple trees along the road – also for taxes.

When the Browns' son, Alvah, was married the second time, William and the boys [his two sons] built a new house on the site of the old overseer's house across the road from the Brodie house. In 1963, this is the residence of Richard D. Brown.

In 1883, they were living with their son and daughter-in-law, Charles Hiram and Martha Brown on the Brodie farm. William and Charles continued to farm the Brodie place until William sold the Brodie house and the land around it on the north side of the road on August 21, 1883 to Gideon (Gid) and Mary Allen Freeman for $4000. They had lived there sixteen years, 1867-1883. On November 27, 1883, William and Nancy and their grandson, Sherman [son of Alvah Brown by his first wife] who was living with them, moved in with Alvah across the road. They remained with him [except for a period of time in 1905 that they lived with Clarence, Carrie, and Donald Brown] until their deaths in 1909 [Nancy] and 1914 [William].

For at least the last ten years of William's life he was blind. He was blind in April, 1901 when he attended the funeral of his brother, John Brown, with Mabel Brown Clark. William's funeral services were conducted by Reverend Barrett of Hermon, NY.

Nancy Brown was a strong, active woman until the winter of 1908-9 when her health began to fail. She had cancer and suffered much, though she bore it all cheerfully. She was a Baptist [her parents, Charles Alvah and Rachel Pratt Viall Johnson, were some of the first members of the Russell Baptist Church according to the list of members that began in 1809]. Her funeral services were conducted by Reverend Hugh Kane. It is said that Nancy did not particularly care for her given name [Nancy]. She wore a black bonnet in later life. Only Nancy and William knew that she had cancer until just before her death. It was kept a secret. She bore it with Spartan-like determination.

The genealogy of the William and Nancy A. Johnson Brown family can be found in the Genealogy Section of this book, and the *Diaries of Nancy A. Johnson Brown and William H. Brown* is available from Heritage Books, Inc., Bowie, MD.

THE AUTOBIOGRAPHY OF HIRAM ALVAH JOHNSON, SENIOR

I was born in the town of Russell, St. Lawrence County, State of New York, on the 18th day of February, 1819. My father's name was Charles Alvah Johnson. My mother maiden name was Rachel Pratt. She had been married to a man by the name of Samson Viall before she became the wife of my father, and had four daughters by

Viall. My father and mother had seven children, four sons and three daughters. My oldest sister, Eliza, died when she was about two years old; she was scalded by turning a tub of hot water upon herself. Three of my half-sisters, two of my whole sisters, and three brothers are still living (in July, 1874). When I was eight years old, my father moved to Edwards, NY about eight miles from Russell. I was raised to hard work on a farm. My father was a hard working, industrious farmer and considered at that time as very well off. My parents were strictly moral and religious, belonging to the Baptist Church. When I was 20, I started out for myself working for my brother-in-law, Dr. James Foster, who had married Susan Viall, my half-sister. They lived in Jefferson County, New York. The fall before this I went to Lewis County, New York to work, but soon became homesick and went back home. In the fall of 1839, I went back to Russell and lived with my brother-in-law, Elihu Phelps, husband of my half-sister, Phila Viall, and attended school during the winter. In the spring, I concluded I would buy a piece of land and go to work on it. I made a partial contract for a piece of timberland with my brother-in-law and went to work chopping off the underbrush for a clearing. I followed this for a few days and became discouraged and told the folks I was going West to Illinois. I had a brother living in Pike County, Illinois. I started for that county in May, 1840. I took a steamer at Ogdensburg, NY which was the first one I had ever traveled on (never having seen one until the winter before.) The first night we had a severe storm and I became very seasick and concluded if I ever got on land again I would keep off the water in the future. We landed at Rochester, NY and I took the canal boat for Florence, Pike County, Illinois. I arrived at my brother's about the middle of May and afterwards worked some of the time for a man nearby. The next winter, I attend school about three months each year from the time I was four years old until I was twenty-two; consequently, my education was what might be called tolerably good. When I arrived in Illinois I had no property except my clothes.

On the 25th of July, 1841, I was married to Elizabeth Jane Whitley and went to keeping house on forty acres of land that she had partly paid for. Remaining there two years, I sold that place and took up a quarter section of land on Bay Creek in the same county [Pike]. I

15

worked hard, fenced and broke a small field, built a house, raised a crop of corn, but took the ague (illness), got discouraged and sold out in the fall and went back on Honey Creek and contracted for another quarter section of land and went to work improving it. In the fall of 1845, I sold out with the calculation of going to Texas in the following spring. During the winter I made my arrangements for the trip but a short time previous to the time for starting, one of my horses was accidentally killed and consequently, I could not go. This I have always considered a great blessing, for had I gone to Texas I am satisfied that I would not have been satisfied with the country and would have left it soon and then come to Oregon as others did who went at that time. In the spring of 1846, I moved to Pittsfield, Illinois and followed teaming with an ox-team. In June I went on a visit to my people in New York, calculating to start to Oregon the next spring. I went by the way of St. Louis up the Ohio River, thence across by stage Erie, thence down Lake Erie, Lake Ontario, and the St. Lawrence River. Had a pleasant visit with my father's family and returned home in July. I remained in Pittsfield until the following April 5, 1847 when we started overland with an ox-team for Oregon. Everything considered, we had a very pleasant journey. We crossed the Missouri River on May 1 and arrived at Fort Laramie on June 4, the Green River on July 4, Fort Hall about the first of August, The Dalles on September 4, and reached Oregon City on September 10.

We stopped in Clackamas County a few days and then came to Marion County and took up a claim one and half miles north of the Santiam River. The claim had been taken before and abandoned. There was a small cabin on it and we moved into it and went to work. I followed making rails that winter and worked in rain and shine. I could not get wheat for work but could get plenty of beef and potatoes. I used to walk to my work three miles and back and cut and split three hundred rails a day. I fenced and broke ten acres and put in wheat and have always had plenty of everything since. In the fall of 1848, I went to the California gold mines, working 38 days and made about $2,000. Then left the mines and went to San Francisco and waited a long time for a passage home, and then took a sailing vessel for the Columbia River. [I] Arrived home the first of March. I worked on the farm that season and in the fall started to the mines again but when I got to Shasta Peak, I met a good many men coming back disgusted with the mines and I returned home myself. Continued on the farm until January 1863 when I bought out a stock of goods in Jefferson and moved there the following fall. Sold goods for about five years, then sold out and removed back to the farm and built a new house and barn. I sold a portion of my land and bought a house and lot in East Salem and have remained there since.

Politically I was a Democrat until the democracy went into the rebellion and I did not go with them. I have been a Republican ever since. I have assessed Marion County twice and assisted to assess it once more. Have been a Justice of the Peace the most of the time for twenty-two years.

I united with the M. E. [Methodist Episcopal] Church when I was about 15 years of age and was baptized by them. At the age of twenty-two after I came to Illinois, I became acquainted with the Christian Church and united with them and have continued a firm believer in the New Testament Christianity ever since. I never played a game of cards for anything – don't even know how they count cards. Never was on the floor to dance. Have been strictly temperate, yet never belonging to any temperance organization since I was a boy. Never used tobacco except to smoke a cigar occasionally and am not guilty of any of the bad habits that most men indulge in. This may look like boasting, but I may as well tell the truth. In the summer of 1863, I joined the A.F. & A. M. and have never regretted it. I think next to Christianity, it is the best institution now in operation. I have always endeavored to live in peace with all men and now in my 57th year I have not an enemy on earth that I would not do a favor to if possible. In 1876, my wife and I went on a trip to Philadelphia, New York visiting my brother in Illinois and my friends and relatives in New York. Returning home in July about 1878, I bought a place on Church Street and in 1883 built a new house on the same lot and moved into it. The next summer I bought a small place two miles east of town and moved there. We remained nine months, when we got lonesome and rented the place and moved back to Salem and are still staying here. Continued to act as Justice of the Peace, assistant County Treasurer and Assessor until 1888.

17

Since that time have retired from business and am taking the world easy. In the winter of 1890, I had a very sick spell. The doctors gave me up to die. Before that time I always had a kind of fear of death. But I became perfectly reconciled to the matter and death had no terrors to me but as I commenced to get better, that love of life returned and while death has no particular terror, still I am in no hurry to leave this beautiful world.

BIOGRAPHY OF JOHN CHARLES JOHNSON

John Charles Johnson, a representative citizen of Marion County, Oregon, has been a resident of the Pacific Coast from childhood, and since arriving at mature years has been prominently identified with the agricultural interest of this section. He is a native of Illinois and was born May 29, 1842. He came with his parents, Hiram Alvah Johnson and Elizabeth Jane Whitley Johnson, across the plains on the Oregon Trail with he was five years old. He received his education in the schools of Jefferson, Oregon and was reared to the occupation of a farmer. When he came of age, his father gave him 160 acres of land devoting four years to the cultivation and improvement of this section of land. After disposing of the farm, he purchased 900 acres in Linn County, Oregon which he cultivated and improved for a period of four years. He sold this Linn County land and embarked in mercantile trade in Scio in Linn County.

He formed a partnership with J. C. Brown and they did a successful business until 1890 at which time John Charles Johnson sold his interest and moved to Salem, Oregon. He invested in city and county property and engaged in real estate transactions on his own account. He was very fortunate in his operations, and had become possessed of much valuable property. He was married in 1863 to Miss Violetta Gunsaules, a native of Illinois but a resident of Oregon since 1853.

Mr. Johnson cast his first presidential vote for Abraham Lincoln and has since been a member of the Republican Party doing active and efficient service. He has been a delegate to many conventions and while a citizen of Scio was twice elected Mayor of that city. In 1890, he was elected a member of the City Council in Salem, Oregon. He is a member of the A.O.U.W. and of the Masonic fraternity, belonging both to the blue lodge and chapter of the latter order. He is a man of excellent business judgment and by energy and perseverance, has achieved success in all of his undertakings.

BIOGRAPHY OF GEORGE WASHINGTON JOHNSON

George Washington Johnson, a prominent member of commercial circles in Marion County, Oregon, is one of the pioneers of the State of Oregon. He was born at Pittsfield, Pike County, Illinois on July 19, 1844, a son of Hiram A. Johnson and Elizabeth Jane Whitley Johnson. He was three years of age when his parents crossed the plains to Oregon in 1847. He received his education in the common schools and was a farmer on his own lands from the time he came of age until 1875. He then embarked in the general mercantile business in Scio, Linn County, Oregon and had a very successful and profitable trade there until 1882. In that year he sold out and came to Salem, Oregon and purchased the business established by E. Myre & Company, which he since conducted with a marked ability. He carries a stock of furnishing goods, hats, caps, trunks, and valises, all well selected with a special view to the demands of the public. The patronage is drawn from a territory whose radius is twenty-five miles. In addition to his mercantile interests, Mr. Johnson has invested in county and city property, and is doing a real estate business of his own account. He owns a pleasant residence in the City of Salem where he lives with his family in the enjoyment of many of the comforts of this civilization. He was a soldier in the late Civil War having enlisted in 1863 and serving until its close.

He was united in marriage in 1866 to Miss Mary Parthena Jones, a native of Missouri, and a daughter of Louis Jones who migrated to Oregon in 1852.

Mr. Johnson is a worthy member of the Masonic fraternity belonging both to the blue lodge and chapter. He cast his first presidential vote for the world renowned soldier and patriot, General U.S. Grant, and has since affiliated with the Republican Party. He is a man of quiet, thoughtful manner, strictly honorable in business, and a liberal supporter of those enterprises which tend to advance the interests of the city, county, and state.

BIOGRAPHY OF WILLIAM WARREN JOHNSON OF OREGON

William Warren Johnson, later known as "Broady" was the third son of Hiram Alvah Johnson, Sr. and Elizabeth Jane Whitley Johnson. Warren, which is the name his parents called him, was born May 20, 1847 on the Oregon Trail while the family was en route to Oregon from Pittsfield, Illinois. The exact birthplace was near the site of Fort Hall [*probably Ft. Laramie*] on the Platte River in Nebraska. The birth occurred in a covered wagon and held up the wagon train for one day.

The Hiram Alvah Johnson family settled on a donation land claim near Santiam City, Oregon which is in the vicinity of Jefferson, Oregon and is called Jefferson, Oregon instead of Santiam City. Santiam City was washed always in the middle 1800s by a flood of the Santiam River. Warren spent more time in school than his brothers, according to Hiram Alvah Johnson, because he had a crippled right hand which somewhat limited his usefulness as a farm hand as a teenager. At the age of eighteen, William Warren Johnson apprenticed to Benjamin Van Buren to learn the blacksmith trade. On February 25, 1869, Warren married Caroline Harris, daughter of David and Hester Harris. William Warren and Caroline lived in Jefferson, Oregon where he continued his blacksmith trade until 1873. In 1873 the William Warren Johnsons moved to the vicinity of Mitchell, Oregon in Wheeler County. William Warren Johnson named the town of Mitchell for ex-senator Mitchell. Mr. Johnson operated a blacksmith shop and handled his cattle until 1875. At that time he sold out his cattle and blacksmith shop and returned to Marion County. He next accepted a position as agency blacksmith on the Malheur Indian Reservation and remained there until 1878. This year marked the outbreak of the Bannock and Paiute Indians and Mr. Johnson returned to Canyon City, Oregon with his family.

20

Upon his return to the Indian Agency he found that all people had fled. He then returned to Canyon City and accepted a position as blacksmith to shoe the government horses and accompanied the soldiers in the expeditions. He witnessed some fighting, especially at Castle Rock, Oregon. Following the Indian Wars of the 1880s, Warren was engaged as post blacksmith at Camp Harney until that was abandoned in 1882. In 1882, Warren, who by now was "Broady," joined with John Robinson and built the first structure in Burns, Oregon. It was located where the Burns Hotel now stands and his structure was a hotel and saloon called Egan Saloon. Since 1882, William Warren Johnson was identified with the town of Burns and the County of Harney. He was deputy United States Marshal and was always known as a progressive, energetic, fair, and unselfish man.

Caroline and William Warren Johnson had seven children all of whom are cited within the genealogical section of this book.

CAROLINE HARRIS JOHNSON

Written by Caroline Harris Johnson in a diary

I was born in Washington County, Iowa, in the year 1849. In the year 1864, I crossed the plains in a covered wagon with my parents. We crossed with a train of ten wagons, some of which were drawn by ox teams.

On the way, we were attacked by a band of Native Americans and all the wagons formed a circle which acted as a fort. Painted warriors were hiding and firing from behind every tree but we finally succeeded in driving them away. Every woman helped to fight.

We came to Oregon in 1868 as I had an aunt living in Jefferson, Oregon. Her name was Curtis. I made my home with them. They ran the hotel there. In 1869, I was married to Mr. William Warren Johnson of Jefferson. He was a blacksmith by trade. In 1873, we went up the Columbia River with a wagon and fifty head of cattle to

21

Bridge Creek which is now called Mitchell. Mr. Johnson named the town in the year 1875. In 1875 we moved back to Jefferson and in 1876 we went to the Malheur Agency among those Piute Indians who were hostile at that time.

We were there when they [Native Americans] went on the warpath in 1878. Old Chief Winnemucca and three other chiefs had their big talk in my kitchen as they didn't want the other natives to hear them. Winnemucca tried to get them not to go on the warpath but he could not do anything with them. Five days after he went home, on a Saturday, they came after their rations as usual. Egan and all his warriors rode in front of our house, got off their ponies, and shook hands with me. They said they were going hunting and would be back to gather the vegetables. They went twenty miles from there where they met the Bannocks and had their war dance. The interpreter sent to Harney [County] for the soldiers. All the women and children packed and we went to John Day, Oregon. Part of the men stayed. Four of them took their blankets and slept on the hill that night: Dr. Dodson, Mr. Regan, Reinhart, and Frank Johnson [William Warren Johnson's brother]. My husband had to take the team and wagon back from John Day and when he got there, the men were gone and he thought they had been killed by the natives. He left the team and wagon and rode back to John Day on a horse. When he started there were two Native Americans as spies across the Malheur River and when they saw him the ran and jumped on their horses and went to tell the others. The Native Americans came back and stole all the horses and cattle that were left. Mr. Johnson met the soldiers going in from Harney to the agency. The natives came to Happy Valley and killed Rye Smith's father and brother. At the P Ranch they killed a Chinaman. From there they went to Silver Creek and destroyed houses and burned fields. Then they went across the Mountains to Silvies River and still further until they reached the John Day River. A runner was dispatched to John Day with the news that the Indians were coming. So all of us packed our belongings and moved to the mining tunnels where we hid for three days. While we were there, one of the scouts, whose wife was with us in the tunnel, was killed and cut all to pieces. They had been married only three months and we felt so sorry for his poor little wife.

22

Captain Bernard told about one battle he was in. He said that the bullets whizzed by his ears pretty close from Indians' guns but when they turned the gatling guns loose, how they did run. They carried their dead off with them. The soldiers took possession of what they left. There was everything you could think of.

I did not hear of Captain Bernard for six weeks after that. Just he and another went by horseback to overtake the soldiers. I just supposed that the natives had killed them. But after the war, he came to Camp Harney.

The winter following was a hard one. There was more snow than I have ever seen. In the spring the water formed a lack from Harney to Burns, Oregon.

The next year the post was abandoned and the Indians sent to Yakima as prisoners. My husband made iron shackles and put two together and when the soldiers went they took the Indians in those big government wagons. The Native Americans were in Yakima for four years. This was nothing but stock country then and there were very few people in the whole country. There was lots of range and we did not have to feed the range stock at all.

My husband and John Robinson built the first hotel in Burns, Oregon. It is where the new Burns Hotel now stands. Grandma Caldwell and Mrs. Stinger first ran it.

We lived in Burns from that date until 1906 when Mr. Johnson died. In 1909, we moved to Albany, Oregon and from there to Edmonds, Washington where my boys, Eldon and Leon and I built a home. We lived there until 1916. We moved back to Burns, Oregon in 1916. I could see a lot of changes and from then on I have seen the pioneer dream slowly coming true.

BIOGRAPHY OF ARCHIE JAMES JOHNSON

To a greater or lesser degree, a man is measured by the success which he achieves in his undertakings, the circle of his influence widening in proportion to the height which he attains among his associates, his words carrying weight as his actions have previously proven his ability to command respect and confidence. It is no discredit to the other section of the Union that the great Northwest should, so early in its infancy, have reason to name with pride a large percentage of its citizens as those who have risen to more than local prominence, whose hands have upheld the Western states through the trying period of growth and consequent power, for they are natives or sons of natives of the Middle and Eastern states which have passed on some of their brightest and most enterprising men to aid in the advancement of civilization of the Pacific slope.

Among these men, none hold or more merit a higher position of both local and state prominence than Archie J. Johnson, the son and grandson of pioneers, and the representative of a New York family which has made its way with true pioneer instinct to a locality where men of ability and earnestness of purpose are required to cement the union of a then remote territory, and develop the possibilities which nature has so plentifully bestowed upon it. That these three, father, son, and native son; have faithfully fulfilled their duties as citizens, a brief biographical resume' will quickly show, and it will be interesting reading to those who have watched the beginning, growth and triumphal lead in the van of progress of this Western Commonwealth.

The grandfather, Hiram Alvah Johnson, Senior, was born in St. Lawrence County, New York on February 18, 1819, and after his emigration to the middle west, he remained in Illinois until 1847 when he crossed the plains with ox teams, and at once took up a donation land claim near Jefferson, Marion County, Oregon. For twenty-eight years he made his home upon this farm of 640 acres, and in the town of Jefferson, where he engaged in a general merchandise business, and at the close of that period he removed to

Salem and made his home there until his death in February, 1896 at the age of 77 years. He was a man of strong independent ideas, and as such he influenced more or less the affairs of the community in which he resided.

He was a Republican in politics and for twelve years he served as Justice of the Peace in Salem, Oregon.

He was a member of the Christian Church and into this work he carried the same traits dominant in his political and social life. His son, John Charles, the father of Archie James Johnson, was a native of Illinois, being born on May 29, 1842, and he came with his father and mother into the West, living upon the latter's farm until 1869 when he bought property located three miles north of Scio, Linn County, consisting of a thousand acres. There he successfully engaged in farming and stock raising until 1874 when he decided to venture into the commercial life of the City of Scio by engaging in a general mercantile business with one J. M. Brown, with home he remained for one year. The firm was afterward known as "Johnson Brothers" for four years, after which John C. Johnson sold out and lived retired for a couple of years, when he again became connected with the general merchandise business of the same city, his partner being Riley Shelton. This connection occupied another four years, and for a like period after that he lived retired. In 1889, he engaged for one year with his son, Archie J., of this review, and then selling his interest in the business to Ross E. Hibler. He then removed to Salem where he now makes his home, though each summer finds him with his family upon his 240 acre farm near Stayton, Marion County, Oregon.

In 1864, John Charles Johnson married Violetta Gunsaules, a native of Illinois, who was born in 1846, the daughter of Manuel Gunsaules, who was a native of Pennsylvania, moving first to Ohio and later, at the age of fifteen, to Illinois, and came across the plains to Oregon in 1853 locating one and a half mile east of Jefferson, Marion County where he died in 1878 at the age of sixty-four. Of the four sons and three daughters, five children are now living. [see Genealogy of John Charles Johnson within this book]

25

Archie James Johnson, was born three miles northwest of Jefferson, Oregon on September 18, 1867. He received a preliminary education in the common schools and upon the completion of the course, he entered the Portland Business College in the spring of 1885 where he made a phenomenal record in his studies in comparison to preceding scholars. He had also developed early a decided talent for business and at the age of fourteen years acted as clerk in a general merchandise establishment at Scio. Oregon. At age sixteen, he took the position of bookkeeper and head salesman for Johnson & Shelton and maintained the same credibility until 1887. He then became timekeeper for the Oregon Pacific Railway but gave this up from which he removed to Seattle, Washington in the spring of 1888 and engaged in the real estate business. The next year found him again a resident of Scio, and in connection with his father, herein previously mentioned, he engaged in the general merchandise business, and later continued with Mr. Hibler, who is now the owner of the store. In 1891, he sold out his interest in the business and in January, 1892 he removed to Salem where he lived until November of the same year, but seemingly not satisfied to live any place but in the city where he had spent his boyhood days and had met with success in all his business dealings, he returned to Scio and with Thomas J. Munkers [who was an uncle of his sister-in-law, Maud Rundlett Johnson] purchased the controlling interest in the Bank of Scio and at once assumed the active management of it. In 1894, he purchased Mr. Munkers' interest in the bank and became president and conducted the business until the fall of 1900. His brother, Charles Virgil Johnson, husband of Maud Rundlett Johnson named above, joined the Bank of Scio as cashier in 1896. Archie James Johnson sold the bank in 1900 and engaged in stock raising, having bought 4,160 acres of land in Benton and Polk Counties and began the stock business on extensive plans, in connection with his brother, Charles Virgil Johnson and his brother-in-law, John C. Simpson, husband of Archie's sister, Etta Johnson Simpson. Their specialty was registered stock and they had a fine herd of Shorthorn and a few choice Hereford cattle along with their grade cattle, sheep and goats. In partnership with Ross E. Hibler, he is extensively engaged in buying mohair and wool throughout the Willamette Valley, a far-reaching business in this State of Oregon. Mr. Johnson has certainly made a success of his business interests in the City of Scio and elsewhere, and his connection with the various commercial and industrial enterprises of this city, his chief prominence in the latter being in the flouring mill business having purchased a one-half interest in 1895 in the fine flouring mill located in Scio. He disposed of the business in 1900 working up a large export business in flour during this period and he is rightly named as one of the principals in the prominent work of the community.

Mr. Johnson was married in January 1888 to Miss Linnie Young, a native of Minnesota, and they were the parents of six children [see Genealogy section]. Fraternally, Archie James Johnson was a member of the Encampment, subordinate and Rebekah lodges of the I.O.O.F. and the Modern Woodmen of America. He belongs to the Cumberland Presbyterian Church. Even among the busy hours of his business life, Mr. Johnson has found time to take an active interest in all public and political movements, as an ardent Republican, serving his party in various positions of trust and honor. In June 1894, he was elected to the State Senate to represent Linn County for four years carrying by a large majority a previously Democratic county. In this position he became a prominent factor in the affairs of the State of Oregon serving on various important committees. He was the promoter of the bill at the 1897 Session to tax foreign companies when carrying on business in the State, but which could not be considered on account of the failure in the organization of the House during the entire Session. He has also been a member of the State Central Committee, for years a member of the County Central Committee of his party, and has served several terms as Councilman of the City of Scio as well as its mayor. Archie Johnson was a school director for two terms and was Chairman of the Board when the Scio school building was erected. The chief business interest of Mr. Johnson at the present time is the position to which he was appointed in March 1899, that of National Bank examiner for the Northwest District including the States of Oregon, Washington, Montana, Idaho and Wyoming. This position he has held with the success which has characterized all of his efforts and which win for him the respect of all who appreciate the business sagacity and untiring energy of their fellow townsman. He is a very busy man, for all his time not given to his official duties is taken up with his large personal interests. Mr. Johnson is esteemed among his associates for an exceptionally pleasing personality and intrinsic worth of character, which has made him a valuable citizen to all communities in which he has in the past resided, and especially to the town wherein most of his life has been passed, that of Scio, Linn County, Oregon. In July 1903, Mr. Johnson removed to Corvallis [Johnson's brother, Charles Virgil Johnson, was mayor of Corvallis] where he has taken up his permanent residence, being near his farm and livestock interests and is at home in this beautiful college city on the banks of the Willamette River.

AUTOBIOGRAPHY OF CHARLES VIRGIL JOHNSON

Edited by Gerald Garth Johnson

I believe one of the most interesting articles I have ever read was one written by my grandfather, Hiram Alvah Johnson, Sr., many years ago. This article contained a sketch of my grandfather's life after he crossed the plains from Illinois to Oregon in 1847 and settled with his family on a Donation Land Claim about two miles north of Jefferson, Oregon. The story was of such interest to me I have wondered if, perhaps, it would be of interest to my grandchildren if I should leave such a sketch of my life. So, on this 59th birthday, I write this article with the one thought only in my mind, that it may be of interest to those who follow me.

My father, John Charles Johnson, was the son of Hiram Alvah Johnson and Elizabeth Jane Whitley Johnson, who crossed the plains from Pike County, Illinois, to Oregon by ox team in the year 1847. They were on the Oregon trail for six months and four days taking the Barlow Trail from The Dalles rather than the Columbia River route by water. John Charles Johnson was five years old, having been born in Pike County, Illinois on May 29, 1842. The Johnson family settled near Jefferson, Oregon, previously known as Santiam City.

The actual patent for the Donation Land Claim [*Hiram and Elizabeth's*] was not signed until President Andrew Johnson signed it on the 27th day of November 1865 on certificate number 769 that had been issued previously in 1850 from the Oregon City Land Office under an act approved by Congress September 27, 1850 and provided for making land of public lands available to those who would migrate and improve their donated land. The land grand is for one section of 640 acres designated as claim No. 55 being a part of sections 25, 26, 35, and 36 in township 9, south of range 3, west of the Willamette Meridian. Said grant sets forth the fact that Hiram A. Johnson and his heirs are to have the north one-half and Elizabeth J. Johnson and heirs, the south one-half. The grant is attested by Edward D. Neill, Secretary, and I. N. Granger, recorder, of the General Land Office at Washington, D.C.

The Johnsons moved into a primitive log cabin that had been built but abandoned by the first grantee. Once it was repaired, the family moved in and Grandfather [Hiram] started for the mines in California having been carried away by the Gold Rush of 1849. After a winter spent in the mines and he had accumulated considerable gold, Grandfather returned to his Oregon home, built a new house on the farm, stocked and equipped the place and again started for the mines. Upon arriving in Southern Oregon [actually Shasta County, California] he met many people returning from the mines with the report that an incurable sickness was prevalent and it was dangerous to stay in California. Grandfather returned home to Santiam City.

Farming was their principal occupation, but in 1862, Grandfather purchased a stock of general merchandise goods at Jefferson and turned his farm, which at that included over 1,200 acres, over to his sons to run. He built a house about one mile north of Jefferson and conducted his general merchandise business in Jefferson.

Steamboat navigation at times came up the Santiam River to Jefferson, but freight was ordinarily transported by team and wagon from Portland, a distance of seventy miles. In the fall and winter of 1862, Father [John Charles] hauled the freight, driving a six horse team. He would take a load of produce to Portland and return with a load of merchandise. During the year 1863, Father taught school in what was then called the Jefferson Institute. He then returned to the farm and was married on March 13, 1864 to Miss Violetta Gunsaules.

Mother [*Violetta*] was the daughter of Manuel and Mary [Cox] Gunsaules. She crossed the plains with her parents in 1853 from Fayette, Stark County, Illinois by ox team, being on the road about seven months. They settled on a Donation Land Claim about one mile south of Jefferson. Mother was born in Knox County, Illinois on April 19, 1845 and lived with her parents on their farm until her marriage to John Charles Johnson.

After the marriage of this young couple, Hiram Alvah Johnson gave them 100 acres of the old Donation Land Claim and they moved onto the farm, living in the house built by my Grandfather. With their own 100 acres, they also farmed a part of Grandfather's place. In 1865, Father purchased from his father [Hiram] an additional 100 acres and until 1869, he farmed the 200 acres until he sold this land and purchased a large stock farm three miles north of Scio, Linn County, Oregon. They farmed and raised stock on this place until 1875 when they sold and traded their holdings for a stock of general merchandise goods at Scio. On March 4, 1875, they moved to Scio where Father embarked in the general mercantile business and continued in this business until 1890 when he disposed of his business in Scio and moved to Salem, Oregon where he expected to retire from active business life.

The genealogy of John Charles Johnson and Violetta Gunsaules Johnson is in the Genealogy section of this book. John Charles Johnson died December 3, 1920 and Violetta Johnson died on November 15, 1930.

Now we come to the subject of this sketch, Charles Virgil Johnson, the fifth child and third son of John Charles and Violetta Gunsaules Johnson, who was born March 18, 1875 in Scio, Oregon. He lived an uneventful life as a boy in a town of about three hundred people.

When I look back, with the knowledge I now have of the actual population of Scio, it seems impossible to me for in my childhood, I thought Scio was a city of at least a thousand people. It was at least a mile up to the old swimming hole at the dam, and down to the manhole through the pasture of Uncle Jimmie Williams. From our home to the store was not less than eight blocks and when we used to go down to the Morris home and then on to the warehouse, it was a mile to the Morris place and two miles to the warehouse. The Christian and Methodist Churches were large with a seating capacity of several hundred. The Christmas trees [services] we had at the church were attended by at least 500 people. The houses were large; the bridge over Thomas Creek was large; the creek was a wide stream; in fact, everything was on a large scale. Now what are the facts? When I go to Scio now I find the old swimming hole at the dam is not more than six or seven blocks from the main part of town; the manhole through Uncle Jimmie Williams' is about four blocks; down to the Morris place is just around the corner; and to the old warehouse, nothing to it. From our home to the store is actually three city blocks, but what a time we children would have in the summertime, starting for the swimming hole with all our clothes on, consisting of a shirt and a pair of overalls. Who would be first in? The shirt and overalls were off by the time we reached the water's edge!

Speaking of the old swimming hole, let it be recorded here that in my boyhood days, a bathing suit was unknown. When as boys we went swimming, we went in to the water in the raw garbed in Nature's all outdoors. The girls had a swimming hole at some distance down the creek and they were all garbed in old Mother Hubbard dresses or coverage of some sort, but swimming, as I recall it in those days, was a man's sport. Every boy knee high to a duck learned to swim. Girls did not. In fact, as I recall, girls and grown women did not go swimming as the boys and men did. I do not remember one girl in Scio in those days who could swim.

We always kept a milch cow and at the age of seven years, it feel to my lot to drive the cow to pasture after milking – Father always

31

doing the milking – in the morning and to drive her home in the evening. This chore fell to my lot at this early age on account of the death of my brother, Elmer, who was two years old than I was. I recall three difference pastures used during the eight years I drove the cow back and forth while living in Scio. One pasture was down past the old slaughter house in a property owned by Jimmie Williams; another was on the Munkers' property and say, were there thistles in this pasture and did we get them in our feet. We were always barefoot of course. How sore a foot could get with those sharp thistles! Many, many times both feet were infected at the same time. I well recall the poultice Mother would mix up to pull the thistles and believe me it would pull. (Brown sugar and brown soap.) Father acquired a farm out the Old West Scio Road and the cow had to be driven to this pasture. I recall I had to go all the way to the Cary place before I reached the gate, almost to West Scio, at least one and one-half miles. Now when this had to be done before school, you see we could not stay in bed until near school time, but I was up pretty early.

In the summertime, it was sore feet from stone bruises and thistles and sore backs from sunburn. Cold cream was used on the backs which were so bad at times that boils covered them. This was from going barefoot and lying out of the water in the sun after a day's swim.

Another chore which fell to my lot the next winter was building fires, two each morning; one in the cook stove and one in the living room. The parlor fire was built only on occasions. I remember distinctly that immediately after the fires were built I had to grind coffee for breakfast. The old fashioned coffee mill was used. Coffee in those days was bought green and Mother used to parch her own coffee and grind it for the pot.

Another thing was very provoking. We had to carry water from a pump and the pump was about twenty feet from the back door. So no matter what kind of weather, we had to go out to the pump to get a bucket of water and on wash days it was my task to carry the wash water. Did those sisters of mine use lots of water? Well, I should say! This water near the house was not good drinking water so we had another pump about one hundred yards from the house across the street in our barn lot. Water also had to be pumped here for the cow and horse. And by the way, right where this old pump stood was where my first home in Scio was located.

Oh, those days of inconvenience! Kerosene lamps were the thing, and tallow candles were used in the bedrooms. There was one chore I recall I did not have to do. However, Father bought his wood in four foot lengths and he always had Sam Howell saw this wood. I put it in the shed. Sam used a buck saw and sawed otherwise than by buck saw. Abe Powell, who lived near Scio, ran a threshing machine by horsepower and in the fall of the year would rig up his horsepower to a circular saw and saw the wood in Scio. Sam had to step aside for progress. The circular saw took lots of space. If wood was sawed in a city street, traffic was stopped as the horsepower took several horses and was circular so space was necessary.

Life at Scio as I recall was spent by the children as children will spend their time. In the winter it was school. I recall when I was eleven years old, Uncle Ike Witherite, a farmer at Jefferson, sent word to Father that if I wanted to come over to his place and go with the threshers, he would let me have a horse and I could get a job bucking straw. I did that very thing. I remember my horse was Old Kate. I worked the year through threshing at fifty cents a day. I believed they allowed Uncle Ike fifty cents per day for the horse. Say, we would go to work at daylight and quit at dusk. The next summer I worked for my brother-in-law, J. H. Daniel, harrowing. He was running a farm Father purchased out in the West Scio area and at one time I harrowed for fifteen days at fifty cents a day and the $7.50 made on this job was invested in an overcoat. I recall sending the money by Father to Salem where he purchased the overcoat. My first one, and was I proud. I had a girl friend by this time but I still went barefoot although I was twelve years old!

The summer I was thirteen I again went with Uncle Ike and the threshers, and the summer I was fourteen I worked in Father's store, counting eggs, cooping chickens, packing dried apples, plums, etc.

33

On the 18th of March, 1890 I was fifteen years old and on the 21st of March we moved to Salem, Oregon.

Father owned some lots about a block north on Winter Street and started building a house so we lived in the Waldo house until our new home was completed. After moving to Salem, I again started driving the cow to pasture (we always had a cow) and it always fell to my lot to drive this cow to and from pasture. The pasture this time was out by the Oregon State Hospital and was a distance of about two miles.

In 1891, I started school in Salem, attending what at that time was known as the East Salem School. I attended this school during the years 1891 and 1892 and in 1893 I started at Willamette University and attended there during 1893 and 1894. I worked for my brother-in-law, J. H. Daniels, during haying time, by working with his hay baler. After the haying season was over I would go with the threshing crew. During the summer of 1894, Dr. L. L. Rowland, who was superintendent at the Oregon State Insane Asylum, gave me a job as an attendant at that institution. I started work there in June 1894 and quit in September 1897 to accept a position as bookkeeper at the Scio Roller Mills. I was bookkeeper at the mill from September 1897 to March 1898 when I was elected cashier at the Bank of Scio. I retained this position until May 1902 when my brother, Archie, traded for a large stock ranch in Polk and Benton Counties, a co-partnership was formed consisting of my brother Archie, my brother-in-law John C. Simpson, and myself. Our purpose, of course, was to get rich by raising stock. Did we? I got out while I yet had a shirt on my back! In 1902, we moved to the stock farm in Polk and Benton Counties. [King's Valley and Airlie].

You will note I said "we." In October of 1898, I was married to Maud E. Rundlett at Salem, Oregon. Maud was the daughter of Mrs. Harriette Rundlett to whom I referred when I said we. My family lived in the Waldo house just across the street from Mrs. Rundlett so my acquaintance with the Rundlett family started when I was fifteen years of age.

During the years 1893, 1894, and 1895, I was on the football team of Willamette University. I played the position of center all three years. During 1893 and 1894, I was attending school and in 1895, I was working at the Asylum but arrangements were made so that I played with the team for that year also. This team was undefeated during the season of 1894 and for the first and only time, we defeated the Oregon State Agricultural College [now Oregon State University]. During these years at the Willamette University, I developed into a runner, a jumper, and a boxer. As a 100 yard dash man, my time for 100 yards was ten and two-fifth seconds. As a running broad jumper, my records was 22 feet, 3 inches and for two hops and a jump my records was 30 feet, 2 inches. Some of you youngsters try to equal this record! In those days it was up among the best. My closest competitor in this latter jump was one of the professors, W.C. Hawley. Mr. Hawley was afterwards President of Willamette University and in 1908 was elected as a Representative to the US Congress, holding that position until 1932. As a boxer I met all comers during the year 1893.

In the spring of 1897, I purchased two lots on a corner just across the street from the Riley Shelton home in Scio. When I was a boy, in fact when we moved from Scio to Salem in 1890, we moved from this property occupied at this time by Riley Shelton and the lots I purchased were part of our own cow lot. Tom J. Munkers had just completed a new house so I purchased his old house and had it moved and set up on my newly purchased lots and had the house reconditioned. Furniture was purchased, so when I took my bride to Scio on October 16, 1898, we moved into our own home. After our marriage in Salem, Oregon on October 12, 1898, we went to Portland and stopped at the Imperial Hotel which was operated by Phil Metschan, ex-state treasurer, and we stayed in Portland until October 16. Then we took the train for Scio, going up over the eastside from Woodburn to West Scio and from West Scio by stage coach to Scio where I held the position of cashier of the Bank of Scio. After two or three days spent at my brother's home in Scio while our house was being finished, the rugs laid and furniture placed, we moved into our own home.

In 1899, I was elected as a member of the City Council of Scio for a two-year term and was re-elected in 1901, but we moved from Scio in the spring of 1902.

The stock farm we acquired consisted of 4,300 acres, and at one time we ran more than 1,000 head of sheep and about 400 head of cattle. While living on this ranch, our first child, Dorothy, was born on March 26, 1904. During the summer of 1904, not having found ranching to my liking, I purchased an interest in a general merchandise store in Airlie, Oregon. Early in the Fall of that year we moved to Airlie where I conducted said business. In the winter of 1904, I was appointed postmaster by President Theodore Roosevelt. I conducted this store until 1907 when I opened a men's clothing store [The Toggery] in Corvallis, Oregon and in the fall of that year we moved to Corvallis to manage this business leaving my clerk, Mr. A. N. Newbill in charge of the Airlie store. While living at Airlie, in fact, June 21, 1905, our second child, Charles Garth, was born, so there were four of us in our move to Corvallis.

During 1908, Mr. W. C. Hawley came to me and asked me to accept the chairmanship of the Congressional Committee for the First Congressional District as he expected to be a candidate for Congress. I was a delegate to this convention and was elected its chairman. So, I managed the first Congressional campaign of W. C. Hawley for Congress. He was elected. I also managed his second campaign and he was again elected. Mr. A. W. Prescott was my secretary. Prescott was a graduate of Willamette University and we had attended school at the same time. Mr. Hawley was our teacher there.

In 1910, I was elected to the City Council of Corvallis, Oregon. Mr. Virgil Waters at that time the elected mayor. He was not in good health and resigned as mayor and I was elected. My term of office expired in November, 1911. We moved to Portland, Oregon in October 1911 as I had been appointed United States Appraiser of Merchandise. Mr. Hawley asked President William Howard Taft to appoint me to this position for the Port of Portland as General Owen Summers died while hold this position.

I succeeded him, taking office in October 1911 but in November, 1912, Woodrow Wilson, a Democrat, was elected President and on April 1, 1913, Mr. Wheeler, a Democrat, was appointed in my place. I returned to Airlie in June 1913, purchased the interest of my partner in the general mercantile business there (I had always retained my interest in this business) and managed the business. I took an examination for postmaster, passed the examination, and was appointed by President Woodrow Wilson. So I have served as a Federal Officer under three Presidents: postmaster under Theodore Roosevelt, U.S. Appraiser under William Howard Taft, and postmaster under Woodrow Wilson.

The business at Airlie was conducted by me until December 19, 1918 when fire broke out in the store building and not only destroyed the store building and our stock of goods but our home and many of our household effects. Our loss was heavy as insurance premiums were high, having no fire protection, and we were not fully covered. We did a large credit business and when discontinuing business, collections could not be made, and from a financial standpoint, we were broke.

The Oregon State Legislature met that winter and so I came to Salem for a job. Due to the efforts of Senator Patterson, I was appointed as chief clerk of the engrossed bills committee of the Senate at a salary of $7.50 per day. This enabled us to move to Salem, which we did in the spring of 1919. We purchased a home [still standing on Commercial Street] on contract on North Commercial.

Soon after the adjournment of the Legislature, Ben Olcott, my friend who was then Governor, called me to his office and informed me that a bill had passed providing for the licensing and regulation of real estate brokers, said its administration was under the State Insurance Commissioner, Harvey Wells, and if I wanted the job of getting this law in order and enforcing same, he would call Mr. Wells and arrange it. Did I want it? My decision was given at once. So on May 27, 1919, I went on the payroll of the State of Oregon as deputy real estate commissioner. Capt. A. C. Barber succeeded Mr. Wells as Insurance Commissioner and I was appointed deputy real estate commissioner by Mr. Barber.

Walter Pierce was elected Governor to succeed Ben Olcott in the fall of 1922 and appointed Will Moore the insurance commissioner to succeed Mr. Barber. I served under Mr. Moore until June, 1923 when William A. Mullen was appointed to act as deputy.

In July, 1923, we sold our property on North Commercial Street and moved to Portland where I opened a real estate office on the corner of Second and Stark streets and continued in the real estate business until the first of the year 1927. In the fall of 1926, I. L. Patterson was elected as Governor to succeed Walter Pierce and Mr. Patterson asked me to come back to Salem and take charge of the real estate license law. Patterson appointed Mr. Clare A. Lee the Insurance Commissioner, and I was appointed on March 1, 1927, and again came to Salem. Maud did not move to Salem until May 1928. You see, the family had gotten back to two of us again. Dorothy has a position with the Federal Government and lives in Washington, D.C. and Garth has a position with the W. P. Fuller Paint Company and lives in Portland with his wife, Violette. [Violette Marie Brewer]

I am still holding the position of deputy real estate commissioner. Mr. Patterson died in the fall of 1929 and Mr. A. W. Norblad became Governor by reason of the fact that he was President of the Senate. No change was made in either the insurance commissioner or deputy real estate commissioner by Governor Norblad. In the fall of 1930, Julius L. Meier was elected Governor. Governor Meier appointed Mr. A. H. Averill the insurance commissioner and I was retained as deputy real estate commissioner, so up to date I have served the state under five governors: Olcott, Pierce, Patterson, Norblad and Meier. I called attention to having served under three presidents. This was a period of about ten years and my service under five governors has been about twelve years as of my 59th year. I have put in twenty-two years with the Federal and State Governments, however, nine years of this time with the Federal Government I was conducting my own business.

One very important matter which I failed to record was that during World War I, I was appointed as one of the seven regional directors of Polk County. These directors had to pass on all men drafted into service, all war loans and stamp sales, Red Cross drives, and in fact, all war activities carried on at home were under the supervision of the seven regional directors in each county. These seven were drafted for service during the duration of the war and it was considered the same as any other war service, and without remuneration. The directors met in Dallas, Oregon, the county seat of Polk, every two weeks and when the war was over, we were discharged. Each was given a medal for distinguished service by the United States Government. This is the nearest I have ever been to service in the United States Army.

I have been in every county in this state and in every city in the state of more than 1,000 population. I have traveled every highway in the state except the Yellowstone Highway from Burns to Lakeview. In 1920, I spent a week in Kansas City, MO going there to Chicago where I attended the Republican National Convention which nominated Warren Harding for President and Calvin Coolidge for vice-president. I have been affiliated with the Republican Party since I became of voting age, casting my first vote for William McKinley for president in that memorable campaign between McKinley and William Jennings Bryan in 1896. After leaving Chicago, in company with realtors from Portland, Oregon and the States of Washington, Wyoming, Montana, and Idaho, we covered every prominent city in each of the states. Meetings were held and discussions took place with reference to state license laws for the regulation of the real estate business, with the result that each of these states enacted such law at the next Legislative assemblies. I have made several trips East, visited many states in the Union, and also spent a week in Toronto, Canada.

I am very well acquainted in every part of our state and count my acquaintances as my friends. I have never betrayed a friend. I believe a person can be and should be honest politically as well as from a business standpoint. In my numerous public positions, I have at all times attempted to do my duty, let the chips fall where they may. Neither politics, religion, nor friendship has had any thought in my mind in performing my duty. I recall politically, I have had several opportunities to hold positions or to aspire to office which I turned down; some on account of my word having been given, and I would not break it. When W. C. Hawley was Congressman from the state, he was called upon to fill the position of Postmaster at Corvallis. A fight for the appointment was on between A. W. Lafferty and B. W. Johnson. Mr. Hawley could not decide between them. I had acted as campaign manager for Mr. Hawley in his election so he asked me to accept the appointment. His argument was that no person could take exception to his giving this appointment to his campaign manager. But I refused as I had endorsed B. W. Johnson for the position and promised him my support. B. W. Johnson was finally appointed.

I recall another incident in 1922. I was called upon by a delegation of five persons, two from Salem and three from Portland. I do not recall the names of two but there was Senator I. L. Patterson, Senator C. W. Bishop, and W. D. Ayers, a capitalist of Portland. Mr. O. P. Hoff was state treasurer. He had just completed his first term of four years in office and had announced his candidacy for re-election. While there was quite a bit of opposition to Mr. Hoff, he had made a good treasurer in my opinion and was entitled to re-election so Mr. Hoff and I had talked over the campaign and I promised him my support. In fact, Mr. Hoff was looking to me to help Mr. J.W. Crawford, his chief deputy (now Circuit Judge of Multnomah County) to carry on his campaign. The committee above referred to wanted me to become a candidate for State Treasurer, promising me the Republican Central Committee would be with me and that my campaign expenses would be donated. I turned it down, explaining to this committee that I had promised my support to Mr. Hoff.

After Walter Pierce succeeded Mr. Ben Olcott as Governor and W. A. Mullen succeeded me as deputy real estate commissioner, Mr. Hoff, state treasurer, asked me to accept the position of secretary of the Board of Control. This appointment is made by the Governor, State Treasurer, and Secretary of State. The secretary of the Board

40

of Control at that time was a Mr. Goodin, and Secretary of State Kozer was in favor of retaining Mr. Goodin, but Treasurer Hoff and Governor Pierce wanted a change. Mr. Hoff informed me that Governor Pierce wanted to change the superintendent at the State Reform School in Woodburn, Oregon. I told him I would accept, and then I was called upon by a committee of an organization known as the Ku Klux Klan, an anti-Catholic and anti-Negro organization in the state that had quite a little to do with the election of Governor Pierce. This committee consisted of three, one of whom I do not recall, but the other two were A. A. Slaughter and Herbert Rowley. I was informed that Governor Pierce wanted to support me for Secretary of the Board of Control but before doing so he wanted to know if I was a member of the Ku Klux Klan. I politely told them they could go to H— with their organization and that I would never subscribe to it. Well, needless to say, I did not receive the appointment, as the Governor went back on his word to Treasurer Hoff after Hall supported the Governor's choice for Superintendent of the Reform School. So strange things happen politically!

Mr. Hoff passed away while in office in 1924. Governor Pierce appointed Jefferson Myers to fill out his term and in the general election in 1925, Thomas B. Kay was elected and in 1928, Mr. Kay was a very sick man, going to New York for treatment. There were weeks and weeks when he was not expected to live. It was reported that he was afflicted with an incurable disease and it was just a question of time, as he could not get well. Governor Patterson (we were close friends) talked with me on several occasions as to whom he would appoint in case Mr. Kay died. Several names were suggested and secret investigations made, but no final decision was made until one day I said, "Governor, do you recall coming to me in 1922 with a committee, asking me to become a candidate for State Treasurer?" He said he did, and I said, "Well, if you thought me competent then, am I not competent now?"

He said, "Yes, you shall have the appointment." So time went on, but Mr. Kay got better and Mr. Patterson passed away. Mr. Kay lived until after Governor Meier took office and when Mr. Kay passed away, he appointed Rufus Holman.

41

I have been successful, not in a financial way but in a moral way. I am afraid I have not laid away enough finances for support in our old age, I afraid, but I have stored up a host of friendships or real and true friends. Maud and I have lived a happy life. Our children have grown to be a fine man and a fine woman, healthy and strong. They both have good positions and are getting along in the world as all good citizens should. They are of fine dispositions and reputations above reproach.

It would be wrong for me to close this article without saying something of my companion. I became acquainted with the Rundlett family upon moving to Salem in 1890. I was then fifteen years old. While I was working at the State Asylum, Maud worked there also and during the years 1895-1897, we were together a great deal. We became engaged in 1897 I believe, and were married on October 12, 1898, so we have been traveling in double harness more than thirty-five years. A more faithful, patient wife, kind and loving mother, has never been. Not one of the nagging kind, but always putting up with my shortcomings, happy and loving, always helpful with advice and never looking on the dark side. She has lived a life of the Golden Rule. To my knowledge she has never done one of her fellow man a wrong and always is ready and willing to lend a helping hand. I can truthfully call her "Blessed." Now,

> "Let me grow lovely growing old
> So many fine things do.
> Laces and ivory and gold,
> And silks need not be new;
> There is a healing in old trees,
> Old streets a glamour hold;
> Why may not I, as well as these,
> Grow lovely, growing old?"

In 1934, just ten years ago and in my 59th year, I wrote the preceding account of my life. I am now in my 69th year and will try and account for some of the things that have happened since that time. Guess I will make this a regular ten accounting. [He did not do so] I was State Deputy Real Estate Commissioner ten years ago in 1934. I held that office until November, 1936. Charles A. Martin, a Democrat, was elected Governor of the State, and many Democrats were seeking positions as state employees, and the Governor, in order to keep peace in his own ranks, had to remove several Republicans from office and appoint faithful Democrats in their places. So in 1936, I walked the plank as they say. I was succeeded by William L. Graham, a very good friend. Graham was a realtor in Portland, had served as president of the Portland Realty Board, and two sessions in the Legislature from Multnomah County. In fact, he was a State Representative at the time of his appointment.

Donald Woodard, a young man in Portland who had just succeeded his father as head of the Woodard Realty Company of Portland, one of the older firms of the city, was negotiating for the purchase of the Wakefield-Fries Realty and Insurance business. Wakefield-Fries Company was the oldest realty organization in the City of Portland. After my resignation as Real Estate Commissioner, I was in Portland and Mr. Donald Woodard asked me to his office for a conversation at which time he told me he was negotiating for the purchase of the Wakefield-Fries Realty and Insurance Company and if the deal went through he would like to have me come with him as his sales manager with the understanding that I would close all deals made in his office. This was a new venture but was perfectly sound. The closing of a deal is sometimes very difficult, and all parties to a deal must have their interests protected both from a legal as well as an ethical standpoint. So Mr. Woodard thought I was just the man for this place. Salary was not mentioned but we went ahead on the assumption that the salary would be ample. Woodard finally closed his deal; I had waited too long in January, 1937 for him to get ready for business, and when things were finally arranged we talked salary. The best I could do with him was $100 per month and commission, which would have netted me about $200 per month and after years would not have been more than $300 per month and with no chance of buying into the firm. I finally turned his offer down, took out a Real Estate Brokers License and went into the office of J. F. Ulrich Company in Salem, Oregon. I had been acquainted with Ulrich for years; he had been in business for about fifteen years and had a very

43

nice little business worked up. I did not buy into the business, as he did not care to sell, but went in with the agreement that he was to furnish the room, pay all expenses, including advertising, and that I was to pay him 25 % of whatever commissions I earned. Should I make any money other than commissions, by reason of my real estate business, it was to be my money.

While I was in the office of Real Estate Commissioner, I made a special study of methods of appraisals, feeling at some time I might put out my shingle as an appraiser of lands. I believe it was sometime in February that I made my connections with J. F. Ulrich Company, and for the first months things were pretty slow but early in April of that year, 1937, Mr. and Mrs. Walter Walling came to Oregon the from East and Mrs. Walling had inherited quite a sum of money from her father's estate. She was anxious to make some investments. They came to me and I had them look over an apartment which could be purchased for $50,000 and was a good investment at that price. Well, believe it or not, I took them over to the apartment at about 2:30 in the afternoon and at 3:30 p.m. they had given me a down payment of $5,000. I made up the papers in the deal and Mr. and Mrs. Fisher, the owners, signed and I had that deal in escrow that afternoon. My commission was $2,500 and things began to look up.

But that did not last; it was just one of those things. On the whole I made some very good deals while I was with the J. F. Ulrich Company, and on the side, I did quite a bit of appraisal work which was good pay. My charge for appraising was $25.00 per day, and if it was necessary for me to appear in court with reference to the value of property, my charge was $25.00 as expert testimony. I have done a lot of appraisal work since I left the State Real Estate Office. From 1938 up until the time I closed my real estate office in Salem, I was a member of the Appraisal Committee of the Salem Realty board and for four years of that time, Chairman of the Board. It was during my term as Chairman that we drafted a new form of appraisal report for our customers, and this form was so well thought of that it was adopted by the State Association of Real Estate Boards and also the California State Association.

44

While I was with the State and the Real Estate Department, I was particularly interested in organization work. In every community where there were a few brokers, I worked with them to organize a Realty Board. So when I left the office we had twenty-three realty organizations in the State of Oregon. I found after I had been with the J.F. Ulrich Company for a short time that the Salem Realty Board was not functioning as an organization. I was surprised, as I had helped to organize this board back in 1923. It was then known as the Marion-Polk Counties Realty Board. This was due to the fact that there were very few brokers in Polk County and they wanted to affiliate. This ran along for a few years and the name was finally changed to the Salem Realty Board. They functioned for some time, but in 1937 when I began to check into the situation, I found they had not had a meeting since 1934. Well, needless to say, I got busy and a meeting was called and arrangements made for a meeting in the near future for the purpose of electing new officers. I made application for membership, was accepted, and we were set to go.

The meeting day arrived and William McGilchrist was elected President (I do not recall who the other officers were), and from that time to the present, Salem has had one of the most active Realty Boards in the State of Oregon. Their Constitution and By-laws were outdated; first they were organized as the Marion-Polk Counties Realty Board; afterward as the Salem Realty Board. They had changed their name only, so they appointed me chairman of a committee to draft a new Constitution and By-Laws. I made my draft and presented it to the Board and it was adopted making us up to date. I was elected President by the Board in 1938 and again in 1939.

During my administration, the State Association had at their annual meeting concluded to ask for a new Real Estate License Law, one calling for examination and issuing licenses on merit only, and there were several new and progressive features they desired the new law to contain. I was appointed chairman of a committee to draft this new law. The law was finally drafted and presented to the Legislature of 1939. This was a very progressive Act and was so different in viewpoint that several members of the Legislature doubted whether or not they should support the measure. We were having hard sledding as we did not have any lobby support; all was volunteer work and work only when one could spend the time. So the Association asked me to go to work and see that the bill passed, paying me $300 to do the work. Well, the result was that we got the bill through both Houses and was signed by Governor Charles A. Sprague on June 15, 1939. There have been a few amendments since its original passage, but Oregon now has one of the best Real Estate License Laws now functioning in the United States of America.

On April 21, 1939, a resolution was offered to the Salem Realty Board, and adopted also by the State Association of Real Estate Boards, commending me for my untiring effort in the preparation of and passage of the new Real Estate Licensing Law, copies of which were given to me. Well, it just goes to show that a fellow can accumulate a vast number of friendships as he goes through this life's journey.

When I stepped down as president of the Salem Realty Board I was elected Treasurer of the Board, which position I head until I resigned from Board membership. I was also a Director of the Board at the time I resigned, which office I had held since I was first elected President of the Board. I remained with the J. F. Ulrich Company until 1940 when War was declared on Germany and Japan, World War II, at which time the U.S. Government built a encampment in Benton County, acquiring some 60,000 acres of land in both Polk and Benter Counties. I was selected as one of the appraisers of these lands and put in a straight 60 days at the work. They were in a hurry so wanted us to work Sundays and every day until the job was completed. There were seven appraisers and it took us just 60 days to complete the job for which we received the sum of $25.00 per day. This was in the fall of 1940. I think we finished our work about November.

When I returned to the Ulrich office, Mr. Ulrich had acquired a gravel company and was devoting his time to the gravel and sand business, so I purchased an undivided one-half interest in the real estate business of N. J. Lindgren and formed the co-partnership of Lindgren and Johnson. We did a good business, much better than I was doing with the J. F. Ulrich Company. In fact, I acquired a very nice business from people living in the Benton and Polk County areas taking them to find another farm. My acquaintance with them brought us quite a bit of business. My part of the real estate business was handling farm property, but I had made a study of farm appraisals during our work for the Government. We attended night school at the Corvallis College [Oregon State University] making a study of soils, so I was considered an expert on farm soils and farm prices. So, when a farm listing was given to us, I always went out over the farm, studied the soil, and fixed the value. Then when we had a customer, I really knew what I was talking to him about.

I continued this until the fall of 1943 when the work of going over the farm lands was a hardship as I was not as young as I once was, so I applied to my friend Governor Earl Snell, for an appointment at which I could make a fair living and yet not be tied down; outside work preferred. Mr. Snell told me he thought there was a position under the State Board of Control that I would like, that he would look into the matter and let me know. The Board of Control, being made up of the Governor, Secretary of State and State Treasurer, is so much more satisfactory because the position does not change at the whim of an election. One of these officers might be succeeded by a Democrat but that would make no difference with my position as long as the work was done to the satisfaction of the Board. Well, Mr. Roy Mills, Secretary of the Board of Control, called me the next day and asked if I could come up to his office for a talk. I did, and he informed me that he had a position open that called for considerable travel and if I did not mind that he was sure I could do the work. They were to furnish me a car, typewriter, and whatever other necessary things I needed, such as bags, briefcases, pay all my expenses, and also pay me $200 per month for the first year, $225 for the second year, and $250 for the third and remaining years. I was to stop at the best hotels, and eat at the best eating places. Well, this sounded good to me, so I told Mr. Mills that I would be ready to go to work on October 15, 1944. I have just completed my first year, like the work, and am practically my own boss. I spend the weekends at home unless I make a trip to Southern or Eastern Oregon; then I am away for three weeks. But on these trips Mother [Maud, his wife] goes with me. In fact, we have been at home but very little since I went on the job. She has nothing but her flowers and yard to keep her home so away we go and have enjoyed the past year immensely. We have covered every county in the State this last year and have driven a distance of more than 16,000 miles and proud to say without an accident.

When I accepted this job with the State, I informed some of the boys at the Salem Realty Board that I intended resigning as a member of the Board as of November 15. That was at least one month away. We of the Board had been for some time working on a plan with the National Association of Real Estate Boards to change the name of our board from Salem Realty Board to The Salem Board of Realtors. This more definitely fixed the term realtor in the mind of the public. The national association wants all the boards to do this. But in order to do so the Constitution and By-laws of each board has to be changed to conform to the rules of the National Association. Another thing was bothering Board members and that was under War regulations, cities throughout the land were being bothered by set up of the Government whereby the Government through its agents regulated the rental and sale of real estate, and this was working a hardship on persons having property to sell as well as the purchasers of property. The rental situation was bad, very bad, when the Government took over to regulate. So these two things bothered the boys very much and they asked that I stay on the Board until both of these matters were fixed. So I was again appointed to change the Constitution and By-laws of the Salem Realty Board to the Salem Board of Realtors. After drawing same, submitting to the Board for their approval, it was sent to the National Association for their approval; and some few slight changes made, came back, and were adopted. So Salem now has the only Board recognized by the National Association in the Northwest as a Board of Realtors. Well, the next matter to fix up was the rental situation. I was appointed chairman of a committee to interview Mr. Gague, agent in Portland representing the Government. The committee called on Mr. Gague to see if we might not work out some plan whereby the City Council would take the matter over and regulate the matter as a local concern. We were informed that this had been tried but it was impossible to get the Council to make an appropriation to take care of expenses, as it would take the work of one person continually. He said that might work out but doubted it. Well, sir, we came back home, I drew up a City Ordinance that levied a fee of from fifty cents to five dollars on all properties, rooms, etc. for rent and after fighting this through three meetings of the City Council, it passed. The Ordinance was known as the Fair Rents Committee, and this committee had the authority to either raise or lower rents in the City of Salem. The fee charged was small but brought in something more than $3000 per year. A good clerk was employed and Salem has been free from any trouble on account of the Government control.

Time passed on and October 15th came. I resigned and went to work for the State. Mr. Lindgren purchased my undivided one-half interest in the business of Lindgren & Johnson. [The office had been located in what was known as the Hollywood District in North Salem on Capitol Street] At the next meeting of the Board, and in my absence, the Board voted me a Life Membership in the Salem Board of Realtors sending me a copy of my Honorary Membership. I surely appreciate this action on the part of my fellow members and friends.

I am now on a trip to Southern Oregon. Mother is not with me at this time as she felt that she should stay at home and can some fruit. I will return to Salem about the first week of October and then prepare for a trip into Eastern Oregon and will be there three weeks or a month. I want to clean up Eastern Oregon before the winter weather sets in. Mother will accompany me on this trip.

The genealogy of Charles Virgil Johnson is included in the Genealogy Section of this book.

AN ORAL HISTORY BY LULU JOHNSON McHARGUE

A Harney County, Oregon Historical
Society History Project

PAULINE BRAYMEN [LATER AS PB]: This is Pauline Braymen, and I'm interviewing Lulu McHargue on December 14, 1979 at the Presbyterian Nursing Home in Ontario, Oregon. Were you born in Harney County?

LULU McHARGUE: [LATER AS LM]: I was born in Burns, Oregon [now Harney County, previously Grant County].

PB: In Burns. And what were your parent's names?

LM: W. W. Johnson, they called him "Broady."

PB: Okay, I was wondering when Mr. Jones told me about you if Broady Johnson was your father.

LM: And my mother was Carolyn and her maiden name was Harris.

PB: Were they married in Burns, or did they come to Burns from somewhere else?

LM: No, they were married in Jefferson [Oregon].

PB: Do you know when they came to Harney County?

LM: Well about '49 in 19 and 48 or 49. [She meant 1848-9]

PB: What year were you born?

LM: I was born in 1887.

PB: So they probably came in about 1884 then.

LM: Yeah, they probably did. They by, you know, the wagon train. And there was a lot of them came together. And I heard my mother talk about being in the train, and where they had to go in a circle, you know, when they camped at night. And then they had different problems with the Native Americans on their way, and even after they was in Harney County [OR]. I guess I must have been a small girl, whey they had Native problems there to, the Paiute Indians.

PB: But they came to Harney County from Jefferson County on the coast? [She meant Jefferson, Oregon in the Willamette Valley, not the Coast]

LM: Uh huh.

PB: Did they grow up there or had they come from somewhere else.

LM: Yes, and I think they were born in Jefferson County. [wrong]

PB: They were raised in that part of the country. Well tell me about your father, I know the name. What did he do, what was his business?

LM: He was a saloon man. He had a saloon, and he was a gambler too.

PB: Was that the Red Front Saloon, or do you remember the name of the saloon that he...

LM: No, I think it was the White Front.

PB: White Front.

LM: Uh huh.

PB: You went to school in Burns?

LM: Yes, I went to school in Burns. And I married when I was quite young. Yeah, I was 16 when I married, and that was when I was out of the eighth grade.

PB: Were you married at home, or in a church?

LM: Yes, we were married in our home, in our own home.

PB: Do you remember the minister's name?

LM: I've forgotten it right now.

PB: Did you have a special dress that you wore for the wedding?

LM: Well, I had my Fourth of July dress, but it had to be lengthened. So they took the ruffle off of the top and put it on the bottom. So I had the wedding dress out of my Fourth of July dress. And my husband was in the Red Front delivery stable at that time.

PB: Well, that where I got the Red Front idea I knew that......

LM: Uh huh. Well this was ....where my Dad's saloon was, it was a saloon. Do you live in Burns now?

PB: I live about three miles out of Burns on a ranch. My dad was Henry Ausmus. Do you remember the Ausmus name?

LM: Yes, I remember. And do you remember Lloyd Johnson?

PB: I don't. The name sounds familiar, but I don't.

LB: Well, he was in Lawen, he lived in Lawen.

PB: Okay, I know. Was he related to Wayne Johnson?

LM: No, no there were other Johnsons, but ....

PB: My dad would probably know, because that's where he grew up.

LM: LeRoy Johnson probably graduated with your Dad.

PB: Yeah, I know LeRoy.

LM: Uh huh. LeRoy was out to see me one day...and did you know Hester Goodman?

PB: I know the name.

LM: He was the sheriff, you know, of Harney County for ten years.

PB: Was he the one that was shot at the Chautauqua? Were you there at the time?

LM: No, we wasn't in Burns. We was on a homestead. We weren't very far from where he was shot though.

PB: Where did you homestead?

LM: In the Barren Valley, or Crowley. They name it after we [who] homesteaded there. It was just a barren valley at that time.

PB: Well, that's quite a ways from Burns, that about eight.....

LM: Well, we went by wagon, and we had mules, you know.

PB: How many....

LM: We had two little children at that time, two little boys.

PB: How many days did it take to go from Burns to Crowley?

LM: Just about three days. We stopped at the Visher Ranch the first night, and then on to the Turnbull Ranch, and then home. The Turnbull Ranch was what they call Moreville afterward.

53

PB: Moreville, that's a new name to me, I don't remember hearing that before.

LM: Do you know where the Tom Turnbull Ranch was, did you?

PB: I think so. How long did you live at Crowley, or Barren Valley?

LM: I think it was about twenty years we lived there.

PB: Did you have cattle?

LM: U huh, we ran cattle.

PB: Did you put any crops in at all, or did you have meadow hay?

LM: Yes, we didn't have very good luck with some of them though. We had to go out and buy hay. He had to take, my husband had to take the cattle across, to you know, to the Owyhee and buy hay. And at that time he had to pay $35 a ton for it.

PB: That was a good price for those days.

LM: That was a big price. Then he brought the cattle home, and ....we had to borrow money, you know, to feed the cattle. And of course why we didn't have them very long until they come and took our cattle away from us, because we couldn't make our payments.

PB: Was this during the depression?

LM: Uh huh, one depression.

PB: One depression. So are we talking about 1930, or before that?

LM: No. Then we moved to Vale, and we had two more children then, Marilyn and Jim. They were born at Vale. One of them was born, Jim was born in 1930 and Marilyn was born in 1933. Of

54

course, I had eight children to start in with. Warren was the oldest one.

PB: He was born in Harney County? Warren was the oldest?

LM: Uh huh. Yeah, he was born in Harney County, and so was my other son. And then of course when we moved over to Crowley, why we were in Malheur County.

PB: I think so. The line goes right through over there somewhere.

LM: My thinker isn't as good as it ought to be ....but I was 92 my last birthday. I will be 93 on February the 14th.

PB: A Valentine's baby?

LM: Uh huh. My oldest sister [Ada] was born on Valentine's Day, too. She's seventeen years older than I was. And they were all the Johnson bunch.

PB: I've heard of lots of people mention Broady Johnson, especially as one of the early ...

LM: Old pioneers.

PB: Old pioneers in Burns.

LM: Well I have his Dad's biography, and I have ours. But I got everything all mixed up after I came up here, so I don't know where anything is.

PB: Do you have a daughter, or a son that lives in Ontario or Vale?

LM: I have five that live right around here close. Jim and Nellie, and Gretchen, Lynn, and Tim.

PB: You are very lucky to have them so close to you.

LM: Oh, I am. And my oldest daughter though lives in San Diego.

PB: Do you remember what the town of Burns looked like when you were a girl growing up?

LM: Is that recording now?

PB: Uh huh, uh huh.

LM: I wanted to hear you ask that?

PB: Okay.

LM: (Laughter) I remember a long time ago….at that time, and she had one of them. And oh, we had so much fun with it. She played the piano, and then they said, Now then, Lulu, sit there and why don't you sing? It was terrible when I listened at it, after I sang. Because I'm afraid to come home in the dark, and it was dark! (Laughter)

PB: We don't sound to one another, I mean, we don't sound to ourselves as we sound to other people. And it really is a shock when we hear yourselves the first time. Because you don't hear yourself the same way that you sound to other people.

LM: (Laughter) We really had a ball with that thing. We still talk about it whenever we are together. We remember the things that we said, and it was so silly. But we were quite a bunch anyway. We always liked to laugh and joke.

PB: That's what keeps you young.

LM: Yes, I think so.

PB: You were talking about your Fourth of July dress. I've heard some other people tell me about their Fourth of July dress. This was a special occasion, wasn't it?

LM: Oh yes, uh huh. My mother sat up probably until midnight making it.

PB: Was it white?

LM: Uh huh.

PB: Did it have a sash?

LM: Well, it had ruffles all down.

PB: It had ruffles.

LM: Yes, and it had a blouse and the sash around the waist, just like they are wearing now.

PB: Do you remember Vela Richardson?

LM: Uh I....

PB: I can't remember what her maiden name was now. She lived out, they lived out by Wright's Point when they were children, and she had a Fourth of July dress, a special dress to wear then.

LM: I remember the name very well, but I can't place just who she was. But I went over to Pioneer Days this last time, and well, really the only ones that was young, was we grew up together, was Frankie Pelton, and her name used to be Shelley. And Grandma Mace, and her name was McQueen. And then I met Frank King, he used to be out on the farm. But there wasn't very many.

PB: No, the people from your era are thinning down, there aren't so many anymore.

LM: No.

PB: I remember now, I knew I had seen you before. That's where I saw you, at the Pioneer Day.

57

LM: Uh huh. And that's where I remember seeing you, too. Well, did you speak or something?

PB: Oh, I think they probably introduced me, because I was there for publicity purposes. In fact, I record the program every year, so that they have a record of that.

LM: Well, that's nice.

PB: And it will be in the library, and you know, years from now people can listen to it and know what it was like. So I usually get introduced, and that's probably why you saw me.

LM: Uh huh, probably was. Well I think you are doing just very well, and it's nice to think of our young people to remember.

PB: Well, it's interesting to find out what it was like when things weren't quite so convenient. Now we jump in our car and we drive to Crowley in a couple of hours, where it took you three days to go. I think it's important to remember these things.

LM: I think we were all happy. I don't know why, but we were.

PB: Well life, the face of life, was much slower. I think everyone had more time to enjoy.

LM: Of course, we lost a little boy, he was killed with a run away horse. And later, lost another baby. Then later my oldest boy died. But the rest of them are alive.

PB: What was your husband's first name?

LM: Rush.

PB: Rush McHargue?

LM: Uh huh. McHargue.

PB: When did he come to Harney County?

LM: Well, he was about, he was 21 I think, when he came.

PB: He was 21 when he came. And you were married shortly thereafter, after he came?

LM: Yes.

PB: You were 16 when you were married?

LM: Uh huh. Would you like a drink of grape juice?

PB: Well, thank you, I just finished lunch. We ate at the Charolais Restaurant, and they serve a really nice buffet. It was really good.

[At this point, Lulu Johnson McHargue's nursing home roommate was involved and that portion has been eliminated in this account. What follows is a comment that Lula Johnson McHargue made at the end of the oral interview]:

LM: I didn't see a train until I was 22 years old.

[Lulu Belle Johnson McHargue died July 29, 1986 in Ontario, Oregon at the age of 99.]

BIOGRAPHY OF ALVAH PERCIVAL BROWN

Alvah Percival Brown was one of three children of William H. Brown and Nancy A. Johnson Brown and was born in Pitcairn, NY on September 16, 1846. Later, he was joined by his brother, Charles Hiram Brown and a sister, Clara E. Brown.

The naming of Alvah Percival by his parents was typical of Nineteenth Century practices where children were named after

59

relatives. Alvah Percival Brown's grandfather and uncle [Charles Alvah Johnson and Hiram Alvah Johnson] both had "Alvah" as a middle name, and "Percival" was the name of one of William H. Brown's brothers, Percival H. Brown.

In young adulthood, Alvah P. Brown learned the farming trade from his father, and from 1877 to 1884 he farmed his father's farm. Later, his son, Sherman William Brown by Alvah's first wife, Manie Cleland, farmed the same farm from 1884 to 1897.

Alvah married Manie Cleland, on March 23, 1870 but she died July 22, 1875 from what some believe were complications from childbirth of Sherman William Brown who was born July 31, 1873 in Edwards, New York. Manie Cleland was the daughter of William Cleland and Jane Kerr Cleland. Following the death of his mother, Manie Cleland Brown, Sherman was raised by Alvah's brother and sister-in-law, Charles H. and Martha Noble Brown, until Alvah's marriage to Sarah Grant, daughter of Thomas Grant and Julia Rushton Grant of Russell, NY, on June 20, 1877.

Alvah P. Brown was an enterprising young man, and after 1884, after buying the West Edwards cheese factory, he became a cheese maker and later had businesses in Fowler, and Little York, all in Northern New York. In 1885, Alvah rented his York factory to his cousin, Sidney Brown, son of Robert Brown, William H. Brown's brother.

Beginning in January of 1885, Alvah and his family moved in with his parents to stay until spring. Sometime between 1884 and 1896, Alvah and Sarah lived in Fowler, NY. However, Alvah Brown owned the Little York Cheese Factory and adjoining lands in 1894 so it is believed that the Browns lived in Little York, NY. In later years his residence was in Edwards, NY where Alvah owned and managed the Cheese Factory that he had previously rented to his cousin, Sidney Brown.

Alvah died of diabetes at age sixty after a year's illness. At the end, he was in a coma the last twenty-four hours. He died at 6:30 a.m. on

Saturday, March 3, 1906. He was a member of the F & A.M. Lodge from 1867 and was a member of the [Methodist] Union Church in Edwards, New York.

Sarah Grant Brown's parents, Thomas Grant and Julia Rushton were among the first settlers of the Edwards-Russell, New York area where they cleared land and built a log cabin. Sarah Brown was formerly a seamstress and was especially active during World War II with the Red Cross. Even after her eyesight failed, she continued crocheting and knitting for her family. She died in her sleep on January 1, 1954 in Gouverneur, NY where she lived with her daughter, Rose [Mary Rose] Dulack-Maloy. Sarah was a member of the Methodist Church and the Order of the Eastern Star and Rebeccas.

GENEALOGY

Ancestors of Ira Johnson

Generation One

1. IRA[1] JOHNSON (*Jonathan,* #2) was born on 7 Jun 1753 at Sturbridge, Worcester Co., MA. He married Abigail Furbush, daughter of Benjamin Forbush and Elizabeth Marble, in Sep 1784. He died at NY. He began military service at MA in the Revolutionary War. He appeared on the census of 1800 at Stillwater, Saratoga Co., NY. [see #26, page 95]

Generation Two

2. JONATHAN[2] JOHNSON (*Nathaniel,* #4) was born on 30 Jan 1710. He married Jerusha Green (see #3) after 9 Sep 1739 at Leicester, Worcester Co., Massaschusetts Bay Colony. He married Abigail Goodale, daughter of John Goodale and Hannah Colburn, on 16 Jun 1756. He died on 30 Aug 1776 at Sturbridge, Worcester Co., Massaschusetts Bay Colony, at age 66.

Children of Jonathan[2] Johnson and Jerusha Green (see #3) were as follows:

    i.   NATHANIEL[1]; baptized 12 Oct 1740 at Sturbridge, MA.

    ii.   JONATHAN; born 21 Oct 1742 at Leicester, MA.

    iii.   JERUSHA; born 26 Nov 1744 at Grafton; she and Asa Humphrey obtained a marriage license 28 Feb 1767 at Sturbridge, MA; married Asa Humphrey 5 Apr 1767; died 27 Mar 1808 at age 63.

iv.   MARTHA; born 31 Oct 1749 at Woodstock, CT; she and Jason Allen obtained a marriage license 4 Mar 1773 at Sturbridge, MA.

1.   v.   IRA.

3. JERUSHA[2] GREEN was born before 1719. She and Jonathan Johnson obtained a marriage license on 9 Sep 1739 at Leicester, Worcester Co., Massaschusetts Bay Colony. She married Jonathan Johnson (see #2), son of Nathaniel Johnson II and Mary Haven, after 9 Sep 1739 at Leicester, Worcester Co., Massaschusetts Bay Colony. She died on 18 Aug 1754 at Woodstock, Windham Co., CT.

Generation Three

4. NATHANIEL[3] JOHNSON II (*Nathaniel*, #6) was born in 1680. He married Mary Haven (see #5), daughter of John Haven and Hannah Hitchins, on 23 Nov 1708. He died on 21 Jul 1733.

Children of Nathaniel[3] Johnson II and Mary Haven (see #5) were as follows:

2.   i.   JONATHAN[2].

ii.   JAMES; born 21 Jul 1711; married Susanna Waters; married Sarah Holbrook; married Anna Bishop.

iii.   JOHN; born 20 Oct 1714; married Abigail (--?--). He was a physician.

iv.   HANNAH; born 21 Feb 1717.

v.   NATHANIEL III; born 4 Oct 1718; died 21 Jul 1733 at age 14.

5. MARY[3] HAVEN (*John*, #8) was born before 1685. She married Nathaniel Johnson II (see #4), son of Nathaniel Johnson and Abigail May, on 23 Nov 1708.

She lived before 23 Nov 1708 at Lynn, MA.

6. NATHANIEL^4 JOHNSON (*Humphrey*, #10) was born on 21 Mar 1666 at Hingham, Plymouth Colony (now MA). He married Abigail May (see #7) circa 1682 at Hingham, Plymouth Colony (now MA). He died on 4 May 1755 at Pomfret, Windham Co., CT, at age 89.

He began military service in 1690 Canada Expedition under Capt. Andrews.

Children of Nathaniel^4 Johnson and Abigail May (see #7) were as follows:

- 4.   i.   NATHANIEL^3 II.
- ii.   ABIGAIL; born Jul 1683; died young.
- iii.   JOSEPH; born 9 Sep 1685; married Lydia Twitchell, daughter of Joseph TWITCHELL and Lydia (--?--), 13 May 1709 at Sherborn, MA; died 25 Mar 1745 at Holliston, MA, at age 59.
- iv.   ABIGAIL; born 1 Apr 1687; died 15 Jan 1782 at Promfret, CT, at age 94.
- v.   ELISHA; born 12 Mar 1688; married Abigail Weld between 25 May 1708 and 1709.
  He lived at Sutton, MA.
- vi.   THOMAS; born 12 Mar 1690.
- vii.   MARY; born 11 Mar 1691; married Noah Morse 12 Jul 1705.
- viii.   JONATHAN; born 16 Mar 1692; died 6 Jan 1702 at Sherborn, MA, at age 9.
- ix.   MARTHA; born 19 Feb 1696/97 at Sherborn, Middlesex Co., MA; married Timothy Sabin, son of Benjamin Sabin and Sarah Parker, 5 Feb 1717/18 at Pomfret, Windham Co., CT; died 2 Oct 1745 at Pomfret, Windham Co., CT, at age 48.
- x.   MEHITABLE; born 15 Oct 1699; married Humphrey Goodell, son of Thomas Goodell and Sarah (--?--), 12 Jan 1727.

7. ABIGAIL^4 MAY was born in Jul 1666 at Hingham, Plymouth Co., MA. She married Nathaniel Johnson (see #6), son of Humphrey

Johnson and Ellen Cheney, circa 1682 at Hingham, Plymouth Colony (now MA). She died on 9 Apr 1745 at Pomfret, Windham Co., CT, at age 78.

8. JOHN[4] HAVEN was born before 1665. He married Hannah Hitchins (see #9).

Children of John[4] Haven and Hannah Hitchins (see #9) were:

    5.   i.   MARY[3].

9. HANNAH[4] HITCHINS was born before 1665. She married John Haven (see #8).

Generation Five

10. HUMPHREY[5] JOHNSON (*John*, #12) was baptized on 5 Nov 1620 at St. John the Baptist Church, Great Amwell, Co. Hertfordshire, England. He married Ellen Cheney (see #11), daughter of William Cheney and Margaret (or Margery) Mason, on 20 Mar 1641/42 at Roxbury, Suffolk Co., Massachusetts Bay Colony. He married Abigail Stansfull on 6 Dec 1678 at Roxbury, Suffolk Co., MA. He died on 24 Jul 1692 at Hingham, Plymouth Co., MA, at age 71.

He was an ancestor of Franklin D. Roosevelt. He emigrated on 8 Apr 1630. He lived in 1651 at Scituate, Massachusetts Bay Colony. He began military service King Philip's War in Capt. Isaac Johnson's Company.

Children of Humphrey[5] Johnson and Ellen Cheney (see #11) were as follows:

    i.   MEHITABLE[4]; born Sep 1644; married Samuel Hinsdale 31 Oct 1660; married John Root; married John Coleman 11 Mar 1679; died 4 Aug 1689 at age 44.

    ii.   MARTHA; baptized 12 Sep 1647 at Roxbury, MA; married Obadiah Morse, son of Daniel Morse and Lydia Fisher; died 1714.

    iii.   DEBORAH; baptized 20 Jan 1650.

iv. JOHN; born Mar 1653 at Roxbury, MA; died 12 Jun 1674 at Hingham, MA, at age 21.

v. JOSEPH; born 24 Jun 1655; died 6 Sep 1676 at Hingham, MA, at age 21.

vi. BENJAMIN; born 27 Aug 1657; married Rebecca Hershey, daughter of William Hershey and Rebecca Chubbock, 11 Jun 1683; died 26 Mar 1707 at age 49.

He was Blacksmith.

vii. MARGARET; born 22 Dec 1659 at Scituate, MA; married Josiah Leavitt 20 Oct 1676; died 5 Jun 1739 at age 79.

viii. MARY; born 19 Apr 1663 at Scituate, MA.

6. ix. NATHANIEL.

x. ISAAC; born 18 Feb 1667/68 at Hingham, MA; married Abigail Leavitt, daughter of John Leavitt, circa 1690; died 1735.

11. ELLEN[5] CHENEY (*William*, #14) was born circa 1626 at England. She married Humphrey Johnson (see #10), son of Capt. John Johnson and Mary Heath, on 20 Mar 1641/42 at Roxbury, Suffolk Co., Massachusetts Bay Colony. She died on 29 Sep 1678 at Hingham, Plymouth Co., MA.

She was also known as Elinor Cheney.

Generation Six

12. CAPT. JOHN[6] JOHNSON was born before 1593 at England. He married Mary Heath (see #13), daughter of William Heath and Agnes Cheney, on 21 Sep 1613 at St. Mary the Virgin Church, Ware, Co. Hertfordshire, England. He married Margery (--?--) at England. He married Grace Negus before Oct 1656. He died on 30 Sep 1659 at Roxbury, Suffolk Co., Massachusetts Bay Colony. Johnson lived in Ware and Great Amwell before coming to the Massachusetts Bay Colony. He left on 6 Apr 1630 from Isle of Wight, (South Hampton), England. He immigrated on 22 Jun 1630 to

Massachusetts Bay Colony (now MA). He lived at Roxbury, Massachusetts Bay Colony.

Children of Capt. John[6] Johnson and Mary Heath (see #13) were as follows:

    i.   MARY[5]; baptized 31 Jul 1614 at Ware, Co. Hertfordshire, England; married Roger Mowry circa 1644; married John Kingsley 16 Mar 1673/74; died 29 Jan 1678/79 at Reboboth, MA, at age 64.

    ii. ISAAC; baptized 11 Feb 1615 at St. John the Baptist Church, Great Amwell, Co. Hertfordshire, England; married Elizabeth Porter, daughter of Adrian Porter and Margaret Plomer, 20 Jan 1636/37 at Roxbury, MA; died 19 Dec 1675 at "Great Swamp", North Kingston, RI, at age 60.

    iii. JOHN; baptized 5 Apr 1618 at St. John the Baptist Church, Great Amwell, Co. Hertfordshire, England; buried 8 Jul 1627 at St. Mary the Virgin Church, Ware, Co. Hertfordshire, England.

    iv. ELIZABETH; baptized 22 Aug 1619 at St. John the Baptist Church, Great Amwell, Co. Hertfordshire, England; married Robert Pepper, son of Richard Pepper and Mary (--?--), 14 Mar 1642/43.

10.   v.   HUMPHREY.

    vi. JOSEPH; baptized 20 Apr 1622 at St. John the Baptist Church, Great Amwell, Co. Hertfordshire, England.

    vii. SUSAN; baptized 16 Jul 1623 at St. John the Baptist Church, Great Amwell, Co. Hertfordshire, England; died before 15 Aug 1629 at Ware, England; buried 15 Aug 1629 at St. Mary the Virgin Church Cemetery, Ware, Co. Hertfordshire, England.

viii. SARAH; baptized 12 Nov 1624 at St. Mary the Virgin Church, Ware, Co. Hertfordshire, England; married Hugh Burt circa 1645; married William Bartram circa 1653 at Lynn, Essex Co., MA; died before 6 Nov 1694 at Swansey, MA.

ix. JOSEPH; baptized 6 Mar 1626/27 at St. Mary the Virgin Church, Ware, Co. Hertfordshire, England; died before 30 Mar 1627 at Ware, England; buried 30 Mar 1627 at St. Mary the Virgin Church Cemetery, Ware, Co. Hertfordshire, England.

x. HANNAH; baptized 23 Mar 1627/28.

13. MARY[6] HEATH (*William,* #16) was baptized on 24 Mar 1593/94 at Ware, Co. Hertfordshire, England. She married Capt. John Johnson (see #12) on 21 Sep 1613 at St. Mary the Virgin Church, Ware, Co. Hertfordshire, England. She died before 15 May 1629 at Ware, Co. Hertfordshire, England. She was buried on 15 May 1629 at St. Mary the Virgin Church Cemetery, Ware, Co. Hertfordshire, England.

14. WILLIAM[6] CHENEY (*Lawrence,* #18) was born before 1605 at England. He married Margaret (or Margery) Mason (see #15). He died on 2 May 1667 at Roxbury, MA.

He lived at Roxbury, Massachusetts Bay Colony. He was an assessor on 21 Feb 1648.

Children of William[6] Cheney and Margaret (or Margery) Mason (see #15) were as follows:

11. i. ELLEN[5].

ii. MARGARET; married Thomas Hastings Apr 1650.

iii. THOMAS.

iv. WILLIAM; died Sep 1681.

v. JOHN; born 29 Sep 1639 at Roxbury, MA; died 1671.

vi. MEHITABEL; born 1 Jun 1643.

15. MARGARET (OR MARGERY)[6] MASON was born before 1606. She married William Cheney (see #14), son of Lawrence Cheney and Julian Waldren. She died 2 or 3 May 1686 at Boston, Suffolk Co.,

Massachusetts Bay Colony (now MA). She was buried on 3 Jul 1686 at Roxbury, MA.

Generation Seven

16. WILLIAM[7] HEATH (*Edward*, #20) was born ca 1550-55 at England. He married Agnes Cheney (see #17), daughter of Robert Cheney III and Joan Harrison, on 9 Jun 1580 at Parish of Waltham Abbey, Co. Essex, England. He died before 7 Jan 1624/25 at Ware, England. He was buried on 7 Jan 1624/25 at Ware, England.

Children of William[7] Heath and Agnes Cheney (see #17) were:

13.   i.   MARY[6].

17. AGNES[7] CHENEY (*Robert*, #22) was born circa 1560 at Waltham Abbey, Co. Essex, England. She married William Heath (see #16), son of Edward Heath and Alice (--?--), on 9 Jun 1580 at Parish of Waltham Abbey, Co. Essex, England.

18. LAWRENCE[7] CHENEY (*John*, #24) married Julian Waldren (see #19).

Children of Lawrence[7] Cheney and Julian Waldren (see #19) were:

14.   i.   WILLIAM[6].

19. JULIAN[7] WALDREN married Lawrence Cheney (see #18), son of John Cheney and Agnes (--?--).

Generation Eight

20. EDWARD[8] HEATH (*Robert*, #26) was born circa 1530 at England. He married Alice (--?--) (see #21) circa 1550 at England. He died before 8 Mar 1592/93 at Little Amwell, Ware, Co. Hertfordshire, England. He was buried on 8 Mar 1592/93 at Little Amwell, Ware Parish, Co. Hertfordshire, England.

Children of Edward[8] Heath and Alice (--?--) (see #21) were as follows:

        i.   MARGARET[7]; died before 6 Mar 1592/93.

16.   ii.   WILLIAM.

       iii.   ROBERT.

       iv.   JOAN; died after 6 Mar 1592/93.

       v.   ELIZABETH; married John King 3 Dec 1582 at Ware, England; died after 6 Mar 1592/93.

      vi.   THOMAS; married Agnes Woodburne 29 Nov 1599 at Ware, England.

     vii.   JAMES; baptized between 9 Mar 1560 and 1561 at Ware, England; buried 21 Sep 1562.

    viii.   JOHN; baptized between 28 Feb 1563 and 1564 at Great Amwell, England.

      ix.   ELLEN; baptized 9 Jul 1565 at Ware, England.

       x.   KATHERINE; baptized 20 Aug 1568 at Ware, England.

      xi.   RICHARD; baptized 20 Aug 1568 at Ware, England; died before 6 Mar 1592/93.

21. ALICE[8] (--?--) was born before 1530. She married Edward Heath (see #20), son of Robert Heath, circa 1550 at England. She died on 24 Dec 1593 at Ware, England. She was buried on 24 Dec 1593 at Ware, England.

22. ROBERT[8] CHENEY III (*Robert*, #27) married Joan Harrison (see #23), daughter of John Harrison and Agnes (--?--), Before 4 Jan 1549/50. He died after 1 Oct 1567.   He lived on 4 Jan 1550 at Waltham Abbey, Co. Essex, England.

Children of Robert[8] Cheney III and Joan Harrison (see #23) were as follows:

       i.   JOHN[7]

      ii. RALPH

     iii. WILLIAM; buried 1 Apr 1610 at Waltam Abbey.

17.   iv. AGNES.

      v. ROBERT

23. JOAN[8] HARRISON (*John*, #28) was born circa 1525. She married Robert Cheney III (see #22), son of Robert Cheney Jr, before 4 Jan 1549/50. She married John Hanford on 3 Jun 1568 at Waltham

Abbey, Essex, England. She died in 1597. She was buried on 14 May 1597 at Waltam Abbey, Essex, England.

24. JOHN[8] CHENEY married Agnes (--?--) (see #25).

Children of John[8] Cheney and Agnes (--?--) (see #25) were:

    18.   i.   LAWRENCE[7].

25. AGNES[8] (--?--) married John Cheney (see #24).

Generation Nine

26. ROBERT[9] HEATH was born circa 1510.

Children of Robert[9] Heath and an unknown spouse were:

    20.   i.   EDWARD[8].

27. ROBERT[9] CHENEY JR. (*Robert*, #30).

Children of Robert[9] Cheney Jr. and an unknown spouse were as follows:

    22.   i.   ROBERT[8] III.
            ii.   AGNES.

28. JOHN[9] HARRISON married Agnes (--?--) (see #29). He died between 4 Jan 1549 and 28 Apr 1551.

Children of John[9] Harrison and Agnes (--?--) (see #29) were as follows:

    23.   i.   JOAN[8].
            ii.   WILLIAM.
           iii.   ELIZABETH.
           iv.   MARGARET.

29. AGNES[9] (--?--) married John Harrison (see #28). She married (--?--) Britten.

Generation Ten

30. ROBERT[10] CHENEY SR..

Children of Robert[10] Cheney Sr. and an unknown spouse were:

    27.   i.   ROBERT[9] JR..

Ancestors of Abigail Furbush

"Furbush" and "Forbush/Forbes" are derived from Furbusher for those who were in the employment of the Royalty in England who "furbushed" the silver in the castle.

Generation One

1. ABIGAIL[1] FURBUSH (*Benjamin Forbush,* #2) was born on 19 Oct 1761. She and Ira Johnson obtained a marriage license in Sep 1784 at Sturbridge, MA. She lived before Sep 1784 at Brookfield, MA.

Generation Two

2. BENJAMIN[2] FORBUSH (*Aaron,* #4) was born on 23 Jan 1723. He married Elizabeth Marble (see #3), daughter of Nathaniel Marble and Susannah Woodcock.

He began military service on 1 Jan 1779 at Third Precinct, Brookfield, MA, Capt. Nathan Hamilton's Company, Rev. War.

Children of Benjamin[2] Forbush and Elizabeth Marble (see #3) were:

    1.   i.   ABIGAIL[1].

3. ELIZABETH[2] MARBLE (*Nathaniel,* #6) was born on 20 Apr 1736 at Hingham, MA. She married Benjamin Forbush (see #2), son of Aaron Forbush and Susanna Morse.

She lived at Brookfield, MA.

Generation Three

4. AARON[3] FORBUSH (*Thomas,* #8) was born on 3 Apr 1693 at Marlboro, Essex Co., MA. He married Susanna Morse (see #5), daughter of Samuel Morse and Grace (--?--), on 13 Jan 1719. He married Joanna or Suzanna (--?--). He died in Oct 1752 at age 59.

Children of Aaron[3] Forbush and Susanna Morse (see #5) were:

    2.   i.   BENJAMIN[2].

5. SUSANNA[3] MORSE (*Samuel*, #10) was born on 22 Dec 1698 at Watertown, Middlesex Co., MA. She married Aaron Forbush (see #4), son of Thomas Forbush and Dorcas Rice, on 13 Jan 1719. She died on 23 Jun 1790 at Wilmington, Windham Co., VT, at age 91.

6. NATHANIEL[3] MARBLE married Susannah Woodcock (see #7).

Children of Nathaniel[3] Marble and Susannah Woodcock (see #7) were:

    3.   i.   ELIZABETH[2].

7. SUSANNAH[3] WOODCOCK married Nathaniel Marble (see #6).

Generation Four

8. THOMAS[4] FORBUSH (*Daniel Forbes*, #12) was born on 6 Mar 1667 at Cambridge, MA. He married Dorcas Rice (see #9), daughter of Edward Rice and Anna (--?--). He died in May 1738 at age 71.

He lived at Westboro, MA. He was Deacon on 28 Oct 1724 at Westboro, MA.

Children of Thomas[4] Forbush and Dorcas Rice (see #9) were:

    4.   i.   AARON[3].

9. DORCAS[4] RICE (*Edward Rice*, #14) was born on 29 Jan 1664. She married Thomas Forbush (see #8), son of Daniel Forbes and Rebecca Perriman. She died on 24 Mar 1753 at age 89.

She was member of the Westboro Church.

10. SAMUEL[4] MORSE (*Joseph*, #16) was born on 4 Sep 1670 at Groton, Middlesex Co., MA. He married Grace (--?--) (see #11). He died on 10 Jul 1758 at Watertown or Marlborough, MA, at age 87.

Children of Samuel[4] Morse and Grace (--?--) (see #11) were:

    5.   i.   SUSANNA[3].

11. GRACE[4] (--?--) married Samuel Morse (see #10), son of Joseph Morse Jr. and Susanna Shattuck. She died on 10 Jul 1758 at Watertown, MA.

12. DANIEL[5] FORBES was born circa 1620 at Kinellar (probably), Scotland. He married Rebecca Perriman (see #13) on 26 Mar 1660 at Cambridge, Middlesex Co., Massachusetts Bay Colony. He married an unknown person on 23 May 1679 at Concord, MA. He died in Oct 1687 at Marlboro, MA.

Children of Daniel[5] Forbes and Rebecca Perriman (see #13) were:

      8.   i.   THOMAS[4].

13. REBECCA[5] PERRIMAN was born before 1640. She married Daniel Forbes (see #12) on 26 Mar 1660 at Cambridge, Middlesex Co., Massachusetts Bay Colony. She died on 3 May 1677.

14. EDWARD[5] RICE (*Edmund Rice*, #18) was baptized on 26 Oct 1622 at Co. Suffolk, England. He married Anna (--?--) (see #15). He married Agnes Bent. He died on 15 Aug 1712 at Marlbrough, MA, at age 89.

Children of Edward[5] Rice and Anna (--?--) (see #15) were:

      9.   i.   DORCAS[4].

15. ANNA[5] (--?--) was born before 1645. She married Edward Rice (see #14), son of Edmund Rice and Thomasine Frost.

16. JOSEPH[5] MORSE JR. (*Joseph*, #20) was born on 30 Apr 1637 at Watertown, Middlesex Co., Massachusetts Bay Colony. He married Susanna Shattuck (see #17), daughter of William Shattuck and Susanna (--?--), on 12 Apr 1661 at Watertown, MA. He died in 1677 at Watertown, Middlesex Co., Massachusetts Bay Colony.

Children of Joseph[5] Morse Jr. and Susanna Shattuck (see #17) were as follows:

          i.   an unknown person.
      10.   ii.   SAMUEL.

17. SUSANNA[5] SHATTUCK (*William*, #22) was born circa 1643 at Watertown, Middlesex Co., MA. She married Joseph Morse Jr. (see #16), son of Joseph Morse Sr. and Hester Pierce, on 12 Apr 1661 at Watertown, MA. She died on 16 Mar 1716 at Marlborough, MA.

18. EDMUND[6] RICE (*Henry*, #24) was born circa 1594 at Barkhamstead, Co. Hertfordshire, England. He married Thomasine Frost (see #19), daughter of Edward Frost and Thomasine Belgrave, on 15 Oct 1618 at Bury St. Edmunds, England. He died on 3 May 1663 at Marlborough, Middlesex Co., MA.   He lived in 1639 at Sudbury, MA.

Children of Edmund[6] Rice and Thomasine Frost (see #19) were as follows:

> i. HENRY[5]; born before 1619 at England; married Elizabeth Moore, daughter of Joseph Morse, 1643/4 (or 1642) at Sudbury, MA; died 10 Feb 1710/11 at Farmingham, MA.
>
> 14. ii. EDWARD.

19. THOMASINE[6] FROST (*Edward*, #26) was baptized on 11 Aug 1600. She married Edmund Rice (see #18), son of Henry Rice and Margaret Baker, on 15 Oct 1618 at Bury St. Edmunds, England. She died on 13 Jun 1654 at Sudbury, Middlesex Co., MA, at age 53.

20. JOSEPH[6] MORSE SR. (*Joseph*, #28) was born circa 1610/11 at Ipswich, Co. Suffolk, England. He married Hester Pierce (see #21), daughter of John Pierce and Elizabeth Trull, in 1636. He died on 4 Mar 1690/91 at Massachusetts Bay Colony (now MA).

He emigrated. He lived at Watertown, MA.

Children of Joseph[6] Morse Sr. and Hester Pierce (see #21) were:

> 16. i. JOSEPH[5] JR..

21. HESTER[6] PIERCE (*John*, #30) was born before 1620 at England. She married Joseph Morse Sr. (see #20), son of Joseph Morse and Dorothy (--?--), in 1636.

22. WILLIAM[6] SHATTUCK was born circa 1621/22 at England. He married Susanna (--?--) (see #23) circa 1642 at Watertown, Middlesex Co., Massachusetts Bay Colony (now MA). He died on 14 Aug 1672 at Watertown, Middlesex, Massachusetts Bay Colony (now MA).

Children of William[6] Shattuck and Susanna (--?--) (see #23) were:

    17.   i.   SUSANNA[5].

23. SUSANNA[6] (--?--) was born circa 1621. She married William Shattuck (see #22), son of Demarus (--?--), circa 1642 at Watertown, Middlesex Co., Massachusetts Bay Colony (now MA). She died on 11 Dec 1686.

Generation Seven

24. HENRY[7] RICE was born circa 1555 at Midlesex, England. He married Margaret Baker (see #25), daughter of Thomas Baker and Agnes Goldhop, on 22 Jun 1579.

    Children of Henry[7] Rice and Margaret Baker (see #25) were:

    18.   i.   EDMUND[6].

25. MARGARET[7] BAKER (*Thomas*, #33) was born circa 1558 at Co. Suffolk, England. She married Henry Rice (see #24) on 22 Jun 1579.

26. EDWARD[7] FROST (*John*, #35) was born between 13 Mar 1560 and 1561 at Glemsford, England. He married Thomasine Belgrave (see #27), daughter of John Belgrave and Joanna Strut, on 26 Jul 1585 at Glemsford, England. He died before 3 Aug 1616 at Stanstead, England. He was buried on 3 Aug 1616 at Stanstead, England.

    Children of Edward[7] Frost and Thomasine Belgrave (see #27) were:

    19.   i.   THOMASINE[6].

27. THOMASINE[7] BELGRAVE (*John*, #37) was christened between 1 Feb 1561 and 1562 at Leverington, England. She married Edward Frost (see #26), son of John Frost and Ann Scott, on 26 Jul 1585 at Glemsford, England.

28. JOSEPH[7] MORSE was born ca 1576 or 1587 at Co. Suffolk, England. He married Dorothy (--?--) (see #29) circa 1610. He died on 29 Sep 1646.

Children of Joseph[7] Morse and Dorothy (--?--) (see #29) were:

  20. i. JOSEPH[6] SR..

29. DOROTHY[7] (--?--) was born before 1590. She married Joseph Morse (see #28), son of Richard Morse, circa 1610.

30. JOHN[7] PIERCE was born before 1600. He married Elizabeth Trull (see #31).

Children of John[7] Pierce and Elizabeth Trull (see #31) were:

  21. i. HESTER[6].

31. ELIZABETH[7] TRULL was born before 1600. She married John Pierce (see #30).

32. DEMARUS[7] (--?--) was born circa 1610 at England. She married [?Samuel?] Shattuck.

Generation Eight

33. THOMAS[8] BAKER married Agnes Goldhop (see #34).

Children of Thomas[8] Baker and Agnes Goldhop (see #34) were:

  25. i. MARGARET[7].

34. AGNES[8] GOLDHOP married Thomas Baker (see #33).

35. JOHN[8] FROST (*William*, #40) was born circa 1535. He married Ann Scott (see #36), daughter of Richard Scott and Joanna (--?--), between 29 Jan 1558 and 1559 at Glemsford, England. He died on 9 Feb 1609/10 at Hardtest, England.

Children of John[8] Frost and Ann Scott (see #36) were:

  26. i. EDWARD[7].

36. ANN[8] SCOTT (*Richard*, #42) was born before 1540. She married John Frost (see #35), son of William Frost and Phillippa (--?--), between 29 Jan 1558 and 1559 at Glemsford, England. She died on 30 Jul 1588 at Hardtest, England.

37. JOHN[8] BELGRAVE married Joanna Strut (see #38), daughter of John Strut and Catherine (--?--), on 22 Sep 1560 at Glemsford, England. He died before 12 Feb 1590/91 at Leverington, England.

Children of John[8] Belgrave and Joanna Strut (see #38) were:

   27.   i.   THOMASINE[7].

38. JOANNA[8] STRUT (*John*, #44) married John Belgrave (see #37) on 22 Sep 1560 at Glemsford, England. She was buried on 14 Aug 1577.

39. RICHARD[8] MORSE (*Thomas*, #46) was born ca 1540/42 at Stoke by Nyland, Suffolk, England. He died on 30 Jun 1603 at Dedham, England.

Generation Nine

40. WILLIAM[9] FROST married Phillippa (--?--) (see #41). He died in 1549 at Glemsford, England.

Children of William[9] Frost and Phillippa (--?--) (see #41) were:

   35.   i.   JOHN[8].

41. PHILLIPPA[9] (--?--) was born before 1515 at England (probably). She married William Frost (see #40). She died between 20 Jan 1557 and 1558 at Lidgate, England.

42. RICHARD[9] SCOTT (*Richard*, #48) was born before 1520 at England (probably). He married Joanna (--?--) (see #43). He died between 1565 and 1565.

Children of Richard[9] Scott and Joanna (--?--) (see #43) were:

   36.   i.   ANN[8].

43. JOANNA[9] (--?--) was born before 1520 at England (probably). She married Richard Scott (see #42), son of Richard Scott. She died on 23 Aug 1556 at Glemsford, England.

44. JOHN[9] STRUT (*Thomas*, #49) married Catherine (--?--) (see #45). He died before 22 Apr 1591 at Glemsford, Co. Suffolk, England. He was buried on 22 Apr 1591 at Glemsford, Co. Suffolk, England.

Children of John[9] Strut and Catherine (--?--) (see #45) were:

    38.   i.   JOANNA[8].

45. CATHERINE[9] (--?--) married John Strut (see #44), son of Thomas Strut and Johane (--?--). She died before 18 Aug 1578 at Glemsford, England.

46. THOMAS[9] MORSE (*Robert*, #51) was born before 1520 at Stoke by Nayland, England. He married Agnes (--?--) (see #47). He died before 15 Feb 1577 at Stoke by Nayland, England. He was buried on 15 Feb 1577 at Stokes by Nayland, England.

Children of Thomas[9] Morse and Agnes (--?--) (see #47) were:

    39.   i.   RICHARD[8].

47. AGNES[9] (--?--) was born before 1520. She married Thomas Morse (see #46), son of Robert Morse and Agnes.

Generation Ten

48. RICHARD[10] SCOTT (*William*, #53) was born circa 1476 at Boxstead, Co. Suffolk, England. He died in Apr 1560.

Children of Richard[10] Scott and an unknown spouse were:

    42.   i.   RICHARD[9].

49. THOMAS[10] STRUT (*John*, #55) was born before 1501. He married Johane (--?--) (see #50). He died circa 1548 at Melford, England.

Children of Thomas[10] Strut and Johane (--?--) (see #50) were:

    44.   i.   JOHN[9].

50. JOHANE[10] (--?--) married Thomas Strut (see #49), son of John Strut and Isabelle [aka Elisabeth] (--?--).

51. ROBERT[10] MORSE (*John*, #57) married Agnes (see #52). He died ca 1551/2 at Stoke by Nayland, Co. Suffolk, England.

Children of Robert[10] Morse and Agnes (see #52) were:

    46.   i.   THOMAS[9].

52. AGNES[10] ? MOSSE ? was born in 1499 at Stoke by Nayland, Co. Suffolk, England. She married Robert Morse (see #51), son of John Morse. She died before 17 Jan 1578 at Stoke By Nayland, England. She was buried on 17 Jan 1578 at Stokes by Nayland, England.

Generation Eleven

53. WILLIAM[11] SCOTT was born circa 1450 at Glemsford, Co. Suffolk, England. He married Clemence (--?--) (see #54).

Children of William[11] Scott and Clemence (--?--) (see #54) were:

    48.   i.   RICHARD[10].

54. CLEMENCE[11] (--?--) married William Scott (see #53).

55. JOHN[11] STRUT was born before 1481. He married Isabelle [aka Elisabeth] (--?--) (see #56). He died after 12 Sep 1516 at Glemsford, Co. Suffolk, England. He was buried at Glemsford, England.

Children of John[11] Strut and Isabelle [aka Elisabeth] (--?--) (see #56) were:

    49.   i.   THOMAS[10].

56. ISABELLE [AKA ELISABETH][11] (--?--) was born before 1481. She married John Strut (see #55). She died in 1526 at Glemsford, England.

57. JOHN[11] MORSE (*Robert*, #58) was born circa 1452 at Stratford, Co. Suffolk, England. He died at England.

Children of John[11] Morse and an unknown spouse were:

    51.   i.   ROBERT[10].

Generation Twelve

58. ROBERT[12] MORSE was born before 1430. He died at England.

Children of Robert[12] Morse and an unknown spouse were:

    57.   i.   JOHN[11].

Descendants of Capt. John Johnson

The following genealogy of Capt. John Johnson contained herein only includes the direct line from Capt. John Johnson to Ira Johnson. From Ira Johnson forward, all known descendants are shown.

Generation One

1. CAPT. JOHN [1] JOHNSON was born before 1593 at England. He married Mary Heath, daughter of William Heath and Agnes Cheney, on 21 Sep 1613 at St. Mary the Virgin Church, Ware, Co. Hertfordshire, England. He married Margery (--?--) at England. He married Grace Negus before Oct 1656. He died on 30 Sep 1659 at Roxbury, Suffolk Co., Massachusetts Bay Colony. Johnson lived in Ware and Great Amwell before coming to the Massachusetts Bay Colony. He left on 6 Apr 1630 from Isle of Wight, (South Hampton), England. He arrived on 22 Jun 1630 at Massachusetts Bay Colony (now MA). He lived at Roxbury, Massachusetts Bay Colony. John Johnson was an ancestor of Presidents Franklin Pierce (14th President) and Franklin Delano Roosevelt (32nd President).

Children of Capt. John[1] Johnson and Mary Heath were as follows:

2.   i.   MARY[2], baptized 31 Jul 1614 at Ware, Co. Hertfordshire, England; married Roger Mowry; married John Kingsley.

3.   ii.   ISAAC, baptized 11 Feb 1615 at St. John the Baptist Church, Great Amwell, Co. Hertfordshire, England; married Elizabeth Porter.

     iii.   JOHN; baptized 5 Apr 1618 at St. John the Baptist Church, Great Amwell, Co. Hertfordshire, England; buried 8 Jul 1627 at St.

Mary the Virgin Church, Ware, Co. Hertfordshire, England.

iv. ELIZABETH; baptized 22 Aug 1619 at St. John the Baptist Church, Great Amwell, Co. Hertfordshire, England; married Robert Pepper, son of Richard Pepper and Mary (--?--), 14 Mar 1642/43.

4. v. HUMPHREY, baptized 5 Nov 1620 at St. John the Baptist Church, Great Amwell, Co. Hertfordshire, England; married Ellen Cheney; married Abigail Stansfull.

vi. JOSEPH; baptized 20 Apr 1622 at St. John the Baptist Church, Great Amwell, Co. Hertfordshire, England.

vii. SUSAN; baptized 16 Jul 1623 at St. John the Baptist Church, Great Amwell, Co. Hertfordshire, England; died before 15 Aug 1629 at Ware, England; buried 15 Aug 1629 at St. Mary the Virgin Church Cem., Ware, Co. Hertfordshire, England.

5. viii. SARAH, baptized 12 Nov 1624 at St. Mary the Virgin Church, Ware, Co. Hertfordshire, England; married Hugh Burt; married William Bartram.

ix. JOSEPH; baptized 6 Mar 1626/27 at St. Mary the Virgin Church, Ware, Co. Hertfordshire, England; died before 30 Mar 1627 at Ware, England; buried 30 Mar 1627 at St. Mary the Virgin Church Cemetery, Ware, Co. Hertfordshire, England.

x. HANNAH; baptized 23 Mar 1627/28.

Generation Two

2. MARY[2] JOHNSON (*John[1]*) was baptized on 31 Jul 1614 at Ware, Co. Hertfordshire, England. She married Roger Mowry circa 1644.

She married John Kingsley on 16 Mar 1673/74. She died on 29 Jan 1678/79 at Rehoboth, MA, at age 64.   Children of Mary[2] Johnson and Roger Mowry were as follows:

    i.   ROGER[3]; died.

    ii.   JONATHON; born 2 May 1637; married Mary Bartlett, daughter of Robert Bartlett and Mary Warren, 8 Jul 1659; married Hannah (--?--).
He lived at Plymouth.

    iii.   BETHIAH; baptized 17 Jul 1638; married George Palmer 30 Sep 1662.

    iv.   MARY; baptized 16 Feb 1639.

    v.   ELIZABETH; baptized 27 Mar 1642.

    vi.   NATHANIEL; born 10 Jan 1644; married Johanna Inman, daughter of Edward Inman, 1666; died 24 Mar 1717/18 at age 74.

    vii.   JOHN; born 1645; married Mary (--?--); died 7 Jul 1690.

    viii.   MEHITABLE; born 1646; married Eldad Kingsley, son of John Kingsley, 9 May 1662.

    ix.   JOSEPH; born 1647; married Mary Wilbur; died 27 May 1716.

    x.   BENJAMIN; born 8 May 1649; married Martha Hazard, daughter of Thomas Hazard and Martha (--?--).

    xi.   THOMAS; born 19 Jul 1652; married Susanna Newell, daughter of Abraham Newell and Susanna Rand; died 27 Dec 1717 at age 65.

    xii.   HANNAH; born 23 Sep 1656; married Benjamin Sherman, son of Philip Sherman and Sarah Odding, 3 Dec 1674; died 1718.

3. ISAAC[2] JOHNSON (*John[1]*) was baptized on 11 Feb 1615 at St. John the Baptist Church, Great Amwell, Co. Hertfordshire, England. He married Elizabeth Porter, daughter of Adrian Porter and Margaret Plomer, on 20 Jan 1636/37 at Roxbury, MA. He died on 19 Dec 1675 at "Great Swamp", North Kingston, RI, at age 60.

Children of Isaac[2] Johnson and Elizabeth Porter were as follows:

6.   i.   ELIZABETH^3, born 24 Dec 1637 at Roxbury, MA; married Henry Bowen.

      ii.   JOHN; born 3 Nov 1639; 18 Dec 1661 at Roxbury, MA.

      iii.   MARY; born 10 Apr 1642 at Roxbury, MA; married William Bartholemew Jr. 17 Dec 1663 at Roxbury, MA.

      iv.   ISAAC; born 7 Nov 1643 at Roxbury, MA; married Mary Harris, daughter of Daniel Harris and Mary Weld, 26 Oct 1669; died 3 Feb 1719/20 at age 76; buried at Riverside Cemetery, Middletown, CT.

      v.   JOSEPH.

      vi.   NATHANIEL.

4. HUMPHREY^2 JOHNSON (*John^1*) was baptized on 5 Nov 1620 at St. John the Baptist Church, Great Amwell, Co. Hertfordshire, England. He married Ellen Cheney, daughter of William Cheney and Margaret (or Margery) Mason, on 20 Mar 1641/42 at Roxbury, Suffolk Co., Massachusetts Bay Colony. He married Abigail Stansfull on 6 Dec 1678 at Roxbury, Suffolk Co., MA. He died on 24 Jul 1692 at Hingham, Plymouth Co., MA, at age 71. He was Ancestor of Franklin D. Roosevelt. He emigrated on 8 Apr 1630. He lived in 1651 at Scituate, Massachusetts Bay Colony. He began military service King Philip's War in Capt. Isaac Johnson's Company.

      Children of Humphrey^2 Johnson and Ellen Cheney were as follows:

7.   i.   MEHITABLE^3, born April, 1643/4 at Roxbury, MA; married Samuel Hinsdale; married John Root; married John Coleman.

8.   ii.   MARTHA, baptized 12 Sep 1647 at Roxbury, MA; married Obadiah Morse.

      iii.   DEBORAH; baptized 20 Jan 1650.

      iv.   JOHN; born Mar 1653 at Roxbury, MA; died 12 Jun 1674 at Hingham, MA, at age 21.

      v.   JOSEPH; born 24 Jun 1655; died 6 Sep 1676 at Hingham, MA, at age 21.

9.   vi.   BENJAMIN, born 27 Aug 1657; married Rebecca Hershey.

10.   vii.   MARGARET, born 22 Dec 1659 at Scituate, MA; married Josiah Leavitt.

    viii.   MARY; born 19 Apr 1663 at Scituate, MA.

11.   ix.   NATHANIEL, born 21 Mar 1666 at Hingham, Plymouth Colony (now MA); married Abigail May.

12.   x.   ISAAC, born 18 Feb 1667/68 at Hingham, MA; married Abigail Leavitt.

Children of Humphrey[2] Johnson and Abigail Stansfull were as follows:

    i.   JOHN[3].

    ii.   JOHN; born 8 Jun 1680; married Mary Ramsey 26 May 1702; died 7 Aug 1755 at Colchester, CT, at age 75.

    iii.   DEBORAH; born 19 Feb 1682/83 at Suitate, MA; married Isaac Davis 19 Dec 1705.

5. SARAH[2] JOHNSON (*John[1]*) was baptized on 12 Nov 1624 at St. Mary the Virgin Church, Ware, Co. Hertfordshire, England. She married Hugh Burt circa 1645. She married William Bartram circa 1653 at Lynn, Essex Co., MA. She died before 6 Nov 1694 at Swansey, MA.

Children of Sarah[2] Johnson and William Bartram were as follows:

    i.   MARY[3]; born 6 Apr 1654 at Lynn, Essex Co., MA.

    ii.   REBECCA.

    iii.   ESTER.

    iv.   ELLEN.

    v.   ELIZABETH.

    vi.   HANNAH.

    vii.   SUSANNA.

6. ELIZABETH[3] JOHNSON (*Isaac*[2], *John*[1]) was born on 24 Dec 1637 at Roxbury, MA. She married Henry Bowen, son of Griffith Bowen and Margaret Fleming, on 20 Dec 1658 at Roxbury, MA. She died on 20 Apr 1701 at Woodstock, CT, at age 63.

Children of Elizabeth[3] Johnson and Henry Bowen were:

13.   i.   JOHN[4], born 1 Sep 1662 at Roxbury, MA; married Hannah Brewer.

7. MEHITABLE[3] JOHNSON (*Humphrey*[2], *John*[1]) was born in Sep 1643/4. She married Samuel Hinsdale on 31 Oct 1660. She married John Root. She married John Coleman on 11 Mar 1679. She died on 4 Aug 1689 at age 46.

Children of Mehitable[3] Johnson and Samuel Hinsdale were as follows:

    i.   MEHITABLE[4]; born 18 Oct 1663; married Obadiah Dickinson; died before 1702 at Weathersfield, CT.

14.   ii.   MARY, born 22 Jul 1665; married Thomas Sheldon.

    iii.   ANN; born 22 Feb 1667; married Martin Kellogg 10 Dec 1684; died 19 Jul 1689 at age 22.

    iv.   SARAH; married Samuel Janes; died 13 May 1704.

    v.   MEHUMAN; born 1673 at Deerfield, MA; married Susanna Rockwood; died 1694.

        He was the first white child born in Deerfield, MA.

Children of Mehitable[3] Johnson and John Root were:

    i.   THANKFUL, B. 1677, Northampton, Hampshire Co., MA. She married Thomas Welles, 7 Jan 1697 in Weatherfield, Hartford Co., CT.

Children of Mehitable[3] Johnson and John Coleman were as follows:

    i.   EBENEZER, born 29 Aug 1680. Married Ruth Niles on March 11, 1705, Colchester, New London Co., CT. He died 1741.

ii.   NATHANIEL, born 18 Oct 1684. He
married Mary Ely. He died 7 Apr 1755,
Hatfield, MA.

8. MARTHA[3] JOHNSON (*Humphrey[2], John[1]*) was baptized on 12
Sep 1647 at Roxbury, MA. She married Obadiah Morse, son of
Daniel Morse and Lydia Fisher. She died in 1714.

Children of Martha[3] Johnson and Obadiah Morse were:

i.   OBADIAH[4]; died young.

9. BENJAMIN[3] JOHNSON (*Humphrey[2], John[1]*) was born on 27 Aug
1657. He married Rebecca Hershey, daughter of William Hershey
and Rebecca Chubbock, on 11 Jun 1683. He died on 26 Mar 1707 at
age 49.

He was a blacksmith.

Children of Benjamin[3] Johnson and Rebecca Hershey were as
follows:

i.   REBECCA[4]; born 28 Jun 1684; died 28 Sep 1684.

ii.   BENJAMIN; born 15 Jul 1685; died 5 Dec 1685.

iii.   REBECCA; born 31 Jul 1687; married Jonathan
Washburn 17 Dec 1719 at Boston, MA.

iv.   JOSHUA; born 9 Aug 1689; died 21 Mar 1694 at
age 4.

v.   RUTH; born 10 Jan 1692; died 8 Mar 1713 at age
21.

vi.   SARAH; born 7 Feb 1694; married Nathaniel
Fearing 25 Jan 1716 at Hingham, MA; died 15
May 1736 at age 42.

vii.   DAUGHTER; born 1 Dec 1695; died 8 Dec 1695.

viii. BENJAMIN; born 3 Jun 1696; married Ruth Beale
4 Feb 1720; died 30 Mar 1760 at Sharon, MA, at
age 63.

ix.   MARY; born 28 Jul 1699; married Barnabus
Seabury 11 Oct 1722; died 29 Oct 1723 at age
24.

x.   JOSHUA; born 28 Sep 1701; married Lydia Ward
29 Apr 1730; died 8 Aug 1789 at Stoughton,
MA, at age 87.

He moved circa 1740 to Stoughton, MA.

xi. DEBORAH; born 8 Sep 1703; married Benjamin Perry between 27 May 1722 and 1723 at Bridgewater, MA.

10. MARGARET[3] JOHNSON (*Humphrey[2]*, *John[1]*) was born on 22 Dec 1659 at Scituate, MA. She married Josiah Leavitt on 20 Oct 1676. She died on 5 Jun 1739 at age 79.

Children of Margaret[3] Johnson and Josiah Leavitt were as follows:

i. JOSIAH[4]; born 28 Jul 1679; married Abigail Gill 1 Apr 1706; died 19 Sep 1717 at age 38.

ii. JOSEPH; born 23 Jul 1681; married Judith Hobart 10 Jan 1711.

iii. MARGARET; born 20 Oct 1683; married Caleb Lincoln 17 Nov 1709.

iv. JEREMIAH; born 21 Aug 1685; married Jael Hobart 10 Sep 1712.

v. JOSHUA; born 1 Aug 1687; married Hannah Devotion 22 Jan 1713; died 22 Oct 1732 at age 45.

vi. DAVID; born 16 Aug 1691.
He lived at Meriden, CT.

vii. ASAPH; born 31 Jul 1695; married Ruth Devotion 28 Mar 1717; married Margaret Bissell 30 Aug 1722.

viii. HEZEKIAH; born 17 Sep 1697; married Mary Beale 31 Jan 1723.

ix. MARY; born 7 Oct 1699; married Matthew Cushing 1717.
She lived at Rehoboth, MA.

11. NATHANIEL[3] JOHNSON (*Humphrey[2]*, *John[1]*) was born on 21 Mar 1666 at Hingham, Plymouth Colony (now MA). He married Abigail May circa 1682 at Hingham, Plymouth Colony (now MA). He died on 4 May 1755 at Pomfret, Windham Co., CT, at age 89.

He began military service in 1690 Canada Expedition under Capt. Andrews.

Children of Nathaniel[3] Johnson and Abigail May were as follows:

15.   i.   NATHANIEL[4] II, born 1680; married Mary Haven.

     ii.   ABIGAIL; born Jul 1683; died young.

16.   iii.   JOSEPH, born 9 Sep 1685; married Lydia Twitchell.

     iv.   ABIGAIL; born 1 Apr 1687; died 15 Jan 1782 at Promfret, CT, at age 94.

17.   v.   ELISHA, born 12 Mar 1688; married Abigail Weld.

     vi.   THOMAS; born 12 Mar 1690.

18.   vii.   MARY, born 11 Mar 1691; married Noah Morse.

     viii.   JONATHAN; born 16 Mar 1692; died 6 Jan 1702 at Sherborn, MA, at age 9.

19.   ix.   MARTHA, born 19 Feb 1696/97 at Sherborn, Middlesex Co., MA; married Timothy Sabin.

20.   x.   MEHITABLE, born 15 Oct 1699; married Humphrey Goodell.

12.   ISAAC[3] JOHNSON (*Humphrey[2]*, *John[1]*) was born on 18 Feb 1667/68 at Hingham, MA. He married Abigail Leavitt, daughter of John Leavitt, circa 1690. He died in 1735.

Children of Isaac[3] Johnson and Abigail Leavitt were as follows:

     i.   ABIGAIL[4]; born 28 Apr 1689.

     ii.   DAVID; born 16 Oct 1692 at Hingham, MA; married Rebecca Washburn.

     iii.   HANAH; born 17 Jan 1694/95 at Hingham, MA; married Joseph Washburn Jr. 1716; died 1780 at Leicester, MA.

     iv.   SOLOMON; born 9 Mar 1696/97 at Hingham, MA.

     v.   JAMES; married Jane Harris.

     vi.   DEBORAH; born at Hingham, MA.

     vii.   DANIEL; born 20 Apr 1700 at Hingham, MA; married Betty Latham.

     viii.   REBECCA; born at Hingham, MA.

ix. SARAH; born 1 Jul 1702 at Bridgewater, MA; married Solomon Pratt Deacon.

x. JOHN; born 11 Jun 1705 at Bridgewater, MA; married Margaret Holman 21 Oct 1731; died 12 Nov 1770 at age 65.

xi. JOSEPH; born 17 Dec 1707 at Bridgewater, MA; died 6 Nov 1730 at age 22.

xii. BENJAMIN; born 6 Mar 1711 at Bridgewater, MA; married Ruth Holman.

xiii. MARY; born 18 Jun 1716 at Bridgewater, MA; married James Hooper 10 Feb 1737; died 28 Dec 1757 at age 41.

Generation Four

13. JOHN[4] BOWEN (*Elizabeth[3]Johnson, Isaac[2], John[1]*) was born on 1 Sep 1662 at Roxbury, MA. He married Hannah Brewer.

Children of John[4] Bowen and Hannah Brewer were:

21. i. ABIGAIL[5], born 5 Jul 1700 at Roxbury, MA; married Caleb Kendrick.

14. MARY[4] HINSDALE (*Mehitable[3]Johnson, Humphrey[2], John[1]*) was born on 22 Jul 1665. She married Thomas Sheldon.

Children of Mary[4] Hinsdale and Thomas Sheldon were:

22. i. BENJAMIN[5], married Mary Strong.

15. NATHANIEL[4] JOHNSON II (*Nathaniel[3], Humphrey[2], John[1]*) was born in 1680. He married Mary Haven, daughter of John Haven and Hannah Hitchins, on 23 Nov 1708. He died on 21 Jul 1733.

Children of Nathaniel[4] Johnson II and Mary Haven were as follows:

23. i. JONATHAN[5], born 30 Jan 1710; married Jerusha Green; married Abigail Goodale.

ii. JAMES; born 21 Jul 1711; married Susanna Waters; married Sarah Holbrook; married Anna Bishop.

iii. JOHN; born 20 Oct 1714; married Abigail (--?--). He was a physician.

iv. HANNAH; born 21 Feb 1717.

v. NATHANIEL III; born 4 Oct 1718; died 21 Jul 1733 at age 14.

16. JOSEPH[4] JOHNSON (*Nathaniel[3], Humphrey[2], John[1]*) was born on 9 Sep 1685. He married Lydia Twitchell, daughter of Joseph Twitchell and Lydia (--?--), on 13 May 1709 at Sherborn, MA. He died on 25 Mar 1745 at Holliston, MA, at age 59.

Children of Joseph[4] Johnson and Lydia Twitchell were as follows:

i. LYDIA[5]; born 27 Jul 1709.

ii. MOSES; born 18 Nov 1711; married Sabilla Plympton 1732.

iii. ISAAC; born 28 Mar 1714; married Abigail Leland 1737; married Elizabeth (--?--) 1749.

iv. JOSEPH; born 22 May 1716; died young.

v. DAVID; born 8 Jul 1719 at Sherborn, MA; died 7 Feb 1719/20.

vi. ELISHA; born 20 Nov 1720; married Mary Gay 1741.

vii. DAVID; born 28 Jul 1723.

viii. SARAH; born 18 Jul 1727.

ix. JOSEPH; born 1729; died 3 Jan 1929.

x. JOSEPH; born 30 Jan 1731 at Holliston, MA.

17. ELISHA[4] JOHNSON (*Nathaniel[3] Johnson, Humphrey[2], John[1]*) was born on 12 Mar 1688. He married Abigail Weld between 25 May 1708 and 1709.

He lived at Sutton, MA.

Children of Elisha[4] Johnson and Abigail Weld were as follows:

i. ELEANOR[5]; born 24 Jun 1710 at Roxbury, MA.

ii. ABIGAIL; born 15 Sep 1714; died 26 Nov 1714 at Roxbury, MA.

18. MARY[4] JOHNSON (*Nathaniel[3], Humphrey[2], John[1]*) was born on 11 Mar 1691. She married Noah Morse on 12 Jul 1705.

Children of Mary[4] Johnson and Noah Morse were as follows:

i.   TABATHA[5]; born 1706.

ii. JEMIMA; born 1707; died circa 1714.

iii. HEPSEBAH; born 2 Apr 1708; married Jonathan Mason.

iv. EXPERIENCE; born 15 Apr 1710; married Joseph Morse 17 May 1735.

v.   CYPRIAN; born 15 Jun 1712.

19. MARTHA[4] JOHNSON (*Nathaniel[3]*, *Humphrey[2]*, *John[1]*) was born on 19 Feb 1696/97 at Sherborn, Middlesex Co., MA. She married Timothy Sabin, son of Benjamin Sabin and Sarah Parker, on 5 Feb 1717/18 at Pomfret, Windham Co., CT. She died on 2 Oct 1745 at Pomfret, Windham Co., CT, at age 48.

Children of Martha[4] Johnson and Timothy Sabin were as follows:

i.   HULDAH[5]; born 21 Jun 1719.

ii.   NATHANIEL; born 18 May 1721; married Elizabeth Stone 27 Dec 1744; died 17 Nov 1747 at age 26.

iii. TIMOTHY; born 11 Oct 1723 at Pomfret, Windham Co., CT; died 7 Oct 1743 at Pomfret, Windham Co., CT, at age 19.

iv.   ICHABOD; born 25 May 1726; married Sarah Cole 24 Aug 1749; died 23 Apr 1783 at age 56.

v.   MARTHA; born 30 Aug 1728; died Jul 1805 at age 76.

vi.   JOSIAH; born 8 Feb 1730/31; married Anna Davis 10 Jul 1750; died 21 Apr 1806 at age 75.

vii. DANIEL; born 31 Jan 1734/35 at Pomfret, Windham Co., CT; died 7 Feb 1753 at Thompson, Windham Co., CT, at age 18.

viii. SARAH; born 4 May 1737 at Pomfret, Windham Co., CT; died 26 Dec 1749 at Pomfret, Windham Co., CT, at age 12.

20. MEHITABLE[4] JOHNSON (*Nathaniel[3]*, *Humphrey[2]*, *John[1]*) was born on 15 Oct 1699. She married Humphrey Goodell, son of Thomas Goodell and Sarah (--?--), on 12 Jan 1727.

Children of Mehitable[4] Johnson and Humphrey Goodell were as follows:

    i. MARY[5]; born 2 Nov 1727; married Zechariah Keys 20 Sep 1750; married Thomas Coe.

    ii. ELENOR; born 4 Oct 1729; married Joel Taylor 5 Jul 1758.

    iii. EUNICE; born 6 Mar 1732.

    iv. MEHITABLE; born 9 Jun 1734; married Jacob Goodell Jr. 1 Dec 1756.

    v. LYDIA; born 26 Mar 1736; married Joseph Davison Jr. 5 Jan 1757.

    vi. KEZIAH; born 26 Mar 1736; married Timothy Robinson 5 Jan 1757.

    vii. LUCE; born 16 Mar 1739; died 9 Aug 1741 at age 2.

Generation Five

21. ABIGAIL[5] BOWEN (*John[4]*, *Elizabeth[3]Johnson*, *Isaac[2]*, *John[1]*) was born on 5 Jul 1700 at Roxbury, MA. She married Caleb Kendrick. She died on 16 Sep 1775 at Groton at age 75.

Children of Abigail[5] Bowen and Caleb Kendrick were:

24.   i. BENJAMIN[6], born 30 Jan 1723/24 at Newton, MA; married Sarah Harris.

22. BENJAMIN[5] SHELDON (*Mary[4]Hinsdale*, *Mehitable[3]Johnson*, *Humphrey[2]*, *John[1]*) married Mary Strong.

Children of Benjamin[5] Sheldon and Mary Strong were:

25.   i. MARY[6], married "Capt" Joseph Lyman.

23. JONATHAN[5] JOHNSON (*Nathaniel[4]*, *Nathaniel[3]*, *Humphrey[2]*, *John[1]*) was born on 30 Jan 1710. He married Jerusha Green after 9 Sep 1739 at Leicester, Worcester Co., Massachusetts Bay Colony. He married Abigail Goodale, daughter of John Goodale and Hannah Colburn, on 16 Jun 1756. He died on 30 Aug 1776 at Sturbridge, Worcester Co., Massachusetts Bay Colony, at age 66.

Children of Jonathan[5] Johnson and Jerusha Green were as follows:

    i.   NATHANIEL[6]; baptized 12 Oct 1740 at Sturbridge, MA.

    ii. JONATHAN; born 21 Oct 1742 at Leicester, MA.

    iii. JERUSHA; born 26 Nov 1744 at Grafton; she and Asa Humphrey obtained a marriage license 28 Feb 1767 at Sturbridge, MA; married Asa Humphrey 5 Apr 1767; died 27 Mar 1808 at age 63.

    iv. MARTHA; born 31 Oct 1749 at Woodstock, CT; she and Jason Allen obtained a marriage license 4 Mar 1773 at Sturbridge, MA.

26.   v. IRA, born 7 Jun 1753 at Sturbridge, Worcester Co., MA; married Abigail Furbush.

There were no children of Jonathan[5] Johnson and Abigail Goodale.

Generation Six

24.   BENJAMIN[6] KENDRICK (*Abigail[5]Bowen*, *John[4]*, *Elizabeth[3]Johnson*, *Isaac[2]*, *John[1]*) was born on 30 Jan 1723/24 at Newton, MA. He married Sarah Harris, daughter of Stephen Harris and Mary (--?--), on 1 Mar 1750 at Probably Hollis, NH. He died on 13 Nov 1812 at Amherst, NH, at age 88.

Children of Benjamin[6] Kendrick and Sarah Harris were:

27.   i. ANNA[7], born 30 Oct 1768 at Amherst, NH; married Benjamin Pierce Jr.

25.   MARY[6] SHELDON (*Benjamin[5]*, *Mary[4]Hinsdale*, *Mehitable[3]Johnson*, *Humphrey[2]*, *John[1]*) married "Capt" Joseph Lyman.

Children of Mary[6] Sheldon and "Capt" Joseph Lyman were:

28.   i. JOSEPH[7], married Anne ROBBINS.

26. IRA[6] JOHNSON (*Jonathan*[5], *Nathaniel*[4], *Nathaniel*[3], *Humphrey*[2], *John*[1]) was born on 7 Jun 1753 at Sturbridge, Worcester Co., MA. He married Abigail Furbush, daughter of Benjamin Forbush and Elizabeth Marble, in Sep 1784. He died at NY.

He began military service at MA in the Revolutionary War. He appeared on the census of 1800 at Saratoga, NY.

Children of Ira[6] Johnson and Abigail Furbush were as follows:

- 29.   i.   CHARLES ALVAH[7], born 26 Feb 1785 at Brookfield, Worcester Co., MA; married Rachel Pratt.
- 30.   ii.   WARREN
- 31.   iii.   GEORGE JOHN, born circa 1800; married Sarah Turnbaugh.
-      iv.   LORICA.
-      v.   JOSHUA; married (--?--) Gibbons.
-      vi.   ABRAHAM; died at Washington Co., PA.

Generation Seven

27. ANNA[7] KENDRICK (*Benjamin*[6], *Abigail*[5]*Bowen*, *John*[4], *Elizabeth*[3]*Johnson*, *Isaac*[2], *John*[1]) was born on 30 Oct 1768 at Amherst, NH. She married Benjamin Pierce Jr., son of Benjamin Pierce and Elizabeth Merrill, on 1 Feb 1790.

Children of Anna[7] Kendrick and Benjamin Pierce Jr. were:

-      i.   FRANKLIN[8]; born 23 Nov 1804 at Hillsboro, NH; married Jane Means Appleton 19 Nov 1834 at Amherst, NH; died 8 Oct 1869 at Concord, NH, at age 64. He was the 14th US President.

28. JOSEPH[7] LYMAN (*Mary*[6]*Sheldon*, *Benjamin*[5], *Mary*[4]*Hinsdale*, *Mehitable*[3]*Johnson*, *Humphrey*[2], *John*[1]) married Anne Robbins.

Children of Joseph[7] Lyman and Anne Robbins were:

- 32.   i.   CATHERINE[8], married Warren Delano.

29. CHARLES ALVAH[7] JOHNSON (*Ira[6], Jonathan[5], Nathaniel[4], Nathaniel[3], Humphrey[2], John[1]*) was born on 26 Feb 1785 at Brookfield, Worcester Co., MA. He married Rachel Pratt, daughter of Abel Pratt Jr. and Rachel Payne, on 16 Dec 1813 at Russell, St. Lawrence, NY. He died on 20 Apr 1847 at Edwards, St. Lawrence Co., NY, at age 62. He was buried at Payne Cemetery, Edwards, St. Lawrence Co., NY.

Children of Samson Viall and Rachel Pratt were as follows:

33.   i.   HARRIETT C.[8], born 8 Nov 1805 at Russell, St. Lawrence Co., NY; married Wesley Porter Harmon.

35.   ii.   SUSAN, born 9 Feb 1808 at Russell, St. Lawrence Co., NY; married James Foster.

36.   iii.   LEVITIA (LOUISA), born 15 May 1810 at Russell, St. Lawrence Co., NY; married Elihu Phelps.

38.   iv.   PHILA, born 26 May 1813; married Ebenezer Harmon.

Children of Charles Alvah[7] Johnson and Rachel Pratt were as follows:

34.   i.   CHARLES VICTOR[8], born 11 May 1814 at Russell, St. Lawrence Co., NY; married Emily Spann.

      ii.   ELIZA B.; born 22 Feb 1817 at Russell, St. Lawrence Co., NY; died 22 May 1818 at Russell, St. Lawrence Co., NY, at age 1.

37.   iii.   HIRAM ALVAH, born 18 Feb 1819 at Russell, St. Lawrence Co., NY; married Elizabeth Jane Whitley.

39.   iv.   ABEL PRATT, born 7 Jun 1821 at Russell, St. Lawrence Co., NY; married Lucy E. Haile.

40.   v.   WILLIAM WARREN, born 1 Dec 1823 at Russell, St. Lawrence Co., NY; married Hannah Maria Merrill.

41.   vi.   NANCY A., born 7 Nov 1825 at Russell, St. Lawrence Co., NY; married William Harry Brown.

42. vii. EMMORANCY, born 22 May 1827 at Pitcairn, St. Lawrence Co., NY; married Alfred Brooks Hall.

30. WARREN[7] JOHNSON (*Ira[6], Jonathan[5], Nathaniel[4], Nathaniel[3], Humphrey[2], John[1]*).

Children of Warren[7] Johnson and an unknown spouse were:

43. i. IRA[8]

31. GEORGE JOHN[7] JOHNSON (*Ira[6], Jonathan[5], Nathaniel[4], Nathaniel[3], Humphrey[2], John[1]*) was born circa 1800. He married Sarah Turnbaugh, daughter of John Turnbaugh and Barbara Ann Robinson. He died in 1824 at Galena, IL.

He lived in 1823 at Lincoln Co., MO.

Children of George John[7] Johnson and Sarah Turnbaugh were as follows:

44. i. LUTILIA[8], born 17 Apr 1823 at Lincoln Co., MO; married Andrew Main.

45. ii. RUFUS E., born 1 Jan 1825 at Pike Co., IL; married Anna Moomau.

Generation Eight

32. CATHERINE[8] LYMAN (*Joseph[7], Mary[6]Sheldon, Benjamin[5], Mary[4]Hinsdale, Mehitable[3]Johnson, Humphrey[2], John[1]*) married Warren Delano.

Children of Catherine[8] Lyman and Warren Delano were:

46. i. SARAH[9], married James Roosevelt.

33. HARRIETT C.[8] VIALL (*Charles[7]Johnson, Ira[6], Jonathan[5], Nathaniel[4], Nathaniel[3], Humphrey[2], John[1]*) was born on 8 Nov 1805 at Russell, St. Lawrence Co., NY. She married Wesley Porter Harmon on 25 Feb 1823. She died on 10 Feb 1884 at Edwards, St. Lawrence Co., NY, at age 78. She was buried at Payne Cemetery near Edwards, St. Lawrence Co., NY.

Children of Harriett C.[8] Viall and Wesley Porter Harmon were as follows:

47. i. EUNICE[9], born 16 May 1824; married Sardine S. Van Ornum.

ii. SUSAN V.; born 7 Dec 1825; married Clauncey Gibbons 1 Jan 1855; died 29 Aug 1901 at age 75.

48. iii. PAUL OSGOOD, born 21 Jun 1828; married Mary Elizabeth Titus.

49. iv. ALTHA, born 23 Jul 1830; married John Wallace Laidlaw; married Milton Thompson.

v. ADONIRAM J.; born 3 Aug 1832; died 3 Aug 1832.

vi. SOPHRONIA M.; born 26 Jan 1834; married Al Laidlaw, son of (--?--) Laidlaw and Theresa Eliza Blood, 11 Dec 1857.

50. vii. WESLEY PORTER JR., born 15 Oct 1837 at Edwards, St. Lawrence Co., NY; married Nancy Laidlaw.

34. CHARLES VICTOR[8] JOHNSON (*Charles[7]*, *Ira[6]*, *Jonathan[5]*, *Nathaniel[4]*, *Nathaniel[3]*, *Humphrey[2]*, *John[1]*) was born on 11 May 1814. He married Emily Spann, daughter of Jesse Spann and Mary Leighton, on 1 Jul 1838 at Pike Co., IL. He died on 12 Nov 1888 at Hardin Township, Pike Co., IL, at age 74.

Children of Charles Victor[8] Johnson and Emily Spann were as follows:

51. i. MARY LEIGHTON[9], born 2 Oct 1839 at Pike Co., IL; married John Nicholson.

ii. ABEL PRATT; born 15 Jun 1841 at Pike Co., IL; died 5 May 1863 at Pt. Gibson, Grand Gulf Co., MS, at age 21.

iii. RACHEL P.; born 20 Jan 1842 at Pike Co., IL; buried at Johnson Cemetery, Hardin, IL.

52. iv. REBECCA EMILY, born 28 Nov 1845 at Pike Co., IL; married Samuel Wiley Miller.

53. v. PHILA VIOLET, born 2 Jul 1849 at Independence, Pike Co., IL; married Richard Thornton.

vi. HIRAM; born 24 Oct 1852 at Pike Co., IL; died 25 Apr 1853; buried at Johnson Cemetery, Hardin, IL.

54. vii. EMMA NANCY, born 1854 at Pike Co., IL; married Monroe D. Ransom.

viii. MINERVA A.; born 14 Mar 1858 at Pike Co., IL; died 25 Mar 1859 at Pike Co., IL, at age 1; buried at Johnson Cemetery, Hardin, IL.

35. SUSAN[8] VIALL (*Charles[7]Johnson, Ira[6], Jonathan[5], Nathaniel[4], Nathaniel[3], Humphrey[2], John[1]*) was born on 9 Feb 1808 at Russell, St. Lawrence Co., NY. She married James Foster. She died on 19 Apr 1887 at Kingston, DeKalb Co., IL, at age 79. She was buried on 21 Apr 1887 at Kingston, DeKalb Co., IL.

Children of Susan[8] Viall and James Foster were as follows:

i. PETER[9]; born 1834 at Canada.

ii. JOHN; born 1836 at Canada.

iii. JOSEPH; born 1838 at Canada.

iv. SAMUEL; born 1840 at Canada.

v. MARY; born 1841 at NY.

vi. ELIZABETH; born 1843 at NY.

vii. JANE; born 1845 at NY.

viii. SALLY; born 1846 at NY.

ix. JULIA; born 1848 at NY.

36. LEVITIA (LOUISA)[8] VIALL (*Charles[7]Johnson, Ira[6], Jonathan[5], Nathaniel[4], Nathaniel[3], Humphrey[2], John[1]*) was born on 15 May 1810 at Russell, St. Lawrence Co., NY. She married Elihu Phelps. She died on 30 Nov 1872 at age 62.

She appeared on the census of 1850 at Russell, St. Lawrence Co., NY.

Children of Levitia (Louisa)[8] Viall and Elihu Phelps were as follows:

i. MARY L.[9]; born circa 1832.

ii. CORNELIA; born circa 1834; married James Rushton.

iii. ELIHU V. JR.; born circa 1836.

iv. SYLVIA; born 1838; married (--?--) White.

She was the mother of five children.

    v.   GEORGE W.; born circa 1844.

37.   HIRAM ALVAH[8] JOHNSON (*Charles*[7], *Ira*[6], *Jonathan*[5], *Nathaniel*[4], *Nathaniel*[3], *Humphrey*[2], *John*[1]) was born on 18 Feb 1819 at Russell, St. Lawrence Co., NY. He married Elizabeth Jane Whitley, daughter of Samuel Whitley Jr. and Catherine L. McNary, on 25 Jul 1841 at Highland, Pike Co., IL. He died on 4 Feb 1896 at Salem, Marion Co., OR, at age 76. He was buried at Pioneer Cemetery, Salem, Marion Co., OR.

He was a member of the Christian Church. He arrived in a wagon train via the Oregon Trail on 10 Sep 1847 at Oregon City, OR. He appeared on the census of 1 Jun 1850 at Marion Co., OR Territory. He was Justice of the Peace on 1 Jun 1880.

Children of Hiram Alvah[8] Johnson and Elizabeth Jane Whitley were as follows:

55.   i.   JOHN CHARLES[9], born 29 May 1842 at Pike Co., IL; married Violetta Gunsaules.

56.   ii.   GEORGE WASHINGTON SR., born 19 Jul 1844 at Pike Co., IL; married Mary Parthena Jones.

57.   iii.   WILLIAM WARREN, born 20 May 1847 on a "Wagon Train", along the Platte River, NE; married Caroline E. Harris.

58.   iv.   HIRAM ALVAH JR., born 3 Mar 1849 at Jefferson, Marion Co., OR.

59.   v.   SAMUEL THURSTON, born 18 Mar 1850 at Jefferson, Marion Co., OR; married Mary Jane "Mollie" Elliott.

       vi.   RACHEL C.; born 12 Nov 1852 at Jefferson, Marion Co., OR; married John Earl 3 Oct 1876; married John W. Harritt 20 Sep 1892; died 15 May 1933 at Salem, Marion Co., OR, at age 80.

            She appeared on the census of 1 Jun 1860 at Southern Precinct, Santiam City, Marion Co., OR.

60.   vii.   FRANCIS "FRANK" M., born 16 Dec 1855 at Jefferson, Marion Co., OR; married Emma Cosper.

viii. HARVEY W.; born 26 Aug 1858 at Jefferson, Marion Co., OR; died 7 May 1861 at Jefferson, Marion Co., OR, at age 2; buried at Jefferson Cemetery, Jefferson, Marion Co., OR.

He appeared on the census of 1 Jun 1860 at Southern Precinct, Santiam City, Marion Co., OR.

38. PHILA[8] VIALL (*Charles[7]Johnson, Ira[6], Jonathan[5], Nathaniel[4], Nathaniel[3], Humphrey[2], John[1]*) was born on 26 May 1813. She married Ebenezer Harmon. She died on 6 Mar 1898 at age 84.

Children of Phila[8] Viall and Ebenezer Harmon were as follows:

61. i. CHARLES VIALL[9], born 1836; married Maryette Maltby.
    ii. HIRAM H.; born circa 1838; died 1839.
    iii. EMMA A.; born circa 1841; died 1842.
    iv. JAMES.

39. ABEL PRATT[8] JOHNSON (*Charles[7], Ira[6], Jonathan[5], Nathaniel[4], Nathaniel[3], Humphrey[2], John[1]*) was born on 7 Jun 1821 at Russell, St. Lawrence Co., NY. He married Lucy E. Haile on 15 Sep 1846 at Edwards, St. Lawrence Co., NY. He died on 12 Apr 1920 at South Hampton, NY, at age 98.

He appeared on the census of 1 Jun 1850 at Edwards Township, St. Lawrence Co., NY.

Children of Abel Pratt[8] Johnson and Lucy E. Haile were as follows:

62. i. ELGIN ABEL[9], born 15 Aug 1849 at Edwards, St. Lawrence Co., NY; married Phoebe J. Hall.
    ii. WILLIAM H.; born 9 Mar 1848 at Edwards, St. Lawrence Co., NY; died 12 May 1848 at Edwards, St. Lawrence Co., NY.
    iii. LUCY A.; born 6 Mar 1852 at Edwards, St. Lawrence Co., NY; married Edward Perry 25 Apr 1876.

She appeared on the census of 1 Jun 1860 at Edwards Township, St. Lawrence Co., NY.

iv.   JOHN C.; born 13 Sep 1853 at NY; married Mary Bilings at Pine Valley, NY; died 1927 at Edwards, St. Lawrence Co., NY.

He appeared on the census of 1 Jun 1860 at Edwards Township, St. Lawrence Co., NY.

v.   HAIDEE ADELL; born 27 Dec 1857 at Edwards, St. Lawrence Co., NY; died 26 Dec 1859 at Edwards, St. Lawrence Co., NY, at age 1.

vi.   STELLA M.; born 12 Apr 1863 at Edwards, St. Lawrence Co., NY; married Charles Ward 27 Dec 1882.

vii.   DORA A.; born 20 Sep 1865 at Edwards, St. Lawrence Co., NY; married Malvin Stevens 12 Feb 1890.

viii.   JESSIE E.; born 3 Jun 1868 at Edwards, St. Lawrence Co., NY; married Will E. Hummel 31 Dec 1894; died 1944.

40.   WILLIAM WARREN[8] JOHNSON (*Charles[7]*, *Ira[6]*, *Jonathan[5]*, *Nathaniel[4]*, *Nathaniel[3]*, *Humphrey[2]*, *John[1]*) was born on 1 Dec 1823 at Russell, St. Lawrence Co., NY. He married Hannah Maria Merrill on 15 Sep 1846. He died on 4 Jun 1883 at Russell, St. Lawrence Co., NY, at age 59. He was buried at Payne Cemetery, Edwards, St. Lawrence Co., NY.

He appeared on the census of 1 Jun 1850 at Edwards Township, St. Lawrence Co., NY.

Children of William Warren[8] Johnson and Hannah Maria Merrill all born at Edwards, St. Lawrence Co., NY, were as follows:

63.   i.   ELIZA ANN[9], born 8 Jul 1847; married Allen Payne.

64.   ii.   CHARLES VIALL, born 30 Oct 1849.

iii.   EMMA A.; born 23 Sep 1852; married Eugene M. Harrington 4 May 1874; died 16 Oct 1897 at Pitcairn, NY, at age 45.

She appeared on the census of 1 Jun 1860 at Edwards Township, St. Lawrence Co., NY.

    iv.   ALVARETTA A.; born 22 Mar 1855; married Warren L. Allen 3 Jul 1876 at Methodist Church, Hermon, St. Lawrence Co., NY.

            She appeared on the census of 1 Jun 1860 at Edwards Township, St. Lawrence Co., NY.

    v.   GEORGE RUGGLES; born 24 Oct 1857; died 21 Oct 1916 at age 58.

            He appeared on the census of 1 Jun 1860 at Edwards Township, St. Lawrence Co., NY.

    vi.   FREDERICK WARREN; born 10 Aug 1863; married Ora McAllester.

    vii.   FRANK R.; born 26 Feb 1868; married Mary Jennie Winslow; died 10 Feb 1906 at VT at age 37.

41. NANCY A.[8] JOHNSON (*Charles*[7], *Ira*[6], *Jonathan*[5], *Nathaniel*[4], *Nathaniel*[3], *Humphrey*[2], *John*[1]) was born on 7 Nov 1825 at Russell, St. Lawrence Co., NY. She married William Harry Brown on 19 Sep 1844 at Edwards, St. Lawrence Co., NY. She died on 23 Mar 1909 at Edwards, St. Lawrence Co., NY, at age 83. She was buried at Edwards, St. Lawrence Co., NY.

She appeared on the census of 1 Jun 1900 at Edwards, St. Lawrence Co., NY.

Children of Nancy A.[8] Johnson and William Harry Brown were as follows:

  65.   i.   ALVAH PERCIVAL[9], born 16 Sep 1846 at Pitcairn, St. Lawrence Co., NY; married Marian "Manie" Cleland; married Sarah J. Grant.

  66.   ii.   CHARLES HIRAM, born 30 Nov 1848 at Edwards, St. Lawrence Co., NY; married Martha Eliza Noble.

        iii.   CLARA E.; born 22 Jul 1859 at Edwards, St. Lawrence Co., NY; died 17 Nov 1868 at Edwards, St. Lawrence Co., NY, at age 9.

42. EMMORANCY[8] JOHNSON (*Charles*[7], *Ira*[6], *Jonathan*[5], *Nathaniel*[4], *Nathaniel*[3], *Humphrey*[2], *John*[1]) was born on 22 May 1827 at Pitcairn, St. Lawrence Co., NY. She married Alfred Brooks

Hall, son of Gardner A. Hall and Lutheria Nott, on 1 Jan 1845 at Edwards, St. Lawrence Co., NY. She died on 12 Feb 1890 at Edwards, St. Lawrence Co., NY, at age 62. She was buried at Riverside Cemetery, Edwards, St. Lawrence Co., NY. She was also known as Emmarancie, Emma, Emmah, and Em.

Children of Emmorancy[8] Johnson and Alfred Brooks Hall all born at Edwards, St. Lawrence Co., NY, were as follows:

67.   i.   HIRAM JUDSON[9], born 4 May 1852; married Ellison Louisa Barnes.

68.   ii.   JOSEPHINE, born 9 Jun 1854; married Albert Wight; married (--?--) Youngs.

69.   iii.   VENILA EDITH, born 14 Jun 1855; married Jasper Leonard Ward.

70.   iv.   MYRON, born May 1860; married Anna Winslow.

71.   v.   VENIRA A., born Apr 1862; married Morris E. Pratt.

72.   vi.   EMMA D., born 1864; married William Clark.

    vii.   CHARLES S.; born 10 Jan 1867; married Mary or Hattie Fuller; married Lois Wells 11 Mar 1890 at Gouverneur, St. Lawrence Co., NY; died 1 Sep 1943 at Canton, NY, at age 76.

43.   IRA[8] JOHNSON (*Warren[7], Ira[6], Jonathan[5], Nathaniel[4], Nathaniel[3], Humphrey[2], John[1]*) lived at IA.

Children of Ira[8] Johnson and an unknown spouse were:

    i.   ELDER[9] lived at OR.

44.   LUTILIA[8] JOHNSON (*George[7], Ira[6], Jonathan[5], Nathaniel[4], Nathaniel[3], Humphrey[2], John[1]*) was born on 17 Apr 1823 at Lincoln Co., MO. She married Andrew Main, son of Solomon Main, on 27 Sep 1838. She died on 9 Aug 1892 at Pike Co., IL, at age 69. She was buried at Petty Cemetery, Martinsburg Township, Pike Co., IL.

Children of Lutilia[8] Johnson and Andrew Main were as follows:

73. i. JOHN[9], born 1839 at Pike Co., IL; married Mary Walker.

ii. RUFUS; born 1842; died 1864.
He was unmarried.

74. iii. ALVIN NYE, born 1844; married Lydia Sarah Foote.

75. iv. PHILLIP MELVIN, born 1847 at Pike Co., IL; married Amilia Baker.

76. v. ANDREW PARKER, born 1849 at Pike Co., IL; married Elizabeth Hack.

vi. COLONEL; born 1850.
He was unmarried.

77. vii. SARAH JANE, born 1852 at Pike Co., IL; married Theodore Colvin.

78. viii. MINERVA ANN, born 1857; married Mason Lawson.

79. ix. GEORGE WASHINGTON, born 1859; married Emma Faris.

x. HENRY; born 1861; died 1863.

80. xi. WILLIAM H., born 1864; married Della Davidson.

81. xii. THOMAS JEFFERSON, born 1866; married Zella Bennett.

45. RUFUS E.[8] JOHNSON (*George[7]*, *Ira[6]*, *Jonathan[5]*, *Nathaniel[4]*, *Nathaniel[3]*, *Humphrey[2]*, *John[1]*) was born on 1 Jan 1825 at Pike Co., IL. He married Anna Moomau on 26 Sep 1846 at Pike Co., IL. He died on 14 Sep 1879 at Pike Co., IL, at age 54.

Children of Rufus E.[8] Johnson and Anna Moomau all born at Pike Co., IL, were as follows:

82. i. ALVIN RICHARD[9], born 6 Aug 1849; married Mary Harper; married Delila Gallaway.

83. ii. GEORGE HARDIN, born 15 Nov 1851; married Sarah Kisire Harper; married Sarah Emma Britain.

84. iii. LEWIS OSCAR, born 5 Jan 1854; married Sarah A. Cooper.

85.   iv.   ISAAC BENTON, born 16 Aug 1867; married Nellie Grace Long.

Generation Nine

46. SARAH[9] DELANO (*Catherine[8]Lyman, Joseph[7], Mary[6]Sheldon, Benjamin[5], Mary[4]Hinsdale, Mehitable[3]Johnson, Humphrey[2], John[1]*) married James Roosevelt.

Children of Sarah[9] Delano and James Roosevelt were:

    i.   FRANKLIN DELANO[10] was the 32nd US President.

47. EUNICE[9] HARMON (*Harriett[8]Viall, Charles[7]Johnson, Ira[6], Jonathan[5], Nathaniel[4], Nathaniel[3], Humphrey[2], John[1]*) was born on 16 May 1824. She married Sardine S. Van Ornum on 2 Sep 1843.

Children of Eunice[9] Harmon and Sardine S. Van Ornum were:

    i.   LEWIS[10].

48. PAUL OSGOOD[9] HARMON (*Harriett[8]Viall, Charles[7]Johnson, Ira[6], Jonathan[5], Nathaniel[4], Nathaniel[3], Humphrey[2], John[1]*) was born on 21 Jun 1828. He married Mary Elizabeth Titus, daughter of Sylvanus Jenison Titus and Harriett Maria Snow, on 22 Mar 1853. He died on 25 Apr 1864 at age 35.

Children of Paul Osgood[9] Harmon and Mary Elizabeth Titus were as follows:

    i.   WESLEY O.[10]; born 21 Jun 1855; died 2 Jan 1868 at age 12; buried at Payne Cemetery near Edwards, St. Lawrence Co., NY.

    ii.   HARRIETT ADALINE; born 17 Jul 1857; married John Austin Wood 3 Jul 1875; died 3 May 1941 at age 83; buried at Sedwards Cemetery.

49. ALTHA[9] HARMON (*Harriett[8]Viall, Charles[7]Johnson, Ira[6], Jonathan[5], Nathaniel[4], Nathaniel[3], Humphrey[2], John[1]*) was born on 23 Jul 1830. She married John Wallace Laidlaw, son of (--?--) Laidlaw and Theresa Eliza Blood, on 7 Jan 1851. She married Milton Thompson. She died on 28 Apr 1906 at age 75.

Children of Altha[9] Harmon and an unknown spouse were:

    i.   FRANCILIA[10]; born 25 Dec 1853.

50. WESLEY PORTER[9] HARMON JR. (*Harriett*[8]*Viall*, *Charles*[7]*Johnson*, *Ira*[6], *Jonathan*[5], *Nathaniel*[4], *Nathaniel*[3], *Humphrey*[2], *John*[1]) was born on 15 Oct 1837 at Edwards, St. Lawrence Co., NY. He married Nancy Laidlaw, daughter of (--?--) Laidlaw and Theresa Eliza Blood, on 4 Sep 1860. He died on 19 Apr at Edwards, St. Lawrence Co., NY. He was buried at Payne Cemetery.

Children of Wesley Porter[9] Harmon Jr. and Nancy Laidlaw were as follows:

    i.   ALTHA[10]; born 1863; died 1886 at Edwards, St. Lawrence Co., NY.

    ii.   ANN ELIZA; born 1863; died 1956 at Edwards, St. Lawrence Co., NY.

    iii.   EDWARD P.; born 1865.
        He was the father of eight children.

    iv.   LILLY M.; born 1870; died 1898 at Edwards, St. Lawrence Co., NY.

51. MARY LEIGHTON[9] JOHNSON (*Charles*[8], *Charles*[7], *Ira*[6], *Jonathan*[5], *Nathaniel*[4], *Nathaniel*[3], *Humphrey*[2], *John*[1]) was born on 2 Oct 1839 at Pike Co., IL. She married John Nicholson on 7 Oct 1858 at Independence, Pike Co., IL. She died on 22 Nov 1908 at Jackson Co., MO, at age 69. She was buried at Greenwood Cemetery, West Pittsfield, Pike Co., IL.

Children of Mary Leighton[9] Johnson and John Nicholson were as follows:

86.   i.   CHARLES VIAL[10], born 1 Mar 1861 at Pike Co., IL; married Lena Watson.

        ii.   FLORENCE ANN; born 14 Jun 1862 at Pike Co., IL; married J. R. Sears.

87.   iii.   MARY EMILY, born 20 Aug 1864 at Pike Co., IL; married James Garnsey.

        iv.   REBECCA MAY; born 18 May 1866 at Pike Co., IL; married David Clauser.

v. HARRIETT EVA; born 30 Oct 1868 at Pike Co., IL; married Charles Douglas Jeffers.

vi. PHILA VIOLET; born 6 Aug 1870 at Pike Co., IL; died young; buried at Johnson Cemetery, Hardin, IL.

vii. JESSIE VIVIAN; born 7 Sep 1871 at Pike Co., IL; married James R. Moore.

viii. JOHN ROBERT; born 18 Oct 1874; died young; buried at Greenwood Cemetery, West Pittsfield, Pike Co., IL.

52. REBECCA EMILY[9] JOHNSON (*Charles*[8], *Charles*[7], *Ira*[6], *Jonathan*[5], *Nathaniel*[4], *Nathaniel*[3], *Humphrey*[2], *John*[1]) was born on 28 Nov 1845. She married Samuel Wiley Miller, son of James B. Miller and Mary Griffin, on 21 Aug 1867 at Pike Co., IL. She died on 8 Sep 1916 at Pike Co., IL, at age 70. She was buried at Glasgow Cemetery, Scott Co., IL.

Children of Rebecca Emily[9] Johnson and Samuel Wiley Miller were as follows:

88. i. MARY EMILY[10], born 21 Feb 1869; married "Doc" Lawrence Killebrew.

ii. CHARLES VIAL; born 26 Nov 1870; married Laura (--?--); died 12 Feb 1927 at age 56; buried at Huntington, WV.

He was also known as JOHN CHARLES VIAL MILLER.

89. iii. ETHEL WAYNE, born 17 Sep 1873; married Thomas Spencer Killebrew.

90. iv. WILLIAM BAIRD RICHARD, born 27 Nov 1876; married Lucy Potter.

53. PHILA VIOLET[9] JOHNSON (*Charles*[8], *Charles*[7], *Ira*[6], *Jonathan*[5], *Nathaniel*[4], *Nathaniel*[3], *Humphrey*[2], *John*[1]) was born on 2 Jul 1849 at Independence, Pike Co., IL. She married Richard Thornton on 16 Mar 1875 at Pike Co., IL. She died on 18 Nov 1919 at Spring Creek, Pike Co., IL, at age 70.

Children of Phila Violet[9] Johnson and Richard Thornton were as follows:

        i.   ANNIE[10]; born 4 Jan 1877 at Hardin Township, Pike Co., IL; died 4 Jan 1877; buried at Johnson Cemetery, Pike Co., IL.

91.   ii.   RICHARD STANLEY, born 10 Feb 1879 at Pike Co., IL; married Sarah Allison.

92.   iii.   BERTHA MAHALA, born 12 Dec 1880 at Pike Co., IL; married Luther E. Smith.

93.   iv.   HERBERT DOSS, born 31 Mar 1885 at Newburg Township, Pike Co., IL; married Lora Alice Scranton.

54.   EMMA NANCY[9] JOHNSON (*Charles*[8], *Charles*[7], *Ira*[6], *Jonathan*[5], *Nathaniel*[4], *Nathaniel*[3], *Humphrey*[2], *John*[1]) was born in 1854. She married Monroe D. Ransom in 1876. She died on 30 Mar 1943 at Pike Co., IL.

Children of Emma Nancy[9] Johnson and Monroe D. Ransom were:

94.   i.   WARREN G.[10], born 1877 at Pike Co., IL; married Pearl St John; married Cora Weaver.

55.   JOHN CHARLES[9] JOHNSON (*Hiram*[8], *Charles*[7], *Ira*[6], *Jonathan*[5], *Nathaniel*[4], *Nathaniel*[3], *Humphrey*[2], *John*[1]) was born on 29 May 1842 at Pike Co., IL. He married Violetta Gunsaules, daughter of Manuel Gunsaules and Easter Ann Cox, on 3 Mar 1864. He died on 3 Dec 1920 at Salem, Marion Co., OR, at age 78.

He appeared on the census of 1 Jun 1850 at Marion Co., OR Territory. As of 1 Jun 1850, he was also known as Charles Johnson.

Children of John Charles[9] Johnson and Violetta Gunsaules were as follows:

95.   i.   ELIZABETH ANNA "LIZZIE"[10], born 11 Feb 1865 at Scio, Linn Co., OR; married John Daniel.

96.   ii.   ARCHIE JAMES SR, born 18 Sep 1867; married Linnie Young; married Jennie Young.

97.   iii.   ETTA ARZELLA, born 4 Jan 1871; married John C. Simpson.

iv. JOHN ELMER; born 22 Mar 1873 at Scio, Linn Co., OR; died 27 Oct 1882 at Scio, Linn Co., OR, at age 9.

98. v. CHARLES VIRGIL, born 18 Mar 1875 at Scio, Linn Co., OR; married Maud Ethel Rundlett.

vi. CLARENCE ELVA; born 14 Apr 1881 at Scio, Linn Co., OR; died 3 Nov 1882 at Scio, Linn Co., OR, at age 1.

99. vii. PEARL INEZ, born 5 Nov 1883 at Scio, Linn Co., OR; married Albert S. Shaw; married Wiley Stuart.

56. GEORGE WASHINGTON[9] JOHNSON SR. (*Hiram[8]*, *Charles[7]*, *Ira[6]*, *Jonathan[5]*, *Nathaniel[4]*, *Nathaniel[3]*, *Humphrey[2]*, *John[1]*) was born on 19 Jul 1844 at Pike Co., IL. He married Mary Parthena Jones on 14 Oct 1866. He died on 16 Oct 1919 at Salem, Marion Co., OR, at age 75.

He appeared on the census of 1 Jun 1870 at Jefferson, Marion Co., OR.

Children of George Washington[9] Johnson Sr. and Mary Parthena Jones were as follows:

100. i. OSCAR M.[10], born 16 Jul 1867; married Mrytle (--?--).

101. ii. ROSE E., born 26 Jan 1869 at Scio, Linn Co., OR; married Willis E. McElroy.

102. iii. LULU B., born Jul 1870; married Frank Albert Baker.

103. iv. GEORGE WASHINGTON JR, born 24 Feb 1876; married Verda Belle Valet.

104. v. CLYDE E., born 2 Jan 1881; married Grace VanWagner.

105. vi. PAUL VAYNE, born 19 Jan 1888 at Salem, Marion Co., OR; married Leona Graham.

57. WILLIAM WARREN[9] JOHNSON (*Hiram[8]*, *Charles[7]*, *Ira[6]*, *Jonathan[5]*, *Nathaniel[4]*, *Nathaniel[3]*, *Humphrey[2]*, *John[1]*) was born on 20 May 1847 at a "Wagon Train", along the Platte River, NE. He married Caroline E. Harris, daughter of David Harris and Hester

Wood, on 25 Feb 1869 at Jefferson, Marion Co., OR. He died on 12 May 1906 at Burns, Harney Co., OR, at age 58. He was buried at Blk 20 Lot 8 IOOF Section, Burns, Harney Co., OR.

As of 1 Jun 1850, he was also known as Warren Johnson. He was the person who named Mittchell, Wheeler Co., OR in 1875. He appeared on the census of 1880 at Harney Prec., Grant Co., OR. He was Blacksmith in 1880.

Children of William Warren[9] Johnson and Caroline E. Harris were as follows:

106. i. ADA MAY[10], born 14 Feb 1870 at Jefferson, Marion Co., OR; married Charles Schlenker Iaeger; divorced Charles Schlenker Iaeger; married Stonewall Jackson Mothershead.

107. ii. CHARLES W., born 29 May 1871 at OR; married Minnie R. Reed.

 iii. ANNA; born 20 May 1872; died 14 Aug 1887 at age 15.

108. iv. LLOYD LEROY, born 4 Jul 1875; married Bertha Clark.

109. v. HESTER ELIZABETH, born 19 Oct 1876 at Indian Agency, Vale, OR; married William Austin Goodman.

 vi. ELDON C.; born 9 Aug 1881 at Camp Harney, Grant Co. (now Harney Co.), OR; married Betsy Anderson 28 Jun 1917 at Seattle, King Co., WA; died 19 Oct 1953 at Burns, Harney Co., OR, at age 72; buried at Blk 20 Lot 9 IOOF Sec, Burns Cemetery, Burns, Harney Co., OR.

  He appeared on the census of 1900 at Burns Prec., Burns, Harney Co., OR.

 vii. WILLIAM "WILLIE"; born 5 Mar 1885; died at Burns, Harney Co., OR.

 viii. (--?--).

110. ix. LULU BELLE, born 14 Feb 1887 at Burns, Harney Co., OR; married Rush McHargue Sr.

x. LEON M.; born 23 Feb 1891; died 30 Oct 1916 at MT at age 25; buried at Edmonds Cemetery, Edmonds, Snohomish Co., WA.

He appeared on the census of 1900 at Burns Precinct, Burns, Harney Co., OR.

58. HIRAM ALVAH[9] JOHNSON JR. (*Hiram*[8], *Charles*[7], *Ira*[6], *Jonathan*[5], *Nathaniel*[4], *Nathaniel*[3], *Humphrey*[2], *John*[1]) was born on 3 Mar 1849 at Jefferson, Marion Co., OR. He died on 12 Dec 1917 at Salem, Marion Co., OR, at age 68.

He appeared on the census of 1 Jun 1850 at Marion Co., OR Territory. As of 1 Jun 1850, he was also known as Alva Johnson.

Children of Hiram Alvah[9] Johnson Jr. and Amanda Savanna Jones were as follows:

111. i. CLAUDE A.[10], born 8 May 1874; married Lucy A. (--?--); divorced Lucy A. (--?--).

112. ii. MYRTLE J., born 24 Apr 1876; married Arthur H. Williams; married Edward Hamer; divorced Edward Hamer.

113. iii. HIRAM ALVAH III, born 31 Dec 1878 at Salem, Marion Co., OR; married Anna Adaline Grabenhorst; married Mary A. Edwards; divorced Mary A. Edwards.

114. iv. CRETA J., born May 1889; married Orville Stubbs; married Charles W. Stege; married (--?--) Green.

59. SAMUEL THURSTON[9] JOHNSON (*Hiram*[8], *Charles*[7], *Ira*[6], *Jonathan*[5], *Nathaniel*[4], *Nathaniel*[3], *Humphrey*[2], *John*[1]) was born on 18 Mar 1850 at Jefferson, Marion Co., OR. He married Mary Jane "Mollie" Elliott on 20 Aug 1876 at Marion Co., OR. He died on 28 Oct 1919 at Portland, Multnomah Co., OR, at age 69. He was buried at Belle Passi Cemetery, Woodburn, Marion Co., OR.

He appeared on the census of 1 Jun 1860 at Southern Precinct, Santiam City, Marion Co., OR.

Children of Samuel Thurston[9] Johnson and Mary Jane "Mollie" Elliott were as follows:

115. i. FRED LEROY[10], born 31 Jul 1877 at Jefferson, Marion Co., OR; married Lettie Elloda Watkinds.

ii. ROYAL HERBERT; born 28 Mar 1879 at Jefferson, Marion Co., OR; died 24 Sep 1904 at Jefferson, Marion Co., OR, at age 25.

iii. EDWARD NORTON; born 4 Dec 1880 at Jefferson, Marion Co., OR; married Nettie E. Broyles 7 Jun 1916; died 6 Aug 1935 at Woodburn, Marion Co., OR, at age 54.

116. iv. EDYTHE MADILLA, born 9 Apr 1882 at Jefferson, Marion Co., OR; married James Henry Wagenblast.

v. GERTRUDE NELLIE; born 19 Nov 1884 at Jefferson, Marion Co., OR; died 15 Apr 1905 at Jefferson, Marion Co., OR, at age 20.

vi. JAMES MCQUAID; born 18 Jun 1887 at Jefferson, Marion Co., OR; died 9 Oct 1890 at Jefferson, Marion Co., OR, at age 3.

vii. JESSIE LEETTA; born 3 Aug 1891 at Jefferson, Marion Co., OR; died 20 Aug 1892 at age 1.

viii. FRANCES BERNEICE; born 2 Sep 1894 at Jefferson, Marion Co., OR; died 4 May 1912 at Jefferson, Marion Co., OR, at age 17.

ix. EUGENE DAYLE; born 17 Apr 1897 at Jefferson, Marion Co., OR; died 2 Oct 1918 at France at age 21; buried 15 Sep 1920 at Belle Passi Cemetery, Woodburn, Marion Co., OR.

x. (--?--); born 1900; died young.

60. FRANCIS "FRANK" M.[9] JOHNSON (*Hiram*[8], *Charles*[7], *Ira*[6], *Jonathan*[5], *Nathaniel*[4], *Nathaniel*[3], *Humphrey*[2], *John*[1]) was born on 16 Dec 1855 at Jefferson, Marion Co., OR. He married Emma Cosper, daughter of William Cosper, on 11 Apr 1881. He died on 18 Jun 1913 at Moscow, ID, at age 57.

He appeared on the census of 1 Jun 1860 at Southern Precinct, Santiam City, Marion Co., OR. He was a teacher circa 1876 at Indian Agency School, Vale, OR.

Children of Francis "Frank" M.[9] Johnson and Emma Cosper were:

    i.   HERBERT DE LOS[10]; born 19 Nov 1882 at ID; married Nellie E. Bradley, daughter of F. William Bradley and Margarett Fossett; died 17 Apr 1964 at Yakima, Yakima Co., WA, at age 81.

61. CHARLES VIALL[9] HARMON (*Phila*[8]*Viall*, *Charles*[7]*Johnson*, *Ira*[6], *Jonathan*[5], *Nathaniel*[4], *Nathaniel*[3], *Humphrey*[2], *John*[1]) was born in 1836. He married Maryette Maltby. He died in 1903.

Children of Charles Viall[9] Harmon and Maryette Maltby were as follows:

    i.   ALBERT G.[10]; born 1871; died 1872.
    ii. GERTIE C.; died 26 Mar

62. ELGIN ABEL[9] JOHNSON (*Abel*[8], *Charles*[7], *Ira*[6], *Jonathan*[5], *Nathaniel*[4], *Nathaniel*[3], *Humphrey*[2], *John*[1]) was born on 15 Aug 1849 at Edwards, St. Lawrence Co., NY. He married Phoebe J. Hall on 28 May 1873 at Millport, NY. He died at CA.

He appeared on the census of 1 Jun 1850 at Edwards Township, St. Lawrence Co., NY. He lived at OR.

Children of Elgin Abel[9] Johnson and Phoebe J. Hall were as follows:

    i.   HAIDEE[10]; born 15 Dec 1874 at Edwards, St. Lawrence Co., NY; died 15 Dec 1874 at Edwards, St. Lawrence Co., NY.
117. ii. SAPHRONIA L., married Arthur L. Dilmore.
    iii. HARRY A.; born 26 Feb 1878 at Scio, Linn Co., OR; married May Penn.
    iv. ELNORA M.; born 24 Nov 1880 at Scio, Linn Co., OR; married William Walker Jul 1906; died 1947; buried at Pine Valley, NY.
    v. FRED S.; born 17 Aug 1886 at Hillside, Linn Co., OR; married Maud Crouter 27 Mar 1910.
118. vi. ABEL PRATT II, born 29 Dec 1889 at Elmira, Chemung Co., NY; married Clara Ray Penny.

63. ELIZA ANN[9] JOHNSON (*William*[8], *Charles*[7], *Ira*[6], *Jonathan*[5], *Nathaniel*[4], *Nathaniel*[3], *Humphrey*[2], *John*[1]) was born on 8 Jul 1847 at Edwards, St. Lawrence Co., NY. She married Allen Payne on 25 Mar 1868 at Hermon, St. Lawrence Co., NY. She died on 14 Jan 1879 at age 31.

She appeared on the census of 1 Jun 1850 at Edwards Township, St. Lawrence Co., NY.

Children of Eliza Ann[9] Johnson and Allen Payne were as follows:

      i.   ERNEST[10]; born 1868; married (--?--) ?

     ii.   ELMER A.; born Jan 1869; married Nora Ward 21 Mar 1894; died 1937.

64. CHARLES VIALL[9] JOHNSON (*William*[8], *Charles*[7], *Ira*[6], *Jonathan*[5], *Nathaniel*[4], *Nathaniel*[3], *Humphrey*[2], *John*[1]) was born on 30 Oct 1849 at Edwards, St. Lawrence Co., NY. He died on 15 Sep 1908 at Hermon, St. Lawrence Co., NY, at age 58.

He appeared on the census of 1 Jun 1850 at Edwards Township, St. Lawrence Co., NY.

Children of Charles Viall[9] Johnson and Celia A. Laidlaw all born at Edwards, St. Lawrence Co., NY, were as follows:

       i.   OLIE ALTHA[10]; born 12 Aug 1881; died 20 Dec 1933 at Hermon, St. Lawrence Co., NY, at age 52.

           She appeared on the census of 1 Jun 1900 at Edwards Township, St. Lawrence Co., NY.

119.   ii.   ETHEL MORIAH, born 23 Sep 1883; married Rollin Clark Noble.

120.   iii.   FERNE HELEN, born 1 May 1886; married Floyd Noble.

     iv.   MABEL E.; born 3 Dec 1888; died 30 Oct 1890 at age 1.

      v.   VONNE "VAUGHN" RUTH; born 5 Sep 1890; died 27 Jun 1903 at age 12.

           She appeared on the census of 1 Jun 1900 at Edwards Township, St. Lawrence Co., NY.

121.   vi.   JOHN WARREN, born 20 Jun 1893; married Orabell Chase.

65. ALVAH PERCIVAL[9] BROWN (*Nancy*[8]*Johnson*, *Charles*[7], *Ira*[6], *Jonathan*[5], *Nathaniel*[4], *Nathaniel*[3], *Humphrey*[2], *John*[1]) was born on 16 Sep 1846 at Pitcairn, St. Lawrence Co., NY. He married Marian "Manie" Cleland, daughter of William Cleland and Jane Kerr, on 23 Mar 1870. He married Sarah J. Grant, daughter of Thomas Grant and Julia A. Rushton, on 20 Jun 1877 at Edwards, St. Lawrence Co., NY. He died on 3 Mar 1906 at Edwards, St. Lawrence Co., NY, at age 59.

He appeared on the census of 1 Jun 1900 at Edwards, St. Lawrence Co., NY.

Children of Alvah Percival[9] Brown and Marian "Manie" Cleland were:

122.   i.   SHERMAN WILLIAM[10], born 31 Jul 1873 at Edwards, St. Lawrence Co., NY; engaged Lena May Ward; married Gertrude Backus; engaged Florence Raycraft.

Children of Alvah Percival[9] Brown and Sarah J. Grant were as follows:

123.   i.   MANIE ELNORA[10], born 10 Jun 1879 at Edwards, St. Lawrence Co., NY; married Earle S. Johnson.

　　ii.   MARY ROSE; born 22 Feb 1881 at Edwards, St. Lawrence Co., NY; married Arthur Dulack, son of Joseph Dulack and Catherine O'Shea, 22 Feb 1905 at Edwards, St. Lawrence Co., NY; married Joseph B. Maloy, son of John Maloy and Elizabeth Colgan; died 5 Feb 1975 at Gouverneur, St. Lawrence Co., NY, at age 93.

　　　　She appeared on the census of 1 Jun 1900 at Edwards, St. Lawrence Co., NY.

　　iii.   HAROLD ELMER; born 30 Aug 1890 at Little York, St. Lawrence Co., NY; died 1 Sep 1964 at Gouverneur, St. Lawrence Co., NY, at age 74; buried 4 Sep 1964 at Riverside Cemetery, Edwards, St. Lawrence Co., NY.

He appeared on the census of 1 Jun 1900 at Edwards, St. Lawrence Co., NY. He was unmarried.

iv. CLARA PEARL; born 3 Mar 1896 at Edwards, St. Lawrence Co., NY; died 21 Feb 1969 at Memorial Hospital, Hollywood, Broward Co., FL, at age 72; buried 24 Feb 1969 at Riverside Cemetery, Edwards, St. Lawrence Co., NY.

She was unmarried.

66. CHARLES HIRAM[9] BROWN (*Nancy*[8]*Johnson, Charles*[7], *Ira*[6], *Jonathan*[5], *Nathaniel*[4], *Nathaniel*[3], *Humphrey*[2], *John*[1]) was born on 30 Nov 1848 at Edwards, St. Lawrence Co., NY. He married Martha Eliza Noble on 26 Dec 1869 at Harrisville, NY. He died on 31 Mar 1929 at Edwards, St. Lawrence Co., NY, at age 80.

He appeared on the census of 1 Jun 1900 at Edwards, St. Lawrence Co., NY.

Children of Charles Hiram[9] Brown and Martha Eliza Noble all born at Edwards, St. Lawrence Co., NY, were as follows:

124. i. CLARENCE CHARLES[10], born 2 Jun 1872; married Carrie Pearl Cleland.

125. ii. OSWALD BOWER, born 4 Mar 1874; married Pearl Theresa Baldwin; married Nellie Morrosey.

126. iii. MABEL E., born 1 Jan 1876; married Charles Milton Clark.

67. HIRAM JUDSON[9] HALL (*Emmorancy*[8]*Johnson, Charles*[7], *Ira*[6], *Jonathan*[5], *Nathaniel*[4], *Nathaniel*[3], *Humphrey*[2], *John*[1]) was born on 4 May 1852 at Edwards, St. Lawrence Co., NY. He married Ellison Louisa Barnes, daughter of Horace Barnes and Ellison Eldora Dunn, in 1871. He died on 11 Jan 1913 at Edwards, St. Lawrence Co., NY, at age 60. He was buried on 14 Jan 1913 at Riverside Cemetery, Edwards, St. Lawrence Co., NY.

He appeared on the census of 1 Jun 1900 at Edwards, St. Lawrence Co., NY.

Children of Hiram Judson[9] Hall and Ellison Louisa Barnes all born at Edwards, St. Lawrence Co., NY, were as follows:

127.   i.   LETA E.[10], born 24 Jun 1874; married Eddy R. Beach.

128.   ii.   LEON HORACE, born 4 Mar 1876; married Mayme Gertrude Clary.

129.   iii.   FLORENCE E., born 20 Apr 1880; married Gilbert Hughes; married Jacob O. Davis.

130.   iv.   LOTTIE MAE, born 23 Jun 1882; married Arthur Isidore Boulet.

131.   v.   FRANK EMERY SR, born 7 Oct 1884; married Bernice Mari Lillis.

68.   JOSEPHINE[9] HALL (*Emmorancy[8]Johnson, Charles[7], Ira[6], Jonathan[5], Nathaniel[4], Nathaniel[3], Humphrey[2], John[1]*) was born on 9 Jun 1854 at Edwards, St. Lawrence Co., NY. She married Albert Wight on 13 Aug 1873. She married (--?--) Youngs. She died on 2 Mar 1909 at Pitcairn, St. Lawrence Co., NY, at age 54. She was buried at Riverside Cemetery, Edwards, St. Lawrence Co., NY.

Children of Josephine[9] Hall and Albert Wight were as follows:

   i.   LETTIE[10]; born 22 Jun 1875.

   ii.   LONA; born 14 Feb 1879.

There were no children of Josephine[9] Hall and (--?--) Youngs.

69.   VENILA EDITH[9] HALL (*Emmorancy[8]Johnson, Charles[7], Ira[6], Jonathan[5], Nathaniel[4], Nathaniel[3], Humphrey[2], John[1]*) was born on 14 Jun 1855 at Edwards, St. Lawrence Co., NY. She married Jasper Leonard Ward, son of Leonard Ward and Angeline Winslow, circa 1875. She died on 23 Jun 1934 at Gouverneur, St. Lawrence Co., NY, at age 79. She was buried at Payne Cemetery, Edwards, St. Lawrence Co., NY.

She was also known as Nillie. She appeared on the census of 1 Jun 1900 at Edwards, St. Lawrence Co., NY. As of 1 Jun 1900, she was also known as Edith V. Ward.

Children of Venila Edith[9] Hall and Jasper Leonard Ward all born at Edwards, St. Lawrence Co., NY, were as follows:

132.   i.   BRUCE THERON[10], born 16 Jul 1875; married Carrie Elizabeth Creighton.

133.	ii.	LENA MAY, born 8 Jul 1877; married Webster Maybee.
134.	iii.	MARGARET M., born 12 Mar 1880; married Perley Shampine.
	iv.	LEONARD; born 11 Jun 1883; died 28 Aug 1911 at Gouverneur, St. Lawrence Co., NY, at age 28; buried at Payne Cemetery, Edwards, St. Lawrence Co., NY.
135.	v.	GRACE, born 5 Sep 1886; married Burton Maybee.
136.	vi.	BLANCHE, born 23 Oct 1888; married Horace Alfred Brotherton; married Wilbur Cunningham.
	vii.	CLARENCE B.; born 19 Jun 1891; married Mayfred L. Coloney 18 Dec 1915 at Gouverneur, St. Lawrence Co., NY; died 30 Jul 1946 at Ogdensburg, St. Lawrence Co., NY, at age 55; buried at Payne Cemetery, Edwards, St. Lawrence Co., NY.

He appeared on the census of 1 Jun 1900 at Edwards Township, St. Lawrence Co., NY. He was separated from Mayfred circa 1932.

137.	viii.	HOWARD "DICK", born 7 Oct 1893; married Mina Dart.
138.	ix.	EDITH LURA, born 28 Nov 1895; married Ralph Marshall Morgan.
	x.	EVA; born 23 Apr 1899; died before 23 Aug 1949.

She was unmarried. She appeared on the census of 1 Jun 1900 at Edwards Township, St. Lawrence Co., NY.

| | xi. | EARL; born 20 Jun 1901; died 1 Oct 1910 at Edwards, St. Lawrence Co., NY, at age 9; buried at Payne Cemetery, Edwards, St. Lawrence Co., NY. |

70. MYRON[9] HALL (*Emmorancy*[8]*Johnson, Charles*[7], *Ira*[6], *Jonathan*[5], *Nathaniel*[4], *Nathaniel*[3], *Humphrey*[2], *John*[1]) was born in May 1860 at Edwards, St. Lawrence Co., NY. He married Anna

Winslow circa 1885. He died in 1902 at Edwards, St. Lawrence Co., NY. He was buried at Riverside Cemetery, Edwards, St. Lawrence Co., NY.

He appeared on the census of 1 Jun 1900 at Edwards, St. Lawrence Co., NY.

Children of Myron[9] Hall and Anna Winslow were as follows:

    i.   HAZEL J.[10]; born Oct 1889 at NY.

          She appeared on the census of 1 Jun 1900 at Edwards, St. Lawrence Co., NY.

    ii. (--?--); died before 1900.

    iii. MYRTLE J.; born Jun 1893 at NY.

          She appeared on the census of 1 Jun 1900 at Edwards, St. Lawrence Co., NY.

    iv. GLADYS B.; born Oct 1895 at NY.

          She appeared on the census of 1 Jun 1900 at Edwards, St. Lawrence Co., NY.

71.   VENIRA A.[9] HALL (*Emmorancy*[8]*Johnson*, *Charles*[7], *Ira*[6], *Jonathan*[5], *Nathaniel*[4], *Nathaniel*[3], *Humphrey*[2], *John*[1]) was born in Apr 1862 at Edwards, St. Lawrence Co., NY. She married Morris E. Pratt, son of Henry T. Pratt, circa 1881. She died on 8 Mar 1934 at Edwards, St. Lawrence Co., NY, at age 71. She was buried at Riverside Cemetery, Edwards, St. Lawrence Co., NY.

She was also known as Nearie. She appeared on the census of 1 Jun 1900 at Edwards, St. Lawrence Co., NY.

Children of Venira A.[9] Hall and Morris E. Pratt were as follows:

139.   i.   HARRISON L.[10], born 6 Aug 1882 at Edwards, St. Lawrence Co., NY; married Mary Gotham.

140.   ii. CECILE EVA, born 20 May 1884 at Edwards, St. Lawrence Co., NY; married Arthur Henry Newvine.

141.   iii. HARLEY THERON, born 3 Apr 1885 at Edwards, St. Lawrence Co., NY; married Mary Caroline Lennon.

        iv. (--?--); born circa 6 Jul 1886; died 20 Jul 1886.

        v.   CHARLES; born 19 Jul 1887; died 14 Oct 1893 at age 6.

72. EMMA D.^{9} HALL (*Emmorancy*^{8}*Johnson*, *Charles*^{7}, *Ira*^{6}, *Jonathan*^{5}, *Nathaniel*^{4}, *Nathaniel*^{3}, *Humphrey*^{2}, *John*^{1}) was born in 1864 at Edwards, St. Lawrence Co., NY. She married William Clark.

Children of Emma D.^{9} Hall and William Clark were:

    i.   MILDRED^{10}; married (--?--) Redmond.

73. JOHN^9 MAIN (*Lutilia*^{8}*Johnson*, *George*^{7}, *Ira*^{6}, *Jonathan*^{5}, *Nathaniel*^{4}, *Nathaniel*^{3}, *Humphrey*^{2}, *John*^{1}) was born in 1839 at Pike Co., IL. He married Mary Walker. He died at MO.

Children of John^9 Main and Mary Walker were as follows:

142.   i.   ALICE^{10}, born 1862; married Thomas Burbridge.
143.   ii. ALVIN, born 1864; married Ella Johnson; married Anne Sheppard.
        iii. LUTILIA; born 1869; died 1945.
144.   iv. LENA OPAL, born 1872; married Ora Johnson.

74. ALVIN NYE^9 MAIN (*Lutilia*^{8}*Johnson*, *George*^{7}, *Ira*^{6}, *Jonathan*^{5}, *Nathaniel*^{4}, *Nathaniel*^{3}, *Humphrey*^{2}, *John*^{1}) was born in 1844. He married Lydia Sarah Foote. He died in 1929.

Children of Alvin Nye^9 Main and Lydia Sarah Foote were as follows:

    i.   CLARA MONDAN^{10}; born 1866; died 1953.
145.   ii. RUFUS HENRY, born 1868; married Helen Chrysup.
146.   iii. JOSIAH, born 1870; married Emily Triplet.
147.   iv. BLANCH MARGRET, born 1874; married William Gay.
148.   v. ROSE IDA, born 1874; married Luther Lawrence Warden.
        vi. GEORGIANA JANE; born 1879.
149.   vii. ROSCOE CONKLING, born 1882; married Ruth Flower Stafford.
150.   viii. FRANCIS ALVIN, born 1884; married Iva Woolfolk Scanland.

75. PHILLIP MELVIN[9] MAIN (*Lutilia*[8]*Johnson, George*[7], *Ira*[6], *Jonathan*[5], *Nathaniel*[4], *Nathaniel*[3], *Humphrey*[2], *John*[1]) was born in 1847 at Pike Co., IL. He married Amilia Baker. He died in 1946 at CA.

Children of Phillip Melvin[9] Main and Amilia Baker were as follows:

	i.	NOLY[10]; born 1871; died 1899.
151.	ii.	LOTTIE, born 1875; married Alex Sutherland.
	iii.	JENNIE; born 1878; died 1937.
152.	iv.	DAISY, born 1880; married M. William McDonald.
	v.	MELVIN PHILIP; born 1882; died 1947.
153.	vi.	CLYDE, born 1884; married Margaret Alexander.
	vii.	NELL; born 1889; married George Dick.

76. ANDREW PARKER[9] MAIN (*Lutilia*[8]*Johnson, George*[7], *Ira*[6], *Jonathan*[5], *Nathaniel*[4], *Nathaniel*[3], *Humphrey*[2], *John*[1]) was born in 1849 at Pike Co., IL. He married Elizabeth Hack.

Children of Andrew Parker[9] Main and Elizabeth Hack were as follows:

154.	i.	ODUS OLEN[10], born 1875; married Virdie May Hughs; married Katherine Halverson.
155.	ii.	LONNIE LOREN, born 1877; married Alma V. Hunter.
156.	iii.	BYARD BOLEN, born 1879; married Iva E. Johnson; married Coy Doyle.
157.	iv.	TADE MARION, born 1881; married James L. Wood.
158.	v.	HARRY HERMAN, born 1883; married Ruby Opal Brannon.
159.	vi.	CARRIE CLIFFORD, born 1885; married Lillie Jones.
160.	vii.	FLO FOUNTAIN, born 1888; married Helen Johnson; married Lizzie Shott.
161.	viii.	NINA NOBLE, born 1891; married John William Walkey; married William Henry Thiele.

ix. RELL RTENCIE; born 1893; married Blanche Gore; married Dorothy Owens; married Edna Hesseman.

162. x. MUDD MARBLE, born 1895; married Alma McCormick.

xi. EELA ELAS; born 1897; married Frank Reardon.

77. SARAH JANE[9] MAIN (*Lutilia[8]Johnson, George[7], Ira[6], Jonathan[5], Nathaniel[4], Nathaniel[3], Humphrey[2], John[1]*) was born in 1852 at Pike Co., IL. She married Theodore Colvin. She died in 1937.

Children of Sarah Jane[9] Main and Theodore Colvin were as follows:

163. i. MINNERVA ALICE[10], born 1881 at Pike Co., IL; married Joseph A. MaLee.

164. ii. BEULAH AUDRY, born 1883 at Pike Co., IL; married Edward C. Kulmus.

165. iii. SIDNEY ORVILLE, born 1885; married Pearl Naoma Colby.

166. iv. ANTHONEY BEN, born 1887; married Eva Borg.

167. v. GLADYS CARRIE, born 1890; married Alvah E. Williams.

78. MINERVA ANN[9] MAIN (*Lutilia[8]Johnson, George[7], Ira[6], Jonathan[5], Nathaniel[4], Nathaniel[3], Humphrey[2], John[1]*) was born in 1857. She married Mason Lawson. She died in 1897.

Children of Minerva Ann[9] Main and Mason Lawson were as follows:

i. DAISEY E.[10]; born 1879; married L. C. Schecklelsworth.

ii. ROSE E.; born 1881; died 1912.

168. iii. PANSY A., born 1883; married A. J. Koenig.

79. GEORGE WASHINGTON[9] MAIN (*Lutilia[8]Johnson, George[7], Ira[6], Jonathan[5], Nathaniel[4], Nathaniel[3], Humphrey[2], John[1]*) was born in 1859. He married Emma Faris. He died in 1948.

Children of George Washington[9] Main and Emma Faris were as follows:

169.   i.   LELA[10], born 1885; married Edward Shriver.

170.   ii.   FARIS, born 1890; married Susan Long.

        iii.   L. CARL; born 1895; married Elizabeth Dutton.

80.   WILLIAM H.[9] MAIN (*Lutilia*[8]*Johnson*, *George*[7], *Ira*[6], *Jonathan*[5], *Nathaniel*[4], *Nathaniel*[3], *Humphrey*[2], *John*[1]) was born in 1864. He married Della Davidson. He died in 1948.

Children of William H.[9] Main and Della Davidson were as follows:

        i.   WENDELL[10]; born 1891.

        ii.   WALTER; born 1895.

        iii.   KEITH; born 1899.

81.   THOMAS JEFFERSON[9] MAIN (*Lutilia*[8]*Johnson*, *George*[7], *Ira*[6], *Jonathan*[5], *Nathaniel*[4], *Nathaniel*[3], *Humphrey*[2], *John*[1]) was born in 1866. He married Zella Bennett. He died in 1947.

Children of Thomas Jefferson[9] Main and Zella Bennett were:

171.   i.   EUGENE[10], born 1899; married Margaret Niles.

82.   ALVIN RICHARD[9] JOHNSON (*Rufus*[8], *George*[7], *Ira*[6], *Jonathan*[5], *Nathaniel*[4], *Nathaniel*[3], *Humphrey*[2], *John*[1]) was born on 6 Aug 1849 at Pike Co., IL. He married Mary Harper on 11 Oct 1870 at Pike Co., IL. He married Delila Gallaway on 25 May 1899. He died on 8 Dec 1923 at Pike Co., IL, at age 74.

Children of Alvin Richard[9] Johnson and Mary Harper were as follows:

172.   i.   EVA M.[10], born 22 Apr 1872 at Pike Co., IL; married Otto Main.

173.   ii.   ANNA P., born 20 Mar 1875 at Pike Co., IL; married Melvin Troutner.

174.   iii.   LEWIS ARTHUR, born 3 Jul 1877 at Pike Co., IL; married Lucinda Gant.

175.   iv.   IVA E., born 26 Mar 1880 at Pike Co., IL; married Byard Bolen Main.

        v.   (--?--); born 5 May 1883; died 30 Sep 1883.

Children of Alvin Richard[9] Johnson and Delila Gallaway were:

176.   i.   EVA[10], born 2 Sep 1900 at Pike Co., IL; married William Porter Jeffries.

83.   GEORGE HARDIN[9] JOHNSON (*Rufus*[8], *George*[7], *Ira*[6], *Jonathan*[5], *Nathaniel*[4], *Nathaniel*[3], *Humphrey*[2], *John*[1]) was born on 15 Nov 1851 at Pike Co., IL. He married Sarah Kisire Harper on 8 Nov 1876 at Pike Co., IL. He married Sarah Emma Britain on 21 Apr 1921. He died on 22 Mar 1923 at Mulvane, Ness Co., KS, at age 71.

He moved in Sep 1879 to Ness Co., KS.

Children of George Hardin[9] Johnson and Sarah Kisire Harper were as follows:

    i.   MINNIE MAUD[10]; born 11 May 1878 at Martinsberg Township, Pike Co., IL; died 4 Mar 1969 at Wichita, KS, at age 90.

177.   ii.   FLOY BENTON, born 16 Jan 1880 at Ness Co., KS; married Mabel Smith.

178.   iii.   GEORGE RUFUS, born 18 Sep 1882 at Ness Co., KS; married Della Quimby.

    iv.   ELMER VERNON; born 30 Mar 1885 at Ness Co., KS; died 10 May 1888 at Ness Co., KS, at age 3.

    v.   LAURA ANNA; born 7 Jun 1887 at Ness Co., KS; married Walter F. Messinger 31 Dec 1913; died 1 Oct 1981 at Ness Co., KS, at age 94.

    vi.   (--?--); born Oct 1889; died Oct 1889.

    vii.   CLARENCE ELISHA; born 12 Sep 1891 at Francis Township, Ness Co., KS; married Maisy Huey 16 Mar 1921; died 2 Jul 1989 at Wichita, KS, at age 97.

179.   viii.   RALPH CLETUS, born 13 Jun 1897 at Francis Township, Ness Co., KS; married Hazel Marie Smith.

84.   LEWIS OSCAR[9] JOHNSON (*Rufus*[8], *George*[7], *Ira*[6], *Jonathan*[5], *Nathaniel*[4], *Nathaniel*[3], *Humphrey*[2], *John*[1]) was born on 5 Jan 1854 at Pike Co., IL. He married Sarah A. Cooper on 8 Nov 1874 at Pike Co., IL. He died on 27 Mar 1931 at Los Angeles, Los Angeles Co., CA, at age 77.

Children of Lewis Oscar[9] Johnson and Sarah A. Cooper were as follows:

180.   i.   JOHN IRA[10], born 28 Aug 1875 at Pike Co., IL; married May Hyde.

        ii.   MARY; born 16 Dec 1878; married (--?--) Dent. She lived at St. Louis, MO.

181.   iii.   LAURA MAY, born 17 May 1885 at Austin, TX; married Frank Hubert Miller.

182.   iv.   OSCA ALVIN, born 22 Nov 1887 at Pearl, IL; married Hattie Hess; married Helen B Boyle.

85. ISAAC BENTON[9] JOHNSON (*Rufus[8]*, *George[7]*, *Ira[6]*, *Jonathan[5]*, *Nathaniel[4]*, *Nathaniel[3]*, *Humphrey[2]*, *John[1]*) was born on 16 Aug 1867 at Pike Co., IL. He married Nellie Grace Long on 25 Feb 1894 at Pike Co., IL. He died on 29 Jun 1955 at Pike Co., IL, at age 87.

Children of Isaac Benton[9] Johnson and Nellie Grace Long were as follows:

183.   i.   IVIS BENTON[10], born 21 Dec 1894 at Pike Co., IL; married Fay Marie Atwood.

184.   ii.   ICEL FERN, born 6 Aug 1896 at Pike Co., IL; married William Crist Brown.

185.   iii.   RUFUS WINFIELD, born 28 Sep 1899 at Pittsfield, Pike Co., IL; married Vernice Mary Atwood.

        iv.   RUBY MARIE; born 1 Aug 1901 at Pike Co., IL; died 17 Feb 1993 at age 91.

        v.   FRED ESTIL; born 29 Jul 1903; died 15 Oct 1966 at age 63.

186.   vi.   WENDELL ALVIN, born 27 Apr 1906; married Helen Mildred Mink.

Generation Ten

86. CHARLES VIAL[10] NICHOLSON (*Mary[9] Johnson*, *Charles[8]*, *Charles[7]*, *Ira[6]*, *Jonathan[5]*, *Nathaniel[4]*, *Nathaniel[3]*, *Humphrey[2]*, *John[1]*) was born on 1 Mar 1861 at Pike Co., IL. He married Lena

Watson on 1 Feb 1893 at Pike Co., IL. He died on 4 Apr 1944 at Pike Co., IL, at age 83. He was buried at Pittsfield West Cemetery, Pittsfield, Pike Co., IL.

Children of Charles Vial[10] Nicholson and Lena Watson were as follows:

187.   i.   OREN HARVEY[11], born 24 Jul 1895 at Kings Co., CA; married Meleta Harris.

188.   ii.   SUSAN GLADYS, born 9 Mar 1897 at Kings Co., CA; married Paul Niebur.

189.   iii.   MARY MYRTLE, born 25 Aug 1899 at Pike Co., IL; married Robert A. Shive.

190.   iv.   BERYL LOIS, born 6 Jul 1901 at Pike Co., IL; married Joseph Hiram Sanderson.

191.   v.   JESSIE V., born 25 Jul 1905 at Pike Co., IL; married William Paul Rader.

       vi.   JOHN WATSON; born 25 Mar 1909 at Pittsfield, Pike Co., IL.

He lived at Mountain Home, AR.

192.   vii.   CHARLES MYRON, born 7 Jun 1912 at Pittsfield, Pike Co., IL; married Martha Bagby.

       viii.   MARJORIE LEONA; born 29 Mar 1915 at Pittsfield, Pike Co., IL; married Charles Lane 26 Nov 1955.

She lived at Bethalto, IL.

87.   MARY EMILY[10] NICHOLSON (*Mary*[9]*Johnson, Charles*[8], *Charles*[7], *Ira*[6], *Jonathan*[5], *Nathaniel*[4], *Nathaniel*[3], *Humphrey*[2], *John*[1]) was born on 20 Aug 1864 at Pike Co., IL. She married James Garnsey.

Children of Mary Emily[10] Nicholson and James Garnsey were as follows:

       i.   EDITH[11].

       ii.   FAITH DOROTHY; born 1894.

88.   MARY EMILY[10] MILLER (*Rebecca*[9]*Johnson, Charles*[8], *Charles*[7], *Ira*[6], *Jonathan*[5], *Nathaniel*[4], *Nathaniel*[3], *Humphrey*[2],

John[1]) was born on 21 Feb 1869. She married "Doc" Lawrence Killebrew on 7 Feb 1892. She died on 9 May 1957 at age 88.

Children of Mary Emily[10] Miller and "Doc" Lawrence Killebrew were as follows:

      i.   JESSIE ELEANORE[11]; born 1 Jun 1893; died 11 Sep 1893.

193.   ii.   REBECCA ELVA, born 24 Jun 1894; married Jessie L. Sherwin.

      iii. LAWRENCE MILLER; born 22 Aug 1896; died 1 Oct 1906 at age 10.

194.   iv. MARY EDITH, born 5 Nov 1899 at Scott Co., IL; married Charles William Jones.

195.   v.   NORENE FRANCES, born 7 Oct 1901; married ? (--?--).

196.   vi. ETHEL MILDRED, born 13 Sep 1904; married Ernest Newingham.

197.   vii. THEODORE RANDALL, born 2 Aug 1908; married Verna Abrahams.

89.   ETHEL WAYNE[10] MILLER (*Rebecca[9]Johnson, Charles[8], Charles[7], Ira[6], Jonathan[5], Nathaniel[4], Nathaniel[3], Humphrey[2], John[1]*) was born on 17 Sep 1873. She married Thomas Spencer Killebrew on 3 Jul 1892. She died on 22 Feb 1954 at age 80. She was buried at Glasgow Cemetery, Scott Co., IL.

She was also known as Florence Anna Ethel Wayne Miller.

Children of Ethel Wayne[10] Miller and Thomas Spencer Killebrew were as follows:

198.   i.   CHARLES EDWARD[11], born 11 Jun 1893; married Faye Ransom.

199.   ii.   WILLIAM LEE, born 20 Feb 1896; married Deborah Sherwin.

200.   iii. FLORENCE ANNA, born 4 Jan 1899; married Henry Schafer.

201.   iv. SAMUEL LAWRENCE, born 12 Oct 1906; married Elsie Evans.

      v.   HOWARD EDWIN; born 29 Jul 1908.

202. vi. ROBERT WILEY, born 12 Jul 1911; married Viola Hepworth.

90. WILLIAM BAIRD RICHARD[10] MILLER (*Rebecca[9]Johnson, Charles[8], Charles[7], Ira[6], Jonathan[5], Nathaniel[4], Nathaniel[3], Humphrey[2], John[1]*) was born on 27 Nov 1876. He married Lucy Potter on 24 Dec 1906. He died on 4 Aug 1961 at Springfield, IL, at age 84. He was buried at Oak Ridge Cemetery, Springfield, Sangamon Co., IL.

Children of William Baird Richard[10] Miller and Lucy Potter were:

203. i. WILLIAM BAIRD[11] JR, born 15 Nov 1907; married Doris Sleeter; divorced Doris Sleeter.

91. RICHARD STANLEY[10] THORNTON (*Phila[9]Johnson, Charles[8], Charles[7], Ira[6], Jonathan[5], Nathaniel[4], Nathaniel[3], Humphrey[2], John[1]*) was born on 10 Feb 1879 at Pike Co., IL. He married Sarah Allison. He died in 1928 at Alton, Pike Co., IL.

Children of Richard Stanley[10] Thornton and Sarah Allison were:

204. i. RUSSELL E.[11], born 2 Sep 1904 at Pittsfield, Pike Co., IL; married Mary Brace.

92. BERTHA MAHALA[10] THORNTON (*Phila[9]Johnson, Charles[8], Charles[7], Ira[6], Jonathan[5], Nathaniel[4], Nathaniel[3], Humphrey[2], John[1]*) was born on 12 Dec 1880 at Pike Co., IL. She married Luther E. Smith on 24 Dec 1898 at Pike Co., IL. She died on 18 Jan 1953 at Pike Co., IL, at age 72.

Children of Bertha Mahala[10] Thornton and Luther E. Smith were as follows:

205. i. GLADYS[11], married (--?--) Byrne; married (--?--) Dodge.
206. ii. IOLA, married Clair Schone.
207. iii. JESSIE EVELYN, born 6 Apr 1906 at Nebo, Pike Co., IL; married Leslie Durbin.
iv. TRAVIS.

93. HERBERT DOSS[10] THORNTON (*Phila[9]Johnson, Charles[8], Charles[7], Ira[6], Jonathan[5], Nathaniel[4], Nathaniel[3], Humphrey[2], John[1]*) was born on 31 Mar 1885 at Newburg Township, Pike Co., IL. He married Lora Alice Scranton on 1 Jul 1912 at Los Angeles, Los Angeles Co., CA. He died on 14 Nov 1943 at Arlington, Riverside Co., CA, at age 58.

Children of Herbert Doss[10] Thornton and Lora Alice Scranton were as follows:

208.   i.   RUSSEL IVY[11], born 4 Jul 1913 at Fresno, Fresno Co., CA; married Garnie E. Dorman.

       ii.   LELIA MAY; born 7 May 1917 at San Pedro, Los Angeles Co., CA; died 7 Nov 1923 at Artesia, Los Angeles Co., CA, at age 6; buried at Fairhaven Cemetery, Santa Ana, CA.

209.   iii.   WILBUR VERLE, born 7 Oct 1919 at Hynes, Los Angeles Co., CA; married Frances Maria Skarich.

94. WARREN G.[10] RANSOM (*Emma[9]Johnson, Charles[8], Charles[7], Ira[6], Jonathan[5], Nathaniel[4], Nathaniel[3], Humphrey[2], John[1]*) was born in 1877 at Pike Co., IL. He married Pearl St John. He married Cora Weaver in 1903. He died in 1961 at Pike Co., IL.

Children of Warren G.[10] Ransom and Cora Weaver all born at Pike Co., IL, were as follows:

       i.   EMMA JEANNETTE[11]; born 29 Jun 1905; died 12 Oct 1906 at age 1; buried at Watson Cemetery, Pike Co., IL.

       ii.   EVELYN; born 31 May 1906.
She lived in 1985 at the Charles V. Johnson Homestead, Independence, IL.

210.   iii.   BERNICE, born 20 Jan 1911; married Wayland R. Swanson M.D.

95. ELIZABETH ANNA "LIZZIE"[10] JOHNSON (*John[9], Hiram[8], Charles[7], Ira[6], Jonathan[5], Nathaniel[4], Nathaniel[3], Humphrey[2], John[1]*) was born on 11 Feb 1865. She married John Daniel on 14

Aug 1883 at Scio, Linn Co., OR. She died in 1942 at Eugene, Lane Co., OR.

She was also known as Lizzie Johnson.

Children of Elizabeth Anna "Lizzie"[10] Johnson and John Daniel were as follows:

      i.   CHESTER[11]; born 27 Apr 1884 at Albany, Linn Co., OR; died 22 Jun 1964 at Eugene, Lane Co., OR, at age 80.

      ii.   ARCHIE CARLYLE; born 2 Jun 1889.

      iii.   (--?--); born 27 Jun 1890; died young.

      iv.   TEMPA VIOLETTA; born 20 Aug 1895.

96. ARCHIE JAMES[10] JOHNSON SR (*John*[9], *Hiram*[8], *Charles*[7], *Ira*[6], *Jonathan*[5], *Nathaniel*[4], *Nathaniel*[3], *Humphrey*[2], *John*[1]) was born on 18 Sep 1867. He married Linnie Young on 31 Jan 1888. He married Jennie Young on 18 Sep 1928 at Multnomah Co., OR. He died in Feb 1939 at Lebanon, Linn Co., OR, at age 71.

Children of Archie James[10] Johnson Sr and Linnie Young were as follows:

211.   i.   CLEO[11], born 13 Aug 1888 at Seattle, King Co., WA; married John F. Porter.

      ii.   ZETA ELMA; born 12 Dec 1889 at Portland, Multnomah Co., OR; married Floyd Bogue 8 Jan 1913 at Benton Co., OR; died 19 Jan 1919 at Corvallis, Benton Co., OR, at age 29.

212.   iii.   ELMO ELTON, born 19 Nov 1891 at Scio, Linn Co., OR; married Linnie Durell.

213.   iv.   DARRELL DELOS, born 10 Jul 1897 at Scio, Linn Co., OR; married Bertha McHenry.

214.   v.   ORLO ORTON, born 2 Jul 1900 at Scio, Linn Co., OR; married Frances Watkins; married Kathleen Wied.

      vi.   WANDA LINN; born 31 Jan 1905 at Corvallis, Benton Co., OR; married J. C. Woodbury 6 Jun 1935 at Benton Co., OR.

215.   vii.   ARCHIE JAMES JR, born 20 Oct 1912 at Corvallis, Benton Co., OR; married Bonnie Jane

Harris; married June (--?--); married Glenna Bessie Johnston; married Edmonda Fisher.

97. ETTA ARZELLA[10] JOHNSON (*John[9]*, *Hiram[8]*, *Charles[7]*, *Ira[6]*, *Jonathan[5]*, *Nathaniel[4]*, *Nathaniel[3]*, *Humphrey[2]*, *John[1]*) was born on 4 Jan 1871. She married John C. Simpson on 1 Dec 1890 at Scio, Linn Co., OR. She died on 2 Jan 1967 at Corvallis, Benton Co., OR, at age 95.

Children of Etta Arzella[10] Johnson and John C. Simpson were as follows:

216.   i.   ZELMA[11], born 18 Feb 1892; married William E. Williams.

    ii.   RUTH; born 18 Dec 1897; married Charles M. Wagner 15 Jun 1920 at Kalama, Cowlitz Co., WA; died 26 Oct 1990 at age 92.

98. CHARLES VIRGIL[10] JOHNSON (*John[9]*, *Hiram[8]*, *Charles[7]*, *Ira[6]*, *Jonathan[5]*, *Nathaniel[4]*, *Nathaniel[3]*, *Humphrey[2]*, *John[1]*) was born on 18 Mar 1875 at Scio, Linn Co., OR. He married Maud Ethel Rundlett, daughter of Samuel S. Rundlett and Harriette S. Gesner, on 12 Oct 1898 at Salem, Marion Co., OR. He died on 25 Oct 1961 at Salem, Marion Co., OR, at age 86.

He appeared on the census of 1 Apr 1930 at Salem, Marion Co., OR.

Children of Charles Virgil[10] Johnson and Maud Ethel Rundlett were as follows:

    i.   DOROTHY ETHEL[11]; born 26 Mar 1904 at Kings Valley, Benton Co., OR; died 4 Aug 1984 at Hillsborough Co., FL, at age 80.

217.   ii.   CHARLES GARTH, born 21 Jun 1905 at Airlie, Benton Co., OR; married Violette Marie Brewer; married Enid Cleek.

99. PEARL INEZ[10] JOHNSON (*John[9]*, *Hiram[8]*, *Charles[7]*, *Ira[6]*, *Jonathan[5]*, *Nathaniel[4]*, *Nathaniel[3]*, *Humphrey[2]*, *John[1]*) was born on 5 Nov 1883 at Scio, Linn Co., OR. She married Albert S. Shaw on 29 Sep 1900. She married Wiley Stuart on 28 Oct 1914 at

Multnomah Co., OR. She died on 1 May 1948 at Portland, Multnomah Co., OR, at age 64.

Children of Pearl Inez[10] Johnson and Albert S. Shaw were:

218.   i.   DORIS V.[11], born 16 May 1904; married Jack Charles Parsons.

There were no children of Pearl Inez[10] Johnson and Wiley Stuart.

100.   OSCAR M.[10] JOHNSON (*George*[9], *Hiram*[8], *Charles*[7], *Ira*[6], *Jonathan*[5], *Nathaniel*[4], *Nathaniel*[3], *Humphrey*[2], *John*[1]) was born on 16 Jul 1867. He married Mrytle (--?--). He died on 14 Feb 1914 at Salem, Marion Co., OR, at age 46.

He appeared on the census of 1 Jun 1870 at Jefferson, Marion Co., OR.

Children of Oscar M.[10] Johnson and Mrytle (--?--) were:

    i.   LEE STUART[11]; born 9 Aug 1911; died 9 Aug 1911.

101.   ROSE E.[10] JOHNSON (*George*[9], *Hiram*[8], *Charles*[7], *Ira*[6], *Jonathan*[5], *Nathaniel*[4], *Nathaniel*[3], *Humphrey*[2], *John*[1]) was born on 26 Jan 1869 at Scio, Linn Co., OR. She married Willis E. McElroy on 24 Jun 1890 at Salem, Marion Co., OR. She died on 25 Feb 1915 at Portland, OR, at age 46.

She appeared on the census of 1 Jun 1870 at Jefferson, Marion Co., OR.

Children of Rose E.[10] Johnson and Willis E. McElroy were as follows:

    i.   GEORGE EBEN[11]; born 10 Mar 1893 at Salem, Marion Co., OR; married Clara (--?--) at Seattle, King Co., WA; died 1969.

219.   ii.   AGNES MARIE, born 27 Feb 1898 at Chicago, Cook Co., IL; married Carroll Hanson.

220.   iii.   EARLE JOHNSON, born 25 Jun 1904 at Salem, Marion Co., OR; married Ann Owen.

102.   LULU B.[10] JOHNSON (*George*[9], *Hiram*[8], *Charles*[7], *Ira*[6], *Jonathan*[5], *Nathaniel*[4], *Nathaniel*[3], *Humphrey*[2], *John*[1]) was born in Jul 1870. She married Frank Albert Baker on 18 Dec 1894 at Marion Co., OR.

Children of Lulu B.[10] Johnson and Frank Albert Baker were:

    i.   ALICE M.[11]; born Mar 1898.

103. GEORGE WASHINGTON[10] JOHNSON JR (*George*[9], *Hiram*[8], *Charles*[7], *Ira*[6], *Jonathan*[5], *Nathaniel*[4], *Nathaniel*[3], *Humphrey*[2], *John*[1]) was born on 24 Feb 1876. He married Verda Belle Valet circa 1911.

He appeared on the census of 1 Apr 1930 at 355 North Church St., Salem, Marion Co., OR.

Children of George Washington[10] Johnson Jr and Verda Belle Valet were:

221.   i.   GEORGE LESLIE[11], born 1913 at OR; married Vera Geraldine Tanner.

104. CLYDE E.[10] JOHNSON (*George*[9], *Hiram*[8], *Charles*[7], *Ira*[6], *Jonathan*[5], *Nathaniel*[4], *Nathaniel*[3], *Humphrey*[2], *John*[1]) was born on 2 Jan 1881. He married Grace VanWagner. He died on 6 Dec 1928 at Salem, Marion Co., OR, at age 47.

Children of Clyde E.[10] Johnson and Grace VanWagner were:

222.   i.   PAULINE EDITH[11], born 12 Apr 1909 at Salem, Marion Co., OR; married Howard Keeling.

105. PAUL VAYNE[10] JOHNSON (*George*[9], *Hiram*[8], *Charles*[7], *Ira*[6], *Jonathan*[5], *Nathaniel*[4], *Nathaniel*[3], *Humphrey*[2], *John*[1]) was born on 19 Jan 1888 at Salem, Marion Co., OR. He married Leona Graham, daughter of John B. Graham and Minnie Jones, circa 1908. He died on 18 Dec 1936 at Salem, Marion Co., OR, at age 48.

He appeared on the census of 1 Apr 1930 at 455 High St., Salem, Marion Co., OR.

Children of Paul Vayne[10] Johnson and Leona Graham were:

    i.   JULIA GRAHAM[11]; born 17 May 1915 at OR; died 15 Feb 2001 at Marion Co., OR, at age 85.

106. ADA MAY[10] JOHNSON (*William*[9], *Hiram*[8], *Charles*[7], *Ira*[6], *Jonathan*[5], *Nathaniel*[4], *Nathaniel*[3], *Humphrey*[2], *John*[1]) was born on 14 Feb 1870 at Jefferson, Marion Co., OR. She married Charles Schlenker Iaeger, son of Charles L. Iaeger and Sarah A. Schlenker, on 13 Jan 1886 at Burns, Grant Co. (now Harney Co.), OR. She and Charles Schlenker Iaeger were divorced circa 1892. She married Stonewall Jackson Mothershead, son of Charles Mothershead and Nancy Jane Cheatham, on 17 Dec 1895 at Olympic Hotel, Edmonds, Snohomish Co., WA. She died on 27 Feb 1964 at Central Point, Jackson Co., OR, at age 94. She was buried on 3 Mar 1964 at Edmonds Cemetery, Edmonds, Snohomish Co., WA.

She appeared on the census of 1 Jun 1880 at Harney Prec., Grant Co., OR. She was an assistant postmaster in 1913 at Edmonds, Snohomish Co., WA.

Children of Ada May[10] Johnson and Charles Schlenker Iaeger were:

> 223.　　i.　GEORGE JOHNSON[11], born 21 Sep 1886 at Burns, Harney Co., OR; married Laura "Maye" Arrowood.

There were no children of Ada May[10] Johnson and Stonewall Jackson Mothershead.

107.　CHARLES W.[10] JOHNSON (*William*[9], *Hiram*[8], *Charles*[7], *Ira*[6], *Jonathan*[5], *Nathaniel*[4], *Nathaniel*[3], *Humphrey*[2], *John*[1]) was born on 29 May 1871. He married Minnie R. Reed on 13 Jan 1892 at Harney Co., OR. He died on 7 May 1929 at age 57.

He appeared on the census of 1880 at Harney Prec., Grant Co., OR. He was a saloon keeper in 1900 at Burns, Harney Co., OR.

Children of Charles W.[10] Johnson and Minnie R. Reed were:

> 224.　　i.　TOILEY[11], born Oct 1892; married Fred Williams.

108.　LLOYD LEROY[10] JOHNSON (*William*[9], *Hiram*[8], *Charles*[7], *Ira*[6], *Jonathan*[5], *Nathaniel*[4], *Nathaniel*[3], *Humphrey*[2], *John*[1]) was born on 4 Jul 1875. He married Bertha Clark on 11 Nov 1900 at Harney Co., OR. He died in 1951.

He appeared on the census of 1 Jun 1880 at Harney Prec., Grant Co., OR.

Children of Lloyd Leroy[10] Johnson and Bertha Clark were as follows:

225.   i.   JAMES "LEROY"[11], born 25 Apr 1902 at Burns, Harney Co., OR; married Lutha Marie Parker.

226.   ii.   ADA IRENE, born 1904; married Harold Pickens; married John McGovern.

        iii.   WINNIE; born 14 Oct 1907; died 31 Jul 1910 at age 2.

109.   HESTER ELIZABETH[10] JOHNSON (*William*[9], *Hiram*[8], *Charles*[7], *Ira*[6], *Jonathan*[5], *Nathaniel*[4], *Nathaniel*[3], *Humphrey*[2], *John*[1]) was born on 19 Oct 1876 at Indian Agency, Vale, OR. She married William Austin Goodman on 15 Dec 1895 at Harney Co., OR. She died on 29 Dec 1958 at Harney Co., OR, at age 82.

She appeared on the census of 1880 at Harney Precinct, Grant Co., OR.

Children of Hester Elizabeth[10] Johnson and William Austin Goodman were as follows:

        i.   WARREN KENNY[11]; born 1896; died 17 Nov 1896.

227.   ii.   FLORABEL, born Oct 1897 at OR; married Harry Z. Smith.

228.   iii.   AUSTIN EDWARD, born 8 Feb 1900 at OR; married Mary McCrea.

229.   iv.   BLANCHE, born 1904 at OR; married James McCulloch.

110.   LULU BELLE[10] JOHNSON (*William*[9], *Hiram*[8], *Charles*[7], *Ira*[6], *Jonathan*[5], *Nathaniel*[4], *Nathaniel*[3], *Humphrey*[2], *John*[1]) was born on 14 Feb 1887. She married Rush McHargue Sr. on 14 Oct 1903 at Burns, Harney Co., OR. She died on 29 Jul 1986 at Malheur Co., OR, at age 99.

She appeared on the census of 1900 at Burns Prec., Burns, Harney Co., OR. She lived before Jul 1986 at Ontario, Malheur Co., OR.

Children of Lulu Belle[10] Johnson and Rush McHargue Sr. were as follows:

230.   i.   WARREN TAYLOR[11], born 12 Apr 1904 at OR; married Ruby South; married Dorothy Patnude Adams.

           ii.   RAYMOND "DAWSON"; born 21 Aug 1905; died 15 Jul 1914 at age 8; buried in the Burns Cemetery, Burns, Harney Co., OR.

231.   iii.   FRANCIS CAROLINE, born 21 Jan 1911 at OR; married Larry S. Smith.

232.   iv.   RUSH GOODMAN, born 28 Oct 1912 at Burns, Harney Co., OR; married Emily Ermina Maupin.

233.   v.   LEON OTTO, born 27 Jun 1915 at OR; married Lena McKinney.

           vi.   GEORGE THOMAS; born 16 Apr 1926; died 8 May 1926; buried in the Burns Cemetery, Burns, Harney Co., OR.

234.   vii.   JAMES WILLIAM, born 25 Nov 1930; married Grace Mae Lawrence.

235.   viii.   MARILYN JOE, born 3 Oct 1933; married Kenneth Goul.

111. CLAUDE A.[10] JOHNSON (*Hiram*[9], *Hiram*[8], *Charles*[7], *Ira*[6], *Jonathan*[5], *Nathaniel*[4], *Nathaniel*[3], *Humphrey*[2], *John*[1]) was born on 8 May 1874. He married Lucy A. (--?--). He and Lucy A. (--?--) were divorced. He died on 5 Nov 1933 at Salem, Marion Co., OR, at age 59.

He appeared on the census of 1 Jun 1880 at Scio, Linn Co., OR.

Children of Claude A.[10] Johnson and Lucy A. (--?--) were:

236.   i.   EDWIN CLAUDE[11], born 1917; married Kathryn Lucille Boyle.

112. MYRTLE J.[10] JOHNSON (*Hiram*[9], *Hiram*[8], *Charles*[7], *Ira*[6], *Jonathan*[5], *Nathaniel*[4], *Nathaniel*[3], *Humphrey*[2], *John*[1]) was born on 24 Apr 1876. She married Arthur H. Williams on 12 May 1897 at Marion Co., OR. She married Edward Hamer. She and Edward Hamer were divorced. She died on 17 Nov 1932 at Salem, Marion Co., OR, at age 56.

She appeared on the census of 1 Jun 1880 at Scio, Linn Co., OR.

There were no children of Myrtle J.^{10} Johnson and Arthur H. Williams.

Children of Myrtle J.^{10} Johnson and Edward Hamer were as follows:

            i.   MARJORIE^{11}; born 19 Jun 1907 at Linn Co., OR; died 18 Jul 1926 at Salem, Marion Co., OR, at age 19.

237.   ii.   ALVIN KANZLER, born 15 Sep 1913 at Portland, Multnomah Co., OR; married Delma Alene Brown.

113. HIRAM ALVAH^{10} JOHNSON III (*Hiram*^{9}, *Hiram*^{8}, *Charles*^{7}, *Ira*^{6}, *Jonathan*^{5}, *Nathaniel*^{4}, *Nathaniel*^{3}, *Humphrey*^{2}, *John*^{1}) was born on 31 Dec 1878 at Salem, Marion Co., OR. He married Anna Adaline Grabenhorst, daughter of William H Grabenhorst and Eva Haight, on 24 Apr 1908 at Salem, Marion Co., OR. He married Mary A. Edwards on 17 Oct 1914 at Salem, Marion Co., OR. He and Mary A. Edwards were divorced on 5 Aug 1920 at Salem, Marion Co., OR. He died on 11 Aug 1959 at San Diego, San Diego Co., CA, at age 80.

He appeared on the census of 1 Jun 1880 at Scio, Linn Co., OR.

Children of Hiram Alvah^{10} Johnson III and Anna Adaline Grabenhorst were:

238.   i.   ROBERT ALLEN^{11}, born 15 Apr 1913 at Salem, Marion Co., OR; married Frances Ostrin; married Donna Lee Klein.

Children of Hiram Alvah^{10} Johnson III and Mary A. Edwards were:

239.   i.   LEO DELBERT^{11}, born 14 Apr 1916; married Margaret Jacqueline McGhee.

114. CRETA J.^{10} JOHNSON (*Hiram*^{9}, *Hiram*^{8}, *Charles*^{7}, *Ira*^{6}, *Jonathan*^{5}, *Nathaniel*^{4}, *Nathaniel*^{3}, *Humphrey*^{2}, *John*^{1}) was born in May 1889. She married Orville Stubbs on 11 Oct 1906 at Salem, Marion Co., OR. She married Charles W. Stege on 20 Apr 1909 at Polk Co., OR. She married (--?--) Green. She died in 1934.

Children of Creta J.[10] Johnson and Orville Stubbs were:

240.   i.   EVELYN M.[11], born 16 May 1907 at Salem, Marion Co., OR; married Emile F. Aufranc; married Addison Lane. She was also known as Evelyn Johnson.

There were no children of Creta J.[10] Johnson and Charles W. Stege.

Children of Creta J.[10] Johnson and (--?--) Green were:

        i.   BILLY[11]; died at India.

115. FRED LEROY[10] JOHNSON (*Samuel[9]*, *Hiram[8]*, *Charles[7]*, *Ira[6]*, *Jonathan[5]*, *Nathaniel[4]*, *Nathaniel[3]*, *Humphrey[2]*, *John[1]*) was born on 31 Jul 1877 at Jefferson, Marion Co., OR. He married Lettie Elloda Watkinds, daughter of Thomas Morgan Kirckpatrick Watkinds and Lucilla Elvia Abbott, on 8 Mar 1899 at Salem, Marion Co., OR. He died on 23 Jan 1948 at Portland, Multnomah Co., OR, at age 70. He was buried at Portland Memorial Mauseleum, Portland, Multnomah Co., OR.

Children of Fred Leroy[10] Johnson and Lettie Elloda Watkinds were as follows:

241.   i.   VERYL LEROSE[11], born 30 Mar 1900 at Jefferson, Marion Co., OR; married Vern Loren Drager.

242.   ii.   ACLE FRANCIS, born 10 Aug 1902 at Jefferson, Marion Co., OR; married Josephine Louisa Sanders.

243.   iii. NELLIE LUCILLE, born 21 Jun 1904 at Jefferson, Marion Co., OR; married Earl Henbest.

244.   iv.   GERTRUDE LAVERN, born 9 May 1906 at Jefferson, Marion Co., OR; married Alva Jess Williams.

        v.   GLADYS MAY; born 5 Feb 1908 at Portland, Multnomah Co., OR; died Oct 1996 at age 88; buried at Portland Memorial Mauseleum, Portland, Multnomah Co., OR. She was also known as HELEN CATHERINE JOHNSON. She was unmarried in 1985.

245.   vi.   SAMUEL THURSTON II, born 26 Apr 1912 at Portland, Multnomah Co., OR; married Barbara Lee Kopsland.

116. EDYTHE MADILLA[10] JOHNSON (*Samuel*[9], *Hiram*[8], *Charles*[7], *Ira*[6], *Jonathan*[5], *Nathaniel*[4], *Nathaniel*[3], *Humphrey*[2], *John*[1]) was born on 9 Apr 1882 at Jefferson, Marion Co., OR. She married James Henry Wagenblast on 21 Jun 1900. She died on 15 May 1961 at Portland, Multnomah Co., OR, at age 79.

Children of Edythe Madilla[10] Johnson and James Henry Wagenblast were as follows:

246.   i.   GENEVA BERNICE[11], born 9 Nov 1902 at Roseburg, OR; married Adolph Mathiesen.
247.   ii.   JAMES EDWARD, born 16 Apr 1904 at Roseburg, OR; married Genevive Luedinkok.
248.   iii.   MAURICE JOHNSON, born 19 Oct 1906 at Roseburg, OR; married Betty Altishin.
249.   iv.   MABEL ELIZABETH, born 16 May 1908 at Silverton, Marion Co., OR; married Dolph Falkenhagen.

117. SAPHRONIA L.[10] JOHNSON (*Elgin*[9], *Abel*[8], *Charles*[7], *Ira*[6], *Jonathan*[5], *Nathaniel*[4], *Nathaniel*[3], *Humphrey*[2], *John*[1]) married Arthur L. Dilmore on 12 Jul 1897. She died at Pine Valley, NY.

Children of Saphronia L.[10] Johnson and Arthur L. Dilmore were as follows:

250.   i.   SAYRE ALBERT[11], born 1906 at Laceyville, PA; married Ester Catherine Soper.
        ii.   KENNETH; married Catherine (--?--).
        iii.   ROBERT.
        iv.   RICHARD.
        v.   THOMAS.
        vi.   (--?--).
        vii.   (--?--).

118. ABEL PRATT^{10} JOHNSON II (*Elgin^9*, *Abel^8*, *Charles^7*, *Ira^6*, *Jonathan^5*, *Nathaniel^4*, *Nathaniel^3*, *Humphrey^2*, *John^1*) was born on 29 Dec 1889 at Elmira, Chemung Co., NY. He married Clara Ray Penny, daughter of Jacob R. Penny and Elsie G. Barhydt, on 6 Nov 1912 at Schenectady, NY. He died on 21 Feb 1925 at Syracuse, Onondoga Co., NY, at age 35.

Children of Abel Pratt^{10} Johnson II and Clara Ray Penny were as follows:

251.	i.	DONALD ALFRED^{11}, born 17 Jul 1915 at Elmira, Chemung Co., NY; married Myrtle Helena Beckley; married Katherine Ferguson.
252.	ii.	CARL EVERETT, born 10 Dec 1915 at Syracuse, Onondoga Co., NY; married Nona Jean Clark.
253.	iii.	RUTH WINIFRED, born 11 Mar 1917 at Elmira, NY; married William Herbert Sahm II.
254.	iv.	ABEL PHILLIP SR., born 4 Mar 1920 at Syracuse, Onondoga Co., NY; married Rita Caroline Ditch.
255.	v.	ROBERT EARL, born 10 Jul 1922 at Syracuse, Onondoga Co., NY; married Florence Kathleen Taylor; married Mildred Yost; married Doris Glee Windsor.
256.	vi.	MILDRED VIOLET, born 17 Oct 1924 at Syracuse, Onondoga Co., NY; married Dale Byran Caughey.

119. ETHEL MORIAH^{10} JOHNSON (*Charles^9*, *William^8*, *Charles^7*, *Ira^6*, *Jonathan^5*, *Nathaniel^4*, *Nathaniel^3*, *Humphrey^2*, *John^1*) was born on 23 Sep 1883 at Edwards, St. Lawrence Co., NY. She married Rollin Clark Noble on 11 Sep 1907. She died on 24 Jun 1964 at age 80.

She appeared on the census of 1 Jun 1900 at Edwards Township, St. Lawrence Co., NY.

Children of Ethel Moriah^{10} Johnson and Rollin Clark Noble were:

	i.	IRENE V.^{11}; born 8 Jul 1911; married Pratt Fairchild MacWhorter 1937; died 1958.

120. FERNE HELEN[10] JOHNSON (*Charles*[9], *William*[8], *Charles*[7], *Ira*[6], *Jonathan*[5], *Nathaniel*[4], *Nathaniel*[3], *Humphrey*[2], *John*[1]) was born on 1 May 1886 at Edwards, St. Lawrence Co., NY. She married Floyd Noble on 26 Sep 1906. She died on 4 Sep 1954 at Lisbon, NY, at age 68.

She appeared on the census of 1 Jun 1900 at Edwards Township, St. Lawrence Co., NY.

Children of Ferne Helen[10] Johnson and Floyd Noble were as follows:

257.   i.   DONALD RUPERT[11], born 29 Mar 1913; married Joanna Caranossios.

258.   ii.   WORTH, born 14 Nov 1922; married Margaret Mitchell.

121. JOHN WARREN[10] JOHNSON (*Charles*[9], *William*[8], *Charles*[7], *Ira*[6], *Jonathan*[5], *Nathaniel*[4], *Nathaniel*[3], *Humphrey*[2], *John*[1]) was born on 20 Jun 1893 at Edwards, St. Lawrence Co., NY. He married Orabell Chase on 3 Dec 1919 at Fine, St. Lawrence Co., NY. He died on 20 Nov 1952 at age 59.   He appeared on the census of 1 Jun 1900 at Edwards Township, St. Lawrence Co., NY.

Children of John Warren[10] Johnson and Orabell Chase were as follows:

259.   i.   CHARLES VANCE[11] SR, born 12 Apr 1921 at Hermon, St. Lawrence Co., NY; married Barbara Esther Woods.

260.   ii.   JOHN WARREN JR., born 10 Dec 1923 at Hermon, St. Lawrence Co., NY; married Rita Marie Roy.

        iii.   HARRIET ELIZABETH; born 21 Feb 1925 at Hermon, St. Lawrence Co., NY; married Roy E. Jenne 10 Nov 1946 at Hermon, St. Lawrence Co., NY; Divorced Roy E. Jenne.

              She lived in 2003 at Hermon, St. Lawrence Co., NY.

261.   iv.   ELEANOR BELLE, born 21 Nov 1927 at Hermon, St. Lawrence Co., NY; married James J. Kilmer.

262. v.   PHYLLIS IRENE, born 8 Jan 1931 at Hermon, St. Lawrence Co., NY; married Athol Glynn Edwards.

263. vi.   NANCY JEAN, born 9 Aug 1937 at Ogdensburg, NY; married James P. Sayer; married Kenneth Richard Johnson; divorced Kenneth Richard Johnson.

122.   SHERMAN WILLIAM^{10} BROWN (*Alvah^9*, *Nancy^{8}Johnson*, *Charles^7*, *Ira^6*, *Jonathan^5*, *Nathaniel^4*, *Nathaniel^3*, *Humphrey^2*, *John^1*) was born on 31 Jul 1873 at Edwards, St. Lawrence Co., NY. He and Lena May Ward were engaged. He married Gertrude Backus on 3 Dec 1895 at Russell, St. Lawrence Co., NY. He and Florence Raycraft were engaged. He died on 8 Feb 1957 at Canton, St. Lawrence Co., NY, at age 83. He was buried on 11 Feb 1957 at Canton, St. Lawrence Co., NY.

He appeared on the census of 1 Jun 1900 at Edwards, St. Lawrence Co., NY.

Children of Sherman William^{10} Brown and Lena May Ward were:

  i.   MYRTLE^{11}; born 18 Jul 1893 at Edwards, St. Lawrence Co., NY.

There were no children of Sherman William^{10} Brown and Gertrude Backus.

There were no children of Sherman William^{10} Brown and Florence Raycraft.

123.   MANIE ELNORA^{10} BROWN (*Alvah^9*, *Nancy^{8}Johnson*, *Charles^7*, *Ira^6*, *Jonathan^5*, *Nathaniel^4*, *Nathaniel^3*, *Humphrey^2*, *John^1*) was born on 10 Jun 1879 at Edwards, St. Lawrence Co., NY. She married Earle S. Johnson, son of Acil Comfort Johnson and Mary Ann Bierman, before 1899. She died in Jul 1965 at age 86.

Children of Manie Elnora^{10} Brown and Earle S. Johnson were as follows:

264. i.   MILDRED^{11}, born circa 1899; married Robert Hill.

265.   ii.   MIRIAM, born circa 1907 at Gouverneur, St. Lawrence Co., NY; married Gerald Leonard; married Jack Hayden.

266.   iii.   DOROTHY JEAN, born circa 1910 at Gouverneur, St. Lawrence Co., NY; married Michael Kennedy; married Howard Hitsman.

124. CLARENCE CHARLES[10] BROWN (*Charles*[9], *Nancy*[8]*Johnson*, *Charles*[7], *Ira*[6], *Jonathan*[5], *Nathaniel*[4], *Nathaniel*[3], *Humphrey*[2], *John*[1]) was born on 2 Jun 1872 at Edwards, St. Lawrence Co., NY. He married Carrie Pearl Cleland on 15 Sep 1898 at Edwards, St. Lawrence Co., NY. He died on 13 Apr 1922 at Edwards, St. Lawrence Co., NY, at age 49.

He appeared on the census of 1 Jun 1900 at Edwards, St. Lawrence Co., NY.

Children of Clarence Charles[10] Brown and Carrie Pearl Cleland both born at Edwards, St. Lawrence Co., NY, were as follows:

267.   i.   CLARENCE DONALD[11], born 30 Apr 1900; married Inez Lucille Noble.

       ii.   HELEN MARTHA; born 28 Sep 1905; married Robert Harmon 21 Feb 1931 at White Plains, NY; she and Robert Harmon were divorced Aug 1944; married Charles Clark Adams 23 Apr 1955 at White Plains, NY; died 1 Aug 1997 at Southbury, CT, at age 91.

125. OSWALD BOWER[10] BROWN (*Charles*[9], *Nancy*[8]*Johnson*, *Charles*[7], *Ira*[6], *Jonathan*[5], *Nathaniel*[4], *Nathaniel*[3], *Humphrey*[2], *John*[1]) was born on 4 Mar 1874 at Edwards, St. Lawrence Co., NY. He married Pearl Theresa Baldwin on 24 Oct 1901 at Gouverneur, St. Lawrence Co., NY. He married Nellie Morrosey on 21 Apr 1917 at Edwards, St. Lawrence Co., NY. He died on 10 Dec 1930 at Edwards, St. Lawrence Co., NY, at age 56.

He appeared on the census of 1 Jun 1900 at Edwards, St. Lawrence Co., NY.

Children of Oswald Bower[10] Brown and Nellie Morrosey were:

i.   CHARLES MACLYN[11]; born 7 May 1921; married Katherine (--?--); died circa 1978.

126.   MABEL E.[10] BROWN (*Charles*[9], *Nancy*[8]*Johnson*, *Charles*[7], *Ira*[6], *Jonathan*[5], *Nathaniel*[4], *Nathaniel*[3], *Humphrey*[2], *John*[1]) was born on 1 Jan 1876 at Edwards, St. Lawrence Co., NY. She married Charles Milton Clark on 4 Jul 1906 at Mexico Pt., NY. She died on 31 Oct 1963 at Manlius, NY, at age 87. She was buried at Canton, NY.

She appeared on the census of 1 Jun 1900 at Edwards, St. Lawrence Co., NY.

Children of Mabel E.[10] Brown and Charles Milton Clark were as follows:

268.   i.   MARTHA ELIZABETH[11], born 30 Jun 1915 at Canton, St. Lawrence Co., NY; married Carson Perry Buck.

269.   ii.   HARRIET ISABEL, born 9 Apr 1918 at Canton, St. Lawrence Co., NY; married Richard H. Connors.

270.   iii.   CHARLES ROLLIN SR, born 13 Jul 1920 at Canton, NY; married Evelyne Frances Flannagen.

127.   LETA E.[10] HALL (*Hiram*[9], *Emmorancy*[8]*Johnson*, *Charles*[7], *Ira*[6], *Jonathan*[5], *Nathaniel*[4], *Nathaniel*[3], *Humphrey*[2], *John*[1]) was born on 24 Jun 1874 at Edwards, St. Lawrence Co., NY. She married Eddy R. Beach, son of William Martin Jackson Beach and Lucy Maria Thomas, on 26 Jun 1891 at Fowler, St. Lawrence Co., NY. She died on 9 Nov 1953 at Ogdensburg Hospital, Ogdensburg, St. Lawrence Co., NY, at age 79. She was buried on 12 Nov 1953 at Riverside Cemetery, Edwards, St. Lawrence Co., NY.

Children of Leta E.[10] Hall and Eddy R. Beach all born at Edwards, St. Lawrence Co., NY, were as follows:

271.   i.   EVERETT E.[11], born 11 Mar 1892; married Marguerite Hawes.

272.   ii.   VIVIAN, born 18 Jan 1896; married David L. Gardner.

iii.   NINA LUCIE; born 28 Jun 1897; married Stanley Dygert; died at New York City, NY.

128. LEON HORACE[10] HALL (*Hiram*[9], *Emmorancy*[8]*Johnson*, *Charles*[7], *Ira*[6], *Jonathan*[5], *Nathaniel*[4], *Nathaniel*[3], *Humphrey*[2], *John*[1]) was born on 4 Mar 1876 at Edwards, St. Lawrence Co., NY. He married Mayme Gertrude Clary, daughter of James Clary and Agnes Jewel Clark, on 9 Nov 1909 at Fowler, St. Lawrence Co., NY. He died on 11 Jan 1955 at Gouverneur, St. Lawrence Co., NY, at age 78. He was buried at Hailesboro Cemetery, Gouverneur, St. Lawrence Co., NY.

He appeared on the census of 1 Jun 1900 at Edwards, St. Lawrence Co., NY.

Children of Leon Horace[10] Hall and Mayme Gertrude Clary all born at Edwards, St. Lawrence Co., NY, were as follows:

      i.   (--?--)[11]; born 24 Mar 1910; died 24 Mar 1910 at Edwards, St. Lawrence Co., NY; buried at Edwards, St. Lawrence Co., NY.

      ii. GLENN L.; born 30 May 1911; married Isabelle June Savage, daughter of Edmond Savage and Louisa June Lavancha, 5 Aug 1940 at Spragueville Methodist Church, Gouverneur, St. Lawrence Co., NY; died 21 Dec 1981 at Edward John Noble Hospital, Gouverneur, St. Lawrence Co., NY, at age 70; buried 24 Dec 1981 at Hailesboro Cemetery, NY.

273. iii. REATHA MARIE, born 2 Mar 1914; married Edwin Nelson Boprey.

274. iv. ELLISON, born 3 Jun 1915; married Douglas J. Fredenburg Sr.

275. v. CLIFFORD HIRAM, born 26 Mar 1917; married Isabel Yaddow.

129. FLORENCE E.[10] HALL (*Hiram*[9], *Emmorancy*[8]*Johnson*, *Charles*[7], *Ira*[6], *Jonathan*[5], *Nathaniel*[4], *Nathaniel*[3], *Humphrey*[2], *John*[1]) was born on 20 Apr 1880 at Edwards, St. Lawrence Co., NY. She married Gilbert Hughes, son of John Hughes Sr. and Mary Jane Gallagher, on 28 Jan 1901 at Edwards, St. Lawrence Co., NY. She married Jacob O. Davis on 20 Mar 1907 at Edwards, St. Lawrence Co., NY. She died on 10 Mar 1911 at Fowler, St.

Lawrence Co., NY, at age 30. She was buried at Riverside Cemetery, Edwards, St. Lawrence Co., NY.

She appeared on the census of 1 Jun 1900 at Edwards, St. Lawrence Co., NY.

Children of Florence E.[10] Hall and Gilbert Hughes both born at Edwards, St. Lawrence Co., NY, are as follows:

276.   i.   LEE ETHEL[11], born 22 Aug 1901; married Sarah (--?--).

277.   ii.   LYLE GILBERT, born 24 Oct 1903; married Edna Mae Meldrim.

Children of Florence E.[10] Hall and Jacob O. Davis were:

         i.   (--?--)[11]; born 10 Mar 1911.

130.   LOTTIE MAE[10] HALL (*Hiram*[9], *Emmorancy*[8]*Johnson*, *Charles*[7], *Ira*[6], *Jonathan*[5], *Nathaniel*[4], *Nathaniel*[3], *Humphrey*[2], *John*[1]) was born on 23 Jun 1882 at Edwards, St. Lawrence Co., NY. She married Arthur Isidore Boulet, son of Victor Boulet and Helene Martin, on 19 Feb 1901 at Edwards, St. Lawrence Co., NY. She died on 24 Apr 1956 at Edwards, St. Lawrence Co., NY, at age 73. She was buried at Fairview Cemetery, Edwards, St. Lawrence Co., NY.

She appeared on the census of 1 Jun 1900 at Edwards, St. Lawrence Co., NY.

Children of Lottie Mae[10] Hall and Arthur Isidore Boulet all born at Edwards, St. Lawrence Co., NY, were as follows:

278.   i.   GERALD LINDEN[11], born 21 Jun 1902; married Alice Kauffman.

         ii.   LAWRENCE EDWARD; born 28 Jan 1904; married Madeline Kauffman; died 8 Jul 1989 at age 85; buried at Holy Ghost Cemetery, Chili, NY.

279.   iii.   GERVAISE ISADORE, born 24 May 1906; married Hazel M. Wheeler.

280.   iv.   ARTHUR OLNEY, born 25 Aug 1907; married Oneita May French.

281.   v.   LOUISE FLORENCE, born 30 Sep 1913; married Leon Dewey Typhair.

282. vi. BERNARD PHILIP, born 9 Oct 1919; married Mary Jean Brown.

131. FRANK EMERY[10] HALL SR (*Hiram*[9], *Emmorancy*[8]*Johnson*, *Charles*[7], *Ira*[6], *Jonathan*[5], *Nathaniel*[4], *Nathaniel*[3], *Humphrey*[2], *John*[1]) was born on 7 Oct 1884 at Edwards, St. Lawrence Co., NY. He married Bernice Mari Lillis, daughter of George Lillis and Anna Cole, on 28 Oct 1906 at Antwerp, St. Lawrence Co., NY. He died on 7 Mar 1940 at Ogdensburg Hospital, Ogdensburg, St. Lawrence Co., NY, at age 55. He was buried at Fairview Cemetery, Edwards, St. Lawrence Co., NY.

He appeared on the census of 1 Jun 1900 at Edwards, St. Lawrence Co., NY.

Children of Frank Emery[10] Hall Sr and Bernice Mari Lillis all born at Edwards, St. Lawrence Co., NY, were as follows:

283. i. KATHLEEN MARIE[11], born 28 Dec 1907; married John Arnold.

284. ii. GERALDINE LOUISE, born 7 Aug 1910; married Wesley Brailey; divorced Wesley Brailey.

iii. FRED; born 23 Jul 1912; died 24 Jul 1912 at Edwards, St. Lawrence Co., NY; buried at Riverside Cemetery, Edwards, St. Lawrence Co., NY.

iv. FRANK EMERY JR.; born 23 Jul 1912; died 25 Jul 1912 at Edwards, St. Lawrence Co., NY; buried at Riverside Cemetery, Edwards, St. Lawrence Co., NY.

285. v. CHERRY LILLIS, born 7 May 1917; married Philip Franklin McCarthy.

286. vi. FREDERICK GEORGE, born 22 Jul 1924; married Doris Jones.

vii. PATRICIA GLADYS; born 29 Nov 1926. She was unmarried.

132. BRUCE THERON[10] WARD (*Venila*[9]*Hall*, *Emmorancy*[8]*Johnson*, *Charles*[7], *Ira*[6], *Jonathan*[5], *Nathaniel*[4], *Nathaniel*[3], *Humphrey*[2], *John*[1]) was born on 16 Jul 1875 at Edwards, St. Lawrence Co., NY. He married Carrie Elizabeth

Creighton, daughter of James Creighton and Harriet Curtis, on 23 Feb 1900 at Gouverneur, St. Lawrence Co., NY. He died on 23 Aug 1949 at Noble Foundation Hospital, Gouverneur, St. Lawrence Co., NY, at age 74. He was buried on 27 Aug 1949 at Fairview Cemetery, Edwards, St. Lawrence Co., NY.

He appeared on the census of 1 Jun 1900 at Edwards Township, St. Lawrence Co., NY.

Children of Bruce Theron[10] Ward and Carrie Elizabeth Creighton were as follows:

287.   i.   SETH ALFRED[11], born 26 Aug 1901 at Edwards, St. Lawrence Co., NY; married Gladys McLeod.

288.   ii.   MARY ROSE, born 30 Jan 1903 at Fine, St. Lawrence Co., NY; married Durward Eugene Cole.

289.   iii.   BOWER WILLIAM, born 15 Feb 1905 at Fine, St. Lawrence Co., NY; married Hilda Cockayne.

290.   iv.   GERALD BERT, born 27 Jan 1907 at Fine, St. Lawrence Co., NY; married Lucille Reed.

291.   v.   IRENE MILDRED, born 2 May 1920 at Edwards, St. Lawrence Co., NY; married Paul Mullaney; married Earl Reed Jr; married Silas Woodrow Whitford.

133.   LENA MAY[10] WARD (*Venila[9]Hall, Emmorancy[8]Johnson, Charles[7], Ira[6], Jonathan[5], Nathaniel[4], Nathaniel[3], Humphrey[2], John[1]*) was born on 8 Jul 1877 at Edwards, St. Lawrence Co., NY. She married Webster Maybee, son of Nelson Maybee and Eliza Poole, on 4 May 1898 at Gouverneur, St. Lawrence Co., NY. She died in 1916 at Antwerp, Jefferson Co., NY. She was buried at Hillside Cemetery, Antwerp, Jefferson Co., NY.

Children of Lena May[10] Ward and Webster Maybee were as follows:

292.   i.   MYRTLE MAY[11], born 18 Jul 1893 at Edwards, St. Lawrence Co., NY; married Roy John Mason.

      ii.   ARTHUR; born 17 Sep 1896 at Fine, St. Lawrence Co., NY; died 5 Jun 1897 at Fine, St.

Lawrence Co., NY; buried at Fine, St. Lawrence Co., NY.

293.   iii.   EVELYN VENILA, born 27 Apr 1900 at Newton Falls, St. Lawrence Co., NY; married Meryl Bradigan.

        iv.   LESTER ROY; born 1912; died 1925 at Russell, St. Lawrence Co., NY; buried at Hillside Cemetery, Antwerp, Jefferson Co., NY.

134. MARGARET M.^{10} WARD (*Venila^{9}Hall, Emmorancy^{8}Johnson, Charles^7, Ira^6, Jonathan^5, Nathaniel^4, Nathaniel^3, Humphrey^2, John^1*) was born on 12 Mar 1880 at Edwards, St. Lawrence Co., NY. She married Perley Shampine, son of Peter Shampine and Jane Thomas, on 12 Jun 1899 at Hermon, St. Lawrence Co., NY. She died on 4 Jul 1909 at Antwerp, Jefferson Co., NY, at age 29. She was buried at Hillside Cemetery, Antwerp, Jefferson Co., NY.

Children of Margaret M.^{10} Ward and Perley Shampine were as follows:

        i.   EARL^{11}; born 1901 at Edwards, St. Lawrence Co., NY.

        ii.   RUTH; born 1903.

294.   iii.   MAUDE ESTHER, born 29 Apr 1906 at Antwerp, Jefferson Co., NY; married Edward Spalding Smingler.

        iv.   MAY; born Jul 1909 at Antwerp, Jefferson Co., NY; died Jul 1909 at Antwerp, Jefferson Co., NY; buried at Hillside Cemetery, Antwerp, Jefferson Co., NY.

135. GRACE^{10} WARD (*Venila^{9}Hall, Emmorancy^{8}Johnson, Charles^7, Ira^6, Jonathan^5, Nathaniel^4, Nathaniel^3, Humphrey^2, John^1*) was born on 5 Sep 1886 at Edwards, St. Lawrence Co., NY. She married Burton Maybee, son of Nelson Maybee and Eliza Poole, on 1 Jan 1907 at Edwards, St. Lawrence Co., NY. She died on 22 Oct 1950 at home, Russell, St. Lawrence Co., NY, at age 64. She was buried at Woodland Cemetery, Fine, St. Lawrence Co., NY.

She appeared on the census of 1 Jun 1900 at Edwards Township, St. Lawrence Co., NY.

Children of Grace[10] Ward and Burton Maybee were as follows:

 i. INEZ[11]; born 13 Jun 1907 at Fine, St. Lawrence Co., NY; died 21 Jul 1980 at home, Russell, St. Lawrence Co., NY, at age 73; buried at Hermon Cemetery, Hermon, St. Lawrence Co., NY.
  She was never married.

 ii. (--?--).

 iii. IRENE; born 28 Mar 1909 at Fine, St. Lawrence Co., NY; married Hubert Beaulieu 1942; died 9 Aug 1985 at Mercy Hospital, Watertown, Jefferson Co., NY, at age 76; buried at Hermon Cemetery, Hermon, St. Lawrence Co., NY.

136. BLANCHE[10] WARD (*Venila[9]Hall, Emmorancy[8]Johnson, Charles[7], Ira[6], Jonathan[5], Nathaniel[4], Nathaniel[3], Humphrey[2], John[1]*) was born on 23 Oct 1888 at Edwards, St. Lawrence Co., NY. She married Horace Alfred Brotherton, son of Clark Brotherton and Elizabeth LeFleur, in Sep 1906. She married Wilbur Cunningham. She died on 20 Sep 1948 at age 59. She was buried at Hillside Cemetery, Antwerp, Jefferson Co., NY.

She appeared on the census of 1 Jun 1900 at Edwards Township, St. Lawrence Co., NY.

Children of Blanche[10] Ward and Horace Alfred Brotherton were as follows:

 i. MERTON[11]; born 28 Nov 1909; married Ella Clifton 2 Aug 1946.

 ii. MILTON; born 10 Feb 1912 at Edwards, St. Lawrence Co., NY; married Elizabeth Hill Dec 1934; died 28 Oct 1947 at age 35; buried at Hillside Cemetery, Antwerp, Jefferson Co., NY.

 iii. MARIAH; born 28 Dec 1913; married Lloyd Phair 1 Oct 1931; died 10 Jun 1932 at age 18; buried at Hillside Cemetery, Antwerp, Jefferson Co., NY.

 iv. MYRTLE; born 18 Aug 1916; married Stanley Belmore 25 Jan 1939.
  She lived in 1979 at Gouverneur, St. Lawrence Co., NY.

v.   MELVIN; born 25 Nov 1918; married Ruth Delles 20 Nov 1941.

There were no children of Blanche[10] Ward and Wilbur Cunningham.

137.   HOWARD   "DICK"[10]   WARD   (*Venila[9]Hall, Emmorancy[8]Johnson, Charles[7], Ira[6], Jonathan[5], Nathaniel[4], Nathaniel[3], Humphrey[2], John[1]*) was born on 7 Oct 1893 at Edwards, St. Lawrence Co., NY. He married Mina Dart, daughter of Daniel Dart and Adelia Dygert, on 2 Jan 1916 at St. Edwards Church, Talcville, NY. He died on 13 Mar 1960 at Clifton-Fine Hospital, Star Lake, St. Lawrence Co., NY, at age 66. He was buried on 16 Mar 1960 at Fairview Cemetery, Edwards, St. Lawrence Co., NY.

He appeared on the census of 1 Jun 1900 at Edwards Township, St. Lawrence Co., NY.

Children of Howard "Dick"[10] Ward and Mina Dart were as follows:

	i.	FLOYD[11].
	ii.	VERA.
	iii.	(--?--).
	iv.	CARL. .
	v.	CLARA.
295.	vi.	EDWARD LAWRENCE, born 24 May 1916 at Edwards, St. Lawrence Co., NY; married Mildred Dorothy Maxiner.

138.   EDITH LURA[10]   WARD (*Venila[9]Hall, Emmorancy[8]Johnson, Charles[7], Ira[6], Jonathan[5], Nathaniel[4], Nathaniel[3], Humphrey[2], John[1]*) was born on 28 Nov 1895 at Edwards, St. Lawrence Co., NY. She married Ralph Marshall Morgan on 28 May 1932 at Watertown, Jefferson Co., NY. She died on 3 Jan 1989 at Canton-Potsdam Hospital, Potsdam, St. Lawrence Co., NY, at age 93. She was buried at Brookdale Cemetery.

She appeared on the census of 1 Jun 1900 at Edwards Township, St. Lawrence Co., NY. She lived on 16 Mar 1960 at Massena, St. Lawrence Co., NY.

Children of Edith Lura[10] Ward and Ralph Marshall Morgan were as follows:

> i.   RALPH[11].
> ii. RETA.

296.   iii. RUTH, born 26 Sep 1932 at Syracuse, Onondaga Co., NY; married Armand Dumont.

297.   iv. JEANNINE, born 7 Nov 1933 at Syracuse, Onondaga Co., NY; married Leo Lynch.

298.   v. CHARLOTTE ANNE, born 30 Jan 1936 at Syracuse, Onondoga Co., NY; married Donald Posewitz.

139. HARRISON L.[10] PRATT (*Venira*[9]*Hall, Emmorancy*[8]*Johnson, Charles*[7], *Ira*[6], *Jonathan*[5], *Nathaniel*[4], *Nathaniel*[3], *Humphrey*[2], *John*[1]) was born on 6 Aug 1882 at Edwards, St. Lawrence Co., NY. He married Mary Gotham on 12 Nov 1926 at Carthage, NY.

He appeared on the census of 1 Jun 1900.

Children of Harrison L.[10] Pratt and Mary Gotham were as follows:

> i.   (--?--)[11].
> ii. IRENE VERGA; born 6 Jun 1914.

140. CECILE EVA[10] PRATT (*Venira*[9]*Hall, Emmorancy*[8]*Johnson, Charles*[7], *Ira*[6], *Jonathan*[5], *Nathaniel*[4], *Nathaniel*[3], *Humphrey*[2], *John*[1]) was born on 20 May 1884 at Edwards, St. Lawrence Co., NY. She married Arthur Henry Newvine on 1 Jun 1904 at Edwards, St. Lawrence Co., NY. She died on 3 Nov 1961 at Edwards, St. Lawrence Co., NY, at age 77.

She appeared on the census of 1 Jun 1900 at Edwards, St. Lawrence Co., NY.

Children of Cecile Eva[10] Pratt and Arthur Henry Newvine all born at Edwards, St. Lawrence Co., NY, were as follows:

> i.   RUTH MAMIE[11]; born 18 Dec 1904; married Frank Cayea 19 Apr 1923 at Gouverneur, St. Lawrence Co., NY.

ii. IDA MAE; born 8 Jun 1909; married George Garvis 18 Jul 1931 at Edwards, St. Lawrence Co., NY; married Philip C. Smith 8 Oct 1973 at Madrid, NY.

299. iii. FRIEDA LOUISE, born 24 Apr 1913; married Ralph Boni.

141. HARLEY THERON[10] PRATT (*Venira[9]Hall, Emmorancy[8]Johnson, Charles[7], Ira[6], Jonathan[5], Nathaniel[4], Nathaniel[3], Humphrey[2], John[1]*) was born on 3 Apr 1885 at Edwards, St. Lawrence Co., NY. He married Mary Caroline Lennon on 25 Sep 1919 at Star Lake, NY. He died on 29 Nov 1961 at Star Lake, NY, at age 76.

He appeared on the census of 1 Jun 1900 at Edwards, St. Lawrence Co., NY.

Children of Harley Theron[10] Pratt and Mary Caroline Lennon are as follows:

300. i. WILLIAM[11], born 19 Sep 1920 at Benson Mines, NY; married Frances Morgan.

ii. THERON; born Dec 1921 at Edwards, St. Lawrence Co., NY.

301. iii. DONALD, born Apr 1923 at Edwards, St. Lawrence Co., NY; married Pauline Briggs.

302. iv. CLIFFORD, born Apr 1925 at Edwards, St. Lawrence Co., NY; married Faye Iaria.

142. ALICE[10] MAIN (*John[9], Lutilia[8]Johnson, George[7], Ira[6], Jonathan[5], Nathaniel[4], Nathaniel[3], Humphrey[2], John[1]*) was born in 1862. She married Thomas Burbridge at Hardin Township, Pike Co., IL. She died in 1947.

Children of Alice[10] Main and Thomas Burbridge were as follows:

303. i. NOLA ESTELLA[11], married Bert Havener.

304. ii. FLOYD, born 1885; married Sadie Klenine.

305. iii. ROSS, born 1887; married Eva Yaeger.

306. iv. OPAL, born 1889; married Arthur Foster.

143. ALVIN[10] MAIN (*John[9], Lutilia[8]Johnson, George[7], Ira[6], Jonathan[5], Nathaniel[4], Nathaniel[3], Humphrey[2], John[1]*) was born in 1864. He married Ella Johnson. He married Anne Sheppard. He died in 1919.

Children of Alvin[10] Main and Ella Johnson were as follows:

      i.   VIRGIL[11].
      ii. GRACE.

Children of Alvin[10] Main and Anne Sheppard were as follows:

      i.   OZIE[11].
      ii. IVA.
      iii. EVA.
      iv. ZELMA.

144. LENA OPAL[10] MAIN (*John[9], Lutilia[8]Johnson, George[7], Ira[6], Jonathan[5], Nathaniel[4], Nathaniel[3], Humphrey[2], John[1]*) was born in 1872. She married Ora Johnson. She died in 1936.

Children of Lena Opal[10] Main and Ora Johnson were as follows:

307.   i.   RAYMOND EARL[11], born 1892; married Daisy Moore; married Lena Reeder.

308.   ii. COY, born 2 Feb 1901; married H. Gay Wassell.

145. RUFUS HENRY[10] MAIN (*Alvin[9], Lutilia[8]Johnson, George[7], Ira[6], Jonathan[5], Nathaniel[4], Nathaniel[3], Humphrey[2], John[1]*) was born in 1868. He married Helen Chrysup. He died in 1955.

Children of Rufus Henry[10] Main and Helen Chrysup were as follows:

309.   i.   GEORGE CHRYSUP[11], born 1897; married Helen Margaret Kubesch.

      ii. ALVIN NYE; born 1900; died 1946.

310.   iii. RUTH NYE, born 1908; married Alfred Koeler.

311.   iv. JOSEPHINE BARNEY, born 13 Feb 1912; married Harry Budd Atkinson.

      v. PHILIP ANDREW; born 1917.

146. JOSIAH[10] MAIN (*Alvin*[9], *Lutilia*[8]*Johnson*, *George*[7], *Ira*[6], *Jonathan*[5], *Nathaniel*[4], *Nathaniel*[3], *Humphrey*[2], *John*[1]) was born in 1870. He married Emily Triplet. He died in 1948 at Hemet, CA.

Children of Josiah[10] Main and Emily Triplet are:

  i. NORMAN FRANCIS[11]; born 1901; married Fay Helm; married Clarisse Revis.

147. BLANCH MARGRET[10] MAIN (*Alvin*[9], *Lutilia*[8]*Johnson*, *George*[7], *Ira*[6], *Jonathan*[5], *Nathaniel*[4], *Nathaniel*[3], *Humphrey*[2], *John*[1]) was born in 1874. She married William Gay.

Children of Blanch Margret[10] Main and William Gay were:

312. i. ELIZABETH[11], born 1895; married Frank Lewis.

148. ROSE IDA[10] MAIN (*Alvin*[9], *Lutilia*[8]*Johnson*, *George*[7], *Ira*[6], *Jonathan*[5], *Nathaniel*[4], *Nathaniel*[3], *Humphrey*[2], *John*[1]) was born in 1874. She married Luther Lawrence Warden.

Children of Rose Ida[10] Main and Luther Lawrence Warden are as follows:

  i. L. LAWRENCE[11] JR.; born 1904; married Eleanor Leach.
313. ii. ALVIN MAIN, born 1908; married Sylvia Callahan; married Grace Eileen Joseph.
314. iii. JOHN SEVIER, born 1914; married Helen Louise McCrory.

149. ROSCOE CONKLING[10] MAIN (*Alvin*[9], *Lutilia*[8]*Johnson*, *George*[7], *Ira*[6], *Jonathan*[5], *Nathaniel*[4], *Nathaniel*[3], *Humphrey*[2], *John*[1]) was born in 1882. He married Ruth Flower Stafford.

Children of Roscoe Conkling[10] Main and Ruth Flower Stafford were as follows:

315. i. ALVIN NYE[11] II, born 1918; married June Kelly.
  ii. EDWARD STAFFORD; born 1918.
316. iii. NATHANIEL FOOTE, born 1920; married Barbara Jean Cheda; married Davney Olson.
317. iv. PETER SWINEFORD, born 1922; married Estella Ashley.

157

        v.   ROBERT ANDREW; born 1923.

318.   vi.   RUFUS WILLIAM, born 1925; married Mary Lou Murphy.

       vii. CAROLINE; born 1927; died 1927.

319.   viii. SARAH FLOWER, born 1928; married Carl Emil Johnson.

150. FRANCIS ALVIN^{10} MAIN (*Alvin*^{9}, *Lutilia*^{8}*Johnson*, *George*^{7}, *Ira*^{6}, *Jonathan*^{5}, *Nathaniel*^{4}, *Nathaniel*^{3}, *Humphrey*^{2}, *John*^{1}) was born in 1884. He married Iva Woolfolk Scanland. He died in 1954.

Children of Francis Alvin^{10} Main and Iva Woolfolk Scanland are as follows:

320.   i.   MARGURITE^{11}, born 1906; married John Zimmerman.

321.   ii. BERNEICE SCANLAND, born 1908; married Cecile W. Martin.

151. LOTTIE^{10} MAIN (*Phillip*^{9}, *Lutilia*^{8}*Johnson*, *George*^{7}, *Ira*^{6}, *Jonathan*^{5}, *Nathaniel*^{4}, *Nathaniel*^{3}, *Humphrey*^{2}, *John*^{1}) was born in 1875. She married Alex Sutherland. She died in 1954.

Children of Lottie^{10} Main and Alex Sutherland were as follows:

322.   i.   ROSS^{11}, born 1897; married Mary Hook; married Dorothy Kanady; married Rita (--?--).

323.   ii. STELLA, born 1908; married Derrill Angst.

152. DAISY^{10} MAIN (*Phillip*^{9}, *Lutilia*^{8}*Johnson*, *George*^{7}, *Ira*^{6}, *Jonathan*^{5}, *Nathaniel*^{4}, *Nathaniel*^{3}, *Humphrey*^{2}, *John*^{1}) was born in 1880. She married M. William McDonald. She died in 1937.

Children of Daisy^{10} Main and M. William McDonald are:

        i.   MILDRED^{11}; born 1908.

153. CLYDE^{10} MAIN (*Phillip*^{9}, *Lutilia*^{8}*Johnson*, *George*^{7}, *Ira*^{6}, *Jonathan*^{5}, *Nathaniel*^{4}, *Nathaniel*^{3}, *Humphrey*^{2}, *John*^{1}) was born in 1884. He married Margaret Alexander. He died in 1953.

Children of Clyde^{10} Main and Margaret Alexander were as follows:

        i.   FARIS^{11}; born 1920; died 1942.

ii.   BEVERLY; born 1926; married W. V. Spencer.

154.   ODUS OLEN[10] MAIN (*Andrew*[9], *Lutilia*[8]*Johnson*, *George*[7], *Ira*[6], *Jonathan*[5], *Nathaniel*[4], *Nathaniel*[3], *Humphrey*[2], *John*[1]) was born in 1875. He married Virdie May Hughs. He married Katherine Halverson. He died in 1948.

Children of Odus Olen[10] Main and Virdie May Hughs were as follows:

324.   i.   SYLVIA MABLE[11], born 1897; married William Andrew Morgan.

325.   ii.   EMMET ARNOLD, born 1901; married Lulu E. Skinner.

326.   iii.   AGEE GALE, born 1903; married Lavillea Gillian.

327.   iv.   SUSIE ELIZABETH, born 1906; married Earl Ruby; married Glenn Allen; married All Crews.

There were no children of Odus Olen[10] Main and Katherine Halverson.

155.   LONNIE LOREN[10] MAIN (*Andrew*[9], *Lutilia*[8]*Johnson*, *George*[7], *Ira*[6], *Jonathan*[5], *Nathaniel*[4], *Nathaniel*[3], *Humphrey*[2], *John*[1]) was born in 1877. He married Alma V. Hunter. He died in 1929.

Children of Lonnie Loren[10] Main and Alma V. Hunter were as follows:

i.   PAUL[11]; born 1901; died 1931.

328.   ii.   VAUGHN, born 1903; married Lottie M. Wood.

329.   iii.   ERNEST W., born 1906; married Frances Martin.

330.   iv.   RAY O., born 1908; married Evelyn Frances Clough.

331.   v.   AARON, born 1910; married Ella Pearl Woods.

332.   vi.   PARKER EMERY, born 1912; married Hazel Osburn.

333.   vii.   TRACY L., born 1914; married Virginia Zamboni.

156.   BYARD BOLEN[10] MAIN (*Andrew*[9], *Lutilia*[8]*Johnson*, *George*[7], *Ira*[6], *Jonathan*[5], *Nathaniel*[4], *Nathaniel*[3], *Humphrey*[2], *John*[1]) was born in 1879. He married Iva E. Johnson, daughter of Alvin Richard

Johnson and Mary Harper. He married Coy Doyle. He died in 1922 at Pike Co., IL.

Children of Byard Bolen[10] Main and Iva E. Johnson are as follows:

334.   i.   CLEDA[11], born 1900; married Martin R. Hoover.

335.   ii.   EVELYN, born 30 Apr 1902 at Nebo, Pike Co., IL; married Emil Hobbs.

336.   iii.   GEORGIA, born 1904; married Coy Doyle; married Wayne Harpole.

Children of Byard Bolen[10] Main and Coy Doyle are as follows:

337.   i.   LOTTIE[11], born 1914; married Floyd Flowers.

338.   ii.   BERTRAM, born 1916; married Ellen Morrison; married Helen Kelly.

157. TADE MARION[10] MAIN (*Andrew*[9], *Lutilia*[8]*Johnson, George*[7], *Ira*[6], *Jonathan*[5], *Nathaniel*[4], *Nathaniel*[3], *Humphrey*[2], *John*[1]) was born in 1881. She married James L. Wood. She died in 1946.

Children of Tade Marion[10] Main and James L. Wood were as follows:

i.   ELIZABETH[11]; born 1913.
She was married and divorced.

ii.   MARION; born 1915; died 1947.

158. HARRY HERMAN[10] MAIN (*Andrew*[9], *Lutilia*[8]*Johnson, George*[7], *Ira*[6], *Jonathan*[5], *Nathaniel*[4], *Nathaniel*[3], *Humphrey*[2], *John*[1]) was born in 1883. He married Ruby Opal Brannon. He died in 1955.

Children of Harry Herman[10] Main and Ruby Opal Brannon are as follows:

339.   i.   ZENNA B.[11], born 1913; married Burley Bohannon; married James Culbertson.

340.   ii.   ELSIE ELLA, born 1921; married William E. Childres.

341.   iii.   DOROTHY ISABELLE, born 1923; married Oliver E. Phillips.

342.   iv.   IDA RHEA, born 1926; married Robert V. Callen.

159. CARRIE CLIFFORD[10] MAIN (*Andrew*[9], *Lutilia*[8]*Johnson*, *George*[7], *Ira*[6], *Jonathan*[5], *Nathaniel*[4], *Nathaniel*[3], *Humphrey*[2], *John*[1]) was born in 1885. He married Lillie Jones. He died in 1943.

Children of Carrie Clifford[10] Main and Lillie Jones were as follows:

343.	i.	CECIL[11], born 1908; married Arley Shelton.
344.	ii.	JOHN, born 1910; married Madeline McLean.
345.	iii.	KENNETH, born 1912; married Thelma Goetz.
346.	iv.	GLADYS, born 1914; married Harry Owen.
	v.	CLARENCE; born 1918; died 1925.
347.	vi.	CLAUDIA, born 1920; married Roy Duncan.
348.	vii.	ELMER, born 1921; married Norma Haffey.
349.	viii.	LAURA BETH, born 1923; married Oswald Mueller.
350.	ix.	PEARL, born 1924; married Albert Benner.
351.	x.	CLIFFORD JR., born 1928; married Estella Lassick.
352.	xi.	EDITH, born 1929; married Richard L. Phillips.
	xii.	BEULAH; born 1933; died 1934.

160. FLO FOUNTAIN[10] MAIN (*Andrew*[9], *Lutilia*[8]*Johnson*, *George*[7], *Ira*[6], *Jonathan*[5], *Nathaniel*[4], *Nathaniel*[3], *Humphrey*[2], *John*[1]) was born in 1888. He married Helen Johnson. He married Lizzie Shott. He died in 1938.

Children of Flo Fountain[10] Main and Helen Johnson are as follows:

353.	i.	HAMPTON RANZY[11] SR., born 1907; married Carsie Congleton.
354.	ii.	WILBERT RICHARD OGAL, born 1909; married Eloise Wallace.
355.	iii.	JESSIE OGAL RICHARD, born 1911; married Helen Driscoll; married Lizzie Shott.

There were no children of Flo Fountain[10] Main and Lizzie Shott.

161. NINA NOBLE[10] MAIN (*Andrew*[9], *Lutilia*[8]*Johnson*, *George*[7], *Ira*[6], *Jonathan*[5], *Nathaniel*[4], *Nathaniel*[3], *Humphrey*[2], *John*[1]) was born in 1891. She married John William Walkey. She married William Henry Thiele.

Children of Nina Noble[10] Main and John William Walkey were as follows:

356.   i.   MERTON MAIN[11], born 1908; married Mildred Schmidt.
            ii.   JAMES WESLEY; born 1912; married Lorraine Laughlin.
           iii.   MAURCIE NELSON; born 1914; died 1914.
           iv.   ERWIN OSWALD; born 1916; married Kay Baer; died 1944.

There were no children of Nina Noble[10] Main and William Henry Thiele.

162.   MUDD MARBLE[10] MAIN (*Andrew*[9], *Lutilia*[8]*Johnson*, *George*[7], *Ira*[6], *Jonathan*[5], *Nathaniel*[4], *Nathaniel*[3], *Humphrey*[2], *John*[1]) was born in 1895. He married Alma McCormick.

Children of Mudd Marble[10] Main and Alma McCormick are:

357.   i.   MAX M.[11], born 1920; married Mary Boyles.

163.   MINNERVA ALICE[10] COLVIN (*Sarah*[9]*Main*, *Lutilia*[8]*Johnson*, *George*[7], *Ira*[6], *Jonathan*[5], *Nathaniel*[4], *Nathaniel*[3], *Humphrey*[2], *John*[1]) was born in 1881 at Pike Co., IL. She married Joseph A. MaLee. She died in 1951 at Oak Grove, MO.

Children of Minnerva Alice[10] Colvin and Joseph A. MaLee are as follows:

358.   i.   THEODORE[11], born 1911; married Mamie M. Schroeder; married Aleene Adams.
359.   ii.   MARGARET LOUISE, born 1916; married David C. Calhoun.

164.   BEULAH AUDRY[10] COLVIN (*Sarah*[9]*Main*, *Lutilia*[8]*Johnson*, *George*[7], *Ira*[6], *Jonathan*[5], *Nathaniel*[4], *Nathaniel*[3], *Humphrey*[2], *John*[1]) was born in 1883 at Pike Co., IL. She married Edward C. Kulmus.

Children of Beulah Audry[10] Colvin and Edward C. Kulmus were as follows:

 i. JANE AUDRIE[11]; born 1910; died 1933.
360. ii. EARL EDWARD, born 1912; married Margaret Catherine Johnson.
 iii. VIRGINIA MAY; born 1917; married Everatt Edgar Hancock.

165. SIDNEY ORVILLE[10] COLVIN (*Sarah*[9]*Main, Lutilia*[8]*Johnson, George*[7], *Ira*[6], *Jonathan*[5], *Nathaniel*[4], *Nathaniel*[3], *Humphrey*[2], *John*[1]) was born in 1885. He married Pearl Naoma Colby. He died in 1954.

Children of Sidney Orville[10] Colvin and Pearl Naoma Colby are as follows:

361. i. RICHARD ORVILLE[11], born 1908; married Helen Cross.
362. ii. SIDNEY ROBERT, born 1913; married Ruth Smith.

166. ANTHONEY BEN[10] COLVIN (*Sarah*[9]*Main, Lutilia*[8]*Johnson, George*[7], *Ira*[6], *Jonathan*[5], *Nathaniel*[4], *Nathaniel*[3], *Humphrey*[2], *John*[1]) was born in 1887. He married Eva Borg in 1913 at Dallas, TX.

Children of Anthoney Ben[10] Colvin and Eva Borg were as follows:

363. i. THOMAS B.[11], born 1915; married Edmore Engle.
 ii. DORIS ELLEN; born 1918; died 1919 at Dallas, TX.
364. iii. WINFRED A., born 1921; married Dorothy Snyder.
365. iv. AUDREY MAE, born 1925; married Alva Lincoln Hysom.

167. GLADYS CARRIE[10] COLVIN (*Sarah*[9]*Main, Lutilia*[8]*Johnson, George*[7], *Ira*[6], *Jonathan*[5], *Nathaniel*[4], *Nathaniel*[3], *Humphrey*[2], *John*[1]) was born in 1890. She married Alvah E. Williams in 1929.

Children of Gladys Carrie[10] Colvin and Alvah E. Williams are:

      i.   JAMES ALVAH[11]; born 1931.

168.   PANSY A.[10] LAWSON (*Minerva[9]Main*, *Lutilia[8]Johnson*, *George[7]*, *Ira[6]*, *Jonathan[5]*, *Nathaniel[4]*, *Nathaniel[3]*, *Humphrey[2]*, *John[1]*) was born in 1883. She married A. J. Koenig. She died in 1910.

    Children of Pansy A.[10] Lawson and A. J. Koenig are:

366.   i.   MARIE[11], born 1904; married Walter M. Pine; married Herman Engleman.

169.   LELA[10] MAIN (*George[9]*, *Lutilia[8]Johnson*, *George[7]*, *Ira[6]*, *Jonathan[5]*, *Nathaniel[4]*, *Nathaniel[3]*, *Humphrey[2]*, *John[1]*) was born in 1885. She married Edward Shriver.

    Children of Lela[10] Main and Edward Shriver are as follows:

367.   i.   JOSEPHINE[11], born 1907; married Edwin C. Miller.

368.   ii.   MARY ALICE, married Edwin M. Strom.

170.   FARIS[10] MAIN (*George[9]*, *Lutilia[8]Johnson*, *George[7]*, *Ira[6]*, *Jonathan[5]*, *Nathaniel[4]*, *Nathaniel[3]*, *Humphrey[2]*, *John[1]*) was born in 1890. He married Susan Long. He died in 1921.

    Children of Faris[10] Main and Susan Long are:

      i.   FARIS[11]; born 1921.

171.   EUGENE[10] MAIN (*Thomas[9]*, *Lutilia[8]Johnson*, *George[7]*, *Ira[6]*, *Jonathan[5]*, *Nathaniel[4]*, *Nathaniel[3]*, *Humphrey[2]*, *John[1]*) was born in 1899. He married Margaret Niles.

    Children of Eugene[10] Main and Margaret Niles are as follows:

      i.   THOMAS FREDRICK[11]; born 1934.
      ii.   MARALYN MARGARET; born 1937.
     iii. CORAL JEANNETTE; born 1944.

172.   EVA M.[10] JOHNSON (*Alvin[9]*, *Rufus[8]*, *George[7]*, *Ira[6]*, *Jonathan[5]*, *Nathaniel[4]*, *Nathaniel[3]*, *Humphrey[2]*, *John[1]*) was born on 22 Apr 1872 at Pike Co., IL. She married Otto Main on 27 Dec

1894 at Pike Co., IL. She died on 5 Nov 1902 at Pike Co., IL, at age 30. She was buried in the Watson Cemetery.

Children of Eva M.[10] Johnson and Otto Main were as follows:

    i.   JAMES[11]; died 1945.

    ii. CARSON ESTLE; born 23 Feb 1895; died 11 Apr 1960 at age 65; buried 14 Apr 1960 at Rosehill Cemetery, Chicago, Cook Co., IL.

    iii. EDITH; married Ed Berger at Morton, MI.

    iv. LOLAND; born 7 Aug 1901 at Nebo, Pike Co., IL; married Dorothy Helen Sanford 21 Nov 1922 at Centralia, Marion Co., IL; died 13 Jul 1964 at Royal Oak, Oakland Co., MI, at age 62; buried 16 Jul 1964 at White Chapel Memorial Cemetery, Troy, Oakland Co., MI.

        His name was legally changed to LOLAND SPEPPARD.

173. ANNA P.[10] JOHNSON (*Alvin*[9], *Rufus*[8], *George*[7], *Ira*[6], *Jonathan*[5], *Nathaniel*[4], *Nathaniel*[3], *Humphrey*[2], *John*[1]) was born on 20 Mar 1875 at Pike Co., IL. She married Melvin Troutner.

Children of Anna P.[10] Johnson and Melvin Troutner were as follows:

  369.   i.   BLANCHE[11], born 2 Aug 1896; married Floyd M. Taylor.

  370.   ii. OPAL, born 1897; married William Hunt; divorced William Hunt; married Homer Rhoades.

         iii. ROSS; born 1902; married Esther Gerard.

        He was merchant and farmer at Alma, KS.

174. LEWIS ARTHUR[10] JOHNSON (*Alvin*[9], *Rufus*[8], *George*[7], *Ira*[6], *Jonathan*[5], *Nathaniel*[4], *Nathaniel*[3], *Humphrey*[2], *John*[1]) was born on 3 Jul 1877 at Pike Co., IL. He married Lucinda Gant. He died on 25 May 1937 at Pike Co., IL, at age 59. He was buried at Crescent Heights Cemetery, Pleasant Hill, Pike Co., IL.

Children of Lewis Arthur[10] Johnson and Lucinda Gant were as follows:

371.   i.   MARY HAZEL[11], born 8 Nov 1901; married Thomas Shellhorse.

372.   ii.   LEWIS HAYWARD, born 12 Nov 1903 at Nebo, Pike Co., IL; married Iva Lillian Goltz.

iii.   RAYMOND AMOS; born 1917; died 1943.

iv.   JAMES LOWELL was unmarried. He lived at Hallsville, MO.

175.   IVA E.[10] JOHNSON (*Alvin*[9], *Rufus*[8], *George*[7], *Ira*[6], *Jonathan*[5], *Nathaniel*[4], *Nathaniel*[3], *Humphrey*[2], *John*[1]) was born on 26 Mar 1880 at Pike Co., IL. She married Byard Bolen Main, son of Andrew Parker Main and Elizabeth Hack. She died on 24 Jan 1912 at Pike Co., IL, at age 31. She was buried in the Nebo Cemetery, Nebo, IL.

Children of Iva E.[10] Johnson and Byard Bolen Main are as follows:

i.   CLEDA[11], born 1900; married Martin R. Hoover. (see # 334.).

ii.   EVELYN, born 30 Apr 1902 at Nebo, Pike Co., IL; married Emil Hobbs. (see # 335.).

iii.   GEORGIA, born 1904; married Coy Doyle; married Wayne Harpole. (see # 336.).

176.   EVA[10] JOHNSON (*Alvin*[9], *Rufus*[8], *George*[7], *Ira*[6], *Jonathan*[5], *Nathaniel*[4], *Nathaniel*[3], *Humphrey*[2], *John*[1]) was born on 2 Sep 1900 at Pike Co., IL. She married William Porter Jeffries on 16 Dec 1917. She died on 13 Jul 1976 at age 75. She was buried at Pittsfield West Cemetery, Pittsfield, Pike Co., IL.

Children of Eva[10] Johnson and William Porter Jeffries are:

373.   i.   RICHARD LEE[11], born 28 Feb 1919 at Perry, IL; married Lois Eleanor Nicholson.

177.   FLOY BENTON[10] JOHNSON (*George*[9], *Rufus*[8], *George*[7], *Ira*[6], *Jonathan*[5], *Nathaniel*[4], *Nathaniel*[3], *Humphrey*[2], *John*[1]) was born on 16 Jan 1880 at Ness Co., KS. He married Mabel Smith. He died at CA.

Children of Floy Benton[10] Johnson and Mabel Smith are:

i.   WALTER[11].

178.   GEORGE RUFUS[10] JOHNSON (*George*[9], *Rufus*[8], *George*[7], *Ira*[6], *Jonathan*[5], *Nathaniel*[4], *Nathaniel*[3], *Humphrey*[2], *John*[1]) was born on 18 Sep 1882 at Ness Co., KS. He married Della Quimby on 10 Aug 1908. He died on 31 Jul 1961 at Erie, KS, at age 78.

Children of George Rufus[10] Johnson and Della Quimby were as follows:

374.   i.   HARLEY ROBERT[11], born 16 Oct 1911 at Albert, KS; married Edith Lucille Padley.

375.   ii.   AUDREY DELLA, born 5 Apr 1913 at Albert, KS; married Ray Rufenacht.

376.   iii.   WARREN HARDIN, born 5 Mar 1915 at Bazine, KS; married Nita Evelyn Grassfield.

iv.   REVA MARGARET; born 29 Aug 1917 at Ness Co., KS; married Glen Singleton; married Richard Rainey; died 1 Aug 1952 at Miami, FL, at age 34.

377.   v.   LOY LEE, born 16 Jul 1920 at Ness Co., KS; married Glennella Bourdet.

378.   vi.   DANA MARGARET, born 29 Jul 1924 at Ness Co., KS; married Joe Cook.

179.   RALPH CLETUS[10] JOHNSON (*George*[9], *Rufus*[8], *George*[7], *Ira*[6], *Jonathan*[5], *Nathaniel*[4], *Nathaniel*[3], *Humphrey*[2], *John*[1]) was born on 13 Jun 1897 at Francis Township, Ness Co., KS. He married Hazel Marie Smith on 24 Dec 1918. He died on 4 Apr 1985 at Wichita, KS, at age 87.

Children of Ralph Cletus[10] Johnson and Hazel Marie Smith were as follows:

i.   RAY C.[11]; born 21 Apr 1922 at Mulvane, KS; died 20 Aug 1942 at Belle Plaine, KS, at age 20. He was unmarried.

ii.   GEORGE HUBERT; born 11 May 1928 at Mulvane, KS; married Norma Mae Mahan 12 Jun 1953.

379.   iii.   HELEN MARIE, born 20 Dec 1930 at Mulvane, KS; married David Hill.

380.   iv.   DONALD EARL, born 24 Dec 1936; married Theresa Florine Kern.

180. JOHN IRA[10] JOHNSON (*Lewis*[9], *Rufus*[8], *George*[7], *Ira*[6], *Jonathan*[5], *Nathaniel*[4], *Nathaniel*[3], *Humphrey*[2], *John*[1]) was born on 28 Aug 1875 at Pike Co., IL. He married May Hyde. He died at Baldwin Park, CA.

Children of John Ira[10] Johnson and May Hyde are as follows:

    i.   HELEN[11].

    ii.   EARL.

    iii.   MILDRED.

181. LAURA MAY[10] JOHNSON (*Lewis*[9], *Rufus*[8], *George*[7], *Ira*[6], *Jonathan*[5], *Nathaniel*[4], *Nathaniel*[3], *Humphrey*[2], *John*[1]) was born on 17 May 1885 at Austin, TX. She married Frank Hubert Miller on 31 Dec 1905. She died on 17 May 1980 at age 95.

Children of Laura May[10] Johnson and Frank Hubert Miller were as follows:

381.   i.   MILDRED "LUCILLE"[11], born 14 Oct 1906 at Pearl, IL; married Oren Keith Smith.

382.   ii.   BLANCHE ELIZABETH, born 16 Mar 1910 at Pearl, IL; married Frank Brown Elston.

    iii.   OLIFFE MARIE; born 24 Jan 1914; married Ardell Earl Adams 4 Jul 1937.

383.   iv.   FRANCES MAY, born 1 Aug 1919 at Pearl, IL; married Charles Cleo Inskip.

384.   v.   LOIS DEAN, born 6 Jul 1922 at Pearl, IL; married Joseph Lambert.

182. OSCA ALVIN[10] JOHNSON (*Lewis*[9], *Rufus*[8], *George*[7], *Ira*[6], *Jonathan*[5], *Nathaniel*[4], *Nathaniel*[3], *Humphrey*[2], *John*[1]) was born on 22 Nov 1887 at Pearl, IL. He married Hattie Hess. He married Helen B Boyle on 10 Jun 1936. He died on 16 Feb 1991 at Bethaldo, IL, at age 103.

Children of Osca Alvin[10] Johnson and Hattie Hess were as follows:

385.   i.   KATHRYN[11], born 1912; married Heridin Verdin Battershell.

           ii.   OSCA LEWIS.

Children of Osca Alvin[10] Johnson and Helen B Boyle are:

           i.   CHARLES[11].

183.   IVIS BENTON[10] JOHNSON (*Isaac*[9], *Rufus*[8], *George*[7], *Ira*[6], *Jonathan*[5], *Nathaniel*[4], *Nathaniel*[3], *Humphrey*[2], *John*[1]) was born on 21 Dec 1894 at Pike Co., IL. He married Fay Marie Atwood in Mar 1924 at Carthage, IL. He died on 31 May 1955 at Denver, Denver Co., CO, at age 60. He was buried at Denver, Denver Co., CO.

Children of Ivis Benton[10] Johnson and Fay Marie Atwood are as follows:

386.   i.   MAVIS MARIE[11], born 30 Mar 1926 at Carthage, IL; married Moses Lewis.

387.   ii.   NELLIE DALE, born 17 Jun 1927 at Pittsfield, Pike Co., IL; married Clarence Rozie Crum; married George Oscar Baugh.

184.   ICEL FERN[10] JOHNSON (*Isaac*[9], *Rufus*[8], *George*[7], *Ira*[6], *Jonathan*[5], *Nathaniel*[4], *Nathaniel*[3], *Humphrey*[2], *John*[1]) was born on 6 Aug 1896 at Pike Co., IL. She married William Crist Brown on 28 Jul 1928 at Quincy, Adams Co., IL.

Children of Icel Fern[10] Johnson and William Crist Brown are as follows:

388.   i.   JANET ELLEN[11], born 28 Apr 1929 at Cedar Rapids, IA; married Robert Edward Thune.

389.   ii.   JOY ELAINE, born 19 Feb 1931 at Cedar Rapids, IA; married Ralph Edward Kane.

390.   iii.   WILMA FERN, born 20 Jul 1932 at Cedar Rapids, IA; married Arlyn Lynuer Wendell Clark.

391.   iv.   WILLIAM BENTON, born 8 Oct 1933 at Cedar Rapids, IA; married Marlys Ann Brock.

392.   v.   MARY ANN, born 25 Sep 1935 at Iowa City, Johnson Co., IA; married John Alvin Gregory Jr.

185. RUFUS WINFIELD^{10} JOHNSON (*Isaac^9, Rufus^8, George^7, Ira^6, Jonathan^5, Nathaniel^4, Nathaniel^3, Humphrey^2, John^1*) was born on 28 Sep 1899 at Pittsfield, Pike Co., IL. He married Vernice Mary Atwood on 13 Mar 1926 at Pittsfield, Pike Co., IL.

Children of Rufus Winfield^{10} Johnson and Vernice Mary Atwood are as follows:

- 393.   i.   LOIS AILEEN^{11}, born 28 Mar 1927 at Pittsfield, Pike Co., IL; married John Robert "Bob" McKenna.
- 394.   ii.   VERNON WENDELL, born 25 Jan 1930; married Helen Pearl Wilkins.
- 395.   iii.   PHYLLIS LEE, born 16 Sep 1931 at Pittsfield, Pike Co., IL; married Daniel Duran Rose.

186. WENDELL ALVIN^{10} JOHNSON (*Isaac^9, Rufus^8, George^7, Ira^6, Jonathan^5, Nathaniel^4, Nathaniel^3, Humphrey^2, John^1*) was born on 27 Apr 1906. He married Helen Mildred Mink on 18 Aug 1934. He died on 13 Apr 1991 at age 84.

Children of Wendell Alvin^{10} Johnson and Helen Mildred Mink both born at Quincy, Adams Co., IL, were as follows:

- 396.   i.   RONALD WENDELL^{11}, born 14 Dec 1937; married Billie Kay Knapp; divorced Billie Kay Knapp; married Connie Bowers.
- 397.   ii.   BEN RAY, born 23 Jun 1939; married Joyce Mardell Pearson.

Generation Eleven

187. OREN HARVEY^{11} NICHOLSON (*Charles^{10}, Mary^{9}Johnson, Charles^8, Charles^7, Ira^6, Jonathan^5, Nathaniel^4, Nathaniel^3, Humphrey^2, John^1*) was born on 24 Jul 1895 at Kings Co., CA. He married Meleta Harris. He died in May 1935 at Pittsfield, Pike Co., IL, at age 39.

Children of Oren Harvey[11] Nicholson and Meleta Harris all born at Pittsfield, Pike Co., IL, are as follows:

    i. KATHERINE LOUISE[12]; born 17 Sep 1917; married Raymond Browning 1938; married Robert Arnold 1961.

398. ii. LOIS ELEANOR, born 11 Feb 1920; married Richard Lee Jeffries.

399. iii. ANNA LEE, born 27 Mar 1923; married Howard Mann.

    iv. JAMES ROBERT; born 10 Aug 1927; married Kathleen Chambers.

188. SUSAN GLADYS[11] NICHOLSON (*Charles*[10], *Mary*[9]*Johnson*, *Charles*[8], *Charles*[7], *Ira*[6], *Jonathan*[5], *Nathaniel*[4], *Nathaniel*[3], *Humphrey*[2], *John*[1]) was born on 9 Mar 1897 at Kings Co., CA. She married Paul Niebur on 6 Dec 1916 at Pittsfield, Pike Co., IL.

Children of Susan Gladys[11] Nicholson and Paul Niebur are as follows:

    i. PHILIP LORING[12]; born 1 May 1917 at Pittsfield, Pike Co., IL.

400. ii. CHARLES WILLIAM, born 7 Oct 1918 at Pittsfield, Pike Co., IL; married Mildred Virginia Williams.

401. iii. PAUL EVART, born 20 May 1921; married Nola Waltrip; married Leoline Willard.

    iv. WARREN DEAN; born 3 Jan 1923 at Pittsfield, Pike Co., IL.

402. v. ROBERT FREDERICK, born 21 Sep 1931; married Marilyn Northern.

189. MARY MYRTLE[11] NICHOLSON (*Charles*[10], *Mary*[9]*Johnson*, *Charles*[8], *Charles*[7], *Ira*[6], *Jonathan*[5], *Nathaniel*[4], *Nathaniel*[3], *Humphrey*[2], *John*[1]) was born on 25 Aug 1899 at Pike Co., IL. She married Robert A. Shive on 25 Jul 1919 at Bowling Green, Pike Co., MO. She died on 24 May 1968 at Pittsfield, Pike Co., IL, at age 68. She was buried at Winchester Cemetery, Scott Co., IL.

Children of Mary Myrtle[11] Nicholson and Robert A. Shive are as follows:

403. i. VERA ORLENA[12], born 17 Jul 1920 at Pittsfield, Pike Co., IL; married William Havens.

404. ii. MARY FRANCES, born 10 Nov 1921 at Pittsfield, Pike Co., IL; married Donald Wilday Giger.

405. iii. BERNICE "BETTY", born 19 Jul 1923 at Pittsfield, Pike Co., IL; married Clarence Lidstrom; married Elmer Kurth.

406. iv. MABEL LEONA, born 13 Feb 1925 at Pittsfield, Pike Co., IL; married Arthur Lewis Chapman.

407. v. LOUIS RICHARD, born 23 Dec 1926 at Pittsfield, Pike Co., IL; married Ethel Marie Wilkins.

408. vi. JAMES WILLIAM, born 10 Jan 1929 at Pittsfield, Pike Co., IL; married Betty Jean Ross.

409. vii. HENRY JOSEPH, born 14 May 1930 at Pittsfield, Pike Co., IL; married Edith Looper; married Mary Mae Cox.

410. viii. ALICE JEANETTE, born 29 Jun 1931 at Montezuma Township, Milton, Pike Co., IL; married Duane Eldon Guth.

411. ix. DOROTHY JANE, born 10 Jan 1933 at Montezuma Township, Milton, Pike Co., IL; married Harlan Albert Nevius.

412. x. JOHN C., born 11 Feb 1935 at Montezuma Township, Pike Co., IL; married Shirley Ann Bryant.

413. xi. JACK FRANKLIN, born 27 Jul 1936 at Montezuma Township, Pike Co., IL; married Janice Settles.

414. xii. NORMA JEAN, born 3 Sep 1939 at Montezuma Township, Pike Co., IL; married Arthur Clay Reel.

415. xiii. THOMAS LEE, born 8 May 1941 at Montezuma Township, Pike Co., IL; married Linda Sue Kieth.

190. BERYL LOIS[11] NICHOLSON (*Charles*[10], *Mary*[9]*Johnson*, *Charles*[8], *Charles*[7], *Ira*[6], *Jonathan*[5], *Nathaniel*[4], *Nathaniel*[3],

Humphrey[2], *John*[1]) was born on 6 Jul 1901 at Pike Co., IL. She married Joseph Hiram Sanderson. She died on 12 May 1993 at age 91.

Children of Beryl Lois[11] Nicholson and Joseph Hiram Sanderson are as follows:

416.　　i.　WILMA EVELYN[12], born 13 May 1921; married Joel Marian Worley.

417.　　ii.　NORMA CHARLENE, born 1 Mar 1923; married Lewis Abram Souders.

418.　　iii.　CARRIE JOSEPHINE, born 18 Mar 1926; married Lloyd Leonard Long Jr.

419.　　iv.　BETTY JEAN, born 16 Apr 1931; married Leslie Farrell Hamilton.

191.　JESSIE V.[11] NICHOLSON (*Charles*[10], *Mary*[9]*Johnson*, *Charles*[8], *Charles*[7], *Ira*[6], *Jonathan*[5], *Nathaniel*[4], *Nathaniel*[3], *Humphrey*[2], *John*[1]) was born on 25 Jul 1905 at Pike Co., IL. She married William Paul Rader at Pike Co., IL. She died on 12 Jun 1983 at age 77.

Children of Jessie V.[11] Nicholson and William Paul Rader were as follows:

420.　　i.　CAROLYN LOUISE[12], born 10 Oct 1924; married Thomas Gates.

421.　　ii.　JOHN WILLIAM, born 28 Mar 1930; married Elizabeth (--?--).

422.　　iii.　RALPH EDWARD, born 21 Apr 1941; married Virginia Maybe.

192.　CHARLES MYRON[11] NICHOLSON (*Charles*[10], *Mary*[9]*Johnson*, *Charles*[8], *Charles*[7], *Ira*[6], *Jonathan*[5], *Nathaniel*[4], *Nathaniel*[3], *Humphrey*[2], *John*[1]) was born on 7 Jun 1912 at Pittsfield, Pike Co., IL. He married Martha Bagby on 16 Oct 1936 at Springfield, IL. He died on 5 Jun 1979 at Indianapolis, IN, at age 66.

Children of Charles Myron[11] Nicholson and Martha Bagby are as follows:

　　　i.　NANCY SUE[12]; born 30 Aug 1937.

423.   ii.   CHARLES ROY, born 24 Feb 1940; married Phyliss (--?--).

424.   iii.   MARY ANN, born 12 Aug 1943; married Charles DeLong.

      iv.   MARTHA KAY; born 13 Jun 1945 at Pike Co., IL. Married unknown person.

193.   REBECCA ELVA[11] KILLEBREW (*Mary[10]Miller, Rebecca[9]Johnson, Charles[8], Charles[7], Ira[6], Jonathan[5], Nathaniel[4], Nathaniel[3], Humphrey[2], John[1]*) was born on 24 Jun 1894. She married Jessie L. Sherwin on 18 Aug 1916 at Scott Co., IL. She died on 15 Feb 1973 at age 78.

Children of Rebecca Elva[11] Killebrew and Jessie L. Sherwin are as follows:

425.   i.   JOHN LAWRENCE[12], born 11 Jan 1918; married Marjorie Spencer.

      ii.   WINIFRED; born 10 Apr 1921.

      iii.   WILMA; born 26 Jul 1922.

426.   iv.   JESSIE EUGENE, born 9 Sep 1923; married Mary Louise Ward.

      v.   MARY ELVA; born 21 May 1932; married Donald Butcher 22 Jun 1952.

194.   MARY EDITH[11] KILLEBREW (*Mary[10]Miller, Rebecca[9]Johnson, Charles[8], Charles[7], Ira[6], Jonathan[5], Nathaniel[4], Nathaniel[3], Humphrey[2], John[1]*) was born on 5 Nov 1899 at Scott Co., IL. She married Charles William Jones on 4 Sep 1918 at Pearl, IL.

Children of Mary Edith[11] Killebrew and Charles William Jones are as follows:

      i.   ELOISE[12]; born 9 Jul 1920; married Marvin Tholen 16 Jun 1946.

427.   ii.   LAVERN, born 15 Dec 1922; married Betty E. Duncan; divorced Betty E. Duncan; married Vivian Willner.

195. NORENE FRANCES[11] KILLEBREW (*Mary[10]Miller, Rebecca[9]Johnson, Charles[8], Charles[7], Ira[6], Jonathan[5], Nathaniel[4], Nathaniel[3], Humphrey[2], John[1]*) was born on 7 Oct 1901. She married ? (--?--). She died on 31 Oct 1974 at age 73.

Children of Norene Frances[11] Killebrew and ? (--?--) are:

> 428.　i.　VIRGINIA "BERNADINE"[12], born 11 Apr 1923; married Wilbur German.

196. ETHEL MILDRED[11] KILLEBREW (*Mary[10]Miller, Rebecca[9]Johnson, Charles[8], Charles[7], Ira[6], Jonathan[5], Nathaniel[4], Nathaniel[3], Humphrey[2], John[1]*) was born on 13 Sep 1904. She married Ernest Newingham on 10 Dec 1924.

Children of Ethel Mildred[11] Killebrew and Ernest Newingham were as follows:

> 　　i.　LYNDLE ERNEST[12]; born 24 Apr 1925; died 29 Mar 1945 at age 19.
> 429.　ii.　NADINE, born 8 Aug 1926; married Harry Arnold.
> 430.　iii.　BERNARD RANDALL, born 6 Feb 1932; married Ann Sweet; divorced Ann Sweet; married Joan Leach Hulick.
> 431.　iv.　NAOMI NORENE, born 10 Jul 1933; married Harold E. Wright.
> 432.　v.　CAROL DEAN, born 25 Oct 1934; married Elizabeth Agger.

197. THEODORE RANDALL[11] KILLEBREW (*Mary[10]Miller, Rebecca[9]Johnson, Charles[8], Charles[7], Ira[6], Jonathan[5], Nathaniel[4], Nathaniel[3], Humphrey[2], John[1]*) was born on 2 Aug 1908. He married Verna Abrahams on 26 Nov 1930.

Children of Theodore Randall[11] Killebrew and Verna Abrahams are:

> 433.　i.　RANDALL ABRAMS[12], born 11 Aug 1935; married Sue Ann Coultas.

There were no children of Theodore Randall[11] Killebrew and Daisy Clark.

198.   CHARLES   EDWARD[11]   KILLEBREW   (*Ethel[10]Miller*, *Rebecca[9]Johnson*,   *Charles[8]*,   *Charles[7]*,   *Ira[6]*,   *Jonathan[5]*, *Nathaniel[4]*, *Nathaniel[3]*, *Humphrey[2]*, *John[1]*) was born on 11 Jun 1893. He married Faye Ransom on 21 Nov 1920. He died on 25 Nov 1972 at age 79.

Children of Charles Edward[11] Killebrew and Faye Ransom are as follows:

    434.   i.   HELEN[12], born 4 Feb 1923; married Stuart Loyd.

    435.   ii.   CHARLES DALE, born 30 May 1924; married Betty Jo Hollembrek.

199.   WILLIAM   LEE[11]   KILLEBREW   (*Ethel[10]Miller*, *Rebecca[9]Johnson*,   *Charles[8]*,   *Charles[7]*,   *Ira[6]*,   *Jonathan[5]*, *Nathaniel[4]*, *Nathaniel[3]*, *Humphrey[2]*, *John[1]*) was born on 20 Feb 1896. He married Deborah Sherwin on 20 Jun 1919. He died on 5 Mar 1975 at age 79.

Children of William Lee[11] Killebrew and Deborah Sherwin are as follows:

    436.   i.   DOROTHY[12], born 25 Sep 1920; married David Haldane.

    437.   ii.   WILLIAM RUSSELL, born 23 Jan 1922; married Mildred Harshbarger.

    438.   iii.   VERA, born 1 Jul 1925; married Lyle H. Schertz.

    439.   iv.   GLEN SHERWIN, born 16 Jun 1931; married Audrey Stice.

200.   FLORENCE   ANNA[11]   KILLEBREW   (*Ethel[10]Miller*, *Rebecca[9]Johnson*,   *Charles[8]*,   *Charles[7]*,   *Ira[6]*,   *Jonathan[5]*, *Nathaniel[4]*, *Nathaniel[3]*, *Humphrey[2]*, *John[1]*) was born on 4 Jan 1899. She married Henry Schafer on 22 Sep 1924. She died on 21 Feb 1984 at age 85.

Children of Florence Anna[11] Killebrew and Henry Schafer are as follows:

440.   i.   CHARLES H.[12], born 21 Oct 1928; married Elvira Haley; divorced Elvira Haley.

           ii.   JAMES; born 1933.

201. SAMUEL LAWRENCE[11] KILLEBREW (*Ethel[10]Miller, Rebecca[9]Johnson, Charles[8], Charles[7], Ira[6], Jonathan[5], Nathaniel[4], Nathaniel[3], Humphrey[2], John[1]*) was born on 12 Oct 1906. He married Elsie Evans on 25 Jun 1927.

Children of Samuel Lawrence[11] Killebrew and Elsie Evans are as follows:

441.   i.   SAMUEL ROBERT[12], born 18 Nov 1932; married Rita Savage.

442.   ii.   LAWRENCE EVANS, born 7 Dec 1937; married Shirley B. Sweetin.

202. ROBERT WILEY[11] KILLEBREW (*Ethel[10]Miller, Rebecca[9]Johnson, Charles[8], Charles[7], Ira[6], Jonathan[5], Nathaniel[4], Nathaniel[3], Humphrey[2], John[1]*) was born on 12 Jul 1911. He married Viola Hepworth on 28 Jul 1945. He died on 11 Mar 1982 at age 70.

Children of Robert Wiley[11] Killebrew and Viola Hepworth are:

443.   i.   ROBERT LEE[12], born 7 Nov 1945; married Gloria Costello.

203. WILLIAM BAIRD[11] MILLER JR (*William[10], Rebecca[9]Johnson, Charles[8], Charles[7], Ira[6], Jonathan[5], Nathaniel[4], Nathaniel[3], Humphrey[2], John[1]*) was born on 15 Nov 1907. He married Doris Sleeter on 8 Oct 1932. He and Doris Sleeter were divorced on 15 Jun 1946. He died on 5 May 1951 at age 43. He was buried at Oak Ridge Cemetery, Springfield, Sangamon Co., IL.

Children of William Baird[11] Miller Jr and Doris Sleeter are as follows:

444.   i.   SANDRA KAY[12], born 4 Jul 1937; married David Lee Ummel.

445.   ii.   DONALD BAIRD, born 3 Dec 1942; married Sharon Kay Ackland.

204. RUSSELL E.[11] THORNTON (*Richard*[10], *Phila*[9]*Johnson*, *Charles*[8], *Charles*[7], *Ira*[6], *Jonathan*[5], *Nathaniel*[4], *Nathaniel*[3], *Humphrey*[2], *John*[1]) was born on 2 Sep 1904 at Pittsfield, Pike Co., IL. He married Mary Brace on 4 Jan 1921. He died on 29 Nov 1974 at age 70. He was buried at Green Pond Cemetery, Pearl, Pike Co., IL.

Children of Russell E.[11] Thornton and Mary Brace are:

446.   i.   STEWART[12], married (--?--) ?

205. GLADYS[11] SMITH (*Bertha*[10]*Thornton*, *Phila*[9]*Johnson*, *Charles*[8], *Charles*[7], *Ira*[6], *Jonathan*[5], *Nathaniel*[4], *Nathaniel*[3], *Humphrey*[2], *John*[1]) married (--?--) Byrne. She married (--?--) Dodge.

Children of Gladys[11] Smith and (--?--) Byrne are:

     i.   BETTY[12].

There were no children of Gladys[11] Smith and (--?--) Dodge.

206. IOLA[11] SMITH (*Bertha*[10]*Thornton*, *Phila*[9]*Johnson*, *Charles*[8], *Charles*[7], *Ira*[6], *Jonathan*[5], *Nathaniel*[4], *Nathaniel*[3], *Humphrey*[2], *John*[1]) married Clair Schone.

Children of Iola[11] Smith and Clair Schone are as follows:

     i.   MELVIN[12].
     ii.   SHARON.

207. JESSIE EVELYN[11] SMITH (*Bertha*[10]*Thornton*, *Phila*[9]*Johnson*, *Charles*[8], *Charles*[7], *Ira*[6], *Jonathan*[5], *Nathaniel*[4], *Nathaniel*[3], *Humphrey*[2], *John*[1]) was born on 6 Apr 1906 at Nebo, Pike Co., IL. She married Leslie Durbin. She died on 5 Jul 1981 at Pittsfield, Pike Co., IL, at age 75.

Children of Jessie Evelyn[11] Smith and Leslie Durbin are as follows:

     i.   DONALD[12].
     ii.   BARBARA.
     iii.   SANDRA was married.

208. RUSSEL IVY[11] THORNTON (*Herbert*[10], *Phila*[9]*Johnson*, *Charles*[8], *Charles*[7], *Ira*[6], *Jonathan*[5], *Nathaniel*[4], *Nathaniel*[3], *Humphrey*[2], *John*[1]) was born on 4 Jul 1913. He married Garnie E. Dorman on 26 Nov 1936 at Los Angeles, Los Angeles Co., CA. He died on 6 Mar 1995 at age 81.

He lived in 1985 at Hemet, CA.

Children of Russel Ivy[11] Thornton and Garnie E. Dorman are as follows:

447.   i.   ROLLAND RUSSEL[12], born 21 Aug 1938; married Patricia Jo Lowman.

448.   ii.   MARILYN ESTHER, born 25 Sep 1941; married Alfred Ray Boggs; divorced Alfred Ray Boggs.

209. WILBUR VERLE[11] THORNTON (*Herbert*[10], *Phila*[9]*Johnson*, *Charles*[8], *Charles*[7], *Ira*[6], *Jonathan*[5], *Nathaniel*[4], *Nathaniel*[3], *Humphrey*[2], *John*[1]) was born on 7 Oct 1919 at Hynes, Los Angeles Co., CA. He married Frances Maria Skarich on 18 Jul 1948 at Los Angeles, Los Angeles Co., CA.

Children of Wilbur Verle[11] Thornton and Frances Maria Skarich are:

i.   LISA MARIA[12]; born 8 Jul 1957.

210. BERNICE[11] RANSOM (*Warren*[10], *Emma*[9]*Johnson*, *Charles*[8], *Charles*[7], *Ira*[6], *Jonathan*[5], *Nathaniel*[4], *Nathaniel*[3], *Humphrey*[2], *John*[1]) was born on 20 Jan 1911 at Pike Co., IL. She married Wayland R. Swanson.

Children of Bernice[11] Ransom and Wayland R. Swanson M.D. were as follows:

449.   i.   JOHN HAGOOD[12], born 19 Feb 1938; married Renee Ahmed Series.

450.   ii.   JUDITH ELAINE, born 1 Jun 1942; married Joseph Block.

iii.   JAMES ROBERT; born 4 Jan 1945; died 28 Jul 1979 at age 34.

211. CLEO[11] JOHNSON (*Archie*[10], *John*[9], *Hiram*[8], *Charles*[7], *Ira*[6], *Jonathan*[5], *Nathaniel*[4], *Nathaniel*[3], *Humphrey*[2], *John*[1]) was born on 13 Aug 1888 at Seattle, King Co., WA. She married John F. Porter on 5 Oct 1910 at Benton Co., OR. She died on 15 Apr 1961 at Corvallis, Benton Co., OR, at age 72.

Children of Cleo[11] Johnson and John F. Porter were:

> 451.   i.   ZETA LYLE[12], born 12 Dec 1914 at Corvallis, Benton Co., OR; married Bruce M. Beardsley; married Zee Floyd Earl.

212. ELMO ELTON[11] JOHNSON (*Archie*[10], *John*[9], *Hiram*[8], *Charles*[7], *Ira*[6], *Jonathan*[5], *Nathaniel*[4], *Nathaniel*[3], *Humphrey*[2], *John*[1]) was born on 19 Nov 1891 at Scio, Linn Co., OR. He married Linnie Durell on 17 Jun 1914 at Benton Co., OR. He died on 10 Feb 1969 at Corvallis, Benton Co., OR, at age 77.

Children of Elmo Elton[11] Johnson and Linnie Durell both born at Corvallis, Benton Co., OR, were as follows:

> 452.   i.   DONALD ELTON[12], born 8 Jul 1915; married Madge Marshall.
>
> 453.   ii.   CHARLES CLAIR, born 4 Jan 1917; married Kay Thomas; married (--?--) ?

213. DARRELL DELOS[11] JOHNSON (*Archie*[10], *John*[9], *Hiram*[8], *Charles*[7], *Ira*[6], *Jonathan*[5], *Nathaniel*[4], *Nathaniel*[3], *Humphrey*[2], *John*[1]) was born on 10 Jul 1897 at Scio, Linn Co., OR. He married Bertha McHenry on 15 Nov 1917 at Benton Co., OR. He died on 1 Mar 1927 at Corvallis, Benton Co., OR, at age 29.

Children of Darrell DeLos[11] Johnson and Bertha McHenry both born at Corvallis, Benton Co., OR, were as follows:

> 454.   i.   RICHARD DARREL[12], born 29 Jan 1920; married Elizabeth L. Peake.
>
> 455.   ii.   MURIEL ANN, born 19 Jan 1923; married F. Robert Preece.

214. ORLO ORTON[11] JOHNSON (*Archie*[10], *John*[9], *Hiram*[8], *Charles*[7], *Ira*[6], *Jonathan*[5], *Nathaniel*[4], *Nathaniel*[3], *Humphrey*[2],

John[1]) was born on 2 Jul 1900 at Scio, Linn Co., OR. He married Frances Watkins on 2 Jul 1921 at Benton Co., OR. He married Kathleen Wied in 1941 at Vancouver, WA. He died on 11 Feb 1988 at Benton Co., OR, at age 87.

Children of Orlo Orton[11] Johnson and Frances Watkins were:

456.   i.   ALLEN[12], born 19 Jul 1922; married Jessie Mae Jones.

Children of Orlo Orton[11] Johnson and Kathleen Wied are:

457.   i.   KATHLEEN MAY[12], born 19 Jun 1943; married Jerry Holland; married Murl Starr.

215. ARCHIE JAMES[11] JOHNSON JR (*Archie[10]*, *John[9]*, *Hiram[8]*, *Charles[7]*, *Ira[6]*, *Jonathan[5]*, *Nathaniel[4]*, *Nathaniel[3]*, *Humphrey[2]*, *John[1]*) was born on 20 Oct 1912 at Corvallis, Benton Co., OR. He married Bonnie Jane Harris. He married June (--?--). He married Glenna Bessie Johnston. He married Edmonda Fisher.

Children of Archie James[11] Johnson Jr and Bonnie Jane Harris are:

458.   i.   JANET[12], born 30 Dec 1933 at Portland, Multnomah Co., OR; married Richard B. Simons.

Children of Archie James[11] Johnson Jr and June (--?--) are:

          i.   SHARRYL[12].

Children of Archie James[11] Johnson Jr and Glenna Bessie Johnston are as follows:

459.   i.   JEANNIE LINN[12], born 14 Jul 1949 at Auburn, CA; married Harold Vietti.

460.   ii.   CHRISTOPHER JAMES, born 18 Jun 1951 at Auburn, CA; married Michelle Cary.

461.   iii.   GERALDINE ANNE, born 2 Jun 1952 at Auburn, CA; married Worth Havens Dikeman.

        iv.   DARREL GLENN; born 20 Dec 1955 at Eugene, Lane Co., OR; married Mary Ann Nihart 16 Apr 1983 at Washington, IA.

216. ZELMA[11] SIMPSON (*Etta[10]Johnson, John[9], Hiram[8], Charles[7], Ira[6], Jonathan[5], Nathaniel[4], Nathaniel[3], Humphrey[2], John[1]*) was born on 18 Feb 1892. She married William E. Williams on 28 Apr 1912 at Independence, OR. She died on 1 Dec 1938 at age 46.

Children of Zelma[11] Simpson and William E. Williams were as follows:

        i.   MAXINE[12]; born 14 Oct 1923 at Airlie, OR; married Walter Franklin Watson 11 Sep 1949 at Shedd, OR.

462.   ii.   DORICE, born 6 Aug 1926 at Airlie, OR; married Russell Laubner Stewart.

217. CHARLES GARTH[11] JOHNSON (*Charles[10], John[9], Hiram[8], Charles[7], Ira[6], Jonathan[5], Nathaniel[4], Nathaniel[3], Humphrey[2], John[1]*) was born on 21 Jun 1905 at Airlie, OR. He married Violette Marie Brewer, daughter of Edger Joseph Brewer and Grace Magdelena Wilson, on 18 Jun 1927 at Portland, Multnomah Co., OR. He married Enid Cleek at Medford, Jackson Co., OR. He died on 4 May 1966 at Albuquerque, NM, at age 60.

Children of Charles Garth[11] Johnson and Violette Marie Brewer are as follows:

463.   i.   KARLENE MAE[12], born 6 Dec 1933 at Portland, Multnomah Co., OR; married James Edward Messer.

464.   ii.   GERALD GARTH, born 13 Mar 1937 at Portland, Multnomah Co., OR; married Nancy Anne Ticknor.

218. DORIS V.[11] SHAW (*Pearl[10]Johnson, John[9], Hiram[8], Charles[7], Ira[6], Jonathan[5], Nathaniel[4], Nathaniel[3], Humphrey[2], John[1]*) was born on 16 May 1904. She married Jack Charles Parsons. She died on 7 Jul 1991 at Portland, Multnomah Co., OR, at age 87.

Children of Doris V.[11] Shaw and Jack Charles Parsons are:

465.   i.   BETTY JEANNINE[12], born 14 Feb 1928; married William Babeckos.

219. AGNES MARIE[11] MCELROY (*Rose*[10]*Johnson*, *George*[9], *Hiram*[8], *Charles*[7], *Ira*[6], *Jonathan*[5], *Nathaniel*[4], *Nathaniel*[3], *Humphrey*[2], *John*[1]) was born on 27 Feb 1898 at Chicago, Cook Co., IL. She married Carroll Hanson. She died on 7 Dec 1984 at Austin, TX, at age 86.

Children of Agnes Marie[11] McElroy and Carroll Hanson are:

466.   i.   WILLIS[12]

220. EARLE JOHNSON[11] MCELROY (*Rose*[10]*Johnson*, *George*[9], *Hiram*[8], *Charles*[7], *Ira*[6], *Jonathan*[5], *Nathaniel*[4], *Nathaniel*[3], *Humphrey*[2], *John*[1]) was born on 25 Jun 1904 at Salem, Marion Co., OR. He married Ann Owen at Leavenworth, WA.

Children of Earle Johnson[11] McElroy and Ann Owen are:

467.   i.   ALICIA ANN[12], born 16 May 1927; married Monte Craig Smalley.

221. GEORGE LESLIE[11] JOHNSON (*George*[10], *George*[9], *Hiram*[8], *Charles*[7], *Ira*[6], *Jonathan*[5], *Nathaniel*[4], *Nathaniel*[3], *Humphrey*[2], *John*[1]) was born in 1913 at OR. He married Vera Geraldine Tanner.

Children of George Leslie[11] Johnson and Vera Geraldine Tanner are as follows:

468.   i.   ROY LESLIE[12], born 16 Feb 1944 at Salem, Marion Co., OR; married Lieselotte Curfrass; married Adele Stack.

469.   ii.   DOROTHY ALICE, born 1 Sep 1946; married Victor Lee Nelson; married Larry Lowder.

470.   iii.   RAY WESLEY, born 17 May 1947 at Salem, Marion Co., OR; married E. Antoinette Cowan.

471.   iv.   ROSS EDWARD, born 20 May 1952 at Salem, Marion Co., OR; married Debra Adele Meacham.

       v.   DARLENE CAROL; born 10 Jan 1954.

472.   vi.   DELORES JEAN, born 4 Nov 1957 at Gold Beach, OR; married Jimie Dean Richmond.

222. PAULINE EDITH[11] JOHNSON (*Clyde*[10], *George*[9], *Hiram*[8], *Charles*[7], *Ira*[6], *Jonathan*[5], *Nathaniel*[4], *Nathaniel*[3], *Humphrey*[2], *John*[1]) was born on 12 Apr 1909 at Salem, Marion Co., OR. She married Howard Keeling. She died on 20 Mar 1983 at Salem, Marion Co., OR, at age 73.

Children of Pauline Edith[11] Johnson and Howard Keeling are:

473.　　i.　MELINDA MAE[12], born 1943; married Richard Floyd Armstrong.

223. GEORGE JOHNSON[11] IAEGER (*Ada*[10]*Johnson*, *William*[9], *Hiram*[8], *Charles*[7], *Ira*[6], *Jonathan*[5], *Nathaniel*[4], *Nathaniel*[3], *Humphrey*[2], *John*[1]) was born on 21 Sep 1886 at Burns, Harney Co., OR. He married Laura "Maye" Arrowood, daughter of William Morris Arrowood and Lena Newman, on 24 Oct 1910 at Arlington Hotel, Seattle, King Co., WA. He died on 18 Mar 1965 at Medford, Jackson Co., OR, at age 78. He was buried at Edmonds Cemetery, Edmonds, Snohomish Co., WA.

He moved in 1895 to the Olympic Hotel, Edmonds, Snohomish Co., WA. He appeared on the census of 1 Jan 1920 at Main St., 3rd Ward, Edmonds, Snohomish Co., WA.

Children of George Johnson[11] Iaeger and Laura "Maye" Arrowood were as follows:

　　　　i.　ADA MAY[12]; born 12 Jun 1911 at Echo Lake, Snohomish Co., WA; died 14 Apr 1916 at Edmonds, Snohomish Co., WA, at age 4; buried 16 Jun 1916 at Edmonds Cemetery, Edmonds, Snohomish Co., WA.

474.　　ii.　GEORGIE CATHERINE, born 20 Jun 1912 at Edmonds, Snohomish Co., WA; married Lawrence Earl Gamey; divorced Lawrence Earl Gamey.

475.　　iii.　HAZEL MARIE LENORA, born 5 Dec 1913 at Edmonds, Snohomish Co., WA; married George Nils Naslund; married Harold Julius Skutvik.

476. iv. LOIS LEONA, born 22 Jul 1916 at Edmonds, Snohomish Co., WA; married Charles Edwin Hill.

477. v. CHARLES ARROWOOD, born 14 Jan 1919 at Edmonds, Snohomish Co., WA; married Virginia Breuser.

vi. WILLIAM STONEWALL; born 16 Dec 1919 at Edmonds, Snohomish Co., WA; died 14 Dec 1942 at Japan at age 22; buried at Manila American Cemetery and Memorial, Republic of the Philippines.

He appeared on the census of 1 Jan 1920 at Main St., 3rd Ward, Edmonds, Snohomish Co., WA. He began military service circa 1941 at Hdq Bat,, 60th C. A. (A A), Fort Mills, Republic of the Philippines. He lived on 30 Aug 1941 at Manila, Republic of the Philippines.

478. vii. JACKSON MOTHERSHEAD, born 24 Jul 1921 at South Bend, Pacific Co., WA; married Bettie Ross.

479. viii. VIRGINIA ANN, born 26 Feb 1923 at Baleville, South Bend, Pacific Co, WA; married Albert Arthur Blandin.

480. ix. LULUBELLE CAROLINE, born 29 Jan 1925 at Mrs. Fricketts on Sunset Ave., Edmonds, Snohomish Co., WA; married Carl Strasser; divorced Carl Strasser; married Eldon Lewis; divorced Eldon Lewis; married Leonard Earl Norris Sr.

481. x. KATHLEEN IRENE, born 29 Mar 1927 at Edmonds Hospital, Edmonds, Snohomish Co., WA; married Howard Gary Dean Poole.

482. xi. GEORGE JOHNSON JR., born 27 Mar 1931 at Snohomish Hospital, Snohomish, Snohomish Co., WA; married Virginia Merise Dickson.

224. TOILEY[11] JOHNSON (*Charles*[10], *William*[9], *Hiram*[8], *Charles*[7], *Ira*[6], *Jonathan*[5], *Nathaniel*[4], *Nathaniel*[3], *Humphrey*[2], *John*[1]) was born in Oct 1892. She married Fred Williams.

She appeared on the census of 1 Jun 1900 at Burns Prec., Burns, Harney Co., OR.

Children of Toiley[11] Johnson and Fred Williams are as follows:

    i.   PETRUNELLA[12].
    ii. JENEVIEVE.
    iii. DARREL.
    iv. CLIFFORD.

225. JAMES "LEROY"[11] JOHNSON (*Lloyd*[10], *William*[9], *Hiram*[8], *Charles*[7], *Ira*[6], *Jonathan*[5], *Nathaniel*[4], *Nathaniel*[3], *Humphrey*[2], *John*[1]) was born on 25 Apr 1902 at Burns, Harney Co., OR. He married Lutha Marie Parker on 7 Jun 1924 at Burns, Harney Co., OR. He died on 31 Oct 1980 at Tacoma, Pierce Co., WA, at age 78.

Children of James "Leroy"[11] Johnson and Lutha Marie Parker are as follows:

483.   i.   ORLAND LEROY[12], born 30 Jul 1925 at Burns, Harney Co., OR; married Norma Jane Carper.

484.   ii. LLOYD ALLEN, born 22 Jun 1927 at Newbridge, OR; married Virgie Jewel Vanderpool.

485.   iii. LOUEL MARIE, born 14 Apr 1937 at Burns, Harney Co., OR; married James Edward Anderson.

486.   iv. RICHARD BARRY, born 15 Dec 1943 at La Grande, OR; married Alberta Margarita Avila.

487.   v. GARETH JAMES, born 3 Aug 1952 at Idaho Falls, ID; married Martha Elaine Holmen.

226. ADA IRENE[11] JOHNSON (*Lloyd*[10], *William*[9], *Hiram*[8], *Charles*[7], *Ira*[6], *Jonathan*[5], *Nathaniel*[4], *Nathaniel*[3], *Humphrey*[2], *John*[1]) was born in 1904. She married Harold Pickens. She married John McGovern. She died in Dec 1984 at Spokane, WA.

Children of Ada Irene[11] Johnson and Harold Pickens were as follows:

488.   i.   GERALDINE LUCILLE[12], married Lyall Byers.

489.   ii. JOHN LLOYD, born 3 Feb 1930; married Clara Sue Ledbetter.

227. FLORABEL[11] GOODMAN (*Hester[10]Johnson, William[9], Hiram[8], Charles[7], Ira[6], Jonathan[5], Nathaniel[4], Nathaniel[3], Humphrey[2], John[1]*) was born in Oct 1897 at OR. She married Harry Z. Smith on 17 Jun 1916 at Burns, Harney Co., OR.

She appeared on the census of 1900 at Burns Prec., Burns, Harney Co., OR.

Children of Florabel[11] Goodman and Harry Z. Smith are as follows:

      i.   NORMA[12]; married Robert Witherell.
      ii.   ROBERT; married Norma (--?--).

228. AUSTIN EDWARD[11] GOODMAN (*Hester[10]Johnson, William[9], Hiram[8], Charles[7], Ira[6], Jonathan[5], Nathaniel[4], Nathaniel[3], Humphrey[2], John[1]*) was born on 8 Feb 1900 at OR. He married Mary McCrea. He died on 2 Jul 1946 at Portland, Multnomah Co., OR, at age 46.

He appeared on the census of 1 Jun 1900 at Burns Prec., Burns, Harney Co., OR.

Children of Austin Edward[11] Goodman and Mary McCrea both born at Burns, Harney Co., OR, are as follows:

490.   i.   BETTY JEAN[12], born 9 May 1923; married Paul C. Brown.
491.   ii.   WILLIAM AUSTIN "AUTIE", born 4 Aug 1925; married Mildred Perry.

229. BLANCHE[11] GOODMAN (*Hester[10]Johnson, William[9], Hiram[8], Charles[7], Ira[6], Jonathan[5], Nathaniel[4], Nathaniel[3], Humphrey[2], John[1]*) was born in 1904 at OR. She married James McCulloch.

She appeared on the census of 1 Jan 1920 at Harney Precinct, Burns, Harney Co., OR.

Children of Blanche[11] Goodman and James McCulloch are as follows:

      i.   J. W. "BILL"[12].
      ii.   RICHARD R.; married Bernice Laythe.

230. WARREN TAYLOR[11] MCHARGUE (*Lulu*[10]*Johnson, William*[9], *Hiram*[8], *Charles*[7], *Ira*[6], *Jonathan*[5], *Nathaniel*[4], *Nathaniel*[3], *Humphrey*[2], *John*[1]) was born on 12 Apr 1904 at OR. He married Ruby South in May 1929. He married Dorothy Patnude Adams on 18 Apr 1950. He died on 24 May 1960 at age 56.

He appeared on the census of 1 Jan 1920 at Crowley Precinct, Malheur Co., OR.

Children of Warren Taylor[11] McHargue and Ruby South were as follows:

492. i. WARREN "GENE"[12], born 17 May 1929 at Ontario, OR; married Louise Scholl; divorced Louise Scholl.

493. ii. CARL WESLEY, born 17 Sep 1930 at Owhyee Dam, OR; married LuAnn Lamborn; divorced LuAnn Lamborn; married Patricia Hine.

iii. FRED ONEIL; born 1 Aug 1932; died 1 Jul 2002 at age 69; buried at Mt. View Cemetery, View (La Central), WA.

He was unmarried in 1985.

494. iv. DELORES IRENE, born 23 Feb 1934; married Raymond McPherson; divorced Raymond McPherson.

495. v. LLOYD JOSEPH, born 25 Sep 1938 at Aberdeen, Grays Harbor Co., WA; married Anne M. Lambert.

231. FRANCIS CAROLINE[11] MCHARGUE (*Lulu*[10]*Johnson, William*[9], *Hiram*[8], *Charles*[7], *Ira*[6], *Jonathan*[5], *Nathaniel*[4], *Nathaniel*[3], *Humphrey*[2], *John*[1]) was born on 21 Jan 1911 at OR. She married Larry S. Smith. She died on 12 Jan 1987 at age 75. She was buried at Greenwood Memorial Park, San Diego, San Diego CO., CA.

Children of Francis Caroline[11] McHargue and Larry S. Smith are:

496.   i.   ROBERT AMBER[12], born 28 Jul 1939 at San Diego, CA; married Sandra Keller; married Tina Mason; married Claudia Uzzell.

232. RUSH GOODMAN[11] MCHARGUE (*Lulu*[10]*Johnson, William*[9], *Hiram*[8], *Charles*[7], *Ira*[6], *Jonathan*[5], *Nathaniel*[4], *Nathaniel*[3], *Humphrey*[2], *John*[1]) was born on 28 Oct 1912 at Burns, Harney Co., OR. He married Emily Ermina Maupin on 16 Jun 1934. He died on 1 Dec 1991 at age 79. He was buried at Crowley, OR.

Children of Rush Goodman[11] McHargue and Emily Ermina Maupin were as follows:

        i.   ROBERT LEON[12]; born 8 Feb 1936; died 21 Jan 1954 at age 17.

497.   ii.   WILLIAM RAY, born 7 Mar 1942 at Ontario, Malheur Co., OR; married Sandra Lee Gill.

498.   iii.   JACK MERRELL, born 12 Sep 1945 at Ontario, Malheur Co., OR; married Judy Stewart.

499.   iv.   JOSEPH ELDON, born 9 Jul 1947 at Ontario, Malheur Co., OR; married Linda Ann Skinner; divorced Linda Ann Skinner; married Mary Potter.

233. LEON OTTO[11] MCHARGUE (*Lulu*[10]*Johnson, William*[9], *Hiram*[8], *Charles*[7], *Ira*[6], *Jonathan*[5], *Nathaniel*[4], *Nathaniel*[3], *Humphrey*[2], *John*[1]) was born on 27 Jun 1915 at OR. He married Lena McKinney on 24 May 1937. He died on 19 Aug 1996 at age 81. He was buried at Crowley, OR.

He lived in 1996 at Vale, Malheur Co., OR.

Children of Leon Otto[11] McHargue and Lena McKinney all born at Ontario, OR, were as follows:

500.   i.   RICHARD LEON[12], born 23 Aug 1937; married Beverly Hall; divorced Beverly Hall; married LaNeeta (--?--); married Barbara Robertson;.

501.   ii.   FRANCIS MARIE, born 27 Oct 1940; married Frances Leroy McKinney; divorced Frances Leroy McKinney.

502. iii. MELVINA "LOUISE", born 10 Nov 1941; married Larry Roland Holmes; divorced Larry Roland Holmes.

503. iv. DONNA JEAN, born 22 May 1943; married William C. Caughell; divorced William C. Caughell; married John Buckinger.

v. PATRICK JOSEPH; born 21 Mar 1946; died 15 Jul 1946 at Vale, OR.

234. JAMES WILLIAM[11] MCHARGUE (*Lulu*[10]*Johnson, William*[9], *Hiram*[8], *Charles*[7], *Ira*[6], *Jonathan*[5], *Nathaniel*[4], *Nathaniel*[3], *Humphrey*[2], *John*[1]) was born on 25 Nov 1930. He married Grace Mae Lawrence on 6 Aug 1952.

He lived in 2000 at Fruitland, ID.

Children of James William[11] McHargue and Grace Mae Lawrence were as follows:

504. i. JANICE KAY[12], born 16 Apr 1955 at Ontario, OR; married James William Grimes; divorced James William Grimes; married David Stone.

ii. ELLEN SUE; born 21 Jun 1956 at Ontario, OR; died 25 Jun 1956.

505. iii. PAMELA ANN, born 22 Jul 1957 at Ontario, OR; married Daniel Amos Stephens; divorced Daniel Amos Stephens.

iv. (--?--); born 29 May 1963; died 29 May 1963.

235. MARILYN JOE[11] MCHARGUE (*Lulu*[10]*Johnson, William*[9], *Hiram*[8], *Charles*[7], *Ira*[6], *Jonathan*[5], *Nathaniel*[4], *Nathaniel*[3], *Humphrey*[2], *John*[1]) was born on 3 Oct 1933. She married Kenneth Goul.

She lived in 2000 at Payette, ID.

Children of Marilyn Joe[11] McHargue and Kenneth Goul both born at Ontario, OR, are as follows:

i. KENNETH MICHAEL[12]; born 29 Dec 1955; married Sandra Hall.

He lived in 2000 at Mesa, AZ.

506.   ii.   THOMAS BRADLEY, born 28 Jul 1961; married Jacqueline Chadwick.

236.   EDWIN CLAUDE[11] JOHNSON (*Claude*[10], *Hiram*[9], *Hiram*[8], *Charles*[7], *Ira*[6], *Jonathan*[5], *Nathaniel*[4], *Nathaniel*[3], *Humphrey*[2], *John*[1]) was born in 1917. He married Kathryn Lucille Boyle. He died at Salem, Marion Co., OR.

Children of Edwin Claude[11] Johnson and Kathryn Lucille Boyle are as follows:

507.   i.   LAURENCE EDWIN[12], born 31 Jul 1941; married Sharon Kaye Diemert.

508.   ii.   GLENN EARLE, born 30 Sep 1944; married Carolyn Louise Grignon.

237.   ALVIN KANZLER[11] HAMER (*Myrtle*[10]*Johnson*, *Hiram*[9], *Hiram*[8], *Charles*[7], *Ira*[6], *Jonathan*[5], *Nathaniel*[4], *Nathaniel*[3], *Humphrey*[2], *John*[1]) was born on 15 Sep 1913 at Portland, Multnomah Co., OR. He married Delma Alene Brown on 20 May 1933. He died on 27 Dec 1987 at Salem, Marion Co., OR, at age 74.

Children of Alvin Kanzler[11] Hamer and Delma Alene Brown are:

509.   i.   RONALD KANZLER[12], born 24 Aug 1938; married Linda Mae Greenwood.

238.   ROBERT ALLEN[11] JOHNSON (*Hiram*[10], *Hiram*[9], *Hiram*[8], *Charles*[7], *Ira*[6], *Jonathan*[5], *Nathaniel*[4], *Nathaniel*[3], *Humphrey*[2], *John*[1]) was born on 15 Apr 1913 at Salem, Marion Co., OR. He married Frances Ostrin. He married Donna Lee Klein. He died on 6 Sep 2000 at Longview, Cowlitz Co., WA, at age 87. He was buried at City View Cemetery, Salem, Marion Co., OR.

He lived at Rainier, OR.

There were no children of Robert Allen[11] Johnson and Frances Ostrin.

Children of Robert Allen[11] Johnson and Donna Lee Klein are as follows:

i. LORRAINE M.^{12}; born 24 May 1962; married Brian Timothy Jennings 16 Apr 1983 at Rainier, OR.

She lived on 6 Sep 2000 at Longview, Cowlitz Co., WA.

510. ii. LYN ANN, born 11 Jan 1965; married Gary Lee Scott.

iii. LISA E.; born 2 Mar 1969; married (--?--) Taylor.

She lived on 6 Sep 2000 at Scappoose, OR.

239. LEO DELBERT^{11} JOHNSON (*Hiram*^{10}, *Hiram*^{9}, *Hiram*^{8}, *Charles*^{7}, *Ira*^{6}, *Jonathan*^{5}, *Nathaniel*^{4}, *Nathaniel*^{3}, *Humphrey*^{2}, *John*^{1}) was born on 14 Apr 1916. He married Margaret Jacqueline McGhee on 15 Apr 1941 at Silver Spring, MD. He died on 12 Oct 1982 at Warren Co., MD, at age 66.

Children of Leo Delbert^{11} Johnson and Margaret Jacqueline McGhee are as follows:

511. i. SUSAN ANNE^{12}, married Howard Rucker Keister III; divorced Howard Rucker Keister III.

512. ii. JACQUELINE MARIE, married David Peale.

513. iii. KAREN LEA, married Robert Powell.

240. EVELYN M.^{11} JOHNSON (*Creta*^{10}, *Hiram*^{9}, *Hiram*^{8}, *Charles*^{7}, *Ira*^{6}, *Jonathan*^{5}, *Nathaniel*^{4}, *Nathaniel*^{3}, *Humphrey*^{2}, *John*^{1}) was born on 16 May 1907 at Salem, Marion Co., OR. She married Emile F. Aufranc. She married Addison Lane. She died on 24 Jun 1979 at Curry Co., OR, at age 72.

Children of Evelyn M.^{11} Johnson and Emile F. Aufranc are:

514. i. RICHARD EMILE^{12}, born 7 Dec 1936; married Doris Lavonne Reynolds; married Ava Dean Peterson.

241. VERYL LEROSE^{11} JOHNSON (*Fred*^{10}, *Samuel*^{9}, *Hiram*^{8}, *Charles*^{7}, *Ira*^{6}, *Jonathan*^{5}, *Nathaniel*^{4}, *Nathaniel*^{3}, *Humphrey*^{2}, *John*^{1}) was born on 30 Mar 1900 at Jefferson, Marion Co., OR. She married Vern Loren Drager on 27 Dec 1918 at Britenbush, OR. She died in 1990 at Mesa, AZ. She was buried at Portland Memorial Mauseleum, Portland, Multnomah Co., OR.

Children of Veryl LeRose[11] Johnson and Vern Loren Drager are as follows:

  i.   JACK LEROY[12]; born 6 Jan 1921 at Grants Pass, OR.
  ii. VERN LOREN JR.; born 18 Oct 1926 at Salem, Marion Co., OR.

242. ACLE FRANCIS[11] JOHNSON (*Fred*[10], *Samuel*[9], *Hiram*[8], *Charles*[7], *Ira*[6], *Jonathan*[5], *Nathaniel*[4], *Nathaniel*[3], *Humphrey*[2], *John*[1]) was born on 10 Aug 1902 at Jefferson, Marion Co., OR. He married Josephine Louisa Sanders on 4 Sep 1924 at Salem, Marion Co., OR. He died in 1961 at Portland, Multnomah Co., OR.

Children of Acle Francis[11] Johnson and Josephine Louisa Sanders are as follows:

  515. i.   ACLE FRANCIS[12] JR., born 26 Oct 1925 at Okanogan, Okanogan Co., WA; married Ann Agnes Cody.
  516. ii. MARVIN ELLIOTT, born 5 Oct 1928 at Eugene, OR; married Marcia Quisenberry.

243. NELLIE LUCILLE[11] JOHNSON (*Fred*[10], *Samuel*[9], *Hiram*[8], *Charles*[7], *Ira*[6], *Jonathan*[5], *Nathaniel*[4], *Nathaniel*[3], *Humphrey*[2], *John*[1]) was born on 21 Jun 1904 at Jefferson, Marion Co., OR. She married Earl Henbest on 7 Dec 1922 at Roseburg, Douglas Co., OR. She died in 1960 at Roseburg, Douglas Co., OR.

Children of Nellie Lucille[11] Johnson and Earl Henbest are as follows:

  517. i.   VIRGINIA MAY[12], born 14 Jul 1923; married Dick Sour.
  518. ii.   RICHARD EARL, born 16 Oct 1925; married ? (--?--).
        iii. BEVERLY JEAN; born 10 Jul 1933.

244. GERTRUDE LAVERN[11] JOHNSON (*Fred*[10], *Samuel*[9], *Hiram*[8], *Charles*[7], *Ira*[6], *Jonathan*[5], *Nathaniel*[4], *Nathaniel*[3], *Humphrey*[2],

John[1]) was born on 9 May 1906 at Jefferson, Marion Co., OR. She married Alva Jess Williams on 14 Jan 1924 at Roseburg, Douglas Co., OR. She died on 20 Oct 1964 at age 58.

Children of Gertrude Lavern[11] Johnson and Alva Jess Williams were as follows:

> i. EUGENE DAYLE[12]; born 18 Mar 1925 at Roseburg, Douglas Co., OR; died 19 Nov 1936 at Dunsmore, CA, at age 11.

519. ii. DONALD ALVA, born 16 Aug 1926 at Roseburg, Douglas Co., OR; married Laurel Anne Sherar.

520. iii. CAROLYN JANE, born 15 Aug 1931 at Yreka, CA; married Philip Perry Hickman.

245. SAMUEL THURSTON[11] JOHNSON II (*Fred*[10], *Samuel*[9], *Hiram*[8], *Charles*[7], *Ira*[6], *Jonathan*[5], *Nathaniel*[4], *Nathaniel*[3], *Humphrey*[2], *John*[1]) was born on 26 Apr 1912 at Portland, Multnomah Co., OR. He married Barbara Lee Kopsland on 20 Oct 1936 at Portland, Multnomah Co., OR. He died on 8 Jan 1994 at Mesa, AZ, at age 81. He was buried at Portland Memorial Mauseleum, Portland, Multnomah Co., OR.

Children of Samuel Thurston[11] Johnson II and Barbara Lee Kopsland both born at Colville, Stevens Co., WA, are as follows:

521. i. SHARON LEE[12], born 30 May 1939; married William Clayton Lacey.

522. ii. RONALD DAYLE, born 31 Aug 1940; married Modena Joyce Lane.

246. GENEVA BERNICE[11] WAGENBLAST (*Edythe*[10]*Johnson*, *Samuel*[9], *Hiram*[8], *Charles*[7], *Ira*[6], *Jonathan*[5], *Nathaniel*[4], *Nathaniel*[3], *Humphrey*[2], *John*[1]) was born on 9 Nov 1902 at Roseburg, OR. She married Adolph Mathiesen on 24 Jun 1924. She died on 2 Sep 1979 at age 76.

Children of Geneva Bernice[11] Wagenblast and Adolph Mathiesen both born at Portland, Multnomah Co., OR, are as follows:

523. i. PATRICIA LOU[12], born 11 Jan 1928; married Theodore Crandall; married Harvey Simmelink.

524. ii. JAMES PETER, born 30 Dec 1932; married Sandra Burton.

247. JAMES EDWARD[11] WAGENBLAST (*Edythe[10]Johnson, Samuel[9], Hiram[8], Charles[7], Ira[6], Jonathan[5], Nathaniel[4], Nathaniel[3], Humphrey[2], John[1]*) was born on 16 Apr 1904 at Roseburg, OR. He married Genevive Luedinkok on 25 Dec 1928. He died on 10 Aug 1940 at Klamath Falls, OR, at age 36.

Children of James Edward[11] Wagenblast and Genevive Luedinkok are as follows:

525. i. KATHRYNE JOAN[12], born 24 Dec 1929; married Ernest Vernon Risberg.

526. ii. JAMES EDWARD II, born 10 Apr 1933; married Sheila Mathis; married Mary Kingsley.

248. MAURICE JOHNSON[11] WAGENBLAST (*Edythe[10]Johnson, Samuel[9], Hiram[8], Charles[7], Ira[6], Jonathan[5], Nathaniel[4], Nathaniel[3], Humphrey[2], John[1]*) was born on 19 Oct 1906 at Roseburg, OR. He married Betty Altishin on 26 Jan 1946 at Beaverton, OR. He died on 7 May 1959 at Portland, Multnomah Co., OR, at age 52.

Children of Maurice Johnson[11] Wagenblast and Betty Altishin are as follows:

527. i. GEORGE MICHAEL[12], born 1 May 1947; married Susan Jensen; married Gloria Jean Stringham.

528. ii. MARY KATHRYN, born 13 May 1953; married Clark Alan Hockstetler.

249. MABEL ELIZABETH[11] WAGENBLAST (*Edythe[10]Johnson, Samuel[9], Hiram[8], Charles[7], Ira[6], Jonathan[5], Nathaniel[4], Nathaniel[3], Humphrey[2], John[1]*) was born on 16 May 1908 at Silverton, Marion Co., OR. She married Dolph Falkenhagen on 3 Nov 1934.

Children of Mabel Elizabeth[11] Wagenblast and Dolph Falkenhagen are:

529. i. SUSAN CAROL[12], born 3 Oct 1942 at Tacoma, Pierce Co., WA; married Marcus Policar.

250. SAYRE ALBERT[11] DILMORE (*Saphronia*[10]*Johnson, Elgin*[9], *Abel*[8], *Charles*[7], *Ira*[6], *Jonathan*[5], *Nathaniel*[4], *Nathaniel*[3], *Humphrey*[2], *John*[1]) was born in 1906 at Laceyville, PA. He married Ester Catherine Soper at Watkins Glen, NY. He died in 1967. He was buried at Pine Valley, NY.

Children of Sayre Albert[11] Dilmore and Ester Catherine Soper are as follows:

	i.	GERALD IVAN[12].
530.	ii.	JACQUE RODNEY, born 5 Aug 1931; married Joyce Ina Burgess.
	iii.	ESTHER ELIZABETH.
	iv.	JAMES ROGER.
	v.	MARY ANN.
	vi.	SAYRE HALBERT II.
	vii.	CYNTHIA JOY.
	viii.	DONALD EDWARD.
	ix.	CAROLINE JEAN.

251. DONALD ALFRED[11] JOHNSON (*Abel*[10], *Elgin*[9], *Abel*[8], *Charles*[7], *Ira*[6], *Jonathan*[5], *Nathaniel*[4], *Nathaniel*[3], *Humphrey*[2], *John*[1]) was born on 17 Jul 1915 at Elmira, Chemung Co., NY. He married Myrtle Helena Beckley, daughter of John Hazard Beckley and Louisa Bell Crocker, on 14 Feb 1940 at North Syracuse, Onondoga Co., NY. He married Katherine Ferguson circa 1989. He died on 7 Apr 2000 at St. Petersburg, Pinellas Co., FL, at age 84.

Children of Donald Alfred[11] Johnson and Myrtle Helena Beckley both born at Syracuse, Onondaga Co., NY, are as follows:

531.	i.	ELEANOR LOUISE[12], born 5 May 1935; married Wendel Dwight Lilly.
532.	ii.	DONNA LEE, born 17 Nov 1944; married Richard Arnold Hall.

252. CARL EVERETT[11] JOHNSON (*Abel*[10], *Elgin*[9], *Abel*[8], *Charles*[7], *Ira*[6], *Jonathan*[5], *Nathaniel*[4], *Nathaniel*[3], *Humphrey*[2], *John*[1]) was born on 10 Dec 1915 at Syracuse, Onondoga Co., NY. He married Nona Jean Clark on 22 Feb 1947.

Children of Carl Everett[11] Johnson and Nona Jean Clark are as follows:

> i. JEFFREY RICHARD[12]; born 19 Mar 1953 at St. Petersburg, FL; married Maria Eisenbarth 5 Oct 1974 at Berlin, Germany.
>
> ii. CARL GREGORY; born 2 Dec 1955 at Syracuse, Onondoga Co., NY.

253. RUTH WINIFRED[11] JOHNSON (*Abel[10]*, *Elgin[9]*, *Abel[8]*, *Charles[7]*, *Ira[6]*, *Jonathan[5]*, *Nathaniel[4]*, *Nathaniel[3]*, *Humphrey[2]*, *John[1]*) was born on 11 Mar 1917 at Elmira, NY. She married William Herbert Sahm II on 11 Jun 1938. She died on 20 Mar 1998 at Bedford, Bedford Co., VA, at age 81.

Children of Ruth Winifred[11] Johnson and William Herbert Sahm II were as follows:

> 533. i. WILLIAM HERBERT[12] III, born 14 Apr 1939; married Ludmila Jandolenko.
>
> 534. ii. RUTH ANN, born 1 Feb 1943 at Syracuse, Onondoga Co., NY; married Cleo A. Dorpinghaus.
>
> 535. iii. LARRY GENE, born 6 Feb 1945 at Syracuse, Onondoga Co., NY; married Cheryl Hoar.
>
> 536. iv. LUELLA JEAN, born 6 Feb 1945 at Syracuse, Onondoga Co., NY; married David Arthur Klotz.
>
> 537. v. JOYCE SANDRA, born 17 Aug 1946; married Paul Herbert Opolski.
>
> 538. vi. BEVERLY JOY, born 29 Jul 1949 at Syracuse, Onondoga Co., NY; married Milton Earl Oakley.
>
> vii. STEPHEN PAUL; born 1 Apr 1953 at Syracuse, Onondoga Co., NY; married Brenda Knight 27 Nov 1977 at Brooklyn, NY.
>
> viii. FRANCIS JAMES; born 27 Aug 1956 at Syracuse, Onondoga Co., NY; married Lorraine Kay Munger 12 Nov 1977.

254. ABEL PHILLIP[11] JOHNSON SR. (*Abel[10]*, *Elgin[9]*, *Abel[8]*, *Charles[7]*, *Ira[6]*, *Jonathan[5]*, *Nathaniel[4]*, *Nathaniel[3]*, *Humphrey[2]*,

John[1]) was born on 4 Mar 1920 at Syracuse, Onondoga Co., NY. He married Rita Caroline Ditch, daughter of Walter Raymond Ditch and Caroline Norton, on 19 Apr 1947 at North Syracuse, Onondoga Co., NY.

Children of Abel Phillip[11] Johnson Sr. and Rita Caroline Ditch were as follows:

539.   i.   GLORIA JEAN[12], born 7 Jun 1948 at Syracuse, Onondoga Co., NY; married Richard Rudolph Yenny.

540.   ii.   JEANINE MARIE, born 19 Jul 1949 at Syracuse, Onondoga Co., NY; married Keith Nelson Zinsmeyer.

541.   iii.   ABEL PHILLIP JR., born 26 Apr 1951 at Syracuse, Onondoga Co., NY; married Melody Lynn Dove; divorced Melody Lynn Dove; married Karen Sue Hayamker.

542.   iv.   ILENE SUZANNE, born 27 Nov 1953 at Syracuse, Onondoga Co., NY; married Herbert Forrest Marshall Jr.

       v.   MARY LARENA; born 15 Feb 1955 at Syracuse, Onondaga Co., NY; died 16 Feb 1955 at Syracuse, Onondaga Co., NY; buried at Syracuse, Onondaga Co., NY.

543.   vi.   PATRICIA CLARE, born 13 Jun 1957 at Syracuse, Onondoga Co., NY; married Richard Welcome Gearsbeck II.

       vii.   ROBERT MATHEW; born 11 Jul 1958 at Syracuse, Onondoga Co., NY; died 26 Jul 1958 at Syracuse, Onondoga Co., NY; buried at Syracuse, Onondaga Co., NY.

       viii.   DANIEL MARK; born 8 Oct 1959 at Syracuse, Onondoga Co., NY.

544.   ix.   LANETTE ANN, born 8 Jan 1964 at Syracuse, Onondoga Co., NY; married Darryl John Buist Sr; divorced Darryl John Buist Sr; married William Olmstead.

x.　EDWARD ANTHONY; born 31 Jan 1967 at Syracuse, Onondaga Co., NY.

255. ROBERT EARL[11] JOHNSON (*Abel*[10], *Elgin*[9], *Abel*[8], *Charles*[7], *Ira*[6], *Jonathan*[5], *Nathaniel*[4], *Nathaniel*[3], *Humphrey*[2], *John*[1]) was born on 10 Jul 1922 at Syracuse, Onondoga Co., NY. He married Florence Kathleen Taylor on 22 Jun 1942 at N. Syracuse, Onondoga Co., NY. He married Mildred Yost at N. Syracuse, Onondoga Co., NY. He married Doris Glee Windsor. He died on 27 Apr 1998 at Crystal River, Citrus Co., FL, at age 75.

Children of Robert Earl[11] Johnson and Florence Kathleen Taylor are as follows:

545.　　i.　KATHLEEN MARIE[12], born 12 May 1943 at Rome, Onieda Co., NY; married Bradford James Pettit.

546.　　ii.　ROBERT EARL, born 6 Nov 1945; married Sharon Yvette Chapman.

　　　　iii.　DAVID EDWARD; born 27 Jan 1947 at Syracuse, Onondaga Co., NY; married Cheryl Lou Stewart; he and Cheryl Lou Stewart were divorced Dec 1968; married Phyllis Marie Kinard 16 Jun 1992 at Atlanta, Fulton Co., FL; he and Phyllis Marie Kinard were divorced Mar 1998.

Children of Robert Earl[11] Johnson and Mildred Yost are:

　　　　i.　REBECCA SUE[12]; born 1960.

There were no children of Robert Earl[11] Johnson and Doris Glee Windsor.

256. MILDRED VIOLET[11] JOHNSON (*Abel*[10], *Elgin*[9], *Abel*[8], *Charles*[7], *Ira*[6], *Jonathan*[5], *Nathaniel*[4], *Nathaniel*[3], *Humphrey*[2], *John*[1]) was born on 17 Oct 1924 at Syracuse, Onondaga Co., NY. She married Dale Byran Caughey.

Children of Mildred Violet[11] Johnson and Dale Byran Caughey all born at Syracuse, Onondaga Co., NY, were as follows:

　　　　i.　BONNIE JEAN[12]; born 3 May 1949; died 5 May 1949 at Syracuse, Onondaga Co., NY.

ii. LOIS ANN; born 6 Apr 1950; married Steven LeRoy Heiden; she and Steven LeRoy Heiden were divorced; married just prior to her death to Robert Facto Sep 1988 at St. Petersburg, Pinellas Co., FL; died 4 Sep 1988 at St. Petersburg, Pinellas Co., FL, at age 38; buried 7 Sep 1988 at All Faiths Cemetery, St. Petersburg, Pinellas Co., FL.

iii. JOHN PAUL; born 24 Dec 1966.

257. DONALD RUPERT[11] NOBLE (*Ferne[10]Johnson, Charles[9], William[8], Charles[7], Ira[6], Jonathan[5], Nathaniel[4], Nathaniel[3], Humphrey[2], John[1]*) was born on 29 Mar 1913. He married Joanna Caranossios on 1 Dec 1940 at Yonkers, NY. He died on 27 Apr 1997 at age 84.

Children of Donald Rupert[11] Noble and Joanna Caranossios are as follows:

547. i. DONALD RUPERT[12] JR., born 11 Dec 1941; married Glee Gillies.

548. ii. CONSTANCE FAITH, born 6 Jan 1950; married Eugene Thomas Kesicke.

258. WORTH[11] NOBLE (*Ferne[10]Johnson, Charles[9], William[8], Charles[7], Ira[6], Jonathan[5], Nathaniel[4], Nathaniel[3], Humphrey[2], John[1]*) was born on 14 Nov 1922. He married Margaret Mitchell on 20 Feb 1946. He died on 29 Dec 2000 at Lisbon, NY, at age 78.

Children of Worth[11] Noble and Margaret Mitchell both born at Ogdensburg, NY, are as follows:

549. i. PHYLLIS[12], born 14 Jul 1953; married Wayne Brock.

ii. PATRICIA; born 29 Dec 1955.

259. CHARLES VANCE[11] JOHNSON SR (*John[10], Charles[9], William[8], Charles[7], Ira[6], Jonathan[5], Nathaniel[4], Nathaniel[3], Humphrey[2], John[1]*) was born on 12 Apr 1921 at Hermon, St. Lawrence Co., NY. He married Barbara Esther Woods on 26 Jan 1947 at Hermon Methodist Church. He died on 5 Feb 2003 at

Hermon, St. Lawrence Co., NY, at age 81. He was buried at Maple Grove Cemetery, Richville, St. Lawrence Co., NY. He began military service in 1942 at Fourth Marine Division.

Children of Charles Vance[11] Johnson Sr and Barbara Esther Woods are as follows:

550.   i.   GLORIA JEAN[12], born 16 Mar 1948; married Arthur Alexander; married Donald Jones.

551.   ii.   CHARLES VANCE JR., born 10 Feb 1953; married Cynthia Brice; married Michele Gail Wahlers.

260. JOHN WARREN[11] JOHNSON JR. (*John[10]*, *Charles[9]*, *William[8]*, *Charles[7]*, *Ira[6]*, *Jonathan[5]*, *Nathaniel[4]*, *Nathaniel[3]*, *Humphrey[2]*, *John[1]*) was born on 10 Dec 1923 at Hermon, St. Lawrence Co., NY. He married Rita Marie Roy on 27 Aug 1954. He died on 27 Jun 1977 at Gouverneur, St. Lawrence Co., NY, at age 53.

Children of John Warren[11] Johnson Jr. and Rita Marie Roy are as follows:

552.   i.   DEBORAH ANN[12], born 7 Aug 1955 at Canton, St. Lawrence Co., NY; married Dale E. Matthews; divorced Dale E. Matthews.

553.   ii.   CHRISTINE MARION, born 19 Dec 1956 at Canton, St. Lawrence Co., NY; married Dwayne Ronald Blandin.

554.   iii.   JOHN WARREN III, born 29 Apr 1960 at Gouverneur, St. Lawrence Co., NY; married Sondra Goodnough.

        iv.   KAREN MARIE; born 3 May 1968 at Watertown, Jefferson Co., NY.

555.   v.   KATHERINE MARGIE, born 3 May 1968 at Watertown, Jefferson Co., NY; married Robert Beauchamp.

261. ELEANOR BELLE[11] JOHNSON (*John[10]*, *Charles[9]*, *William[8]*, *Charles[7]*, *Ira[6]*, *Jonathan[5]*, *Nathaniel[4]*, *Nathaniel[3]*, *Humphrey[2]*, *John[1]*) was born on 21 Nov 1927. She married James J. Kilmer on 19 Apr 1947 at Hermon, St. Lawrence Co., NY.

She lived in 2003 at FL.

Children of Eleanor Belle[11] Johnson and James J. Kilmer are as follows:

      i.   ANTOINETTE MARIE[12]; born 26 Oct 1949 at Gouverneur, St. Lawrence Co., NY; married William Joseph Mathies 17 Apr 1981 at Reno, NV.

556.   ii. SANDRA JEAN, born 4 Mar 1951 at Guam; married Theodore Ralph Pfeiffer.

      iii. JAMES J.; born 4 Jul 1952 at Gouverneur, St. Lawrence Co., NY.

262. PHYLLIS IRENE[11] JOHNSON (*John*[10], *Charles*[9], *William*[8], *Charles*[7], *Ira*[6], *Jonathan*[5], *Nathaniel*[4], *Nathaniel*[3], *Humphrey*[2], *John*[1]) was born on 8 Jan 1931 at Hermon, St. Lawrence Co., NY. She married Athol Glynn Edwards on 20 Feb 1953 at Northport, IL.

She lived in 2003 at FL.

Children of Phyllis Irene[11] Johnson and Athol Glynn Edwards are as follows:

      i.   JOAN ANN[12]; born 11 Jun 1954; married Michael William DeRoo 17 Oct 1987.

557.   ii. JEAN MARIE, born 21 Jun 1955; married Paul Francis Merithew.

558.   iii. JAQUELINE KAY, born 14 Mar 1957; married Edward C. Gauthier.

559.   iv. TERRY LYNN, born 4 Jul 1958; married Blane Harding.

560.   v. TONI LEA, born 21 May 1968; married Darren Brabaw; married Bartle Canny.

263. NANCY JEAN[11] JOHNSON (*John*[10], *Charles*[9], *William*[8], *Charles*[7], *Ira*[6], *Jonathan*[5], *Nathaniel*[4], *Nathaniel*[3], *Humphrey*[2], *John*[1]) was born on 9 Aug 1937 at Ogdensburg, NY. She married James P. Sayer on 14 Sep 1957. She married Kenneth Richard Johnson on 21 Sep 1986 at FL. She and Kenneth Richard Johnson were divorced circa 1988.

Children of Nancy Jean[11] Johnson and James P. Sayer all born at Canton, NY, are as follows:

      i.   KIM^{12}; born 16 Jul 1958.

561.   ii. BARBARA JEAN, born 6 Jul 1959; married James Blackburn; married Gary Butler.

      iii. JAMES WARREN; born 18 Feb 1965.

264.   MILDRED^{11} JOHNSON (*Manie^{10}Brown*, *Alvah^9*, *Nancy^{8}Johnson*, *Charles^7*, *Ira^6*, *Jonathan^5*, *Nathaniel^4*, *Nathaniel^3*, *Humphrey^2*, *John^1*) was born circa 1899. She married Robert Hill circa 1920. She died in 1971 at Norfolk, St. Lawrence Co., NY.

She appeared on the census of 1 Apr 1930 at Norfolk, St. Lawrence Co., NY.

Children of Mildred^{11} Johnson and Robert Hill are as follows:

      i.   (--?--)^{12}.

562.   ii. JAMES S., born circa 1922 at NY.

563.   iii. SARAH

265.   MIRIAM^{11} JOHNSON (*Manie^{10}Brown*, *Alvah^9*, *Nancy^{8}Johnson*, *Charles^7*, *Ira^6*, *Jonathan^5*, *Nathaniel^4*, *Nathaniel^3*, *Humphrey^2*, *John^1*) was born circa 1907 at Gouverneur, St. Lawrence Co., NY. She married Gerald Leonard. She married Jack Hayden. She died at Norfolk, St. Lawrence Co., NY.

Children of Miriam^{11} Johnson and Gerald Leonard are:

564.   i.   ELIZABETH^{12}, married Harold Bell.

There were no children of Miriam^{11} Johnson and Jack Hayden.

266.   DOROTHY JEAN^{11} JOHNSON (*Manie^{10}Brown*, *Alvah^9*, *Nancy^{8}Johnson*, *Charles^7*, *Ira^6*, *Jonathan^5*, *Nathaniel^4*, *Nathaniel^3*, *Humphrey^2*, *John^1*) was born circa 1910 at Gouverneur, St. Lawrence Co., NY. She married Michael Kennedy. She married Howard Hitsman. She died at Gouverneur, St. Lawrence Co., NY.

Children of Dorothy Jean^{11} Johnson and Michael Kennedy are as follows:

      i.   (--?--)^{12}.

ii. (--?--).

Children of Dorothy Jean[11] Johnson and Howard Hitsman are:

i. (--?--)[12].

267. CLARENCE DONALD[11] BROWN (*Clarence[10]*, *Charles[9]*, *Nancy[8]Johnson*, *Charles[7]*, *Ira[6]*, *Jonathan[5]*, *Nathaniel[4]*, *Nathaniel[3]*, *Humphrey[2]*, *John[1]*) was born on 30 Apr 1900 at Edwards, St. Lawrence Co., NY. He married Inez Lucille Noble on 28 Jun 1924. He died on 25 Nov 1971 at Edwards, St. Lawrence Co., NY, at age 71.

He appeared on the census of 1 Jun 1900 at Edwards, St. Lawrence Co., NY. As of 1 Jun 1900, he was also known as Donald C. Brown.

Children of Clarence Donald[11] Brown and Inez Lucille Noble both born at Gouverneur, St. Lawrence Co., NY, are as follows:

565. i. RICHARD DONALD[12], born 14 Jul 1930; married Barbara Ruth Fulton.

566. ii. CONSTANCE LUCILLE, born 25 Oct 1931; married Burton George McElwain.

268. MARTHA ELIZABETH[11] CLARK (*Mabel[10]Brown*, *Charles[9]*, *Nancy[8]Johnson*, *Charles[7]*, *Ira[6]*, *Jonathan[5]*, *Nathaniel[4]*, *Nathaniel[3]*, *Humphrey[2]*, *John[1]*) was born on 30 Jun 1915 at Canton, St. Lawrence Co., NY. She married Carson Perry Buck on 8 Jun 1936 at St. Lawrence University Chapel, Canton, St. Lawrence Co., NY. She died on 12 May 1997 at Manlius, Onondaga Co., NY, at age 81. She was buried on 15 May 1997 at Manlius Village Cemetery, Manlius, NY.

Children of Martha Elizabeth[11] Clark and Carson Perry Buck are as follows:

567. i. MARY ELIZABETH[12], born 1 Feb 1940 at St. Joseph Hospital, South Bend, St. Joseph Co., IN; married Joseph Anthony Spadaro.

568. ii. HARRIET GERTRUDE, born 11 Dec 1941 at St. Joseph Hospital, South Bend, St. Joseph Co., IN; married Charles Michael Connelly.

569.   iii.   NANCY MADELINE, born 19 Mar 1945 at St. Joseph Hospital, South Bend, St. Joseph Co., IN; married Frank Bradford Simpson III.

570.   iv.   FREDERICK JOHN, born 27 Sep 1950 at St. Joseph Hospital, South Bend, St. Joseph Co., IN; married Gloria Ann Lemke; divorced Gloria Ann Lemke; engaged Anne Munz.

571.   v.   KATHERINE MARIE, born 7 Nov 1951 at St. Joseph Hospital, South Bend, St. Joseph Co., IN; married Daniel Robert Siegfried; married Winfrey Dean Waits.

572.   vi.   WILLIAM JOHN PAUL, born 23 Jun 1958 at Syracuse, Onondoga Co., NY; married Elizabeth Ann Beltowski.

269.   HARRIET ISABEL[11] CLARK (*Mabel*[10]*Brown, Charles*[9], *Nancy*[8]*Johnson, Charles*[7], *Ira*[6], *Jonathan*[5], *Nathaniel*[4], *Nathaniel*[3], *Humphrey*[2], *John*[1]) was born on 9 Apr 1918 at Canton, St. Lawrence Co., NY. She married Richard H. Connors on 5 Sep 1942 at Hemlock, Ontario Co., NY. She died on 14 Mar 1967 at Rochester, Monroe Co., NY, at age 48.

Children of Harriet Isabel[11] Clark and Richard H. Connors all born at Rochester, Monroe Co., NY, were as follows:

          i.   CHARLES RICHARD[12]; born 18 Mar 1944; died 4 Oct 1953 at Rochester, Monroe Co., NY, at age 9.

573.   ii.   ELIZABETH BROWN, born 7 Feb 1946; married Dort Albert Cameron III.

574.   iii.   THOMAS CLARK, born 10 Oct 1950; married Mary Lucille Ennist; divorced Mary Lucille Ennist; married Deborah Jean Cravens.

          iv.   WILLIAM RICHARD; born 29 Dec 1955; married Anne Marie Lawson 23 Oct 1999 at Lake George, Washington Co., NY.

Richard H. Connors married Gwendolyn A. Russell on 4 May 1968 at Penfield, Monroe Co., NY. She was born 22 Aug 1923 at Staten Island, NY. She married William Macellven.

Children of Gwendolyn A.[1] Russell and Richard H. Connors all born at Rochester, Monroe Co., NY, are as follows:

i.   SUSAN MARKS[2] MACELLVEN

(Gwendolyn[1] Russell) was born on 24 Jul 1946 at Rochester, Monroe Co., NY. She married Lance Foster on 23 Apr 1971 at Tampa, FL.

Children of Susan Marks[2] MACELLVEN and Lance Foster both born at Tampa, FL, are as follows:

i.TANYA[3]; born 20 Jun 1972.
ii.ERIKA; born 28 May 1975.

ii.   ERIC RUSSELL[2] MACELLVEN

(Gwendolyn[1] Russell) was born on 6 Jun 1949 at Rochester, Monroe Co., NY. He married Linda O'Donnell on 25 Jan 1994 at Bath, ME.

Children of Eric Russell[2] Macellven and Linda O'Donnell are:

i. MORGAN[3]; born 9 Jun 1986 at Portland, ME.

iii.   DAVID MOORE[2] MACELLVEN

(Gwendolyn[1] Russell) was born on 6 Oct 1955 at Rochester, Monroe Co., NY. He married Tamara Dolhun on 12 Aug 1978 at Long Grove, IL.

Children of David Moore[2] Macellven and Tamara Dolhun are as follows:

i. LAUREN[3]; born 5 Aug 1985 at Rochester, Monroe Co., NY

ii. KIRSTEN, born 4 April 1988 at Rochester, Monroe Co., NY

270. CHARLES ROLLIN[11] CLARK SR (*Mabel[10]Brown, Charles[9], Nancy[8]Johnson, Charles[7], Ira[6], Jonathan[5], Nathaniel[4], Nathaniel[3], Humphrey[2], John[1]*) was born on 13 Jul 1920 at Canton, NY. He married Evelyne Frances Flannagen on 29 May 1943 at Walla Walla, WA. He died on 13 Dec 1985 at Canton, NY, at age 65.

Children of Charles Rollin[11] Clark Sr and Evelyne Frances Flannagen were as follows:

> 575.   i.   JAMES MILTON[12], born 16 Sep 1945 at Canton, NY; married Linda St Louis.
>
> 576.   ii.   CHARLES ROLLIN II, born 16 May 1947 at Canton, NY; married Linda Jean Rosinski.
>
>   iii.   JOHN EVERT; born 21 Jul 1948 at Potsdam, NY; died 20 Jul 1976 at Canton, NY, at age 27.
>
>   iv.   DAVID BROWN; born 14 Jan 1951 at Canton, NY.

271. EVERETT E.[11] BEACH (*Leta[10]Hall, Hiram[9], Emmorancy[8]Johnson, Charles[7], Ira[6], Jonathan[5], Nathaniel[4], Nathaniel[3], Humphrey[2], John[1]*) was born on 11 Mar 1892 at Edwards, St. Lawrence Co., NY. He married Marguerite Hawes on 30 Jun 1920 at Harrisville, NY. He died on 29 Jul 1962 at Ogdensburg, NY, at age 70. He was buried at Morrisville Rural Cemetery, Morrisville, NY.

Children of Everett E.[11] Beach and Marguerite Hawes were as follows:

>   i.   MADELYN LUCILLE[12]; born 7 Apr 1922 at Utica, NY; married Donald Johns; died 5 May 1975 at Atlanta, GA, at age 53.
>
>   ii.   HELEN ARLENE; born 13 Apr 1924 at Watertown, NY; married John Owens; married Thomas Flynn; married George Loughrey; died 20 Oct 1978 at Syracuse, Onondaga Co., NY, at age 54.

577.   iii.   JANE MARIE, born 2 Jun 1932 at Theresa, Jefferson Co., NY; married George Augustus Grappotte Sr.

578.   iv.   JANICE CORNELIA, born 18 Aug 1935; married William G. Backus; married (--?--) Daley.

272.   VIVIAN[11] BEACH (*Leta*[10]*Hall*, *Hiram*[9], *Emmorancy*[8]*Johnson*, *Charles*[7], *Ira*[6], *Jonathan*[5], *Nathaniel*[4], *Nathaniel*[3], *Humphrey*[2], *John*[1]) was born on 18 Jan 1896 at Edwards, St. Lawrence Co., NY. She married David L. Gardner on 1 Oct 1919 at Washington, DC. She died in Oct 1964 at Harrisville, Lewis Co., NY, at age 68. She was buried at St. Francis Cemetery, Harrisville, Lewis Co., NY.

Children of Vivian[11] Beach and David L. Gardner were as follows:

    i.   EDWARD[12]; died circa 1977 at Harrisville, Lewis Co., NY.

    ii.   ELIZABETH; married (--?--) Connors; married (--?--) Thomas.

    iii.   MARY; married Arthur Dooley.

273.   REATHA MARIE[11] HALL (*Leon*[10], *Hiram*[9], *Emmorancy*[8]*Johnson*, *Charles*[7], *Ira*[6], *Jonathan*[5], *Nathaniel*[4], *Nathaniel*[3], *Humphrey*[2], *John*[1]) was born on 2 Mar 1914 at Edwards, St. Lawrence Co., NY. She married Edwin Nelson Boprey, son of John Franklin Boprey and Lillian May Blair, on 25 May 1936 at Gouverneur, St. Lawrence Co., NY. She died on 15 Jun 1989 at Potsdam Hospital, St. Lawrence Co., NY, at age 75. She was buried on 17 Jun 1989 at Riverside Cemetery, Norwood, NY.

Children of Reatha Marie[11] Hall and Edwin Nelson Boprey were as follows:

579.   i.   RICHARD JOSEPH[12], born 8 Jan 1937 at Gouverneur, St. Lawrence Co., NY; married Marlene Mary Scott.

580.   ii.   JACQUELINE JANET, born 14 Jun 1938 at Gouverneur, St. Lawrence Co., NY; married George Charles Spencer.

581.   iii.   BONNIE KAY, born 16 May 1940 at Gouverneur, St. Lawrence Co., NY; married Keith Francis Barnes.

582.   iv.   MICHAEL LEON SR., born 20 Mar 1942 at Norwood, St. Lawrence Co., NY; married Rosemary Orologio.

583.   v.   ROBERT EDWIN, born 30 Mar 1944 at Potsdam, St. Lawrence Co., NY; married Linda Frances LaClair.

274. ELLISON[11] HALL (*Leon*[10], *Hiram*[9], *Emmorancy*[8]*Johnson*, *Charles*[7], *Ira*[6], *Jonathan*[5], *Nathaniel*[4], *Nathaniel*[3], *Humphrey*[2], *John*[1]) was born on 3 Jun 1915 at Edwards, St. Lawrence Co., NY. She married Douglas J. Fredenburg Sr., son of Judd M. Fredenburg and Alberta Thayer. She died on 28 Sep 1989 at Gouverneur, St. Lawrence Co., NY, at age 74. She was buried at Hailesboro Cemetery, NY.

Children of Ellison[11] Hall and Douglas J. Fredenburg Sr. were as follows:

   i.   DOUGLAS[12] JR.; born 9 Feb 1936 at Gouverneur, St. Lawrence Co., NY; died 5 Jul 1978 at Gouverneur, St. Lawrence Co., NY, at age 42; buried at Hailesboro Cemetery, St. Lawrence Co., NY

   ii.   GARY; married Carolyn Knight.

   iii.   KIM SLEEMAN.

275. CLIFFORD HIRAM[11] HALL (*Leon*[10], *Hiram*[9], *Emmorancy*[8]*Johnson*, *Charles*[7], *Ira*[6], *Jonathan*[5], *Nathaniel*[4], *Nathaniel*[3], *Humphrey*[2], *John*[1]) was born on 26 Mar 1917 at Edwards, St. Lawrence Co., NY. He married Isabel Yaddow in 1940 at Gouverneur, St. Lawrence Co., NY.

Children of Clifford Hiram[11] Hall and Isabel Yaddow are as follows:

584.   i.   GWENDOLYN MAE[12], born 2 Nov at Gouverneur, St. Lawrence Co., NY; married Dean Bressette.

ii.   CONNIE ELLEN.

iii.   CLIFFORD MARK; married Jane Markwick.

iv.   DIXIE MARIE; born 6 Nov 1957 at Gouverneur, St. Lawrence Co., NY.

276.   LEE ETHEL[11] HUGHES (*Florence[10]Hall, Hiram[9], Emmorancy[8]Johnson, Charles[7], Ira[6], Jonathan[5], Nathaniel[4], Nathaniel[3], Humphrey[2], John[1]*) was born on 22 Aug 1901 at Edwards, St. Lawrence Co., NY. He married Sarah (--?--).

Children of Lee Ethel[11] Hughes and Sarah (--?--) are as follows:

i.   ROBERT[12].

ii.   DANNY.

277.   LYLE GILBERT[11] HUGHES (*Florence[10]Hall, Hiram[9], Emmorancy[8]Johnson, Charles[7], Ira[6], Jonathan[5], Nathaniel[4], Nathaniel[3], Humphrey[2], John[1]*) was born on 24 Oct 1903 at Edwards, St. Lawrence Co., NY. He married Edna Mae Meldrim on 26 Aug 1927 at Edwards, St. Lawrence Co., NY.

Children of Lyle Gilbert[11] Hughes and Edna Mae Meldrim are:

585.   i.   KENNETH GILBERT[12], born 2 Nov 1931 at Gouverneur, St. Lawrence Co., NY; married Dolores F. Youngs.

278.   GERALD LINDEN[11] BOULET (*Lottie[10]Hall, Hiram[9], Emmorancy[8]Johnson, Charles[7], Ira[6], Jonathan[5], Nathaniel[4], Nathaniel[3], Humphrey[2], John[1]*) was born on 21 Jun 1902 at Edwards, St. Lawrence Co., NY. He married Alice Kauffman on 31 Oct. He died on 6 Jan 1963 at St. Mary's Hospital, Rochester, NY, at age 60. He was buried at Holy Ghost Cemetery, Chili, NY.

Children of Gerald Linden[11] Boulet and Alice Kauffman are as follows:

586.   i.   GERALD[12], born 15 Jun 1931; married Mary Ann Fahey.

ii.   GEORGE; born 24 Mar 1933; married Carol Scheich.

587.   iii.   JAMES, born 28 Jun 1934; married Betty Colley.

279. GERVAISE ISADORE[11] BOULET (*Lottie[10]Hall*, *Hiram[9]*, *Emmorancy[8]Johnson*, *Charles[7]*, *Ira[6]*, *Jonathan[5]*, *Nathaniel[4]*, *Nathaniel[3]*, *Humphrey[2]*, *John[1]*) was born on 24 May 1906 at Edwards, St. Lawrence Co., NY. He married Hazel M. Wheeler on 12 Dec 1936 at Harrisville, Lewis Co., NY. He died on 29 Dec 1955 at Edwards, St. Lawrence Co., NY, at age 49. He was buried at Fairview Cemetery, Edwards, St. Lawrence Co., NY.

Children of Gervaise Isadore[11] Boulet and Hazel M. Wheeler are as follows:

      i.   CONNIE[12]; born 1944; married Theodore Bostick.

588.   ii. DONNA, born 1947; married Theodore Bostick.

280. ARTHUR OLNEY[11] BOULET (*Lottie[10]Hall*, *Hiram[9]*, *Emmorancy[8]Johnson*, *Charles[7]*, *Ira[6]*, *Jonathan[5]*, *Nathaniel[4]*, *Nathaniel[3]*, *Humphrey[2]*, *John[1]*) was born on 25 Aug 1907 at Edwards, St. Lawrence Co., NY. He married Oneita May French on 16 Dec 1933 at Antwerp, NY. He died on 16 Sep 1967 at Painted Post, NY, at age 60. He was buried at Fairview Cemetery, Edwards, St. Lawrence Co., NY.

Children of Arthur Olney[11] Boulet and Oneita May French were as follows:

589.   i.   CAROLYN ANN[12], born 1 Dec 1934 at Gouverneur, St. Lawrence Co., NY; married Leo Everett Averill.

590.   ii. KAY ONALEE, born 7 Jul 1936 at Edwards, St. Lawrence Co., NY; married Murray A. Hartley.

591.   iii. JOAN MARIE, born 31 Jan 1943 at Edwards, St. Lawrence Co., NY; married Jack Ward.

281. LOUISE FLORENCE[11] BOULET (*Lottie[10]Hall*, *Hiram[9]*, *Emmorancy[8]Johnson*, *Charles[7]*, *Ira[6]*, *Jonathan[5]*, *Nathaniel[4]*, *Nathaniel[3]*, *Humphrey[2]*, *John[1]*) was born on 30 Sep 1913 at Edwards, St. Lawrence Co., NY. She married Leon Dewey Typhair, son of Charles Typhair, on 21 Dec 1935 at Fine Methodist parsonage, Fine, NY. She died on 6 Dec 1982 at Thompson

Hospital, Canadaigua, NY, at age 69. She was buried on 10 Dec 1982 at Fairview Cemetery, Edwards, St. Lawrence Co., NY.

Children of Louise Florence[11] Boulet and Leon Dewey Typhair are:

    592.   i.   DOLORES[12], married Paul Osborne.

282.   BERNARD PHILIP[11] BOULET (*Lottie[10]Hall*, *Hiram[9]*, *Emmorancy[8]Johnson*, *Charles[7]*, *Ira[6]*, *Jonathan[5]*, *Nathaniel[4]*, *Nathaniel[3]*, *Humphrey[2]*, *John[1]*) was born on 9 Oct 1919 at Edwards, St. Lawrence Co., NY. He married Mary Jean Brown on 30 Oct 1942. He died on 13 Jun 1997 at age 77. He was buried on 17 Jun 1997 at Falls Cemetery, Greece, NY.

Children of Bernard Philip[11] Boulet and Mary Jean Brown were as follows:

    i.   BARBARA ANN[12]; born 21 Dec 1944; married (--?--) Goodridge.
    ii.   THOMAS BERNARD; born 8 Jun 1947.
    iii. JULIA ELLEN; born 30 Aug 1952; married (--?--) Quadrozzi.
    iv. STEPHEN HALL; born 9 Apr 1959.

283.   KATHLEEN MARIE[11] HALL (*Frank[10]*, *Hiram[9]*, *Emmorancy[8]Johnson*, *Charles[7]*, *Ira[6]*, *Jonathan[5]*, *Nathaniel[4]*, *Nathaniel[3]*, *Humphrey[2]*, *John[1]*) was born on 28 Dec 1907 at Edwards, St. Lawrence Co., NY. She married John Arnold on 16 Dec 1928 at DeKalb Junction, St. Lawrence Co., NY.

Children of Kathleen Marie[11] Hall and John Arnold are as follows:

    i.   JOHN[12] II; born at Gouverneur, St. Lawrence Co., NY; married Anna (--?--).
    ii.   LAWRENCE PHILIP.
    iii. JOAN JULIA.
    iv. CHARLOTTE; married Donald McWilliams.
    v.   WINSTON GEORGE.
    vi. CONNIE; married Thomas Whittle.

284.   GERALDINE   LOUISE[11]   HALL   (*Frank*[10], *Hiram*[9], *Emmorancy*[8]*Johnson*, *Charles*[7], *Ira*[6], *Jonathan*[5], *Nathaniel*[4], *Nathaniel*[3], *Humphrey*[2], *John*[1]) was born on 7 Aug 1910 at Edwards, St. Lawrence Co., NY. She married Wesley Brailey on 17 Oct 1928 at Johnsburg, Warren Co., NY. She and Wesley Brailey were divorced. She died on 24 Aug 1964 at Watertown, Jefferson Co., NY, at age 54.

Children of Geraldine Louise[11] Hall and Wesley Brailey both born at Edwards, St. Lawrence Co., NY, were as follows:

> i.   ROBERTA JUNE[12]; born 28 Nov 1929; died 30 Nov 1929 at Edwards, St. Lawrence Co., NY.
>
> ii.   WESLEY JUNIOR; born 31 Jul 1932; married Margaret (--?--); died 21 Aug 1982 at Modesto, CA, at age 50.

285.   CHERRY   LILLIS[11]   HALL   (*Frank*[10], *Hiram*[9], *Emmorancy*[8]*Johnson*, *Charles*[7], *Ira*[6], *Jonathan*[5], *Nathaniel*[4], *Nathaniel*[3], *Humphrey*[2], *John*[1]) was born on 7 May 1917 at Edwards, St. Lawrence Co., NY. She married Philip Franklin McCarthy on 6 Apr 1934 at Harrisville, Lewis Co., NY.

Children of Cherry Lillis[11] Hall and Philip Franklin McCarthy are as follows:

> i.   PHILIP FRANKLIN[12] JR.; born 5 Jul 1935 at Harrisville, NY; married Diane Boyd.
>
> 593.   ii.   RICHARD GEORGE SR., born 9 Mar 1937 at Pitcairn, NY; married Hildegarde Specht.
>
> iii.   MARILYN JUNE; born 14 Jan 1941 at Harrisville, NY; married Jay Stevens.
>
> iv.   MARIE LOUISE; born 28 Oct 1949 at Cathage, NY.
>
> She was unmarried.

286.   FREDERICK   GEORGE[11]   HALL   (*Frank*[10], *Hiram*[9], *Emmorancy*[8]*Johnson*, *Charles*[7], *Ira*[6], *Jonathan*[5], *Nathaniel*[4], *Nathaniel*[3], *Humphrey*[2], *John*[1]) was born on 22 Jul 1924 at Edwards, St. Lawrence Co., NY. He married Doris Jones.

Children of Frederick George[11] Hall and Doris Jones are as follows:

    i.   MICHAEL[12].

    ii.   MARK.

287.   SETH ALFRED[11] WARD (*Bruce[10]*, *Venila[9]Hall*, *Emmorancy[8]Johnson*, *Charles[7]*, *Ira[6]*, *Jonathan[5]*, *Nathaniel[4]*, *Nathaniel[3]*, *Humphrey[2]*, *John[1]*) was born on 26 Aug 1901 at Edwards, St. Lawrence Co., NY. He married Gladys McLeod, daughter of George McLeod and Amy (--?--), on 5 Jul 1930 at Rochester, Monroe Co., NY.

Children of Seth Alfred[11] Ward and Gladys McLeod are as follows:

    i.   NORMAN[12] lived in 1980 at Black River.

    ii.   ERWIN lived in 1980 at Goleta, CA.

288.   MARY ROSE[11] WARD (*Bruce[10]*, *Venila[9]Hall*, *Emmorancy[8]Johnson*, *Charles[7]*, *Ira[6]*, *Jonathan[5]*, *Nathaniel[4]*, *Nathaniel[3]*, *Humphrey[2]*, *John[1]*) was born on 30 Jan 1903 at Fine, St. Lawrence Co., NY. She married Durward Eugene Cole on 27 Nov 1924 at Gouverneur, St. Lawrence Co., NY.

Children of Mary Rose[11] Ward and Durward Eugene Cole are as follows:

  594.   i.   DORIS RUTH[12], born 6 Oct 1926 at Pitcairn, NY; married Melvin Anthony Hurley.

         ii.   HELEN LOUISE; born 17 Jun 1931 at Edwards, St. Lawrence Co., NY; married Myron K. Exford 29 Apr 1951 at Russell, St. Lawrence Co., NY.

289.   BOWER WILLIAM[11] WARD (*Bruce[10]*, *Venila[9]Hall*, *Emmorancy[8]Johnson*, *Charles[7]*, *Ira[6]*, *Jonathan[5]*, *Nathaniel[4]*, *Nathaniel[3]*, *Humphrey[2]*, *John[1]*) was born on 15 Feb 1905 at Fine, St. Lawrence Co., NY. He married Hilda Cockayne on 20 Nov 1941 at Massena, St. Lawrence Co., NY. He died on 7 Apr 1978 at House of Good Samaritan Hospital, Watertown, Jefferson Co., NY, at age 73. He was buried at Clare Cemetery, Clare, NY.

Children of Bower William[11] Ward and Hilda Cockayne are:

    i.   BARBARA[12]; married Willis Hence.

290.   GERALD BERT[11] WARD (*Bruce[10]*, *Venila[9]Hall*, *Emmorancy[8]Johnson*, *Charles[7]*, *Ira[6]*, *Jonathan[5]*, *Nathaniel[4]*, *Nathaniel[3]*, *Humphrey[2]*, *John[1]*) was born on 27 Jan 1907 at Fine, St. Lawrence Co., NY. He married Lucille Reed on 28 Oct 1944 at Richville, St. Lawrence Co., NY. He died on 27 Dec 1966 at Edward John Noble Hospital, Gouverneur, St. Lawrence Co., NY, at age 59. He was buried on 30 Dec 1966 at Fairview Cemetery, Edwards, St. Lawrence Co., NY.

Children of Gerald Bert[11] Ward and Lucille Reed were as follows:

  595.   i.   BONNIE[12], married Gary Hall.
  596.   ii.   MAXINE, married Larry Folsom.
         iii.   ESTHER; born Nov 1948; died 1948; buried at Fairview Cemetery, Edwards, St. Lawrence Co., NY.

291.   IRENE MILDRED[11] WARD (*Bruce[10]*, *Venila[9]Hall*, *Emmorancy[8]Johnson*, *Charles[7]*, *Ira[6]*, *Jonathan[5]*, *Nathaniel[4]*, *Nathaniel[3]*, *Humphrey[2]*, *John[1]*) was born on 2 May 1920 at Edwards, St. Lawrence Co., NY. She married Paul Mullaney. She married Earl Reed Jr. She married Silas Woodrow Whitford.

Children of Irene Mildred[11] Ward and Paul Mullaney are as follows:

  597.   i.   PATRICK PAUL[12], born 21 May 1939; married Dawn Fuller.
  598.   ii.   PATRICIA, born 19 Jul 1941; married Wayne LaPlante.

Children of Irene Mildred[11] Ward and Earl Reed Jr. are as follows:

  599.   i.   EARLENE[12], married Gary Bigeral.
  600.   ii.   RONALD, born 24 Jul 1943; married Sally Schryer.

Children of Irene Mildred[11] Ward and Silas Woodrow Whitford were as follows:

601. i. WILLIAM[12], born 21 Aug 1953; married Sherry Burnett.
602. ii. JAMES, born 7 Mar 1955; married Crystal Saur.
603. iii. VICKI, born 4 Oct 1957; married William Church.
604. iv. KENNETH, born 25 Aug 1961; married Donna Thornton.
605. v. RICKY, born 20 Jun 1964; married JoAnn Harrington.

292. MYRTLE MAY[11] MAYBEE (*Lena*[10]*Ward*, *Venila*[9]*Hall*, *Emmorancy*[8]*Johnson*, *Charles*[7], *Ira*[6], *Jonathan*[5], *Nathaniel*[4], *Nathaniel*[3], *Humphrey*[2], *John*[1]) was born on 18 Jul 1893 at Edwards, St. Lawrence Co., NY. She married Roy John Mason, son of Bion Mason and Anna Smith, on 27 Dec 1911 at Antwerp, Jefferson Co., NY. She died on 28 Oct 1985 at Canton United Helpers Home, Canton, St. Lawrence Co., NY, at age 92. She was buried on 31 Oct 1985 at Hillside Cemetery, Antwerp, Jefferson Co., NY.

Children of Myrtle May[11] Maybee and Roy John Mason are as follows:

606. i. ALBERT BION[12], born 16 Jan 1920 at Ogdensburg, St. Lawrence Co., NY; married Florence Gary; married Thelma Bellinger.
      ii. AZA MAY; born 15 Jun 1922 at Gouverneur, St. Lawrence Co., NY; married Walter Allen 3 Oct 1959 at Harrisville, Jefferson Co., NY.
607. iii. BETTIE VENILA, born 4 Jun 1924 at Gouverneur, St. Lawrence Co., NY; married Louis Hardy.
608. iv. WEBSTER ROY, born 16 Dec 1926; married Mary Currier.
609. v. EARL LESTER, born 5 May 1929 at Antwerp, Jefferson Co., NY; married Shirley Curr; married Donna Flight.

610.   vi.   CHARLES ROY, born 18 Feb 1942 at Gouverneur, St. Lawrence Co., NY; married Sally Hendrick.

293.   EVELYN VENILA[11] MAYBEE (*Lena[10]Ward, Venila[9]Hall, Emmorancy[8]Johnson, Charles[7], Ira[6], Jonathan[5], Nathaniel[4], Nathaniel[3], Humphrey[2], John[1]*) was born on 27 Apr 1900 at Newton Falls, St. Lawrence Co., NY. She married Meryl Bradigan.

Children of Evelyn Venila[11] Maybee and Meryl Bradigan are as follows:

    i.   LENA[12].
    ii. EILEEN.
    iii. (--?--).
    iv. (--?--).

294.   MAUDE ESTHER[11] SHAMPINE (*Margaret[10]Ward, Venila[9]Hall, Emmorancy[8]Johnson, Charles[7], Ira[6], Jonathan[5], Nathaniel[4], Nathaniel[3], Humphrey[2], John[1]*) was born on 29 Apr 1906 at Antwerp, Jefferson Co., NY. She married Edward Spalding Smingler on 2 May 1937 at Syracuse, Onondaga Co., NY.

She lived in 1979 at Erie, PA.

Children of Maude Esther[11] Shampine and Edward Spalding Smingler are:

    i.   JANETTE WARD[12]; born 5 Feb 1939 at Utica, Oneida Co., NY.
       She was unmarried.

295.   EDWARD LAWRENCE[11] WARD (*Howard[10], Venila[9]Hall, Emmorancy[8]Johnson, Charles[7], Ira[6], Jonathan[5], Nathaniel[4], Nathaniel[3], Humphrey[2], John[1]*) was born on 24 May 1916 at Edwards, St. Lawrence Co., NY. He married Mildred Dorothy Maxiner, daughter of Ira Maxiner, on 20 Jun 1934 at Edwards, St. Lawrence Co., NY. He died on 1 May 1936 at St. Joseph's Zinc Mine, Edwards, St. Lawrence Co., NY, at age 19. He was buried on 4 May 1936 at Fairview Cemetery, Edwards, St. Lawrence Co., NY.

Children of Edward Lawrence[11] Ward and Mildred Dorothy Maxiner were:

    i.   DONALD[12]; born circa 1935; died 1936.

217

He lived on 16 Mar 1960 at Clinton, Oneida Co., NY.

296. RUTH[11] MORGAN (*Edith[10]Ward, Venila[9]Hall, Emmorancy[8]Johnson, Charles[7], Ira[6], Jonathan[5], Nathaniel[4], Nathaniel[3], Humphrey[2], John[1]*) was born on 26 Sep 1932 at Syracuse, Onondaga Co., NY. She married Armand Dumont on 3 Jan 1953. She died on 6 Feb 1990 at NY at age 57.

She lived in 1979 at Syracuse, Onondaga Co., NY.

Children of Ruth[11] Morgan and Armand Dumont are as follows:

       i.   JOANNA[12]; born 9 Sep 1955.

611.   ii. DONNA, born 29 Jan 1957; married Charles Richard Emler.

      iii. PAUL; born 27 Jun 1967.

297. JEANNINE[11] MORGAN (*Edith[10]Ward, Venila[9]Hall, Emmorancy[8]Johnson, Charles[7], Ira[6], Jonathan[5], Nathaniel[4], Nathaniel[3], Humphrey[2], John[1]*) was born on 7 Nov 1933 at Syracuse, Onondaga Co., NY. She married Leo Lynch on 28 Aug 1954.

She lived in 1979 at Brookdale, St. Lawrence Co., NY.

Children of Jeannine[11] Morgan and Leo Lynch are as follows:

612.   i. NANCY JEAN[12], born 8 Oct 1955 at Massena, St. Lawrence Co., NY; married Gary Ross Wells.

613.   ii. MICHAEL LEO, born 15 Aug 1956 at Massena, NY; married Brenda Deleel.

      iii. PATRICK JAMES; born 9 Jan 1958 at Massena, NY; married Sarah Lynn Stevens 29 Sep 1984 at Brasher Falls, NY.

614.   iv. CONSTANCE ANN, born 31 Jan 1959 at Massena, St. Lawrence Co., NY; married Allen David Pike.

      v. MARY JANE; born 8 Mar 1961 at Massena, St. Lawrence Co., NY; married Bruce Wayne Watkins 26 Mar 1983 at Brasher Falls, St. Lawrence Co., NY.

      vi. MAUREEN ELIZABETH; born 21 Aug 1962 at Massena, St. Lawrence Co., NY.

vii.   DENNIS CHARLES; born 13 Feb 1965 at Massena, NY.

298.   CHARLOTTE ANNE[11] MORGAN (*Edith*[10]*Ward, Venila*[9]*Hall, Emmorancy*[8]*Johnson, Charles*[7], *Ira*[6], *Jonathan*[5], *Nathaniel*[4], *Nathaniel*[3], *Humphrey*[2], *John*[1]) was born on 30 Jan 1936 at Syracuse, Onondoga Co., NY. She married Donald Posewitz on 19 Feb 1955 at Massena, St. Lawrence Co., NY.

She lived at Clay, Onondaga Co., NY.

Children of Charlotte Anne[11] Morgan and Donald Posewitz both born at Massena, St. Lawrence Co., NY, are as follows:

i.   RAY E.[12]; born 23 Oct 1961.

ii.   RACHAEL A.; born 3 Dec 1962.

299.   FRIEDA LOUISE[11] NEWVINE (*Cecile*[10]*Pratt, Venira*[9]*Hall, Emmorancy*[8]*Johnson, Charles*[7], *Ira*[6], *Jonathan*[5], *Nathaniel*[4], *Nathaniel*[3], *Humphrey*[2], *John*[1]) was born on 24 Apr 1913 at Edwards, St. Lawrence Co., NY. She married Ralph Boni. She died in Jan 1963 at Syracuse, Onondoga Co., NY, at age 49.

Children of Frieda Louise[11] Newvine and Ralph Boni are as follows:

615.   i.   CORINNE ANN[12], born 19 May 1935 at Gouverneur, St. Lawrence Co., NY; married Kenny Jones.

616.   ii.   JANET KAY, born 20 Nov 1938 at Gouverneur, St. Lawrence Co., NY; married Robert Manning.

300.   WILLIAM[11] PRATT (*Harley*[10], *Venira*[9]*Hall, Emmorancy*[8]*Johnson, Charles*[7], *Ira*[6], *Jonathan*[5], *Nathaniel*[4], *Nathaniel*[3], *Humphrey*[2], *John*[1]) was born on 19 Sep 1920 at Benson Mines, NY. He married Frances Morgan on 24 Nov 1944 at Edwards, St. Lawrence Co., NY.

Children of William[11] Pratt and Frances Morgan are as follows:

617.   i.   JOY[12], born 5 Jan 1947 at Geneva, NY; married Marcel Massenet.

618.   ii.   JOSEPH, born 23 Aug 1948 at Gouverneur, St. Lawrence Co., NY; married Carol McIntosh.

iii. JILL; born 8 Feb 1950 at Gouverneur, St. Lawrence Co., NY; married David Schaefer at Lowville, NY.

619. iv. JOHN, born 14 Nov 1953 at Gouverneur, St. Lawrence Co., NY; married Rochelle Seovey.

620. v. JENNIFER, born 8 Sep 1955 at Gouverneur, St. Lawrence Co., NY; married Brent Yaple.

621. vi. JEFFREY, born 30 Sep 1957 at Gouverneur, St. Lawrence Co., NY; married Romona Normand.

622. vii. JACQUELINE THERESA, born 8 Aug 1959 at Gouverneur, St. Lawrence Co., NY; married Thomas Gates.

viii. JASON; born 22 Feb 1965 at Gouverneur, St. Lawrence Co., NY.

301. DONALD[11] PRATT (*Harley*[10], *Venira*[9]*Hall*, *Emmorancy*[8]*Johnson*, *Charles*[7], *Ira*[6], *Jonathan*[5], *Nathaniel*[4], *Nathaniel*[3], *Humphrey*[2], *John*[1]) was born in Apr 1923 at Edwards, St. Lawrence Co., NY. He married Pauline Briggs at Edwards, St. Lawrence Co., NY.

Children of Donald[11] Pratt and Pauline Briggs are:

i. RICHARD[12].

302. CLIFFORD[11] PRATT (*Harley*[10], *Venira*[9]*Hall*, *Emmorancy*[8]*Johnson*, *Charles*[7], *Ira*[6], *Jonathan*[5], *Nathaniel*[4], *Nathaniel*[3], *Humphrey*[2], *John*[1]) was born in Apr 1925 at Edwards, St. Lawrence Co., NY. He married Faye Iaria at Auburn, NY.

Children of Clifford[11] Pratt and Faye Iaria are as follows:

i. KENT[12].
ii. DIANE.

303. NOLA ESTELLA[11] BURBRIDGE (*Alice*[10]*Main*, *John*[9], *Lutilia*[8]*Johnson*, *George*[7], *Ira*[6], *Jonathan*[5], *Nathaniel*[4], *Nathaniel*[3], *Humphrey*[2], *John*[1]) married Bert Havener.

Children of Nola Estella[11] Burbridge and Bert Havener are as follows:

623.   i.   FOREST B.[12] SR., born 1901; married Louise Bodine.

        ii.   VIOLET; born 1907; married Fredrick D. Mitchell.

304. FLOYD[11] BURBRIDGE (*Alice*[10]*Main, John*[9], *Lutilia*[8]*Johnson, George*[7], *Ira*[6], *Jonathan*[5], *Nathaniel*[4], *Nathaniel*[3], *Humphrey*[2], *John*[1]) was born in 1885. He married Sadie Klenine.

He was also known as Lloyd Burbridge.

Children of Floyd[11] Burbridge and Sadie Klenine are as follows:

        i.   LYNDLE[12]; born 1907; married Maude Galloway.

624.   ii.   CHARLES EUGENE, born 1909; married Alline Marshall.

625.   iii.   THUMAN PAUL, born 1911; married Mildred Davey.

626.   iv.   FLOYD JR., born 1913; married Evelyn Guthrie.

        v.   IRVIN LEROY; born 1917; married Helen Anderson 1938.

305. ROSS[11] BURBRIDGE (*Alice*[10]*Main, John*[9], *Lutilia*[8]*Johnson, George*[7], *Ira*[6], *Jonathan*[5], *Nathaniel*[4], *Nathaniel*[3], *Humphrey*[2], *John*[1]) was born in 1887. He married Eva Yaeger.

Children of Ross[11] Burbridge and Eva Yaeger are:

627.   i.   DONNA[12], born 1917; married Wallace Brown.

306. OPAL[11] BURBRIDGE (*Alice*[10]*Main, John*[9], *Lutilia*[8]*Johnson, George*[7], *Ira*[6], *Jonathan*[5], *Nathaniel*[4], *Nathaniel*[3], *Humphrey*[2], *John*[1]) was born in 1889. She married Arthur Foster.

Children of Opal[11] Burbridge and Arthur Foster are:

628.   i.   GLEN[12], born 1919; married Lillian Lee.

307. RAYMOND EARL[11] JOHNSON (*Lena*[10]*Main, John*[9], *Lutilia*[8]*Johnson, George*[7], *Ira*[6], *Jonathan*[5], *Nathaniel*[4], *Nathaniel*[3], *Humphrey*[2], *John*[1]) was born in 1892. He married Daisy Moore. He married Lena Reeder.

Children of Raymond Earl[11] Johnson and Daisy Moore are as follows:

629.   i.   ORA RICHARD[12], born 1915; married Edna Harris.

630.   ii.   VERNA IONE, born 1917; married Patrick Malone.

631.   iii.   CHARLES RAYMOND, born 1919; married Helen Krause.

632.   iv.   MAYNARD EARL, born 1923; married Gladys Henry.

       v.   LONNIE EDWARD; born 1923; married Joyce Williams; married Lena Reeder.

Children of Raymond Earl[11] Johnson and Lena Reeder are as follows:

       i.   MARILYN JEAN[12]; born 1932.

       ii.   EARL RAY; born 1933.

       iii.   ALLEN WAYNE; born 1939.

308.   COY[11] JOHNSON (*Lena*[10]*Main, John*[9], *Lutilia*[8]*Johnson, George*[7], *Ira*[6], *Jonathan*[5], *Nathaniel*[4], *Nathaniel*[3], *Humphrey*[2], *John*[1]) was born on 2 Feb 1901. She married H. Gay Wassell in 1917 at Pittsfield, IL. She died on 26 Aug 1980 at age 79.

Children of Coy[11] Johnson and H. Gay Wassell are as follows:

633.   i.   WANNA[12], born 1918; married Vick Welton.

634.   ii.   OLIN, born 1921; married Shirley Rample.

       iii.   MARION; born 1926; married Rose Rample.
He lived in 2000 at Pittsfield, IL.

       iv.   DWAUN; born 1928; married Marjorie Schaffer.
He lived in 2000 at Pittsfield, IL.

       v.   TWYLA; born 1932; married (--?--) Brends; married (--?--) Kreigel.
She lived in 2000 at Jacksonville, IL.

309.   GEORGE CHRYSUP[11] MAIN (*Rufus*[10], *Alvin*[9], *Lutilia*[8]*Johnson, George*[7], *Ira*[6], *Jonathan*[5], *Nathaniel*[4],

Nathaniel[3], *Humphrey*[2], *John*[1]) was born in 1897. He married Helen Margaret Kubesch. He died in 1936.

Children of George Chrysup[11] Main and Helen Margaret Kubesch were as follows:

  i.   GEORGE CARLTON[12]; born 1927; married Opal McKee.
  ii. HENRY FRANK; born 1932; died 1946.

310. RUTH NYE[11] MAIN (*Rufus*[10], *Alvin*[9], *Lutilia*[8]*Johnson*, *George*[7], *Ira*[6], *Jonathan*[5], *Nathaniel*[4], *Nathaniel*[3], *Humphrey*[2], *John*[1]) was born in 1908. She married Alfred Koeler.

Children of Ruth Nye[11] Main and Alfred Koeler are as follows:

  i.   BARBARA JOSEPHINE[12]; born 1936.
  ii. ROBERT MARION; born 1940.

311. JOSEPHINE BARNEY[11] MAIN (*Rufus*[10], *Alvin*[9], *Lutilia*[8]*Johnson*, *George*[7], *Ira*[6], *Jonathan*[5], *Nathaniel*[4], *Nathaniel*[3], *Humphrey*[2], *John*[1]) was born on 13 Feb 1912. She married Harry Budd Atkinson.

Children of Josephine Barney[11] Main and Harry Budd Atkinson are as follows:

  i.   HENRY[12]; born 1938.
  ii. ELIZABETH; born 1940.

312. ELIZABETH[11] GAY (*Blanch*[10]*Main*, *Alvin*[9], *Lutilia*[8]*Johnson*, *George*[7], *Ira*[6], *Jonathan*[5], *Nathaniel*[4], *Nathaniel*[3], *Humphrey*[2], *John*[1]) was born in 1895. She married Frank Lewis.

Children of Elizabeth[11] Gay and Frank Lewis are:

  635.   i.   GENEVIEVE GAY[12], born 1915; married Robert William DeWolf.

313. ALVIN MAIN[11] WARDEN (*Rose*[10]*Main*, *Alvin*[9], *Lutilia*[8]*Johnson*, *George*[7], *Ira*[6], *Jonathan*[5], *Nathaniel*[4], *Nathaniel*[3], *Humphrey*[2], *John*[1]) was born in 1908. He married Sylvia Callahan. He married Grace Eileen Joseph.

Children of Alvin Main[11] Warden and Sylvia Callahan are:

i. LINDA JEAN^{12}; born 1943.

There were no children of Alvin Main^{11} Warden and Grace Eileen Joseph.

314. JOHN SEVIER^{11} WARDEN (*Rose^{10}Main, Alvin^9, Lutilia^{8}Johnson, George^7, Ira^6, Jonathan^5, Nathaniel^4, Nathaniel^3, Humphrey^2, John^1*) was born in 1914. He married Helen Louise McCrory.

Children of John Sevier^{11} Warden and Helen Louise McCrory are:

i. ROSALIE JOAN^{12}; born 1943.

315. ALVIN NYE^{11} MAIN II (*Roscoe^{10}, Alvin^9, Lutilia^{8}Johnson, George^7, Ira^6, Jonathan^5, Nathaniel^4, Nathaniel^3, Humphrey^2, John^1*) was born in 1918. He married June Kelly.

Children of Alvin Nye^{11} Main II and June Kelly are as follows:

i. ANDREW KELLY^{12}; born 1943.
ii. BARBARA RUTH; born 1945.
iii. CARL DOUGLAS; born 1947.

316. NATHANIEL FOOTE^{11} MAIN (*Roscoe^{10}, Alvin^9, Lutilia^{8}Johnson, George^7, Ira^6, Jonathan^5, Nathaniel^4, Nathaniel^3, Humphrey^2, John^1*) was born in 1920. He married Barbara Jean Cheda. He married Davney Olson.

There were no children of Nathaniel Foote^{11} Main and Barbara Jean Cheda.

Children of Nathaniel Foote^{11} Main and Davney Olson are as follows:

i. DERRICK OLSON^{12}; born 1951.
ii. DARREN CHRISTIAN; born 1956.

317. PETER SWINEFORD^{11} MAIN (*Roscoe^{10}, Alvin^9, Lutilia^{8}Johnson, George^7, Ira^6, Jonathan^5, Nathaniel^4, Nathaniel^3, Humphrey^2, John^1*) was born in 1922. He married Estella Ashley.

Children of Peter Swineford[11] Main and Estella Ashley are as follows:

    i.   CHRISTOPHER ALVIN[12]; born 1948.

    ii.   CAROL ANN; born 1950.

    iii.   WILLIAM EDWARD; born 1954.

318. RUFUS WILLIAM[11] MAIN (*Roscoe[10]*, *Alvin[9]*, *Lutilia[8]Johnson*, *George[7]*, *Ira[6]*, *Jonathan[5]*, *Nathaniel[4]*, *Nathaniel[3]*, *Humphrey[2]*, *John[1]*) was born in 1925. He married Mary Lou Murphy.

Children of Rufus William[11] Main and Mary Lou Murphy are as follows:

    i.   KAREN LOUISE[12]; born 1950.

    ii.   ROBERT KEVIN; born 1952.

    iii.   DAVID STAFFORD; born 1953.

319. SARAH FLOWER[11] MAIN (*Roscoe[10]*, *Alvin[9]*, *Lutilia[8]Johnson*, *George[7]*, *Ira[6]*, *Jonathan[5]*, *Nathaniel[4]*, *Nathaniel[3]*, *Humphrey[2]*, *John[1]*) was born in 1928. She married Carl Emil Johnson.

Children of Sarah Flower[11] Main and Carl Emil Johnson are as follows:

    i.   ERIC STAFFORD[12]; born 1954.

    ii.   LISA RUTH; born 1956.

320. MARGURITE[11] MAIN (*Francis[10]*, *Alvin[9]*, *Lutilia[8]Johnson*, *George[7]*, *Ira[6]*, *Jonathan[5]*, *Nathaniel[4]*, *Nathaniel[3]*, *Humphrey[2]*, *John[1]*) was born in 1906. She married John Zimmerman.

Children of Margurite[11] Main and John Zimmerman are:

    i.   ROGER FRANK[12]; born 1936.

321. BERNEICE SCANLAND[11] MAIN (*Francis[10]*, *Alvin[9]*, *Lutilia[8]Johnson*, *George[7]*, *Ira[6]*, *Jonathan[5]*, *Nathaniel[4]*, *Nathaniel[3]*, *Humphrey[2]*, *John[1]*) was born in 1908. She married Cecile W. Martin.

Children of Berneice Scanland[11] Main and Cecile W. Martin are:

    i.   MURRAY[12]; born 1934.

322.   ROSS[11]   SUTHERLAND   (*Lottie*[10]*Main,   Phillip*[9], *Lutilia*[8]*Johnson,   George*[7],   *Ira*[6],   *Jonathan*[5],   *Nathaniel*[4], *Nathaniel*[3], *Humphrey*[2], *John*[1]) was born in 1897. He married Mary Hook. He married Dorothy Kanady. He married Rita (--?--).

Children of Ross[11] Sutherland and Mary Hook are as follows:

i.   PHYLLIS[12];   born   1926;   married   Walter Pendergast.

ii.   ANNE; born 1930.

323.   STELLA[11]   SUTHERLAND   (*Lottie*[10]*Main,   Phillip*[9], *Lutilia*[8]*Johnson,   George*[7],   *Ira*[6],   *Jonathan*[5],   *Nathaniel*[4], *Nathaniel*[3], *Humphrey*[2], *John*[1]) was born in 1908. She married Derrill Angst.

Children of Stella[11] Sutherland and Derrill Angst are as follows:

i.   PHILIP[12]; born 1940.

ii.   DAVID; born 1943.

324. SYLVIA MABLE[11] MAIN (*Odus*[10], *Andrew*[9], *Lutilia*[8]*Johnson, George*[7], *Ira*[6], *Jonathan*[5], *Nathaniel*[4], *Nathaniel*[3], *Humphrey*[2], *John*[1]) was born in 1897. She married William Andrew Morgan.

Children of Sylvia Mable[11] Main and William Andrew Morgan are as follows:

i.   LOIS MURIEL RUBY[12]; born 1926.

ii.   WILLIAM ANDREW ROLLAND; born 1945.

325.   EMMET   ARNOLD[11]   MAIN   (*Odus*[10],   *Andrew*[9], *Lutilia*[8]*Johnson,   George*[7],   *Ira*[6],   *Jonathan*[5],   *Nathaniel*[4], *Nathaniel*[3], *Humphrey*[2], *John*[1]) was born in 1901. He married Lulu E. Skinner.

Children of Emmet Arnold[11] Main and Lulu E. Skinner are as follows:

636.   i.   KENNETH R.[12], born 1923; married Mildred Smith.

637.   ii.   EUGENE I., born 1925; married Evelyn Reynold.

iii.   WILMA; born 1927; married James Louthan.

638. iv. EMMET E., born 1930; married Thelma Horton.

v. ROBERT M.; born 1933; married Dean Mills.

639. vi. DORIS J., born 1936; married Raymond Reimer.

326. AGEE GALE[11] MAIN (*Odus*[10], *Andrew*[9], *Lutilia*[8]*Johnson*, *George*[7], *Ira*[6], *Jonathan*[5], *Nathaniel*[4], *Nathaniel*[3], *Humphrey*[2], *John*[1]) was born in 1903. He married Lavillea Gillian.

Children of Agee Gale[11] Main and Lavillea Gillian are as follows:

i. ROBERT[12]; born 1925.

ii. DONALD; born 1926.

327. SUSIE ELIZABETH[11] MAIN (*Odus*[10], *Andrew*[9], *Lutilia*[8]*Johnson*, *George*[7], *Ira*[6], *Jonathan*[5], *Nathaniel*[4], *Nathaniel*[3], *Humphrey*[2], *John*[1]) was born in 1906. She married Earl Ruby. She married Glenn Allen. She married All Crews.

Children of Susie Elizabeth[11] Main and Earl Ruby are as follows:

i. BRANSFORD M.[12]; born 1924 at Liberty, KS.

640. ii. LOIS MURIEL, born 1926; married Thadeus Elkins.

Children of Susie Elizabeth[11] Main and Glenn Allen are as follows:

641. i. JOY MABLE[12], born 1929; married Ronald Niles.

642. ii. LOLITA MAY, married Julius Earl Long.

643. iii. JAMES M., born 1933; married Velma Lee Skidmore.

644. iv. INA MARGO, born 1941; married Edward Roy.

Children of Susie Elizabeth[11] Main and All Crews are:

i. ALICE A.[12]; born 1945.

328. VAUGHN[11] MAIN (*Lonnie*[10], *Andrew*[9], *Lutilia*[8]*Johnson*, *George*[7], *Ira*[6], *Jonathan*[5], *Nathaniel*[4], *Nathaniel*[3], *Humphrey*[2], *John*[1]) was born in 1903. He married Lottie M. Wood.

Children of Vaughn[11] Main and Lottie M. Wood are:

i. VERNON G.[12]; born 1944.

329. ERNEST W.[11] MAIN (*Lonnie*[10], *Andrew*[9], *Lutilia*[8]*Johnson*, *George*[7], *Ira*[6], *Jonathan*[5], *Nathaniel*[4], *Nathaniel*[3], *Humphrey*[2], *John*[1]) was born in 1906. He married Frances Martin.

Children of Ernest W.[11] Main and Frances Martin are as follows:

    i.   JOAN E.[12]; born 1937.
    ii. MARY JANE; born 1939.
    iii. FRANKLIN E.; born 1941.
    iv. RUTH E.; born 1942.

330. RAY O.[11] MAIN (*Lonnie*[10], *Andrew*[9], *Lutilia*[8]*Johnson*, *George*[7], *Ira*[6], *Jonathan*[5], *Nathaniel*[4], *Nathaniel*[3], *Humphrey*[2], *John*[1]) was born in 1908. He married Evelyn Frances Clough.

Children of Ray O.[11] Main and Evelyn Frances Clough are as follows:

    i. SUSAN DOROTHY[12]; born 1937.
    ii. ROBERT RAY; born 1939.

331. AARON[11] MAIN (*Lonnie*[10], *Andrew*[9], *Lutilia*[8]*Johnson*, *George*[7], *Ira*[6], *Jonathan*[5], *Nathaniel*[4], *Nathaniel*[3], *Humphrey*[2], *John*[1]) was born in 1910. He married Ella Pearl Woods. He died in 1936.

Children of Aaron[11] Main and Ella Pearl Woods are as follows:

    i. ELMER[12]; born 1932.
    ii. ANDA; born 1933.

332. PARKER EMERY[11] MAIN (*Lonnie*[10], *Andrew*[9], *Lutilia*[8]*Johnson*, *George*[7], *Ira*[6], *Jonathan*[5], *Nathaniel*[4], *Nathaniel*[3], *Humphrey*[2], *John*[1]) was born in 1912. He married Hazel Osburn.

Children of Parker Emery[11] Main and Hazel Osburn are:

    i. FRED EMERY[12]; born 1937.

333. TRACY L.[11] MAIN (*Lonnie*[10], *Andrew*[9], *Lutilia*[8]*Johnson*, *George*[7], *Ira*[6], *Jonathan*[5], *Nathaniel*[4], *Nathaniel*[3], *Humphrey*[2], *John*[1]) was born in 1914. He married Virginia Zamboni.

Children of Tracy L.[11] Main and Virginia Zamboni are as follows:

    i.   RICHARD MARION[12]; born 1937.

         He was also known as RICHARD MARVIN MAIN.

    ii. LORNA JEAN; born 1940.

334. CLEDA[11] MAIN (*Byard*[10], *Andrew*[9], *Lutilia*[8]*Johnson*, *George*[7], *Ira*[6], *Jonathan*[5], *Nathaniel*[4], *Nathaniel*[3], *Humphrey*[2], *John*[1]) was born in 1900. She married Martin R. Hoover.

Children of Cleda[11] Main and Martin R. Hoover are:

    i.   JOHN[12].

335. EVELYN[11] MAIN (*Byard*[10], *Andrew*[9], *Lutilia*[8]*Johnson*, *George*[7], *Ira*[6], *Jonathan*[5], *Nathaniel*[4], *Nathaniel*[3], *Humphrey*[2], *John*[1]) was born on 30 Apr 1902 at Nebo, Pike Co., IL. She married Emil Hobbs on 9 Oct 1923.

Children of Evelyn[11] Main and Emil Hobbs are as follows:

  645.   i.   LAVON[12], born 1924; married Gertrude Roberts; divorced Gertrude Roberts; married Peggy Dacey Morris.

         ii. ELDONNA; born 1929.

336. GEORGIA[11] MAIN (*Byard*[10], *Andrew*[9], *Lutilia*[8]*Johnson*, *George*[7], *Ira*[6], *Jonathan*[5], *Nathaniel*[4], *Nathaniel*[3], *Humphrey*[2], *John*[1]) was born in 1904. She married Coy Doyle. She married Wayne Harpole at Nebo, IL.

There were no children of Georgia[11] Main and Coy Doyle.

Children of Georgia[11] Main and Wayne Harpole are:

  646.   i.   LILLIAN[12], born 1927; married Dallas Barton.

337. LOTTIE[11] MAIN (*Byard*[10], *Andrew*[9], *Lutilia*[8]*Johnson*, *George*[7], *Ira*[6], *Jonathan*[5], *Nathaniel*[4], *Nathaniel*[3], *Humphrey*[2], *John*[1]) was born in 1914. She married Floyd Flowers.

Children of Lottie[11] Main and Floyd Flowers are as follows:

      i.   LILLIAN IRENE[12]; born 1939.

     ii.   DOROTHY JEAN; born 1940.

    iii.   WAYNE; born 1944.

    iv.   PATRICIA ANN; born 1945.

     v.   GLADYS; born 1947.

    vi.   CAROL MAY; born 1950.

   vii.   RAYMOND EUGENE; born 1951.

  viii.   KENNETH LEE; born 1954.

338.   BERTRAM[11] MAIN (*Byard[10]*, *Andrew[9]*, *Lutilia[8]Johnson*, *George[7]*, *Ira[6]*, *Jonathan[5]*, *Nathaniel[4]*, *Nathaniel[3]*, *Humphrey[2]*, *John[1]*) was born in 1916. He married Ellen Morrison. He married Helen Kelly.

Children of Bertram[11] Main and Ellen Morrison are as follows:

     i.   STEPHANIE[12]; born 1939.

     ii.   MICHAEL; born 1941.

Children of Bertram[11] Main and Helen Kelly are as follows:

     i.   LARRY DENNIS[12]; born 1947.

     ii.   GREGORY FRANKLIN; born 1949.

    iii.   GLENDON CALVIN; born 1949.

    iv.   BYRON CLAVIN; born 1954.

339.   ZENNA B.[11] MAIN (*Harry[10]*, *Andrew[9]*, *Lutilia[8]Johnson*, *George[7]*, *Ira[6]*, *Jonathan[5]*, *Nathaniel[4]*, *Nathaniel[3]*, *Humphrey[2]*, *John[1]*) was born in 1913. She married Burley Bohannon. She married James Culbertson.

Children of Zenna B.[11] Main and Burley Bohannon are as follows:

     i.   RALPH[12]; born 1932.

     ii.   PHYLIS; born 1935.

Children of Zenna B.[11] Main and James Culbertson are:

     i.   JAMES ERNEST[12]; born 1953.

340.   ELSIE ELLA[11] MAIN (*Harry[10]*, *Andrew[9]*, *Lutilia[8]Johnson*, *George[7]*, *Ira[6]*, *Jonathan[5]*, *Nathaniel[4]*, *Nathaniel[3]*, *Humphrey[2]*, *John[1]*) was born in 1921. She married William E. Childres.

Children of Elsie Ella[11] Main and William E. Childres were as follows:

    i.   GARY WILLIAM[12]; born 1941.

    ii.   JAN KATHLEEN; born 1944; died 1944.

    iii.   WAYNE; born 1946.

341.   DOROTHY ISABELLE[11] MAIN (*Harry*[10], *Andrew*[9], *Lutilia*[8]*Johnson*, *George*[7], *Ira*[6], *Jonathan*[5], *Nathaniel*[4], *Nathaniel*[3], *Humphrey*[2], *John*[1]) was born in 1923. She married Oliver E. Phillips.

Children of Dorothy Isabelle[11] Main and Oliver E. Phillips are as follows:

    i.   LARRY OLIVER[12]; born 1943.

        He was also known as LARRY ALVIN PHILLIPS.

    ii.   RICHARD MARSHALL; born 1945.

    iii.   MARJORIE DOROTHY; born 1949.

342.   IDA RHEA[11] MAIN (*Harry*[10], *Andrew*[9], *Lutilia*[8]*Johnson*, *George*[7], *Ira*[6], *Jonathan*[5], *Nathaniel*[4], *Nathaniel*[3], *Humphrey*[2], *John*[1]) was born in 1926. She married Robert V. Callen.

Children of Ida Rhea[11] Main and Robert V. Callen are as follows:

    i.   ROBERT RHEA[12]; born 1945.

    ii.   JAMES VINCENT; born 1948.

    iii.   MARIANNE; born 1954.

343.   CECIL[11] MAIN (*Carrie*[10], *Andrew*[9], *Lutilia*[8]*Johnson*, *George*[7], *Ira*[6], *Jonathan*[5], *Nathaniel*[4], *Nathaniel*[3], *Humphrey*[2], *John*[1]) was born in 1908. She married Arley Shelton.

Children of Cecil[11] Main and Arley Shelton were as follows:

647.   i.   MILDRED[12], born 1930; married (--?--) LeBrun.

       ii.   LYLE NORVEL; born 1931; died 1933.

       iii.   LILLIE; born 1934; married Carol Nelson.

       iv.   JO'AN; born 1936.

       v.   JACK; born 1938.

vi.   BETTY; born 1940.

344.   JOHN[11] MAIN (*Carrie*[10], *Andrew*[9], *Lutilia*[8]*Johnson*, *George*[7], *Ira*[6], *Jonathan*[5], *Nathaniel*[4], *Nathaniel*[3], *Humphrey*[2], *John*[1]) was born in 1910. He married Madeline McLean.

Children of John[11] Main and Madeline McLean are as follows:

    i.   ROBERT[12]; born 1944.
   ii.   ANNE; born 1945.

345.   KENNETH[11] MAIN (*Carrie*[10], *Andrew*[9], *Lutilia*[8]*Johnson*, *George*[7], *Ira*[6], *Jonathan*[5], *Nathaniel*[4], *Nathaniel*[3], *Humphrey*[2], *John*[1]) was born in 1912. He married Thelma Goetz.

Children of Kenneth[11] Main and Thelma Goetz are as follows:

648.   i.   PHYLLIS[12], born 1932; married Richard Potuzak.
       ii.   EARL; born 1933.
     iii.   SHIRLEY; born 1935; married Robert Siever.
     iv.   FRANCIS; born 1937.
      v.   CARRY; born 1938.
     vi.   HELEN; born 1940.
    vii.   BARBARA; born 1944.
   viii.   THEODORE; born 1945.
     ix.   LINDA; born 1947.

346.   GLADYS[11] MAIN (*Carrie*[10], *Andrew*[9], *Lutilia*[8]*Johnson*, *George*[7], *Ira*[6], *Jonathan*[5], *Nathaniel*[4], *Nathaniel*[3], *Humphrey*[2], *John*[1]) was born in 1914. She married Harry Owen.

Children of Gladys[11] Main and Harry Owen were as follows:

    i.   MELVIN[12]; born 1933; died 1954.
   ii.   ROBERT; born 1935; died 1954.
  iii.   JOYCE MARIE; born 1949.

347.   CLAUDIA[11] MAIN (*Carrie*[10], *Andrew*[9], *Lutilia*[8]*Johnson*, *George*[7], *Ira*[6], *Jonathan*[5], *Nathaniel*[4], *Nathaniel*[3], *Humphrey*[2], *John*[1]) was born in 1920. She married Roy Duncan.

Children of Claudia[11] Main and Roy Duncan are as follows:

    i.   RONALD ROY[12]; born 1955.

ii.   DOUGLAS DARRELL; born 1956.

348.   ELMER[11] MAIN (*Carrie*[10], *Andrew*[9], *Lutilia*[8]*Johnson*, *George*[7], *Ira*[6], *Jonathan*[5], *Nathaniel*[4], *Nathaniel*[3], *Humphrey*[2], *John*[1]) was born in 1921. He married Norma Haffey.

Children of Elmer[11] Main and Norma Haffey are as follows:

i.   LOREN[12]; born 1947.
ii.   DONALD DEAN; born 1948.
iii. CECILIA; born 1950.
iv.   SANDRA; born 1953.

349.   LAURA BETH[11] MAIN (*Carrie*[10], *Andrew*[9], *Lutilia*[8]*Johnson*, *George*[7], *Ira*[6], *Jonathan*[5], *Nathaniel*[4], *Nathaniel*[3], *Humphrey*[2], *John*[1]) was born in 1923. She married Oswald Mueller.

Children of Laura Beth[11] Main and Oswald Mueller are as follows:

i.   FREDDIE[12]; born 1944.
ii.   LARRY; born 1946.
iii. LORNE; born 1950.
iv.   LINDA; born 1952.

350.   PEARL[11] MAIN (*Carrie*[10], *Andrew*[9], *Lutilia*[8]*Johnson*, *George*[7], *Ira*[6], *Jonathan*[5], *Nathaniel*[4], *Nathaniel*[3], *Humphrey*[2], *John*[1]) was born in 1924. She married Albert Benner.

Children of Pearl[11] Main and Albert Benner are as follows:

i.   SHARON[12]; born 1943.
ii.   ALBERTA; born 1945.
iii. RICHARD; born 1947.
iv.   JAMES JACOB; born 1948.
v.   MARY; born 1949.
vi.   GARY.
vii. RODNEY; born 1953.

351.   CLIFFORD[11] MAIN JR. (*Carrie*[10], *Andrew*[9], *Lutilia*[8]*Johnson*, *George*[7], *Ira*[6], *Jonathan*[5], *Nathaniel*[4], *Nathaniel*[3], *Humphrey*[2], *John*[1]) was born in 1928. He married Estella Lassick.

Children of Clifford[11] Main Jr. and Estella Lassick are as follows:

    i.   CLIFFORD[12] III; born 1948.
    ii.   FRANCES; born 1949.
    iii.   CLAUDIA; born 1952.
    iv.   STEVE; born 1953.

352. EDITH[11] MAIN (*Carrie*[10], *Andrew*[9], *Lutilia*[8]*Johnson*, *George*[7], *Ira*[6], *Jonathan*[5], *Nathaniel*[4], *Nathaniel*[3], *Humphrey*[2], *John*[1]) was born in 1929. She married Richard L. Phillips.

Children of Edith[11] Main and Richard L. Phillips are as follows:

    i.   RICHARD L.[12]; born 1951.
    ii.   DAVID LARRY; born 1951.
    iii.   DANIEL PAUL; born 1954.

353. HAMPTON RANZY[11] MAIN SR. (*Flo*[10], *Andrew*[9], *Lutilia*[8]*Johnson*, *George*[7], *Ira*[6], *Jonathan*[5], *Nathaniel*[4], *Nathaniel*[3], *Humphrey*[2], *John*[1]) was born in 1907. He married Carsie Congleton.

Children of Hampton Ranzy[11] Main Sr. and Carsie Congleton were as follows:

649.   i.   DAISY[12], born 1929; married Spencer Ray Woolard.
650.   ii.   FLO DARLES, born 1931; married Peggy Ann Cutler.
    iii.   CLIFFTON RAY; born 1933; married Betty Ruth Maden.
    iv.   LOUISE; born 1935; married Mitchel Jackson Robins.
    v.   DONNIE RUTH; born 1935.
    vi.   HAMPTON RANZY JR.; born 1939; died 1939.
    vii.   RICHARD GRAY; born 1941.

354. WILBERT RICHARD OGAL[11] MAIN (*Flo*[10], *Andrew*[9], *Lutilia*[8]*Johnson*, *George*[7], *Ira*[6], *Jonathan*[5], *Nathaniel*[4], *Nathaniel*[3], *Humphrey*[2], *John*[1]) was born in 1909. He married Eloise Wallace.

Children of Wilbert Richard Ogal[11] Main and Eloise Wallace are as follows:

    i.   HELEN ISOBELL[12]; born 1932.
    ii. RUTH; born 1934.
    iii. WILLIAM DAVID; born 1935.
    iv. JEANETTE; born 1937.
    v.   HARRY HAMPTON; born 1938.
    vi. WILBERT WALLACE; born 1942.

355. JESSIE OGAL RICHARD[11] MAIN (*Flo[10]*, *Andrew[9]*, *Lutilia[8]Johnson*, *George[7]*, *Ira[6]*, *Jonathan[5]*, *Nathaniel[4]*, *Nathaniel[3]*, *Humphrey[2]*, *John[1]*) was born in 1911. He married Helen Driscoll in 1936. He married Lizzie Shott.

Children of Jessie Ogal Richard[11] Main and Helen Driscoll are:

    i.   VIRGINIA[12]; born 1938.

356. MERTON MAIN[11] WALKEY (*Nina[10]Main*, *Andrew[9]*, *Lutilia[8]Johnson*, *George[7]*, *Ira[6]*, *Jonathan[5]*, *Nathaniel[4]*, *Nathaniel[3]*, *Humphrey[2]*, *John[1]*) was born in 1908. He married Mildred Schmidt.

Children of Merton Main[11] Walkey and Mildred Schmidt are:

    i.   GENE NELSON[12]; born 1928.

357. MAX M.[11] MAIN (*Mudd[10]*, *Andrew[9]*, *Lutilia[8]Johnson*, *George[7]*, *Ira[6]*, *Jonathan[5]*, *Nathaniel[4]*, *Nathaniel[3]*, *Humphrey[2]*, *John[1]*) was born in 1920. He married Mary Boyles.

Children of Max M.[11] Main and Mary Boyles are as follows:

    i.   CHERYL ANN[12]; born 1948.
    ii. SUSAN KAY; born 1952.

358. THEODORE[11] MALEE (*Minnerva[10]Colvin*, *Sarah[9]Main*, *Lutilia[8]Johnson*, *George[7]*, *Ira[6]*, *Jonathan[5]*, *Nathaniel[4]*, *Nathaniel[3]*, *Humphrey[2]*, *John[1]*) was born in 1911. He married Mamie M. Schroeder in 1934. He married Aleene Adams in 1949.

Children of Theodore[11] MaLee and Mamie M. Schroeder are:

    i.   CONNIE SUE[12]; born 1938 at MO.

There were no children of Theodore[11] MaLee and Aleene Adams.

359.   MARGARET   LOUISE[11]   MALEE   (*Minnerva[10]Colvin*, *Sarah[9]Main*, *Lutilia[8]Johnson*, *George[7]*, *Ira[6]*, *Jonathan[5]*, *Nathaniel[4]*, *Nathaniel[3]*, *Humphrey[2]*, *John[1]*) was born in 1916. She married David C. Calhoun in 1943.

Children of Margaret Louise[11] MaLee and David C. Calhoun are:

    i.   CORAL C.[12]; born 1944.

360. EARL EDWARD[11] KULMUS (*Beulah[10]Colvin*, *Sarah[9]Main*, *Lutilia[8]Johnson*, *George[7]*, *Ira[6]*, *Jonathan[5]*, *Nathaniel[4]*, *Nathaniel[3]*, *Humphrey[2]*, *John[1]*) was born in 1912. He married Margaret Catherine Johnson.

Children of Earl Edward[11] Kulmus and Margaret Catherine Johnson are as follows:

    i.   LINDA KAY[12]; born 1940.
    ii.   STEVEN EDWARD; born 1947.

361. RICHARD ORVILLE[11] COLVIN (*Sidney[10]*, *Sarah[9]Main*, *Lutilia[8]Johnson*, *George[7]*, *Ira[6]*, *Jonathan[5]*, *Nathaniel[4]*, *Nathaniel[3]*, *Humphrey[2]*, *John[1]*) was born in 1908. He married Helen Cross.

Children of Richard Orville[11] Colvin and Helen Cross are as follows:

    i.   SARA JO[12]; born 1942 at St. Louis, MO.
    ii.   NANCY RUTH; born 1945 at Cinncinatti, OH.

362.   SIDNEY   ROBERT[11]   COLVIN   (*Sidney[10]*, *Sarah[9]Main*, *Lutilia[8]Johnson*, *George[7]*, *Ira[6]*, *Jonathan[5]*, *Nathaniel[4]*, *Nathaniel[3]*, *Humphrey[2]*, *John[1]*) was born in 1913. He married Ruth Smith in 1940.

Children of Sidney Robert[11] Colvin and Ruth Smith are as follows:

    i.   SHARON KAY[12]; born 1947.
    ii.   ROBERT LEE; born 1953.

363.   THOMAS B.[11] COLVIN (*Anthoney*[10], *Sarah*[9]*Main*, *Lutilia*[8]*Johnson*,   *George*[7],   *Ira*[6],   *Jonathan*[5],   *Nathaniel*[4], *Nathaniel*[3], *Humphrey*[2], *John*[1]) was born in 1915. He married Edmore Engle in 1946.

Children of Thomas B.[11] Colvin and Edmore Engle all born at Hutchinson, KS, are as follows:

    i.   THOMAS ENGLE[12]; born 1947.
    ii. MICHAEL ALBERT; born 1948.
    iii. PATRICA ANN; born 1950.
    iv. WILLIAM ANTHONY; born 1952.

364.   WINFRED A.[11] COLVIN (*Anthoney*[10], *Sarah*[9]*Main*, *Lutilia*[8]*Johnson*,   *George*[7],   *Ira*[6],   *Jonathan*[5],   *Nathaniel*[4], *Nathaniel*[3], *Humphrey*[2], *John*[1]) was born in 1921. He married Dorothy Snyder in 1941.

Children of Winfred A.[11] Colvin and Dorothy Snyder both born at Hutchinson, KS, are as follows:

    i.   DAVID ALLEN[12]; born 1942.
    ii. RICHARD STANLEY; born 1949.

365.   AUDREY MAE[11] COLVIN (*Anthoney*[10], *Sarah*[9]*Main*, *Lutilia*[8]*Johnson*,   *George*[7],   *Ira*[6],   *Jonathan*[5],   *Nathaniel*[4], *Nathaniel*[3], *Humphrey*[2], *John*[1]) was born in 1925. She married Alva Lincoln Hysom in 1943.

Children of Audrey Mae[11] Colvin and Alva Lincoln Hysom all born at Hutchinson, KS, are as follows:

    i.   SUE ELLEN[12]; born 1946.
    ii. STEVEN LARRY; born 1946.
    iii. SANDRA; born 1948.
    iv. JERRY LEE; born 1950.

366.   MARIE[11] KOENIG (*Pansy*[10]*Lawson*, *Minerva*[9]*Main*, *Lutilia*[8]*Johnson*,   *George*[7],   *Ira*[6],   *Jonathan*[5],   *Nathaniel*[4], *Nathaniel*[3], *Humphrey*[2], *John*[1]) was born in 1904. She married Walter M. Pine. She married Herman Engleman.

Children of Marie[11] Koenig and Walter M. Pine are as follows:

651.   i.   EILEEN[12], born 1922; married Thomas Alvin Gill.

652.   ii.   ELIZABETH, born 1924; married Telford Thorenson.

653.   iii.   MARDELL, born 1926; married William F. Smith.

367.   JOSEPHINE[11] SHRIVER (*Lela*[10]*Main*, *George*[9], *Lutilia*[8]*Johnson*, *George*[7], *Ira*[6], *Jonathan*[5], *Nathaniel*[4], *Nathaniel*[3], *Humphrey*[2], *John*[1]) was born in 1907. She married Edwin C. Miller.

Children of Josephine[11] Shriver and Edwin C. Miller are as follows:

       i.   MARVIN[12]; born 1931.

       ii.   JUDITH ANN; born 1935.

368.   MARY ALICE[11] SHRIVER (*Lela*[10]*Main*, *George*[9], *Lutilia*[8]*Johnson*, *George*[7], *Ira*[6], *Jonathan*[5], *Nathaniel*[4], *Nathaniel*[3], *Humphrey*[2], *John*[1]) married Edwin M. Strom.

Children of Mary Alice[11] Shriver and Edwin M. Strom are:

       i.   PETER[12]; born 1942.

369.   BLANCHE[11] TROUTNER (*Anna*[10]*Johnson*, *Alvin*[9], *Rufus*[8], *George*[7], *Ira*[6], *Jonathan*[5], *Nathaniel*[4], *Nathaniel*[3], *Humphrey*[2], *John*[1]) was born on 2 Aug 1896. She married Floyd M. Taylor. She died on 1 Aug 1992 at age 95.

Children of Blanche[11] Troutner and Floyd M. Taylor were:

       i.   MARY CATHERINE[12]; born 1916; died 1937.

370.   OPAL[11] TROUTNER (*Anna*[10]*Johnson*, *Alvin*[9], *Rufus*[8], *George*[7], *Ira*[6], *Jonathan*[5], *Nathaniel*[4], *Nathaniel*[3], *Humphrey*[2], *John*[1]) was born in 1897. She married William Hunt. She and William Hunt were divorced. She married Homer Rhoades.

Children of Opal[11] Troutner and William Hunt are as follows:

654.   i.   WILLIAM[12] JR., born 1918 at KS; married Mary Beth Shaw; divorced Mary Beth Shaw.

655.   ii.   FLORIENE, born 1921; married Harry Stout.

371. MARY HAZEL[11] JOHNSON (*Lewis*[10], *Alvin*[9], *Rufus*[8], *George*[7], *Ira*[6], *Jonathan*[5], *Nathaniel*[4], *Nathaniel*[3], *Humphrey*[2], *John*[1]) was born on 8 Nov 1901. She married Thomas Shellhorse on 15 Nov 1918. She died on 8 Jul 1989 at age 87. She was buried at Crescent Heights Cemetery, Pleasant Hill, IL.

Children of Mary Hazel[11] Johnson and Thomas Shellhorse are as follows:

    i.   LORAINE[12].

    ii.   GLEN.

    iii.   ARVILLE lived at Louisiana, MO.

372. LEWIS HAYWARD[11] JOHNSON (*Lewis*[10], *Alvin*[9], *Rufus*[8], *George*[7], *Ira*[6], *Jonathan*[5], *Nathaniel*[4], *Nathaniel*[3], *Humphrey*[2], *John*[1]) was born on 12 Nov 1903 at Nebo, Pike Co., IL. He married Iva Lillian Goltz on 16 Sep 1923. He died on 25 Nov 1974 at Pike Co., IL, at age 71. He was buried at Crescent Heights Cemetery, Pleasant Hill, IL. He was a farmer.

Children of Lewis Hayward[11] Johnson and Iva Lillian Goltz are as follows:

  656.   i.   ONETA FERN[12], born 6 Jun 1924; married Donald Clair McBride.

  657.   ii.   CHARLES LYNDLE, born 15 Mar 1926 at Nebo (near), IL; married Imogene Smith.

  658.   iii.   HAYWARD LAVON, born 16 Apr 1927 at Nebo (near), IL; married Edna Eilene Carlton.

  659.   iv.   OTELA FAY, born 12 Nov 1928; married Thomas M. Burke.

373. RICHARD LEE[11] JEFFRIES (*Eva*[10]*Johnson*, *Alvin*[9], *Rufus*[8], *George*[7], *Ira*[6], *Jonathan*[5], *Nathaniel*[4], *Nathaniel*[3], *Humphrey*[2], *John*[1]) was born on 28 Feb 1919 at Perry, IL. He married Lois Eleanor Nicholson, daughter of Oren Harvey Nicholson and Meleta Harris, on 28 Sep 1940.

Children of Richard Lee[11] Jeffries and Lois Eleanor Nicholson are as follows:

660.   i.   JEANNE ANN[12], born 31 Jan 1945 at Long Beach, CA; married Gary Lee Personett.

661.   ii.   GARY LEE, born 8 Jan 1946 at Pittsfield, Pike Co., IL; married Kazulo Sato.

662.   iii.   DIANA LYNN, born 17 Feb 1948 at Pittsfield, Pike Co., IL; married Michael Dennis McCartney.

374. HARLEY ROBERT[11] JOHNSON (*George*[10], *George*[9], *Rufus*[8], *George*[7], *Ira*[6], *Jonathan*[5], *Nathaniel*[4], *Nathaniel*[3], *Humphrey*[2], *John*[1]) was born on 16 Oct 1911 at Albert, KS. He married Edith Lucille Padley on 16 Oct 1964. He died on 7 Sep 1966 at Erie, KS, at age 54.

Children of Harley Robert[11] Johnson and Edith Lucille Padley were:

      i.   (--?--)[12].

375. AUDREY DELLA[11] JOHNSON (*George*[10], *George*[9], *Rufus*[8], *George*[7], *Ira*[6], *Jonathan*[5], *Nathaniel*[4], *Nathaniel*[3], *Humphrey*[2], *John*[1]) was born on 5 Apr 1913 at Albert, KS. She married Ray Rufenacht.

Children of Audrey Della[11] Johnson and Ray Rufenacht are as follows:

      i.   DALE[12] was a lawyer at Amarillo, TX.

      ii.   HOWARD.

      iii.   DELLA; married Jerome Steffan.
            She lived at Chase, KS.

376. WARREN HARDIN[11] JOHNSON (*George*[10], *George*[9], *Rufus*[8], *George*[7], *Ira*[6], *Jonathan*[5], *Nathaniel*[4], *Nathaniel*[3], *Humphrey*[2], *John*[1]) was born on 5 Mar 1915 at Bazine, KS. He married Nita Evelyn Grassfield on 16 Dec 1942.

Children of Warren Hardin[11] Johnson and Nita Evelyn Grassfield are as follows:

663.   i.   WARREN LEE[12], born 18 Oct 1943 at Anamosa, IA; married Gloria Bristol.

ii. MARVIN GLENN; born 2 May 1946.

377. LOY LEE[11] JOHNSON (*George*[10], *George*[9], *Rufus*[8], *George*[7], *Ira*[6], *Jonathan*[5], *Nathaniel*[4], *Nathaniel*[3], *Humphrey*[2], *John*[1]) was born on 16 Jul 1920 at Ness Co., KS. He married Glennella Bourdet on 5 Dec 1942 at Kansas City, MO.

Children of Loy Lee[11] Johnson and Glennella Bourdet are as follows:

664.   i. BILLY[12], married Karl Cox.
       ii. MARILYN.

378. DANA MARGARET[11] JOHNSON (*George*[10], *George*[9], *Rufus*[8], *George*[7], *Ira*[6], *Jonathan*[5], *Nathaniel*[4], *Nathaniel*[3], *Humphrey*[2], *John*[1]) was born on 29 Jul 1924 at Ness Co., KS. She married Joe Cook. She died on 1 Jan 1965 at Crane, MO, at age 40.

Children of Dana Margaret[11] Johnson and Joe Cook are as follows:

665.   i. JOE ELLEN[12], married Terry Davidson.
       ii. DANE SUE; married Fred Mehl.
       iii. JANICE KAY; married Dale Farrington.
       iv. DAVID.

379. HELEN MARIE[11] JOHNSON (*Ralph*[10], *George*[9], *Rufus*[8], *George*[7], *Ira*[6], *Jonathan*[5], *Nathaniel*[4], *Nathaniel*[3], *Humphrey*[2], *John*[1]) was born on 20 Dec 1930 at Mulvane, KS. She married David Hill on 12 Nov 1955.

Children of Helen Marie[11] Johnson and David Hill are as follows:

       i. TIMOTHY DAVID[12].
       ii. MICHAEL RALPH.

380. DONALD EARL[11] JOHNSON (*Ralph*[10], *George*[9], *Rufus*[8], *George*[7], *Ira*[6], *Jonathan*[5], *Nathaniel*[4], *Nathaniel*[3], *Humphrey*[2], *John*[1]) was born on 24 Dec 1936. He married Theresa Florine Kern on 3 Oct 1959 at Belle Plaine, KS.

Children of Donald Earl[11] Johnson and Theresa Florine Kern are as follows:

i. BRENDA KAY[12].

ii. DEBORAH.

381. MILDRED "LUCILLE"[11] MILLER (*Laura*[10]*Johnson, Lewis*[9], *Rufus*[8], *George*[7], *Ira*[6], *Jonathan*[5], *Nathaniel*[4], *Nathaniel*[3], *Humphrey*[2], *John*[1]) was born on 14 Oct 1906 at Pearl, IL. She married Oren Keith Smith on 22 Mar 1930.

Children of Mildred "Lucille"[11] Miller and Oren Keith Smith were as follows:

666.   i.   DORIS JEAN[12], born 21 Feb 1932; married Jerry Dean Akers.

667.   ii.   KEITH LEE, born 13 Mar 1934; married Linda Lou Capps.

382. BLANCHE ELIZABETH[11] MILLER (*Laura*[10]*Johnson, Lewis*[9], *Rufus*[8], *George*[7], *Ira*[6], *Jonathan*[5], *Nathaniel*[4], *Nathaniel*[3], *Humphrey*[2], *John*[1]) was born on 16 Mar 1910 at Pearl, IL. She married Frank Brown Elston on 26 Aug 1939. She died on 23 Sep 1982 at Kirkwood, MO, at age 72.

Children of Blanche Elizabeth[11] Miller and Frank Brown Elston were as follows:

i.   JANE FRANCES[12]; born 13 Mar 1941 at Kirkwood, MO; died 1 Mar 1947 at Webster Grove, MO, at age 5.

668.   ii.   DAVID GEORGE, born 7 Mar 1944; married Helen Anita Wells.

383. FRANCES MAY[11] MILLER (*Laura*[10]*Johnson, Lewis*[9], *Rufus*[8], *George*[7], *Ira*[6], *Jonathan*[5], *Nathaniel*[4], *Nathaniel*[3], *Humphrey*[2], *John*[1]) was born on 1 Aug 1919 at Pearl, IL. She married Charles Cleo Inskip on 26 Jan 1945.

Children of Frances May[11] Miller and Charles Cleo Inskip are:

669.   i.   LINDA SUE[12], born 12 Jul 1949; married Terry Feig.

384. LOIS DEAN[11] MILLER (*Laura*[10]*Johnson, Lewis*[9], *Rufus*[8], *George*[7], *Ira*[6], *Jonathan*[5], *Nathaniel*[4], *Nathaniel*[3], *Humphrey*[2],

$John^1$) was born on 6 Jul 1922 at Pearl, IL. She married Joseph Lambert on 16 Oct 1941.

Children of Lois Dean[11] Miller and Joseph Lambert are as follows:

    670.   i.   SANDRA KAY[12], born 4 Aug 1943 at Kansas City, MO; married Garth Dunlap.

    671.   ii.   RONNIE JOE, born 28 Sep 1946 at Woodriver, IL; married Deborah Kenrick.

385. KATHRYN[11] JOHNSON (*Osca*[10], *Lewis*[9], *Rufus*[8], *George*[7], *Ira*[6], *Jonathan*[5], *Nathaniel*[4], *Nathaniel*[3], *Humphrey*[2], *John*[1]) was born in 1912. She married Heridin Verdin Battershell.

Children of Kathryn[11] Johnson and Heridin Verdin Battershell are as follows:

    672.   i.   LINDA SUE[12], born 23 Jun 1937 at Bethalto, Madison Co., IL; married Frank Spencer Long.

        ii.   BETTIE LOUISE; married Bert R. Hamblin.

386. MAVIS MARIE[11] JOHNSON (*Ivis*[10], *Isaac*[9], *Rufus*[8], *George*[7], *Ira*[6], *Jonathan*[5], *Nathaniel*[4], *Nathaniel*[3], *Humphrey*[2], *John*[1]) was born on 30 Mar 1926 at Carthage, IL. She married Moses Lewis on 24 Dec 1947 at Denver, Denver Co., CO.

Children of Mavis Marie[11] Johnson and Moses Lewis are as follows:

    673.   i.   FAYE KATHLEEN[12], born 4 Oct 1949 at Denver, Denver Co., CO; married Larry LuRue Axtell.

    674.   ii.   REX IVIS, born 5 Aug 1951 at Denver, Denver Co., CO; married Vicki Reba Harris.

        iii.   JEFFREY LEE; born 4 Apr 1961.

387. NELLIE DALE[11] JOHNSON (*Ivis*[10], *Isaac*[9], *Rufus*[8], *George*[7], *Ira*[6], *Jonathan*[5], *Nathaniel*[4], *Nathaniel*[3], *Humphrey*[2], *John*[1]) was born on 17 Jun 1927 at Pittsfield, Pike Co., IL. She married Clarence Rozie Crum. She married George Oscar Baugh.

Children of Nellie Dale[11] Johnson and Clarence Rozie Crum all born at Denver, Denver Co., CO, are as follows:

i. GREGORY[12]; born 12 Jun 1952; married Linda Ann Whitehouse; married Pamela Jo Kenneby.

ii. VICKIE DIANE; born 2 Jul 1954; married Charles Michael McCarthy.

iii. GARY EUGENE; born 5 Mar 1956; married Margaret Helen Simpson.

Children of Nellie Dale[11] Johnson and George Oscar Baugh are as follows:

i. MICHAEL STEPHEN[12]; born 22 Dec 1958 at Denver, Denver Co., CO; married Selma Marlene Knight.

ii. DAVID WAYNE; born 22 Dec 1965.

388. JANET ELLEN[11] BROWN (*Icel*[10]*Johnson, Isaac*[9], *Rufus*[8], *George*[7], *Ira*[6], *Jonathan*[5], *Nathaniel*[4], *Nathaniel*[3], *Humphrey*[2], *John*[1]) was born on 28 Apr 1929 at Cedar Rapids, IA. She married Robert Edward Thune on 26 Mar 1950 at Cedar Rapids, IA.

Children of Janet Ellen[11] Brown and Robert Edward Thune all born at Cedar Rapids, IA, are as follows:

675. i. REBECCA ELLEN[12], born 2 Jan 1951; married Douglas J. Gleason.

ii. ROBERT EDWARD; born 14 Nov 1953; married Bonnie Catherine Dean 5 May 1979; he and Bonnie Catherine Dean were divorced; married Debbie (--?--).

iii. WILLIAM SCOTT; born 11 Jun 1956; married Mary Jane Ford 9 Jun 1979.

iv. MARGARET ANNE; born 2 Jul 1958; married Brad Williams 6 Jun 1982.

She lived at Denver, Denver Co., CO.

389. JOY ELAINE[11] BROWN (*Icel*[10]*Johnson, Isaac*[9], *Rufus*[8], *George*[7], *Ira*[6], *Jonathan*[5], *Nathaniel*[4], *Nathaniel*[3], *Humphrey*[2], *John*[1]) was born on 19 Feb 1931 at Cedar Rapids, IA. She married Ralph Edward Kane on 1 Jul 1950.

Children of Joy Elaine[11] Brown and Ralph Edward Kane were as follows:

676.   i.   LINDA KAY[12], born 19 Jun 1953 at Denver, Denver Co., CO; married Dennis Wayne Stick.

        ii.   NANCY JOY; born 14 Jun 1954; died 14 Aug 1954.

677.   iii.   JOY-ANNE, born 5 Nov 1956 at Cedar Rapids, IA; married Wayne Nederhoff.

678.   iv.   RALPH EDWARD JR., born 14 Oct 1957 at Cedar Rapids, IA; married Cynthia Bowers.

        v.   CYNTHIA LEE; born 3 Nov 1961.

        vi.   RACHEL SUE; born 21 Sep 1972.

390. WILMA FERN[11] BROWN (*Icel*[10]*Johnson, Isaac*[9], *Rufus*[8], *George*[7], *Ira*[6], *Jonathan*[5], *Nathaniel*[4], *Nathaniel*[3], *Humphrey*[2], *John*[1]) was born on 20 Jul 1932 at Cedar Rapids, IA. She married Arlyn Lynuer Wendell Clark on 5 Jun 1953 at Cedar Rapids, IA.

Children of Wilma Fern[11] Brown and Arlyn Lynuer Wendell Clark are as follows:

        i.   MICHAEL DAVID[12]; born 13 Jan 1957.

679.   ii.   WILLIAM KYLE WENDELL, born 19 Mar 1959 at Enid, Garfield Co., OK; married Bonnie Tanner.

        iii.   CATHY LYNNE; born 13 Nov 1960.

        iv.   STEPHEN ARLYN; born 28 Jun 1964.

391. WILLIAM BENTON[11] BROWN (*Icel*[10]*Johnson, Isaac*[9], *Rufus*[8], *George*[7], *Ira*[6], *Jonathan*[5], *Nathaniel*[4], *Nathaniel*[3], *Humphrey*[2], *John*[1]) was born on 8 Oct 1933 at Cedar Rapids, IA. He married Marlys Ann Brock on 25 Jul.

Children of William Benton[11] Brown and Marlys Ann Brock are as follows:

680.   i.   WILLIAM DAVID[12], born 21 Feb 1961; married Janet Ann Howard.

        ii.   JULIE RENEE; born 8 Mar 1963; married Bret Allan Knockle 10 Sep 1988.

iii. MARIANNE LYNETTE; born 7 Jun 1967; married Jimmy E. Casas 18 May 1991.

392. MARY ANN[11] BROWN (*Icel*[10]*Johnson, Isaac*[9], *Rufus*[8], *George*[7], *Ira*[6], *Jonathan*[5], *Nathaniel*[4], *Nathaniel*[3], *Humphrey*[2], *John*[1]) was born on 25 Sep 1935 at Iowa City, Johnson Co., IA. She married John Alvin Gregory Jr. on 26 Dec 1955.

Children of Mary Ann[11] Brown and John Alvin Gregory Jr. are as follows:

681.   i.   JOHN BENTON[12], born 10 Sep 1958 at Council Bluffs, IA; married Shari Kay Richter.
682.   ii.   JENNIFER LYNN, born 14 Oct 1960 at Council Bluffs, IA; married John Williams.
         iii.   NICHOLAS RAY; born 16 Jan 1964; married Lori Deneen Roenfeldt 17 Dec 1988.

393. LOIS AILEEN[11] JOHNSON (*Rufus*[10], *Isaac*[9], *Rufus*[8], *George*[7], *Ira*[6], *Jonathan*[5], *Nathaniel*[4], *Nathaniel*[3], *Humphrey*[2], *John*[1]) was born on 28 Mar 1927 at Pittsfield, Pike Co., IL. She married John Robert "Bob" McKenna on 9 Apr 1948 at Clarksville, MS.

Children of Lois Aileen[11] Johnson and John Robert "Bob" McKenna were as follows:

683.   i.   SHERRY[12], born 14 May 1947; married Conrad Keil.
684.   ii.   TERRY LYNN, born 20 May 1948 at Forest City, AR; married Robert Allen Feltman.
685.   iii.   LYNDA PHYLLIS, born 10 Nov 1949; married George Oakley.
686.   iv.   MICHAEL JAY, born 3 Oct 1952; married Wendy (--?--); divorced Wendy (--?--); married Kathy (--?--).
687.   v.   SANDRA DELPHINE, born 12 Nov 1954 at Pittsfield, Pike Co., IL; married Steven George Strohl.
         vi.   (--?--);
688.   vii.   ROBIN EUGENE, born 28 Jul 1959; married Catherine Rose O'Leary.

689.   viii.   JILL DENISE, born 17 Jul 1960 at St. Louis, MO; married Allen Duane Huffman.

394. VERNON WENDELL[11] JOHNSON (*Rufus*[10], *Isaac*[9], *Rufus*[8], *George*[7], *Ira*[6], *Jonathan*[5], *Nathaniel*[4], *Nathaniel*[3], *Humphrey*[2], *John*[1]) was born on 25 Jan 1930. He married Helen Pearl Wilkins, daughter of Russell Wilkins and Stella Howell.

He lived at CA.

Children of Vernon Wendell[11] Johnson and Helen Pearl Wilkins were as follows:

690.   i.   JOSLIN JANE[12], born 28 May 1954.

ii.   DENNIS JAMES; born Apr 1956; died Apr 1956.

iii.   SUSAN MONETTE; born 20 Dec 1960; married Glen Alsesen 19 Mar 1988.

395. PHYLLIS LEE[11] JOHNSON (*Rufus*[10], *Isaac*[9], *Rufus*[8], *George*[7], *Ira*[6], *Jonathan*[5], *Nathaniel*[4], *Nathaniel*[3], *Humphrey*[2], *John*[1]) was born on 16 Sep 1931 at Pittsfield, Pike Co., IL. She married Daniel Duran Rose on 22 Apr 1951.

Children of Phyllis Lee[11] Johnson and Daniel Duran Rose both born at Pittsfield, Pike Co., IL, are as follows:

691.   i.   WENDY LEIGH[12], born 28 Aug 1953; married Brian Lowe.

692.   ii.   TIMOTHY DAN, born 17 Jul 1956; married Moyra Simpson; divorced Moyra Simpson.

396. RONALD WENDELL[11] JOHNSON (*Wendell*[10], *Isaac*[9], *Rufus*[8], *George*[7], *Ira*[6], *Jonathan*[5], *Nathaniel*[4], *Nathaniel*[3], *Humphrey*[2], *John*[1]) was born on 14 Dec 1937 at Quincy, Adams Co., IL. He married Billie Kay Knapp on 29 Jul 1962. He and Billie Kay Knapp were divorced in 1977. He married Connie Bowers on 18 Jan 1991. He died on 29 Mar 1999 at age 61.

Children of Ronald Wendell[11] Johnson and Billie Kay Knapp are as follows:

693.   i.   TIM R.[12], born 23 May 1963; married Pamela Lord.

694.   ii.   TAMMY KAY, born 5 Oct 1964; married James Dean Hardin.

        iii.   SUZANNE RENEE; born 31 Dec 1969; married Shannon Norton 15 Jun 1991 at Kansas City, MO.

397. BEN RAY[11] JOHNSON (*Wendell[10], Isaac[9], Rufus[8], George[7], Ira[6], Jonathan[5], Nathaniel[4], Nathaniel[3], Humphrey[2], John[1]*) was born on 23 Jun 1939 at Quincy, Adams Co., IL. He married Joyce Mardell Pearson, daughter of Ralph D. Pearson and Annie L. Kirk, on 9 Nov 1958.   He lived in 2000 at Pittsfield, IL.

Children of Ben Ray[11] Johnson and Joyce Mardell Pearson are as follows:

695.   i.   KATHLEEN YUVONNE[12], born 29 May 1959 at Pittsfield, Pike Co., IL; married Paul Opie; divorced Paul Opie; married James Buranosky; married (--?--) McMahon.

696.   ii.   BEN RAY JR., born 23 Dec 1960; married Brook Shinn.

697.   iii.   MICHAEL WENDELL, born 11 May 1965; married Sonia Wittland; divorced Sonia Wittland.

        iv.   HOLLY ANN; born 5 Jan 1973; married (--?--) Rumple.

Generation Twelve

398. LOIS ELEANOR[12] NICHOLSON (*Oren[11], Charles[10], Mary[9]Johnson, Charles[8], Charles[7], Ira[6], Jonathan[5], Nathaniel[4], Nathaniel[3], Humphrey[2], John[1]*) was born on 11 Feb 1920 at Pittsfield, Pike Co., IL. She married Richard Lee Jeffries, son of William Porter Jeffries and Eva Johnson, on 28 Sep 1940.

Children of Lois Eleanor[12] Nicholson and Richard Lee Jeffries are as follows:

> i. JEANNE ANN[13], born 31 Jan 1945 at Long Beach, CA; married Gary Lee Personett. (see # 660.).
> ii. GARY LEE, born 8 Jan 1946 at Pittsfield, Pike Co., IL; married Kazulo Sato. (see # 661.).
> iii. DIANA LYNN, born 17 Feb 1948 at Pittsfield, Pike Co., IL; married Michael Dennis McCartney. (see # 662.).

399. ANNA LEE[12] NICHOLSON (*Oren[11]*, *Charles[10]*, *Mary[9]Johnson*, *Charles[8]*, *Charles[7]*, *Ira[6]*, *Jonathan[5]*, *Nathaniel[4]*, *Nathaniel[3]*, *Humphrey[2]*, *John[1]*) was born on 27 Mar 1923 at Pittsfield, Pike Co., IL. She married Howard Mann on 27 Feb 1943.

Children of Anna Lee[12] Nicholson and Howard Mann are as follows:

> i. BARBARA ANN[13]; born 13 Aug 1944; married John Eugene Hinds 6 Apr 1968.
> ii. MARY JEAN; born 5 Feb 1947; married Michael Barker 29 Jun 1977.

400. CHARLES WILLIAM[12] NIEBUR (*Susan[11]Nicholson*, *Charles[10]*, *Mary[9]Johnson*, *Charles[8]*, *Charles[7]*, *Ira[6]*, *Jonathan[5]*, *Nathaniel[4]*, *Nathaniel[3]*, *Humphrey[2]*, *John[1]*) was born on 7 Oct 1918 at Pittsfield, Pike Co., IL. He married Mildred Virginia Williams on 28 Jun 1941.

Children of Charles William[12] Niebur and Mildred Virginia Williams are as follows:

> 698. i. LORETTA SUE[13], born 20 Mar 1942; married Gerald Eberly.
> 699. ii. MARSHA KAY, born 23 Nov 1944; married John Young.
> 700. iii. CAROLINE JOAN, born 29 Jan 1949; married James Palerino; divorced James Palerino; married William Maier.
> 701. iv. CHERYL ANN, born 13 Mar 1951; married Paul Lapinski.

401. PAUL EVART^{12} NIEBUR (*Susan^{11}Nicholson, Charles^{10}, Mary^{9}Johnson, Charles^8, Charles^7, Ira^6, Jonathan^5, Nathaniel^4, Nathaniel^3, Humphrey^2, John^1*) was born on 20 May 1921. He married Nola Waltrip in 1944. He married Leoline Willard on 10 Nov 1950.

Children of Paul Evart^{12} Niebur and Nola Waltrip are:

   702.   i.   JULIE ANN^{13}, born 13 Oct 1945; married Thomas Ellis.

Children of Paul Evart^{12} Niebur and Leoline Willard are as follows:

   i.   PAUL MICHAEL^{13}; born 1 Feb 1954.
   ii.   RONDA KAY; born 18 Nov 1955; married Jeff Blake 7 Oct 1978; she and Jeff Blake were divorced.
   iii.   JILL MARIE; born 22 Dec 1961; married Jeffrey Allen Jesberg.

402. ROBERT FREDERICK^{12} NIEBUR (*Susan^{11}Nicholson, Charles^{10}, Mary^{9}Johnson, Charles^8, Charles^7, Ira^6, Jonathan^5, Nathaniel^4, Nathaniel^3, Humphrey^2, John^1*) was born on 21 Sep 1931. He married Marilyn Northern on 2 Mar 1953.

Children of Robert Frederick^{12} Niebur and Marilyn Northern are as follows:

   703.   i.   BRETT BORDEN^{13}, born 16 Oct 1953; married Cindy Bishop.
   ii.   ANGELA LEE; born 26 Feb 1959; married John Chester McGrath 3 Apr 1982.

403. VERA ORLENA^{12} SHIVE (*Mary^{11}Nicholson, Charles^{10}, Mary^{9}Johnson, Charles^8, Charles^7, Ira^6, Jonathan^5, Nathaniel^4, Nathaniel^3, Humphrey^2, John^1*) was born on 17 Jul 1920 at Pittsfield, Pike Co., IL. She married William Havens, son of James Havens and Bertha Hoots, on 12 Jan 1939.

Children of Vera Orlena^{12} Shive and William Havens were as follows:

704.   i.   JAMES WILLIAM[13], born 27 Aug 1939 at Scott
               Co., IL; married Phyllis Ann Akers; divorced
               Phyllis Ann Akers; married Carolyn Ralph
               Young.
705.   ii.   BETTY ANN, born 12 Aug 1941; married Keith
               Jefferson.
706.   iii. ROBERT EUGENE, born 3 Feb 1943; married
               Karla Elaine Jarvis.
707.   iv.   THOMAS EARL, born 24 May 1945; married
               Joyce K. Davis.
         v.   DANIEL LEE; born 12 Oct 1947; married Judith
               E. Stinebaker 26 Nov 1965; died 28 Dec 1967 at
               Viet Nam at age 20.

404. MARY FRANCES[12] SHIVE (*Mary[11]Nicholson, Charles[10],
Mary[9]Johnson, Charles[8], Charles[7], Ira[6], Jonathan[5], Nathaniel[4],
Nathaniel[3], Humphrey[2], John[1]*) was born on 10 Nov 1921 at
Pittsfield, Pike Co., IL. She married Donald Wilday Giger on 6 Sep
1939.

Children of Mary Frances[12] Shive and Donald Wilday Giger are
as follows:

708.   i.   ELIZABETH SUZANNE[13], born 22 Sep 1940.
709.   ii.   DAVID RAY, born 23 Sep 1942; married Donna
               Jean Douglas.
710.   iii. DONNA MARIE, born 24 Nov 1945; married
               Floyd Irvin Pursley.
         iv.   DONALD WAYNE; born 13 Aug 1948.

405. BERNICE "BETTY"[12] SHIVE (*Mary[11]Nicholson, Charles[10],
Mary[9]Johnson, Charles[8], Charles[7], Ira[6], Jonathan[5], Nathaniel[4],
Nathaniel[3], Humphrey[2], John[1]*) was born on 19 Jul 1923 at
Pittsfield, Pike Co., IL. She married Clarence Lidstrom on 8 Apr
1944. She married Elmer Kurth on 30 Jan 1965.

Children of Bernice "Betty"[12] Shive and Clarence Lidstrom are
as follows:

711.   i.   JANICE CAROL[13], born 24 Sep 1945; married
               Howard Earl Zimmerman.

712.   ii.   JOYCE ANN, born 8 Apr 1949; married Jessie Tabbert.

406.   MABEL LEONA^{12} SHIVE (*Mary^{11}Nicholson, Charles^{10}, Mary^{9}Johnson, Charles^{8}, Charles^{7}, Ira^{6}, Jonathan^{5}, Nathaniel^{4}, Nathaniel^{3}, Humphrey^{2}, John^{1}*) was born on 13 Feb 1925 at Pittsfield, Pike Co., IL. She married Arthur Lewis Chapman on 19 Jan 1951.

Children of Mabel Leona^{12} Shive and Arthur Lewis Chapman are as follows:

713.   i.   ARTHUR LEWIS^{13} JR., born 9 Dec 1951 at RI; married Diane Meeks.

714.   ii.   SANDRA LYNN, born 25 Jan 1955 at ID; married Keith Bonn.

407.   LOUIS RICHARD^{12} SHIVE (*Mary^{11}Nicholson, Charles^{10}, Mary^{9}Johnson, Charles^{8}, Charles^{7}, Ira^{6}, Jonathan^{5}, Nathaniel^{4}, Nathaniel^{3}, Humphrey^{2}, John^{1}*) was born on 23 Dec 1926 at Pittsfield, Pike Co., IL. He married Ethel Marie Wilkins on 27 May 1951.

Children of Louis Richard^{12} Shive and Ethel Marie Wilkins were as follows:

i.   LARRY RICHARD^{13}; born 9 Mar 1952; died 20 May 1960 at age 8; buried at Winchester, Scott Co., IL.

ii.   JEFFERY ALAN; born 25 Mar 1956. He lived in 1985 at Springfield, IL.

iii.   PANELA SUE; born 21 Apr 1963; married Laurence Michael Hembrough 23 Oct 1982 at Winchester, IL.

408.   JAMES WILLIAM^{12} SHIVE (*Mary^{11}Nicholson, Charles^{10}, Mary^{9}Johnson, Charles^{8}, Charles^{7}, Ira^{6}, Jonathan^{5}, Nathaniel^{4}, Nathaniel^{3}, Humphrey^{2}, John^{1}*) was born on 10 Jan 1929 at Pittsfield, Pike Co., IL. He married Betty Jean Ross on 21 Jun 1953 at Macomb, IL.

Children of James William[12] Shive and Betty Jean Ross are as follows:

715.　　i.　JAMES WILLIAM[13] JR., born 9 Mar 1955 at Macomb, IL; married Mary Jo Scott.

　　　　　ii.　DANIEL LEE; born 28 Dec 1956.

　　　　　iii.　STEVEN GENE; born 16 Sep 1960.

409.　HENRY JOSEPH[12] SHIVE (*Mary*[11]*Nicholson, Charles*[10], *Mary*[9]*Johnson, Charles*[8], *Charles*[7], *Ira*[6], *Jonathan*[5], *Nathaniel*[4], *Nathaniel*[3], *Humphrey*[2], *John*[1]) was born on 14 May 1930 at Pittsfield, Pike Co., IL. He married Edith Looper on 25 Jan 1951 at AR. He married Mary Mae Cox on 19 Jul 1969.

Children of Henry Joseph[12] Shive and Edith Looper were as follows:

716.　　i.　JOAN[13], born 8 Dec 1951; married Charles Lakin.

　　　　　ii.　MICHAEL ALLEN; born 29 Jun 1953; died 14 Jul 1954 at age 1.

717.　　iii.　JERRY LEE, born 26 Jun 1954; married Cindy Dann.

718.　　iv.　NANCY ELAINE, born 30 Jul 1958; married Tony Eugene Crain.

719.　　v.　STEVE WILLIAM, born 22 Sep 1959; married Sherry Sue Piper.

720.　　vi.　CONNIE SUE, born 7 Jun 1964; married Larry Z. DePue.

410.　ALICE JEANETTE[12] SHIVE (*Mary*[11]*Nicholson, Charles*[10], *Mary*[9]*Johnson, Charles*[8], *Charles*[7], *Ira*[6], *Jonathan*[5], *Nathaniel*[4], *Nathaniel*[3], *Humphrey*[2], *John*[1]) was born on 29 Jun 1931 at Montezuma Township, Milton, Pike Co., IL. She married Duane Eldon Guth on 19 Nov 1949.

Children of Alice Jeanette[12] Shive and Duane Eldon Guth were as follows:

　　　　　i.　KATHLEEN MARIE[13]; born 10 Aug 1950; died 11 Aug 1950.

    ii.   BRENDA JEANNE; born 13 Jun 1952; married Stephen Edward Hart 11 Jun 1983.

    iii. RONALD DUANE; born 14 Dec 1955.

    iv. DAVID BRIAN; born 17 Dec 1957; married Lenora Catherine Stewart 16 Oct 1982 at Bloomington, IL.

    v.   KAREN JANET; born 26 Feb 1959.

411. DOROTHY JANE^{12} SHIVE (*Mary*^{11}*Nicholson, Charles*^{10}, *Mary*^{9}*Johnson, Charles*^{8}, *Charles*^{7}, *Ira*^{6}, *Jonathan*^{5}, *Nathaniel*^{4}, *Nathaniel*^{3}, *Humphrey*^{2}, *John*^{1}) was born on 10 Jan 1933 at Montezuma Township, Milton, Pike Co., IL. She married Harlan Albert Nevius on 24 Apr 1952.

Children of Dorothy Jane^{12} Shive and Harlan Albert Nevius are as follows:

721.   i.   MARY JEAN^{13}, born 2 Jan 1954 at Peoria, IL; married Donald Ray Kupferschmid.

    ii. LINDA DIANE; born 3 Feb 1957.

    iii. DEBRA LYNN; born 4 Aug 1964.

412. JOHN C.^{12} SHIVE (*Mary*^{11}*Nicholson, Charles*^{10}, *Mary*^{9}*Johnson, Charles*^{8}, *Charles*^{7}, *Ira*^{6}, *Jonathan*^{5}, *Nathaniel*^{4}, *Nathaniel*^{3}, *Humphrey*^{2}, *John*^{1}) was born on 11 Feb 1935 at Montezuma Township, Pike Co., IL. He married Shirley Ann Bryant on 5 May 1963.

Children of John C.^{12} Shive and Shirley Ann Bryant were as follows:

    i.   JOHN CHARLES^{13}; born 26 Dec 1963; died 26 Dec 1963.

    ii. TERESA SUE; born 26 Dec 1963.

    iii. DARIN WAYNE; born 7 Apr 1968.

    iv. AMY ELAINE; born 3 Jun 1972.

413. JACK FRANKLIN^{12} SHIVE (*Mary*^{11}*Nicholson, Charles*^{10}, *Mary*^{9}*Johnson, Charles*^{8}, *Charles*^{7}, *Ira*^{6}, *Jonathan*^{5}, *Nathaniel*^{4}, *Nathaniel*^{3}, *Humphrey*^{2}, *John*^{1}) was born on 27 Jul 1936 at

Montezuma Township, Pike Co., IL. He married Janice Settles on 18 Aug 1957.

Children of Jack Franklin[12] Shive and Janice Settles are as follows:

    i.   CYNTHIA JO[13]; born 30 Jan 1959.
    ii. SALLY ANN; born 9 Aug 1960.
    iii. DOUGLAS JAY; born 29 Dec 1963.
    iv. KARLA JOANN; born 9 Oct 1970.

414. NORMA JEAN[12] SHIVE (*Mary*[11]*Nicholson*, *Charles*[10], *Mary*[9]*Johnson*, *Charles*[8], *Charles*[7], *Ira*[6], *Jonathan*[5], *Nathaniel*[4], *Nathaniel*[3], *Humphrey*[2], *John*[1]) was born on 3 Sep 1939 at Montezuma Township, Pike Co., IL. She married Arthur Clay Reel on 26 Jul 1959.

Children of Norma Jean[12] Shive and Arthur Clay Reel are as follows:

722.   i.   WILLIAM RODNEY[13], born 12 Jun 1960; married Mary Neely.
723.   ii. REBECCA JEAN, born 19 Aug 1962; married Berlyn Dean Thomas Jr.
    iii. RHONDA BETH; born 3 Sep 1966.
    iv. ROBERT CLAY; born 31 Oct 1968.

415. THOMAS LEE[12] SHIVE (*Mary*[11]*Nicholson*, *Charles*[10], *Mary*[9]*Johnson*, *Charles*[8], *Charles*[7], *Ira*[6], *Jonathan*[5], *Nathaniel*[4], *Nathaniel*[3], *Humphrey*[2], *John*[1]) was born on 8 May 1941 at Montezuma Township, Pike Co., IL. He married Linda Sue Kieth on 18 Dec 1960.

Children of Thomas Lee[12] Shive and Linda Sue Kieth are as follows:

    i.   DONALD EUGENE[13]; born 29 Jul 1961; married Lori Ann Fox 12 Dec 1981 at Beardstown, IL.
    ii. RUTH ANN; born 14 Aug 1962.
    iii. THOMAS PAUL; born 15 Apr 1970.

416. WILMA EVELYN[12] SANDERSON (*Beryl*[11]*Nicholson*, *Charles*[10], *Mary*[9]*Johnson*, *Charles*[8], *Charles*[7], *Ira*[6], *Jonathan*[5],

Nathaniel[4], *Nathaniel*[3], *Humphrey*[2], *John*[1]) was born on 13 May 1921. She married Joel Marian Worley circa 1942.

Children of Wilma Evelyn[12] Sanderson and Joel Marian Worley are as follows:

    i.   WILLIAM J.[13]; born 11 Aug 1948.

    ii.   GEOFFREY DEAN; born 11 Mar 1952; married (--?--) ? Mar 1980.

417. NORMA CHARLENE[12] SANDERSON (*Beryl*[11]*Nicholson*, *Charles*[10], *Mary*[9]*Johnson*, *Charles*[8], *Charles*[7], *Ira*[6], *Jonathan*[5], *Nathaniel*[4], *Nathaniel*[3], *Humphrey*[2], *John*[1]) was born on 1 Mar 1923. She married Lewis Abram Souders circa 1946.

Children of Norma Charlene[12] Sanderson and Lewis Abram Souders are as follows:

724.   i.   JUDY KAY[13], born 1 Aug 1947; married James George Leinen; divorced James George Leinen.

725.   ii.   MARCIA LEE, born 9 Jun 1950; married Robert Wayne Henry.

    iii.   LARRY KENT; born 6 Jul 1951; married Vickie Dickson.

418. CARRIE JOSEPHINE[12] SANDERSON (*Beryl*[11]*Nicholson*, *Charles*[10], *Mary*[9]*Johnson*, *Charles*[8], *Charles*[7], *Ira*[6], *Jonathan*[5], *Nathaniel*[4], *Nathaniel*[3], *Humphrey*[2], *John*[1]) was born on 18 Mar 1926. She married Lloyd Leonard Long Jr circa 1946.

Children of Carrie Josephine[12] Sanderson and Lloyd Leonard Long Jr are as follows:

    i.   PHILIP ALLEN[13]; born 21 Jun 1947.

726.   ii.   DAVID LLOYD, born 21 Mar 1953; married Linda Kay Buckingham.

    iii.   ROGER MURPHY; born 15 Oct 1956; married Amelia Hogan 16 Jun 1983.

    iv.   MARK ANDREW; born 28 Apr 1961.

419. BETTY JEAN[12] SANDERSON (*Beryl*[11]*Nicholson*, *Charles*[10], *Mary*[9]*Johnson*, *Charles*[8], *Charles*[7], *Ira*[6], *Jonathan*[5], *Nathaniel*[4],

Nathaniel[3], *Humphrey*[2], *John*[1]) was born on 16 Apr 1931. She married Leslie Farrell Hamilton circa 1949.

Children of Betty Jean[12] Sanderson and Leslie Farrell Hamilton are as follows:

727.　　i.　LESLIE STEVEN[13], born 7 Mar 1950; married Ann Shields.

728.　　ii.　JOE GLEN, born 15 Dec 1953; married Kathleen Merrill.

420.　CAROLYN LOUISE[12] RADER (*Jessie*[11]*Nicholson, Charles*[10], *Mary*[9]*Johnson, Charles*[8], *Charles*[7], *Ira*[6], *Jonathan*[5], *Nathaniel*[4], *Nathaniel*[3], *Humphrey*[2], *John*[1]) was born on 10 Oct 1924. She married Thomas Gates circa 1944. She died on 3 Jan 1970 at age 45.

Children of Carolyn Louise[12] Rader and Thomas Gates are:

729.　　i.　THOMAS NICHOL[13], born 30 Sep 1945; married Lindy (--?--); married Louise (--?--).

421.　JOHN WILLIAM[12] RADER (*Jessie*[11]*Nicholson, Charles*[10], *Mary*[9]*Johnson, Charles*[8], *Charles*[7], *Ira*[6], *Jonathan*[5], *Nathaniel*[4], *Nathaniel*[3], *Humphrey*[2], *John*[1]) was born on 28 Mar 1930. He married Elizabeth (--?--) on 29 Mar.

Children of John William[12] Rader and Elizabeth (--?--) were as follows:

　　　　i.　STEVEN[13]; born 12 Nov 1951.

730.　　ii.　JOYCE, born 27 Mar 1953; married Kenneth Martin; divorced Kenneth Martin.

　　　　iii.　THOMAS.

　　　　iv.　ROBERT; born 7 Jan 1954; died 8 Jul 1961 at age 7.

422.　RALPH EDWARD[12] RADER (*Jessie*[11]*Nicholson, Charles*[10], *Mary*[9]*Johnson, Charles*[8], *Charles*[7], *Ira*[6], *Jonathan*[5], *Nathaniel*[4], *Nathaniel*[3], *Humphrey*[2], *John*[1]) was born on 21 Apr 1941. He married Virginia Maybe on 26 Jan at NJ.

Children of Ralph Edward[12] Rader and Virginia Maybe are as follows:

i. CHISTY[13]; born 1971.

ii. KAREN; born 26 Jul 1975.

423. CHARLES ROY[12] NICHOLSON (*Charles[11]*, *Charles[10]*, *Mary[9]Johnson*, *Charles[8]*, *Charles[7]*, *Ira[6]*, *Jonathan[5]*, *Nathaniel[4]*, *Nathaniel[3]*, *Humphrey[2]*, *John[1]*) was born on 24 Feb 1940. He married Phyliss (--?--).

Children of Charles Roy[12] Nicholson and Phyliss (--?--) are as follows:

i. BEN DAVID[13]; born 1 Feb 1962.

ii. DANIEL; born 28 May 1964.

iii. ELIZABETH ANN; born 5 Sep 1967.

424. MARY ANN[12] NICHOLSON (*Charles[11]*, *Charles[10]*, *Mary[9]Johnson*, *Charles[8]*, *Charles[7]*, *Ira[6]*, *Jonathan[5]*, *Nathaniel[4]*, *Nathaniel[3]*, *Humphrey[2]*, *John[1]*) was born on 12 Aug 1943. She married Charles DeLong circa 1966.

Children of Mary Ann[12] Nicholson and Charles DeLong are as follows:

i. BRETT[13]; born 1 Nov 1967.

ii. JENNIE; born 10 May 1970.

425. JOHN LAWRENCE[12] SHERWIN (*Rebecca[11]Killebrew*, *Mary[10]Miller*, *Rebecca[9]Johnson*, *Charles[8]*, *Charles[7]*, *Ira[6]*, *Jonathan[5]*, *Nathaniel[4]*, *Nathaniel[3]*, *Humphrey[2]*, *John[1]*) was born on 11 Jan 1918. He married Marjorie Spencer on 6 Jul 1947.

Children of John Lawrence[12] Sherwin and Marjorie Spencer are as follows:

i. NANCY JEAN[13]; born 4 Apr 1950; married Peter VanDenHonert 11 Aug 1973.

ii. MARILYN KAY; born 28 Feb 1953.

iii. JOHN NEAL; born 21 Mar 1957.

426. JESSIE EUGENE[12] SHERWIN (*Rebecca[11]Killebrew*, *Mary[10]Miller*, *Rebecca[9]Johnson*, *Charles[8]*, *Charles[7]*, *Ira[6]*, *Jonathan[5]*, *Nathaniel[4]*, *Nathaniel[3]*, *Humphrey[2]*, *John[1]*) was born on 9 Sep 1923. He married Mary Louise Ward on 21 Sep 1952.

Children of Jessie Eugene[12] Sherwin and Mary Louise Ward are as follows:

    i.   CAROLYN SUE[13]; born 13 Sep 1953.

    ii. GARY EUGENE; born 25 Nov 1958; married Carolyn Kay Kerr 19 Jun 1982.

    iii. RONALD LYNN; born 13 Jul 1962.

427. LAVERN[12] JONES (*Mary*[11]*Killebrew, Mary*[10]*Miller, Rebecca*[9]*Johnson, Charles*[8], *Charles*[7], *Ira*[6], *Jonathan*[5], *Nathaniel*[4], *Nathaniel*[3], *Humphrey*[2], *John*[1]) was born on 15 Dec 1922. He married Betty E. Duncan on 3 Jun 1945. He and Betty E. Duncan were divorced in Dec 1949. He married Vivian Willner on 11 Jul 1954.

Children of LaVern[12] Jones and Betty E. Duncan are as follows:

731.   i.   LARRY LAVERN[13], born 20 Jul 1946; married Jane Richardson; divorced Jane Richardson.

732.   ii. TERESA ANN "TERRI", born 27 Mar 1948; married Terry E. Milton.

Children of LaVern[12] Jones and Vivian Willner are as follows:

    i.   LOY LAVERN[13]; born 27 Apr 1955; married Alice Colleen Finch 16 May 1982.

    ii. LYNN LAVERN; born 24 May 1958; married Barbara Myers 3 Feb 1979; he and Barbara Myers were divorced 1981.

733.   iii. LYLE LAVERN, born 20 Nov 1960; married Ann Denise Ballard.

428. VIRGINIA "BERNADINE"[12] KILLEBREW (*Norene*[11], *Mary*[10]*Miller, Rebecca*[9]*Johnson, Charles*[8], *Charles*[7], *Ira*[6], *Jonathan*[5], *Nathaniel*[4], *Nathaniel*[3], *Humphrey*[2], *John*[1]) was born on 11 Apr 1923. She married Wilbur German on 27 Nov 1940.

Children of Virginia "Bernadine"[12] Killebrew and Wilbur German are as follows:

734.   i.   LINDA KAY[13], born 3 May 1942; married Donald Lawrence Dennis; divorced Donald Lawrence Dennis; married George Manchester;

divorced George Manchester; married Kenneth Erickson.

735.   ii.   WILBUR LEE, born 11 Nov 1946; married Alice Marie Culp.

429.   NADINE[12] NEWINGHAM (*Ethel[11]Killebrew, Mary[10]Miller, Rebecca[9]Johnson, Charles[8], Charles[7], Ira[6], Jonathan[5], Nathaniel[4], Nathaniel[3], Humphrey[2], John[1]*) was born on 8 Aug 1926. She married Harry Arnold on 17 Mar 1952.

Children of Nadine[12] Newingham and Harry Arnold were as follows:

736.   i.   CARMEN S.[13], born 18 May 1954; married Rick Garland II.

737.   ii.   GREG, born 11 Sep 1958; married Kathy (--?--).

         iii.   KATHY; born 16 Feb 1959; died 16 Feb 1959.

430.   BERNARD RANDALL[12] NEWINGHAM (*Ethel[11]Killebrew, Mary[10]Miller, Rebecca[9]Johnson, Charles[8], Charles[7], Ira[6], Jonathan[5], Nathaniel[4], Nathaniel[3], Humphrey[2], John[1]*) was born on 6 Feb 1932. He married Ann Sweet on 25 Aug 1951. He and Ann Sweet were divorced in Aug 1974. He married Joan Leach Hulick on 7 Dec 1979.

Children of Bernard Randall[12] Newingham and Ann Sweet were as follows:

         i.   PATSY ANN[13]; born 9 Feb 1952; married Thomas Sherman 9 Apr 1980.

738.   ii.   CHARLOTTE, born 26 Mar 1954; married Michael Baker.

739.   iii.   JULIE RENEE, born 16 Jul 1955; married Darrell Wright.

         iv.   REBECCA SUE; born 12 Jan 1957; died 13 Jan 1957.

431.   NAOMI NORENE[12] NEWINGHAM (*Ethel[11]Killebrew, Mary[10]Miller, Rebecca[9]Johnson, Charles[8], Charles[7], Ira[6], Jonathan[5], Nathaniel[4], Nathaniel[3], Humphrey[2], John[1]*) was born on 10

Jul 1933. She married Harold E. Wright on 11
Apr 1954.

Children of Naomi Norene[12] Newingham and Harold E. Wright
were as follows:

    i.   DEBBIE[13]; born 17 Jan 1959.

    ii. BARBARA; born 31 Jan 1964.

    iii. STEPHEN EUGENE; born 6 Jul 1966; died 6 Jul
       1966.

432.   CAROL DEAN[12] NEWINGHAM (*Ethel[11]Killebrew,
Mary[10]Miller, Rebecca[9]Johnson, Charles[8], Charles[7], Ira[6],
Jonathan[5], Nathaniel[4], Nathaniel[3], Humphrey[2], John[1]*) was born
on 25 Oct 1934. He married Elizabeth Agger on 25 Nov 1954.

Children of Carol Dean[12] Newingham and Elizabeth Agger are
as follows:

740.   i.   TONA JEAN[13], born 15 Jul 1955; married
           Randall Cree Smith.

    ii. CHRIS; born 10 Feb 1957; married Teresa Jo
       Kenderman 12 Sep 1983.

    iii. TAMARA ELAINE; born 10 Jul 1959; married
       Mark William Joseph 8 Aug 1981.

    iv. TERESA SUE; born 27 Sep 1961; married Mark
       Russell Bettis 9 Jul 1983.
       She was also known as TERRY NEWINGHAN.

433.   RANDALL ABRAMS[12] KILLEBREW (*Theodore[11],
Mary[10]Miller, Rebecca[9]Johnson, Charles[8], Charles[7], Ira[6],
Jonathan[5], Nathaniel[4], Nathaniel[3], Humphrey[2], John[1]*) was born
on 11 Aug 1935. He married Sue Ann Coultas on 8 Jun 1959.

Children of Randall Abrams[12] Killebrew and Sue Ann Coultas
are as follows:

    i.   CARRIE ELLEN[13]; born 1 Oct 1960.

    ii. SARAH ANN; born 2 Jun 1962.

    iii. LESLIE ERIN; born 1 Mar 1972.

434.   HELEN[12] KILLEBREW (*Charles[11], Ethel[10]Miller,
Rebecca[9]Johnson, Charles[8], Charles[7], Ira[6], Jonathan[5],*

Nathaniel[4], *Nathaniel*[3], *Humphrey*[2], *John*[1]) was born on 4 Feb 1923. She married Stuart Loyd on 28 Aug 1941.

Children of Helen[12] Killebrew and Stuart Loyd are as follows:

741.   i.   EARL WAYNE[13], born 8 May 1943; married Sharon Kay Dawkins.

742.   ii.   BARBARA, born 5 Dec 1946; married Larry Joe Dunham.

743.   iii.   EVELYN, born 17 Jan 1949; married Rodney Lee Dehart.

744.   iv.   HAROLD, born 20 Jan 1951; married Janie Armistead.

745.   v.   DIANNA, born 19 Dec 1955; married Donnie W. Foster.

435. CHARLES DALE[12] KILLEBREW (*Charles*[11], *Ethel*[10]*Miller*, *Rebecca*[9]*Johnson*, *Charles*[8], *Charles*[7], *Ira*[6], *Jonathan*[5], *Nathaniel*[4], *Nathaniel*[3], *Humphrey*[2], *John*[1]) was born on 30 May 1924. He married Betty Jo Hollembrek on 5 Jul 1947.

Children of Charles Dale[12] Killebrew and Betty Jo Hollembrek are as follows:

746.   i.   REBECCA DALE[13], born 12 Mar 1949; married (--?--) ?

      ii.   SHARON FAYE; born 30 May 1951.

436. DOROTHY[12] KILLEBREW (*William*[11], *Ethel*[10]*Miller*, *Rebecca*[9]*Johnson*, *Charles*[8], *Charles*[7], *Ira*[6], *Jonathan*[5], *Nathaniel*[4], *Nathaniel*[3], *Humphrey*[2], *John*[1]) was born on 25 Sep 1920. She married David Haldane on 22 Feb 1942.

Children of Dorothy[12] Killebrew and David Haldane are as follows:

747.   i.   CAROLYN JUNE[13], born 3 May 1943; married Kenneth Evridge.

748.   ii.   LINDA SUE, born 17 Jul 1946; married Ed Stauber.

      iii.   NANCY; born 6 Jun 1950.

437. WILLIAM RUSSELL[12] KILLEBREW (*William*[11], *Ethel*[10]*Miller*, *Rebecca*[9]*Johnson*, *Charles*[8], *Charles*[7], *Ira*[6], *Jonathan*[5], *Nathaniel*[4], *Nathaniel*[3], *Humphrey*[2], *John*[1]) was born on 23 Jan 1922. He married Mildred Harshbarger on 30 Mar 1946.

Children of William Russell[12] Killebrew and Mildred Harshbarger are:

749. i. WILLIAM ALLEN[13], born 8 Aug 1950; married Sharon Larson.

438. VERA[12] KILLEBREW (*William*[11], *Ethel*[10]*Miller*, *Rebecca*[9]*Johnson*, *Charles*[8], *Charles*[7], *Ira*[6], *Jonathan*[5], *Nathaniel*[4], *Nathaniel*[3], *Humphrey*[2], *John*[1]) was born on 1 Jul 1925. She married Lyle H. Schertz on 17 Aug 1946.

Children of Vera[12] Killebrew and Lyle H. Schertz are:

 i. DEBORAH JANE[13]; born 9 Dec 1950.

439. GLEN SHERWIN[12] KILLEBREW (*William*[11], *Ethel*[10]*Miller*, *Rebecca*[9]*Johnson*, *Charles*[8], *Charles*[7], *Ira*[6], *Jonathan*[5], *Nathaniel*[4], *Nathaniel*[3], *Humphrey*[2], *John*[1]) was born on 16 Jun 1931. He married Audrey Stice on 5 Aug 1951.

Children of Glen Sherwin[12] Killebrew and Audrey Stice are as follows:

 i. GAYLE[13]; born 26 Apr 1952.

750. ii. MICHAEL, born 24 Nov 1953; married Rhonda Lou Smith.

 iii. KEVIN; born 14 Oct 1960.

440. CHARLES H.[12] SCHAFER (*Florence*[11]*Killebrew*, *Ethel*[10]*Miller*, *Rebecca*[9]*Johnson*, *Charles*[8], *Charles*[7], *Ira*[6], *Jonathan*[5], *Nathaniel*[4], *Nathaniel*[3], *Humphrey*[2], *John*[1]) was born on 21 Oct 1928. He married Elvira Haley on 8 Sep 1951. He and Elvira Haley were divorced in 1983.

Children of Charles H.[12] Schafer and Elvira Haley are as follows:

751. i. JO[13], born 6 Jul 1952; married Steve Messner.

752.   ii.   DALE, born 31 May 1954; married Kerry Leick; divorced Kerry Leick; married Katherine Sewell.

753.   iii.   DIANE, born 10 Jan 1956; married Joseph Ansbro.

There were no children of Charles H.^{12} Schafer and (--?--) ?.

441.   SAMUEL ROBERT^{12} KILLEBREW (*Samuel^{11}*, *Ethel^{10}Miller*, *Rebecca^{9}Johnson*, *Charles^8*, *Charles^7*, *Ira^6*, *Jonathan^5*, *Nathaniel^4*, *Nathaniel^3*, *Humphrey^2*, *John^1*) was born on 18 Nov 1932. He married Rita Savage on 16 Jun 1956.

Children of Samuel Robert^{12} Killebrew and Rita Savage are as follows:

   i.   GRAIG ALLEN^{13}; born 20 Mar 1960.
   ii.   DAVID ROBERT; born 10 Sep 1962.
   iii.   JEREMY JACOB; born 7 Nov 1971.

442.   LAWRENCE EVANS^{12} KILLEBREW (*Samuel^{11}*, *Ethel^{10}Miller*, *Rebecca^{9}Johnson*, *Charles^8*, *Charles^7*, *Ira^6*, *Jonathan^5*, *Nathaniel^4*, *Nathaniel^3*, *Humphrey^2*, *John^1*) was born on 7 Dec 1937. He married Shirley B. Sweetin on 22 Dec 1956.

Children of Lawrence Evans^{12} Killebrew and Shirley B. Sweetin are as follows:

   i.   MICHAEL LAWRENCE^{13}; born 10 Mar 1958.
   ii.   JAMES "PATRICK"; born 2 Oct 1963.

443.   ROBERT LEE^{12} KILLEBREW (*Robert^{11}*, *Ethel^{10}Miller*, *Rebecca^{9}Johnson*, *Charles^8*, *Charles^7*, *Ira^6*, *Jonathan^5*, *Nathaniel^4*, *Nathaniel^3*, *Humphrey^2*, *John^1*) was born on 7 Nov 1945. He married Gloria Costello on 25 Jun 1966.

Children of Robert Lee^{12} Killebrew and Gloria Costello are as follows:

   i.   DEBRA^{13}; born 20 Oct 1968.
   ii.   BARBARA; born 4 Jul 1970.
   iii.   BEVERLY; born 1 Mar 1972.

444.   SANDRA KAY^{12} MILLER (*William^{11}*, *William^{10}*, *Rebecca^{9}Johnson*, *Charles^8*, *Charles^7*, *Ira^6*, *Jonathan^5*,

Nathaniel[4], *Nathaniel*[3], *Humphrey*[2], *John*[1]) was born on 4 Jul 1937. She married David Lee Ummel on 13 Sep 1958.

Children of Sandra Kay[12] Miller and David Lee Ummel are as follows:

      i. ERIC BRIAN[13]; born 9 Jan 1962; married Renee Thacker 30 Mar 1985.

      ii. JON DAVID; born 28 Jul 1963.

      iii. SCOTT BAIRD; born 13 Apr 1965.

445. DONALD BAIRD[12] MILLER (*William*[11], *William*[10], *Rebecca*[9]*Johnson*, *Charles*[8], *Charles*[7], *Ira*[6], *Jonathan*[5], *Nathaniel*[4], *Nathaniel*[3], *Humphrey*[2], *John*[1]) was born on 3 Dec 1942. He married Sharon Kay Ackland on 28 Apr 1962.

Children of Donald Baird[12] Miller and Sharon Kay Ackland are as follows:

754.   i. KRISTINE DAWN[13], born 15 Sep 1962; married Robert Dalldorf.

755.   ii. KENNETH CHANDLER, born 21 Apr 1965; married (--?--) ?

446. STEWART[12] THORNTON (*Russell*[11], *Richard*[10], *Phila*[9]*Johnson*, *Charles*[8], *Charles*[7], *Ira*[6], *Jonathan*[5], *Nathaniel*[4], *Nathaniel*[3], *Humphrey*[2], *John*[1]) married (--?--) ?

Children of Stewart[12] Thornton and (--?--) ? are:

      i. PAT[13]; married Byran Glenn 19 Jun 1982.

447. ROLLAND RUSSEL[12] THORNTON (*Russel*[11], *Herbert*[10], *Phila*[9]*Johnson*, *Charles*[8], *Charles*[7], *Ira*[6], *Jonathan*[5], *Nathaniel*[4], *Nathaniel*[3], *Humphrey*[2], *John*[1]) was born on 21 Aug 1938. He married Patricia Jo Lowman, daughter of Andrew Ray Lowman and Bernice Christine Sells, on 21 Feb 1959 at Maywood, Los Angeles Co., CA.

Children of Rolland Russel[12] Thornton and Patricia Jo Lowman are as follows:

      i. RONALD RUSSEL[13] JR.; born 18 Sep 1959.

  ii. TRACY LYN; born 9 Jul 1962; married Gregory James Moore 13 Sep 1986 at Fullerton, CA.

  iii. DONALD PATRICK; born 7 Sep 1965.

448. MARILYN ESTHER[12] THORNTON (*Russel*[11], *Herbert*[10], *Phila*[9]*Johnson, Charles*[8], *Charles*[7], *Ira*[6], *Jonathan*[5], *Nathaniel*[4], *Nathaniel*[3], *Humphrey*[2], *John*[1]) was born on 25 Sep 1941. She married Alfred Ray Boggs on 20 Feb 1965. She and Alfred Ray Boggs were divorced in 1979.

Children of Marilyn Esther[12] Thornton and Alfred Ray Boggs are as follows:

756. i. STEVEN MARK[13], born 26 Oct 1960; married Jennie Brunner.

  ii. DAVID MARTIN; born 9 May 1962.
   He was also known as DAVID MARTIN VELKOV.

  iii. JAMES RAY; born 22 Oct 1964.

  iv. LINDA SUZANNE; born 8 Dec 1965.

449. JOHN HAGOOD[12] SWANSON (*Bernice*[11]*Ransom, Warren*[10], *Emma*[9]*Johnson, Charles*[8], *Charles*[7], *Ira*[6], *Jonathan*[5], *Nathaniel*[4], *Nathaniel*[3], *Humphrey*[2], *John*[1]) was born on 19 Feb 1938. He married Renee Ahmed Series in 1970 at NY.

He lived at Seacliff, NY.

Children of John Hagood[12] Swanson and Renee Ahmed Series were as follows:

  i. MONICA MARIE[13]; born 11 Jun 1971.

  ii. CATHERINE; born 26 May 1979.

  iii. PETER WARREN; born 20 Oct 1981; died 28 Dec 1999 at age 18.

450. JUDITH ELAINE[12] SWANSON (*Bernice*[11]*Ransom, Warren*[10], *Emma*[9]*Johnson, Charles*[8], *Charles*[7], *Ira*[6], *Jonathan*[5], *Nathaniel*[4], *Nathaniel*[3], *Humphrey*[2], *John*[1]) was born on 1 Jun 1942. She married Joseph Block.

She lived in 2000 at Washington, DC.

Children of Judith Elaine[12] Swanson and Joseph Block are as follows:

    i.   STEPHEN[13]; born 14 Nov 1976.

    ii. CAROLYN; born 6 Aug 1979.

451. ZETA LYLE[12] PORTER (*Cleo*[11]*Johnson*, *Archie*[10], *John*[9], *Hiram*[8], *Charles*[7], *Ira*[6], *Jonathan*[5], *Nathaniel*[4], *Nathaniel*[3], *Humphrey*[2], *John*[1]) was born on 12 Dec 1914 at Corvallis, Benton Co., OR. She married Bruce M. Beardsley in 1937 at Benton Co., OR. She married Zee Floyd Earl on 13 Jun 1950 at Washington Co., OR. She died on 25 Sep 1999 at Corvallis, Benton Co., OR, at age 84.

Children of Zeta Lyle[12] Porter and Bruce M. Beardsley are:

  757.   i.   JOHN PARKE[13], born 23 Sep 1940 at Portland, Multnomah Co., OR; married Janet Norrine Travis.

Children of Zeta Lyle[12] Porter and Zee Floyd Earl both born at Portland, Multnomah Co., OR, are as follows:

  758.   i.   THOMAS ROBERT[13], born 4 Oct 1952; married Carrie Groomer.

    ii. JAMES FREDERICK; born 28 Jan 1957; married Sandra Seidman 17 Apr 1983 at Boston, MA.

452. DONALD ELTON[12] JOHNSON (*Elmo*[11], *Archie*[10], *John*[9], *Hiram*[8], *Charles*[7], *Ira*[6], *Jonathan*[5], *Nathaniel*[4], *Nathaniel*[3], *Humphrey*[2], *John*[1]) was born on 8 Jul 1915 at Corvallis, Benton Co., OR. He married Madge Marshall on 14 Nov 1937 at Portland, Multnomah Co., OR.

Children of Donald Elton[12] Johnson and Madge Marshall are as follows:

    i.   DONALD MACRAE[13]; born 14 Jul 1941; married Michelle Morgenroth 29 Aug 1965 at Santa Barbara, CA.

    ii. DEBORAH LYNN; born 29 Nov 1948; married Russell Reininger 18 Oct 1980 at Corvallis, Benton Co., OR.

453. CHARLES CLAIR[12] JOHNSON (*Elmo*[11], *Archie*[10], *John*[9], *Hiram*[8], *Charles*[7], *Ira*[6], *Jonathan*[5], *Nathaniel*[4], *Nathaniel*[3], *Humphrey*[2], *John*[1]) was born on 4 Jan 1917 at Corvallis, Benton Co., OR. He married Kay Thomas. He married (--?--) ? He died on 17 Aug 1966 at Corvallis, Benton Co., OR, at age 49.

Children of Charles Clair[12] Johnson and Kay Thomas are:

    i.   ROBERT[13]; his name was legally changed to ROBERT WELLS.

454. RICHARD DARREL[12] JOHNSON (*Darrell*[11], *Archie*[10], *John*[9], *Hiram*[8], *Charles*[7], *Ira*[6], *Jonathan*[5], *Nathaniel*[4], *Nathaniel*[3], *Humphrey*[2], *John*[1]) was born on 29 Jan 1920 at Corvallis, Benton Co., OR. He married Elizabeth L. Peake on 1 Sep 1946 at Grants Pass, OR. He died on 3 Dec 1976 at Salem, Marion Co., OR, at age 56.

Children of Richard Darrel[12] Johnson and Elizabeth L. Peake are as follows:

    i.   LON STEPHEN[13]; born 13 Oct 1948; married Christine R. Schultz.

    ii.   DARREL CRAIG; born 23 Feb 1950 at Lebanon, Linn Co., OR; married Bettye Atkinson 14 Apr 1984 at Washington, DC.

    iii.   LYNNE LORAINE; born 14 Nov 1951 at Lebanon, Linn Co., OR; married Lou Barkley 1982.

    iv.   SCOTT CARL; born 24 Sep 1954 at Lebanon, Linn Co., OR.

455. MURIEL ANN[12] JOHNSON (*Darrell*[11], *Archie*[10], *John*[9], *Hiram*[8], *Charles*[7], *Ira*[6], *Jonathan*[5], *Nathaniel*[4], *Nathaniel*[3], *Humphrey*[2], *John*[1]) was born on 19 Jan 1923 at Corvallis, Benton Co., OR. She married F. Robert Preece on 14 May 1949 at Corvallis, Benton Co., OR.

Children of Muriel Ann[12] Johnson and F. Robert Preece are as follows:

    i.   ROBERT DWIGHT[13]; born 14 Jul 1953 at Los Angeles, Los Angeles Co., CA.

ii. CAROL ANN; born 26 Sep 1956 at Concord, CA.

456. ALLEN[12] HUNNEYCUTT (*Orlo[11]Johnson, Archie[10], John[9], Hiram[8], Charles[7], Ira[6], Jonathan[5], Nathaniel[4], Nathaniel[3], Humphrey[2], John[1]*) was born on 19 Jul 1922. He married Jessie Mae Jones in 1944. He died on 11 Aug 1981 at Corvallis, Benton Co., OR, at age 59.

He was also known as Allen Johnson.

Children of Allen[12] Hunneycutt and Jessie Mae Jones are as follows:

i. DALE A.[13].

ii. GARY A..

iii. PATRICIA.

iv. DIANE.

457. KATHLEEN MAY[12] JOHNSON (*Orlo[11], Archie[10], John[9], Hiram[8], Charles[7], Ira[6], Jonathan[5], Nathaniel[4], Nathaniel[3], Humphrey[2], John[1]*) was born on 19 Jun 1943. She married Jerry Holland. She married Murl Starr.

Children of Kathleen May[12] Johnson and Jerry Holland are:

i. JEFF[13]; born Jun 1962 at ID.

Children of Kathleen May[12] Johnson and Murl Starr are:

i. KRISTI[13]; born Oct 1975 at Reseda, CA.

458. JANET[12] JOHNSON (*Archie[11], Archie[10], John[9], Hiram[8], Charles[7], Ira[6], Jonathan[5], Nathaniel[4], Nathaniel[3], Humphrey[2], John[1]*) was born on 30 Dec 1933 at Portland, Multnomah Co., OR. She married Richard B. Simons.

Her name was legally changed to Janet Johnson-Westfall.

Children of Janet[12] Johnson and Richard B. Simons are as follows:

i. DAVID LYLE[13]; born 22 Sep 1965 at San Diego, San Diego Co., CA.

ii. DRINA KATHLEEN; born 3 Dec 1966 at San Diego, San Diego Co., CA.

iii. PAUL; born 26 Jun 1971 at Portland, Multnomah Co., OR.

459. JEANNIE LINN[12] JOHNSON (*Archie*[11], *Archie*[10], *John*[9], *Hiram*[8], *Charles*[7], *Ira*[6], *Jonathan*[5], *Nathaniel*[4], *Nathaniel*[3], *Humphrey*[2], *John*[1]) was born on 14 Jul 1949 at Auburn, CA. She married Harold Vietti.

Children of Jeannie Linn[12] Johnson and Harold Vietti all born at Anderson, CA, are as follows:

i. PAUL ALAN[13]; born 31 Aug 1971.
ii. SARA MARIE; born 15 Jun 1976.
iii. ANNA KATHLEEN; born 23 Mar 1981.

460. CHRISTOPHER JAMES[12] JOHNSON (*Archie*[11], *Archie*[10], *John*[9], *Hiram*[8], *Charles*[7], *Ira*[6], *Jonathan*[5], *Nathaniel*[4], *Nathaniel*[3], *Humphrey*[2], *John*[1]) was born on 18 Jun 1951 at Auburn, CA. He married Michelle Cary.

Children of Christopher James[12] Johnson and Michelle Cary both born at Redding, CA, are as follows:

i. CHAD PHILIP[13]; born 5 Nov 1980.
ii. AMANDA LYNN; born 28 Oct 1982.

461. GERALDINE ANNE[12] JOHNSON (*Archie*[11], *Archie*[10], *John*[9], *Hiram*[8], *Charles*[7], *Ira*[6], *Jonathan*[5], *Nathaniel*[4], *Nathaniel*[3], *Humphrey*[2], *John*[1]) was born on 2 Jun 1952 at Auburn, CA. She married Worth Havens Dikeman.

Children of Geraldine Anne[12] Johnson and Worth Havens Dikeman are as follows:

i. JENNIFER LYNN DIKEMAN[13]; born 20 Sep 1972.
ii. BONNY JEAN JOHNSON; born 18 Nov 1980 at Berkeley, CA.
iii. ADAM JAMES DIKEMAN; born 27 May 1983 at Albany, CA.

462. DORICE[12] WILLIAMS (*Zelma*[11]*Simpson*, *Etta*[10]*Johnson*, *John*[9], *Hiram*[8], *Charles*[7], *Ira*[6], *Jonathan*[5], *Nathaniel*[4], *Nathaniel*[3], *Humphrey*[2], *John*[1]) was born on 6 Aug 1926. She married Russell Laubner Stewart on 3 Aug 1948. She died on 22 Nov 1996 at Linn Co., OR, at age 70.

Children of Dorice[12] Williams and Russell Laubner Stewart all born at Albany, OR, are as follows:

    i.   SHELLEY DORICE[13]; born 2 Apr 1952.
    ii. MARK RUSSELL; born 29 Jan 1955.
    iii. SCOTT EDWARD; born 15 Jan 1959; married Catherine Ann O'Hare 16 Jul 1983 at Corvallis, Benton Co., OR.

463. KARLENE MAE[12] JOHNSON (*Charles*[11], *Charles*[10], *John*[9], *Hiram*[8], *Charles*[7], *Ira*[6], *Jonathan*[5], *Nathaniel*[4], *Nathaniel*[3], *Humphrey*[2], *John*[1]) was born on 6 Dec 1933. She married James Edward Messer on 29 Jan 1955 at Medford, Jackson Co., OR.

Children of Karlene Mae[12] Johnson and James Edward Messer all born at Medford, Jackson Co., OR, are as follows:

759.   i.   GREGORY JAMES[13], born 16 Dec 1955; married Billie Donnelly; divorced Billie Donnelly; married Donna Adams; married Candace L. Anderson.
          ii. NICKOLE ANNE; born 24 Feb 1958; married Darren Clausen 14 Jun 1980 at Salem, Marion Co., OR; she and Darren Clausen were divorced; married Richard William Quackenbush 22 Mar 1996 at Las Vegas, NV.
          iii. KARLA JEAN; born 27 Apr 1960; married Laird Donald Holt 5 Feb 1984 at Reno, NV.
760.   iv. GRANT EDWARD, born 31 Aug 1962; married Carla Nicole Sherrouse.
761.   v. JOHN ANDREW, born 22 Feb 1966; married Julie Greene. Divorced Julie Greene.
          vi. ANDREA SHAUN; born 27 Dec 1967.
         vii. NEIL PATRICK; born 23 Dec 1968.

464. GERALD GARTH[12] JOHNSON (*Charles*[11], *Charles*[10], *John*[9], *Hiram*[8], *Charles*[7], *Ira*[6], *Jonathan*[5], *Nathaniel*[4], *Nathaniel*[3], *Humphrey*[2], *John*[1]) was born on 13 Mar 1937 at Portland, Multnomah Co., OR. He married Nancy Anne Ticknor, daughter of

Harold Weyburn Ticknor and Edythe Martha Wadley, on 29 Jun 1963 at Silverton, Marion Co., OR.

Children of Gerald Garth[12] Johnson and Nancy Anne Ticknor are as follows:

762.   i.   LEANNE MICHELE[13], born 29 Jul 1965 at Salem, Marion Co., OR; married Michael Andrew Shaw.

763.   ii.   LISA MARIE, born 12 Jan 1968 at Portland, Multnomah Co., OR; married Robert H. Ford.

       iii.   GEOFFREY GARTH; born 30 May 1972 at Portland, Multnomah Co., OR.

465.   BETTY JEANNINE[12] PARSONS (*Doris*[11]*Shaw, Pearl*[10]*Johnson, John*[9], *Hiram*[8], *Charles*[7], *Ira*[6], *Jonathan*[5], *Nathaniel*[4], *Nathaniel*[3], *Humphrey*[2], *John*[1]) was born on 14 Feb 1928. She married William Babeckos.

Children of Betty Jeannine[12] Parsons and William Babeckos are as follows:

764.   i.   MARCELLA DORENE[13], born 16 Aug 1946 at Seattle, King Co., WA; married Wesley Dreyer.

765.   ii.   WILLIAM BRECHT, born 14 Aug 1951 at Portland, Multnomah Co., OR; married Terri Lynn Jensen.

       iii.   JENNIFER LYNN.

466.   WILLIS[12] HANSON (*Agnes*[11]*McElroy, Rose*[10]*Johnson, George*[9], *Hiram*[8], *Charles*[7], *Ira*[6], *Jonathan*[5], *Nathaniel*[4], *Nathaniel*[3], *Humphrey*[2], *John*[1]).

Children of Willis[12] Hanson and ? (--?--) are as follows:

       i.   (--?--)[13].

       ii.   (--?--).

       iii.   (--?--).

       iv.   (--?--).

467.   ALICIA ANN[12] MCELROY (*Earle*[11], *Rose*[10]*Johnson, George*[9], *Hiram*[8], *Charles*[7], *Ira*[6], *Jonathan*[5], *Nathaniel*[4], *Nathaniel*[3], *Humphrey*[2], *John*[1]) was born on 16 May 1927. She married Monte Craig Smalley on 3 Nov 1947.

Children of Alicia Ann[12] McElroy and Monte Craig Smalley are as follows:

766.   i.   CHRISTINE ANN[13], born 9 Oct 1948; married Dennis Stroh.

767.   ii.   GRAIG MITCHELL, born 31 May 1950; married Wendy Johnson.

         iii.   CURTIS EARLE; born 21 Dec 1952; married Diane Ibea.

         iv.   CORY BRENT; born 27 May 1956.

468. ROY LESLIE[12] JOHNSON (*George[11]*, *George[10]*, *George[9]*, *Hiram[8]*, *Charles[7]*, *Ira[6]*, *Jonathan[5]*, *Nathaniel[4]*, *Nathaniel[3]*, *Humphrey[2]*, *John[1]*) was born on 16 Feb 1944 at Salem, Marion Co., OR. He married Lieselotte Curfrass on 18 May 1968 at Badkissinten, Germany. He married Adele Stack on 21 May 1978 at Reno, NV.

Children of Roy Leslie[12] Johnson and Lieselotte Curfrass are:

         i.   BARBARA SABRINA[13]; born 16 Oct 1969 at St. Helens, OR.

469. DOROTHY ALICE[12] JOHNSON (*George[11]*, *George[10]*, *George[9]*, *Hiram[8]*, *Charles[7]*, *Ira[6]*, *Jonathan[5]*, *Nathaniel[4]*, *Nathaniel[3]*, *Humphrey[2]*, *John[1]*) was born on 1 Sep 1946. She married Victor Lee Nelson on 20 Mar 1970 at Portland, Multnomah Co., OR. She married Larry Lowder on 21 Sep 1980 at Vancouver, WA.

Children of Dorothy Alice[12] Johnson and Victor Lee Nelson are:

         i.   JOHN EINER[13]; born 11 Nov 1971 at Portland, Multnomah Co., OR.

470. RAY WESLEY[12] JOHNSON (*George[11]*, *George[10]*, *George[9]*, *Hiram[8]*, *Charles[7]*, *Ira[6]*, *Jonathan[5]*, *Nathaniel[4]*, *Nathaniel[3]*, *Humphrey[2]*, *John[1]*) was born on 17 May 1947 at Salem, Marion Co., OR. He married E. Antoinette Cowan on 2 Sep 1966 at Rainier, OR.

Children of Ray Wesley[12] Johnson and E. Antoinette Cowan are as follows:

> i. MARC WRAY[13]; born 25 Jul 1969 at Longview, Cowlitz Co., WA.
>
> 768. ii. GABRIELLE, born 22 Dec 1971 at Longview, Cowlitz Co., WA.
>
> 769. iii. SHELLEY, born 22 Oct 1979.

471. ROSS EDWARD[12] JOHNSON (*George*[11], *George*[10], *George*[9], *Hiram*[8], *Charles*[7], *Ira*[6], *Jonathan*[5], *Nathaniel*[4], *Nathaniel*[3], *Humphrey*[2], *John*[1]) was born on 20 May 1952 at Salem, Marion Co., OR. He married Debra Adele Meacham on 30 Aug 1971 at Portland, Multnomah Co., OR.

Children of Ross Edward[12] Johnson and Debra Adele Meacham are:

> i. MELLANIE NICOLE[13]; born 31 May 1973 at Pendleton, OR.

472. DELORES JEAN[12] JOHNSON (*George*[11], *George*[10], *George*[9], *Hiram*[8], *Charles*[7], *Ira*[6], *Jonathan*[5], *Nathaniel*[4], *Nathaniel*[3], *Humphrey*[2], *John*[1]) was born on 4 Nov 1957 at Gold Beach, OR. She married Jimie Dean Richmond on 27 May 1977 at Kelso, WA.

Children of Delores Jean[12] Johnson and Jimie Dean Richmond both born at Longview, Cowlitz Co., WA, are as follows:

> i. CHARLES LESLIE[13]; born 13 Aug 1978.
>
> ii. DEJANELL MARIE; born 15 Sep 1980.

473. MELINDA MAE[12] KEELING (*Pauline*[11]*Johnson*, *Clyde*[10], *George*[9], *Hiram*[8], *Charles*[7], *Ira*[6], *Jonathan*[5], *Nathaniel*[4], *Nathaniel*[3], *Humphrey*[2], *John*[1]) was born in 1943. She married Richard Floyd Armstrong.

Children of Melinda Mae[12] Keeling and Richard Floyd Armstrong are as follows:

> i. JENNIFER JO[13]; born 11 Jun 1970.
>
> ii. BRIAN RICHARD; born 9 Jul 1973 at Salem, Marion Co., OR.

474. GEORGIE CATHERINE^{12} IAEGER (*George^{11}, Ada^{10}Johnson, William^9, Hiram^8, Charles^7, Ira^6, Jonathan^5, Nathaniel^4, Nathaniel^3, Humphrey^2, John^1*) was born on 20 Jun 1912 at Edmonds, Snohomish Co., WA. She married Lawrence Earl Gamey, son of Jack Gamey and Agusta (--?--), on 5 Dec 1931. She and Lawrence Earl Gamey were divorced. She died on 30 Oct 1988 at Big Lake, Skagit Co, WA, at age 76. She was buried at Edmonds Cemetery, Edmonds, Snohomish Co., WA.

She appeared on the census of 1 Jan 1920 at Main St., 3rd Ward, Edmonds, Snohomish Co., WA.

Children of Georgie Catherine^{12} Iaeger and Lawrence Earl Gamey were as follows:

> 770. i. LAWRENCE "NEIL"^{13}, born 11 Oct 1935 at Everett, Snohomish Co., WA; married Mary Leake; divorced Mary Leake.
>
> 771. ii. JACK WILLIAM, born 1 May 1942 at Snohomish, Snohomish Co., WA; married Christine "Micky" Weltz; divorced Christine "Micky" Weltz; married Yongsoon Barker; divorced Yongsoon Barker.

475. HAZEL MARIE LENORA^{12} IAEGER (*George^{11}, Ada^{10}Johnson, William^9, Hiram^8, Charles^7, Ira^6, Jonathan^5, Nathaniel^4, Nathaniel^3, Humphrey^2, John^1*) was born on 5 Dec 1913 at Edmonds, Snohomish Co., WA. She married George Nils Naslund, son of Magnus Nils Naslund and Ora Belle Poe, on 27 Nov 1938. She married Harold Julius Skutvik, son of Helmer Skutvik and Hjordis (--?--), on 27 Dec 1958.

She appeared on the census of 1 Jan 1920 at Main St., 3rd Ward, Edmonds, Snohomish Co., WA.

Children of Hazel Marie Lenora^{12} Iaeger and George Nils Naslund are as follows:

> 772. i. GEORGE "DANIEL"^{13}, born 23 May 1942 at Seattle, King Co., WA; married Crystal Lynn Setting.

773. ii. JONATHAN DAVID, born 14 Mar 1946 at Everett, Snohomish Co., WA; married Vicki Lynn Swaim.

774. iii. MARY KAY, born 15 Jan 1952 at Seattle, King Co., WA; married James Russell Lowell; divorced James Russell Lowell; married Bill Carter.

There were no children of Hazel Marie Lenora[12] Iaeger and Harold Julius Skutvik.

476. LOIS LEONA[12] IAEGER (*George[11]*, *Ada[10]Johnson*, *William[9]*, *Hiram[8]*, *Charles[7]*, *Ira[6]*, *Jonathan[5]*, *Nathaniel[4]*, *Nathaniel[3]*, *Humphrey[2]*, *John[1]*) was born on 22 Jul 1916 at Edmonds, Snohomish Co., WA. She married Charles Edwin Hill, son of Coy Dale Hill and Mary Ellen Dowd, on 22 Jun 1940 at Alderwood Manor, Snohomish Co., WA.

She appeared on the census of 1 Jan 1920 at Main St., 3rd Ward, Edmonds, Snohomish Co., WA. She lived on 25 Feb 1998 at Mt Vernon, Skagit Co., WA.

Children of Lois Leona[12] Iaeger and Charles Edwin Hill are as follows:

775. i. JAMES DALE[13], born 23 Aug 1941 at Seattle, King Co., WA; married Carol Ann Shultz; divorced Carol Ann Shultz; married Mary Moericke; divorced Mary Moericke; married Clarice Verlinde; divorced Clarice Verlinde; married Cindee Matthews.

776. ii. MARTHA ANN, born 3 Jan 1946 at Everett, Snohomish Co., WA; married Harley Charles Mann; divorced Harley Charles Mann.

777. iii. KATHLEEN MAY, born 10 Sep 1947 at Scotia, Humboldt Co., CA; married Graig Yost; divorced Graig Yost; married Michael Arther Stevens.

477. CHARLES ARROWOOD[12] IAEGER (*George[11]Iaeger*, *Ada[10]Johnson*, *William[9]*, *Hiram[8]*, *Charles[7]*, *Ira[6]*, *Jonathan[5]*, *Nathaniel[4]*, *Nathaniel[3]*, *Humphrey[2]*, *John[1]*) was born on 14 Jan 1919 at Edmonds, Snohomish Co., WA. He married Virginia Breuser on 21 Mar 1946 at Garberville, Humboldt Co., CA. He died on 9 Nov 1983 at Roseburg, Douglas Co., OR, at age 64.

He appeared on the census of 1 Jan 1920 at Main St., 3rd Ward, Edmonds, Snohomish Co., WA. He began military service circa 1941. He lived on 10 Jan 1944 at Holland.

Children of Charles Arrowood[12] IAEGER and Virginia Breuser are:

> 778.   i.   RICHARD STEPHEN[13], born 21 Nov 1946 at Garberville, Humboldt Co., CA; married Carolyn Ethel Blixseth; divorced Carolyn Ethel Blixseth; married Liana Pearl Cannon; divorced Liana Pearl Cannon; married Barbara Jean Barnett; divorced Barbara Jean Barnett.

478.   JACKSON MOTHERSHEAD[12] IAEGER (*George[11]Iaeger, Ada[10]Johnson, William[9], Hiram[8], Charles[7], Ira[6], Jonathan[5], Nathaniel[4], Nathaniel[3], Humphrey[2], John[1]*) was born on 24 Jul 1921 at South Bend, Pacific Co., WA. He married Bettie Ross, daughter of Dorothy (--?--). He died on 11 Aug 1979 at Shelter Cove, Humboldt Co., CA, at age 58.

He began military service circa 1942.

Children of Jackson Mothershead[12] Iaeger and Bettie Ross were as follows:

> 779.   i.   JUDITH LYNN[13], born 14 May 1943 at Vallejo, CA; married Wayne Beitelspacher; divorced Wayne Beitelspacher; married Rod Kirby; divorced Rod Kirby; married William Migan.
>
>   ii.   JAMES ALTON; born 3 Jul 1947 at Scotia, Humboldt Co., CA; married Tahme (--?--); died 1 Feb 1975 at Bend, OR, at age 27.
>
> 780.   iii.   DENNIS, born 4 Jan 1950 at Garberville, Humboldt Co., CA; married Piper Sue Hamilton; divorced Piper Sue Hamilton; married Peggy Williamson; divorced Peggy Williamson; married Wanda Peck; divorced Wanda Peck.

479. VIRGINIA ANN[12] IAEGER (*George*[11], *Ada*[10]*Johnson*, *William*[9], *Hiram*[8], *Charles*[7], *Ira*[6], *Jonathan*[5], *Nathaniel*[4], *Nathaniel*[3], *Humphrey*[2], *John*[1]) was born on 26 Feb 1923 at Baleville, South Bend, Pacific Co, WA. She married Albert Arthur Blandin, son of Fayette Blandin and Sarah Christina Campbell, on 10 Apr 1943 at Alderwood Manor, Snohomish Co, WA. She died on 20 Feb 1984 at Stevens Hospital, Edmonds, Snohomish Co., WA, at age 60. She was buried on 24 Feb 1984 at Floral Hills Cemetery, Adlerwood Manor, Snohomish Co., WA.

Children of Virginia Ann[12] Iaeger and Albert Arthur Blandin are as follows:

    781.   i.   WILLIAM ARTHUR[13], born 21 Jul 1944 at Providence Hospital, Everett, Snohomish Co., WA; married Alice May Taute.

            ii.   BRUCE ALBERT; born 6 Dec 1948 at Swedish Hospital, Seattle, King Co., WA.

                He began military service in Aug 1969 Joined US Marines (served in Vietnam). He lived at Lake Cavenaugh, Skagit Co., WA.

480. LULUBELLE CAROLINE[12]IAEGER (*George*[11]*Iaeger*, *Ada*[10]*Johnson*, *William*[9], *Hiram*[8], *Charles*[7], *Ira*[6], *Jonathan*[5], *Nathaniel*[4], *Nathaniel*[3], *Humphrey*[2], *John*[1]) was born on 29 Jan 1925 at Mrs. Fricketts on Sunset Ave., Edmonds, Snohomish Co., WA. She married Carl Strasser. She and Carl Strasser were divorced. She married Eldon Lewis. She and Eldon Lewis were divorced. She married Leonard Earl Norris Sr., son of Nathan Edgar Norris and Elizabeth Burge, on 6 Sep at Antinoch, CA. She died on 16 Sep 1988 at Siskiyou Co., CA, at age 63.

Children of Lulubelle Caroline[12] Iaeger and Carl Strasser are:

    782.   i.   ROBERT ALLEN[13], born 23 Apr 1946 at Garberville, Humboldt Co., CA; married Sandra Marie Shields; divorced Sandra Marie Shields; married Carolyn Darline Hopper; divorced Carolyn Darline Hopper; married Joy (--?--).

Children of Lulubelle Caroline[12] IAEGER and Eldon Lewis are:

783.   i.   SUSAN EILEEN[13], born 16 Mar 1948 at Scotia, Humboldt Co., CA; married (--?--) Dean.

Children of Lulubelle Caroline[12] IAEGER and Leonard Earl Norris Sr. were as follows:

784.   i.   LEONARD EARL[13] JR, born 5 Apr 1953 at Arcata, Humboldt Co., CA; married Peggy Ann Cox.

785.   ii.   NANCY LEE, born 22 Oct 1954 at Arcata, Humboldt Co., CA; married Kenneth Eugene Blandin.

786.   iii.   DAVID WARREN, born 26 Jul 1956 at Arcata, Humboldt Co., CA; married Bobbie (--?--).

787.   iv.   WILLIAM GEORGE, born 2 Mar 1959 at Eureka, Humboldt Co., CA; married Rosemary Garcia.

788.   v.   LAURA MAY, born 12 Mar 1961 at Eureka, Humboldt Co., CA; married Earl Conway; divorced Earl Conway.

789.   vi.   TRACY ANN, born 23 Sep 1964 at Arcata, CA; married Bob Nelson.

481.   KATHLEEN IRENE[12] IAEGER (*George[11]Iaeger, Ada[10]Johnson, William[9], Hiram[8], Charles[7], Ira[6], Jonathan[5], Nathaniel[4], Nathaniel[3], Humphrey[2], John[1]*) was born on 29 Mar 1927 at Edmonds Hospital, Edmonds, Snohomish Co., WA. She married Howard Gary Dean Poole, son of Albert Vernon Poole and Violet Mae Howard, on 9 Dec 1946 at Eureka, Humboldt Co., CA.

She lived in 1999 at Wallowa, OR.

Children of Kathleen Irene[12] Ieager and Howard Gary Dean Poole are as follows:

790.   i.   MICHAEL GARY[13], born 27 Jan 1948 at Bend, OR; married Linda (--?--); divorced Linda (--?--); married Susan Marie Polaski.

791.   ii.   PATRICK GEORGE, born 28 Mar 1949 at Bend, OR; married Margaret Ann Grant.

792.   iii.   MARTA GLENN, born 18 May 1952 at Klamath Falls, Klamath Co., OR; married Richard Franklin Anderson.

iv. TIMOTHY GENE; born 8 Apr 1955 at Medford, Jackson Co., OR.

482. GEORGE JOHNSON[12] IAEGER(*George*[11]*Iaeger, Ada*[10]*Johnson, William*[9], *Hiram*[8], *Charles*[7], *Ira*[6], *Jonathan*[5], *Nathaniel*[4], *Nathaniel*[3], *Humphrey*[2], *John*[1]) was born on 27 Mar 1931 at Snohomish Hospital, Snohomish, Snohomish Co., WA. He married Virginia Merise Dickson, daughter of William Harold Dickson and Lola Virginia Swinson, on 4 May 1962 at ElCentro, CA.

He lived on 20 Jun 2000 at Jacksonville, Jackson Co., OR.

Children of George Johnson[12] IAEGER Jr. and Virginia Merise Dickson are as follows:

793. i. MICHAEL DALE[13], born 19 May 1955 at Scotia, Humboldt Co., CA; married Catherine E. MacDonald; divorced Catherine E. MacDonald; married Patricia K. Irvine.

794. ii. CHRISTINA MERISE, born 8 Aug 1957 at Ft. George Meade, MD; married Michael Ronald Russell.

795. iii. VIRGINIA MAYE, born 26 Mar 1963 at San Diego, San Diego Co., CA; married John Pankowski; divorced John Pankowski; married Dennis Allen.

iv. LEE ANN; born 30 Nov 1964 at San Diego, San Diego Co., CA.

She lived in 1997 at Sand Springs, OK.

796. v. KATHLEEN IRENE, born 15 Aug 1967 at San Diego, San Diego Co., CA; married Randy Ryan Shroy.

483. ORLAND LEROY[12] JOHNSON (*James*[11], *Lloyd*[10], *William*[9], *Hiram*[8], *Charles*[7], *Ira*[6], *Jonathan*[5], *Nathaniel*[4], *Nathaniel*[3], *Humphrey*[2], *John*[1]) was born on 30 Jul 1925 at Burns, Harney Co., OR. He married Norma Jane Carper on 20 Nov 1943 at Elgin, OR.

Children of Orland Leroy[12] Johnson and Norma Jane Carper are as follows:

797.   i.   JUDY JANE[13], born 12 Dec 1945 at La Grande, OR; married Richard Dills; married Arthur Lane Staples.

798.   ii.   PATRICIA KAY, born 7 Aug 1952 at Idaho Falls, ID; married Virgil John Jungwirth.

        iii.   DOUGLAS LEROY; born 2 Jun 1955 at Bremerton, WA; married Cathryn Alice Cook 28 Jul 1978 at Tacoma, Pierce Co., WA.

484.   LLOYD ALLEN[12] JOHNSON (*James[11]*, *Lloyd[10]*, *William[9]*, *Hiram[8]*, *Charles[7]*, *Ira[6]*, *Jonathan[5]*, *Nathaniel[4]*, *Nathaniel[3]*, *Humphrey[2]*, *John[1]*) was born on 22 Jun 1927 at Newbridge, OR. He married Virgie Jewel Vanderpool on 2 Sep 1949.

Children of Lloyd Allen[12] Johnson and Virgie Jewel Vanderpool all born at Seattle, King Co., WA, are as follows:

799.   i.   KAREN JEAN[13], born 2 May 1955; married William Howard Erickson.

        ii.   RONALD LLOYD; born 19 Sep 1956.

800.   iii.   ALLEN JAMES, born 19 Sep 1956; married Cathy Varenkamp; divorced Cathy Varenkamp; married Jenifer Lynn Dottram.

        iv.   KEVIN CHARLES; born 18 Feb 1959.

801.   v.   JANET KRISTINE, born 18 Jun 1962; married John Adam Graham.

485.   LOUEL MARIE[12] JOHNSON (*James[11]*, *Lloyd[10]*, *William[9]*, *Hiram[8]*, *Charles[7]*, *Ira[6]*, *Jonathan[5]*, *Nathaniel[4]*, *Nathaniel[3]*, *Humphrey[2]*, *John[1]*) was born on 14 Apr 1937 at Burns, Harney Co., OR. She married James Edward Anderson on 23 Jun 1957 at Boise, ID.

Children of Louel Marie[12] Johnson and James Edward Anderson are as follows:

802.   i.   ANNETTE MARIE[13], born 10 Dec 1961 at Everett, Snohomish Co., WA; married Thomas Michael Ostlie.

        ii.   MELINDA LOUEL; born 28 Mar 1966.

486. RICHARD BARRY[12] JOHNSON (*James*[11], *Lloyd*[10], *William*[9], *Hiram*[8], *Charles*[7], *Ira*[6], *Jonathan*[5], *Nathaniel*[4], *Nathaniel*[3], *Humphrey*[2], *John*[1]) was born on 15 Dec 1943. He married Alberta Margarita Avila.

Children of Richard Barry[12] Johnson and Alberta Margarita Avila both born at San Jaun, Puerto Rico, are as follows:

    i.   MIGUEL RAFAEL[13]; born 10 Oct 1972.

    ii.   GABRIEL RENE; born 4 Oct 1975.

487. GARETH JAMES[12] JOHNSON (*James*[11], *Lloyd*[10], *William*[9], *Hiram*[8], *Charles*[7], *Ira*[6], *Jonathan*[5], *Nathaniel*[4], *Nathaniel*[3], *Humphrey*[2], *John*[1]) was born on 3 Aug 1952 at Idaho Falls, ID. He married Martha Elaine Holmen on 27 Jul 1973 at Darfur, MN.

Children of Gareth James[12] Johnson and Martha Elaine Holmen are as follows:

    i.   HANNAH MARIE[13]; born 12 Sep 1976 at Thief River Falls, MN; married Daniel Koble.

    ii.   JEREMIAH ALLEN; born 1 Sep 1979 at Bagley, MN; married Katrena Westing.

    iii.   JOSHUA JAMES; born 14 May 1982 at Bagley, MN.

488. GERALDINE LUCILLE[12] PICKENS (*Ada*[11]*Johnson*, *Lloyd*[10], *William*[9], *Hiram*[8], *Charles*[7], *Ira*[6], *Jonathan*[5], *Nathaniel*[4], *Nathaniel*[3], *Humphrey*[2], *John*[1]) married Lyall Byers at Cour d' Alene, ID. She died on 10 Jul 1973 at Camas, WA.

Children of Geraldine Lucille[12] Pickens and Lyall Byers are as follows:

  803.   i.   JOAN[13], born 28 Nov 1940 at Grand Coulee, WA; married (--?--) St John.

  804.   ii.   SANDRA, born 25 Apr at Vancouver, WA; married Sam Andrews.

489. JOHN LLOYD[12] PICKENS (*Ada*[11]*Johnson*, *Lloyd*[10], *William*[9], *Hiram*[8], *Charles*[7], *Ira*[6], *Jonathan*[5], *Nathaniel*[4], *Nathaniel*[3],

Humphrey[2], *John*[1]) was born on 3 Feb 1930. He married Clara Sue Ledbetter on 11 Jun 1950 at Heppner, OR.

Children of John Lloyd[12] Pickens and Clara Sue Ledbetter are:

> 805.   i.   THOMAS JAMES[13], born 11 Jan 1954 at Seattle, King Co., WA; married Sandra Lee Wright.

490.   BETTY JEAN[12] GOODMAN (*Austin*[11], *Hester*[10]*Johnson*, *William*[9], *Hiram*[8], *Charles*[7], *Ira*[6], *Jonathan*[5], *Nathaniel*[4], *Nathaniel*[3], *Humphrey*[2], *John*[1]) was born on 9 May 1923 at Burns, Harney Co., OR. She married Paul C. Brown on 4 Feb 1946 at Everett, Snohomish Co., WA.

Children of Betty Jean[12] Goodman and Paul C. Brown are as follows:

> i.   CHRIS EDWARD[13]; born 16 Nov 1946.
> ii.   MARK CHRISTIAN; born 31 Oct 1947.

491.   WILLIAM AUSTIN "AUTIE"[12] GOODMAN (*Austin*[11], *Hester*[10]*Johnson*, *William*[9], *Hiram*[8], *Charles*[7], *Ira*[6], *Jonathan*[5], *Nathaniel*[4], *Nathaniel*[3], *Humphrey*[2], *John*[1]) was born on 4 Aug 1925 at Burns, Harney Co., OR. He married Mildred Perry.

He was a professional singer.

Children of William Austin "Autie"[12] Goodman and Mildred Perry are as follows:

> i.   TERRY PAUL[13].
> ii.   TED J..
> iii.   JILL.
> iv.   KRIS.

492.   WARREN "GENE"[12] MCHARGUE (*Warren*[11], *Lulu*[10]*Johnson*, *William*[9], *Hiram*[8], *Charles*[7], *Ira*[6], *Jonathan*[5], *Nathaniel*[4], *Nathaniel*[3], *Humphrey*[2], *John*[1]) was born on 17 May 1929 at Ontario, OR. He married Louise Scholl. He and Louise Scholl were divorced. He died on 17 Jul 2002 at age 73. He was buried at Mt. View Cemetery, View (La Central), WA.

Children of Warren "Gene"[12] McHargue and Louise Scholl are as follows:

806.　　i.　MELANIE ANN[13], born 28 Apr 1949; married Gary Lane; married Richard John Sayre.

807.　　ii.　GARY STEVEN, born 8 Jun 1950; married Robin Ray Rapplege; divorced Robin Ray Rapplege; married Marla Jean (--?--).

Children of Warren "Gene"[12] McHargue and Kathy Gabrialson are as follows:

808.　　i.　KELLY[13], born 2 Jun 1964.

　　　　ii.　PATTY KAY; born 11 Oct 1966; married Scott Newhouse.

493. CARL WESLEY[12] MCHARGUE (*Warren*[11], *Lulu*[10]*Johnson*, *William*[9], *Hiram*[8], *Charles*[7], *Ira*[6], *Jonathan*[5], *Nathaniel*[4], *Nathaniel*[3], *Humphrey*[2], *John*[1]) was born on 17 Sep 1930 at Owhyee Dam, OR. He married LuAnn Lamborn on 11 Aug 1951. He and LuAnn Lamborn were divorced. He married Patricia Hine on 2 Apr 1957.

He lived in 2002 at Vancouver, Clark Co., WA.

Children of Carl Wesley[12] McHargue and LuAnn Lamborn are:

809.　　i.　KARLUA GAIL[13], born 9 May 1952 at Sacramento, CA; married (--?--) Cessna.

Children of Carl Wesley[12] McHargue and Patricia Hine are as follows:

810.　　i.　CATHRYN PATRICE[13], born 20 Jul 1958 at Swindon, England; married Doug Beseda.

811.　　ii.　CLAUDIA LYNNE, born 19 Mar 1963 at Moses Lake, WA; married Dan McGehee.

494. DELORES IRENE[12] MCHARGUE (*Warren*[11], *Lulu*[10]*Johnson*, *William*[9], *Hiram*[8], *Charles*[7], *Ira*[6], *Jonathan*[5], *Nathaniel*[4], *Nathaniel*[3], *Humphrey*[2], *John*[1]) was born on 23 Feb 1934. She married Raymond McPherson. She and Raymond McPherson were divorced.

She lived in 2002 at Long Beach, CA.

Children of Delores Irene[12] McHargue and Raymond McPherson are as follows:

i.   SEAN[13]; born 10 Feb 1964.

812.   ii.   MICHELLE, born 3 May 1967.

495. LLOYD JOSEPH[12] MCHARGUE (*Warren*[11], *Lulu*[10]*Johnson*, *William*[9], *Hiram*[8], *Charles*[7], *Ira*[6], *Jonathan*[5], *Nathaniel*[4], *Nathaniel*[3], *Humphrey*[2], *John*[1]) was born on 25 Sep 1938 at Aberdeen, Grays Harbor Co., WA. He married Anne M. Lambert on 7 Feb 1960.

He lived in 2003 at Shelton, WA.

Children of Lloyd Joseph[12] McHargue and Anne M. Lambert were as follows:

i.   TERESA MARIE[13]; born 25 Oct 1960 at Burlington, Skagit Co., WA; died 25 Oct 1960 at Burlington, Skagit Co., WA.

813.   ii.   JEFFERY SCOTT, born 21 Nov 1962 at Madigan Army Hospital, Tacoma, Pierce Co., WA; married Debbie A. Brice.

814.   iii.   TAMERA LEIGH, born 15 Jun 1964 at Everett, Snohomish Co., WA; married Glenn A. Wattum.

496. ROBERT AMBER[12] SMITH (*Francis*[11]*McHargue*, *Lulu*[10]*Johnson*, *William*[9], *Hiram*[8], *Charles*[7], *Ira*[6], *Jonathan*[5], *Nathaniel*[4], *Nathaniel*[3], *Humphrey*[2], *John*[1]) was born on 28 Jul 1939. He married Sandra Keller. He married Tina Mason in Jun 1966. He married Claudia Uzzell on 30 Dec 1968.

He lived in 2002 at San Diego, San Diego Co., CA.

Children of Robert Amber[12] Smith and Sandra Keller all born at San Diego, San Diego Co., CA, are as follows:

815.   i.   DIANA[13], born 5 Feb 1958; married Jim Rice.

816.   ii.   PATTY, born 13 Dec 1958; married Verl Craig.

817.   iii.   LORINE, born 5 May 1961; married Randy No.

Children of Robert Amber[12] Smith and Claudia Uzzell are:

i.   LISA[13]; born 22 Nov 1965 at San Diego, San Diego Co., CA.

There were no children of Robert Amber[12] Smith and Tina Mason.

497. WILLIAM RAY[12] MCHARGUE (*Rush*[11], *Lulu*[10]*Johnson*, *William*[9], *Hiram*[8], *Charles*[7], *Ira*[6], *Jonathan*[5], *Nathaniel*[4], *Nathaniel*[3], *Humphrey*[2], *John*[1]) was born on 7 Mar 1942 at Ontario, Malheur Co., OR. He married Sandra Lee Gill on 11 Feb 1963.

He lived in 2002 at Moses Lake, WA.

Children of William Ray[12] McHargue and Sandra Lee Gill are as follows:

818.   i.   SUSAN RENAE[13], born 4 May 1965 at Moscow, Latah Co., ID; married Mohamed Khatouri.

819.   ii.   DANIEL RUSH, born 8 Nov 1966 at Moscow, Latah Co., ID; married Sandra Bonnie Potter; divorced Sandra Bonnie Potter; married Jodi Lyn Miller.

820.   iii.   SHERYL ANN, born 17 Mar 1969 at White Salmon, Klickitat Co., WA; married Billie Lee Swindoll; divorced Billie Lee Swindoll; married Michael John Camporeale.

821.   iv.   LORI LYNN, born 23 Apr 1973 at Twin Falls, Twin Falls Co., ID; married Brad Evers.

822.   v.   LISA DIANE, born 31 Mar 1975 at Ontario, Malheur Co., OR; married Donald Robert Puhlman.

    vi.   RONALD ORIN; born 13 Jan 1980 at Weiser, Washington Co., ID; married Lacey J. Palmer 9 May 2002 at Portland, Multnomah Co., OR.

    He lived in 2000 at Sofia, Bulgaria.

498. JACK MERRELL[12] MCHARGUE (*Rush*[11], *Lulu*[10]*Johnson*, *William*[9], *Hiram*[8], *Charles*[7], *Ira*[6], *Jonathan*[5], *Nathaniel*[4], *Nathaniel*[3], *Humphrey*[2], *John*[1]) was born on 12 Sep 1945 at Ontario, Malheur Co., OR. He married Judy Stewart on 29 Aug 1965.

He lived in 2000 at Troy, ID.

Children of Jack Merrell[12] McHargue and Judy Stewart are as follows:

823.   i.   KRISTINE KAY[13], born 7 Sep 1968 at Spokane, Spokane Co., WA; married Robert Keith Winter.

        ii.   THOMAS O'NEAL; born 4 Oct 1970 at Boise, ID. He lived in 2000 at Troy, ID.

499.   JOSEPH ELDON[12] MCHARGUE (*Rush[11]*, *Lulu[10]Johnson*, *William[9]*, *Hiram[8]*, *Charles[7]*, *Ira[6]*, *Jonathan[5]*, *Nathaniel[4]*, *Nathaniel[3]*, *Humphrey[2]*, *John[1]*) was born on 9 Jul 1947 at Ontario, Malheur Co., OR. He married Linda Ann Skinner on 12 Jun 1966. He and Linda Ann Skinner were divorced. He married Mary Potter on 15 Mar 1985 at Burns, Harney Co., OR.

He lived in 2000 at Hines, Harney Co., OR.

Children of Joseph Eldon[12] McHargue and Linda Ann Skinner were as follows:

824.   i.   RHONDA JO[13], born 8 Jan 1967 at Burns, Harney Co., OR; married Christopher Everhart; divorced Christopher Everhart; married Samuel Perry Kingrey.

        ii.   KEBRA JEAN; born 20 Dec 1968 at Ontario, Malheur Co., OR; died 7 Nov 1983 at Crane, OR, at age 14.

825.   iii.   JOANNA LYN, born 1 Aug 1971 at Ontario, Malheur Co., OR; married Kelly Everhart; divorced Kelly Everhart; engaged Mitch Briggs.

Children of Joseph Eldon[12] McHargue and Mary Potter are as follows:

        i.   NICOLE[13]; born 21 Dec 1981.

        ii.   DAVID 'RYAN'; born 13 Jul 1985 at Redmond, Deschutes Co., OR.

        iii.   WADE THOMAS; born 1 Feb 1987 at Bend, Deschutes Co., OR.

        iv.   ROBERT RUSH; born 20 Oct 1989 at Bend, Deschutes Co., OR.

        v.   MARK TYLER; born 15 Oct 1996 at Moses Lake, Grant Co., WA.

500. RICHARD LEON^{12} MCHARGUE (*Leon^{11}, Lulu^{10}Johnson, William^9, Hiram^8, Charles^7, Ira^6, Jonathan^5, Nathaniel^4, Nathaniel^3, Humphrey^2, John^1*) was born on 23 Aug 1937 at Ontario, OR. He married Beverly Hall on 24 Aug 1957. He married LaNeeta (--?--). He married Barbara Robertson. He and Beverly Hall were divorced.

He lived in 2000 at Boise, ID.

Children of Richard Leon^{12} McHargue and Beverly Hall are:

826.   i.   LINDA JENNANIE^{13}, born 26 Mar 1958; married Robert Brant.

Children of Richard Leon^{12} McHargue and LaNeeta (--?--) are:

i.   MARK^{13}; born 7 Nov 1964.

Children of Richard Leon^{12} McHargue and Barbara Robertson are:

827.   i.   LILLENA JAE^{13}, born 7 Sep 1965; married Brian D. Pitcock.

501. FRANCIS MARIE^{12} MCHARGUE (*Leon^{11}, Lulu^{10}Johnson, William^9, Hiram^8, Charles^7, Ira^6, Jonathan^5, Nathaniel^4, Nathaniel^3, Humphrey^2, John^1*) was born on 27 Oct 1940 at Ontario, OR. She married Frances Leroy McKinney. She and Frances Leroy McKinney were divorced.

She lived in 2000 at Vale, OR.

Children of Francis Marie^{12} McHargue and Frances Leroy McKinney were as follows:

828.   i.   CAROLYN MARIE^{13}, born 22 Jun 1959; married Michael Baltzor.

ii.   SHARON LYNNE; born 7 Oct 1961; died 11 Feb 1969 at age 7.

502. MELVINA "LOUISE"^{12} MCHARGUE (*Leon^{11}, Lulu^{10}Johnson, William^9, Hiram^8, Charles^7, Ira^6, Jonathan^5, Nathaniel^4, Nathaniel^3, Humphrey^2, John^1*) was born on 10 Nov 1941 at Ontario, OR. She married Larry Roland Holmes on 17 Jul 1958. She and Larry Roland Holmes were divorced.

She lived in 2000 at Washougal, WA.

Children of Melvina "Louise"[12] McHargue and Larry Roland Holmes are as follows:

829.   i.   KEBBIE JO[13], born 21 Dec 1958; married Dwight Calhoun.

830.   ii.   RONALD DWAYNE, born 1 Oct 1960; married Machille (--?--).

831.   iii.   BRETT EVANS, born 17 Feb 1967; married (--?--) ?; divorced (--?--) ?

503.   DONNA JEAN[12] MCHARGUE (*Leon*[11], *Lulu*[10]*Johnson*, *William*[9], *Hiram*[8], *Charles*[7], *Ira*[6], *Jonathan*[5], *Nathaniel*[4], *Nathaniel*[3], *Humphrey*[2], *John*[1]) was born on 22 May 1943 at Ontario, OR. She married William C. Caughell on 17 Nov 1967. She and William C. Caughell were divorced. She married John Buckinger.

She lived in 2000 at Vancouver, Clark Co., WA.

Children of Donna Jean[12] McHargue and William C. Caughell are as follows:

i.   WILLIAM NEIL[13]; born 6 Feb 1972.

ii.   CLARA LYNNE; born 11 Jul 1974.

504.   JANICE KAY[12] MCHARGUE (*James*[11], *Lulu*[10]*Johnson*, *William*[9], *Hiram*[8], *Charles*[7], *Ira*[6], *Jonathan*[5], *Nathaniel*[4], *Nathaniel*[3], *Humphrey*[2], *John*[1]) was born on 16 Apr 1955 at Ontario, OR. She married James William Grimes. She and James William Grimes were divorced. She married David Stone.

She lived in 2000 at Goldendale, WA.

Children of Janice Kay[12] McHargue and James William Grimes are:

i.   IKE JAMES[13]; born 22 Nov 1979 at Ontario, OR.

505.   PAMELA ANN[12] MCHARGUE (*James*[11], *Lulu*[10]*Johnson*, *William*[9], *Hiram*[8], *Charles*[7], *Ira*[6], *Jonathan*[5], *Nathaniel*[4], *Nathaniel*[3], *Humphrey*[2], *John*[1]) was born on 22 Jul 1957 at Ontario, OR. She married Daniel Amos Stephens. She and Daniel Amos Stephens were divorced.

She lived in 2000 at Wenatchee, WA.

Children of Pamela Ann[12] McHargue and Daniel Amos Stephens both born at Boise, ID, are as follows:

    i.   ZACHARY AMOS[13]; born 11 Nov 1980.

    ii.   WILLIAM RUSH; born 10 Jun 1982.

506. THOMAS BRADLEY[12] GOUL (*Marilyn*[11]*McHargue, Lulu*[10]*Johnson, William*[9], *Hiram*[8], *Charles*[7], *Ira*[6], *Jonathan*[5], *Nathaniel*[4], *Nathaniel*[3], *Humphrey*[2], *John*[1]) was born on 28 Jul 1961 at Ontario, OR. He married Jacqueline Chadwick on 14 Feb 1987.

He lived in 2000 at Nyssa, OR.

Children of Thomas Bradley[12] Goul and Jacqueline Chadwick are as follows:

    i.   LINDSEY[13]; born 24 Sep 1989.

    ii.   SEAN; born 29 Jun 1992.

    iii.   KRYSTAL; born 3 Nov 1993.

507. LAURENCE EDWIN[12] JOHNSON (*Edwin*[11], *Claude*[10], *Hiram*[9], *Hiram*[8], *Charles*[7], *Ira*[6], *Jonathan*[5], *Nathaniel*[4], *Nathaniel*[3], *Humphrey*[2], *John*[1]) was born on 31 Jul 1941. He married Sharon Kaye Diemert on 23 Feb 1980.

Children of Laurence Edwin[12] Johnson and Sharon Kaye Diemert are:

    i.   ZACKERY EDWIN[13]; born 23 May 1982 at Seattle, King Co., WA.

508. GLENN EARLE[12] JOHNSON (*Edwin*[11], *Claude*[10], *Hiram*[9], *Hiram*[8], *Charles*[7], *Ira*[6], *Jonathan*[5], *Nathaniel*[4], *Nathaniel*[3], *Humphrey*[2], *John*[1]) was born on 30 Sep 1944. He married Carolyn Louise Grignon on 17 Jul 1965.

Children of Glenn Earle[12] Johnson and Carolyn Louise Grignon are as follows:

    i.   SYDNEY LOUISE[13]; born 4 Jul 1966.

    ii.   TODD EARLE; born 10 Sep 1968.

    iii.   ELIZABETH KATHRYN; born 11 Mar 1970.

509. RONALD KANZLER[12] HAMER (*Alvin[11], Myrtle[10]Johnson, Hiram[9], Hiram[8], Charles[7], Ira[6], Jonathan[5], Nathaniel[4], Nathaniel[3], Humphrey[2], John[1]*) was born on 24 Aug 1938. He married Linda Mae Greenwood.

Children of Ronald Kanzler[12] Hamer and Linda Mae Greenwood are as follows:

     i.   TERRI LYN[13]; born 17 Nov 1972.

     ii. ANN MARIE; born 8 Sep 1974.

     iii. TRACY ALENE; born 20 Mar 1976.

510. LYN ANN[12] JOHNSON (*Robert[11], Hiram[10], Hiram[9], Hiram[8], Charles[7], Ira[6], Jonathan[5], Nathaniel[4], Nathaniel[3], Humphrey[2], John[1]*) was born on 11 Jan 1965. She married Gary Lee Scott on 14 Jun 1982 at Longview, Cowlitz Co., WA.

She lived on 6 Sep 2000 at Rainier, OR.

Children of Lyn Ann[12] Johnson and Gary Lee Scott are:

     i.   DOUGLAS LEE[13]; born 15 Jul 1983.

511. SUSAN ANNE[12] JOHNSON (*Leo[11]Johnson, Hiram[10], Hiram[9], Hiram[8], Charles[7], Ira[6], Jonathan[5], Nathaniel[4], Nathaniel[3], Humphrey[2], John[1]*) married Howard Rucker Keister III on 3 Sep 1966 at McLean, VA. She and Howard Rucker Keister III were divorced on 1 Apr 1992 at Roanoke, VA.

Children of Susan Anne[12] JOHNSON and Howard Rucker Keister III are as follows:

     i.   JEFFREY WILLIAM[13]; born 30 Sep 1971.

     ii. LESLIE ANN; born 23 Jan 1974.

512. JACQUELINE MARIE[12] JOHNSON (*Leo[11]Johnson, Hiram[10], Hiram[9], Hiram[8], Charles[7], Ira[6], Jonathan[5], Nathaniel[4], Nathaniel[3], Humphrey[2], John[1]*) married David Peale on 10 Feb 1968 at McLean, VA.

Children of Jacqueline Marie[12] JOHNSON and David Peale are as follows:

     i.   MICHELLE MARIE[13]; born 25 Dec 1970.

ii.   KATHERINE ANNE; born 18 Dec 1972.

513. KAREN LEA^{12} JOHNSON (*Leo*^{11}*Johnson, Hiram*^{10}, *Hiram*^{9}, *Hiram*^{8}, *Charles*^{7}, *Ira*^{6}, *Jonathan*^{5}, *Nathaniel*^{4}, *Nathaniel*^{3}, *Humphrey*^{2}, *John*^{1}) married Robert Powell on 19 Aug 1972 at McLean, VA.

Children of Karen Lea^{12} JOHNSON and Robert Powell are as follows:

i.   JASON ROBERT^{13}.
ii.   COLLIN.
iii.   ALISON.

514. RICHARD EMILE^{12} AUFRANC (*Evelyn*^{11}*Johnson, Creta*^{10}, *Hiram*^{9}, *Hiram*^{8}, *Charles*^{7}, *Ira*^{6}, *Jonathan*^{5}, *Nathaniel*^{4}, *Nathaniel*^{3}, *Humphrey*^{2}, *John*^{1}) was born on 7 Dec 1936. He married Doris Lavonne Reynolds. He married Ava Dean Peterson.

Children of Richard Emile^{12} Aufranc and Doris Lavonne Reynolds are as follows:

832.   i.   JODY^{13}, born 9 Jan 1960; married Mark Rodgers.
833.   ii.   RICHARD EMILE JR., born 4 Oct 1968; married Julie (--?--).

There were no children of Richard Emile^{12} Aufranc and Ava Dean Peterson.

515. ACLE FRANCIS^{12} JOHNSON JR. (*Acle*^{11}, *Fred*^{10}, *Samuel*^{9}, *Hiram*^{8}, *Charles*^{7}, *Ira*^{6}, *Jonathan*^{5}, *Nathaniel*^{4}, *Nathaniel*^{3}, *Humphrey*^{2}, *John*^{1}) was born on 26 Oct 1925 at Okanogan, Okanogan Co., WA. He married Ann Agnes Cody on 9 Apr 1946 at Hartford, CT.

He lived in 2002 at Manchester, CT.

Children of Acle Francis^{12} Johnson Jr. and Ann Agnes Cody are as follows:

834.   i.   MICHAEL SHANNON^{13} SR., born 12 Apr 1948 at Seattle, King Co., WA; married Peggy Lee Golden.

835.   ii.   KATHLEEN ANN, born 3 May 1949 at Seattle, King Co., WA; married Al Augustus Paine Jr.

836.   iii.   STEVEN FRANCIS, born 24 Sep 1951 at Hartford, CT; married Lou Ann Nancy Nicol.

iv.   KEITH THOMAS; born 4 Oct 1954 at Hartford, CT; married Janis Cooper at Hamilton, MT; married Christine Daum 4 Jul 1997 at Stevenville, MT.

He lived in 2003 at Victor, MT.

837.   v.   LAURA LYNN, born 14 Sep 1964 at Manchester Memorial Hospital, Manchester, CT; married David Normand Rossignol; divorced David Normand Rossignol.

838.   vi.   SHELLY MARIE, born 23 Sep 1966 at Manchester Memorial Hospital, Manchester, CT; married Eric Martin Traumuller.

516.   MARVIN ELLIOTT[12] JOHNSON (*Acle*[11], *Fred*[10], *Samuel*[9], *Hiram*[8], *Charles*[7], *Ira*[6], *Jonathan*[5], *Nathaniel*[4], *Nathaniel*[3], *Humphrey*[2], *John*[1]) was born on 5 Oct 1928 at Eugene, OR. He married Marcia Quisenberry.

Children of Marvin Elliott[12] Johnson and Marcia Quisenberry are as follows:

839.   i.   MARC ELLIOTT[13], born 9 Sep 1952 at Oakland, CA; married Shirley Stern.

840.   ii.   MARCY JOANNE, born 13 Jun 1957 at Waukegan, IL; married Mitchell Dale Ragain.

841.   iii.   MARTIN EUGENE, born 27 Mar 1968 at Fremont, CA; married Yvette Marie Solano.

517.   VIRGINIA MAY[12] HENBEST (*Nellie*[11]*Johnson*, *Fred*[10], *Samuel*[9], *Hiram*[8], *Charles*[7], *Ira*[6], *Jonathan*[5], *Nathaniel*[4], *Nathaniel*[3], *Humphrey*[2], *John*[1]) was born on 14 Jul 1923. She married Dick Sour.

Children of Virginia May[12] Henbest and Dick Sour were as follows:

i.   DIANE[13].

ii. SANDRA.

iii. (--?--).

518. RICHARD EARL[12] HENBEST (*Nellie*[11]*Johnson, Fred*[10], *Samuel*[9], *Hiram*[8], *Charles*[7], *Ira*[6], *Jonathan*[5], *Nathaniel*[4], *Nathaniel*[3], *Humphrey*[2], *John*[1]) was born on 16 Oct 1925. He married ? (--?--).

Children of Richard Earl[12] Henbest and ? (--?--) are as follows:

        i. CURTES LYNN[13]; born 1 May 1947 at Roseburg, Douglas Co., OR.

842.   ii. RICHARD EARL II, born 10 Jun 1948 at Oahu, Territory of Hawaii; married Mabel Arlene Wood; married Karen Mullens.

843.   iii. MICHAEL LEE, born 10 Feb 1951 at Roseburg, Douglas Co., OR; married Margaret Waenwright.

        iv. JAMES PATRICK; born 6 Apr 1955 at Oahu, Territory of Hawaii; married Mabel Arlene Wood.

519. DONALD ALVA[12] WILLIAMS (*Gertrude*[11]*Johnson, Fred*[10], *Samuel*[9], *Hiram*[8], *Charles*[7], *Ira*[6], *Jonathan*[5], *Nathaniel*[4], *Nathaniel*[3], *Humphrey*[2], *John*[1]) was born on 16 Aug 1926 at Roseburg, Douglas Co., OR. He married Laurel Anne Sherar. He died on 4 Apr 1986 at Portland, Multnomah Co., OR, at age 59.

Children of Donald Alva[12] Williams and Laurel Anne Sherar are as follows:

844.   i. DONALD DAYLE[13], married Lynn (--?--).

        ii. DEAN ALAN.

520. CAROLYN JANE[12] WILLIAMS (*Gertrude*[11]*Johnson, Fred*[10], *Samuel*[9], *Hiram*[8], *Charles*[7], *Ira*[6], *Jonathan*[5], *Nathaniel*[4], *Nathaniel*[3], *Humphrey*[2], *John*[1]) was born on 15 Aug 1931 at Yreka, CA. She married Philip Perry Hickman on 5 Jan 1949 at Portland, Multnomah Co., OR.

Children of Carolyn Jane[12] Williams and Philip Perry Hickman are as follows:

        i. MARCIA MARIE[13].

ii. MARDELL RAE.

iii. MARGO ANN.

iv. MICHEL PHILIP.

521. SHARON LEE[12] JOHNSON (*Samuel*[11], *Fred*[10], *Samuel*[9], *Hiram*[8], *Charles*[7], *Ira*[6], *Jonathan*[5], *Nathaniel*[4], *Nathaniel*[3], *Humphrey*[2], *John*[1]) was born on 30 May 1939 at Colville, Stevens Co., WA. She married William Clayton Lacey on 2 Jul 1960 at Portland, Multnomah Co., OR.

Children of Sharon Lee[12] Johnson and William Clayton Lacey both born at Burien, King Co., WA, are as follows:

845.   i.   JEFFERY SCOTT[13], born 21 Feb 1963; married Dana Marie Anderson.

846.   ii.   ERIN LEE, born 7 Jan 1967; married Lemont K. Aukland.

522. RONALD DAYLE[12] JOHNSON (*Samuel*[11], *Fred*[10], *Samuel*[9], *Hiram*[8], *Charles*[7], *Ira*[6], *Jonathan*[5], *Nathaniel*[4], *Nathaniel*[3], *Humphrey*[2], *John*[1]) was born on 31 Aug 1940 at Colville, Stevens Co., WA. He married Modena Joyce Lane on 3 Aug 1959 at Portland, Multnomah Co., OR.

He lived in 2002 at Hillsboro, OR.

Children of Ronald Dayle[12] Johnson and Modena Joyce Lane both born at Burien, King Co., WA, are as follows:

847.   i.   DARCEY LYNNE[13], born 11 Feb 1964; married Dirk Theodore Knudsen.

848.   ii.   DARYL LANE, born 20 Dec 1966; married Teresa Elizabeth Lauinger.

523. PATRICIA LOU[12] MATHIESEN (*Geneva*[11]*Wagenblast*, *Edythe*[10]*Johnson*, *Samuel*[9], *Hiram*[8], *Charles*[7], *Ira*[6], *Jonathan*[5], *Nathaniel*[4], *Nathaniel*[3], *Humphrey*[2], *John*[1]) was born on 11 Jan 1928 at Portland, Multnomah Co., OR. She married Theodore Crandall. She married Harvey Simmelink on 21 Aug 1965.

Children of Patricia Lou[12] Mathiesen and Theodore Crandall both born at Portland, Multnomah Co., OR, are as follows:

i.   CLAY MATTHEW[13]; born 22 Feb 1956.

ii. AMY LOUISE; born 4 Oct 1959.

There were no children of Patricia Lou[12] Mathiesen and Harvey Simmelink.

524. JAMES PETER[12] MATHIESEN (*Geneva*[11]*Wagenblast*, *Edythe*[10]*Johnson, Samuel*[9], *Hiram*[8], *Charles*[7], *Ira*[6], *Jonathan*[5], *Nathaniel*[4], *Nathaniel*[3], *Humphrey*[2], *John*[1]) was born on 30 Dec 1932 at Portland, Multnomah Co., OR. He married Sandra Burton on 2 Jan 1955 at Portland, Multnomah Co., OR.

Children of James Peter[12] Mathiesen and Sandra Burton both born at Portland, Multnomah Co., OR, are as follows:

i. DIANE VICTORIA[13]; born 20 Feb 1964.
ii. MATHEW JAMES; born 16 Dec 1965.

525. KATHRYNE JOAN[12] WAGENBLAST (*James*[11], *Edythe*[10]*Johnson, Samuel*[9], *Hiram*[8], *Charles*[7], *Ira*[6], *Jonathan*[5], *Nathaniel*[4], *Nathaniel*[3], *Humphrey*[2], *John*[1]) was born on 24 Dec 1929. She married Ernest Vernon Risberg on 20 Mar 1949 at Reedville, OR.

Children of Kathryne Joan[12] Wagenblast and Ernest Vernon Risberg all born at Portland, Multnomah Co., OR, are as follows:

i. RONALD GARY[13]; born 10 Feb 1950.
ii. KATHRYNE HELEN; born 4 Jul 1953.
iii. BARBARA JOAN; born 27 Mar 1956; married Kevin Harrison 6 Oct 1979.

526. JAMES EDWARD[12] WAGENBLAST II (*James*[11], *Edythe*[10]*Johnson, Samuel*[9], *Hiram*[8], *Charles*[7], *Ira*[6], *Jonathan*[5], *Nathaniel*[4], *Nathaniel*[3], *Humphrey*[2], *John*[1]) was born on 10 Apr 1933. He married Sheila Mathis in Oct 1951. He married Mary Kingsley.

Children of James Edward[12] Wagenblast II and Sheila Mathis were as follows:

i. JAMES E.[13] III; born 1962; died 1976.
ii. RANDI; married Gordon Ledbetter.
iii. CONNIE; married David Jasnock.

iv.   STEWART R..

There were no children of James Edward[12] Wagenblast II and Mary Kingsley.

527.   GEORGE   MICHAEL[12]   WAGENBLAST   (*Maurice*[11], *Edythe*[10]*Johnson, Samuel*[9], *Hiram*[8], *Charles*[7], *Ira*[6], *Jonathan*[5], *Nathaniel*[4], *Nathaniel*[3], *Humphrey*[2], *John*[1]) was born on 1 May 1947. He married Susan Jensen. He married Gloria Jean Stringham.

There were no children of George Michael[12] Wagenblast and Susan Jensen.

Children of George Michael[12] Wagenblast and Gloria Jean Stringham are as follows:

  i.   CHRISTOPHER MICHAEL[13]; born 19 Aug 1966.
  ii.   BROOKE MICHELLE; born 9 Aug 1975.

528.   MARY   KATHRYN[12]   WAGENBLAST   (*Maurice*[11], *Edythe*[10]*Johnson, Samuel*[9], *Hiram*[8], *Charles*[7], *Ira*[6], *Jonathan*[5], *Nathaniel*[4], *Nathaniel*[3], *Humphrey*[2], *John*[1]) was born on 13 May 1953. She married Clark Alan Hockstetler on 28 Jun 1975 at St. Paul, OR.

Children of Mary Kathryn[12] Wagenblast and Clark Alan Hockstetler are:

  i.   MORGAN ELIZABETH[13]; born 26 Apr 1983 at Portland, Multnomah Co., OR.

529.   SUSAN   CAROL[12]   FALKENHAGEN   (*Mabel*[11]*Wagenblast, Edythe*[10]*Johnson, Samuel*[9], *Hiram*[8], *Charles*[7], *Ira*[6], *Jonathan*[5], *Nathaniel*[4], *Nathaniel*[3], *Humphrey*[2], *John*[1]) was born on 3 Oct 1942 at Tacoma, Pierce Co., WA. She married Marcus Policar on 18 Mar 1967.

Children of Susan Carol[12] Falkenhagen and Marcus Policar are as follows:

  i.   JOHN MICHAEL[13]; born 4 Aug 1972.
  ii.   DAVID VICTOR; born 18 May 1976.
  iii.   JAMES MARCUS; born 6 Jul 1977.

530. JACQUE RODNEY[12] DILMORE (*Sayre*[11], *Saphronia*[10]*Johnson*, *Elgin*[9], *Abel*[8], *Charles*[7], *Ira*[6], *Jonathan*[5], *Nathaniel*[4], *Nathaniel*[3], *Humphrey*[2], *John*[1]) was born on 5 Aug 1931. He married Joyce Ina Burgess on 5 Nov 1955 at Lemont, PA.

Children of Jacque Rodney[12] Dilmore and Joyce Ina Burgess are as follows:

    i.   JOHN MARTIN[13]; born 17 Sep 1957.
    ii.   JENNIFER JO; born 6 Mar 1965.

531. ELEANOR LOUISE[12] JOHNSON (*Donald*[11], *Abel*[10], *Elgin*[9], *Abel*[8], *Charles*[7], *Ira*[6], *Jonathan*[5], *Nathaniel*[4], *Nathaniel*[3], *Humphrey*[2], *John*[1]) was born on 5 May 1935 at Syracuse, Onondaga Co., NY. She married Wendel Dwight Lilly, son of George David Lilly and Beulah Geneive Griffin, on 23 Jun 1956 at Syracuse, Onondaga Co., NY.

She was also known as Eleanor Louise Beagle.

Children of Eleanor Louise[12] Johnson and Wendel Dwight Lilly are as follows:

849.   i.   KAREN LOUISE[13], born 17 Apr 1957 at Columbia, Richland Co., SC; married Kenneth Wayne Craven.
850.   ii.   KEVIN DWIGHT, born 9 Feb 1959 at St. Petersburg, Pinellas Co., FL; married Cheryl Ann Toth.
    iii.   KEITH DONALD; born 22 Jan 1970 at St. Petersburg, Pinellas Co., FL.

532. DONNA LEE[12] JOHNSON (*Donald*[11], *Abel*[10], *Elgin*[9], *Abel*[8], *Charles*[7], *Ira*[6], *Jonathan*[5], *Nathaniel*[4], *Nathaniel*[3], *Humphrey*[2], *John*[1]) was born on 17 Nov 1944 at Syracuse, Onondaga Co., NY. She married Richard Arnold Hall, son of Emory Leland Hall and Pauline Doris Beckley, on 5 Feb 1966 at St. Petersburg, Pinellas Co., FL.

Children of Donna Lee[12] Johnson and Richard Arnold Hall are as follows:

851.   i.   DONALD DEAN[13], born 25 Feb 1965 at St. Petersburg, Pinellas Co., FL; married Shannon Reyna Scalf; divorced Shannon Reyna Scalf.

        ii.   DARYL EMORY; born 24 Feb 1967 at St. Petersburg, Pinellas Co., FL.

        iii.   RICHARD ASHLEY; born 8 Jan 1970 at Tallahassee, Leon Co., FL; married Cherylin Seman, daughter of John Karl Seman and Ellen Lynn Chauncey, 6 Jun 1992 at Crossville, Cumberland Co., TN.

852.   iv.   SARAH ELIZABETH, born 20 Jul 1972 at Knoxville, Knox Co., TN; married Raymond Allen Thacker Jr.

        v.   REBECCA GRACE BECKLEY; born 15 Aug 1983 at Knoxville, Knox Co., TN.

533. WILLIAM HERBERT[12] SAHM III (*Ruth*[11]*Johnson, Abel*[10], *Elgin*[9], *Abel*[8], *Charles*[7], *Ira*[6], *Jonathan*[5], *Nathaniel*[4], *Nathaniel*[3], *Humphrey*[2], *John*[1]) was born on 14 Apr 1939. He married Ludmila Jandolenko on 6 Nov 1966 at Syracuse, Onondoga Co., NY.

Children of William Herbert[12] Sahm III and Ludmila Jandolenko are as follows:

        i.   PETER[13]; born 23 Dec 1967.

        ii.   TANIA; born 4 Jan 1970.

534. RUTH ANN[12] SAHM (*Ruth*[11]*Johnson, Abel*[10], *Elgin*[9], *Abel*[8], *Charles*[7], *Ira*[6], *Jonathan*[5], *Nathaniel*[4], *Nathaniel*[3], *Humphrey*[2], *John*[1]) was born on 1 Feb 1943 at Syracuse, Onondoga Co., NY. She married Cleo A. Dorpinghaus.

Children of Ruth Ann[12] Sahm and Cleo A. Dorpinghaus are as follows:

        i.   DOUGLAS JAMES[13]; born 10 Aug 1962.

        ii.   THERESA; born 2 Oct 1963.

        iii.   AMY CHRISTINE; born 19 Mar 1969.

535. LARRY GENE[12] SAHM (*Ruth*[11]*Johnson, Abel*[10], *Elgin*[9], *Abel*[8], *Charles*[7], *Ira*[6], *Jonathan*[5], *Nathaniel*[4], *Nathaniel*[3],

Humphrey[2], *John*[1]) was born on 6 Feb 1945 at Syracuse, Onondoga Co., NY. He married Cheryl Hoar on 19 Jun at Fulton, NY. He died on 11 Feb 1984 at Syracuse, Onondoga Co., NY, at age 39.

Children of Larry Gene[12] Sahm and Cheryl Hoar are as follows:

    i.   TODD[13]; born Jan 1970.

    ii.   FILIP.

    iii.   HANA.

536. LUELLA JEAN[12] SAHM (*Ruth*[11]*Johnson*, *Abel*[10], *Elgin*[9], *Abel*[8], *Charles*[7], *Ira*[6], *Jonathan*[5], *Nathaniel*[4], *Nathaniel*[3], *Humphrey*[2], *John*[1]) was born on 6 Feb 1945 at Syracuse, Onondoga Co., NY. She married David Arthur Klotz on 10 Oct 1966 at Syracuse, Onondoga Co., NY.

Children of Luella Jean[12] Sahm and David Arthur Klotz are as follows:

    i.   DANIEL JAMES[13]; born 20 Sep 1969.

    ii.   DENNIS JOEL; born 6 Mar 1972.

    iii.   DARREN JEFFREY; born 20 Feb 1980.

    iv.   DARCY AMANDA; born 4 Apr 1983.

537. JOYCE SANDRA[12] SAHM (*Ruth*[11]*Johnson*, *Abel*[10], *Elgin*[9], *Abel*[8], *Charles*[7], *Ira*[6], *Jonathan*[5], *Nathaniel*[4], *Nathaniel*[3], *Humphrey*[2], *John*[1]) was born on 17 Aug 1946. She married Paul Herbert Opolski on 8 Jul 1967 at Syracuse, Onondoga Co., NY.

Children of Joyce Sandra[12] Sahm and Paul Herbert Opolski are as follows:

    i.   JAIME MAY[13]; born 10 Jan 1977.

    ii.   JOHANNA PAULA; born 3 Aug 1980.

538. BEVERLY JOY[12] SAHM (*Ruth*[11]*Johnson*, *Abel*[10], *Elgin*[9], *Abel*[8], *Charles*[7], *Ira*[6], *Jonathan*[5], *Nathaniel*[4], *Nathaniel*[3], *Humphrey*[2], *John*[1]) was born on 29 Jul 1949 at Syracuse, Onondoga Co., NY. She married Milton Earl Oakley on 24 Aug 1968 at Syracuse, Onondoga Co., NY.

Children of Beverly Joy[12] Sahm and Milton Earl Oakley are as follows:

     i.   KIMBERLY JOY[13]; born 10 Jan 1970.

    ii.   JONATHAN EARL; born 6 Jun 1971.

539. GLORIA JEAN[12] JOHNSON (*Abel*[11], *Abel*[10], *Elgin*[9], *Abel*[8], *Charles*[7], *Ira*[6], *Jonathan*[5], *Nathaniel*[4], *Nathaniel*[3], *Humphrey*[2], *John*[1]) was born on 7 Jun 1948 at Syracuse, Onondoga Co., NY. She married Richard Rudolph Yenny, son of Rudolph Yenny and Hazel Storrier, on 22 Jul 1972 at North Syracuse, Onondoga Co., NY.

Children of Gloria Jean[12] Johnson and Richard Rudolph Yenny are as follows:

     i.   MATTHEW RICHARD[13]; born 6 Mar 1973.

    ii.   SARA ELIZABETH; born 7 Aug 1978 at Syracuse, Onondaga Co., NY.

540. JEANINE MARIE[12] JOHNSON (*Abel*[11], *Abel*[10], *Elgin*[9], *Abel*[8], *Charles*[7], *Ira*[6], *Jonathan*[5], *Nathaniel*[4], *Nathaniel*[3], *Humphrey*[2], *John*[1]) was born on 19 Jul 1949 at Syracuse, Onondoga Co., NY. She married Keith Nelson Zinsmeyer, son of Henry Alfred Zinsmeyer and Thelma Kathrine Gratzer, on 31 Oct 1969 at North Syracuse, Onondoga Co., NY.

Children of Jeanine Marie[12] Johnson and Keith Nelson Zinsmeyer are:

     i.   JON MICHAEL[13]; born 24 Oct 1978 at Syracuse, Onondaga Co., NY.

541. ABEL PHILLIP[12] JOHNSON JR. (*Abel*[11], *Abel*[10], *Elgin*[9], *Abel*[8], *Charles*[7], *Ira*[6], *Jonathan*[5], *Nathaniel*[4], *Nathaniel*[3], *Humphrey*[2], *John*[1]) was born on 26 Apr 1951 at Syracuse, Onondoga Co., NY. He married Melody Lynn Dove, daughter of Roy Dove and Shirley Ann Robertson, on 21 Sep 1981 at St. Petersburg, Pinellas Co., FL. He and Melody Lynn Dove were divorced. He married Karen Sue Hayamker, daughter of John Schwartz Hayamker Jr. and Catherine Florence Mudd, on 11 Nov 1995 at Orlando, Orange Co., FL.

Children of Abel Phillip[12] Johnson Jr. and Melody Lynn Dove are:

i. ADRIENNE LYNN[13]; born 26 Dec 1982 at St. Petersburg, Pinellas Co., FL.

There were no children of Abel Phillip[12] Johnson Jr. and Karen Sue Hayamker.

542. ILENE SUZANNE[12] JOHNSON (*Abel[11]*, *Abel[10]*, *Elgin[9]*, *Abel[8]*, *Charles[7]*, *Ira[6]*, *Jonathan[5]*, *Nathaniel[4]*, *Nathaniel[3]*, *Humphrey[2]*, *John[1]*) was born on 27 Nov 1953 at Syracuse, Onondoga Co., NY. She married Herbert Forrest Marshall Jr., son of Herbert Forest Marshall Sr. and Agnes Sylvia Gaines, on 6 May 1972 at Syracuse, Onondaga Co., NY.

Children of Ilene Suzanne[12] Johnson and Herbert Forrest Marshall Jr. all born at Syracuse, Onondaga Co., NY, are as follows:

853.   i.   ERIC FORREST[13], born 15 Nov 1972; married Jamie Lynn Fitch.
854.   ii.   JOSEPH MICHAEL, born 9 Oct 1978; married Danielle Nichole Jenkins.
            iii.   GREGORY HERBERT; born 11 Mar 1981.
            iv.   CAROLINE; born 2 Jul 1984.

543. PATRICIA CLARE[12] JOHNSON (*Abel[11]*, *Abel[10]*, *Elgin[9]*, *Abel[8]*, *Charles[7]*, *Ira[6]*, *Jonathan[5]*, *Nathaniel[4]*, *Nathaniel[3]*, *Humphrey[2]*, *John[1]*) was born on 13 Jun 1957 at Syracuse, Onondoga Co., NY. She married Richard Welcome Gearsbeck II, son of Richard Welcome Gearsbeck Sr. and Margaret Ryder, on 8 Mar 1980 at Mattydale, Onondaga Co., NY.

Children of Patricia Clare[12] Johnson and Richard Welcome Gearsbeck II are as follows:

            i.   RICHARD WELCOME[13] III; born 3 Oct 1980 at Syracuse, Onondaga Co., NY.
            ii.   MICHAEL JAMES; born 21 May 1982 at Syracuse, Onondaga Co., NY.
            iii.   KATIE.

544. LANETTE ANN[12] JOHNSON (*Abel[11]*, *Abel[10]*, *Elgin[9]*, *Abel[8]*, *Charles[7]*, *Ira[6]*, *Jonathan[5]*, *Nathaniel[4]*, *Nathaniel[3]*, *Humphrey[2]*, *John[1]*) was born on 8 Jan 1964 at Syracuse, Onondoga Co., NY.

She married Darryl John Buist Sr. on 8 May 1982 at Seminole, Pinellas Co., FL. She and Darryl John Buist Sr. were divorced. She married William Olmstead.

Children of Lanette Ann[12] Johnson and Darryl John Buist Sr. both born at St. Petersburg, Pinellas Co., FL, are as follows:

    i.   DARRYL JOHN[13] JR.; born 16 Jul 1982.

    ii. DAVID ANTHONY; born 1983.

Children of Lanette Ann[12] Johnson and William Olmstead all born at St. Petersburg, Pinellas Co., FL, are as follows:

    i.   JULIE[13]

    ii.   JENIFER

    iii. HEATHER

    iv. CRISTINE;

545. KATHLEEN MARIE[12] JOHNSON (*Robert*[11], *Abel*[10], *Elgin*[9], *Abel*[8], *Charles*[7], *Ira*[6], *Jonathan*[5], *Nathaniel*[4], *Nathaniel*[3], *Humphrey*[2], *John*[1]) was born on 12 May 1943 at Rome, Onieda Co., NY. She married Bradford James Pettit on 27 Oct 1962 at Baldwinsville, NY.

Children of Kathleen Marie[12] Johnson and Bradford James Pettit are as follows:

    i.   LAWRENCE JAMES[13]; born 17 Mar 1964.

    ii. BRADFORD JAMES JR.; born 26 Mar 1965.

    iii. DONALD ALVIN; born 7 Jul 1967.

    iv. DEBORAH RENEE; born 7 Jul 1967.

    v. MICHELLE LYNN; born 2 Mar 1974.

546. ROBERT EARL[12] JOHNSON (*Robert*[11], *Abel*[10], *Elgin*[9], *Abel*[8], *Charles*[7], *Ira*[6], *Jonathan*[5], *Nathaniel*[4], *Nathaniel*[3], *Humphrey*[2], *John*[1]) was born on 6 Nov 1945. He married Sharon Yvette Chapman on 6 Aug 1966 at Baltimore, MD.

Children of Robert Earl[12] Johnson and Sharon Yvette Chapman are:

  855.   i. TRISTAN ALEXANDER[13], born 7 Jun 1978 at Baltimore, MD.

547. DONALD RUPERT[12] NOBLE JR. (*Donald*[11], *Ferne*[10]*Johnson,
Charles*[9], *William*[8], *Charles*[7], *Ira*[6], *Jonathan*[5], *Nathaniel*[4],
Nathaniel[3], *Humphrey*[2], *John*[1]) was born on 11 Dec 1941. He
married Glee Gillies on 5 Sep 1964.

Children of Donald Rupert[12] Noble Jr. and Glee Gillies are as
follows:

    i.   JULIA FERN[13]; born 8 Oct 1971.

   ii.   JENNY CLAIRE; born 24 Sep 1973.

548. CONSTANCE FAITH[12] NOBLE (*Donald*[11], *Ferne*[10]*Johnson,
Charles*[9], *William*[8], *Charles*[7], *Ira*[6], *Jonathan*[5], *Nathaniel*[4],
Nathaniel[3], *Humphrey*[2], *John*[1]) was born on 6 Jan 1950. She
married Eugene Thomas Kesicke on 24 Oct 1974.

Children of Constance Faith[12] Noble and Eugene Thomas
Kesicke are as follows:

    i.   CLAIRE MARIE[13]; born 6 Feb 1980.

   ii.   NICHOLAS PAUL; born 10 Apr 1983.

549. PHYLLIS[12] NOBLE (*Worth*[11], *Ferne*[10]*Johnson, Charles*[9],
William[8], *Charles*[7], *Ira*[6], *Jonathan*[5], *Nathaniel*[4], *Nathaniel*[3],
Humphrey[2], *John*[1]) was born on 14 Jul 1953 at Ogdensburg, NY.
She married Wayne Brock on 17 May 1980.

Children of Phyllis[12] Noble and Wayne Brock are:

    i.   CALLI JOANNE[13]; born 29 Jul 1983.

550. GLORIA JEAN[12] JOHNSON (*Charles*[11], *John*[10], *Charles*[9],
William[8], *Charles*[7], *Ira*[6], *Jonathan*[5], *Nathaniel*[4], *Nathaniel*[3],
Humphrey[2], *John*[1]) was born on 16 Mar 1948. She married Arthur
Alexander on 16 Aug 1969 at Hermon, St. Lawrence Co., NY. She
married Donald Jones on 21 Feb 2000.

Children of Gloria Jean[12] Johnson and Arthur Alexander were as
follows:

    i.   MARK EDWARD[13]; born 8 Feb 1974; married
       Lisa Kimberly Toda 19 Dec 2002.

ii. GARY JONES; born 1984 at Gouverneur, St. Lawrence Co., NY.

There were no children of Gloria Jean[12] Johnson and Donald Jones.

551. CHARLES VANCE[12] JOHNSON JR. (*Charles*[11], *John*[10], *Charles*[9], *William*[8], *Charles*[7], *Ira*[6], *Jonathan*[5], *Nathaniel*[4], *Nathaniel*[3], *Humphrey*[2], *John*[1]) was born on 10 Feb 1953. He married Cynthia Brice on 5 Jul 1975. He married Michele Gail Wahlers.

Children of Charles Vance[12] Johnson Jr. and Cynthia Brice are as follows:

i. JOHN CHARLES[13]; born 1 Nov 1976.
ii. HEATHER ELLEN; born 1 Aug 1980.
iii. TRACEY MAE; born 14 Aug 1982.

Children of Charles Vance[12] Johnson Jr. and Michele Gail Wahlers are as follows:

i. JENNIFER RENE[13]; born 26 Apr 1982.
ii. JULIETTE MARIE; born 2 Jun 1985.

552. DEBORAH ANN[12] JOHNSON (*John*[11], *John*[10], *Charles*[9], *William*[8], *Charles*[7], *Ira*[6], *Jonathan*[5], *Nathaniel*[4], *Nathaniel*[3], *Humphrey*[2], *John*[1]) was born on 7 Aug 1955 at Canton, St. Lawrence Co., NY. She married Dale E. Matthews. She and Dale E. Matthews were divorced in 1980.

Children of Deborah Ann[12] Johnson and Dale E. Matthews are:

i. WENDY MARIE[13]; born 16 Nov 1976 at Watertown, Jefferson Co., NY; married Eric L. Foster 2 Jun 2002.

553. CHRISTINE MARION[12] JOHNSON (*John*[11], *John*[10], *Charles*[9], *William*[8], *Charles*[7], *Ira*[6], *Jonathan*[5], *Nathaniel*[4], *Nathaniel*[3], *Humphrey*[2], *John*[1]) was born on 19 Dec 1956 at Canton, St. Lawrence Co., NY. She married Dwayne Ronald Blandin on 28 Jul 1978.

Children of Christine Marion[12] Johnson and Dwayne Ronald Blandin are as follows:

      i.   ALYSIA ANN[13]; born 30 Aug 1980.

      ii. AUTUM RILEY; born 4 Sep 1999.

554. JOHN WARREN[12] JOHNSON III (*John[11]*, *John[10]*, *Charles[9]*, *William[8]*, *Charles[7]*, *Ira[6]*, *Jonathan[5]*, *Nathaniel[4]*, *Nathaniel[3]*, *Humphrey[2]*, *John[1]*) was born on 29 Apr 1960 at Gouverneur, St. Lawrence Co., NY. He married Sondra Goodnough on 17 Jul 2003.

Children of John Warren[12] Johnson III and Sondra Goodnough are:

      i.   JOHN WARREN[13] IV; born 27 Mar 1999 at Ogdensburg, St. Lawrence Co., NY.

555. KATHERINE MARGIE[12] JOHNSON (*John[11]*, *John[10]*, *Charles[9]*, *William[8]*, *Charles[7]*, *Ira[6]*, *Jonathan[5]*, *Nathaniel[4]*, *Nathaniel[3]*, *Humphrey[2]*, *John[1]*) was born on 3 May 1968 at Watertown, Jefferson Co., NY. She married Robert Beauchamp on 23 Sep 1995.

Children of Katherine Margie[12] Johnson and Robert Beauchamp are:

      i.   TIMOTHY JOHN[13]; born 5 May 2000.

556. SANDRA JEAN[12] KILMER (*Eleanor[11]Johnson*, *John[10]*, *Charles[9]*, *William[8]*, *Charles[7]*, *Ira[6]*, *Jonathan[5]*, *Nathaniel[4]*, *Nathaniel[3]*, *Humphrey[2]*, *John[1]*) was born on 4 Mar 1951 at Guam. She married Theodore Ralph Pfeiffer on 1 Jul 1969 at Arlington, Snohomish Co., WA.

Children of Sandra Jean[12] Kilmer and Theodore Ralph Pfeiffer both born at Arlington, Snohomish Co., WA, are as follows:

  856.   i.   KARIE ANN[13], born 1 May 1970; married Matthew Simmons; divorced Matthew Simmons; married Todd McInturff.

          ii. BRIAN KEITH; born 13 Aug 1972. He lived in 2003 at Seattle, WA.

557. JEAN MARIE[12] EDWARDS (*Phyllis[11]Johnson*, *John[10]*, *Charles[9]*, *William[8]*, *Charles[7]*, *Ira[6]*, *Jonathan[5]*, *Nathaniel[4]*,

*Nathaniel*³, *Humphrey*², *John*¹) was born on 21 Jun 1955. She married Paul Francis Merithew on 11 Jun 1977.

Children of Jean Marie¹² Edwards and Paul Francis Merithew are as follows:

   857.   i.   HOLLI ANN¹³, born 23 Apr 1979.

          ii.   MICHAEL PAUL; born 25 Aug 1980; married Dana Coffey.

         iii.   JESSICA ERIN; born 25 Apr 1982.

558. JAQUELINE KAY¹² EDWARDS (*Phyllis*¹¹*Johnson, John*¹⁰, *Charles*⁹, *William*⁸, *Charles*⁷, *Ira*⁶, *Jonathan*⁵, *Nathaniel*⁴, *Nathaniel*³, *Humphrey*², *John*¹) was born on 14 Mar 1957. She married Edward C. Gauthier on 21 May 1983.

Children of Jaqueline Kay¹² Edwards and Edward C. Gauthier are:

         i.   GRAHAM HUNTER¹³; born 21 Jun 1985 at Canton, NY.

559. TERRY LYNN¹² EDWARDS (*Phyllis*¹¹*Johnson, John*¹⁰, *Charles*⁹, *William*⁸, *Charles*⁷, *Ira*⁶, *Jonathan*⁵, *Nathaniel*⁴, *Nathaniel*³, *Humphrey*², *John*¹) was born on 4 Jul 1958. She married Blane Harding on 19 Jul 1986 at Auburn, NY.

Children of Terry Lynn¹² Edwards and Blane Harding are as follows:

         i.   MARIE THERESA¹³; born 12 Feb 1989 at Auburn, NY.

         ii.   TONI ELIZABETH; born 9 Sep 1992 at Loveland, CO.

         iii.   CHRISTOPHER AARON; born 14 Apr 1994 at Loveland, CO.

         iv.   KYLE ALEXANDER; born 14 Apr 1994 at Loveland, CO.

560. TONI LEA¹² EDWARDS (*Phyllis*¹¹*Johnson, John*¹⁰, *Charles*⁹, *William*⁸, *Charles*⁷, *Ira*⁶, *Jonathan*⁵, *Nathaniel*⁴, *Nathaniel*³,

Humphrey[2], *John*[1]) was born on 21 May 1968. She married Darren Brabaw. She married Bartle Canny.

There were no children of Toni Lea[12] Edwards and Darren Brabaw.

Children of Toni Lea[12] Edwards and Bartle Canny are as follows:

    i.   NICHOLAS GLYNN[13]; born 12 Feb 1999.
    ii.   CHRISTOPHER GRAHAM; born 9 Jul 2001.

561.   BARBARA JEAN[12] SAYER (*Nancy*[11]*Johnson*, *John*[10], *Charles*[9], *William*[8], *Charles*[7], *Ira*[6], *Jonathan*[5], *Nathaniel*[4], *Nathaniel*[3], *Humphrey*[2], *John*[1]) was born on 6 Jul 1959 at Canton, NY. She married James Blackburn on 24 Jul 1977. She married Gary Butler on 13 Mar 1985.

Children of Barbara Jean[12] Sayer and James Blackburn are as follows:

    i.   JAMES NEIL[13] JR.; born 28 Apr 1977.
    ii.   TONIA MARIE; born 11 Sep 1978.

There were no children of Barbara Jean[12] Sayer and Gary Butler.

562.   JAMES S.[12] HILL (*Mildred*[11]*Johnson*, *Manie*[10]*Brown*, *Alvah*[9], *Nancy*[8]*Johnson*, *Charles*[7], *Ira*[6], *Jonathan*[5], *Nathaniel*[4], *Nathaniel*[3], *Humphrey*[2], *John*[1]) was born circa 1922 at NY.

He appeared on the census of 1 Apr 1930 at Norfolk, St. Lawrence Co., NY.

Children of James S.[12] Hill and an unknown person are as follows:

    i.   (--?--)[13].
    ii.   (--?--).
    iii.   (--?--).
    iv.   (--?--).
    v.   (--?--).

563. SARAH[12] HILL (*Mildred*[11]*Johnson*, *Manie*[10]*Brown*, *Alvah*[9], *Nancy*[8]*Johnson*, *Charles*[7], *Ira*[6], *Jonathan*[5], *Nathaniel*[4], *Nathaniel*[3], *Humphrey*[2], *John*[1]).

Children of Sarah[12] Hill and an unknown person are as follows:

    i.   (--?--)[13].

    ii.   (--?--).

564. ELIZABETH[12] LEONARD (*Miriam*[11]*Johnson, Manie*[10]*Brown, Alvah*[9], *Nancy*[8]*Johnson, Charles*[7], *Ira*[6], *Jonathan*[5], *Nathaniel*[4], *Nathaniel*[3], *Humphrey*[2], *John*[1]) married Harold Bell.

Children of Elizabeth[12] Leonard and Harold Bell are as follows:

    i.   APRIL[13]; married (--?--) Feduke.

    ii.   ANNETTE; married (--?--) Kirker.

565. RICHARD DONALD[12] BROWN (*Clarence*[11], *Clarence*[10], *Charles*[9], *Nancy*[8]*Johnson, Charles*[7], *Ira*[6], *Jonathan*[5], *Nathaniel*[4], *Nathaniel*[3], *Humphrey*[2], *John*[1]) was born on 14 Jul 1930 at Gouverneur, St. Lawrence Co., NY. He married Barbara Ruth Fulton on 30 Jun 1954 at Beech Plains, NY.

Children of Richard Donald[12] Brown and Barbara Ruth Fulton all born at Gouverneur, St. Lawrence Co., NY, are as follows:

    i.   GREGORY RICHARD[13]; born 19 Oct 1959. He was unmarried.

858.   ii.   DOUGLAS LEE, born 1 Oct 1961; married Tina Louise Youngs.

    iii.   LISA MARIE; born 8 Feb 1965; married Ricki Lee Harriman 14 Aug 1993 at Gouverneur, St. Lawrence Co., NY; she and Ricki Lee Harriman were divorced 1999.

        She was also known as LISA MARIE HARRIMAN.

566. CONSTANCE LUCILLE[12] BROWN (*Clarence*[11], *Clarence*[10], *Charles*[9], *Nancy*[8]*Johnson, Charles*[7], *Ira*[6], *Jonathan*[5], *Nathaniel*[4], *Nathaniel*[3], *Humphrey*[2], *John*[1]) was born on 25 Oct 1931 at Gouverneur, St. Lawrence Co., NY. She married Burton George McElwain on 24 Jul 1954 at Edwards, St. Lawrence Co., NY.

Children of Constance Lucille[12] Brown and Burton George McElwain are as follows:

859.   i.   EMILY ANNE[13], born 23 Nov 1959 at Potsdam, St. Lawrence Co., NY; married William Joseph Gorton.

860.   ii.   KAREN KAY, born 25 Aug 1962 at Potsdam, St. Lawrence Co., NY; married Mark Frederick Brown.

861.   iii.   DIANE LUCILLE, born 10 Apr 1967 at Malone, Franklin Co., NY; married Christopher Scott Jacob.

567. MARY ELIZABETH[12] BUCK (*Martha*[11]*Clark, Mabel*[10]*Brown, Charles*[9], *Nancy*[8]*Johnson, Charles*[7], *Ira*[6], *Jonathan*[5], *Nathaniel*[4], *Nathaniel*[3], *Humphrey*[2], *John*[1]) was born on 1 Feb 1940 at St. Joseph Hospital, South Bend, St. Joseph Co., IN. She married Joseph Anthony Spadaro on 8 Jul 1967 at Cathedral of the Immaculate Conception, Syracuse, Onondoga Co., NY.

She lived in 1997 at Syracuse, NY.

Children of Mary Elizabeth[12] Buck and Joseph Anthony Spadaro all born at Syracuse, Onondoga Co., NY, are as follows:

862.   i.   ANNE THERESE[13], born 13 Jul 1968; married Mark Christopher Mattus.

863.   ii.   DANIEL JOSEPH, born 24 Sep 1969; married Amee Marie Ravan.

864.   iii.   NINA LOUISE, born 1 Apr 1975; married Robert Walters.

568. HARRIET GERTRUDE[12] BUCK (*Martha*[11]*Clark, Mabel*[10]*Brown, Charles*[9], *Nancy*[8]*Johnson, Charles*[7], *Ira*[6], *Jonathan*[5], *Nathaniel*[4], *Nathaniel*[3], *Humphrey*[2], *John*[1]) was born on 11 Dec 1941 at St. Joseph Hospital, South Bend, St. Joseph Co., IN. She married Charles Michael Connelly on 18 Oct 1969 at St. Ann's Church, Manlius, Onondaga Co., NY.

She lived in 1997 at Sanibel Island, FL.

Children of Harriet Gertrude[12] Buck and Charles Michael Connelly both born at Onondaga Hill, NY, are as follows:

    i.   MARY MARGARET[13]; born 14 Dec 1971.

    ii.   CHARLES PATRICK; born 27 May 1974.

569. NANCY MADELINE[12] BUCK (*Martha[11]Clark, Mabel[10]Brown, Charles[9], Nancy[8]Johnson, Charles[7], Ira[6], Jonathan[5], Nathaniel[4], Nathaniel[3], Humphrey[2], John[1]*) was born on 19 Mar 1945 at St. Joseph Hospital, South Bend, St. Joseph Co., IN. She married Frank Bradford Simpson III on 10 Jun 1967 at St. Ann's Church, Manlius, Onondaga Co., NY.

She lived in 1997 at Villa Hills, NY.

Children of Nancy Madeline[12] Buck and Frank Bradford Simpson III are as follows:

865.   i.   VIRGINIA LEIGH[13], born 23 Apr 1968 at Perrin AFB, Sherman, TX; married Vincent Hawley; divorced Vincent Hawley; engaged Robert Reynolds.

      ii.   RACHEL DENISE; born 26 Jul 1972 at Nuremberg, Germany; married Zane Stewart Muhouen 16 May 2003 at Port Royal Plantation Beach House, Hilton Head Island, SC.

866.   iii.   NATALIE LOUISE, born 15 Dec 1976 at Westchester, PA; married Eric Wayne Schoeppe.

     iv.   CRAIG BRADFORD; born 6 Dec 1978 at Cincinnati, Hamilton Co., OH.

570. FREDERICK JOHN[12] BUCK (*Martha[11]Clark, Mabel[10]Brown, Charles[9], Nancy[8]Johnson, Charles[7], Ira[6], Jonathan[5], Nathaniel[4], Nathaniel[3], Humphrey[2], John[1]*) was born on 27 Sep 1950 at St. Joseph Hospital, South Bend, St. Joseph Co., IN. He married Gloria Ann Lemke on 27 Dec 1975 at Bellevue, NE. He and Gloria Ann Lemke were divorced in Nov 1999. He and Anne Munz were engaged in Aug 2001 at Lancaster, CA.

He lived in 1997 at Lancaster, CA.

Children of Frederick John[12] Buck and Gloria Ann Lemke are:

     i.   HEIDI JEAN[13]; born 13 Oct 1983 at Grand Junction, CO.

Children of Frederick John[12] Buck and Anne Munz are:

i. HEATHER ANNE[13]; born 5 Jul 2002 at Lancaster, CA.

571. KATHERINE MARIE[12] BUCK (*Martha[11]Clark, Mabel[10]Brown, Charles[9], Nancy[8]Johnson, Charles[7], Ira[6], Jonathan[5], Nathaniel[4], Nathaniel[3], Humphrey[2], John[1]*) was born on 7 Nov 1951 at St. Joseph Hospital, South Bend, St. Joseph Co., IN. She married Daniel Robert Siegfried on 10 Aug 1974 at St. Annes Church, Manlius, NY. She married Winfrey Dean Waits on 18 Mar 1978 at Church of the Wildwood, Glenwood Spring, CO.

She lived in 1997 at Bartesville, OK.

There were no children of Katherine Marie[12] Buck and Daniel Robert Siegfried.

Children of Katherine Marie[12] Buck and Winfrey Dean Waits are as follows:

867. i. JUSTIN MARCUS[13], born 23 Dec 1979 at Bayshore Pasadena Hospital, Pasadena, TX; married Rosemary Katherine Pronath.

ii. CHRISTOPHER MICHAEL; born 5 Jun 1983 at Clear Lake Hospital, Webster, TX.

iii. SARAH ELIZABETH; born 1 Aug 1988 at Jane Phillips Medical Center, Bartlesville, OK.

572. WILLIAM JOHN PAUL[12] BUCK (*Martha[11]Clark, Mabel[10]Brown, Charles[9], Nancy[8]Johnson, Charles[7], Ira[6], Jonathan[5], Nathaniel[4], Nathaniel[3], Humphrey[2], John[1]*) was born on 23 Jun 1958 at Syracuse, Onondoga Co., NY. He married Elizabeth Ann Beltowski on 18 Jun 1988 at Camillus, Onondaga Co., NY.

He lived in 1997 at Chittenango, NY.

Children of William John Paul[12] Buck and Elizabeth Ann Beltowski are:

i. WILLIAM JOHN PAUL[13] JR.; born 8 Sep 1994 at Syracuse, Onodaga Co., NY.

573. ELIZABETH BROWN[12] CONNORS (*Harriet[11]Clark, Mabel[10]Brown, Charles[9], Nancy[8]Johnson, Charles[7], Ira[6],*

Jonathan[5], *Nathaniel*[4], *Nathaniel*[3], *Humphrey*[2], *John*[1]) was born on 7 Feb 1946 at Rochester, Monroe Co., NY. She married Dort Albert Cameron III on 9 Oct 1964 at Middlebury, VT.

Children of Elizabeth Brown[12] Connors and Dort Albert Cameron III were as follows:

  i. DORT[13] IV; born Feb 1965; died Feb 1965.

  ii. SARAH BROOKE; born 11 Jun 1970 at North Tarrytown, NY.

  iii. SETH MACALISTAIR; born 25 Apr 1973 at North Tarrytown, NY; married Kirtley Horton 30 Sep 2000.

  iv. MILES ANGUS; born 21 Aug 1977 at North Tarrytown, NY.

  v. ELIZA LINDSAY; born 14 Oct 1982 at Mt. Kisco, NY.

574. THOMAS CLARK[12] CONNORS (*Harriet*[11]*Clark*, *Mabel*[10]*Brown*, *Charles*[9], *Nancy*[8]*Johnson*, *Charles*[7], *Ira*[6], *Jonathan*[5], *Nathaniel*[4], *Nathaniel*[3], *Humphrey*[2], *John*[1]) was born on 10 Oct 1950 at Rochester, Monroe Co., NY. He married Mary Lucille Ennist on 10 Jun 1972 at Kinnelon, NJ. He and Mary Lucille Ennist were divorced in 1977. He married Deborah Jean Cravens on 7 May 1983 at Richardson, TX.

Children of Thomas Clark[12] Connors and Deborah Jean Cravens are as follows:

    i. AMY JEAN KLIMA[13]; born 22 Feb 1973.

  868. ii. LAURIE MARIE KLIMA, born 25 Dec 1977; married Raymond Kelley Richards.

575. JAMES MILTON[12] CLARK (*Charles*[11], *Mabel*[10]*Brown*, *Charles*[9], *Nancy*[8]*Johnson*, *Charles*[7], *Ira*[6], *Jonathan*[5], *Nathaniel*[4], *Nathaniel*[3], *Humphrey*[2], *John*[1]) was born on 16 Sep 1945 at Canton, NY. He married Linda St Louis on 12 Nov 1976.

He and Linda St Louis were separated in 1980.

Children of James Milton[12] Clark and Linda St Louis are:

  i. DAMON[13]; born 10 Jul 1975.

576. CHARLES ROLLIN[12] CLARK II (*Charles[11]*, *Mabel[10]Brown*, *Charles[9]*, *Nancy[8]Johnson*, *Charles[7]*, *Ira[6]*, *Jonathan[5]*, *Nathaniel[4]*, *Nathaniel[3]*, *Humphrey[2]*, *John[1]*) was born on 16 May 1947 at Canton, NY. He married Linda Jean Rosinski on 1 Jun 1974 at Kensington, CT.

Children of Charles Rollin[12] Clark II and Linda Jean Rosinski are as follows:

      i.   CHARLES ROLLIN[13] III; born 16 May 1978 at New Britain, CT.

      ii. BRIAN JOHN; born 4 Nov 1980 at Ogdensburg, NY.

      iii. KEVIN JAN; born 21 Mar 1983 at Ogdensburg, NY.

577. JANE MARIE[12] BEACH (*Everett[11]*, *Leta[10]Hall*, *Hiram[9]*, *Emmorancy[8]Johnson*, *Charles[7]*, *Ira[6]*, *Jonathan[5]*, *Nathaniel[4]*, *Nathaniel[3]*, *Humphrey[2]*, *John[1]*) was born on 2 Jun 1932 at Theresa, Jefferson Co., NY. She married George Augustus Grappotte Sr. on 17 Oct 1953 at Watertown, Jefferson Co., NY. She died on 15 Dec 1989 at Watertown, Jefferson Co., NY, at age 57.

Children of Jane Marie[12] Beach and George Augustus Grappotte Sr. all born at Watertown, Jefferson Co., NY, were as follows:

      i.   DEBORAH ANNE[13]; born 26 Aug 1954; married Bruce Edwin Hoffere.

      ii. SUZANNE MARIE; born 30 Jan 1956; died 5 Nov 1995 at Watertown, Jefferson Co., NY, at age 39. She was unmarried.

      iii. JOAN ELIZABETH; born 3 Mar 1957.

869.   iv. SHARON JANE, born 2 Jun 1958; married (--?--) Danielson.

870.   v.   GEORGE AUGUSTUS JR., born 12 Aug 1961; married Mary Ann Bartels.

578. JANICE CORNELIA[12] BEACH (*Everett[11]*, *Leta[10]Hall*, *Hiram[9]*, *Emmorancy[8]Johnson*, *Charles[7]*, *Ira[6]*, *Jonathan[5]*, *Nathaniel[4]*,

Nathaniel[3], *Humphrey*[2], *John*[1]) was born on 18 Aug 1935. She married William G. Backus. She married (--?--) Daley.

Children of Janice Cornelia[12] Beach and William G. Backus are as follows:

> 871.   i.   AMY LYNN[13], born 31 Dec 1958 at Watertown, NY; married Donald E. Stone; divorced Donald E. Stone.
>
>   ii.   THOMAS WILLIAM; born 22 Jun 1960 at Rochester, Monroe Co., NY.
>
>   iii.   CRAIG PATRICK; born 4 Jul 1967.

579.   RICHARD JOSEPH[12] BOPREY (*Reatha*[11]*Hall*, *Leon*[10], *Hiram*[9], *Emmorancy*[8]*Johnson*, *Charles*[7], *Ira*[6], *Jonathan*[5], *Nathaniel*[4], *Nathaniel*[3], *Humphrey*[2], *John*[1]) was born on 8 Jan 1937 at Gouverneur, St. Lawrence Co., NY. He married Marlene Mary Scott, daughter of Leo Scott and Alice (--?--), on 11 May 1958 at Cohoes, NY.

Children of Richard Joseph[12] Boprey and Marlene Mary Scott both born at Potsdam, St. Lawrence Co., NY, are as follows:

> i.   RICHARD ALAN[13]; born 17 Apr 1959.
>
> ii.   SCOTT LEE; born 9 Jun 1962.

580.   JACQUELINE JANET[12] BOPREY (*Reatha*[11]*Hall*, *Leon*[10], *Hiram*[9], *Emmorancy*[8]*Johnson*, *Charles*[7], *Ira*[6], *Jonathan*[5], *Nathaniel*[4], *Nathaniel*[3], *Humphrey*[2], *John*[1]) was born on 14 Jun 1938 at Gouverneur, St. Lawrence Co., NY. She married George Charles Spencer, son of Chester Louis Spencer and Ineva Dacie Layaw, on 27 Oct 1956 at Schenectady, NY.

Children of Jacqueline Janet[12] Boprey and George Charles Spencer are as follows:

> i.   THOMAS GEORGE[13]; born 7 Jan 1958 at Potsdam, St. Lawrence Co., NY.
>
> 872.   ii.   MARCIA MARIE, born 22 Aug 1961 at General Hospital, Binghamton, Broome Co., NY; married Alexander Martin Satkowski IV.

iii.   COREY JOHN; born 14 Jan 1973 at Binghamton, Broome Co., NY.

581.   BONNIE KAY[12] BOPREY (*Reatha*[11]*Hall, Leon*[10], *Hiram*[9], *Emmorancy*[8]*Johnson, Charles*[7], *Ira*[6], *Jonathan*[5], *Nathaniel*[4], *Nathaniel*[3], *Humphrey*[2], *John*[1]) was born on 16 May 1940 at Gouverneur, St. Lawrence Co., NY. She married Keith Francis Barnes, son of Homer Barnes and Rose LaPage, on 19 Nov 1960 at Syracuse, Onondaga Co., NY.

Children of Bonnie Kay[12] Boprey and Keith Francis Barnes all born at Syracuse, Onondaga Co., NY, are as follows:

873.   i.   KIMBERLY ANN[13], born 31 Jul 1961; married David McNeil.

874.   ii.   CYNTHIA LEIGH, born 15 May 1963; married Donald Poff.

iii.   KEITH JOSEPH; born 19 May 1967; married Tracy Ann Price 28 Aug 1993.

582.   MICHAEL LEON[12] BOPREY SR. (*Reatha*[11]*Hall, Leon*[10], *Hiram*[9], *Emmorancy*[8]*Johnson, Charles*[7], *Ira*[6], *Jonathan*[5], *Nathaniel*[4], *Nathaniel*[3], *Humphrey*[2], *John*[1]) was born on 20 Mar 1942 at Norwood, St. Lawrence Co., NY. He married Rosemary Orologio, daughter of Sebastion (James) Orologio and Carmel Nava, on 21 Jan 1967 at St. Andrews Church, Norwood, St. Lawrence Co., NY.

Children of Michael Leon[12] Boprey Sr. and Rosemary Orologio all born at Potsdam, St. Lawrence Co., NY, are as follows:

875.   i.   BARBARA LOUISE[13], born 6 Aug 1968; married Randal James Phelix.

876.   ii.   MICHAEL LEON JR., born 15 Apr 1970; married Amy Susan Wyley.

877.   iii.   PATRICIA LYNN, born 18 Apr 1971; married Patrick Josiah Colbert.

583.   ROBERT EDWIN[12] BOPREY (*Reatha*[11]*Hall, Leon*[10], *Hiram*[9], *Emmorancy*[8]*Johnson, Charles*[7], *Ira*[6], *Jonathan*[5], *Nathaniel*[4], *Nathaniel*[3], *Humphrey*[2], *John*[1]) was born on 30 Mar 1944 at

Potsdam, St. Lawrence Co., NY. He married Linda Frances LaClair, daughter of Harold Francis LaClair and Lula Grace Tobey, on 18 Jun 1966 at Massena, St. Lawrence Co., NY. He died on 27 Oct 1992 at Binghamton, Broome Co., NY, at age 48. He was buried on 30 Oct 1992 at West Monroe, Oswego Co., NY.

Children of Robert Edwin[12] Boprey and Linda Frances LaClair both born at Syracuse, Onondaga Co., NY, are as follows:

878. i. DAVID BRIAN[13], born 7 Apr 1968; married Deborah Rita Glennon.

879. ii. KELLIE JEAN, born 24 Sep 1969; married Jack William Reakes.

584. GWENDOLYN MAE[12] HALL (*Clifford*[11], *Leon*[10], *Hiram*[9], *Emmorancy*[8]*Johnson*, *Charles*[7], *Ira*[6], *Jonathan*[5], *Nathaniel*[4], *Nathaniel*[3], *Humphrey*[2], *John*[1]) was born on 2 Nov at Gouverneur, St. Lawrence Co., NY. She married Dean Bressette, son of Leonard H. Bressette and Georgiana Patton.

Children of Gwendolyn Mae[12] Hall and Dean Bressette were as follows:

 i. MICHAEL DEAN[13].

880. ii. RICK JAY, born 10 Jun 1963 at Gouverneur, St. Lawrence Co., NY.

 iii. JILL MARIE; married Jeffery Tebo.

585. KENNETH GILBERT[12] HUGHES (*Lyle*[11], *Florence*[10]*Hall*, *Hiram*[9], *Emmorancy*[8]*Johnson*, *Charles*[7], *Ira*[6], *Jonathan*[5], *Nathaniel*[4], *Nathaniel*[3], *Humphrey*[2], *John*[1]) was born on 2 Nov 1931 at Gouverneur, St. Lawrence Co., NY. He married Dolores F. Youngs on 12 May 1956 at Gouverneur, St. Lawrence Co., NY.

Children of Kenneth Gilbert[12] Hughes and Dolores F. Youngs all born at Gouverneur, St. Lawrence Co., NY, are as follows:

 i. PATRICK JOHN[13]; born 20 Nov 1959; married Patricia (--?--) 20 Dec 1981.

 ii. KENDRA LEA; born 15 Aug 1961.

 iii. ELLEN MARIE; born 5 Sep 1963.

iv. GARY LYLE; born 26 Feb 1967; married Sharon Mika 25 Aug 1979.

v. LURA KAY; born 29 Nov 1968.

586. GERALD[12] BOULET (*Gerald[11], Lottie[10]Hall, Hiram[9], Emmorancy[8]Johnson, Charles[7], Ira[6], Jonathan[5], Nathaniel[4], Nathaniel[3], Humphrey[2], John[1]*) was born on 15 Jun 1931. He married Mary Ann Fahey.

Children of Gerald[12] Boulet and Mary Ann Fahey are as follows:

i. ANN MICHELE[13]; born 10 Jun 1957.

ii. EDMUND HERALD; born 25 Sep 1958.

iii. THOMAS JAMES; born 2 Jun 1961.

iv. JANE FRANCES; born 2 Aug 1962.

587. JAMES[12] BOULET (*Gerald[11], Lottie[10]Hall, Hiram[9], Emmorancy[8]Johnson, Charles[7], Ira[6], Jonathan[5], Nathaniel[4], Nathaniel[3], Humphrey[2], John[1]*) was born on 28 Jun 1934. He married Betty Colley.

Children of James[12] Boulet and Betty Colley were as follows:

i. JAMES[13]; born 25 Jan 1958.

ii. JANET; died at Horsehead, NY.

588. DONNA[12] BOULET (*Gervaise[11], Lottie[10]Hall, Hiram[9], Emmorancy[8]Johnson, Charles[7], Ira[6], Jonathan[5], Nathaniel[4], Nathaniel[3], Humphrey[2], John[1]*) was born in 1947. She married Theodore Bostick.

Children of Donna[12] Boulet and Theodore Bostick are:

i. (--?--)[13].

589. CAROLYN ANN[12] BOULET (*Arthur[11], Lottie[10]Hall, Hiram[9], Emmorancy[8]Johnson, Charles[7], Ira[6], Jonathan[5], Nathaniel[4], Nathaniel[3], Humphrey[2], John[1]*) was born on 1 Dec 1934 at Gouverneur, St. Lawrence Co., NY. She married Leo Everett Averill on 9 Aug 1953 at Methodist Church, Edwards, St. Lawrence Co., NY. She died on 8 Mar 2002 at Potsdam Hospital, Canton, NY, at age 67. She was buried at Fairview Cemetery, Edwards, St. Lawrence Co., NY.

Children of Carolyn Ann[12] Boulet and Leo Everett Averill all born at Gouverneur, St. Lawrence Co., NY, were as follows:

	i.	LEE ALAN[13]; born 18 Sep 1955.
881.	ii.	ROGER JOE, born 8 Mar 1957; married Karen Hart.
	iii.	JON BRIAN; born 30 Nov 1959; married Lynette Brassard; married Melissa Whitmarsh; died 30 Jan 2003 at age 43.
882.	iv.	SUZANNE KAY, born 31 Aug 1963; married Wayne Corbine.
	v.	CHISTOPHER PAUL; born 28 Dec 1965; married Becky Bullock.
	vi.	MURRAY GLENN; born 27 Apr 1970.

590. KAY ONALEE[12] BOULET (*Arthur*[11], *Lottie*[10]*Hall*, *Hiram*[9], *Emmorancy*[8]*Johnson*, *Charles*[7], *Ira*[6], *Jonathan*[5], *Nathaniel*[4], *Nathaniel*[3], *Humphrey*[2], *John*[1]) was born on 7 Jul 1936 at Edwards, St. Lawrence Co., NY. She married Murray A. Hartley on 2 Aug 1953 at First Universalist Church, Edwards, St. Lawrence Co., NY. She died on 22 Jan 2000 at Clifton-Fine Hospital, Star Lake, NY, at age 63. She was buried at Fairview Cemetery, Edwards, St. Lawrence Co., NY.

Children of Kay Onalee[12] Boulet and Murray A. Hartley all born at Gouverneur, St. Lawrence Co., NY, are as follows:

883.	i.	SUSAN KAY[13], born 6 Jul 1954; married Frank Solon.
	ii.	STEVEN BASIL; born 3 Aug 1955; married Pamela Zeller.
	iii.	TIMOTHY SCOTT; born 28 Oct 1956; married Terry Tibbits.
884.	iv.	TRUDY ANN, born 2 Dec 1957; married Roger Hatch.

591. JOAN MARIE[12] BOULET (*Arthur*[11], *Lottie*[10]*Hall*, *Hiram*[9], *Emmorancy*[8]*Johnson*, *Charles*[7], *Ira*[6], *Jonathan*[5], *Nathaniel*[4], *Nathaniel*[3], *Humphrey*[2], *John*[1]) was born on 31 Jan 1943 at

Edwards, St. Lawrence Co., NY. She married Jack Ward on 22 Jan 1967 at Edwards, St. Lawrence Co., NY.

Children of Joan Marie^{12} Boulet and Jack Ward are as follows:

    i.   AMY JO^{13}; born 9 Aug 1967 at Gouverneur, St. Lawrence Co., NY.

    ii.   JILL RENEE; born 14 Jul 1970.

592. DOLORES^{12} TYPHAIR (*Louise^{11}Boulet, Lottie^{10}Hall, Hiram^9, Emmorancy^{8}Johnson, Charles^7, Ira^6, Jonathan^5, Nathaniel^4, Nathaniel^3, Humphrey^2, John^1*) married Paul Osborne.

Children of Dolores^{12} Typhair and Paul Osborne are as follows:

    i.   (--?--)^{13}.

    ii.   (--?--).

    iii.   (--?--).

    iv.   (--?--).

    v.   (--?--).

    vi.   (--?--).

593. RICHARD GEORGE^{12} MCCARTHY SR. (*Cherry^{11}Hall, Frank^{10}, Hiram^9, Emmorancy^{8}Johnson, Charles^7, Ira^6, Jonathan^5, Nathaniel^4, Nathaniel^3, Humphrey^2, John^1*) was born on 9 Mar 1937 at Pitcairn, NY. He married Hildegarde Specht.

Children of Richard George^{12} McCarthy Sr. and Hildegarde Specht are as follows:

    i.   RICHARD GEORGE^{13} JR..

    ii.   MICHAEL PATRICK.

    iii.   ROBERT DOUGLAS.

594. DORIS RUTH^{12} COLE (*Mary^{11}Ward, Bruce^{10}, Venila^{9}Hall, Emmorancy^{8}Johnson, Charles^7, Ira^6, Jonathan^5, Nathaniel^4, Nathaniel^3, Humphrey^2, John^1*) was born on 6 Oct 1926 at Pitcairn, NY. She married Melvin Anthony Hurley on 3 Feb 1945 at Edwards, St. Lawrence Co., NY.

Children of Doris Ruth^{12} Cole and Melvin Anthony Hurley both born at Gouverneur, St. Lawrence Co., NY, are as follows:

885.   i.   SHEILA ANN[13], born 10 Apr 1946; married Robert Gary Ingram.

886.   ii.   PHILLIP ANTHONY, born 7 Dec 1948; married Ruth Elaine Thompson.

595.   BONNIE[12] WARD (*Gerald*[11], *Bruce*[10], *Venila*[9]*Hall*, *Emmorancy*[8]*Johnson*, *Charles*[7], *Ira*[6], *Jonathan*[5], *Nathaniel*[4], *Nathaniel*[3], *Humphrey*[2], *John*[1]) married Gary Hall.

Children of Bonnie[12] Ward and Gary Hall are as follows:

887.   i.   GARY[13], married Roxanne (--?--); divorced Roxanne (--?--); married Buffy Matthews.

888.   ii.   PEGGY, married Danny Horne.

889.   iii.   TERRY, married Kim Whitmarsh.

596.   MAXINE[12] WARD (*Gerald*[11], *Bruce*[10], *Venila*[9]*Hall*, *Emmorancy*[8]*Johnson*, *Charles*[7], *Ira*[6], *Jonathan*[5], *Nathaniel*[4], *Nathaniel*[3], *Humphrey*[2], *John*[1]) married Larry Folsom.

Children of Maxine[12] Ward and Larry Folsom are as follows:

   i.   STEVEN[13].

   ii.   BRUCE; married Kim O'Leary.

   iii.   DOUG; married Heather Morehouse.

   iv.   DIANA.

597.   PATRICK PAUL[12] MULLANEY (*Irene*[11]*Ward*, *Bruce*[10], *Venila*[9]*Hall*, *Emmorancy*[8]*Johnson*, *Charles*[7], *Ira*[6], *Jonathan*[5], *Nathaniel*[4], *Nathaniel*[3], *Humphrey*[2], *John*[1]) was born on 21 May 1939. He married Dawn Fuller on 15 Sep 1956.

Children of Patrick Paul[12] Mullaney and Dawn Fuller were as follows:

890.   i.   DAWN PATRICIA[13], born 13 Dec 1956; married Joseph Zacharek.

891.   ii.   PATRICK BRUCE, born 10 Dec 1957; married Julie French; divorced Julie French.

892.   iii.   MICHAEL KEVIN, born 26 Dec 1958; married Kathy Saur.

893. iv. BRIAN KEITH, born 27 Dec 1959; married Janice Ferry; divorced Janice Ferry.

v. BARRY DALTON; born 5 Dec 1960; died 20 Jun 1981 at age 20.

894. vi. EUGENE PAUL, born 12 May 1962; married Brenda Sibley.

895. vii. KATHLEEN ANNETTE, born 1 Mar 1963; married Brian Huber.

viii. JAMES GORDON; born 2 Jul 1965; he and Betty Jones were engaged.

598. PATRICIA^{12} MULLANEY (*Irene^{11}Ward, Bruce^{10}, Venila^{9}Hall, Emmorancy^{8}Johnson, Charles^{7}, Ira^{6}, Jonathan^{5}, Nathaniel^{4}, Nathaniel^{3}, Humphrey^{2}, John^{1}*) was born on 19 Jul 1941. She married Wayne LaPlante in 1959.

Children of Patricia^{12} Mullaney and Wayne LaPlante are as follows:

896. i. STEPHEN WAYNE^{13}, born 27 Sep 1960; married Sherry Oatman.

897. ii. MICHELLE ANNETTE, born 10 May 1962; married Kevin Gagnon.

898. iii. MICHAEL BRUCE, born 1 Nov 1963; engaged Michelle Hale; engaged Penny Fowler.

899. iv. NICHOLE LYNETTE, born 17 Aug 1973; engaged Paul Smith.

599. EARLENE^{12} REED (*Irene^{11}Ward, Bruce^{10}, Venila^{9}Hall, Emmorancy^{8}Johnson, Charles^{7}, Ira^{6}, Jonathan^{5}, Nathaniel^{4}, Nathaniel^{3}, Humphrey^{2}, John^{1}*) married Gary Bigeral.

Children of Earlene^{12} Reed and Gary Bigeral are as follows:

i. AIMEE^{13}; born 22 Jul 1966.

ii. JENNIFER; born Oct 1970.

600. RONALD^{12} REED (*Irene^{11}Ward, Bruce^{10}, Venila^{9}Hall, Emmorancy^{8}Johnson, Charles^{7}, Ira^{6}, Jonathan^{5}, Nathaniel^{4}, Nathaniel^{3}, Humphrey^{2}, John^{1}*) was born on 24 Jul 1943. He married Sally Schryer.

Children of Ronald[12] Reed and Sally Schryer were as follows:

900.   i.   RONALD[13] II, born 9 Jan 1971; married Ladonna (--?--).

901.   ii.   MARTHA, born 12 Feb 1974; married Jack Gonzales.

601. WILLIAM[12] WHITFORD (*Irene[11]Ward*, *Bruce[10]*, *Venila[9]Hall*, *Emmorancy[8]Johnson*, *Charles[7]*, *Ira[6]*, *Jonathan[5]*, *Nathaniel[4]*, *Nathaniel[3]*, *Humphrey[2]*, *John[1]*) was born on 21 Aug 1953. He married Sherry Burnett. He died on 27 Nov 1978 at age 25.

Children of William[12] Whitford and Sherry Burnett are:

i.   WENDY[13]; born 23 Feb 1976.
      She was married and has 2 children.

602. JAMES[12] WHITFORD (*Irene[11]Ward*, *Bruce[10]*, *Venila[9]Hall*, *Emmorancy[8]Johnson*, *Charles[7]*, *Ira[6]*, *Jonathan[5]*, *Nathaniel[4]*, *Nathaniel[3]*, *Humphrey[2]*, *John[1]*) was born on 7 Mar 1955. He married Crystal Saur on 4 Jun 1977.

Children of James[12] Whitford and Crystal Saur are as follows:

902.   i.   JOSHUA JAMES[13], born 27 Jun 1978; engaged Lorissa Weaver.

ii.   JUSTIN WAYNE; born 23 Oct 1980.

iii.   JAMIE LEIGH; born 3 Dec 1982.

603. VICKI[12] WHITFORD (*Irene[11]Ward*, *Bruce[10]*, *Venila[9]Hall*, *Emmorancy[8]Johnson*, *Charles[7]*, *Ira[6]*, *Jonathan[5]*, *Nathaniel[4]*, *Nathaniel[3]*, *Humphrey[2]*, *John[1]*) was born on 4 Oct 1957. She married William Church on 14 May 1977.

She was separated from William.

Children of Vicki[12] Whitford and William Church are as follows:

903.   i.   BRIDGETTE[13], born 14 Jun 1976; engaged John Huckle.

ii.   SUSAN; born 5 Jul 1977; married J. R. Roth.
       She was separated from J. R.

iii.   WILLIAM BRUCE; born 28 Dec 1984.

iv.   WHITNEY; born 20 Oct 1986.

604. KENNETH^{12} WHITFORD (*Irene^{11}Ward, Bruce^{10}, Venila^{9}Hall, Emmorancy^{8}Johnson, Charles^7, Ira^6, Jonathan^5, Nathaniel^4, Nathaniel^3, Humphrey^2, John^1*) was born on 25 Aug 1961. He married Donna Thornton.

Children of Kenneth^{12} Whitford and Donna Thornton are as follows:

	i.	TARA^{13}; born 21 Sep 1979.
904.	ii.	NICOLE, born 2 Feb 1981; married Justin Morehouse.
	iii.	BRIAN; born 13 Jun 1983.
	iv.	HOLLY; born 19 Dec 1988.

605. RICKY^{12} WHITFORD (*Irene^{11}Ward, Bruce^{10}, Venila^{9}Hall, Emmorancy^{8}Johnson, Charles^7, Ira^6, Jonathan^5, Nathaniel^4, Nathaniel^3, Humphrey^2, John^1*) was born on 20 Jun 1964. He married JoAnn Harrington on 20 Aug 1989.

Children of Ricky^{12} Whitford and JoAnn Harrington are as follows:

	i.	SABRINA^{13}; born 14 Jun 1991.
	ii.	CARRIE; born 20 Sep 1993.

606. ALBERT BION^{12} MASON (*Myrtle^{11}Maybee, Lena^{10}Ward, Venila^{9}Hall, Emmorancy^{8}Johnson, Charles^7, Ira^6, Jonathan^5, Nathaniel^4, Nathaniel^3, Humphrey^2, John^1*) was born on 16 Jan 1920 at Ogdensburg, St. Lawrence Co., NY. He married Florence Gary on 6 Sep 1944 at Canton, St. Lawrence Co., NY. He married Thelma Bellinger on 28 Dec 1963.

Children of Albert Bion^{12} Mason and Florence Gary are as follows:

	i.	BION^{13}.
905.	ii.	BARBARA, married (--?--) Graveline.

There were no children of Albert Bion^{12} Mason and Thelma Bellinger.

607. BETTIE VENILA^{12} MASON (*Myrtle^{11}Maybee, Lena^{10}Ward, Venila^{9}Hall, Emmorancy^{8}Johnson, Charles^7, Ira^6, Jonathan^5,*

Nathaniel[4], *Nathaniel*[3], *Humphrey*[2], *John*[1]) was born on 4 Jun 1924 at Gouverneur, St. Lawrence Co., NY. She married Louis Hardy on 6 Jun 1946 at Canton, St. Lawrence Co., NY.

She was also known as Bettie Vinilia Mason.

Children of Bettie Venila[12] Mason and Louis Hardy are as follows:

      i.   Roy[13].
906.   ii. Myrtle, married (--?--) Regan.

608. Webster Roy[12] Mason (*Myrtle*[11]*Maybee*, *Lena*[10]*Ward*, *Venila*[9]*Hall*, *Emmorancy*[8]*Johnson*, *Charles*[7], *Ira*[6], *Jonathan*[5], *Nathaniel*[4], *Nathaniel*[3], *Humphrey*[2], *John*[1]) was born on 16 Dec 1926. He married Mary Currier on 15 Oct 1946 at Brasher Falls, St. Lawrence Co., NY.

Children of Webster Roy[12] Mason and Mary Currier are as follows:

907.   i.   Cathy[13], married (--?--) Deon.
908.   ii. James
      iii. Paul.
      iv. Carol.
      v.   Darlene.

609. Earl Lester[12] Mason (*Myrtle*[11]*Maybee*, *Lena*[10]*Ward*, *Venila*[9]*Hall*, *Emmorancy*[8]*Johnson*, *Charles*[7], *Ira*[6], *Jonathan*[5], *Nathaniel*[4], *Nathaniel*[3], *Humphrey*[2], *John*[1]) was born on 5 May 1929 at Antwerp, Jefferson Co., NY. He married Shirley Curr on 29 Oct 1947 at Lisbon, St. Lawrence Co., NY. He married Donna Flight in 1961.

Children of Earl Lester[12] Mason and Shirley Curr are as follows:

909.   i.   Karen[13], married (--?--) LaLonde.
910.   ii. Cindy, married (--?--) Porter.

There were no children of Earl Lester[12] Mason and Donna Flight.

610. Charles Roy[12] Mason (*Myrtle*[11]*Maybee*, *Lena*[10]*Ward*, *Venila*[9]*Hall*, *Emmorancy*[8]*Johnson*, *Charles*[7], *Ira*[6], *Jonathan*[5],

Nathaniel[4], *Nathaniel*[3], *Humphrey*[2], *John*[1]) was born on 18 Feb 1942 at Gouverneur, St. Lawrence Co., NY. He married Sally Hendrick on 23 Oct 1965 at Canton, St. Lawrence Co., NY.

Children of Charles Roy[12] Mason and Sally Hendrick are as follows:

    i.   JEFFERY[13].
   ii.   MICHELLE.
  iii.   KELLY.

611.   DONNA[12] DUMONT (*Ruth*[11]*Morgan*, *Edith*[10]*Ward*, *Venila*[9]*Hall*, *Emmorancy*[8]*Johnson*, *Charles*[7], *Ira*[6], *Jonathan*[5], *Nathaniel*[4], *Nathaniel*[3], *Humphrey*[2], *John*[1]) was born on 29 Jan 1957. She married Charles Richard Emler on 31 Mar 1978.

Children of Donna[12] Dumont and Charles Richard Emler are as follows:

    i.   CHARLES RICHARD[13]; born 19 Jan 1980.
   ii.   STEPHEN MATTHEW; born 25 Sep 1981.
  iii.   DAVID ALAN; born 27 May 1983.

612. NANCY JEAN[12] LYNCH (*Jeannine*[11]*Morgan*, *Edith*[10]*Ward*, *Venila*[9]*Hall*, *Emmorancy*[8]*Johnson*, *Charles*[7], *Ira*[6], *Jonathan*[5], *Nathaniel*[4], *Nathaniel*[3], *Humphrey*[2], *John*[1]) was born on 8 Oct 1955 at Massena, St. Lawrence Co., NY. She married Gary Ross Wells on 26 Jul 1976 at Brasher Falls, NY.

Children of Nancy Jean[12] Lynch and Gary Ross Wells are as follows:

    i.   KEVIN ROSS[13]; born 24 Jun 1977.
   ii.   MARK EDWARD; born 21 Dec 1978.

613. MICHAEL LEO[12] LYNCH (*Jeannine*[11]*Morgan*, *Edith*[10]*Ward*, *Venila*[9]*Hall*, *Emmorancy*[8]*Johnson*, *Charles*[7], *Ira*[6], *Jonathan*[5], *Nathaniel*[4], *Nathaniel*[3], *Humphrey*[2], *John*[1]) was born on 15 Aug 1956 at Massena, NY. He married Brenda Deleel on 4 Feb 1977 at Hopkinton, NY.

Children of Michael Leo[12] Lynch and Brenda Deleel are as follows:

    i.   BRETT WILLIAM[13]; born 28 Nov 1976.

   ii.   BROOKE MARIE; born 18 Dec 1978.

614.   CONSTANCE ANN[12] LYNCH (*Jeannine[11]Morgan, Edith[10]Ward, Venila[9]Hall, Emmorancy[8]Johnson, Charles[7], Ira[6], Jonathan[5], Nathaniel[4], Nathaniel[3], Humphrey[2], John[1]*) was born on 31 Jan 1959 at Massena, St. Lawrence Co., NY. She married Allen David Pike on 6 Jul 1979 at Brasher Falls, St. Lawrence Co., NY.

Children of Constance Ann[12] Lynch and Allen David Pike are as follows:

    i.   ADRIENNE ELIZABETH[13]; born 9 Apr 1980.

   ii.   DANIEL ALLEN; born 11 Jun 1983.

615.   CORINNE ANN[12] BONI (*Frieda[11]Newvine, Cecile[10]Pratt, Venira[9]Hall, Emmorancy[8]Johnson, Charles[7], Ira[6], Jonathan[5], Nathaniel[4], Nathaniel[3], Humphrey[2], John[1]*) was born on 19 May 1935. She married Kenny Jones.

Children of Corinne Ann[12] Boni and Kenny Jones were as follows:

    i.   KENNETH LEE[13].

   ii.   DEBORAH KAY.

  iii.   BRUCE MICHAEL.

  iv.   BRIAN.

   v.   GARY.

  vi.   RUTH ELLEN.

616.   JANET KAY[12] BONI (*Frieda[11]Newvine, Cecile[10]Pratt, Venira[9]Hall, Emmorancy[8]Johnson, Charles[7], Ira[6], Jonathan[5], Nathaniel[4], Nathaniel[3], Humphrey[2], John[1]*) was born on 20 Nov 1938 at Gouverneur, St. Lawrence Co., NY. She married Robert Manning on 17 Jun 1961.

Children of Janet Kay[12] Boni and Robert Manning are as follows:

    i.   JEFFERY SCOTT[13].

   ii.   JENNIFER.

iii.   JOANNA.

617.   JOY[12] PRATT (*William*[11], *Harley*[10], *Venira*[9]*Hall*, *Emmorancy*[8]*Johnson*, *Charles*[7], *Ira*[6], *Jonathan*[5], *Nathaniel*[4], *Nathaniel*[3], *Humphrey*[2], *John*[1]) was born on 5 Jan 1947 at Geneva, NY. She married Marcel Massenet at France.

Children of Joy[12] Pratt and Marcel Massenet are as follows:

   i.   MICHAEL[13].
   ii.   CAROLINE.
   iii.   MARY ANNE.

618.   JOSEPH[12] PRATT (*William*[11], *Harley*[10], *Venira*[9]*Hall*, *Emmorancy*[8]*Johnson*, *Charles*[7], *Ira*[6], *Jonathan*[5], *Nathaniel*[4], *Nathaniel*[3], *Humphrey*[2], *John*[1]) was born on 23 Aug 1948 at Gouverneur, St. Lawrence Co., NY. He married Carol McIntosh.

Children of Joseph[12] Pratt and Carol McIntosh are as follows:

   i.   JAMES[13].
   ii.   JOANNE.

619.   JOHN[12] PRATT (*William*[11], *Harley*[10], *Venira*[9]*Hall*, *Emmorancy*[8]*Johnson*, *Charles*[7], *Ira*[6], *Jonathan*[5], *Nathaniel*[4], *Nathaniel*[3], *Humphrey*[2], *John*[1]) was born on 14 Nov 1953 at Gouverneur, St. Lawrence Co., NY. He married Rochelle Seovey at Gouverneur, St. Lawrence Co., NY.

Children of John[12] Pratt and Rochelle Seovey are as follows:

   i.   MORGAN ELAINE[13].
   ii.   ERIN.

620.   JENNIFER[12] PRATT (*William*[11], *Harley*[10], *Venira*[9]*Hall*, *Emmorancy*[8]*Johnson*, *Charles*[7], *Ira*[6], *Jonathan*[5], *Nathaniel*[4], *Nathaniel*[3], *Humphrey*[2], *John*[1]) was born on 8 Sep 1955 at Gouverneur, St. Lawrence Co., NY. She married Brent Yaple at Syracuse, Onondoga Co., NY.

Children of Jennifer[12] Pratt and Brent Yaple are as follows:

   i.   TIFFANY[13].
   ii.   BROCK.

621.   JEFFREY[12] PRATT (*William[11]*, *Harley[10]*, *Venira[9]Hall*, *Emmorancy[8]Johnson*, *Charles[7]*, *Ira[6]*, *Jonathan[5]*, *Nathaniel[4]*, *Nathaniel[3]*, *Humphrey[2]*, *John[1]*) was born on 30 Sep 1957 at Gouverneur, St. Lawrence Co., NY. He married Romona Normand at MO.

Children of Jeffrey[12] Pratt and Romona Normand are as follows:

   i.   GENEVIEVE[13].
   ii. ANDREW.
   iii. ROBERT.

622.   JACQUELINE THERESA[12] PRATT (*William[11]*, *Harley[10]*, *Venira[9]Hall*, *Emmorancy[8]Johnson*, *Charles[7]*, *Ira[6]*, *Jonathan[5]*, *Nathaniel[4]*, *Nathaniel[3]*, *Humphrey[2]*, *John[1]*) was born on 8 Aug 1959 at Gouverneur, St. Lawrence Co., NY. She married Thomas Gates at Gouverneur, St. Lawrence Co., NY.

Children of Jacqueline Theresa[12] Pratt and Thomas Gates are as follows:

   i.   RENEE'[13].
   ii. RACHAEL.
   iii. JACOB.

623.   FOREST B.[12] HAVENER SR. (*Nola[11]Burbridge*, *Alice[10]Main*, *John[9]*, *Lutilia[8]Johnson*, *George[7]*, *Ira[6]*, *Jonathan[5]*, *Nathaniel[4]*, *Nathaniel[3]*, *Humphrey[2]*, *John[1]*) was born in 1901. He married Louise Bodine.

Children of Forest B.[12] Havener Sr. and Louise Bodine are:

   i.   FORREST B.[13] JR.; born 1925; married Ester Healy.

624.   CHARLES EUGENE[12] BURBRIDGE (*Floyd[11]*, *Alice[10]Main*, *John[9]*, *Lutilia[8]Johnson*, *George[7]*, *Ira[6]*, *Jonathan[5]*, *Nathaniel[4]*, *Nathaniel[3]*, *Humphrey[2]*, *John[1]*) was born in 1909. He married Alline Marshall.

Children of Charles Eugene[12] Burbridge and Alline Marshall are as follows:

    i.   THOMAS EUGENE[13]; born 1940.

    ii.   LANA MARIE; born 1942.

    iii.   STEVEN KENT; born 1943.

625. THUMAN PAUL[12] BURBRIDGE (*Floyd*[11], *Alice*[10]*Main*, *John*[9], *Lutilia*[8]*Johnson*, *George*[7], *Ira*[6], *Jonathan*[5], *Nathaniel*[4], *Nathaniel*[3], *Humphrey*[2], *John*[1]) was born in 1911. He married Mildred Davey.

Children of Thuman Paul[12] Burbridge and Mildred Davey are as follows:

    i.   PHILIP PAUL[13]; born 1937.

    ii.   RELA JEAN; born 1939.

    iii.   EMIL WAYNE; born 1942.

626. FLOYD[12] BURBRIDGE JR. (*Floyd*[11], *Alice*[10]*Main*, *John*[9], *Lutilia*[8]*Johnson*, *George*[7], *Ira*[6], *Jonathan*[5], *Nathaniel*[4], *Nathaniel*[3], *Humphrey*[2], *John*[1]) was born in 1913. He married Evelyn Guthrie.

Children of Floyd[12] Burbridge Jr. and Evelyn Guthrie are as follows:

    i.   FLOYD ROGER[13]; born 1939.

    ii.   KAREN DIAN; born 1944.

627. DONNA[12] BURBRIDGE (*Ross*[11], *Alice*[10]*Main*, *John*[9], *Lutilia*[8]*Johnson*, *George*[7], *Ira*[6], *Jonathan*[5], *Nathaniel*[4], *Nathaniel*[3], *Humphrey*[2], *John*[1]) was born in 1917. She married Wallace Brown.

Children of Donna[12] Burbridge and Wallace Brown are:

    i.   CAROL LEBRUN[13]; born 1943.

628. GLEN[12] FOSTER (*Opal*[11]*Burbridge*, *Alice*[10]*Main*, *John*[9], *Lutilia*[8]*Johnson*, *George*[7], *Ira*[6], *Jonathan*[5], *Nathaniel*[4], *Nathaniel*[3], *Humphrey*[2], *John*[1]) was born in 1919. He married Lillian Lee.

Children of Glen[12] Foster and Lillian Lee are:

    i.   THOMAS C.[13]; born 1945.

629. ORA RICHARD[12] JOHNSON (*Raymond*[11], *Lena*[10]*Main*, *John*[9], *Lutilia*[8]*Johnson*, *George*[7], *Ira*[6], *Jonathan*[5], *Nathaniel*[4], *Nathaniel*[3], *Humphrey*[2], *John*[1]) was born in 1915. He married Edna Harris.

Children of Ora Richard[12] Johnson and Edna Harris are as follows:

    i.   RICHARD LEE[13]; born 1938.
    ii.   KENNETH WAYNE; born 1940.
   iii.   DONALD EARL; born 1941.
   iv.   DIANNA EILEEN; born 1945.

630. VERNA IONE[12] JOHNSON (*Raymond*[11], *Lena*[10]*Main*, *John*[9], *Lutilia*[8]*Johnson*, *George*[7], *Ira*[6], *Jonathan*[5], *Nathaniel*[4], *Nathaniel*[3], *Humphrey*[2], *John*[1]) was born in 1917. She married Patrick Malone.

Children of Verna Ione[12] Johnson and Patrick Malone are:

    i.   PATRICIA JEAN[13]; born 1939.

631. CHARLES RAYMOND[12] JOHNSON (*Raymond*[11], *Lena*[10]*Main*, *John*[9], *Lutilia*[8]*Johnson*, *George*[7], *Ira*[6], *Jonathan*[5], *Nathaniel*[4], *Nathaniel*[3], *Humphrey*[2], *John*[1]) was born in 1919. He married Helen Krause.

Children of Charles Raymond[12] Johnson and Helen Krause are as follows:

    i.   BARBARA LEE[13]; born 1945.
    ii.   CAROLYN ANN; born 1947.

632. MAYNARD EARL[12] JOHNSON (*Raymond*[11], *Lena*[10]*Main*, *John*[9], *Lutilia*[8]*Johnson*, *George*[7], *Ira*[6], *Jonathan*[5], *Nathaniel*[4], *Nathaniel*[3], *Humphrey*[2], *John*[1]) was born in 1923. He married Gladys Henry.

Children of Maynard Earl[12] Johnson and Gladys Henry are as follows:

    i.   LONNIE MAYNARD[13]; born 1944.
    ii.   ROLAND EARL; born 1947.

633. WANNA[12] WASSELL (*Coy*[11]*Johnson, Lena*[10]*Main, John*[9], *Lutilia*[8]*Johnson, George*[7], *Ira*[6], *Jonathan*[5], *Nathaniel*[4], *Nathaniel*[3], *Humphrey*[2], *John*[1]) was born in 1918. She married Vick Welton.

Children of Wanna[12] Wassell and Vick Welton are:

    i.   RICHARD[13]; born 1939.

634. OLIN[12] WASSELL (*Coy*[11]*Johnson, Lena*[10]*Main, John*[9], *Lutilia*[8]*Johnson, George*[7], *Ira*[6], *Jonathan*[5], *Nathaniel*[4], *Nathaniel*[3], *Humphrey*[2], *John*[1]) was born in 1921. He married Shirley Rample.

He was also known as Alvin Wassell. He lived in 2000 at Mapleton, IL.

Children of Olin[12] Wassell and Shirley Rample are:

    i.   ARLIN[13]; born 1947.

635. GENEVIEVE GAY[12] LEWIS (*Elizabeth*[11]*Gay, Blanch*[10]*Main, Alvin*[9], *Lutilia*[8]*Johnson, George*[7], *Ira*[6], *Jonathan*[5], *Nathaniel*[4], *Nathaniel*[3], *Humphrey*[2], *John*[1]) was born in 1915. She married Robert William DeWolf.

Children of Genevieve Gay[12] Lewis and Robert William DeWolf are as follows:

    i.   JILL[13]; born 1949.
    ii. JOHN ROBERT; born 1950.

636. KENNETH R.[12] MAIN (*Emmet*[11], *Odus*[10], *Andrew*[9], *Lutilia*[8]*Johnson, George*[7], *Ira*[6], *Jonathan*[5], *Nathaniel*[4], *Nathaniel*[3], *Humphrey*[2], *John*[1]) was born in 1923. He married Mildred Smith.

Children of Kenneth R.[12] Main and Mildred Smith are as follows:

    i.   DEVAN[13]; born 1945.
    ii. CHARLENE; born 1947.

637. EUGENE I.[12] MAIN (*Emmet*[11], *Odus*[10], *Andrew*[9], *Lutilia*[8]*Johnson, George*[7], *Ira*[6], *Jonathan*[5], *Nathaniel*[4],

Nathaniel[3], *Humphrey*[2], *John*[1]) was born in 1925. He married Evelyn Reynold.

Children of Eugene I.[12] Main and Evelyn Reynold are:

    i.   JO-ANNE[13].

638.   EMMET E.[12] MAIN (*Emmet*[11], *Odus*[10], *Andrew*[9], *Lutilia*[8]*Johnson*, *George*[7], *Ira*[6], *Jonathan*[5], *Nathaniel*[4], *Nathaniel*[3], *Humphrey*[2], *John*[1]) was born in 1930. He married Thelma Horton.

Children of Emmet E.[12] Main and Thelma Horton are as follows:

    i.   RONALD[13]; born 1949.
    ii. ROY; born 1951.

639.   DORIS J.[12] MAIN (*Emmet*[11], *Odus*[10], *Andrew*[9], *Lutilia*[8]*Johnson*, *George*[7], *Ira*[6], *Jonathan*[5], *Nathaniel*[4], *Nathaniel*[3], *Humphrey*[2], *John*[1]) was born in 1936. She married Raymond Reimer.

Children of Doris J.[12] Main and Raymond Reimer are:

    i.   DELBERT[13]; born 1951.

640.   LOIS MURIEL[12] RUBY (*Susie*[11]*Main*, *Odus*[10], *Andrew*[9], *Lutilia*[8]*Johnson*, *George*[7], *Ira*[6], *Jonathan*[5], *Nathaniel*[4], *Nathaniel*[3], *Humphrey*[2], *John*[1]) was born in 1926. She married Thadeus Elkins.

Children of Lois Muriel[12] Ruby and Thadeus Elkins are as follows:

    i.   THAD ANDREW[13]; born 1944.
    ii. SHARRON LaVONNE; born 1945.
    iii. ROBERT EDWARD; born 1948.

641.   JOY MABLE[12] ALLEN (*Susie*[11]*Main*, *Odus*[10], *Andrew*[9], *Lutilia*[8]*Johnson*, *George*[7], *Ira*[6], *Jonathan*[5], *Nathaniel*[4], *Nathaniel*[3], *Humphrey*[2], *John*[1]) was born in 1929. She married Ronald Niles.

Children of Joy Mable[12] Allen and Ronald Niles are:

i.   PHILLIS JOY MARTION[13]; born 1945.

642.   LOLITA MAY[12] ALLEN (*Susie*[11]*Main*, *Odus*[10], *Andrew*[9], *Lutilia*[8]*Johnson*, *George*[7], *Ira*[6], *Jonathan*[5], *Nathaniel*[4], *Nathaniel*[3], *Humphrey*[2], *John*[1]) married Julius Earl Long.

Children of Lolita May[12] Allen and Julius Earl Long are as follows:

i.   GLEN EARL[13]; born 1945.
ii.   ARTHUR RICKTEE; born 1947.
iii.   EDWARD GENE; born 1955.

643.   JAMES M.[12] ALLEN (*Susie*[11]*Main*, *Odus*[10], *Andrew*[9], *Lutilia*[8]*Johnson*, *George*[7], *Ira*[6], *Jonathan*[5], *Nathaniel*[4], *Nathaniel*[3], *Humphrey*[2], *John*[1]) was born in 1933. He married Velma Lee Skidmore.

Children of James M.[12] Allen and Velma Lee Skidmore were as follows:

i.   JAMES D.[13]; born 1949; died 1953.
ii.   VICTOR C.; born 1950.
iii.   DOUGLAS IVAN; born 1953.
iv.   DEBORAH MARLENE; born 1954.

644.   INA MARGO[12] ALLEN (*Susie*[11]*Main*, *Odus*[10], *Andrew*[9], *Lutilia*[8]*Johnson*, *George*[7], *Ira*[6], *Jonathan*[5], *Nathaniel*[4], *Nathaniel*[3], *Humphrey*[2], *John*[1]) was born in 1941. She married Edward Roy.

Children of Ina Margo[12] Allen and Edward Roy are:

i.   RETTA EVONNE[13].

645.   LAVON[12] HOBBS (*Evelyn*[11]*Main*, *Byard*[10], *Andrew*[9], *Lutilia*[8]*Johnson*, *George*[7], *Ira*[6], *Jonathan*[5], *Nathaniel*[4], *Nathaniel*[3], *Humphrey*[2], *John*[1]) was born in 1924. He married Gertrude Roberts. He and Gertrude Roberts were divorced. He married Peggy Dacey Morris.

Children of Lavon[12] Hobbs and Gertrude Roberts are as follows:

i.   PEGGY[13]; born 1944.

ii.   BEVERLY LYNN; born 1946.

646.   LILLIAN[12] HARPOLE (*Georgia*[11]*Main, Byard*[10], *Andrew*[9], *Lutilia*[8]*Johnson,   George*[7],   *Ira*[6],   *Jonathan*[5],   *Nathaniel*[4], *Nathaniel*[3], *Humphrey*[2], *John*[1]) was born in 1927. She married Dallas Barton.

Children of Lillian[12] Harpole and Dallas Barton are as follows:

    i.   CAROL JOETTE[13]; born 1949.

    ii.   BRENDA LOU; born 1953.

          She was also known as BRENDA LEE BARTON.

647.   MILDRED[12] SHELTON (*Cecil*[11]*Main, Carrie*[10], *Andrew*[9], *Lutilia*[8]*Johnson,   George*[7],   *Ira*[6],   *Jonathan*[5],   *Nathaniel*[4], *Nathaniel*[3], *Humphrey*[2], *John*[1]) was born in 1930. She married (--?--) LeBrun.

Children of Mildred[12] Shelton and (--?--) LeBrun are as follows:

    i.   SUSAN JEANNETTE[13]; born 1949.

    ii.   IRENE DIAN; born 1950.

648.   PHYLLIS[12] MAIN (*Kenneth*[11], *Carrie*[10], *Andrew*[9], *Lutilia*[8]*Johnson,   George*[7],   *Ira*[6],   *Jonathan*[5],   *Nathaniel*[4], *Nathaniel*[3], *Humphrey*[2], *John*[1]) was born in 1932. She married Richard Potuzak.

Children of Phyllis[12] Main and Richard Potuzak are as follows:

    i.   PATRICIA[13]; born 1952.

    ii.   STEVEN; born 1953.

    iii.   DEBORAH; born 1955.

649.   DAISY[12] MAIN (*Hampton*[11], *Flo*[10], *Andrew*[9], *Lutilia*[8]*Johnson,   George*[7],   *Ira*[6],   *Jonathan*[5],   *Nathaniel*[4], *Nathaniel*[3], *Humphrey*[2], *John*[1]) was born in 1929. She married Spencer Ray Woolard.

Children of Daisy[12] Main and Spencer Ray Woolard are as follows:

    i.   INDIA IVE[13]; born 1947.

ii. FAY MARIE; born 1949.

iii. GLORY ANN; born 1951.

iv. DININA MAY; born 1953.

650. FLO DARLES[12] MAIN (*Hampton[11]*, *Flo[10]*, *Andrew[9]*, *Lutilia[8]Johnson*, *George[7]*, *Ira[6]*, *Jonathan[5]*, *Nathaniel[4]*, *Nathaniel[3]*, *Humphrey[2]*, *John[1]*) was born in 1931. He married Peggy Ann Cutler.

Children of Flo Darles[12] Main and Peggy Ann Cutler are:

i. GAYACE ANN[13].

651. EILEEN[12] PINE (*Marie[11]Koenig*, *Pansy[10]Lawson*, *Minerva[9]Main*, *Lutilia[8]Johnson*, *George[7]*, *Ira[6]*, *Jonathan[5]*, *Nathaniel[4]*, *Nathaniel[3]*, *Humphrey[2]*, *John[1]*) was born in 1922. She married Thomas Alvin Gill.

Children of Eileen[12] Pine and Thomas Alvin Gill are as follows:

i. BETHANN OR BERTRAM[13]; born 1942.

ii. CHARLOTTE; born 1944.

652. ELIZABETH[12] PINE (*Marie[11]Koenig*, *Pansy[10]Lawson*, *Minerva[9]Main*, *Lutilia[8]Johnson*, *George[7]*, *Ira[6]*, *Jonathan[5]*, *Nathaniel[4]*, *Nathaniel[3]*, *Humphrey[2]*, *John[1]*) was born in 1924. She married Telford Thorenson.

Children of Elizabeth[12] Pine and Telford Thorenson are:

i. TERRY[13].

653. MARDELL[12] PINE (*Marie[11]Koenig*, *Pansy[10]Lawson*, *Minerva[9]Main*, *Lutilia[8]Johnson*, *George[7]*, *Ira[6]*, *Jonathan[5]*, *Nathaniel[4]*, *Nathaniel[3]*, *Humphrey[2]*, *John[1]*) was born in 1926. She married William F. Smith.

Children of Mardell[12] Pine and William F. Smith are:

i. RONALD L.[13]; born 1945.

654. WILLIAM[12] HUNT JR. (*Opal[11]Troutner*, *Anna[10]Johnson*, *Alvin[9]*, *Rufus[8]*, *George[7]*, *Ira[6]*, *Jonathan[5]*, *Nathaniel[4]*, *Nathaniel[3]*,

Humphrey[2], *John*[1]) was born in 1918 at KS. He married Mary Beth Shaw. He and Mary Beth Shaw were divorced.

Children of William[12] Hunt Jr. and Mary Beth Shaw are as follows:

    i.   CAROLINE SUE[13]; born 1942.

    ii.   BILLIE GAY; born 1945.

655.   FLORIENE[12] HUNT (*Opal*[11]*Troutner*, *Anna*[10]*Johnson*, *Alvin*[9], *Rufus*[8], *George*[7], *Ira*[6], *Jonathan*[5], *Nathaniel*[4], *Nathaniel*[3], *Humphrey*[2], *John*[1]) was born in 1921. She married Harry Stout.

Children of Floriene[12] Hunt and Harry Stout are:

    i.   LESLIE[13]; born 1943.

656. ONETA FERN[12] JOHNSON (*Lewis*[11], *Lewis*[10], *Alvin*[9], *Rufus*[8], *George*[7], *Ira*[6], *Jonathan*[5], *Nathaniel*[4], *Nathaniel*[3], *Humphrey*[2], *John*[1]) was born on 6 Jun 1924. She married Donald Clair McBride, son of Roland McBride and Nellie Oden, on 16 Jun 1944.

Children of Oneta Fern[12] Johnson and Donald Clair McBride are as follows:

  911.   i.   CAROL ANN[13], born 6 Nov 1947; married Carrol Schlieper Jr.

  912.   ii.   NANCY LOUISE, born 22 Jan 1950 at Pike Co., IL; married Robert Curry; married Larry Kunzeman.

  913.   iii. JANET LYNN, born 18 May 1952 at Pike Co., IL; married Rodney Woods.

  914.   iv. ELLEN MARIE, born 1 Jan 1955; married Ronnie Clendenny.

657. CHARLES LYNDLE[12] JOHNSON (*Lewis*[11], *Lewis*[10], *Alvin*[9], *Rufus*[8], *George*[7], *Ira*[6], *Jonathan*[5], *Nathaniel*[4], *Nathaniel*[3], *Humphrey*[2], *John*[1]) was born on 15 Mar 1926 at Nebo (near), IL. He married Imogene Smith, daughter of Nolan Smith and Elizabeth Brown, on 28 Sep 1943.

Children of Charles Lyndle[12] Johnson and Imogene Smith are as follows:

915.   i.   JAMES LYNDLE[13], born 30 Jan 1945; married Susan Marie Hannant.

916.   ii.   LYNDA JEAN, born 14 Jun 1947; married Phillip Dean Crowder.

917.   iii.   WAYNE EUGENE, born 19 Jan 1949; married Donna Bowman; divorced Donna Bowman; married Lorraine Harris.

        iv.   DALE ROY.

658. HAYWARD LAVON[12] JOHNSON (*Lewis*[11], *Lewis*[10], *Alvin*[9], *Rufus*[8], *George*[7], *Ira*[6], *Jonathan*[5], *Nathaniel*[4], *Nathaniel*[3], *Humphrey*[2], *John*[1]) was born on 16 Apr 1927 at Nebo (near), IL. He married Edna Eilene Carlton.

Children of Hayward Lavon[12] Johnson and Edna Eilene Carlton both born at Pike Co., IL, are as follows:

918.   i.   DONNA MARIE[13], born 2 Sep 1946; married Ronald Dale Campbell; divorced Ronald Dale Campbell; married Harold Lamne.

919.   ii.   TERRY LAVON, born 1 Nov 1947; married Janice Nissen.

659. OTELA FAY[12] JOHNSON (*Lewis*[11], *Lewis*[10], *Alvin*[9], *Rufus*[8], *George*[7], *Ira*[6], *Jonathan*[5], *Nathaniel*[4], *Nathaniel*[3], *Humphrey*[2], *John*[1]) was born on 12 Nov 1928. She married Thomas M. Burke, son of Thomas P. Burke and Nora Davis, on 25 Feb 1951.

Children of Otela Fay[12] Johnson and Thomas M. Burke are as follows:

        i.   DIAN OTELA[13]; born 16 Oct 1951.

920.   ii.   MARSHA ANN, born 14 Mar 1953 at Fairmount, WV; married John Price.

        iii.   HOLLY LYNN; born 12 May 1958.

660. JEANNE ANN[12] JEFFRIES (*Richard*[11], *Eva*[10]*Johnson*, *Alvin*[9], *Rufus*[8], *George*[7], *Ira*[6], *Jonathan*[5], *Nathaniel*[4], *Nathaniel*[3], *Humphrey*[2], *John*[1]) was born on 31 Jan 1945 at Long Beach, CA. She married Gary Lee Personett, son of Gilbert Personett and Ethel Johnston, on 18 Dec 1965.

Children of Jeanne Ann[12] Jeffries and Gary Lee Personett were as follows:

  i. STEVEN KENT[13]; born 18 Nov 1970.
  ii. CHAD ERIC; born 29 Jul 1975
  iii. STACY LYNN; born 16 Aug 1976.
  iv. MARK RYAN; born 9 Oct 1977.

661. GARY LEE[12] JEFFRIES (*Richard*[11], *Eva*[10]*Johnson, Alvin*[9], *Rufus*[8], *George*[7], *Ira*[6], *Jonathan*[5], *Nathaniel*[4], *Nathaniel*[3], *Humphrey*[2], *John*[1]) was born on 8 Jan 1946 at Pittsfield, Pike Co., IL. He married Kazulo Sato on 8 Aug 1971.

Children of Gary Lee[12] Jeffries and Kazulo Sato are as follows:

  i. KATHLEEN MARIE[13]; born 24 Jun 1982.
  ii. RYAN TYLER; born 26 Oct 1982.

662. DIANA LYNN[12] JEFFRIES (*Richard*[11], *Eva*[10]*Johnson, Alvin*[9], *Rufus*[8], *George*[7], *Ira*[6], *Jonathan*[5], *Nathaniel*[4], *Nathaniel*[3], *Humphrey*[2], *John*[1]) was born on 17 Feb 1948 at Pittsfield, Pike Co., IL. She married Michael Dennis McCartney, son of Frank McCartney Jr. and Mildred Yokem, on 15 Jul 1967.

Children of Diana Lynn[12] Jeffries and Michael Dennis McCartney are as follows:

  i. LISA ANN[13]; born 10 Jan 1969.
  ii. DEBRA LYNN; born 9 Sep 1971.
  iii. MICHAEL JEFFREY; born 9 Oct 1977.

663. WARREN LEE[12] JOHNSON (*Warren*[11], *George*[10], *George*[9], *Rufus*[8], *George*[7], *Ira*[6], *Jonathan*[5], *Nathaniel*[4], *Nathaniel*[3], *Humphrey*[2], *John*[1]) was born on 18 Oct 1943 at Anamosa, IA. He married Gloria Bristol on 6 May 1974 at Santa Rita Naval Base, Phillipine Islands.

Children of Warren Lee[12] Johnson and Gloria Bristol are as follows:

  i. VIRGINIA BRISTOL[13]; born 2 May 1974.
  ii. LISA ANN BRISTOL; born 6 Mar 1977.
  iii. MATTHEW BRISTOL; born 1 Nov 1978.

664. BILLY[12] JOHNSON (*Loy*[11], *George*[10], *George*[9], *Rufus*[8], *George*[7], *Ira*[6], *Jonathan*[5], *Nathaniel*[4], *Nathaniel*[3], *Humphrey*[2], *John*[1]) married Karl Cox.

Children of Billy[12] Johnson and Karl Cox are as follows:

    i.   (--?--)[13].

    ii. (--?--).

665. JOE ELLEN[12] COOK (*Dana*[11]*Johnson*, *George*[10], *George*[9], *Rufus*[8], *George*[7], *Ira*[6], *Jonathan*[5], *Nathaniel*[4], *Nathaniel*[3], *Humphrey*[2], *John*[1]) married Terry Davidson.

Children of Joe Ellen[12] Cook and Terry Davidson are as follows:

    i.   (--?--)[13].

    ii. (--?--).

666. DORIS JEAN[12] SMITH (*Mildred*[11]*Miller*, *Laura*[10]*Johnson*, *Lewis*[9], *Rufus*[8], *George*[7], *Ira*[6], *Jonathan*[5], *Nathaniel*[4], *Nathaniel*[3], *Humphrey*[2], *John*[1]) was born on 21 Feb 1932. She married Jerry Dean Akers 11 Jul 19.

Children of Doris Jean[12] Smith and Jerry Dean Akers are as follows:

  921.   i.   ROGER DEAN[13], born 6 Jul 1955 at Pittsfield, Pike Co., IL; married Peggy Jo Sibly.

  922.   ii. DEBRA JEAN, born 3 Dec 1956; married John Joseph Dunn II.

667. KEITH LEE[12] SMITH (*Mildred*[11]*Miller*, *Laura*[10]*Johnson*, *Lewis*[9], *Rufus*[8], *George*[7], *Ira*[6], *Jonathan*[5], *Nathaniel*[4], *Nathaniel*[3], *Humphrey*[2], *John*[1]) was born on 13 Mar 1934. He married Linda Lou Capps, daughter of Russell Perry Capps and Elsie Carroll Rodhouse, on 13 Oct 1962. He died in 1993.

Children of Keith Lee[12] Smith and Linda Lou Capps are as follows:

    i.   PAMELA KAY[13]; born 18 Oct 1965.

    ii. STEVEN LEE; born 14 Jul 1970.

668.   DAVID   GEORGE[12]   ELSTON   (*Blanche*[11]*Miller, Laura*[10]*Johnson, Lewis*[9], *Rufus*[8], *George*[7], *Ira*[6], *Jonathan*[5], *Nathaniel*[4], *Nathaniel*[3], *Humphrey*[2], *John*[1]) was born on 7 Mar 1944. He married Helen Anita Wells on 30 Jan 1965.

Children of David George[12] Elston and Helen Anita Wells are as follows:

    i.   FRANK WILLIAM[13]; born 11 Sep 1965.
    ii. NANCY ELIZABETH; born 27 Aug 1968.
    iii. JEANENE ALLISON; born 9 Sep 1970.

669.   LINDA   SUE[12]   INSKIP   (*Frances*[11]*Miller, Laura*[10]*Johnson, Lewis*[9], *Rufus*[8], *George*[7], *Ira*[6], *Jonathan*[5], *Nathaniel*[4], *Nathaniel*[3], *Humphrey*[2], *John*[1]) was born on 12 Jul 1949. She married Terry Feig on 14 Sep 1968.

Children of Linda Sue[12] Inskip and Terry Feig are:

    i.   BRENT WILLIAM[13]; born 28 Dec 1974.

670.   SANDRA   KAY[12]   LAMBERT   (*Lois*[11]*Miller, Laura*[10]*Johnson, Lewis*[9], *Rufus*[8], *George*[7], *Ira*[6], *Jonathan*[5], *Nathaniel*[4], *Nathaniel*[3], *Humphrey*[2], *John*[1]) was born on 4 Aug 1943 at Kansas City, MO. She married Garth Dunlap on 4 May 1968.

Children of Sandra Kay[12] Lambert and Garth Dunlap are as follows:

    i.   KYLE ALLEN[13]; born 24 Sep 1970.
    ii. KEVIN JOSEPH; born 9 Mar 1973.

671.   RONNIE   JOE[12]   LAMBERT   (*Lois*[11]*Miller, Laura*[10]*Johnson, Lewis*[9], *Rufus*[8], *George*[7], *Ira*[6], *Jonathan*[5], *Nathaniel*[4], *Nathaniel*[3], *Humphrey*[2], *John*[1]) was born on 28 Sep 1946 at Woodriver, IL. He married Deborah Kenrick.

Children of Ronnie Joe[12] Lambert and Deborah Kenrick are as follows:

    i.   CHRISTOPHER MICHAEL[13]; born 13 Apr 1972.
    ii. NEIL JOSEPH; born 20 Apr 1975.
    iii. BROOKE MICHELLE; born 26 Jun 1976.

672. LINDA SUE[12] BATTERSHELL (*Kathryn*[11]*Johnson, Osca*[10], *Lewis*[9], *Rufus*[8], *George*[7], *Ira*[6], *Jonathan*[5], *Nathaniel*[4], *Nathaniel*[3], *Humphrey*[2], *John*[1]) was born on 23 Jun 1937 at Bethalto, Madison Co., IL. She married Frank Spencer Long on 7 Jun 1958.

Children of Linda Sue[12] Battershell and Frank Spencer Long both born at Alton, IL, are as follows:

> 923.   i.   BECKY LYNN[13], born 7 Feb 1959; married Jeffrey Scott Alexander.
>
>   ii.   JULIE SUE; born 11 Jul 1961; married Joseph Wayne Horn 7 Jun 1980.

673. FAYE KATHLEEN[12] LEWIS (*Mavis*[11]*Johnson, Ivis*[10], *Isaac*[9], *Rufus*[8], *George*[7], *Ira*[6], *Jonathan*[5], *Nathaniel*[4], *Nathaniel*[3], *Humphrey*[2], *John*[1]) was born on 4 Oct 1949 at Denver, Denver Co., CO. She married Larry LuRue Axtell at Denver, Denver Co., CO.

Children of Faye Kathleen[12] Lewis and Larry LuRue Axtell are as follows:

>   i.   JACQUELINE MARIE[13]; born 19 Apr 1968.
>
>   ii.   PATRICK; born 27 Aug 1971.
>
>   iii.   JENNIFER LEW; born Dec 1972.
>
>   iv.   HEATHER; born 1974.

674. REX IVIS[12] LEWIS (*Mavis*[11]*Johnson, Ivis*[10], *Isaac*[9], *Rufus*[8], *George*[7], *Ira*[6], *Jonathan*[5], *Nathaniel*[4], *Nathaniel*[3], *Humphrey*[2], *John*[1]) was born on 5 Aug 1951 at Denver, Denver Co., CO. He married Vicki Reba Harris, daughter of Willard Harris and Opal Taylor, in Mar 1968.

Children of Rex Ivis[12] Lewis and Vicki Reba Harris are as follows:

>   i.   ERIC SCOTT[13]; born Dec 1969.
>
>   ii.   RYAN IKE; born 28 Nov 1972.
>
>   iii.   REX WADE; born Dec 1977.

675. REBECCA ELLEN[12] THUNE (*Janet*[11]*Brown, Icel*[10]*Johnson, Isaac*[9], *Rufus*[8], *George*[7], *Ira*[6], *Jonathan*[5], *Nathaniel*[4], *Nathaniel*[3], *Humphrey*[2], *John*[1]) was born on 2 Jan 1951 at Cedar Rapids, IA.

She married Douglas J. Gleason, son of Willard E. Gleason and Viola Hazel Anderson, on 29 Aug 1970.

Children of Rebecca Ellen[12] Thune and Douglas J. Gleason are as follows:

    i.   KRISTIN RENEE[13]; born 2 Jun 1971; married Chase Domminic Malara 21 May 1994 at Colorado Springs, CO.

    ii. MICHAEL BENJAMIN; born 31 Aug 1972.

676. LINDA KAY[12] KANE (*Joy[11]Brown, Icel[10]Johnson, Isaac[9], Rufus[8], George[7], Ira[6], Jonathan[5], Nathaniel[4], Nathaniel[3], Humphrey[2], John[1]*) was born on 19 Jun 1953 at Denver, Denver Co., CO. She married Dennis Wayne Stick on 26 Apr 1975.

Children of Linda Kay[12] Kane and Dennis Wayne Stick are as follows:

    i.   SHANNON DENISE[13]; born 21 May 1976.

    ii. SUSAN MARIE; born 21 Aug 1978.

677. JOY-ANNE[12] KANE (*Joy[11]Brown, Icel[10]Johnson, Isaac[9], Rufus[8], George[7], Ira[6], Jonathan[5], Nathaniel[4], Nathaniel[3], Humphrey[2], John[1]*) was born on 5 Nov 1956 at Cedar Rapids, IA. She married Wayne Nederhoff, son of Arthur Nederhoff, on 26 May 1979.

Children of Joy-Anne[12] Kane and Wayne Nederhoff are as follows:

    i.   ANTHONY[13]; born 8 Jun 1980.

    ii. ANDREW; born 26 Aug 1982.

678. RALPH EDWARD[12] KANE JR. (*Joy[11]Brown, Icel[10]Johnson, Isaac[9], Rufus[8], George[7], Ira[6], Jonathan[5], Nathaniel[4], Nathaniel[3], Humphrey[2], John[1]*) was born on 14 Oct 1957 at Cedar Rapids, IA. He married Cynthia Bowers.

Children of Ralph Edward[12] Kane Jr. and Cynthia Bowers are as follows:

    i.   MELISSA[13]; born 14 Jun 1979.

    ii. MICHAEL; born Sep 1980.

679. WILLIAM KYLE WENDELL[12] CLARK (*Wilma*[11]*Brown, Icel*[10]*Johnson, Isaac*[9], *Rufus*[8], *George*[7], *Ira*[6], *Jonathan*[5], *Nathaniel*[4], *Nathaniel*[3], *Humphrey*[2], *John*[1]) was born on 19 Mar 1959 at Enid, Garfield Co., OK. He married Bonnie Tanner, daughter of Rayford Lucian Tanner and Mary Dorothy Hynum, on 10 Mar 1978 at Vicksburg, MS.

Children of William Kyle Wendell[12] Clark and Bonnie Tanner are as follows:

    i.   WILLIAM KYLE[13]; born 24 Oct 1978.
    ii. ROBERT ARLYNN; born 24 Apr 1981.

680. WILLIAM DAVID[12] BROWN (*William*[11], *Icel*[10]*Johnson, Isaac*[9], *Rufus*[8], *George*[7], *Ira*[6], *Jonathan*[5], *Nathaniel*[4], *Nathaniel*[3], *Humphrey*[2], *John*[1]) was born on 21 Feb 1961. He married Janet Ann Howard on 19 Oct 1985.

Children of William David[12] Brown and Janet Ann Howard are as follows:

    i.   WILLIAM RYAN[13]; born 19 Jun 1988.
    ii. WESLEY ADAM; born 28 Dec 1990.

681. JOHN BENTON[12] GREGORY (*Mary*[11]*Brown, Icel*[10]*Johnson, Isaac*[9], *Rufus*[8], *George*[7], *Ira*[6], *Jonathan*[5], *Nathaniel*[4], *Nathaniel*[3], *Humphrey*[2], *John*[1]) was born on 10 Sep 1958 at Council Bluffs, IA. He married Shari Kay Richter, daughter of Marvin Richter, on 1 Aug 1981.

Children of John Benton[12] Gregory and Shari Kay Richter all born at Council Bluffs, IA, are as follows:

    i.   BRADLEY JOHN[13]; born 2 Oct 1984.
    ii. BREANA JOLENE; born 2 Nov 1986.
    iii. SHAILA KAY; born 6 Oct 1988.

682. JENNIFER LYNN[12] GREGORY (*Mary*[11]*Brown, Icel*[10]*Johnson, Isaac*[9], *Rufus*[8], *George*[7], *Ira*[6], *Jonathan*[5], *Nathaniel*[4], *Nathaniel*[3], *Humphrey*[2], *John*[1]) was born on 14 Oct 1960 at Council Bluffs, IA. She married John Williams on 2 Jan 1982.

Children of Jennifer Lynn[12] Gregory and John Williams are:

i.   JORDEN ASHLEY[13]; born 26 Oct 1989 at Council Bluffs, IA.

683. SHERRY[12] MCKENNA (*Lois*[11]*Johnson, Rufus*[10], *Isaac*[9], *Rufus*[8], *George*[7], *Ira*[6], *Jonathan*[5], *Nathaniel*[4], *Nathaniel*[3], *Humphrey*[2], *John*[1]) was born on 14 May 1947. She married Conrad Keil.

Children of Sherry[12] McKenna and Conrad Keil are as follows:

924.   i.   JILL DENISE[13], born 17 Jul 1960; married Herbert Dwayne Kelly.

    ii.   DUANE DANIEL; born 27 Sep 1970; married Amy Louise Casale 11 Feb 1994.

684. TERRY LYNN[12] MCKENNA (*Lois*[11]*Johnson, Rufus*[10], *Isaac*[9], *Rufus*[8], *George*[7], *Ira*[6], *Jonathan*[5], *Nathaniel*[4], *Nathaniel*[3], *Humphrey*[2], *John*[1]) was born on 20 May 1948 at Forest City, AR. She married Robert Allen Feltman, son of William Edward Feltman and Hester Catherine Rable, on 4 Oct 1975.

Children of Terry Lynn[12] McKenna and Robert Allen Feltman are as follows:

i.   PATRICK JASON[13]; born 9 Sep 1976.

ii.   AARON ELLIOTT; born 31 Jan 1980.

iii.   AMANDA; born 27 Dec 1982.

685. LYNDA PHYLLIS[12] MCKENNA (*Lois*[11]*Johnson, Rufus*[10], *Isaac*[9], *Rufus*[8], *George*[7], *Ira*[6], *Jonathan*[5], *Nathaniel*[4], *Nathaniel*[3], *Humphrey*[2], *John*[1]) was born on 10 Nov 1949. She married George Oakley.

Children of Lynda Phyllis[12] McKenna and George Oakley are as follows:

i.   JOHN ROBERT[13]; born 6 Aug 1970.

ii.   DIANA KAY; born 13 Aug 1984.

686. MICHAEL JAY[12] MCKENNA (*Lois*[11]*Johnson, Rufus*[10], *Isaac*[9], *Rufus*[8], *George*[7], *Ira*[6], *Jonathan*[5], *Nathaniel*[4], *Nathaniel*[3], *Humphrey*[2], *John*[1]) was born on 3 Oct 1952. He married Wendy (--?--). He and Wendy (--?--) were divorced. He married Kathy (--?--).

Children of Michael Jay[12] McKenna and an unknown spouse are as follows:

    i.   CHRISTANN KAY[13]; born 8 Jun 1970.
   ii.   STACEY DION; born 12 Aug 1971.
  iii.   LAUREN MICHAEL; born 26 May 1980.
  iv.   JOSHUA MICHAEL; born 15 Sep 1982.
   v.   ALEXIA MICHAEL; born 10 Aug 1984.

687. SANDRA DELPHINE[12] MCKENNA (*Lois*[11]*Johnson, Rufus*[10], *Isaac*[9], *Rufus*[8], *George*[7], *Ira*[6], *Jonathan*[5], *Nathaniel*[4], *Nathaniel*[3], *Humphrey*[2], *John*[1]) was born on 12 Nov 1954 at Pittsfield, Pike Co., IL. She married Steven George Strohl, son of George Edward Strohl and Myrtle Irene Humphrey, on 6 Oct 1978.

Children of Sandra Delphine[12] McKenna and Steven George Strohl are as follows:

    i.   JENNIFER MARIE[13]; born 2 Nov 1988.
   ii.   LUKE GEORGE EDWARD; born 28 Sep 1991.

688. ROBIN EUGENE[12] MCKENNA (*Lois*[11]*Johnson, Rufus*[10], *Isaac*[9], *Rufus*[8], *George*[7], *Ira*[6], *Jonathan*[5], *Nathaniel*[4], *Nathaniel*[3], *Humphrey*[2], *John*[1]) was born on 28 Jul 1959. He married Catherine Rose O'Leary, daughter of Jeremiah Joseph O'Leary and Catherine Moncur Robertson, on 29 May 1976 at Friends Church, Tillson, NY.

Children of Robin Eugene[12] McKenna and Catherine Rose O'Leary are as follows:

    i.   CAITLIN LOIS[13]; born 30 Jun 1980.
   ii.   LAUREL AMY; born 13 Apr 1982.

689. JILL DENISE[12] MCKENNA (*Lois*[11]*Johnson, Rufus*[10], *Isaac*[9], *Rufus*[8], *George*[7], *Ira*[6], *Jonathan*[5], *Nathaniel*[4], *Nathaniel*[3], *Humphrey*[2], *John*[1]) was born on 17 Jul 1960 at St. Louis, MO. She married Allen Duane Huffman, son of James Huffman and Frances Gardner, on 19 Mar 1980.

Children of Jill Denise[12] McKenna and Allen Duane Huffman are:

    i.   LINDSAY[13]; born Sep 1984.

690. JOSLIN JANE[12] JOHNSON (*Vernon*[11], *Rufus*[10], *Isaac*[9], *Rufus*[8], *George*[7], *Ira*[6], *Jonathan*[5], *Nathaniel*[4], *Nathaniel*[3], *Humphrey*[2], *John*[1]) was born on 28 May 1954.

Children of Joslin Jane[12] Johnson and an unknown spouse are:

    i.   KEVIN RUSSEL[13].

691. WENDY LEIGH[12] ROSE (*Phyllis*[11]*Johnson*, *Rufus*[10], *Isaac*[9], *Rufus*[8], *George*[7], *Ira*[6], *Jonathan*[5], *Nathaniel*[4], *Nathaniel*[3], *Humphrey*[2], *John*[1]) was born on 28 Aug 1953 at Pittsfield, Pike Co., IL. She married Brian Lowe, son of Edward Lowe and Florence Elmendorf, on 11 Jun 1977.

Children of Wendy Leigh[12] Rose and Brian Lowe are as follows:

    i.   REBECCA JANE[13]; born 25 Nov 1979.
    ii. DANIEL EDWARD; born 6 Sep 1982.

692. TIMOTHY DAN[12] ROSE (*Phyllis*[11]*Johnson*, *Rufus*[10], *Isaac*[9], *Rufus*[8], *George*[7], *Ira*[6], *Jonathan*[5], *Nathaniel*[4], *Nathaniel*[3], *Humphrey*[2], *John*[1]) was born on 17 Jul 1956 at Pittsfield, Pike Co., IL. He married Moyra Simpson on 10 Jun 1986. He and Moyra Simpson were divorced.

Children of Timothy Dan[12] Rose and Moyra Simpson are as follows:

    i.   JESSICA POLLY[13]; born 28 Sep 1986.
    ii. LORNA ELIZABETH; born 16 Sep 1988.

693. TIM R.[12] JOHNSON (*Ronald*[11], *Wendell*[10], *Isaac*[9], *Rufus*[8], *George*[7], *Ira*[6], *Jonathan*[5], *Nathaniel*[4], *Nathaniel*[3], *Humphrey*[2], *John*[1]) was born on 23 May 1963. He married Pamela Lord.

Children of Tim R.[12] Johnson and Pamela Lord are as follows:

    i.   SHANE ROBERT[13]; born 29 Apr 1985 at Pittsfield, Pike Co., IL.
    ii. KYLE SCOTT; born 24 Feb 1990 at Jacksonville, IL.

694. TAMMY KAY[12] JOHNSON (*Ronald*[11], *Wendell*[10], *Isaac*[9], *Rufus*[8], *George*[7], *Ira*[6], *Jonathan*[5], *Nathaniel*[4], *Nathaniel*[3],

Humphrey[2], *John*[1]) was born on 5 Oct 1964. She married James Dean Hardin on 12 Jun 1982.

Children of Tammy Kay[12] Johnson and James Dean Hardin are:

        i.   ALLISON RENEE[13]; born 27 Jun 1985 at Cameron, MO.

695. KATHLEEN YUVONNE[12] JOHNSON (*Ben*[11], *Wendell*[10], *Isaac*[9], *Rufus*[8], *George*[7], *Ira*[6], *Jonathan*[5], *Nathaniel*[4], *Nathaniel*[3], *Humphrey*[2], *John*[1]) was born on 29 May 1959 at Pittsfield, Pike Co., IL. She married Paul Opie, son of Curtis Mardell Opie and Wilma H. Bertram, on 1 Jan 1981. She and Paul Opie were divorced. She married James Buranosky on 28 May 1988. She married (--?--) McMahon.

She lived in 2000 at Wheatfield, IN.

Children of Kathleen Yuvonne[12] Johnson and Paul Opie are as follows:

        i.   HETHER MARDELL[13]; born 3 Aug 1981.
       ii. STEPHEN PAUL; born 9 Aug 1983.

Children of Kathleen Yuvonne[12] Johnson and James Buranosky are:

        i.   JANE RENEE[13]; born 16 Dec 1988.

696. BEN RAY[12] JOHNSON JR. (*Ben*[11], *Wendell*[10], *Isaac*[9], *Rufus*[8], *George*[7], *Ira*[6], *Jonathan*[5], *Nathaniel*[4], *Nathaniel*[3], *Humphrey*[2], *John*[1]) was born on 23 Dec 1960. He married Brook Shinn on 11 May 1989.

He lived in 2000 at Rockport, IL.

Children of Ben Ray[12] Johnson Jr. and Brook Shinn are:

        i.   JESSIE RAE[13]; born 2 Oct 1990.

697. MICHAEL WENDELL[12] JOHNSON (*Ben*[11], *Wendell*[10], *Isaac*[9], *Rufus*[8], *George*[7], *Ira*[6], *Jonathan*[5], *Nathaniel*[4], *Nathaniel*[3], *Humphrey*[2], *John*[1]) was born on 11 May 1965. He married Sonia Wittland on 5 Aug 1989. He and Sonia Wittland were divorced.

He lived in 2000 at Pittsfield, Pike Co., IL.

Children of Michael Wendell[12] Johnson and Sonia Wittland are:

i.   DILLION RAY[13]; born 17 Apr 1992.

Generation Thirteen

698.   LORETTA SUE[13] NIEBUR (*Charles[12], Susan[11]Nicholson, Charles[10], Mary[9]Johnson, Charles[8], Charles[7], Ira[6], Jonathan[5], Nathaniel[4], Nathaniel[3], Humphrey[2], John[1]*) was born on 20 Mar 1942. She married Gerald Eberly on 23 Mar 1964.

Children of Loretta Sue[13] Niebur and Gerald Eberly are:

i.   MICHAEL EDWARD[14]; born 30 Mar 1965.

699.   MARSHA KAY[13] NIEBUR (*Charles[12], Susan[11]Nicholson, Charles[10], Mary[9]Johnson, Charles[8], Charles[7], Ira[6], Jonathan[5], Nathaniel[4], Nathaniel[3], Humphrey[2], John[1]*) was born on 23 Nov 1944. She married John Young on 24 Apr 1964.

Children of Marsha Kay[13] Niebur and John Young are as follows:

i.   CHRISTINE LYNN[14]; born 5 Nov 1964.

ii.   JOHN CHARLES; born 10 Jan 1966.

iii.   DAVID SCOTT.

iv.   JEFFREY KEITH; born 15 Mar 1972.

700.   CAROLINE JOAN[13] NIEBUR (*Charles[12], Susan[11]Nicholson, Charles[10], Mary[9]Johnson, Charles[8], Charles[7], Ira[6], Jonathan[5], Nathaniel[4], Nathaniel[3], Humphrey[2], John[1]*) was born on 29 Jan 1949. She married James Palerino on 30 Jul 1971. She and James Palerino were divorced in 1974. She married William Maier on 15 Feb 1975.

Children of Caroline Joan[13] Niebur and William Maier are as follows:

i.   JEFFREY THOMAS[14]; born 25 Jul 1975.

ii.   CHRISTOPHER LUCAS; born 20 Jun 1978.

701.   CHERYL ANN[13] NIEBUR (*Charles[12], Susan[11]Nicholson, Charles[10], Mary[9]Johnson, Charles[8], Charles[7], Ira[6], Jonathan[5],*

Nathaniel[4], *Nathaniel*[3], *Humphrey*[2], *John*[1]) was born on 13 Mar 1951. She married Paul Lapinski on 27 Feb 1971.

Children of Cheryl Ann[13] Niebur and Paul Lapinski are as follows:

    i.   JACOB MATHEW[14]; born 20 Feb 1977.

    ii. JAMIE MITCHELLE; born 7 Mar 1979.

702. JULIE ANN[13] NIEBUR (*Paul*[12], *Susan*[11]*Nicholson*, *Charles*[10], *Mary*[9]*Johnson*, *Charles*[8], *Charles*[7], *Ira*[6], *Jonathan*[5], *Nathaniel*[4], *Nathaniel*[3], *Humphrey*[2], *John*[1]) was born on 13 Oct 1945. She married Thomas Ellis on 15 Feb 1964.

Children of Julie Ann[13] Niebur and Thomas Ellis are as follows:

    i.   STEPHANIE[14]; born 5 Mar 1965.

    ii. HOLLY; born 15 Jun 1966.

    iii. THOMAS; born 2 May 1968.

703. BRETT BORDEN[13] NIEBUR (*Robert*[12], *Susan*[11]*Nicholson*, *Charles*[10], *Mary*[9]*Johnson*, *Charles*[8], *Charles*[7], *Ira*[6], *Jonathan*[5], *Nathaniel*[4], *Nathaniel*[3], *Humphrey*[2], *John*[1]) was born on 16 Oct 1953. He married Cindy Bishop on 17 Jan 1976.

Children of Brett Borden[13] Niebur and Cindy Bishop are:

    i.   MICHELE RENEE[14]; born 3 Jul 1980.

704. JAMES WILLIAM[13] HAVENS (*Vera*[12]*Shive*, *Mary*[11]*Nicholson*, *Charles*[10], *Mary*[9]*Johnson*, *Charles*[8], *Charles*[7], *Ira*[6], *Jonathan*[5], *Nathaniel*[4], *Nathaniel*[3], *Humphrey*[2], *John*[1]) was born on 27 Aug 1939 at Scott Co., IL. He married Phyllis Ann Akers on 29 Sep 1961. He and Phyllis Ann Akers were divorced. He married Carolyn Ralph Young on 22 Oct 1979.

Children of James William[13] Havens and Phyllis Ann Akers are as follows:

    i.   LYNETTE ELAINE[14]; born 17 Jun 1964.

    ii. JAMES DANIEL; born 29 Apr 1969.

705. BETTY ANN[13] HAVENS (*Vera*[12]*Shive*, *Mary*[11]*Nicholson*, *Charles*[10], *Mary*[9]*Johnson*, *Charles*[8], *Charles*[7], *Ira*[6], *Jonathan*[5],

Nathaniel⁴, Nathaniel³, Humphrey², John¹) was born on 12 Aug 1941. She married Keith Jefferson on 30 May 1959.

Children of Betty Ann[13] Havens and Keith Jefferson are as follows:

    i.   KENNETH BRUCE[14]; born 15 Feb 1962; married Melanie Sue Dawdy 20 Oct 1984.

    ii. ROBERT KEITH; born 13 Jul 1965.

706. ROBERT EUGENE[13] HAVENS (*Vera¹²Shive, Mary¹¹Nicholson, Charles¹⁰, Mary⁹Johnson, Charles⁸, Charles⁷, Ira⁶, Jonathan⁵, Nathaniel⁴, Nathaniel³, Humphrey², John¹*) was born on 3 Feb 1943. He married Karla Elaine Jarvis circa 1964.

Children of Robert Eugene[13] Havens and Karla Elaine Jarvis are as follows:

    i.   JULIE ANN[14]; born 20 May 1965.

    ii. JILL RENEE; born 19 Sep 1970.

    iii. JODEE LYNN; born 25 Nov 1974.

707. THOMAS EARL[13] HAVENS (*Vera¹²Shive, Mary¹¹Nicholson, Charles¹⁰, Mary⁹Johnson, Charles⁸, Charles⁷, Ira⁶, Jonathan⁵, Nathaniel⁴, Nathaniel³, Humphrey², John¹*) was born on 24 May 1945. He married Joyce K. Davis on 1 Oct 1965.

Children of Thomas Earl[13] Havens and Joyce K. Davis are:

    i.   MICHELLE[14]; born 26 Jul 1969.

708. ELIZABETH SUZANNE[13] GIGER (*Mary¹²Shive, Mary¹¹Nicholson, Charles¹⁰, Mary⁹Johnson, Charles⁸, Charles⁷, Ira⁶, Jonathan⁵, Nathaniel⁴, Nathaniel³, Humphrey², John¹*) was born on 22 Sep 1940.

Children of Elizabeth Suzanne[13] Giger and an unknown person are:

    i.   MARK STEVEN[14]; born 20 Jul 1963.

709. DAVID RAY[13] GIGER (*Mary¹²Shive, Mary¹¹Nicholson, Charles¹⁰, Mary⁹Johnson, Charles⁸, Charles⁷, Ira⁶, Jonathan⁵,*

Nathaniel[4], *Nathaniel*[3], *Humphrey*[2], *John*[1]) was born on 23 Sep 1942. He married Donna Jean Douglas on 20 Aug 1961.

Children of David Ray[13] Giger and Donna Jean Douglas are as follows:

  i. TIMOTHY DAVID[14]; born 9 Sep 1964.
  ii. CRAIG ALAN; born 11 Nov 1966.

710. DONNA MARIE[13] GIGER (*Mary*[12]*Shive*, *Mary*[11]*Nicholson*, *Charles*[10], *Mary*[9]*Johnson*, *Charles*[8], *Charles*[7], *Ira*[6], *Jonathan*[5], *Nathaniel*[4], *Nathaniel*[3], *Humphrey*[2], *John*[1]) was born on 24 Nov 1945. She married Floyd Irvin Pursley on 14 Aug 1963 at Pittsfield, Pike Co., IL.

Children of Donna Marie[13] Giger and Floyd Irvin Pursley were as follows:

925. i. EARL WAYNE[14], born 4 Jun 1964; married Deanna Rains.
  ii. PATRICIA ELAINE; born 2 Feb 1966; died 3 Feb 1966.
  iii. GARY LEE; born 1 Aug 1967.

711. JANICE CAROL[13] LIDSTROM (*Bernice*[12]*Shive*, *Mary*[11]*Nicholson*, *Charles*[10], *Mary*[9]*Johnson*, *Charles*[8], *Charles*[7], *Ira*[6], *Jonathan*[5], *Nathaniel*[4], *Nathaniel*[3], *Humphrey*[2], *John*[1]) was born on 24 Sep 1945. She married Howard Earl Zimmerman on 6 Oct 1962 at Joliet, IL.

Children of Janice Carol[13] Lidstrom and Howard Earl Zimmerman are as follows:

  i. LAWRENCE ALLAN[14]; born 17 May 1963.
  ii. SHERRY LYNN; born 26 Sep 1966.
  iii. SHERYL ANN; born 26 Sep 1966.

712. JOYCE ANN[13] LIDSTROM (*Bernice*[12]*Shive*, *Mary*[11]*Nicholson*, *Charles*[10], *Mary*[9]*Johnson*, *Charles*[8], *Charles*[7], *Ira*[6], *Jonathan*[5], *Nathaniel*[4], *Nathaniel*[3], *Humphrey*[2], *John*[1]) was born on 8 Apr 1949. She married Jessie Tabbert on 20 Jun 1970 at Eldorado, WI.

Children of Joyce Ann[13] Lidstrom and Jessie Tabbert are as follows:

    i.   TANYA MICHELE[14]; born 2 Sep 1974.
   ii.   STACEY LYNN; born 14 Nov 1977.
  iii.   MELISSA NICOLE; born 14 Nov 1977.
  iv.   JEREMY JESSIE; born 4 Oct 1981.

713. ARTHUR LEWIS[13] CHAPMAN JR. (*Mabel*[12]*Shive, Mary*[11]*Nicholson, Charles*[10]*, Mary*[9]*Johnson, Charles*[8]*, Charles*[7]*, Ira*[6]*, Jonathan*[5]*, Nathaniel*[4]*, Nathaniel*[3]*, Humphrey*[2]*, John*[1]*)* was born on 9 Dec 1951 at RI. He married Diane Meeks on 13 Apr 1981. He lived in 1985 at Niceville, FL.

Children of Arthur Lewis[13] Chapman Jr. and Diane Meeks are:

    i.   HEATH[14]; born 14 Jul 1972.

714. SANDRA LYNN[13] CHAPMAN (*Mabel*[12]*Shive, Mary*[11]*Nicholson, Charles*[10]*, Mary*[9]*Johnson, Charles*[8]*, Charles*[7]*, Ira*[6]*, Jonathan*[5]*, Nathaniel*[4]*, Nathaniel*[3]*, Humphrey*[2]*, John*[1]*)* was born on 25 Jan 1955 at ID. She married Keith Bonn on 6 May 1978.

Children of Sandra Lynn[13] Chapman and Keith Bonn were as follows:

    i.   KEITH[14] III; born 5 Jun 1980; died 7 Jun 1980.
   ii.   KRISTINA LYNN; born 22 May 1981.

715. JAMES WILLIAM[13] SHIVE JR. (*James*[12]*, Mary*[11]*Nicholson, Charles*[10]*, Mary*[9]*Johnson, Charles*[8]*, Charles*[7]*, Ira*[6]*, Jonathan*[5]*, Nathaniel*[4]*, Nathaniel*[3]*, Humphrey*[2]*, John*[1]*)* was born on 9 Mar 1955 at Macomb, IL. He married Mary Jo Scott at Champaign, IL.

Children of James William[13] Shive Jr. and Mary Jo Scott are as follows:

    i.   JASON[14]; born 7 Mar 1981.
   ii.   JEREMY; born 7 Mar 1981.

716. JOAN[13] SHIVE (*Henry*[12]*, Mary*[11]*Nicholson, Charles*[10]*, Mary*[9]*Johnson, Charles*[8]*, Charles*[7]*, Ira*[6]*, Jonathan*[5]*, Nathaniel*[4]*,

Nathaniel[3], *Humphrey*[2], *John*[1]) was born on 8 Dec 1951. She married Charles Lakin on 23 May 1970.

Children of Joan[13] Shive and Charles Lakin are as follows:

    i.   PAMELA MARIE[14]; born 7 Jan 1971.

    ii. AMANDA JO; born 10 Nov 1976.

717. JERRY LEE[13] SHIVE (*Henry*[12], *Mary*[11]*Nicholson*, *Charles*[10], *Mary*[9]*Johnson*, *Charles*[8], *Charles*[7], *Ira*[6], *Jonathan*[5], *Nathaniel*[4], *Nathaniel*[3], *Humphrey*[2], *John*[1]) was born on 26 Jun 1954. He married Cindy Dann on 4 Feb 1975.

Children of Jerry Lee[13] Shive and Cindy Dann are as follows:

    i.   AMI ANNETTE[14]; born 19 Jan 1982.

    ii. JEREMY JOSEPH; born 7 Oct 1983.

718. NANCY ELAINE[13] SHIVE (*Henry*[12], *Mary*[11]*Nicholson*, *Charles*[10], *Mary*[9]*Johnson*, *Charles*[8], *Charles*[7], *Ira*[6], *Jonathan*[5], *Nathaniel*[4], *Nathaniel*[3], *Humphrey*[2], *John*[1]) was born on 30 Jul 1958. She married Tony Eugene Crain on 28 May 1977.

Children of Nancy Elaine[13] Shive and Tony Eugene Crain are:

    i.   JASON EUGENE[14]; born 4 Jul 1981.

719. STEVE WILLIAM[13] SHIVE (*Henry*[12], *Mary*[11]*Nicholson*, *Charles*[10], *Mary*[9]*Johnson*, *Charles*[8], *Charles*[7], *Ira*[6], *Jonathan*[5], *Nathaniel*[4], *Nathaniel*[3], *Humphrey*[2], *John*[1]) was born on 22 Sep 1959. He married Sherry Sue Piper on 16 Mar 1980.

Children of Steve William[13] Shive and Sherry Sue Piper are as follows:

    i.   CHRISTY NICOLE[14]; born 18 Jul 1980.

    ii. BRANDY RENEE; born 12 Oct 1981.

720. CONNIE SUE[13] SHIVE (*Henry*[12], *Mary*[11]*Nicholson*, *Charles*[10], *Mary*[9]*Johnson*, *Charles*[8], *Charles*[7], *Ira*[6], *Jonathan*[5], *Nathaniel*[4], *Nathaniel*[3], *Humphrey*[2], *John*[1]) was born on 7 Jun 1964. She married Larry Z. DePue on 4 Sep 1982.

Children of Connie Sue[13] Shive and Larry Z. DePue are:

i.   GRAIG LEWIS[14]; born 22 Mar 1984.

721. MARY JEAN[13] NEVIUS (*Dorothy[12]Shive, Mary[11]Nicholson, Charles[10], Mary[9]Johnson, Charles[8], Charles[7], Ira[6], Jonathan[5], Nathaniel[4], Nathaniel[3], Humphrey[2], John[1]*) was born on 2 Jan 1954 at Peoria, IL. She married Donald Ray Kupferschmid on 29 Sep 1979 at Peoria, IL.

Children of Mary Jean[13] Nevius and Donald Ray Kupferschmid are:

i.   SCOTT ALAN[14]; born 6 Sep 1980.

722. WILLIAM RODNEY[13] REEL (*Norma[12]Shive, Mary[11]Nicholson, Charles[10], Mary[9]Johnson, Charles[8], Charles[7], Ira[6], Jonathan[5], Nathaniel[4], Nathaniel[3], Humphrey[2], John[1]*) was born on 12 Jun 1960. He married Mary Neely on 16 Mar 1979.

Children of William Rodney[13] Reel and Mary Neely are as follows:

i.   AMBER RAMI[14]; born 28 Jul 1979.
ii.   ASHLEY ROBIN; born 3 Oct 1984.

723. REBECCA JEAN[13] REEL (*Norma[12]Shive, Mary[11]Nicholson, Charles[10], Mary[9]Johnson, Charles[8], Charles[7], Ira[6], Jonathan[5], Nathaniel[4], Nathaniel[3], Humphrey[2], John[1]*) was born on 19 Aug 1962. She married Berlyn Dean Thomas Jr. on 19 Jun 1982 at Detroit, IL.

Children of Rebecca Jean[13] Reel and Berlyn Dean Thomas Jr. are:

i.   LILA RENEE[14]; born 20 Nov 1983.

724. JUDY KAY[13] SOUDERS (*Norma[12]Sanderson, Beryl[11]Nicholson, Charles[10], Mary[9]Johnson, Charles[8], Charles[7], Ira[6], Jonathan[5], Nathaniel[4], Nathaniel[3], Humphrey[2], John[1]*) was born on 1 Aug 1947. She married James George Leinen. She and James George Leinen were divorced in 1980.

Children of Judy Kay[13] Souders and James George Leinen are:

i.   JEFFREY JAMES[14]; born 3 Aug 1972.

725. MARCIA LEE[13] SOUDERS (*Norma*[12]*Sanderson,* *Beryl*[11]*Nicholson, Charles*[10], *Mary*[9]*Johnson, Charles*[8], *Charles*[7], *Ira*[6], *Jonathan*[5], *Nathaniel*[4], *Nathaniel*[3], *Humphrey*[2], *John*[1]) was born on 9 Jun 1950. She married Robert Wayne Henry circa 1975.

Children of Marcia Lee[13] Souders and Robert Wayne Henry are as follows:

    i.   SCOTT[14]; born 25 Aug 1976.
    ii. KYLE WAYNE; born 15 May 1979.
    iii. (--?--); born Aug 1980.

726. DAVID LLOYD[13] LONG (*Carrie*[12]*Sanderson,* *Beryl*[11]*Nicholson, Charles*[10], *Mary*[9]*Johnson, Charles*[8], *Charles*[7], *Ira*[6], *Jonathan*[5], *Nathaniel*[4], *Nathaniel*[3], *Humphrey*[2], *John*[1]) was born on 21 Mar 1953. He married Linda Kay Buckingham in 1974.

Children of David Lloyd[13] Long and Linda Kay Buckingham are as follows:

    i.   KATHERINE[14]; born 1976.
    ii. MICHAEL; born 1981.
    iii. DANIEL JOSEPH; born 15 Jul 1983.

727. LESLIE STEVEN[13] HAMILTON (*Betty*[12]*Sanderson,* *Beryl*[11]*Nicholson, Charles*[10], *Mary*[9]*Johnson, Charles*[8], *Charles*[7], *Ira*[6], *Jonathan*[5], *Nathaniel*[4], *Nathaniel*[3], *Humphrey*[2], *John*[1]) was born on 7 Mar 1950. He married Ann Shields.

Children of Leslie Steven[13] Hamilton and Ann Shields are as follows:

    i.   CHADWICH EARL[14]; born 5 Apr 1973.
    ii. DANIEL JOSEPH; born 29 May 1976.

728. JOE GLEN[13] HAMILTON (*Betty*[12]*Sanderson,* *Beryl*[11]*Nicholson, Charles*[10], *Mary*[9]*Johnson, Charles*[8], *Charles*[7], *Ira*[6], *Jonathan*[5], *Nathaniel*[4], *Nathaniel*[3], *Humphrey*[2], *John*[1]) was born on 15 Dec 1953. He married Kathleen Merrill in 1976.

Children of Joe Glen[13] Hamilton and Kathleen Merrill are:

    i.   JUSTIN PAUL[14]; born 28 Dec 1979.

729. THOMAS NICHOL[13] GATES (*Carolyn[12]Rader, Jessie[11]Nicholson, Charles[10], Mary[9]Johnson, Charles[8], Charles[7], Ira[6], Jonathan[5], Nathaniel[4], Nathaniel[3], Humphrey[2], John[1]*) was born on 30 Sep 1945. He married Lindy (--?--). He married Louise (--?--).

Children of Thomas Nichol[13] Gates and Lindy (--?--) are:

    i.   LISA NICHOLETTE[14]; born 7 Nov 1967.

There were no children of Thomas Nichol[13] Gates and Louise (--?--).

730. JOYCE[13] RADER (*John[12], Jessie[11]Nicholson, Charles[10], Mary[9]Johnson, Charles[8], Charles[7], Ira[6], Jonathan[5], Nathaniel[4], Nathaniel[3], Humphrey[2], John[1]*) was born on 27 Mar 1953. She married Kenneth Martin. She and Kenneth Martin were divorced.

Children of Joyce[13] Rader and Kenneth Martin are as follows:

    i.   JULIE[14]; born 1972.

   ii.   DAVID; born 1976.

731. LARRY LAVERN[13] JONES (*LaVern[12], Mary[11]Killebrew, Mary[10]Miller, Rebecca[9]Johnson, Charles[8], Charles[7], Ira[6], Jonathan[5], Nathaniel[4], Nathaniel[3], Humphrey[2], John[1]*) was born on 20 Jul 1946. He married Jane Richardson on 30 Jun 1968. He and Jane Richardson were divorced on 10 Feb 1981.

Children of Larry LaVern[13] Jones and Jane Richardson are as follows:

    i.   MICHELLE[14]; born 30 Jul 1971.

   ii.   MONICA; born 15 Aug 1973.

732. TERESA ANN "TERRI"[13] JONES (*LaVern[12], Mary[11]Killebrew, Mary[10]Miller, Rebecca[9]Johnson, Charles[8], Charles[7], Ira[6], Jonathan[5], Nathaniel[4], Nathaniel[3], Humphrey[2], John[1]*) was born on 27 Mar 1948. She married Terry E. Milton on 3 Mar 1968.

Children of Teresa Ann "Terri"[13] Jones and Terry E. Milton are as follows:

    i.   DEBBIE SUE[14] born 7 Mar 1964.

ii. CATHY JO
iii. KIMBERLY ANN; born 2 Oct 1968.
iv. CHARLES RAY; born 29 Oct 1972.

733. LYLE LAVERN[13] JONES (*LaVern[12]*, *Mary[11]Killebrew*, *Mary[10]Miller*, *Rebecca[9]Johnson*, *Charles[8]*, *Charles[7]*, *Ira[6]*, *Jonathan[5]*, *Nathaniel[4]*, *Nathaniel[3]*, *Humphrey[2]*, *John[1]*) was born on 20 Nov 1960. He married Ann Denise Ballard on 28 Nov 1981.

Children of Lyle LaVern[13] Jones and Ann Denise Ballard are:

i. JEREMY DAVID[14]; born 12 May 1982.

734. LINDA KAY[13] GERMAN (*Virginia[12]Killebrew*, *Norene[11]*, *Mary[10]Miller*, *Rebecca[9]Johnson*, *Charles[8]*, *Charles[7]*, *Ira[6]*, *Jonathan[5]*, *Nathaniel[4]*, *Nathaniel[3]*, *Humphrey[2]*, *John[1]*) was born on 3 May 1942. She married Donald Lawrence Dennis on 10 Jun 1960. She and Donald Lawrence Dennis were divorced. She married George Manchester in Feb 1977. She and George Manchester were divorced. She married Kenneth Erickson on 9 May 1980.

Children of Linda Kay[13] German and Donald Lawrence Dennis are:

926. i. CHERYL LYNN[14], born 4 Jun 1963; married James Dolloff.

735. WILBUR LEE[13] GERMAN (*Virginia[12]Killebrew*, *Norene[11]*, *Mary[10]Miller*, *Rebecca[9]Johnson*, *Charles[8]*, *Charles[7]*, *Ira[6]*, *Jonathan[5]*, *Nathaniel[4]*, *Nathaniel[3]*, *Humphrey[2]*, *John[1]*) was born on 11 Nov 1946. He married Alice Marie Culp on 8 Feb 1964.

Children of Wilbur Lee[13] German and Alice Marie Culp are:

i. MICHAEL[14]; born 11 Jul 1964.

736. CARMEN S.[13] ARNOLD (*Nadine[12]Newingham*, *Ethel[11]Killebrew*, *Mary[10]Miller*, *Rebecca[9]Johnson*, *Charles[8]*, *Charles[7]*, *Ira[6]*, *Jonathan[5]*, *Nathaniel[4]*, *Nathaniel[3]*, *Humphrey[2]*, *John[1]*) was born on 18 May 1954. She married Rick Garland II on 19 Nov 1979.

Children of Carmen S.[13] Arnold and Rick Garland II are as follows:

    i.   JUSTIN TYLER[14]; born 20 Mar 1982.

    ii. JOSHUA AARON; born 21 Jun 1983.

737. GREG[13] ARNOLD (*Nadine[12]Newingham*, *Ethel[11]Killebrew*, *Mary[10]Miller*, *Rebecca[9]Johnson*, *Charles[8]*, *Charles[7]*, *Ira[6]*, *Jonathan[5]*, *Nathaniel[4]*, *Nathaniel[3]*, *Humphrey[2]*, *John[1]*) was born on 11 Sep 1958. He married Kathy (--?--) on 14 Nov 1978.

Children of Greg[13] Arnold and Kathy (--?--) are as follows:

    i.   BROOKE MICHELLE[14]; born 26 Nov 1981.

    ii. SCOTT ROBERT; born 21 Jun 1985.

738. CHARLOTTE[13] NEWINGHAN (*Bernard[12]Newingham*, *Ethel[11]Killebrew*, *Mary[10]Miller*, *Rebecca[9]Johnson*, *Charles[8]*, *Charles[7]*, *Ira[6]*, *Jonathan[5]*, *Nathaniel[4]*, *Nathaniel[3]*, *Humphrey[2]*, *John[1]*) was born on 26 Mar 1954. She married Michael Baker on 4 Jun 1977.

Children of Charlotte[13] Newinghan and Michael Baker are as follows:

    i.   BRIAN MICHAEL[14]; born 1 Jan 1979.

    ii. KEVIN RANDALL; born 11 Feb 1982.

739. JULIE RENEE[13] NEWINGHAN (*Bernard[12]Newingham*, *Ethel[11]Killebrew*, *Mary[10]Miller*, *Rebecca[9]Johnson*, *Charles[8]*, *Charles[7]*, *Ira[6]*, *Jonathan[5]*, *Nathaniel[4]*, *Nathaniel[3]*, *Humphrey[2]*, *John[1]*) was born on 16 Jul 1955. She married Darrell Wright on 7 Jun 1975.

Children of Julie Renee[13] Newinghan and Darrell Wright are as follows:

    i.   JON NICHOLAS[14]; born 8 May 1978.

    ii. NATHANIEL THOMAS; born 11 Aug 1979.

740. TONA JEAN[13] NEWINGHAN (*Carol[12]Newingham*, *Ethel[11]Killebrew*, *Mary[10]Miller*, *Rebecca[9]Johnson*, *Charles[8]*, *Charles[7]*, *Ira[6]*, *Jonathan[5]*, *Nathaniel[4]*, *Nathaniel[3]*, *Humphrey[2]*,

John[1]) was born on 15 Jul 1955. She married Randall Cree Smith on 15 Jun 1975.

Children of Tona Jean[13] Newinghan and Randall Cree Smith are as follows:

    i.   MANDY[14]; born 29 Jul 1976.
    ii. DUSTY JEAN; born 16 May 1978.

741. EARL WAYNE[13] LOYD (*Helen[12]Killebrew, Charles[11], Ethel[10]Miller, Rebecca[9]Johnson, Charles[8], Charles[7], Ira[6], Jonathan[5], Nathaniel[4], Nathaniel[3], Humphrey[2], John[1]*) was born on 8 May 1943. He married Sharon Kay Dawkins on 25 Jul 1970.

Children of Earl Wayne[13] Loyd and Sharon Kay Dawkins are as follows:

    i.   HEIDE KAY[14]; born 21 Dec 1972.
    ii. TIMOTHY EARL; born 23 May 1974.
    iii. ERIN SUE; born 1 Nov 1977.

742. BARBARA[13] LOYD (*Helen[12]Killebrew, Charles[11], Ethel[10]Miller, Rebecca[9]Johnson, Charles[8], Charles[7], Ira[6], Jonathan[5], Nathaniel[4], Nathaniel[3], Humphrey[2], John[1]*) was born on 5 Dec 1946. She married Larry Joe Dunham on 7 Sep 1969.

Children of Barbara[13] Loyd and Larry Joe Dunham are as follows:

    i.   LISA DIANE[14]; born 3 Feb 1970.
    ii. LORI JUNE; born 9 Feb 1973.

743. EVELYN[13] LOYD (*Helen[12]Killebrew, Charles[11], Ethel[10]Miller, Rebecca[9]Johnson, Charles[8], Charles[7], Ira[6], Jonathan[5], Nathaniel[4], Nathaniel[3], Humphrey[2], John[1]*) was born on 17 Jan 1949. She married Rodney Lee Dehart on 5 Oct 1969.

Children of Evelyn[13] Loyd and Rodney Lee Dehart are as follows:

    i.   VALERIE LYNN[14]; born 7 May 1973.
    ii. BRADLEY JAY; born 12 Jan 1975.

744. HAROLD[13] LOYD (*Helen[12]Killebrew, Charles[11], Ethel[10]Miller, Rebecca[9]Johnson, Charles[8], Charles[7], Ira[6], Jonathan[5], Nathaniel[4], Nathaniel[3], Humphrey[2], John[1]*) was born on 20 Jan 1951. He married Janie Armistead on 3 Apr 1982.

Children of Harold[13] Loyd and Janie Armistead are:

    i.   CURT THOMAS[14]; born 4 Jun 1984.

745. DIANNA[13] LOYD (*Helen[12]Killebrew, Charles[11], Ethel[10]Miller, Rebecca[9]Johnson, Charles[8], Charles[7], Ira[6], Jonathan[5], Nathaniel[4], Nathaniel[3], Humphrey[2], John[1]*) was born on 19 Dec 1955. She married Donnie W. Foster on 4 Dec 1977.

Children of Dianna[13] Loyd and Donnie W. Foster are as follows:

    i.   SARAH DIANE[14]; born 17 May 1978.

    ii. MICHAEL RAY; born 19 Jun 1980.

746. REBECCA DALE[13] KILLEBREW (*Charles[12], Charles[11], Ethel[10]Miller, Rebecca[9]Johnson, Charles[8], Charles[7], Ira[6], Jonathan[5], Nathaniel[4], Nathaniel[3], Humphrey[2], John[1]*) was born on 12 Mar 1949. She married (--?--) ?

Children of Rebecca Dale[13] Killebrew and (--?--) ? are:

    i.   CHARLES EDWARD[14]; born 10 Aug 1976.

747. CAROLYN JUNE[13] HALDANE (*Dorothy[12]Killebrew, William[11], Ethel[10]Miller, Rebecca[9]Johnson, Charles[8], Charles[7], Ira[6], Jonathan[5], Nathaniel[4], Nathaniel[3], Humphrey[2], John[1]*) was born on 3 May 1943. She married Kenneth Evridge on 20 Jun 1964.

Children of Carolyn June[13] Haldane and Kenneth Evridge are as follows:

    i.   DAWN[14]; born 23 Mar 1970.

    ii. DAVID; born 15 Nov 1974.

748. LINDA SUE[13] HALDANE (*Dorothy[12]Killebrew, William[11], Ethel[10]Miller, Rebecca[9]Johnson, Charles[8], Charles[7], Ira[6], Jonathan[5], Nathaniel[4], Nathaniel[3], Humphrey[2], John[1]*) was born on 17 Jul 1946. She married Ed Stauber on 29 Jun 1968.

Children of Linda Sue[13] Haldane and Ed Stauber are as follows:

    i.   SANDY[14]; born 11 Nov 1972.

    ii. EDDIE; born 1 Aug 1975.

749. WILLIAM ALLEN[13] KILLEBREW (*William*[12], *William*[11], *Ethel*[10]*Miller*, *Rebecca*[9]*Johnson*, *Charles*[8], *Charles*[7], *Ira*[6], *Jonathan*[5], *Nathaniel*[4], *Nathaniel*[3], *Humphrey*[2], *John*[1]) was born on 8 Aug 1950. He married Sharon Larson on 17 Jan 1969.

Children of William Allen[13] Killebrew and Sharon Larson are:

    i.   MATT GREGORY[14]; born 29 Oct 1975.

750. MICHAEL[13] KILLEBREW (*Glen*[12], *William*[11], *Ethel*[10]*Miller*, *Rebecca*[9]*Johnson*, *Charles*[8], *Charles*[7], *Ira*[6], *Jonathan*[5], *Nathaniel*[4], *Nathaniel*[3], *Humphrey*[2], *John*[1]) was born on 24 Nov 1953. He married Rhonda Lou Smith on 13 Oct 1973.

Children of Michael[13] Killebrew and Rhonda Lou Smith are as follows:

    i.   HEATHER DAWN[14]; born 30 Apr 1974.

    ii. GRAIG ROBERT; born 2 Dec 1976.

751. JO[13] SCHAFER (*Charles*[12], *Florence*[11]*Killebrew*, *Ethel*[10]*Miller*, *Rebecca*[9]*Johnson*, *Charles*[8], *Charles*[7], *Ira*[6], *Jonathan*[5], *Nathaniel*[4], *Nathaniel*[3], *Humphrey*[2], *John*[1]) was born on 6 Jul 1952. She married Steve Messner on 11 Dec 1971.

Children of Jo[13] Schafer and Steve Messner are as follows:

    i.   KIMBERLY[14]; born 14 Dec 1973.

    ii. MICHELLE; born 30 Aug 1977.

752. DALE[13] SCHAFER (*Charles*[12], *Florence*[11]*Killebrew*, *Ethel*[10]*Miller*, *Rebecca*[9]*Johnson*, *Charles*[8], *Charles*[7], *Ira*[6], *Jonathan*[5], *Nathaniel*[4], *Nathaniel*[3], *Humphrey*[2], *John*[1]) was born on 31 May 1954. He married Kerry Leick circa 1975. He and Kerry Leick were divorced. He married Katherine Sewell on 23 Jan 1981.

Children of Dale[13] Schafer and Kerry Leick are as follows:

    i.   HEATHER[14]; born 21 Apr 1976.

    ii. JEREMY; born 10 Jul 1977.

There were no children of Dale[13] Schafer and Katherine Sewell.

753. DIANE[13] SCHAFER (*Charles[12], Florence[11]Killebrew, Ethel[10]Miller, Rebecca[9]Johnson, Charles[8], Charles[7], Ira[6], Jonathan[5], Nathaniel[4], Nathaniel[3], Humphrey[2], John[1]*) was born on 10 Jan 1956. She married Joseph Ansbro on 18 Nov 1972.

Children of Diane[13] Schafer and Joseph Ansbro are as follows:

    i.   ERIC[14]; born 20 May 1973.

    ii. DAVID; born 1 Aug 1980.

754. KRISTINE DAWN[13] MILLER (*Donald[12], William[11], William[10], Rebecca[9]Johnson, Charles[8], Charles[7], Ira[6], Jonathan[5], Nathaniel[4], Nathaniel[3], Humphrey[2], John[1]*) was born on 15 Sep 1962. She married Robert Dalldorf on 18 Apr 1983.

Children of Kristine Dawn[13] Miller and Robert Dalldorf are as follows:

    i.   KIMBERLY K.[14]; born 8 Oct 1983.

    ii. RYAN R.; born 15 May 1985.

755. KENNETH CHANDLER[13] MILLER (*Donald[12], William[11], William[10], Rebecca[9]Johnson, Charles[8], Charles[7], Ira[6], Jonathan[5], Nathaniel[4], Nathaniel[3], Humphrey[2], John[1]*) was born on 21 Apr 1965. He married (--?--) ?

Children of Kenneth Chandler[13] Miller and (--?--) ? are:

    i.   BAIRD[14].

756. STEVEN MARK[13] BOGGS (*Marilyn[12]Thornton, Russel[11], Herbert[10], Phila[9]Johnson, Charles[8], Charles[7], Ira[6], Jonathan[5], Nathaniel[4], Nathaniel[3], Humphrey[2], John[1]*) was born on 26 Oct 1960. He married Jennie Brunner on 1 Feb 1981 at Tulsa, OK.

He was also known as Steven Mark Griffen.

Children of Steven Mark[13] Boggs and Jennie Brunner were as follows:

    i.   ADAM RUSSEL[14]; born 4 Sep 1981; died 6 Nov 1981.

    ii. HANNAH KATHLEEN; born 6 Jan 1983.

757. JOHN PARKE[13] BEARDSLEY (*Zeta*[12]*Porter, Cleo*[11]*Johnson, Archie*[10], *John*[9], *Hiram*[8], *Charles*[7], *Ira*[6], *Jonathan*[5], *Nathaniel*[4], *Nathaniel*[3], *Humphrey*[2], *John*[1]) was born on 23 Sep 1940 at Portland, Multnomah Co., OR. He married Janet Norrine Travis.

Children of John Parke[13] Beardsley and Janet Norrine Travis all born at Corvallis, Benton Co., OR, are as follows:

    i.   LISA LYN[14]; born 5 Apr 1962.

    ii. MICHAEL STUART; born 28 May 1964.

    iii. MARNI KAY; born 13 Jan 1968.

    iv. PAIGE ERIN; born 24 Sep 1970.

758. THOMAS ROBERT[13] EARL (*Zeta*[12]*Porter, Cleo*[11]*Johnson, Archie*[10], *John*[9], *Hiram*[8], *Charles*[7], *Ira*[6], *Jonathan*[5], *Nathaniel*[4], *Nathaniel*[3], *Humphrey*[2], *John*[1]) was born on 4 Oct 1952 at Portland, Multnomah Co., OR. He married Carrie Groomer.

Children of Thomas Robert[13] Earl and Carrie Groomer are as follows:

    i.   ERIN[14]; born 18 Jun 1981 at Salt Lake City, UT.

    ii. BRYCE ANDREW; born 15 May 1982 at Centerville, VT.

759. GREGORY JAMES[13] MESSER (*Karlene*[12]*Johnson, Charles*[11], *Charles*[10], *John*[9], *Hiram*[8], *Charles*[7], *Ira*[6], *Jonathan*[5], *Nathaniel*[4], *Nathaniel*[3], *Humphrey*[2], *John*[1]) was born on 16 Dec 1955 at Medford, Jackson Co., OR. He married Billie Donnelly on 7 May 1976 at ID. He and Billie Donnelly were divorced. He married Donna Adams on 22 Jun 1985 at Reno, NV. He married Candace L. Anderson on 14 Feb 1997 at Josephine Co., OR.

Children of Gregory James[13] Messer and Billie Donnelly are as follows:

    i.   BRIAN JONATHAN[14]; born 11 Sep 1974 at Pocotello, ID.

    ii. KEVIN JAMES; born 12 Feb 1977 at Oahu, HI.

    iii. MICHAEL ALLEN; born 6 Mar 1979 at Shelley, ID.

760. GRANT EDWARD[13] MESSER (*Karlene*[12]*Johnson, Charles*[11], *Charles*[10], *John*[9], *Hiram*[8], *Charles*[7], *Ira*[6], *Jonathan*[5], *Nathaniel*[4], *Nathaniel*[3], *Humphrey*[2], *John*[1]) was born on 31 Aug 1962 at Medford, Jackson Co., OR. He married Carla Nicole Sherrouse on 8 Jan 1990 at Wichita, KS.

Children of Grant Edward[13] Messer and Carla Nicole Sherrouse are as follows:

    i.   JAMES ANTHONY EDWARD[14]; born 27 Nov 1992 at Jackson Co., NC.

    ii.   EVA ELIZABETH; born 21 Jun 1997 at San Antonio, TX.

761. JOHN ANDREW[13] MESSER (*Karlene*[12]*Johnson, Charles*[11], *Charles*[10], *John*[9], *Hiram*[8], *Charles*[7], *Ira*[6], *Jonathan*[5], *Nathaniel*[4], *Nathaniel*[3], *Humphrey*[2], *John*[1]) was born on 22 Feb 1966 at Medford, Jackson Co., OR. He married Julie Greene. Divorced Julie Greene.

Children of John Andrew[13] Messer and Julie Greene are as follows:

    i.   JESSICA LYNN[14]; born 26 Oct 1988 at Salem, Marion Co., OR; died 2 July 2003, Salem, OR; buried 8 July 2003 at City View Cemetery, Salem, Oregon.

    ii.   NATASHA DAWN; born 21 Jul 1995.

762. LEANNE MICHELE[13] JOHNSON (*Gerald*[12], *Charles*[11], *Charles*[10], *John*[9], *Hiram*[8], *Charles*[7], *Ira*[6], *Jonathan*[5], *Nathaniel*[4], *Nathaniel*[3], *Humphrey*[2], *John*[1]) was born on 29 Jul 1965 at Salem, Marion Co., OR. She married Michael Andrew Shaw, son of Herbert Shaw and Barbara "Bobbi" Block, on 23 Jul 1988 at Portland, Multnomah Co., OR.

Children of LeAnne Michele[13] Johnson and Michael Andrew Shaw both born at Salem, Marion Co., OR, are as follows:

    i.   AARON JOHNSON[14]; born 21 May 1993.

    ii.   RYAN MICHAEL; born 5 Dec 1996.

763. LISA MARIE[13] JOHNSON (*Gerald*[12], *Charles*[11], *Charles*[10], *John*[9], *Hiram*[8], *Charles*[7], *Ira*[6], *Jonathan*[5], *Nathaniel*[4], *Nathaniel*[3], *Humphrey*[2], *John*[1]) was born on 12 Jan 1968 at Portland, Multnomah Co., OR. She married Robert H. Ford, son of Robert S. Ford and Judith Bond, on 17 Dec 1988 at Gatlinburg, TN.

She began military service on 24 Nov 1986 Navy Air.

Children of Lisa Marie[13] Johnson and Robert H. Ford all born at Indianapolis, Marion Co., IN, are as follows:

  i.   JAMES ROBERT[14]; born 3 Mar 1994.
  ii. BLAKE HOWLAND; born 3 Nov 1999.
  iii. SAMANTHA JANE; born 11 Feb 2003.

764. MARCELLA DORENE[13] BABECKOS (*Betty*[12]*Parsons*, *Doris*[11]*Shaw*, *Pearl*[10]*Johnson*, *John*[9], *Hiram*[8], *Charles*[7], *Ira*[6], *Jonathan*[5], *Nathaniel*[4], *Nathaniel*[3], *Humphrey*[2], *John*[1]) was born on 16 Aug 1946 at Seattle, King Co., WA. She married Wesley Dreyer on 15 Apr 1966 at Ingleside, TX.

Children of Marcella Dorene[13] Babeckos and Wesley Dreyer are as follows:

  i. KELLY ANN[14]; born 22 Dec 1968.
  ii. PATRICIA ANN; born 23 Jan 1970.

765. WILLIAM BRECHT[13] BABECKOS (*Betty*[12]*Parsons*, *Doris*[11]*Shaw*, *Pearl*[10]*Johnson*, *John*[9], *Hiram*[8], *Charles*[7], *Ira*[6], *Jonathan*[5], *Nathaniel*[4], *Nathaniel*[3], *Humphrey*[2], *John*[1]) was born on 14 Aug 1951 at Portland, Multnomah Co., OR. He married Terri Lynn Jensen on 22 May 1976 at Portland, Multnomah Co., OR.

Children of William Brecht[13] Babeckos and Terri Lynn Jensen are as follows:

  i. KASSANDRA MARIE[14]; born 1 Oct 1978.
  ii. STEPHANIE ANN; born 5 Jan 1981.

766. CHRISTINE ANN[13] SMALLEY (*Alicia*[12]*McElroy*, *Earle*[11], *Rose*[10]*Johnson*, *George*[9], *Hiram*[8], *Charles*[7], *Ira*[6], *Jonathan*[5], *Nathaniel*[4], *Nathaniel*[3], *Humphrey*[2], *John*[1]) was born on 9 Oct 1948. She married Dennis Stroh.

Children of Christine Ann[13] Smalley and Dennis Stroh are:

    i.   NICOLE ANN[14]; born Sep 1972.

767. GRAIG MITCHELL[13] SMALLEY (*Alicia*[12]*McElroy*, *Earle*[11], *Rose*[10]*Johnson*, *George*[9], *Hiram*[8], *Charles*[7], *Ira*[6], *Jonathan*[5], *Nathaniel*[4], *Nathaniel*[3], *Humphrey*[2], *John*[1]) was born on 31 May 1950. He married Wendy Johnson.

Children of Graig Mitchell[13] Smalley and Wendy Johnson are:

    i.   GEOFFREY[14]; born 1970.

768. GABRIELLE[13] JOHNSON (*Ray*[12], *George*[11], *George*[10], *George*[9], *Hiram*[8], *Charles*[7], *Ira*[6], *Jonathan*[5], *Nathaniel*[4], *Nathaniel*[3], *Humphrey*[2], *John*[1]) was born on 22 Dec 1971 at Longview, Cowlitz Co., WA.

Children of Gabrielle[13] Johnson and an unknown spouse are as follows:

    i.   CIARA ANTOINETTE[14]; born 11 May 1991.
    ii. WESLEY ALLEN; born 3 Jun 1998.

769. SHELLEY[13] JOHNSON (*Ray*[12], *George*[11], *George*[10], *George*[9], *Hiram*[8], *Charles*[7], *Ira*[6], *Jonathan*[5], *Nathaniel*[4], *Nathaniel*[3], *Humphrey*[2], *John*[1]) was born on 22 Oct 1979.

Children of Shelley[13] Johnson and an unknown spouse were:

    i.   CAMERON JAMES HILSINGER[14]; born 2 Dec 1999; died 29 Feb 2000.

770. LAWRENCE "NEIL"[13] GAMEY (*Georgie*[12]*Iaeger*, *George*[11], *Ada*[10]*Johnson*, *William*[9], *Hiram*[8], *Charles*[7], *Ira*[6], *Jonathan*[5], *Nathaniel*[4], *Nathaniel*[3], *Humphrey*[2], *John*[1]) was born on 11 Oct 1935 at Everett, Snohomish Co., WA. He married Mary Leake. He and Mary Leake were divorced.

Children of Lawrence "Neil"[13] Gamey and Mary Leake were as follows:

  927.   i.   DAVID GUY[14], born 4 Sep 1957 at San Francisco, CA; married Donna M. Leaverton.

928. ii. SCOTT RAYMOND, married Deana (--?--); divorced Deana (--?--); married Vicki (--?--).

iii. TAMMY LYNN; born 3 Mar 1964.

She lived in 1997 at Federal Way, King Co., WA.

iv. BRIAN NEIL; born 27 Jun 1967 at Yakima, Yakima Co., WA; died 18 Oct 1974 at Yakima, Yakima Co., WA, at age 7.

771. JACK WILLIAM[13] GAMEY (*Georgie[12]Iaeger, George[11], Ada[10]Johnson, William[9], Hiram[8], Charles[7], Ira[6], Jonathan[5], Nathaniel[4], Nathaniel[3], Humphrey[2], John[1]*) was born on 1 May 1942 at Snohomish, Snohomish Co., WA. He married Christine "Micky" Weltz. He and Christine "Micky" Weltz were divorced. He married Yongsoon Barker. He and Yongsoon Barker were divorced. He died on 15 Jul 1987 at Selah, WA, at age 45. He was buried at Snohomish, Snohomish Co., WA.

Children of Jack William[13] Gamey and Christine "Micky" Weltz are:

i. ANTHONY LAWRENCE[14]; born 3 Aug 1965.

There were no children of Jack William[13] Gamey and Yongsoon Barker.

772. GEORGE "DANIEL"[13] NASLUND (*Hazel[12]Iaeger, George[11], Ada[10]Johnson, William[9], Hiram[8], Charles[7], Ira[6], Jonathan[5], Nathaniel[4], Nathaniel[3], Humphrey[2], John[1]*) was born on 23 May 1942 at Seattle, King Co., WA. He married Crystal Lynn Setting, daughter of Joseph Paul Setting and Vivian Lura Billings, on 30 Dec 1964 at Alderwood Manor, Snohomish Co., WA.

He lived in 1980 at Snohomish, Snohomish Co., WA.

Children of George "Daniel"[13] Naslund and Crystal Lynn Setting both born at Seattle, King Co., WA, are as follows:

929. i. CLINTON JOSEPH[14], born 18 May 1964; married Susan Phillips; divorced Susan Phillips; married Sunny Kraft.

930. ii. KEVIN DAVID, born 1 Jul 1966; married Marianne Denise Kessler.

368

773. JONATHAN DAVID[13] NASLUND (*Hazel*[12]*Iaeger*, *George*[11], *Ada*[10]*Johnson*, *William*[9], *Hiram*[8], *Charles*[7], *Ira*[6], *Jonathan*[5], *Nathaniel*[4], *Nathaniel*[3], *Humphrey*[2], *John*[1]) was born on 14 Mar 1946 at Everett, Snohomish Co., WA. He married Vicki Lynn Swaim, daughter of Gerald Swaim and Mary Lou Gillispie, on 30 May 1975 at Thorne Bay, AK.

He moved in 1985 at North Pole, AK.

Children of Jonathan David[13] Naslund and Vicki Lynn Swaim both born at Ketchikan, AK, are as follows:

    i.   KERI RENEE[14]; born 18 Aug 1977.

    ii. KELLI MARIE; born 27 Apr 1980.

774. MARY KAY[13] NASLUND (*Hazel*[12]*Iaeger*, *George*[11], *Ada*[10]*Johnson*, *William*[9], *Hiram*[8], *Charles*[7], *Ira*[6], *Jonathan*[5], *Nathaniel*[4], *Nathaniel*[3], *Humphrey*[2], *John*[1]) was born on 15 Jan 1952 at Seattle, King Co., WA. She married James Russell Lowell on 10 Feb 1972 at Seattle, King Co., WA. She and James Russell Lowell were divorced. She married Bill Carter on 10 Mar 1984 at Cedars Inn, Okanogan, WA.

She lived on 25 Feb 1998 at Mt. Vernon, WA.

Children of Mary Kay[13] Naslund and Bill Carter are:

    i.   JEFFREY JEREMIAH[14]; born 18 Oct 1980 at Omak, WA.

There were no children of Mary Kay[13] Naslund and James Russell Lowell.

775. JAMES DALE[13] HILL (*Lois*[12]*Iaeger*, *George*[11], *Ada*[10]*Johnson*, *William*[9], *Hiram*[8], *Charles*[7], *Ira*[6], *Jonathan*[5], *Nathaniel*[4], *Nathaniel*[3], *Humphrey*[2], *John*[1]) was born on 23 Aug 1941 at Seattle, King Co., WA. He married Carol Ann Shultz, daughter of William Shultz and Ouyda Maddox, on 26 May 1960 at Snohomish, Snohomish Co., WA. He and Carol Ann Shultz were divorced. He married Mary Moericke at Sand Point, ID. He and Mary Moericke were divorced. He married Clarice Verlinde. He and Clarice Verlinde were divorced. He married Cindee Matthews on 14 Sep 1986 at Fairbanks, AK.

He lived on 21 Jul 2001 at Fairbanks, AK.

Children of James Dale[13] Hill and Carol Ann Shultz both born at Seattle, King Co., WA, are as follows:

931.   i.   TERESA MAY[14], born 12 Apr 1961; married James Calvin Bolton; divorced James Calvin Bolton; married Morgan Dellinger III; divorced Morgan Dellinger III; married Charles David Frediani Jr; married (--?--) Milliken.

932.   ii.   JAMES DALE JR, born 16 Nov 1962; married Deborah Fannie Griffith; divorced Deborah Fannie Griffith; married Hillery Jean Prosh; divorced Hillery Jean Prosh; married Susan Beth Korschun; divorced Susan Beth Korschun.

Children of James Dale[13] Hill and an unknown spouse are:

933.   i.   SHERRILL LEE[14], born 15 Feb 1964; married Keith Chew; divorced Keith Chew.

Children of James Dale[13] Hill and Mary Moericke are as follows:

934.   i.   ANNETTE KATHLEEN[14], born 20 Aug 1964 at Central Pt., Jackson Co., OR; married Raymond Frederick Ault; divorced Raymond Frederick Ault; married Kenneth Ray Wells.

935.   ii.   JEFFERY CHARLES WALTER SR., born 21 Sep 1965 at Medford, Jackson Co., OR; married Michele Lynn Brogden; divorced Michele Lynn Brogden; married Lori Ann Chandler.

   iii.   CHARLES EDWIN II; born 14 Jan 1969 at Medford, Jackson Co., OR; married Mary Merrit.

Children of James Dale[13] HILL and Cindee Matthews are:

   i.   TAYLOR NICOLE[14]; born 7 Mar 1991 at Fairbanks, AK.

776.   MARTHA ANN[13] HILL (*Lois*[12]*Iaeger*, *George*[11], *Ada*[10]*Johnson*, *William*[9], *Hiram*[8], *Charles*[7], *Ira*[6], *Jonathan*[5], *Nathaniel*[4], *Nathaniel*[3], *Humphrey*[2], *John*[1]) was born on 3 Jan 1946 at Everett, Snohomish Co., WA. She married Harley Charles Mann, son of Charles Mann and Erma Olson, on 23 Apr 1966 at

Everett, Snohomish Co., WA. She and Harley Charles Mann were divorced.

She lived in 1997 at Seattle, King Co., WA.

Children of Martha Ann[13] Hill and Harley Charles Mann both born at Edmonds, Snohomish Co., WA, are as follows:

> 936. i. BRADLEY CHARLES[14], born 19 Aug 1964; married Gayanna Knutsen; divorced Gayanna Knutsen; married Christy Carter; divorced Christy Carter; married Tammy Lynn Johnson.
>
> 937. ii. KARA MICHELLE, born 15 Oct 1972; married Shawn Michael Hartz.

777. KATHLEEN MAY[13] HILL (*Lois*[12]*Iaeger, George*[11], *Ada*[10]*Johnson, William*[9], *Hiram*[8], *Charles*[7], *Ira*[6], *Jonathan*[5], *Nathaniel*[4], *Nathaniel*[3], *Humphrey*[2], *John*[1]) was born on 10 Sep 1947 at Scotia, Humboldt Co., CA. She married Graig Yost on 23 Sep 1967. She and Graig Yost were divorced. She married Michael Arther Stevens, son of Russel Stevens and Rebecca Travis, on 22 Feb 1976 at Seattle, King Co., WA. She lived in 1997 at Bothell, WA.

Children of Kathleen May[13] Hill and Michael Arther Stevens are:

> i. TREVOR JAMES[14]; born 6 Nov 1980 at Seattle, King Co., WA.

778. RICHARD STEPHEN[13] IAEGER (*Charles*[12], *George*[11]*Iaeger, Ada*[10]*Johnson, William*[9], *Hiram*[8], *Charles*[7], *Ira*[6], *Jonathan*[5], *Nathaniel*[4], *Nathaniel*[3], *Humphrey*[2], *John*[1]) was born on 21 Nov 1946 at Garberville, Humboldt Co., CA. He married Carolyn Ethel Blixseth. He and Carolyn Ethel Blixseth were divorced. He married Liana Pearl Cannon on 9 Apr 1982 at Roseburg, Douglas Co., OR. He and Liana Pearl Cannon were divorced. He married Barbara Jean Barnett. He and Barbara Jean Barnett were divorced.

He lived in 2000 at Roseberg, Douglas Co., OR.

Children of Richard Stephen[13] Iaeger and Liana Pearl Cannon are:

i. KRYSTAL MARIE[14]; born 11 Feb 1983 at Roseburg, Douglas Co., OR.

There were no children of Richard Stephen[13] IAEGER and Barbara Jean Barnett.

779. JUDITH LYNN[13] IAEGER (*Jackson*[12], *George*[11]*Iaeger*, *Ada*[10]*Johnson*, *William*[9], *Hiram*[8], *Charles*[7], *Ira*[6], *Jonathan*[5], *Nathaniel*[4], *Nathaniel*[3], *Humphrey*[2], *John*[1]) was born on 14 May 1943. She married Wayne Beitelspacher in 1962. She and Wayne Beitelspacher were divorced. She married Rod Kirby in 1979. She and Rod Kirby were divorced. She married William Migan in 2000.

She lived in 2000 at Dayton, NV.

Children of Judith Lynn[13] Iaeger and Wayne Beitelspacher are as follows:

i. STACEY LYNN[14]; born 29 Jan 1963 at Hot Springs, Fall River Co., SD.

She lived in 2003 at Bend, Deschutes Co., OR.

938. ii. STEPHEN, born 8 Mar 1967 at Stillwater, MN; married Dawn Milat; divorced Dawn Milat.

780. DENNIS[13] IAEGER (*Jackson*[12], *George*[11]*Iaeger*, *Ada*[10]*Johnson*, *William*[9], *Hiram*[8], *Charles*[7], *Ira*[6], *Jonathan*[5], *Nathaniel*[4], *Nathaniel*[3], *Humphrey*[2], *John*[1]) was born on 4 Jan 1950 at Garberville, Humboldt Co., CA. He married Piper Sue Hamilton in 1971 at Daleville, AL. He and Piper Sue Hamilton were divorced in 1973. He married Peggy Williamson in 1974 at Tacoma, Pierce Co., WA. He and Peggy Williamson were divorced in 1978. He married Wanda Peck in 1984 at Seattle, King Co., WA. He and Wanda Peck were divorced in 1992.

Children of Dennis[13] IAEGER and Wanda Peck are:

i. WILLIAM JACKSON[14]; born 22 Sep 1985 at Seattle, King Co., WA.

He lived in 2001 at Burnsville, MN.

781. WILLIAM ARTHUR[13] BLANDIN (*Virginia*[12]*Iaeger*, *George*[11], *Ada*[10]*Johnson*, *William*[9], *Hiram*[8], *Charles*[7], *Ira*[6], *Jonathan*[5],

$Nathaniel^4$, $Nathaniel^3$, $Humphrey^2$, $John^1$) was born on 21 Jul 1944 at Providence Hospital, Everett, Snohomish Co., WA. He married Alice May Taute, daughter of Zearl Benjamin Taute and Effie Deloris Bye, on 5 Aug 1972 at Edmonds United Methodist Church, Edmonds, Snohomish Co, WA. He was Civil Engineer. He began military service on 28 Aug 1969 at Seattle, King Co., WA, Commissioned in US Army (ROTC). He moved in Aug 2000 at Camano Island, Island Co., WA.

Children of William Arthur^{13} Blandin and Alice May Taute both born at Northwest Hospital, Seattle, King Co., WA, are as follows:

    i.   ERICK WILLIAM^{14}; born 22 Oct 1975.
    ii. ALYNDA DEANNE; born 8 Jul 1979.

782. ROBERT ALLEN^{13} STRASSER (*Lulubelle*^{12}, *George*^{11}*Iaeger*, *Ada*^{10}*Johnson*, *William*^{9}, *Hiram*^{8}, *Charles*^{7}, *Ira*^{6}, *Jonathan*^{5}, *Nathaniel*^{4}, *Nathaniel*^{3}, *Humphrey*^{2}, *John*^{1}) was born on 23 Apr 1946 at Garberville, Humboldt Co., CA. He married Sandra Marie Shields. He and Sandra Marie Shields were divorced. He married Carolyn Darline Hopper in Nov 1969 at Eureka, CA. He and Carolyn Darline Hopper were divorced. He married Joy (--?--).

There were no children of Robert Allen^{13} Strasser and Sandra Marie Shields.

Children of Robert Allen^{13} Strasser and Carolyn Darline Hopper both born at Eureka, CA, are as follows:

    i.   CARL EDWARD^{14}; born 2 Dec 1970.
    ii. ROBERT ALLEN JR; born 28 Jul 1972.

There were no children of Robert Allen^{13} Strasser and Joy (--?--).

783. SUSAN EILEEN^{13} LEWIS (*Lulubelle*^{12}*IAEGER*, *George*^{11}*Iaeger*, *Ada*^{10}*Johnson*, *William*^{9}, *Hiram*^{8}, *Charles*^{7}, *Ira*^{6}, *Jonathan*^{5}, *Nathaniel*^{4}, *Nathaniel*^{3}, *Humphrey*^{2}, *John*^{1}) was born on 16 Mar 1948 at Scotia, Humboldt Co., CA. She married (--?--) Dean.

She lived at Fortuna, CA.

Children of Susan Eileen^{13} LEWIS and (--?--) Dean are:

    i.   CARRIE^{14}.

784. LEONARD EARL[13] NORRIS JR (*Lulubelle*[12], *George*[11]*Iaeger*, *Ada*[10]*Johnson*, *William*[9], *Hiram*[8], *Charles*[7], *Ira*[6], *Jonathan*[5], *Nathaniel*[4], *Nathaniel*[3], *Humphrey*[2], *John*[1]) was born on 5 Apr 1953 at Arcata, Humboldt Co., CA. He married Peggy Ann Cox. He died on 29 Aug 1999 at age 46.

Children of Leonard Earl[13] Norris Jr and Peggy Ann Cox are as follows:

> 939. i. CHRISTINA MARIE[14], born 30 Sep 1974 at Eureka, Humboldt Co., CA.
> 940. ii. DANIEL EARL, born 25 Jan 1976 at Eureka, Humboldt Co., CA.
> 941. iii. TINA KOYE, born 3 Aug 1978 at Eureka, Humboldt Co., CA.

785. NANCY LEE[13] NORRIS (*Lulubelle*[12]*IAEGER*, *George*[11]*Iaeger*, *Ada*[10]*Johnson*, *William*[9], *Hiram*[8], *Charles*[7], *Ira*[6], *Jonathan*[5], *Nathaniel*[4], *Nathaniel*[3], *Humphrey*[2], *John*[1]) was born on 22 Oct 1954 at Arcata, Humboldt Co., CA. She married Kenneth Eugene Blandin, son of Earl Kenneth Blandin and Minnie Eaton Rhoades, on 9 Dec 1972 at Cottonwood, Shasta Co., CA.

She lived in 1996 at Yerrington, NV.

Children of Nancy Lee[13] Norris and Kenneth Eugene Blandin both born at Greeley, Weld Co., CO, are as follows:

> 942. i. SHARON FAYE[14], born 22 Jan 1973; married William Muncy Canterbury.
> ii. SANDRA FAY; born 29 Jul 1976.

786. DAVID WARREN[13] NORRIS (*Lulubelle*[12], *George*[11]*Iaeger*, *Ada*[10]*Johnson*, *William*[9], *Hiram*[8], *Charles*[7], *Ira*[6], *Jonathan*[5], *Nathaniel*[4], *Nathaniel*[3], *Humphrey*[2], *John*[1]) was born on 26 Jul 1956 at Arcata, Humboldt Co., CA. He married Bobbie (--?--). He lived in 2000 at Yreca, CA.

Children of David Warren[13] Norris and Bobbie (--?--) are as follows:

> i. MICHAEL RAY[14]; born 27 Nov 1983.
> ii. MICHELLE FAYE; born 27 Nov 1983.

787. WILLIAM GEORGE^{13} NORRIS (*Lulubelle^{12}, George^{11}Iaeger, Ada^{10}Johnson, William^9, Hiram^8, Charles^7, Ira^6, Jonathan^5, Nathaniel^4, Nathaniel^3, Humphrey^2, John^1*) was born on 2 Mar 1959 at Eureka, Humboldt Co., CA. He married Rosemary Garcia at Greeley, Weld Co., CO.

Children of William George^{13} Norris and Rosemary Garcia are as follows:

> i. WILLIAM GEORGE^{14} JR; born 29 Mar 1981 at Greeley, Weld Co., CO.
>
> ii. JAMIE LEIGH; born 3 Oct 1983 at Redding, CA.

788. LAURA MAY^{13} NORRIS (*Lulubelle^{12}, George^{11}Iaeger, Ada^{10}Johnson, William^9, Hiram^8, Charles^7, Ira^6, Jonathan^5, Nathaniel^4, Nathaniel^3, Humphrey^2, John^1*) was born on 12 Mar 1961 at Eureka, Humboldt Co., CA. She married Earl Conway at Walden, Jackson Co., CO. She and Earl Conway were divorced.

She lived in 1997 at Gazelle, CA.

Children of Laura May^{13} Norris and Earl Conway are as follows:

> i. CLAYTON SCOTT^{14}; born 5 Oct 1983 at Yreka, CA.
>
> ii. AMANDA ALICE; born 26 Oct 1985.

789. TRACY ANN^{13} NORRIS (*Lulubelle^{12}, George^{11}Iaeger, Ada^{10}Johnson, William^9, Hiram^8, Charles^7, Ira^6, Jonathan^5, Nathaniel^4, Nathaniel^3, Humphrey^2, John^1*) was born on 23 Sep 1964 at Arcata, CA. She married Bob Nelson.

She lived at Eureka, CA.

Children of Tracy Ann^{13} Norris and Bob Nelson are as follows:

> 943. i. CRISTIE ANN^{14}, born 8 Jan 1975; married (--?--) Doran.
>
> ii. JEFFREY SCOTT; born 22 Jul 1977.

790. MICHAEL GARY^{13} POOLE (*Kathleen^{12}, George^{11}Iaeger, Ada^{10}Johnson, William^9, Hiram^8, Charles^7, Ira^6, Jonathan^5, Nathaniel^4, Nathaniel^3, Humphrey^2, John^1*) was born on 27 Jan

1948 at Bend, OR. He married Linda (--?--). He and Linda (--?--) were divorced. He married Susan Marie Polaski, daughter of Francis E Tucker and Marjoaie Jane Davis, on 24 Aug 1977 at Vancouver, Clark Co., WA.

He lived in 1997 at Portland, Multnomah Co., OR.

Children of Michael Gary[13] Poole and Linda (--?--) are as follows:

    i.   JACQULINE[14]; born 17 May 1967.

    ii. KENNETH; born 5 Sep.

Children of Michael Gary[13] Poole and Susan Marie Polaski are as follows:

944.   i.   JEFFERY SCOTT[14], born 22 Apr 1973 at Duluth, MN.

    ii. LEON MICHAEL; born 15 May 1973 at Superior, WI.

945. iii. SHAWN PATRICK, born 9 Feb 1977 at Duluth, MN; married Shana Barrett; divorced Shana Barrett.

946. iv. KATHLEEN IRENE, born 22 Apr 1980 at Astoria, Clatsop Co, OR; married Jerred Mack.

791. PATRICK GEORGE[13] POOLE (*Kathleen*[12], *George*[11] *Iaeger*, *Ada*[10] *Johnson*, *William*[9], *Hiram*[8], *Charles*[7], *Ira*[6], *Jonathan*[5], *Nathaniel*[4], *Nathaniel*[3], *Humphrey*[2], *John*[1]) was born on 28 Mar 1949 at Bend, OR. He married Margaret Ann Grant on 26 Dec 1969 at Newberg, OR. He lived in 1997 at Salem, Marion Co., OR.

Children of Patrick George[13] Poole and Margaret Ann Grant are as follows:

947.   i.   JENNY KATHLEEN[14], born 16 Jan 1971 at Hillsboro, OR; married Michael Burns; divorced Michael Burns; married Edward N. Long.

948.   ii. ELIZABETH JUNE, born 19 Mar 1975 at Astoria, Clatsop Co., OR; married Jeremy Glenn Holloway.

    iii. ESTHER MARGARET; born 24 Feb 1980 at Lancaster, PA.

792. MARTA GLENN[13] POOLE (*Kathleen[12], George[11]Iaeger, Ada[10]Johnson, William[9], Hiram[8], Charles[7], Ira[6], Jonathan[5], Nathaniel[4], Nathaniel[3], Humphrey[2], John[1]*) was born on 18 May 1952 at Klamath Falls, Klamath Co., OR. She married Richard Franklin Anderson, son of Robert Anderson and Ardella Jacobson, on 5 Nov 1971 at Virginia City, NV.

She lived at Springfield, OR.

Children of Marta Glenn[13] Poole and Richard Franklin Anderson are as follows:

949.   i.   RICHARD DAVID[14], born 9 Nov 1972 at Bend, OR; married (--?--) ?

950.   ii.   ANDREA MICHELLE, born 19 Nov 1974 at Roseburg, Douglas Co., OR; married Erich McShane Even.

793. MICHAEL DALE[13] CAREY (*George[12], George[11]Iaeger, Ada[10]Johnson, William[9], Hiram[8], Charles[7], Ira[6], Jonathan[5], Nathaniel[4], Nathaniel[3], Humphrey[2], John[1]*) was born on 19 May 1955 at Scotia, Humboldt Co., CA. He married Catherine E. MacDonald on 11 Jul 1976. He and Catherine E. MacDonald were divorced. He married Patricia K. Irvine on 13 Jun 1989 at San Diego, San Diego Co., CA.

Children of Michael Dale[13] Carey and Catherine E. MacDonald are:

     i.   ERIN MERISE[14]; born 1 Sep 1979 at San Diego, San Diego Co., CA.

Children of Michael Dale[13] CAREY and Patricia K. Irvine are as follows:

     i.   ISSAC[14]; born 25 Nov 1975.

     ii.   JACLYN; born 28 Oct 1977.

794. CHRISTINA MERISE[13] CAREY (*George[12], George[11] Iaeger, Ada[10]Johnson, William[9], Hiram[8], Charles[7], Ira[6], Jonathan[5], Nathaniel[4], Nathaniel[3], Humphrey[2], John[1]*) was born on 8 Aug 1957 at Ft. George Meade, MD. She married Michael Ronald Russell on 12 Feb 1977.

She lived in 1997 at Escondido, CA.

Children of Christina Merise[13] Carey and Michael Ronald Russell are as follows:

951.   i.   CIAN MICHAEL[14], born 5 Nov 1976 at San Diego, San Diego Co., CA; married Lissette Murro.

      ii. MIRIAM LEANNE; born 26 Nov 1990 at Kent, King Co., WA.

     iii. SHANNON GRACE; born 23 Jun 1993 at Escondido, CA.

795. VIRGINIA MAYE[13] IAEGER (*George*[12], *George*[11]*Iaeger*, *Ada*[10]*Johnson*, *William*[9], *Hiram*[8], *Charles*[7], *Ira*[6], *Jonathan*[5], *Nathaniel*[4], *Nathaniel*[3], *Humphrey*[2], *John*[1]) was born on 26 Mar 1963 at San Diego, San Diego Co., CA. She married John Pankowski on 22 Aug 1981 at Jacksonville, Jackson Co., OR. She and John Pankowski were divorced. She married Dennis Allen on 6 Apr 2002 at Gold Hill, Jackson Co., OR.

Children of Virginia Maye[13] Iaeger and John Pankowski both born at Rogue Valley Hospital, Medford, Jackson Co., OR, are as follows:

      i. DANIEL JOHN[14]; born 5 Aug 1982.

      ii. SARA MAYE; born 11 Jul 1985.

Children of Virginia Maye[13] IAEGER and Dennis Allen are:

      i. SHELBIE ROSE[14]; born 28 Mar 1992.

796. KATHLEEN IRENE[13] IAEGER (*George*[12], *George*[11]*Iaeger*, *Ada*[10]*Johnson*, *William*[9], *Hiram*[8], *Charles*[7], *Ira*[6], *Jonathan*[5], *Nathaniel*[4], *Nathaniel*[3], *Humphrey*[2], *John*[1]) was born on 15 Aug 1967 at San Diego, San Diego Co., CA. She married Randy Ryan Shroy, son of Larry Shroy and Helen Smoots, on 10 Nov 1990 at Corpus Christe, TX.

Children of Kathleen Irene[13] Iaeger and Randy Ryan Shroy both born at Navy Medical Center, San Diego, San Diego Co., CA, are as follows:

      i. JENIFFER HELEN[14]; born 2 Dec 1992.

ii.   RYAN MICHAEL; born 19 May 1995.

797.   JUDY JANE[13] JOHNSON (*Orland*[12], *James*[11], *Lloyd*[10], *William*[9], *Hiram*[8], *Charles*[7], *Ira*[6], *Jonathan*[5], *Nathaniel*[4], *Nathaniel*[3], *Humphrey*[2], *John*[1]) was born on 12 Dec 1945 at La Grande, OR. She married Richard Dills on 21 May 1964 at Tacoma, Pierce Co., WA. She married Arthur Lane Staples on 19 Apr 1974.

Children of Judy Jane[13] Johnson and Richard Dills all born at Tacoma, Pierce Co., WA, are as follows:

952.   i.   CARY LYNN[14], born 14 Apr 1965; married Danielle Kaasa.

ii.   CORY ALLEN; born 14 Apr 1965.

iii.   RAE ANN; born 12 Sep 1967.

798.   PATRICIA KAY[13] JOHNSON (*Orland*[12], *James*[11], *Lloyd*[10], *William*[9], *Hiram*[8], *Charles*[7], *Ira*[6], *Jonathan*[5], *Nathaniel*[4], *Nathaniel*[3], *Humphrey*[2], *John*[1]) was born on 7 Aug 1952 at Idaho Falls, ID. She married Virgil John Jungwirth on 26 Jun 1971 at Tacoma, Pierce Co., WA.

Children of Patricia Kay[13] Johnson and Virgil John Jungwirth are:

i.   BRETT DAVID[14]; born 28 Nov 1976 at Puyallup, Pierce Co., WA.

799.   KAREN JEAN[13] JOHNSON (*Lloyd*[12], *James*[11], *Lloyd*[10], *William*[9], *Hiram*[8], *Charles*[7], *Ira*[6], *Jonathan*[5], *Nathaniel*[4], *Nathaniel*[3], *Humphrey*[2], *John*[1]) was born on 2 May 1955 at Seattle, King Co., WA. She married William Howard Erickson on 6 Aug 1977 at Everett, Snohomish Co., WA.

Children of Karen Jean[13] Johnson and William Howard Erickson all born at Everett, Snohomish Co., WA, are as follows:

i.   TRISTAN CARL[14]; born 25 May 1985.

ii.   CHRISTOPHER LLOYD; born 31 May 1992.

iii.   CONSTANCE MARIE; born 29 Dec 1996.

800.   ALLEN JAMES[13] JOHNSON (*Lloyd*[12], *James*[11], *Lloyd*[10], *William*[9], *Hiram*[8], *Charles*[7], *Ira*[6], *Jonathan*[5], *Nathaniel*[4],

Nathaniel³, Humphrey², John¹) was born on 19 Sep 1956 at Seattle, King Co., WA. He married Cathy Varenkamp. He and Cathy Varenkamp were divorced in 1997. He married Jenifer Lynn Dottram.

Children of Allen James¹³ Johnson and Cathy Varenkamp are as follows:

    i. RYAN ALLEN¹⁴; born 23 Dec 1981 at Farmington, NM.
    ii. ANDREW JAMES; born 22 Oct 1984 at Portland, Multnomah Co., OR.
    iii. SHANNON BETH; born 9 Apr 1988 at Gulfport, MS.
    iv. LUKE ANTHONY; born Aug 1993 at Tacoma, Pierce Co., WA.

801. JANET KRISTINE¹³ JOHNSON (*Lloyd¹², James¹¹, Lloyd¹⁰, William⁹, Hiram⁸, Charles⁷, Ira⁶, Jonathan⁵, Nathaniel⁴, Nathaniel³, Humphrey², John¹*) was born on 18 Jun 1962 at Seattle, King Co., WA. She married John Adam Graham in Aug 1987 at Everett, Snohomish Co., WA.

Children of Janet Kristine¹³ Johnson and John Adam Graham are as follows:

    i. JEWEL SHAN-MARIE¹⁴; born 15 Jun 1996 at Gaoming City, Guongdong Province, China.
    ii. JOY-MING KRISTINE; born 15 Jan 1999 at Gelu, Yunan Province, China.

802. ANNETTE MARIE¹³ ANDERSON (*Louel¹²Johnson, James¹¹, Lloyd¹⁰, William⁹, Hiram⁸, Charles⁷, Ira⁶, Jonathan⁵, Nathaniel⁴, Nathaniel³, Humphrey², John¹*) was born on 10 Dec 1961 at Everett, Snohomish Co., WA. She married Thomas Michael Ostlie.

Children of Annette Marie¹³ Anderson and Thomas Michael Ostlie both born at Hahn, Germany, are as follows:

    i. TIMOTHY ROBERT¹⁴; born 16 Nov 1986.
    ii. DORI NICOLE; born 22 Jun 1988.

803. JOAN[13] BYERS (*Geraldine[12]Pickens, Ada[11]Johnson, Lloyd[10], William[9], Hiram[8], Charles[7], Ira[6], Jonathan[5], Nathaniel[4], Nathaniel[3], Humphrey[2], John[1]*) was born on 28 Nov 1940 at Grand Coulee, WA. She married (--?--) St John.

Children of Joan[13] Byers and (--?--) St John are as follows:

    i.   DIANNE[14].
    ii. SCOTT.
    iii. DANNY.

804. SANDRA[13] BYERS (*Geraldine[12]Pickens, Ada[11]Johnson, Lloyd[10], William[9], Hiram[8], Charles[7], Ira[6], Jonathan[5], Nathaniel[4], Nathaniel[3], Humphrey[2], John[1]*) was born on 25 Apr at Vancouver, WA. She married Sam Andrews.

Children of Sandra[13] Byers and Sam Andrews are as follows:

    i.   KIMBERLY[14].
    ii. DENISE.
    iii. CHRIS.

805. THOMAS JAMES[13] PICKENS (*John[12], Ada[11]Johnson, Lloyd[10], William[9], Hiram[8], Charles[7], Ira[6], Jonathan[5], Nathaniel[4], Nathaniel[3], Humphrey[2], John[1]*) was born on 11 Jan 1954 at Seattle, King Co., WA. He married Sandra Lee Wright, daughter of Robert Lee Wright and Alice Pauline Davidson, on 31 Oct 1981 at Beaverton, OR.

Children of Thomas James[13] Pickens and Sandra Lee Wright are:

    i.   SARAH LEE[14]; born 13 Mar 1989 at Metro Manila, Philippines.

806. MELANIE ANN[13] MCHARGUE (*Warren[12], Warren[11], Lulu[10]Johnson, William[9], Hiram[8], Charles[7], Ira[6], Jonathan[5], Nathaniel[4], Nathaniel[3], Humphrey[2], John[1]*) was born on 28 Apr 1949. She married Gary Lane. She married Richard John Sayre.

She lived in 2002 at Vancouver, Clark Co., WA.

Children of Melanie Ann[13] McHargue and Gary Lane are as follows:

i. TRACY LOUISE[14]; born 29 Jan 1967.
ii. CHRISTOPHER ERIC; born 22 Jul 1969.
iii. LISA; born 29 Jul 1970.

807. GARY STEVEN[13] MCHARGUE (*Warren[12]*, *Warren[11]*, *Lulu[10]Johnson*, *William[9]*, *Hiram[8]*, *Charles[7]*, *Ira[6]*, *Jonathan[5]*, *Nathaniel[4]*, *Nathaniel[3]*, *Humphrey[2]*, *John[1]*) was born on 8 Jun 1950. He married Robin Ray Rapplege in 1970. He and Robin Ray Rapplege were divorced. He married Marla Jean (--?--).

He lived in 2002 at Portland, Multnomah Co., OR.

Children of Gary Steven[13] McHargue and Robin Ray Rapplege are as follows:

i. JASON LEVI[14]; born 15 Oct 1971.
ii. DARBY SHEA; born 21 Dec 1972.
iii. KEAGEN; born 1982.

Children of Gary Steven[13] McHargue and Marla Jean (--?--) are:

i. HAYLEY K.[14].

808. KELLY[13] MCHARGUE (*Warren[12]*, *Warren[11]*, *Lulu[10]Johnson*, *William[9]*, *Hiram[8]*, *Charles[7]*, *Ira[6]*, *Jonathan[5]*, *Nathaniel[4]*, *Nathaniel[3]*, *Humphrey[2]*, *John[1]*) was born on 2 Jun 1964.

She lived in 2002 at Vancouver, Clark Co., WA.

Children of Kelly[13] McHargue and an unknown spouse are:

i. TAYLOR[14].

809. KARLUA GAIL[13] MCHARGUE (*Carl[12]*, *Warren[11]*, *Lulu[10]Johnson*, *William[9]*, *Hiram[8]*, *Charles[7]*, *Ira[6]*, *Jonathan[5]*, *Nathaniel[4]*, *Nathaniel[3]*, *Humphrey[2]*, *John[1]*) was born on 9 May 1952 at Sacramento, CA. She married (--?--) Cessna.

Children of Karlua Gail[13] McHargue and (--?--) Cessna are as follows:

i. TAYLOR[14].
ii. JESS.

810. CATHRYN PATRICE[13] MCHARGUE (*Carl*[12], *Warren*[11], *Lulu*[10]*Johnson*, *William*[9], *Hiram*[8], *Charles*[7], *Ira*[6], *Jonathan*[5], *Nathaniel*[4], *Nathaniel*[3], *Humphrey*[2], *John*[1]) was born on 20 Jul 1958 at Swindon, England. She married Doug Beseda.

She lived in 2002 at Battle Ground, WA.

Children of Cathryn Patrice[13] McHargue and Doug Beseda are as follows:

    i.   KELSEY[14].
   ii.   EMMY.
  iii.   ANDREA.

811. CLAUDIA LYNNE[13] MCHARGUE (*Carl*[12], *Warren*[11], *Lulu*[10]*Johnson*, *William*[9], *Hiram*[8], *Charles*[7], *Ira*[6], *Jonathan*[5], *Nathaniel*[4], *Nathaniel*[3], *Humphrey*[2], *John*[1]) was born on 19 Mar 1963 at Moses Lake, WA. She married Dan McGehee.

She lived in 2002 at Iowa City, IA.

Children of Claudia Lynne[13] McHargue and Dan McGehee are:

    i.   LUCY[14].

812. MICHELLE[13] MCPHERSON (*Delores*[12]*McHargue*, *Warren*[11], *Lulu*[10]*Johnson*, *William*[9], *Hiram*[8], *Charles*[7], *Ira*[6], *Jonathan*[5], *Nathaniel*[4], *Nathaniel*[3], *Humphrey*[2], *John*[1]) was born on 3 May 1967.

She lived in 2002 at Signal Hill, CA.

Children of Michelle[13] McPherson and an unknown spouse are as follows:

    i.   NATALIE NICOLE[14].
   ii.   MICHAEL ANTHONY.

813. JEFFERY SCOTT[13] MCHARGUE (*Lloyd*[12], *Warren*[11], *Lulu*[10]*Johnson*, *William*[9], *Hiram*[8], *Charles*[7], *Ira*[6], *Jonathan*[5], *Nathaniel*[4], *Nathaniel*[3], *Humphrey*[2], *John*[1]) was born on 21 Nov 1962 at Madigan Army Hospital, Tacoma, Pierce Co., WA. He married Debbie A. Brice.

Children of Jeffery Scott[13] McHargue and Debbie A. Brice are as follows:

i. NICOLE CHRISTINE[14]; born 13 Feb 1994 at Olympia, Thurston Co., WA.

ii. ALEXIS ELIZABETH; born 16 Jun 1998 at Shelton, Mason Co., WA.

814. TAMERA LEIGH[13] MCHARGUE (*Lloyd*[12], *Warren*[11], *Lulu*[10]*Johnson*, *William*[9], *Hiram*[8], *Charles*[7], *Ira*[6], *Jonathan*[5], *Nathaniel*[4], *Nathaniel*[3], *Humphrey*[2], *John*[1]) was born on 15 Jun 1964 at Everett, Snohomish Co., WA. She married Glenn A. Wattum.

She lived in 2002 at Everett, Snohomish Co., WA.

Children of Tamera Leigh[13] McHargue and Glenn A. Wattum both born at Everett, Snohomish Co., WA, are as follows:

i. GABRIELLE ANN[14]; born 26 Jun 1996.

ii. ISAAC JOSEPH; born 18 Apr 1999.

815. DIANA[13] SMITH (*Robert*[12], *Francis*[11]*McHargue*, *Lulu*[10]*Johnson*, *William*[9], *Hiram*[8], *Charles*[7], *Ira*[6], *Jonathan*[5], *Nathaniel*[4], *Nathaniel*[3], *Humphrey*[2], *John*[1]) was born on 5 Feb 1958 at San Diego, San Diego Co., CA. She married Jim Rice.

She lived in 2002 at San Diego, San Diego Co., CA.

Children of Diana[13] Smith and Jim Rice are:

i. ASHLEY[14].

816. PATTY[13] SMITH (*Robert*[12], *Francis*[11]*McHargue*, *Lulu*[10]*Johnson*, *William*[9], *Hiram*[8], *Charles*[7], *Ira*[6], *Jonathan*[5], *Nathaniel*[4], *Nathaniel*[3], *Humphrey*[2], *John*[1]) was born on 13 Dec 1958 at San Diego, San Diego Co., CA. She married Verl Craig.

She lived in 2002 at Merlin, OR.

Children of Patty[13] Smith and Verl Craig are:

953. i. CHERYL[14], married Rick (--?--).

817. LORINE[13] SMITH (*Robert*[12], *Francis*[11]*McHargue*, *Lulu*[10]*Johnson*, *William*[9], *Hiram*[8], *Charles*[7], *Ira*[6], *Jonathan*[5], *Nathaniel*[4], *Nathaniel*[3], *Humphrey*[2], *John*[1]) was born on 5 May 1961 at San Diego, San Diego Co., CA. She married Randy No.

She lived in 2002 at El Cajon, CA.

Children of Lorine[13] Smith and Randy No are as follows:

    i.   AMANDA[14].

    ii. DANYELL.

818.   SUSAN RENAE[13] MCHARGUE (*William[12]*, *Rush[11]*, *Lulu[10]Johnson*, *William[9]*, *Hiram[8]*, *Charles[7]*, *Ira[6]*, *Jonathan[5]*, *Nathaniel[4]*, *Nathaniel[3]*, *Humphrey[2]*, *John[1]*) was born on 4 May 1965 at Moscow, Latah Co., ID. She married Mohamed Khatouri on 16 Jul 1987 at Rabat, Morocco.

She lived in 2002 at Springfield, VA.

Children of Susan Renae[13] McHargue and Mohamed Khatouri are as follows:

    i.   NADIA[14]; born 23 Aug 1989 at Rabat, Morocco.

    ii. LEILA; born 18 Mar 1991 at Rabat, Morocco.

    iii. SAMI; born 31 May 1998 at Rabat, Morocco.

    iv. SARA; born 3 Oct 2000 at Springfield, VA.

819.   DANIEL RUSH[13] MCHARGUE (*William[12]*, *Rush[11]*, *Lulu[10]Johnson*, *William[9]*, *Hiram[8]*, *Charles[7]*, *Ira[6]*, *Jonathan[5]*, *Nathaniel[4]*, *Nathaniel[3]*, *Humphrey[2]*, *John[1]*) was born on 8 Nov 1966 at Moscow, Latah Co., ID. He married Sandra Bonnie Potter on 6 Jun 1987 at Burns, Harney Co., Or. He and Sandra Bonnie Potter were divorced. He married Jodi Lyn Miller on 26 Jun 1993 at Moses Lake, Grant Co., WA.

He lived in 2002 at Wamic, OR.

Children of Daniel Rush[13] McHargue and Sandra Bonnie Potter are as follows:

    i.   KYLA DANIELLE[14]; born 9 Nov 1987 at Redmond, Deschutes Co., OR.

    ii. KATIE LYNN; born 15 May 1989 at Redmond, Deschutes Co., OR.

    iii. TOBY DANIEL JEREMY; born 8 Feb 1992 at Moses Lake, Grant Co., WA.

Children of Daniel Rush[13] McHargue and Jodi Lyn Miller are as follows:

      i.   JORDAN 'RILEY'[14]; born 13 Jan 1988 at La Grande, Union Co., OR.

      ii. JOSIE DANIELLE; born 15 Sep 1993 at The Dalles, Wasco Co., OR.

     iii. DYLAN RUSH; born 2 May 1995 at The Dalles, Wasco Co., OR.

820.   SHERYL ANN[13] MCHARGUE (*William*[12], *Rush*[11], *Lulu*[10]*Johnson*, *William*[9], *Hiram*[8], *Charles*[7], *Ira*[6], *Jonathan*[5], *Nathaniel*[4], *Nathaniel*[3], *Humphrey*[2], *John*[1]) was born on 17 Mar 1969 at White Salmon, Klickitat Co., WA. She married Billie Lee Swindoll on 18 Mar 1989. She and Billie Lee Swindoll were divorced. She married Michael John Camporeale on 2 Jul 2000 at At McHargue Reunion, Moses Lake, Grant Co., WA.　She lived in 2002 at Spokane, Spokane Co., WA.

    Children of Sheryl Ann[13] McHargue and Michael John Camporeale are as follows:

      i.   MICHAEL JOHN[14] JR.; born 7 Mar 1983.

      ii. KEBRA MARIE; born 7 Aug 1990 at Seattle, King Co., WA.

     iii. HAILEY CHRISTINE; born 1 Oct 2001 at Moses Lake, Grant Co., WA.

821.   LORI LYNN[13] MCHARGUE (*William*[12], *Rush*[11], *Lulu*[10]*Johnson*, *William*[9], *Hiram*[8], *Charles*[7], *Ira*[6], *Jonathan*[5], *Nathaniel*[4], *Nathaniel*[3], *Humphrey*[2], *John*[1]) was born on 23 Apr 1973 at Twin Falls, Twin Falls Co., ID. She married Brad Evers on 10 Aug 1996.

    She lived in 2002 at Moses Lake, WA.

    Children of Lori Lynn[13] McHargue and Brad Evers are:

      i.   JORDAN ANTHONY[14]; born 13 Apr 1999 at Spokane, Spokane Co., WA.

822.   LISA DIANE[13] MCHARGUE (*William*[12], *Rush*[11], *Lulu*[10]*Johnson*, *William*[9], *Hiram*[8], *Charles*[7], *Ira*[6], *Jonathan*[5], *Nathaniel*[4], *Nathaniel*[3], *Humphrey*[2], *John*[1]) was born on 31 Mar

1975 at Ontario, Malheur Co., OR. She married Donald Robert Puhlman on 10 Feb 1996 at Seattle, King Co., WA.

She lived in 2000 at Seaside, CA.

Children of Lisa Diane[13] McHargue and Donald Robert Puhlman are as follows:

    i.   CALEB WILLIAM[14]; born 4 Aug 1998 at Spokane, Spokane Co., WA.

    ii. ZACHARY KADIN; born 14 Oct 2001 at Monterey, CA.

    iii. RACHEL LEEANN; born 13 Mar 2003 at Moses Lake, Grant Co., WA.

823. KRISTINE KAY[13] MCHARGUE (*Jack*[12], *Rush*[11], *Lulu*[10]*Johnson*, *William*[9], *Hiram*[8], *Charles*[7], *Ira*[6], *Jonathan*[5], *Nathaniel*[4], *Nathaniel*[3], *Humphrey*[2], *John*[1]) was born on 7 Sep 1968 at Spokane, Spokane Co., WA. She married Robert Keith Winter on 10 May 1986 at Troy, Latah Co., ID.

She lived in 2000 at Sagle, ID.

Children of Kristine Kay[13] McHargue and Robert Keith Winter are as follows:

    i.   SIDNEY RUSH[14].

    ii. STORMI AMBER; born 16 May 1993 at Sandpoint, Bonner Co., ID.

    iii. WINDI SHANIA; born 10 Jun 1995 at Sandpoint, Bonner Co., ID.

824. RHONDA JO[13] MCHARGUE (*Joseph*[12], *Rush*[11], *Lulu*[10]*Johnson*, *William*[9], *Hiram*[8], *Charles*[7], *Ira*[6], *Jonathan*[5], *Nathaniel*[4], *Nathaniel*[3], *Humphrey*[2], *John*[1]) was born on 8 Jan 1967 at Burns, Harney Co., OR. She married Christopher Everhart on 19 Apr 1985 at Harney Co., OR. She and Christopher Everhart were divorced. She married Samuel Perry Kingrey on 27 Mar 1993 at Redmond, Deschutes Co., OR.

She lived in 2000 at Caldwell, ID.

Children of Rhonda Jo[13] McHargue and Christopher Everhart are as follows:

     i.   JOSEPH LEE[14]; born 5 Mar 1986 at Ft. Lewis, Pierce Co., WA.

    ii.   BRETT; born 21 Jun 1989 at Bend, Deschutes Co., OR.

Children of Rhonda Jo[13] McHargue and Samuel Perry Kingrey are:

     i.   JAKE[14]; born 18 Aug 1994 at Boise, Boise Co., ID.

825. JOANNA LYN[13] MCHARGUE (*Joseph[12]*, *Rush[11]*, *Lulu[10] Johnson*, *William[9]*, *Hiram[8]*, *Charles[7]*, *Ira[6]*, *Jonathan[5]*, *Nathaniel[4]*, *Nathaniel[3]*, *Humphrey[2]*, *John[1]*) was born on 1 Aug 1971 at Ontario, Malheur Co., OR. She married Kelly Everhart on 17 Mar 1990 at Crane, Harney Co., OR. She and Kelly Everhart were divorced. She and Mitch Briggs were engaged.

She lived in 2000 at Caldwell, ID.

Children of Joanna Lyn[13] McHargue and Kelly Everhart are as follows:

     i.   ANTHONY GAGE[14]; born 29 Aug 1990 at Burns, Harney Co., OR.

    ii.   IMALEE COSTA; born 14 Feb 1992 at San Diego, San Diego Co., CA.

Children of Joanna Lyn[13] McHargue and Mitch Briggs are:

     i.   JACK BAILEY[14]; born 7 Apr 1996 at Nampa, ID.

826. LINDA JENNANIE[13] MCHARGUE (*Richard[12]*, *Leon[11]*, *Lulu[10] Johnson*, *William[9]*, *Hiram[8]*, *Charles[7]*, *Ira[6]*, *Jonathan[5]*, *Nathaniel[4]*, *Nathaniel[3]*, *Humphrey[2]*, *John[1]*) was born on 26 Mar 1958. She married Robert Brant.

She lived in 2000 at Sparks, NV.

Children of Linda Jennanie[13] McHargue and Robert Brant are as follows:

     i.   MELISSA[14].

    ii.   BENJAMIN.

    iii. JERIMIAH.

827. LILLENA JAE^{13} MCHARGUE (*Richard*^{12}, *Leon*^{11}, *Lulu*^{10}*Johnson*, *William*^{9}, *Hiram*^{8}, *Charles*^{7}, *Ira*^{6}, *Jonathan*^{5}, *Nathaniel*^{4}, *Nathaniel*^{3}, *Humphrey*^{2}, *John*^{1}) was born on 7 Sep 1965. She married Brian D. Pitcock.

She lived in 2000 at Nampa, ID.

Children of Lillena Jae^{13} McHargue and Brian D. Pitcock are as follows:

     i.   MORGAN CALEB^{14}.
    ii.   BRIANNA JAE.

828. CAROLYN MARIE^{13} MCKINNEY (*Francis*^{12}*McHargue*, *Leon*^{11}, *Lulu*^{10}*Johnson*, *William*^{9}, *Hiram*^{8}, *Charles*^{7}, *Ira*^{6}, *Jonathan*^{5}, *Nathaniel*^{4}, *Nathaniel*^{3}, *Humphrey*^{2}, *John*^{1}) was born on 22 Jun 1959. She married Michael Baltzor.

She lived in 2000 at Jordan Valley, OR.

Children of Carolyn Marie^{13} McKinney and Michael Baltzor are as follows:

     i.   SHARI^{14}.
    ii.   MICHELLE.

829. KEBBIE JO^{13} HOLMES (*Melvina*^{12}*McHargue*, *Leon*^{11}, *Lulu*^{10}*Johnson*, *William*^{9}, *Hiram*^{8}, *Charles*^{7}, *Ira*^{6}, *Jonathan*^{5}, *Nathaniel*^{4}, *Nathaniel*^{3}, *Humphrey*^{2}, *John*^{1}) was born on 21 Dec 1958. She married Dwight Calhoun.

She lived in 2000 at Vancouver, Clark Co., WA.

Children of Kebbie Jo^{13} Holmes and Dwight Calhoun are as follows:

     i.   JOSH^{14}.
    ii.   TREVOR.

830. RONALD DWAYNE^{13} HOLMES (*Melvina*^{12}*McHargue*, *Leon*^{11}, *Lulu*^{10}*Johnson*, *William*^{9}, *Hiram*^{8}, *Charles*^{7}, *Ira*^{6}, *Jonathan*^{5}, *Nathaniel*^{4}, *Nathaniel*^{3}, *Humphrey*^{2}, *John*^{1}) was born on 1 Oct 1960. He married Machille (--?--).

Children of Ronald Dwayne^{13} Holmes and Machille (--?--) are as follows:

      i.   BREANNE[14].

     ii. RAINY.

831. BRETT EVANS[13] HOLMES (*Melvina*[12]*McHargue, Leon*[11], *Lulu*[10]*Johnson, William*[9], *Hiram*[8], *Charles*[7], *Ira*[6], *Jonathan*[5], *Nathaniel*[4], *Nathaniel*[3], *Humphrey*[2], *John*[1]) was born on 17 Feb 1967. He married (--?--) ? He and (--?--) ? were divorced.

Children of Brett Evans[13] Holmes and (--?--) ? are as follows:

      i.   JORELL[14].

     ii. CAMERON.

832. JODY[13] AUFRANC (*Richard*[12], *Evelyn*[11]*Johnson, Creta*[10], *Hiram*[9], *Hiram*[8], *Charles*[7], *Ira*[6], *Jonathan*[5], *Nathaniel*[4], *Nathaniel*[3], *Humphrey*[2], *John*[1]) was born on 9 Jan 1960. She married Mark Rodgers.

Children of Jody[13] Aufranc and Mark Rodgers are as follows:

      i.   BRIAN MATHEW[14]; married Candice (--?--) 16 Nov 2001.

     ii. KEVIN MICHAEL; born 21 Jan 1985 at Salem, Marion Co., Or.

833. RICHARD EMILE[13] AUFRANC JR. (*Richard*[12], *Evelyn*[11]*Johnson, Creta*[10], *Hiram*[9], *Hiram*[8], *Charles*[7], *Ira*[6], *Jonathan*[5], *Nathaniel*[4], *Nathaniel*[3], *Humphrey*[2], *John*[1]) was born on 4 Oct 1968. He married Julie (--?--).

He lived in 2002 at Albany, OR.

Children of Richard Emile[13] Aufranc Jr. and Julie (--?--) are:

      i.   (--?--)[14].

834. MICHAEL SHANNON[13] JOHNSON SR. (*Acle*[12], *Acle*[11], *Fred*[10], *Samuel*[9], *Hiram*[8], *Charles*[7], *Ira*[6], *Jonathan*[5], *Nathaniel*[4], *Nathaniel*[3], *Humphrey*[2], *John*[1]) was born on 12 Apr 1948 at Seattle, King Co., WA. He married Peggy Lee Golden on 30 May 1967 at Syracuse, Onondoga Co., NY.

He lived in 2003 at Alexandria, VA.

Children of Michael Shannon[13] Johnson Sr. and Peggy Lee Golden are as follows:

    i.   MICHAEL SHANNON[14] JR.; born 24 Nov 1967 at Coral Gables, FL.

   ii.   KEVIN GLENN; born 12 Dec 1971 at Lake Forest, IL; married Kristen Segenmartin.
       He lived in 2003 at Winter Springs, FL.

835. KATHLEEN ANN[13] JOHNSON (*Acle*[12], *Acle*[11], *Fred*[10], *Samuel*[9], *Hiram*[8], *Charles*[7], *Ira*[6], *Jonathan*[5], *Nathaniel*[4], *Nathaniel*[3], *Humphrey*[2], *John*[1]) was born on 3 May 1949 at Seattle, King Co., WA. She married Al Augustus Paine Jr. on 2 Sep 1972 at Pomfret, CT.

She lived in 2003 at Pomfret Center, CT.

Children of Kathleen Ann[13] Johnson and Al Augustus Paine Jr. are as follows:

    i.   SETH AL[14]; born 29 Oct 1973 at New London, CT.
       He lived in 2003 at Tempe, AZ.

   ii.   TRAVIS MICHAEL; born 20 Aug 1979 at Putnam, CT.

836. STEVEN FRANCIS[13] JOHNSON (*Acle*[12], *Acle*[11], *Fred*[10], *Samuel*[9], *Hiram*[8], *Charles*[7], *Ira*[6], *Jonathan*[5], *Nathaniel*[4], *Nathaniel*[3], *Humphrey*[2], *John*[1]) was born on 24 Sep 1951 at Hartford, CT. He married Lou Ann Nancy Nicol on 4 Aug 1972 at Manchester, CT.

He lived in 2003 at Colchester, CT.

Children of Steven Francis[13] Johnson and Lou Ann Nancy Nicol both born at Manchester, CT, are as follows:

    i.   JENNIFER LYNN[14]; born 10 Jan 1975.
       She lived in 2003 at Waltham, MA.

   ii.   JASON MATTHEW; born 21 Dec 1977.
       He lived in 2003 at Colchester, CT.

837. LAURA LYNN[13] JOHNSON (*Acle*[12], *Acle*[11], *Fred*[10], *Samuel*[9], *Hiram*[8], *Charles*[7], *Ira*[6], *Jonathan*[5], *Nathaniel*[4], *Nathaniel*[3],

Humphrey[2], *John*[1]) was born on 14 Sep 1964 at Manchester Memorial Hospital, Manchester, CT. She married David Normand Rossignol on 20 Jun 1986 at Manchester, CT. She and David Normand Rossignol were divorced.

She lived in 2003 at South Windsor, CT.

Children of Laura Lynn[13] Johnson and David Normand Rossignol are:

        i.   ELYSE MONIQUE[14]; born 13 Apr 1989 at Manchester, CT.

838. SHELLY MARIE[13] JOHNSON (*Acle*[12], *Acle*[11], *Fred*[10], *Samuel*[9], *Hiram*[8], *Charles*[7], *Ira*[6], *Jonathan*[5], *Nathaniel*[4], *Nathaniel*[3], *Humphrey*[2], *John*[1]) was born on 23 Sep 1966 at Manchester Memorial Hospital, Manchester, CT. She married Eric Martin Traumuller on 1 Oct 1988 at Manchester, CT.

She lived in 2003 at Franklin, MA.

Children of Shelly Marie[13] Johnson and Eric Martin Traumuller both born at Manchester, CT, are as follows:

        i.   EVAN CODY[14]; born 2 May 1994.
       ii.   LEAH NICOLE; born 13 Aug 1996.

839. MARC ELLIOTT[13] JOHNSON (*Marvin*[12], *Acle*[11], *Fred*[10], *Samuel*[9], *Hiram*[8], *Charles*[7], *Ira*[6], *Jonathan*[5], *Nathaniel*[4], *Nathaniel*[3], *Humphrey*[2], *John*[1]) was born on 9 Sep 1952 at Oakland, CA. He married Shirley Stern in 1974 at Beaverton, OR.

Children of Marc Elliott[13] Johnson and Shirley Stern are as follows:

        i.   WILLIAM ANTHONY[14]; born 13 Aug 1975 at Portland, Multnomah Co., OR.
       ii.   DANIEL ELLIOTT; born 6 Dec 1983 at Bakersfield, CA.

840. MARCY JOANNE[13] JOHNSON (*Marvin*[12], *Acle*[11], *Fred*[10], *Samuel*[9], *Hiram*[8], *Charles*[7], *Ira*[6], *Jonathan*[5], *Nathaniel*[4], *Nathaniel*[3], *Humphrey*[2], *John*[1]) was born on 13 Jun 1957 at

Waukegan, IL. She married Mitchell Dale Ragain on 27 Jun 1982 at Arcata, CA.

Children of Marcy Joanne[13] Johnson and Mitchell Dale Ragain both born at Fortuna, CA, are as follows:

    i.   STEVEE NYCOLE[14]; born 17 May 1986.
    ii. CAMERON SCOTT; born 29 May 1989.

841. MARTIN EUGENE[13] JOHNSON (*Marvin*[12], *Acle*[11], *Fred*[10], *Samuel*[9], *Hiram*[8], *Charles*[7], *Ira*[6], *Jonathan*[5], *Nathaniel*[4], *Nathaniel*[3], *Humphrey*[2], *John*[1]) was born on 27 Mar 1968 at Fremont, CA. He married Yvette Marie Solano.

Children of Martin Eugene[13] Johnson and Yvette Marie Solano both born at Bakersfield, CA, are as follows:

    i.   COURTNEY RAE[14]; born 20 Dec 1995.
    ii. ANTHONEY WILLIAM; born 19 Oct 2000.

842. RICHARD EARL[13] HENBEST II (*Richard*[12], *Nellie*[11]*Johnson*, *Fred*[10], *Samuel*[9], *Hiram*[8], *Charles*[7], *Ira*[6], *Jonathan*[5], *Nathaniel*[4], *Nathaniel*[3], *Humphrey*[2], *John*[1]) was born on 10 Jun 1948 at Oahu, Territory of Hawaii. He married Mabel Arlene Wood on 15 Jan 1968 at Roseburg, Douglas Co., OR. He married Karen Mullens at Reno, NV.

Children of Richard Earl[13] Henbest II and Mabel Arlene Wood all born at Eugene, Lane Co., OR, are as follows:

    i.   GERALD PATRICK[14]; born 15 Aug 1970; married Teresa (--?--) Aug 1994.
    ii. CHRISTINE ANNETTE; born 22 Feb 1974.
    iii. ANGELIA LYNN; born 26 Apr 1979.

Children of Richard Earl[13] Henbest II and Karen Mullens are:

    i.   KAYLA ELIZABETH[14]; born 21 Jul 1989 at Roseburg, Douglas Co., OR.

843. MICHAEL LEE[13] HENBEST (*Richard*[12], *Nellie*[11]*Johnson*, *Fred*[10], *Samuel*[9], *Hiram*[8], *Charles*[7], *Ira*[6], *Jonathan*[5], *Nathaniel*[4], *Nathaniel*[3], *Humphrey*[2], *John*[1]) was born on 10 Feb 1951 at Roseburg, Douglas Co., OR. He married Margaret Waenwright.

Children of Michael Lee[13] Henbest and Margaret Waenwright are as follows:

  i. RYAN MICHAEL[14]; born 10 Oct 1979 at Orange Co., CA.
  ii. DAVID MATHEW; born 24 Mar 1983 at Santa Anna, CA.
  iii. KEVIN MARK; born 27 Mar 1985 at Eugene, Lane Co., OR.

844. DONALD DAYLE[13] WILLIAMS (*Donald[12], Gertrude[11]Johnson, Fred[10], Samuel[9], Hiram[8], Charles[7], Ira[6], Jonathan[5], Nathaniel[4], Nathaniel[3], Humphrey[2], John[1]*) married Lynn (--?--).

Children of Donald Dayle[13] Williams and Lynn (--?--) are:

  i. LINDA IRENE[14].

845. JEFFERY SCOTT[13] LACEY (*Sharon[12]Johnson, Samuel[11], Fred[10], Samuel[9], Hiram[8], Charles[7], Ira[6], Jonathan[5], Nathaniel[4], Nathaniel[3], Humphrey[2], John[1]*) was born on 21 Feb 1963 at Burien, King Co., WA. He married Dana Marie Anderson on 7 Sep 1990 at Auburn, King Co., WA.

Children of Jeffery Scott[13] Lacey and Dana Marie Anderson are as follows:

  i. JEFFERY COLLINS[14]; born 27 Apr 1994 at Longmont, CO.
  ii. RYAN JOSHUA; born 6 Aug 1997 at Federal Way, King Co., WA.
  iii. QUINN MATTHEW; born 19 Apr 1999 at Auburn, King Co., WA.
  iv. JENNA MARIE; born 30 Jul 2001 at Auburn, King Co., WA.

846. ERIN LEE[13] LACEY (*Sharon[12]Johnson, Samuel[11], Fred[10], Samuel[9], Hiram[8], Charles[7], Ira[6], Jonathan[5], Nathaniel[4], Nathaniel[3], Humphrey[2], John[1]*) was born on 7 Jan 1967 at Burien, King Co., WA. She married Lemont K. Aukland on 9 Apr 1988 at Burien, King Co., WA.

Children of Erin Lee[13] Lacey and Lemont K. Aukland are:

    i.   KYLE CLAYTON[14]; born 21 Oct 1989 at Burien, King Co., WA.

847. DARCEY LYNNE[13] JOHNSON (*Ronald*[12], *Samuel*[11], *Fred*[10], *Samuel*[9],*Hiram*[8],*Charles*[7],*Ira*[6],*Jonathan*[5],*Nathaniel*[4], *Nathaniel*[3], *Humphrey*[2], *John*[1]) was born on 11 Feb 1964 at Burien, King Co., WA. She married Dirk Theodore Knudsen on 7 Sep 1985.

Children of Darcey Lynne[13] Johnson and Dirk Theodore Knudsen are as follows:

    i.   KORD TYLER[14]; born 2 Dec 1988.
    ii. KONNER DIRK; born 29 Dec 1990.
    iii KOLE SPENCER, born 20 Jun 1999.

848. DARYL LANE[13] JOHNSON (*Ronald*[12], *Samuel*[11], *Fred*[10], *Samuel*[9], *Hiram*[8], *Charles*[7], *Ira*[6], *Jonathan*[5], *Nathaniel*[4], *Nathaniel*[3], *Humphrey*[2], *John*[1]) was born on 20 Dec 1966 at Burien, King Co., WA. He married Teresa Elizabeth Lauinger on 19 Jun 1992.

Children of Daryl Lane[13] Johnson and Teresa Elizabeth Lauinger are:

    i.   TUCKER HENRY LANE[14]; born 9 Jun 1999 at Portland, Multnomah Co., OR.

849. KAREN LOUISE[13] LILLY (*Eleanor*[12]*Johnson, Donald*[11], *Abel*[10], *Elgin*[9], *Abel*[8], *Charles*[7], *Ira*[6], *Jonathan*[5], *Nathaniel*[4], *Nathaniel*[3], *Humphrey*[2], *John*[1]) was born on 17 Apr 1957 at Columbia, Richland Co., SC. She married Kenneth Wayne Craven on 3 Sep 1977 at Honey Grove, PA.

Children of Karen Louise[13] Lilly and Kenneth Wayne Craven are as follows:

    i.   JENNIFER LYNN[14]; born 30 Jan 1978 at Dubois, PA.
    ii. AMY MICHELLE; born 12 Jun 1982 at Harriman, Roane Co., TN.

iii. EMILY LAUREN; born 18 Apr 1989 at St. Petersburg, Pinellas Co., FL.

iv. JEREMY WAYNE; born 6 Nov 1995 at St. Petersburg, Pinellas Co., FL.

850. KEVIN DWIGHT[13] LILLY (*Eleanor*[12]*Johnson, Donald*[11], *Abel*[10], *Elgin*[9], *Abel*[8], *Charles*[7], *Ira*[6], *Jonathan*[5], *Nathaniel*[4], *Nathaniel*[3], *Humphrey*[2], *John*[1]) was born on 9 Feb 1959 at St. Petersburg, Pinellas Co., FL. He married Cheryl Ann Toth, daughter of George Toth and Carol (--?--), on 7 Jul 1979 at Johnstown, PA.

Children of Kevin Dwight[13] Lilly and Cheryl Ann Toth both born at St. Petersburg, Pinellas Co., FL, are as follows:

i. KEVIN DWIGHT[14] JR.; born 29 Jan 1981.

ii. MATTHEW DEAN; born 3 Jan 1984.

851. DONALD DEAN[13] HALL (*Donna*[12]*Johnson, Donald*[11], *Abel*[10], *Elgin*[9], *Abel*[8], *Charles*[7], *Ira*[6], *Jonathan*[5], *Nathaniel*[4], *Nathaniel*[3], *Humphrey*[2], *John*[1]) was born on 25 Feb 1965 at St. Petersburg, Pinellas Co., FL. He married Shannon Reyna Scalf, daughter of Gary Thomas Scalf and Betty Jo Graham, on 14 May 1994 at Nashville, Davidson Co., TN. He and Shannon Reyna Scalf were divorced in 2001 at Paducah, KY.

Children of Donald Dean[13] Hall and Shannon Reyna Scalf are:

i. LAUREN ELSIE[14]; born 3 Jan 1998 at Nashville, Davidson Co., TN.

852. SARAH ELIZABETH[13] HALL (*Donna*[12]*Johnson, Donald*[11], *Abel*[10], *Elgin*[9], *Abel*[8], *Charles*[7], *Ira*[6], *Jonathan*[5], *Nathaniel*[4], *Nathaniel*[3], *Humphrey*[2], *John*[1]) was born on 20 Jul 1972 at Knoxville, Knox Co., TN. She married Raymond Allen Thacker Jr., son of Raymond Allen Thacker Sr. and Zena Lois Kerley, on 11 Jul 1992 at Harriman, Roane Co., TN.

Children of Sarah Elizabeth[13] Hall and Raymond Allen Thacker Jr. both born at Knoxville, Knox Co., TN, are as follows:

i. MARY ELISABETH[14]; born 6 Mar 1997.

ii. TIMOTHY NATHANAL; born 14 Aug 1999.

853. ERIC FORREST[13] MARSHALL (*Ilene*[12]*Johnson, Abel*[11], *Abel*[10], *Elgin*[9], *Abel*[8], *Charles*[7], *Ira*[6], *Jonathan*[5], *Nathaniel*[4], *Nathaniel*[3], *Humphrey*[2], *John*[1]) was born on 15 Nov 1972 at Syracuse, Onondaga Co., NY. He married Jamie Lynn Fitch, daughter of Frank Fitch and Sande (--?--), on 18 Apr 1998 at Noblesville, IN.

Children of Eric Forrest[13] Marshall and Jamie Lynn Fitch are as follows:

    i.   ELIA ROSE[14]; born 11 Nov 1996.

    ii. HAYLIE MARIE; born 9 Oct 1999 at Summitville, IN.

854. JOSEPH MICHAEL[13] MARSHALL (*Ilene*[12]*Johnson, Abel*[11], *Abel*[10], *Elgin*[9], *Abel*[8], *Charles*[7], *Ira*[6], *Jonathan*[5], *Nathaniel*[4], *Nathaniel*[3], *Humphrey*[2], *John*[1]) was born on 9 Oct 1978 at Syracuse, Onondaga Co., NY. He married Danielle Nichole Jenkins, daughter of Daniel Funk and Kimberly J. Jenkins, on 28 May 1999 at Anderson, Madison Co., IN.

Children of Joseph Michael[13] Marshall and Danielle Nichole Jenkins both born at Anderson, Madison Co., IN, are as follows:

    i.   JOSEPH THOMAS[14]; born 22 Oct 1999.

    ii. NICHOLAS CHASE; born 8 Jul 2002.

855. TRISTAN ALEXANDER[13] JOHNSON (*Robert*[12], *Robert*[11], *Abel*[10], *Elgin*[9], *Abel*[8], *Charles*[7], *Ira*[6], *Jonathan*[5], *Nathaniel*[4], *Nathaniel*[3], *Humphrey*[2], *John*[1]) was born on 7 Jun 1978 at Baltimore, MD.

Children of Tristan Alexander[13] Johnson and Tonina Moore are:

    i.   HAYLEY MYRIE[14]; born 4 Dec 1995 at Normal, McLean Co., IL.

856. KARIE ANN[13] PFEIFFER (*Sandra*[12]*Kilmer, Eleanor*[11]*Johnson, John*[10], *Charles*[9], *William*[8], *Charles*[7], *Ira*[6], *Jonathan*[5], *Nathaniel*[4], *Nathaniel*[3], *Humphrey*[2], *John*[1]) was born on 1 May 1970 at Arlington, Snohomish Co., WA. She married Matthew Simmons on 27 Feb 1993. She and Matthew Simmons were divorced on 3 Nov 2000. She married Todd McInturff on 26 Jul 2003.

She lived in 2003 at Bothell, WA.

Children of Karie Ann[13] Pfeiffer and Matthew Simmons are as follows:

    i.   COURTNEY BREANNE[14]; born 20 Jun 1994.

    ii. AUSTEN MATHEW; born 31 Mar 1996.

    iii. PRESTON MICHAEL; born 3 Nov 1997.

Children of Karie Ann[13] Pfeiffer and Todd McInturff are:

    i.   AMANDA[14]; born 30 Jun 1994.

857.   HOLLI ANN[13] MERITHEW (*Jean[12]Edwards, Phyllis[11]Johnson, John[10], Charles[9], William[8], Charles[7], Ira[6], Jonathan[5], Nathaniel[4], Nathaniel[3], Humphrey[2], John[1]*) was born on 23 Apr 1979.

Children of Holli Ann[13] Merithew and an unknown spouse are:

    i.   HUNTER CHRISTOPHER[14]; born 9 Jan 2003.

858.   DOUGLAS LEE[13] BROWN (*Richard[12], Clarence[11], Clarence[10], Charles[9], Nancy[8]Johnson, Charles[7], Ira[6], Jonathan[5], Nathaniel[4], Nathaniel[3], Humphrey[2], John[1]*) was born on 1 Oct 1961 at Gouverneur, St. Lawrence Co., NY. He married Tina Louise Youngs on 22 Sep 1990 at Gouverneur, St. Lawrence Co., NY.

Children of Douglas Lee[13] Brown and Tina Louise Youngs both born at Gouverneur, St. Lawrence Co., NY, are as follows:

    i.   SETH DOUGLAS[14]; born 6 Feb 1993.

    ii. AUSTIN LEE; born 11 May 1996.

859. EMILY ANNE[13] MCELWAIN (*Constance[12]Brown, Clarence[11], Clarence[10], Charles[9], Nancy[8]Johnson, Charles[7], Ira[6], Jonathan[5], Nathaniel[4], Nathaniel[3], Humphrey[2], John[1]*) was born on 23 Nov 1959 at Potsdam, St. Lawrence Co., NY. She married William Joseph Gorton on 24 Jul 1982 at Potsdam, St. Lawrence Co., NY.

Children of Emily Anne[13] McElwain and William Joseph Gorton are as follows:

    i.   JACK ALEXANDER[14]; born 30 Apr 1987 at Poughkeepsie, Dutchess Co., NY.

    ii.   KELLY DIANE; born 7 Feb 1989 at Kingston, Ulster Co., NY.

   iii. JOANNA MARIE; born 3 Oct 1991 at Kingston, Ulster Co., NY.

860. KAREN KAY[13] MCELWAIN (*Constance*[12]*Brown, Clarence*[11], *Clarence*[10], *Charles*[9], *Nancy*[8]*Johnson, Charles*[7], *Ira*[6], *Jonathan*[5], *Nathaniel*[4], *Nathaniel*[3], *Humphrey*[2], *John*[1]) was born on 25 Aug 1962 at Potsdam, St. Lawrence Co., NY. She married Mark Frederick Brown on 17 Aug 1985 at Potsdam, St. Lawrence Co., NY.

Children of Karen Kay[13] McElwain and Mark Frederick Brown all born at Geneva, Ontario Co., NY, are as follows:

    i.   ALEXANDRA KATE[14]; born 14 Jul 1989.

    ii.   LAUREN EMILY; born 28 Jun 1991.

   iii. NICHOLAS MARK; born 1 Jun 1993.

   iv. IAN DAVID; born 10 Sep 1996.

861. DIANE LUCILLE[13] MCELWAIN (*Constance*[12]*Brown, Clarence*[11], *Clarence*[10], *Charles*[9], *Nancy*[8]*Johnson, Charles*[7], *Ira*[6], *Jonathan*[5], *Nathaniel*[4], *Nathaniel*[3], *Humphrey*[2], *John*[1]) was born on 10 Apr 1967 at Malone, Franklin Co., NY. She married Christopher Scott Jacob on 5 Oct 1991 at Potsdam, St. Lawrence Co., NY.

Children of Diane Lucille[13] McElwain and Christopher Scott Jacob both born at Albany, Albany Co., NY, are as follows:

    i.   SAMUEL CHRISTOPHER[14]; born 29 Dec 1996.

    ii.   SARAH LOUISE; born 17 Feb 1999.

862. ANNE THERESE[13] SPADARO (*Mary*[12]*Buck, Martha*[11]*Clark, Mabel*[10]*Brown, Charles*[9], *Nancy*[8]*Johnson, Charles*[7], *Ira*[6], *Jonathan*[5], *Nathaniel*[4], *Nathaniel*[3], *Humphrey*[2], *John*[1]) was born on 13 Jul 1968 at Syracuse, Onondoga Co., NY. She married Mark Christopher Mattus on 27 Jul 1991 at Cathedral of the Immaculate Conception, Syracuse, Onondaga Co., NY.

Children of Anne Therese[13] Spadaro and Mark Christopher Mattus all born at Atlanta, Fulton Co., GA, are as follows:

      i.   MICHAEL CHRISTOPHER[14]; born 11 Jan 1997.
      ii. ANTHONY PETER; born 27 Feb 1999.
      iii. MARY LOUISE; born 22 Oct 2000.

863. DANIEL JOSEPH[13] SPADARO (*Mary*[12]*Buck, Martha*[11]*Clark, Mabel*[10]*Brown, Charles*[9], *Nancy*[8]*Johnson, Charles*[7], *Ira*[6], *Jonathan*[5], *Nathaniel*[4], *Nathaniel*[3], *Humphrey*[2], *John*[1]) was born on 24 Sep 1969 at Syracuse, Onondoga Co., NY. He married Amee Marie Ravan on 21 Jul 2001 at Corpus Christi Catholic Church, Colorado Springs, El Paso Co., CO.

Children of Daniel Joseph[13] Spadaro and Amee Marie Ravan are:

      i.   SEMIDA MARIE[14]; born 6 May 2003 at home, Colorado Springs, El Paso Co., CO.

864. NINA LOUISE[13] SPADARO (*Mary*[12]*Buck, Martha*[11]*Clark, Mabel*[10]*Brown, Charles*[9], *Nancy*[8]*Johnson, Charles*[7], *Ira*[6], *Jonathan*[5], *Nathaniel*[4], *Nathaniel*[3], *Humphrey*[2], *John*[1]) was born on 1 Apr 1975 at Syracuse, Onondoga Co., NY. She married Robert Walters on 14 Jun 1997 at Cathedral of the Immaculate Conception, Syracuse, Onondaga Co., NY.

Children of Nina Louise[13] Spadaro and Robert Walters all born at Syracuse, Onondoga Co., NY, are as follows:

      i.   JOSEPH MICHAEL[14]; born 11 Feb 1999.
      ii. REBECCA MARIE; born 15 Jun 2000.
      iii. CLAIRE THERESE; born 17 Mar 2002.

865. VIRGINIA LEIGH[13] SIMPSON (*Nancy*[12]*Buck, Martha*[11]*Clark, Mabel*[10]*Brown, Charles*[9], *Nancy*[8]*Johnson, Charles*[7], *Ira*[6], *Jonathan*[5], *Nathaniel*[4], *Nathaniel*[3], *Humphrey*[2], *John*[1]) was born on 23 Apr 1968 at Perrin AFB, Sherman, TX. She married Vincent Hawley. She and Vincent Hawley were divorced. She and Robert Reynolds were engaged.

Children of Virginia Leigh[13] Simpson and Vincent Hawley are:

i. ALAYNA KATHERINE[14]; born 24 Nov 1993.

Children of Virginia Leigh[13] Simpson and Robert Reynolds are:

i. JESSICA MARIE[14]; born 16 Apr 1988.

866. NATALIE LOUISE[13] SIMPSON (*Nancy[12]Buck, Martha[11]Clark, Mabel[10]Brown, Charles[9], Nancy[8]Johnson, Charles[7], Ira[6], Jonathan[5], Nathaniel[4], Nathaniel[3], Humphrey[2], John[1]*) was born on 15 Dec 1976 at Westchester, PA. She married Eric Wayne Schoeppe on 15 Jul 2000 at Hilton Head Island, SC.

Children of Natalie Louise[13] Simpson and Eric Wayne Schoeppe both born at Hilton Head Island, SC, are as follows:

i. CARSON MACKENZIE[14]; born 4 Oct 1999.
ii. TYLER ANDREW; born 26 Oct 2002.

867. JUSTIN MARCUS[13] WAITS (*Katherine[12]Buck, Martha[11]Clark, Mabel[10]Brown, Charles[9], Nancy[8]Johnson, Charles[7], Ira[6], Jonathan[5], Nathaniel[4], Nathaniel[3], Humphrey[2], John[1]*) was born on 23 Dec 1979 at Bayshore Pasadena Hospital, Pasadena, TX. He married Rosemary Katherine Pronath on 14 Aug 2001 at Church of the Nazarene, Mercer, WI.

Children of Justin Marcus[13] Waits and Rosemary Katherine Pronath both born at Stillwater Medical Center, Stillwater, OK, are as follows:

i. JAMIE CARSON[14]; born 18 Nov 2001.
ii. CIAN DEAN; born 20 Dec 2002.

868. LAURIE MARIE[13] KLIMA (*Thomas[12]Connors, Harriet[11]Clark, Mabel[10]Brown, Charles[9], Nancy[8]Johnson, Charles[7], Ira[6], Jonathan[5], Nathaniel[4], Nathaniel[3], Humphrey[2], John[1]*) was born on 25 Dec 1977. She married Raymond Kelley Richards on 5 Jun 1999 at Austin, TX.

Children of Laurie Marie[13] Klima and Raymond Kelley Richards are:

i. KELLY MARIE[14]; born 2 May 2002 at Houston, TX.

869. SHARON JANE[13] GRAPPOTTE (*Jane[12]Beach, Everett[11], Leta[10]Hall, Hiram[9], Emmorancy[8]Johnson, Charles[7], Ira[6], Jonathan[5], Nathaniel[4], Nathaniel[3], Humphrey[2], John[1]*) was born on 2 Jun 1958 at Watertown, Jefferson Co., NY. She married (--?--) Danielson.

Children of Sharon Jane[13] Grappotte and (--?--) Danielson both born at Buffalo, NY, are as follows:

    i.   JANELLE OLIVIA[14]; born 13 Sep 1988.
    ii. ALLISON; born 16 Aug 1990.

870. GEORGE AUGUSTUS[13] GRAPPOTTE JR. (*Jane[12]Beach, Everett[11], Leta[10]Hall, Hiram[9], Emmorancy[8]Johnson, Charles[7], Ira[6], Jonathan[5], Nathaniel[4], Nathaniel[3], Humphrey[2], John[1]*) was born on 12 Aug 1961 at Watertown, Jefferson Co., NY. He married Mary Ann Bartels.

Children of George Augustus[13] Grappotte Jr. and Mary Ann Bartels both born at New York City, NY, are as follows:

    i.   GEORGE ROSS[14]; born 3 Feb 1997.
    ii. LORRAINE JAQUELYN; born 22 Aug 2001.

871. AMY LYNN[13] BACKUS (*Janice[12]Beach, Everett[11], Leta[10]Hall, Hiram[9], Emmorancy[8]Johnson, Charles[7], Ira[6], Jonathan[5], Nathaniel[4], Nathaniel[3], Humphrey[2], John[1]*) was born on 31 Dec 1958 at Watertown, NY. She married Donald E. Stone. She and Donald E. Stone were divorced.

Children of Amy Lynn[13] Backus and Donald E. Stone both born at Rochester, NY, are as follows:

    i.   KRYSTIE ELAINE[14]; born 1 Mar 1989.
    ii. CATHERINE JANE; born 6 Oct 1990.

872. MARCIA MARIE[13] SPENCER (*Jacqueline[12]Boprey, Reatha[11]Hall, Leon[10], Hiram[9], Emmorancy[8]Johnson, Charles[7], Ira[6], Jonathan[5], Nathaniel[4], Nathaniel[3], Humphrey[2], John[1]*) was born on 22 Aug 1961 at General Hospital, Binghamton, Broome Co., NY. She married Alexander Martin Satkowski IV, son of Alexander

M. Satkowski III and Barbara (--?--), on 24 Jul 1982 at Binghamton, Broome Co., NY.

Children of Marcia Marie[13] Spencer and Alexander Martin Satkowski IV are as follows:

    i.   BRIANNE JANETTE[14]; born 6 May 1983 at Lourdes Hospital, Binghamton, Broome Co., NY; married Andrew Charles Cobb 20 Dec 2002 at Hancock, Delaware Co., NY.

    ii. ARIELLE LYNETTE; born 27 Apr 1984 at Lynchburg, VA.

    iii. ALEXANDER MARTIN V; born 14 Nov 1986 at Lourdes Hospital, Binghamton, Broome Co., NY.

    iv. CODY MICHAEL; born 1 May 1991 at Lourdes Hospital, Binghamton, Broome Co., NY.

873. KIMBERLY ANN[13] BARNES (*Bonnie*[12]*Boprey, Reatha*[11]*Hall, Leon*[10], *Hiram*[9], *Emmorancy*[8]*Johnson, Charles*[7], *Ira*[6], *Jonathan*[5], *Nathaniel*[4], *Nathaniel*[3], *Humphrey*[2], *John*[1]) was born on 31 Jul 1961 at Syracuse, Onondaga Co., NY. She married David McNeil, son of William McNeil and Elizabeth (--?--), on 24 Mar 1984 at Syracuse, Onondaga Co., NY.

Children of Kimberly Ann[13] Barnes and David McNeil all born at Syracuse, Onondaga Co., NY, are as follows:

    i.   BRANDON THOMAS[14]; born 3 Oct 1988.

    ii. TAYLOR DAVID; born 4 Jun 1991.

    iii. CONNOR WILLIAM FRANCIS; born 17 May 1994.

874. CYNTHIA LEIGH[13] BARNES (*Bonnie*[12]*Boprey, Reatha*[11]*Hall, Leon*[10], *Hiram*[9], *Emmorancy*[8]*Johnson, Charles*[7], *Ira*[6], *Jonathan*[5], *Nathaniel*[4], *Nathaniel*[3], *Humphrey*[2], *John*[1]) was born on 15 May 1963 at Syracuse, Onondaga Co., NY. She married Donald Poff in Nov 1982.

Children of Cynthia Leigh[13] Barnes and Donald Poff are as follows:

  954.   i.   KRISTINA MARIE[14], born 2 Feb 1983; married Cody Meachum.

ii. ASHLEIGH; born 1 Dec 1985.

iii. WHITNEY; born 16 Dec 1988.

iv. ZACHARY DONALD; born 2 Jun 1999 at Community General Hospital, Syracuse, Onondaga Co., NY.

875. BARBARA LOUISE[13] BOPREY (*Michael*[12], *Reatha*[11]*Hall*, *Leon*[10], *Hiram*[9], *Emmorancy*[8]*Johnson*, *Charles*[7], *Ira*[6], *Jonathan*[5], *Nathaniel*[4], *Nathaniel*[3], *Humphrey*[2], *John*[1]) was born on 6 Aug 1968 at Potsdam, St. Lawrence Co., NY. She married Randal James Phelix, son of Robert G. Phelix and Marjorie Keerd, on 27 Aug 1988 at St. Andrews Church, Norwood, St. Lawrence Co., NY.

Children of Barbara Louise[13] Boprey and Randal James Phelix are as follows:

i. CORINNA LYNN[14]; born 13 Nov 1991 at Frankfurt, Germany.

ii. BRANDON MICHAEL; born 7 Jun 1995 at Michigan City, IN.

876. MICHAEL LEON[13] BOPREY JR. (*Michael*[12], *Reatha*[11]*Hall*, *Leon*[10], *Hiram*[9], *Emmorancy*[8]*Johnson*, *Charles*[7], *Ira*[6], *Jonathan*[5], *Nathaniel*[4], *Nathaniel*[3], *Humphrey*[2], *John*[1]) was born on 15 Apr 1970 at Potsdam, St. Lawrence Co., NY. He married Amy Susan Wyley, daughter of Lawrence Wyley and Mary Doctuar, on 17 Jan 1989.

Children of Michael Leon[13] Boprey Jr. and Amy Susan Wyley are as follows:

i. CHRISTOPHER DAVID[14]; born 1 Apr 1989 at Massena, St. Lawrence Co., NY.

ii. ANTHONY EDWIN; born 21 Jun 1991 at Elgin Air Force Base, FL.

877. PATRICIA LYNN[13] BOPREY (*Michael*[12], *Reatha*[11]*Hall*, *Leon*[10], *Hiram*[9], *Emmorancy*[8]*Johnson*, *Charles*[7], *Ira*[6], *Jonathan*[5], *Nathaniel*[4], *Nathaniel*[3], *Humphrey*[2], *John*[1]) was born on 18 Apr 1971 at Potsdam, St. Lawrence Co., NY. She married Patrick Josiah

Colbert, son of Allen M. Colbert and Kay Kimpton, on 30 May 1992 at St. Andrews Church, Norwood, St. Lawrence Co., NY.

Children of Patricia Lynn[13] Boprey and Patrick Josiah Colbert all born at Potsdam, St. Lawrence Co., NY, were as follows:

    i.   DANIEL MALCOLM[14]; born 17 Oct 1992.
    ii. SHANNON ROSE; born circa 26 Jul 1995.
    iii. JOSIAH PATRICK; born 1 Dec 1997.

878. DAVID BRIAN[13] BOPREY (*Robert*[12], *Reatha*[11]*Hall, Leon*[10], *Hiram*[9], *Emmorancy*[8]*Johnson, Charles*[7], *Ira*[6], *Jonathan*[5], *Nathaniel*[4], *Nathaniel*[3], *Humphrey*[2], *John*[1]) was born on 7 Apr 1968 at Syracuse, Onondaga Co., NY. He married Deborah Rita Glennon, daughter of Lawrence Kevin Glennon and Maureen Alice Malone, on 4 May 1991 at Constantia, Oswego Co., NY.

Children of David Brian[13] Boprey and Deborah Rita Glennon are as follows:

    i.   COURTNEY ELIZABETH[14]; born 13 Dec 1990.
    ii. JOSHUA ROBERT; born 23 Oct 1992.

879. KELLIE JEAN[13] BOPREY (*Robert*[12], *Reatha*[11]*Hall, Leon*[10], *Hiram*[9], *Emmorancy*[8]*Johnson, Charles*[7], *Ira*[6], *Jonathan*[5], *Nathaniel*[4], *Nathaniel*[3], *Humphrey*[2], *John*[1]) was born on 24 Sep 1969 at Syracuse, Onondaga Co., NY. She married Jack William Reakes, son of Kenneth Reakes, on 4 Jun 1989 at West Monroe, Oswego Co., NY.

Children of Kellie Jean[13] Boprey and Jack William Reakes both born at Syracuse, Onondaga Co., NY, are as follows:

    i.   ASHLEY[14]; born 13 Nov 1987.
    ii. SAMANTHA; born 23 Mar 1992.

880. RICK JAY[13] BRESETT (*Gwendolyn*[12]*Hall, Clifford*[11], *Leon*[10], *Hiram*[9], *Emmorancy*[8]*Johnson, Charles*[7], *Ira*[6], *Jonathan*[5], *Nathaniel*[4], *Nathaniel*[3], *Humphrey*[2], *John*[1]) was born on 10 Jun 1963 at Gouverneur, St. Lawrence Co., NY. He died on 12 Feb 1995 at Gouverneur, St. Lawrence Co., NY, at age 31.

Children of Rick Jay[13] Bresett and an unknown spouse are:

i.   JEREMIAH W.[14]; born circa 1988.

881.   ROGER JOE[13] AVERILL (*Carolyn*[12]*Boulet*, *Arthur*[11], *Lottie*[10]*Hall*, *Hiram*[9], *Emmorancy*[8]*Johnson*, *Charles*[7], *Ira*[6], *Jonathan*[5], *Nathaniel*[4], *Nathaniel*[3], *Humphrey*[2], *John*[1]) was born on 8 Mar 1957 at Gouverneur, St. Lawrence Co., NY. He married Karen Hart.

Children of Roger Joe[13] Averill and Karen Hart are:

i.   TRAVIS[14].

882.   SUZANNE KAY[13] AVERILL (*Carolyn*[12]*Boulet*, *Arthur*[11], *Lottie*[10]*Hall*, *Hiram*[9], *Emmorancy*[8]*Johnson*, *Charles*[7], *Ira*[6], *Jonathan*[5], *Nathaniel*[4], *Nathaniel*[3], *Humphrey*[2], *John*[1]) was born on 31 Aug 1963 at Gouverneur, St. Lawrence Co., NY. She married Wayne Corbine.

Children of Suzanne Kay[13] Averill and an unknown spouse are:

i.   MATTHEW[14]; born 1981.

883.   SUSAN KAY[13] HARTLEY (*Kay*[12]*Boulet*, *Arthur*[11], *Lottie*[10]*Hall*, *Hiram*[9], *Emmorancy*[8]*Johnson*, *Charles*[7], *Ira*[6], *Jonathan*[5], *Nathaniel*[4], *Nathaniel*[3], *Humphrey*[2], *John*[1]) was born on 6 Jul 1954 at Gouverneur, St. Lawrence Co., NY. She married Frank Solon on 18 May 1974 at Gouverneur, St. Lawrence Co., NY.

Children of Susan Kay[13] Hartley and Frank Solon were as follows:

i.   SHANNON KAY[14]; born 2 Mar 1975.
ii.   RYAN FRANK; born 23 Nov 1976 at Starlake, NY; died at Syracuse, Onondoga Co., NY.
iii.   KRISTY LEIGH.
iv.   COREY; born 1983.

884.   TRUDY ANN[13] HARTLEY (*Kay*[12]*Boulet*, *Arthur*[11], *Lottie*[10]*Hall*, *Hiram*[9], *Emmorancy*[8]*Johnson*, *Charles*[7], *Ira*[6], *Jonathan*[5], *Nathaniel*[4], *Nathaniel*[3], *Humphrey*[2], *John*[1]) was born on 2 Dec 1957 at Gouverneur, St. Lawrence Co., NY. She married Roger Hatch in Aug 1976.

Children of Trudy Ann[13] Hartley and Roger Hatch are as follows:

    i.   DEREK JOHN[14]; born 1 Oct 1975.

    ii. (--?--).

885. SHEILA ANN[13] HURLEY (*Doris*[12]*Cole, Mary*[11]*Ward, Bruce*[10], *Venila*[9]*Hall, Emmorancy*[8]*Johnson, Charles*[7], *Ira*[6], *Jonathan*[5], *Nathaniel*[4], *Nathaniel*[3], *Humphrey*[2], *John*[1]) was born on 10 Apr 1946 at Gouverneur, St. Lawrence Co., NY. She married Robert Gary Ingram on 7 Jun 1966 at Edwards, St. Lawrence Co., NY.

Children of Sheila Ann[13] Hurley and Robert Gary Ingram were as follows:

    i.   RICHARD ANTHONY[14]; born 18 Apr 1967; died 28 Aug 1967.

    ii. MICHAEL EUGENE; born 9 Dec 1969.

    iii. LISA ANN; born 21 Jan 1970.

886. PHILLIP ANTHONY[13] HURLEY (*Doris*[12]*Cole, Mary*[11]*Ward, Bruce*[10], *Venila*[9]*Hall, Emmorancy*[8]*Johnson, Charles*[7], *Ira*[6], *Jonathan*[5], *Nathaniel*[4], *Nathaniel*[3], *Humphrey*[2], *John*[1]) was born on 7 Dec 1948 at Gouverneur, St. Lawrence Co., NY. He married Ruth Elaine Thompson on 28 Jul 1973 at Gouverneur, St. Lawrence Co., NY.

Children of Phillip Anthony[13] Hurley and Ruth Elaine Thompson are as follows:

    i.   AMY ROBIN[14]; born 19 Jan 1970.

    ii. ERIN SEANNA; born 12 Aug 1977 at Austin, TX.

887. GARY[13] HALL (*Bonnie*[12]*Ward, Gerald*[11], *Bruce*[10], *Venila*[9]*Hall, Emmorancy*[8]*Johnson, Charles*[7], *Ira*[6], *Jonathan*[5], *Nathaniel*[4], *Nathaniel*[3], *Humphrey*[2], *John*[1]) married Roxanne (--?--). He and Roxanne (--?--) were divorced. He married Buffy Matthews.

Children of Gary[13] Hall and Roxanne (--?--) are as follows:

    i.   JUSTIN[14].

    ii.   MITCH.

    iii.   PATRICK.

Children of Gary[13] Hall and Buffy Matthews are as follows:

    i.   BRITTANY[14].

    ii.   (--?--).

888.   PEGGY[13] HALL (*Bonnie*[12]*Ward*, *Gerald*[11], *Bruce*[10], *Venila*[9]*Hall*, *Emmorancy*[8]*Johnson*, *Charles*[7], *Ira*[6], *Jonathan*[5], *Nathaniel*[4], *Nathaniel*[3], *Humphrey*[2], *John*[1]) married Danny Horne.

Children of Peggy[13] Hall and Danny Horne are as follows:

    i.   RYAN[14].

    ii.   KENDRA.

889.   TERRY[13] HALL (*Bonnie*[12]*Ward*, *Gerald*[11], *Bruce*[10], *Venila*[9]*Hall*, *Emmorancy*[8]*Johnson*, *Charles*[7], *Ira*[6], *Jonathan*[5], *Nathaniel*[4], *Nathaniel*[3], *Humphrey*[2], *John*[1]) married Kim Whitmarsh.

Children of Terry[13] Hall and Kim Whitmarsh are as follows:

    i.   TERRY[14].

    ii.   (--?--).

890.   DAWN PATRICIA[13] MULLANEY (*Patrick*[12], *Irene*[11]*Ward*, *Bruce*[10], *Venila*[9]*Hall*, *Emmorancy*[8]*Johnson*, *Charles*[7], *Ira*[6], *Jonathan*[5], *Nathaniel*[4], *Nathaniel*[3], *Humphrey*[2], *John*[1]) was born on 13 Dec 1956. She married Joseph Zacharek.

Children of Dawn Patricia[13] Mullaney and Joseph Zacharek are as follows:

    i.   MARI[14].

    ii.   JOSEPH; born 13 Dec 1992.

891.   PATRICK BRUCE[13] MULLANEY (*Patrick*[12], *Irene*[11]*Ward*, *Bruce*[10], *Venila*[9]*Hall*, *Emmorancy*[8]*Johnson*, *Charles*[7], *Ira*[6], *Jonathan*[5], *Nathaniel*[4], *Nathaniel*[3], *Humphrey*[2], *John*[1]) was born on 10 Dec 1957. He married Julie French on 4 Nov 1978. He and Julie French were divorced.

Children of Patrick Bruce[13] Mullaney and Julie French are as follows:

    i.   JENNA[14].
    ii. MICHELLE.
    iii. MATTHEW; born 19 May 1986.
    iv. DANIELLE; born 3 Feb 1992.

892. MICHAEL KEVIN[13] MULLANEY (*Patrick*[12], *Irene*[11]*Ward*, *Bruce*[10], *Venila*[9]*Hall*, *Emmorancy*[8]*Johnson*, *Charles*[7], *Ira*[6], *Jonathan*[5], *Nathaniel*[4], *Nathaniel*[3], *Humphrey*[2], *John*[1]) was born on 26 Dec 1958. He married Kathy Saur on 20 Aug 1977.

Children of Michael Kevin[13] Mullaney and Kathy Saur are as follows:

    i. LEIGHANNE[14]; born 2 May 1979.
    ii. JOHN; born 13 Nov 1980.

893. BRIAN KEITH[13] MULLANEY (*Patrick*[12], *Irene*[11]*Ward*, *Bruce*[10], *Venila*[9]*Hall*, *Emmorancy*[8]*Johnson*, *Charles*[7], *Ira*[6], *Jonathan*[5], *Nathaniel*[4], *Nathaniel*[3], *Humphrey*[2], *John*[1]) was born on 27 Dec 1959. He married Janice Ferry on 27 Apr 1979. He and Janice Ferry were divorced.

Children of Brian Keith[13] Mullaney and an unknown spouse are as follows:

    i. STACIA[14].
    ii. CASEY.

894. EUGENE PAUL[13] MULLANEY (*Patrick*[12], *Irene*[11]*Ward*, *Bruce*[10], *Venila*[9]*Hall*, *Emmorancy*[8]*Johnson*, *Charles*[7], *Ira*[6], *Jonathan*[5], *Nathaniel*[4], *Nathaniel*[3], *Humphrey*[2], *John*[1]) was born on 12 May 1962. He married Brenda Sibley.

Children of Eugene Paul[13] Mullaney and Brenda Sibley are as follows:

    i. JESSICA[14]; born 8 Dec 1987.
    ii. JUSTIN; born 27 Feb 1989.
    iii. JEANETTE; born 29 Apr 1990.

895. KATHLEEN ANNETTE[13] MULLANEY (*Patrick*[12], *Irene*[11]*Ward*, *Bruce*[10], *Venila*[9]*Hall*, *Emmorancy*[8]*Johnson*, *Charles*[7], *Ira*[6], *Jonathan*[5], *Nathaniel*[4], *Nathaniel*[3], *Humphrey*[2], *John*[1]) was born on 1 Mar 1963. She married Brian Huber.

Children of Kathleen Annette[13] Mullaney and Brian Huber are as follows:

    i.   ELIZABETH[14].

    ii. GRAHAM.

896. STEPHEN WAYNE[13] LAPLANTE (*Patricia*[12]*Mullaney*, *Irene*[11]*Ward*, *Bruce*[10], *Venila*[9]*Hall*, *Emmorancy*[8]*Johnson*, *Charles*[7], *Ira*[6], *Jonathan*[5], *Nathaniel*[4], *Nathaniel*[3], *Humphrey*[2], *John*[1]) was born on 27 Sep 1960. He married Sherry Oatman.

Children of Stephen Wayne[13] LaPlante and Sherry Oatman are as follows:

    i.   BRANDON[14]; born 9 Sep 1988.

    ii. TYLER; born 5 Jul 1995.

897. MICHELLE ANNETTE[13] LAPLANTE (*Patricia*[12]*Mullaney*, *Irene*[11]*Ward*, *Bruce*[10], *Venila*[9]*Hall*, *Emmorancy*[8]*Johnson*, *Charles*[7], *Ira*[6], *Jonathan*[5], *Nathaniel*[4], *Nathaniel*[3], *Humphrey*[2], *John*[1]) was born on 10 May 1962. She married Kevin Gagnon.

Children of Michelle Annette[13] LaPlante and Kevin Gagnon are as follows:

    i.   CODY[14].

    ii. KAYCEE.

898. MICHAEL BRUCE[13] LAPLANTE (*Patricia*[12]*Mullaney*, *Irene*[11]*Ward*, *Bruce*[10], *Venila*[9]*Hall*, *Emmorancy*[8]*Johnson*, *Charles*[7], *Ira*[6], *Jonathan*[5], *Nathaniel*[4], *Nathaniel*[3], *Humphrey*[2], *John*[1]) was born on 1 Nov 1963. He and Michelle Hale were engaged. He and Penny Fowler were engaged.

Children of Michael Bruce[13] LaPlante and Michelle Hale are as follows:

    i.   MEGAN[14]; born 2 Jul 1988.

    ii. MORGAN; born 21 May 1990.

Children of Michael Bruce[13] LaPlante and Penny Fowler are:

    i.   ALEXIS[14].

899. NICHOLE LYNETTE[13] LAPLANTE (*Patricia*[12]*Mullaney, Irene*[11]*Ward, Bruce*[10]*, Venila*[9]*Hall, Emmorancy*[8]*Johnson, Charles*[7]*, Ira*[6]*, Jonathan*[5]*, Nathaniel*[4]*, Nathaniel*[3]*, Humphrey*[2]*, John*[1]) was born on 17 Aug 1973. She and Paul Smith were engaged.

Children of Nichole Lynette[13] LaPlante and Paul Smith were as follows:

    i.   SAMUEL WAYNE[14]; born 16 Mar 2002.

    ii. MATTHEW PAUL; born 16 Mar 2002; died 16 Mar 2002.

900. RONALD[13] REED II (*Ronald*[12]*, Irene*[11]*Ward, Bruce*[10]*, Venila*[9]*Hall, Emmorancy*[8]*Johnson, Charles*[7]*, Ira*[6]*, Jonathan*[5]*, Nathaniel*[4]*, Nathaniel*[3]*, Humphrey*[2]*, John*[1]) was born on 9 Jan 1971. He married Ladonna (--?--). He died on 10 Jul 1994 at age 23.

Children of Ronald[13] Reed II and Ladonna (--?--) are:

    i.   STEPHANIE[14]; born 21 Jan 1991.

901. MARTHA[13] REED (*Ronald*[12]*, Irene*[11]*Ward, Bruce*[10]*, Venila*[9]*Hall, Emmorancy*[8]*Johnson, Charles*[7]*, Ira*[6]*, Jonathan*[5]*, Nathaniel*[4]*, Nathaniel*[3]*, Humphrey*[2]*, John*[1]) was born on 12 Feb 1974. She married Jack Gonzales.

Martha and Jack have separated.

Children of Martha[13] Reed and Jack Gonzales are as follows:

    i.   RONNIE[14]; born 11 Aug 1995.

    ii. JACK; born 5 Oct 1996.

902. JOSHUA JAMES[13] WHITFORD (*James*[12]*, Irene*[11]*Ward, Bruce*[10]*, Venila*[9]*Hall, Emmorancy*[8]*Johnson, Charles*[7]*, Ira*[6]*, Jonathan*[5]*, Nathaniel*[4]*, Nathaniel*[3]*, Humphrey*[2]*, John*[1]) was born on 27 Jun 1978. He and Lorissa Weaver were engaged.

Children of Joshua James[13] Whitford and Lorissa Weaver are as follows:

 i. NOLAN JAMES[14]; born 3 Feb 2002.
 ii. AVERY JON; born 13 Mar 2003.

903. BRIDGETTE[13] CHURCH (*Vicki*[12]*Whitford, Irene*[11]*Ward, Bruce*[10], *Venila*[9]*Hall, Emmorancy*[8]*Johnson, Charles*[7], *Ira*[6], *Jonathan*[5], *Nathaniel*[4], *Nathaniel*[3], *Humphrey*[2], *John*[1]) was born on 14 Jun 1976. She and John Huckle were engaged.

Children of Bridgette[13] Church and John Huckle are:

 i. CADE[14]; born 2 Feb 2002.

904. NICOLE[13] SHREWSBERRY WHITFORD (*Kenneth*[12]*Whitford, Irene*[11]*Ward, Bruce*[10], *Venila*[9]*Hall, Emmorancy*[8]*Johnson, Charles*[7], *Ira*[6], *Jonathan*[5], *Nathaniel*[4], *Nathaniel*[3], *Humphrey*[2], *John*[1]) was born on 2 Feb 1981. She married Justin Morehouse.

Children of Nicole[13] Shrewsberry Whitford and Justin Morehouse are:

 i. COLE[14]; born 3 Sep 2001.

905. BARBARA[13] MASON (*Albert*[12], *Myrtle*[11]*Maybee, Lena*[10]*Ward, Venila*[9]*Hall, Emmorancy*[8]*Johnson, Charles*[7], *Ira*[6], *Jonathan*[5], *Nathaniel*[4], *Nathaniel*[3], *Humphrey*[2], *John*[1]) married (--?--) Graveline.

Children of Barbara[13] Mason and (--?--) Graveline are as follows:

 i. ANNETTE[14].
 ii. BRETT.

906. MYRTLE[13] HARDY (*Bettie*[12]*Mason, Myrtle*[11]*Maybee, Lena*[10]*Ward, Venila*[9]*Hall, Emmorancy*[8]*Johnson, Charles*[7], *Ira*[6], *Jonathan*[5], *Nathaniel*[4], *Nathaniel*[3], *Humphrey*[2], *John*[1]) married (--?--) Regan.

Children of Myrtle[13] Hardy and (--?--) Regan are:

 i. SCOTT[14].

907. CATHY[13] MASON (*Webster*[12], *Myrtle*[11]*Maybee*, *Lena*[10]*Ward*, *Venila*[9]*Hall*, *Emmorancy*[8]*Johnson*, *Charles*[7], *Ira*[6], *Jonathan*[5], *Nathaniel*[4], *Nathaniel*[3], *Humphrey*[2], *John*[1]) married (--?--) Deon.

Children of Cathy[13] Mason and (--?--) Deon are as follows:

    i.   LISA[14].
    ii. MARK.
    iii. TINA.
    iv. TODD.

908. JAMES[13] MASON (*Webster*[12], *Myrtle*[11]*Maybee*, *Lena*[10]*Ward*, *Venila*[9]*Hall*, *Emmorancy*[8]*Johnson*, *Charles*[7], *Ira*[6], *Jonathan*[5], *Nathaniel*[4], *Nathaniel*[3], *Humphrey*[2], *John*[1]).

Children of James[13] Mason and an unknown spouse are as follows:

    i.   RENAE[14].
    ii. CARRIE.

909. KAREN[13] MASON (*Earl*[12], *Myrtle*[11]*Maybee*, *Lena*[10]*Ward*, *Venila*[9]*Hall*, *Emmorancy*[8]*Johnson*, *Charles*[7], *Ira*[6], *Jonathan*[5], *Nathaniel*[4], *Nathaniel*[3], *Humphrey*[2], *John*[1]) married (--?--) LaLonde.

Children of Karen[13] Mason and (--?--) LaLonde are as follows:

    i.   JEAN[14].
    ii. JUNE.

910. CINDY[13] MASON (*Earl*[12], *Myrtle*[11]*Maybee*, *Lena*[10]*Ward*, *Venila*[9]*Hall*, *Emmorancy*[8]*Johnson*, *Charles*[7], *Ira*[6], *Jonathan*[5], *Nathaniel*[4], *Nathaniel*[3], *Humphrey*[2], *John*[1]) married (--?--) Porter.

Children of Cindy[13] Mason and (--?--) Porter are:

    i.   ALYSSA[14].

911. CAROL ANN[13] MCBRIDE (*Oneta*[12]*Johnson*, *Lewis*[11], *Lewis*[10], *Alvin*[9], *Rufus*[8], *George*[7], *Ira*[6], *Jonathan*[5], *Nathaniel*[4],

Nathaniel[3], *Humphrey*[2], *John*[1]) was born on 6 Nov 1947. She married Carrol Schlieper Jr. on 17 Nov 1966.

Children of Carol Ann[13] McBride and Carrol Schlieper Jr. are as follows:

    i.   BRIAN[14]; born 5 Mar 1970.

    ii. JASON; born 24 Apr 1978.

912. NANCY LOUISE[13] MCBRIDE (*Oneta*[12]*Johnson, Lewis*[11], *Lewis*[10], *Alvin*[9], *Rufus*[8], *George*[7], *Ira*[6], *Jonathan*[5], *Nathaniel*[4], *Nathaniel*[3], *Humphrey*[2], *John*[1]) was born on 22 Jan 1950 at Pike Co., IL. She married Robert Curry on 16 Dec 1967. She married Larry Kunzeman on 12 Jan 1974.

Children of Nancy Louise[13] McBride and Robert Curry are as follows:

    i.   RODNEY[14]; born 26 May 1969.

    ii. DEE ANN; born 3 Apr 1972.

Children of Nancy Louise[13] McBride and Larry Kunzeman are as follows:

    i.   ERIC[14]; born 11 Jun 1974.

    ii. MICAH; born 17 Aug 1980.

913. JANET LYNN[13] MCBRIDE (*Oneta*[12]*Johnson, Lewis*[11], *Lewis*[10], *Alvin*[9], *Rufus*[8], *George*[7], *Ira*[6], *Jonathan*[5], *Nathaniel*[4], *Nathaniel*[3], *Humphrey*[2], *John*[1]) was born on 18 May 1952 at Pike Co., IL. She married Rodney Woods, son of Dale Woods and Virginia Schnepf, on 8 Jul 1979.

Children of Janet Lynn[13] McBride and Rodney Woods are as follows:

    i.   JEFFREY[14]; born 10 Oct 1980.

    ii. KYLE RODNEY; born 6 Jul 1985.

914. ELLEN MARIE[13] MCBRIDE (*Oneta*[12]*Johnson, Lewis*[11], *Lewis*[10], *Alvin*[9], *Rufus*[8], *George*[7], *Ira*[6], *Jonathan*[5], *Nathaniel*[4], *Nathaniel*[3], *Humphrey*[2], *John*[1]) was born on 1 Jan 1955. She married Ronnie Clendenny on 13 Dec 1975.

Children of Ellen Marie[13] McBride and Ronnie Clendenny are as follows:

    i.   ROBYN[14]; born 9 Aug 1977.

    ii.   RICKY; born 2 Dec 1980.

915. JAMES LYNDLE[13] JOHNSON (*Charles*[12], *Lewis*[11], *Lewis*[10], *Alvin*[9], *Rufus*[8], *George*[7], *Ira*[6], *Jonathan*[5], *Nathaniel*[4], *Nathaniel*[3], *Humphrey*[2], *John*[1]) was born on 30 Jan 1945. He married Susan Marie Hannant on 18 Oct 1969.

Children of James Lyndle[13] Johnson and Susan Marie Hannant are as follows:

    i.   AMY CHRISTINE[14]; born 11 Sep 1972.

    ii.   MARK LYNDLE; born 20 Jun 1981.

916. LYNDA JEAN[13] JOHNSON (*Charles*[12], *Lewis*[11], *Lewis*[10], *Alvin*[9], *Rufus*[8], *George*[7], *Ira*[6], *Jonathan*[5], *Nathaniel*[4], *Nathaniel*[3], *Humphrey*[2], *John*[1]) was born on 14 Jun 1947. She married Phillip Dean Crowder on 14 Jun 1970.

Children of Lynda Jean[13] Johnson and Phillip Dean Crowder are as follows:

    i.   CURTIS DALE[14]; born 26 Aug 1968.

    ii.   ANGELA LYNN.

917. WAYNE EUGENE[13] JOHNSON (*Charles*[12], *Lewis*[11], *Lewis*[10], *Alvin*[9], *Rufus*[8], *George*[7], *Ira*[6], *Jonathan*[5], *Nathaniel*[4], *Nathaniel*[3], *Humphrey*[2], *John*[1]) was born on 19 Jan 1949. He married Donna Bowman on 20 Oct 1966. He and Donna Bowman were divorced. He married Lorraine Harris on 9 Nov 1969.

Children of Wayne Eugene[13] Johnson and Donna Bowman are as follows:

    i.   DEBRA LYNN[14]; born 23 Apr 1967.

    ii.   JEFFREY SCOTT; born 14 Mar 1969.

Children of Wayne Eugene[13] Johnson and Lorraine Harris are as follows:

    i.   CARRIE ANN[14]; born 1 Aug 1972.

    ii.   KIMBERLY ANN; born 7 Sep 1977.

iii.   KELLY ALICIA; born 28 Aug 1981.

918. DONNA MARIE[13] JOHNSON (*Hayward*[12], *Lewis*[11], *Lewis*[10], *Alvin*[9], *Rufus*[8], *George*[7], *Ira*[6], *Jonathan*[5], *Nathaniel*[4], *Nathaniel*[3], *Humphrey*[2], *John*[1]) was born on 2 Sep 1946 at Pike Co., IL. She married Ronald Dale Campbell on 1 Jan 1966. She and Ronald Dale Campbell were divorced. She married Harold Lamne on 5 Sep 1981 at Clarksville, MO.

Children of Donna Marie[13] Johnson and Ronald Dale Campbell are as follows:

i.   RONALD SCOTT[14]; born 10 Jun 1969.

ii.   TAMBRA MARIE; born 20 Sep 1971.

919. TERRY LAVON[13] JOHNSON (*Hayward*[12], *Lewis*[11], *Lewis*[10], *Alvin*[9], *Rufus*[8], *George*[7], *Ira*[6], *Jonathan*[5], *Nathaniel*[4], *Nathaniel*[3], *Humphrey*[2], *John*[1]) was born on 1 Nov 1947 at Pike Co., IL. He married Janice Nissen on 16 May 1968.

Children of Terry Lavon[13] Johnson and Janice Nissen are as follows:

i.   MARY JANE[14]; born 6 Aug 1974.

ii.   EDWARD LEWIS; born 28 Nov 1977.

920. MARSHA ANN[13] BURKE (*Otela*[12]*Johnson*, *Lewis*[11], *Lewis*[10], *Alvin*[9], *Rufus*[8], *George*[7], *Ira*[6], *Jonathan*[5], *Nathaniel*[4], *Nathaniel*[3], *Humphrey*[2], *John*[1]) was born on 14 Mar 1953 at Fairmount, WV. She married John Price on 21 May 1977.

Children of Marsha Ann[13] Burke and John Price are as follows:

i.   JERROD[14]; born 28 Oct 1978.

ii.   MATHEW; born 9 Feb 1981.

921. ROGER DEAN[13] AKERS (*Doris*[12]*Smith*, *Mildred*[11]*Miller*, *Laura*[10]*Johnson*, *Lewis*[9], *Rufus*[8], *George*[7], *Ira*[6], *Jonathan*[5], *Nathaniel*[4], *Nathaniel*[3], *Humphrey*[2], *John*[1]) was born on 6 Jul 1955 at Pittsfield, Pike Co., IL. He married Peggy Jo Sibly, daughter of Howard Adair Sibly and Wilma Alberta Elledge.

Children of Roger Dean[13] Akers and Peggy Jo Sibly are as follows:

i. CHRISTOPHER JOSEPH[14]; born 25 Sep 1978.

ii. JENNIFER GAIL; born 30 Mar 1982.

922. DEBRA JEAN[13] AKERS (*Doris*[12]*Smith*, *Mildred*[11]*Miller*, *Laura*[10]*Johnson*, *Lewis*[9], *Rufus*[8], *George*[7], *Ira*[6], *Jonathan*[5], *Nathaniel*[4], *Nathaniel*[3], *Humphrey*[2], *John*[1]) was born on 3 Dec 1956. She married John Joseph Dunn II on 11 Jul 1977.

Children of Debra Jean[13] Akers and John Joseph Dunn II are as follows:

i. KELLIE ELIZABETH[14]; born 8 Nov 1979.

ii. CARRIE LYNN; born 28 Mar 1983.

iii. JOHN JOSEPH III; born 3 Feb 1988.

923. BECKY LYNN[13] LONG (*Linda*[12]*Battershell*, *Kathryn*[11]*Johnson*, *Osca*[10], *Lewis*[9], *Rufus*[8], *George*[7], *Ira*[6], *Jonathan*[5], *Nathaniel*[4], *Nathaniel*[3], *Humphrey*[2], *John*[1]) was born on 7 Feb 1959 at Alton, IL. She married Jeffrey Scott Alexander on 11 Apr 1980.

Children of Becky Lynn[13] Long and Jeffrey Scott Alexander are:

i. ABBY LYNN[14]; born 1 Dec 1988.

924. JILL DENISE[13] KEIL (*Sherry*[12]*McKenna*, *Lois*[11]*Johnson*, *Rufus*[10], *Isaac*[9], *Rufus*[8], *George*[7], *Ira*[6], *Jonathan*[5], *Nathaniel*[4], *Nathaniel*[3], *Humphrey*[2], *John*[1]) was born on 17 Jul 1960. She married Herbert Dwayne Kelly on 21 Dec 1985.

Children of Jill Denise[13] Keil and Herbert Dwayne Kelly are as follows:

i. AMBER JANICE[14]; born 28 Oct 1986.

ii. ASHLEIGH NICOLE; born 11 Mar 1990.

iii. AMY ELIZABETH; born 9 Mar 1992.

Generation Fourteen

925. EARL WAYNE[14] PURSLEY (*Donna*[13]*Giger*, *Mary*[12]*Shive*, *Mary*[11]*Nicholson*, *Charles*[10], *Mary*[9]*Johnson*, *Charles*[8], *Charles*[7],

Ira[6], *Jonathan*[5], *Nathaniel*[4], *Nathaniel*[3], *Humphrey*[2], *John*[1]) was born on 4 Jun 1964. He married Deanna Rains on 5 Nov 1983.

Children of Earl Wayne[14] Pursley and Deanna Rains are:

    i.   JACOB WAYNE[15].

926.   CHERYL LYNN[14] DENNIS (*Linda*[13]*German*, *Virginia*[12]*Killebrew*, *Norene*[11], *Mary*[10]*Miller*, *Rebecca*[9]*Johnson*, *Charles*[8], *Charles*[7], *Ira*[6], *Jonathan*[5], *Nathaniel*[4], *Nathaniel*[3], *Humphrey*[2], *John*[1]) was born on 4 Jun 1963. She married James Dolloff on 9 Apr 1983.

Children of Cheryl Lynn[14] Dennis and James Dolloff are:

    i.   LINDSEY JEAN[15]; born 7 May 1984.

927. DAVID GUY[14] BROCK (*Lawrence*[13], *Georgie*[12]*Iaeger*, *George*[11], *Ada*[10]*Johnson*, *William*[9], *Hiram*[8], *Charles*[7], *Ira*[6], *Jonathan*[5], *Nathaniel*[4], *Nathaniel*[3], *Humphrey*[2], *John*[1]) was born on 4 Sep 1957 at San Francisco, CA. He married Donna M. Leaverton on 16 Jul 1983 at Gretna, LA.

Children of David Guy[14] Brock and Donna M. Leaverton are as follows:

  955.   i.   TAMIE[15], born 26 Sep 1965; married Rodney Dufour.
  956.   ii. KIMBERLY, born 28 Oct 1966; married Christopher Newton.
  957.   iii. ADAM THOMPSON, born 1 Aug 1971; married Jane Marse.

928. SCOTT RAYMOND[14] BROCK (*Lawrence*[13], *Georgie*[12]*Iaeger*, *George*[11], *Ada*[10]*Johnson*, *William*[9], *Hiram*[8], *Charles*[7], *Ira*[6], *Jonathan*[5], *Nathaniel*[4], *Nathaniel*[3], *Humphrey*[2], *John*[1]) married Deana (--?--). He and Deana (--?--) were divorced. He married Vicki (--?--) at Seattle, King Co., WA.

He lived in 1997 at Auburn, WA.

Children of Scott Raymond[14] BROCK and Deana (--?--) are:

    i.   APRIL SUZANNE[15].

929. CLINTON JOSEPH[14] NASLUND (*George[13]Naslund, Hazel[12]Iaeger, George[11], Ada[10]Johnson, William[9], Hiram[8], Charles[7], Ira[6], Jonathan[5], Nathaniel[4], Nathaniel[3], Humphrey[2], John[1]*) was born on 18 May 1964 at Seattle, King Co., WA. He married Susan Phillips on 4 Sep 1987. He and Susan Phillips were divorced in 1995. He married Sunny Kraft on 28 Aug 2000 at Edmonds, Snohomish Co., WA.

He lived in 2001 at Marysville, Snohomish Co., WA.

Children of Clinton Joseph[14] Naslund and Susan Phillips are:

    i.   CHARLES ADAM[15]; born 8 Jun 1980.

Children of Clinton Joseph[14] Naslund and Cynthia Crane are:

    i.   DEBORAH LEANN[15]; born 27 Sep 1985 at Everett, Snohomish Co., WA.

There were no children of Clinton Joseph[14] Naslund and Sunny Kraft.

930. KEVIN DAVID[14] NASLUND (*George[13], Hazel[12]Iaeger, George[11], Ada[10]Johnson, William[9], Hiram[8], Charles[7], Ira[6], Jonathan[5], Nathaniel[4], Nathaniel[3], Humphrey[2], John[1]*) was born on 1 Jul 1966 at Seattle, King Co., WA. He married Marianne Denise Kessler, daughter of John Philip Kessler and Beverly Ann Wright, on 18 Aug 1990 at Reno, NV.

He lived in 2000 at Sulton, Snohomish Co., WA.

Children of Kevin David[14] Naslund and Marianne Denise Kessler are as follows:

    i.   NICKOLAS DAVID[15]; born 16 Mar 1992 at Northwest Hospital, Seattle, King Co., WA.

    ii. JACOB DANIEL; born 4 Jan 1995 at Valley General Hospital, Monroe, Snohomish Co., WA.

931. TERESA MAY[14] HILL (*James[13]Hill, Lois[12]Iaeger, George[11], Ada[10]Johnson, William[9], Hiram[8], Charles[7], Ira[6], Jonathan[5], Nathaniel[4], Nathaniel[3], Humphrey[2], John[1]*) was born on 12 Apr 1961 at Seattle, King Co., WA. She married James Calvin Bolton in Jan 1983 at Amarillo, TX. She and James Calvin Bolton were divorced. She married Morgan Dellinger III on 1 Nov 1986 at Woodbine, GA. She and Morgan Dellinger III were divorced. She married Charles David Frediani Jr. on 30 Oct 1992. She married (--?--) Milliken.

She lived in 1997 at Bedias, TX.

Children of Teresa May[14] Hill and James Calvin Bolton are as follows:

    i.   CALVIN JAMES[15]; born 28 Sep 1984 at Amarillo, TX.

    ii. CHRISTOPHER MICHAEL; born 13 Oct 1985 at Chattanooga, TN.

Children of Teresa May[14] Hill and Morgan Dellinger III are:

    i.   JONATHAN WAYNE[15]; born 19 Sep 1987 at Jacksonville, FL.

There were no children of Teresa May[14] Hill and Charles David Frediani Jr..

There were no children of Teresa May[14] Hill and (--?--) Milliken.

932. JAMES DALE[14] HILL JR (*James*[13]*Hill, Lois*[12]*Iaeger, George*[11]*, Ada*[10]*Johnson, William*[9]*, Hiram*[8]*, Charles*[7]*, Ira*[6]*, Jonathan*[5]*, Nathaniel*[4]*, Nathaniel*[3]*, Humphrey*[2]*, John*[1]) was born on 16 Nov 1962 at Seattle, King Co., WA. He married Deborah Fannie Griffith on 20 May 1982 at Santa Clara, CA. He and Deborah Fannie Griffith were divorced. He married Hillery Jean Prosh on 10 Nov 1983 at San Francisco, CA. He and Hillery Jean Prosh were divorced. He married Susan Beth Korschun on 28 Dec 1987 at Miami, FL. He and Susan Beth Korschun were divorced.

He lived on 15 Mar 2003 at St. Paul, Hennipin Co., MN.

Children of James Dale[14] Hill Jr and Deborah Fannie Griffith are:

    i.   CHRISTINA MARIE[15]; born 2 Jan 1983 at Sacramento, CA.

Children of James Dale[14] Hill Jr and Hillery Jean Prosh are:

    i.   DERICK MONTGOMERY[15]; born 24 Oct 1984.

Children of James Dale[14] Hill Jr and Susan Beth Korschun are:

i. AMY ELIZABETH[15]; born 24 Oct 1988 at Baltimore, MD.

933. SHERRILL LEE[14] THORNBERRY (*James*[13]*Hill*, *Lois*[12]*Iaeger*, *George*[11], *Ada*[10]*Johnson*, *William*[9], *Hiram*[8], *Charles*[7], *Ira*[6], *Jonathan*[5], *Nathaniel*[4], *Nathaniel*[3], *Humphrey*[2], *John*[1]) was born on 15 Feb 1964. She married Keith Chew. She and Keith Chew were divorced.

Children of Sherrill Lee[14] Thornberry and Keith Chew are as follows:

i. CAITLIN NICOLE[15]; born 11 Aug 1990.

ii. KYLE WISON; born 11 Mar 1993.

934. ANNETTE KATHLEEN[14] HILL (*James*[13], *Lois*[12]*Iaeger*, *George*[11], *Ada*[10]*Johnson*, *William*[9], *Hiram*[8], *Charles*[7], *Ira*[6], *Jonathan*[5], *Nathaniel*[4], *Nathaniel*[3], *Humphrey*[2], *John*[1]) was born on 20 Aug 1964 at Central Pt., Jackson Co., OR. She married Raymond Frederick Ault on 14 Apr 1981 at Coeur d' Alene, ID. She and Raymond Frederick Ault were divorced. She married Kenneth Ray Wells on 9 Sep 1989.

She lived in 2002 at Selah, WA.

Children of Annette Kathleen[14] Hill and Raymond Frederick Ault were:

i. CHEZARAE NICHOLE[15]; born 26 Aug 1982 at Yakima, Yakima Co., WA; died 25 Jun 1983 at Portland, Multnomah Co., OR.

Children of Annette Kathleen[14] Hill and Kenneth Ray Wells are:

i. CHARLES JEFFERY RAE[15]; born 5 Oct 1986 at Fairbanks, AK.

935. JEFFERY CHARLES WALTER[14] HILL SR. (*James*[13]*Hill*, *Lois*[12]*Iaeger*, *George*[11], *Ada*[10]*Johnson*, *William*[9], *Hiram*[8], *Charles*[7], *Ira*[6], *Jonathan*[5], *Nathaniel*[4], *Nathaniel*[3], *Humphrey*[2], *John*[1]) was born on 21 Sep 1965 at Medford, Jackson Co., OR. He married Michele Lynn Brogden at Yakima, Yakima Co., WA. He and Michele Lynn Brogden were divorced. He married Lori Ann Chandler on 9 Sep 1999 at Coeur D'Alene, ID.

Children of Jeffery Charles Walter[14] Hill Sr. and Michele Lynn Brogden are:

    i.   STACIE LYNETT[15]; born 28 Sep 1989 at Yakima, Yakima Co., WA.

Children of Jeffery Charles Walter[14] Hill Sr. and Lori Ann Chandler are as follows:

    i.   RYAN LEE[15]; born 11 Sep 1985.

    ii.   JACOB; born 12 Feb 1988.

    iii.   JEFFREY CHARLES WALTER JR.; born 23 Sep 1999 at Yakima, Yakima Co., WA.

Children of Jeffery Charles Walter[14] Hill Sr. and Christine Lynn Wood are:

    i.   GENEVIEVE LYNN[15]; born 19 Jun 1994.

936. BRADLEY CHARLES[14] MANN (*Martha*[13]*Hill, Lois*[12]*Iaeger, George*[11], *Ada*[10]*Johnson, William*[9], *Hiram*[8], *Charles*[7], *Ira*[6], *Jonathan*[5], *Nathaniel*[4], *Nathaniel*[3], *Humphrey*[2], *John*[1]) was born on 19 Aug 1964 at Edmonds, Snohomish Co., WA. He married Gayanna Knutsen on 4 Nov 1984 at Everett, Snohomish Co., WA. He and Gayanna Knutsen were divorced. He married Christy Carter on 12 Apr 1986 at Lake Stevens, Snohomish Co., WA. He and Christy Carter were divorced. He married Tammy Lynn Johnson on 4 Sep 1992 at Reno, NV.

He lived in 2000 at Seabeck, WA.

Children of Bradley Charles[14] Mann and Gayanna Knutsen are:

    i.   TARYN LALEEN[15]; born 24 Apr 1985 at Everett, Snohomish Co., WA.

Children of Bradley Charles[14] Mann and Christy Carter are:

    i.   ZACHERY BLAIR[15]; born 25 Aug 1987 at Everett, Snohomish Co., WA.

Children of Bradley Charles[14] Mann and Tammy Lynn Johnson are as follows:

i. ALEX BRADLEY[15]; born 7 Mar 1995 at Bremerton, WA.

ii. KATELYN LEEANN; born 23 Aug 1997.

937. KARA MICHELLE[14] MANN (*Martha[13]Hill, Lois[12]Iaeger, George[11], Ada[10]Johnson, William[9], Hiram[8], Charles[7], Ira[6], Jonathan[5], Nathaniel[4], Nathaniel[3], Humphrey[2], John[1]*) was born on 15 Oct 1972 at Edmonds, Snohomish Co., WA. She married Shawn Michael Hartz on 5 Jul 1996 at Mt. Vernon, Skagit Co., WA.

Children of Kara Michelle[14] Mann and an unknown spouse are:

i. KYLE CHARLES[15]; born 1993 at Seattle, King Co., WA.

Children of Kara Michelle[14] Mann and Shawn Michael Hartz are:

i. BLAIR DAWN[15]; born 6 Nov 1996.

938. STEPHEN[14] BEITELSPACHER (*Judith[13]Iaeger, Jackson[12], George[11]Iaeger, Ada[10]Johnson, William[9], Hiram[8], Charles[7], Ira[6], Jonathan[5], Nathaniel[4], Nathaniel[3], Humphrey[2], John[1]*) was born on 8 Mar 1967 at Stillwater, MN. He married Dawn Milat in 1991 at Pasco, Franklin Co., WA. He and Dawn Milat were divorced in 1994.

He lived in 2003 at Prineville, Crook Co., OR.

Children of Stephen[14] Beitelspacher and Dawn Milat are:

i. SUNNY[15]; born 23 Dec 1991 at Pasco, WA.

939. CHRISTINA MARIE[14] NORRIS (*Leonard[13]Norris, Lulubelle[12], George[11]Iaeger, Ada[10]Johnson, William[9], Hiram[8], Charles[7], Ira[6], Jonathan[5], Nathaniel[4], Nathaniel[3], Humphrey[2], John[1]*) was born on 30 Sep 1974 at Eureka, Humboldt Co., CA.

Children of Christina Marie[14] Norris and an unknown spouse are:

i. TABAITHA[15].

940. DANIEL EARL[14] NORRIS (*Leonard[13]Norris, Lulubelle[12], George[11]Iaeger, Ada[10]Johnson, William[9], Hiram[8], Charles[7],*

Ira[6], *Jonathan*[5], *Nathaniel*[4], *Nathaniel*[3], *Humphrey*[2], *John*[1]) was born on 25 Jan 1976.

Children of Daniel Earl[14] Norris and an unknown spouse are:

      i.   CHEYANNE[15].

941. TINA KOYE[14] NORRIS (*Leonard*[13]*Norris*, *Lulubelle*[12], *George*[11]*Iaeger*, *Ada*[10]*Johnson*, *William*[9], *Hiram*[8], *Charles*[7], *Ira*[6], *Jonathan*[5], *Nathaniel*[4], *Nathaniel*[3], *Humphrey*[2], *John*[1]) was born on 3 Aug 1978 at Eureka, Humboldt Co., CA.

Children of Tina Koye[14] Norris and an unknown spouse are:

      i.   ELIZABETH[15].

942. SHARON FAYE[14] BLANDIN (*Nancy*[13]*Norris*, *Lulubelle*[12], *George*[11]*Iaeger*, *Ada*[10]*Johnson*, *William*[9], *Hiram*[8], *Charles*[7], *Ira*[6], *Jonathan*[5], *Nathaniel*[4], *Nathaniel*[3], *Humphrey*[2], *John*[1]) was born on 22 Jan 1973 at Greeley, Weld Co., CO. She married William Muncy Canterbury, son of William M. Canterbury, on 11 Dec 1993 at Hawthorne, Mineral Co., NV.

Children of Sharon Faye[14] Blandin and William Muncy Canterbury are:

      i.   CHRISTIFER JAMES[15]; born 18 May 1994 at Hawthorne, Mineral Co., NV.

943. CRISTIE ANN[14] NELSON (*Tracy*[13]*Norris*, *Lulubelle*[12], *George*[11]*Iaeger*, *Ada*[10]*Johnson*, *William*[9], *Hiram*[8], *Charles*[7], *Ira*[6], *Jonathan*[5], *Nathaniel*[4], *Nathaniel*[3], *Humphrey*[2], *John*[1]) was born on 8 Jan 1975. She married (--?--) Doran.

Children of Cristie Ann[14] Nelson and (--?--) Doran are:

      i.   KARYNN NICOLE[15]; born 12 Mar 1995.

944. JEFFERY SCOTT[14] POLASKI (*Michael*[13]*Poole*, *Kathleen*[12], *George*[11]*Iaeger*, *Ada*[10]*Johnson*, *William*[9], *Hiram*[8], *Charles*[7], *Ira*[6], *Jonathan*[5], *Nathaniel*[4], *Nathaniel*[3], *Humphrey*[2], *John*[1]) was born on 22 Apr 1973 at Duluth, MN.

Children of Jeffery Scott[14] Polaski and an unknown spouse both born at Portland, Multnomah Co., OR, are as follows:

    i.   TAYLOR CAMPBELL[15]; born 1 Dec 1992.

    ii. JERAMI; born 24 May 1994.

945. SHAWN PATRICK[14] POOLE (*Michael[13]*, *Kathleen[12]*, *George[11]Iaeger*, *Ada[10]Johnson*, *William[9]*, *Hiram[8]*, *Charles[7]*, *Ira[6]*, *Jonathan[5]*, *Nathaniel[4]*, *Nathaniel[3]*, *Humphrey[2]*, *John[1]*) was born on 9 Feb 1977 at Duluth, MN. He married Shana Barrett on 26 Sep 1998 at Portland, Multnomah Co., OR. He and Shana Barrett were divorced.

Children of Shawn Patrick[14] Poole and Shana Barrett are:

    i.   AUSTIN PATRICK[15]; born 17 Mar 1998.

946. KATHLEEN IRENE[14] POOLE (*Michael[13]* Poole, *Kathleen[12]*, *George[11]Iaeger*, *Ada[10]Johnson*, *William[9]*, *Hiram[8]*, *Charles[7]*, *Ira[6]*, *Jonathan[5]*, *Nathaniel[4]*, *Nathaniel[3]*, *Humphrey[2]*, *John[1]*) was born on 22 Apr 1980 at Astoria, Clatsop Co, OR. She married Jerred Mack on 22 Feb 2000.

Children of Kathleen Irene[14] Poole and Jerred Mack are:

    i.   MAILEA TYANNE[15]; born 17 Oct 2000 at Portland, Multnomah Co., OR.

947. JENNY KATHLEEN[14] POOLE (*Patrick[13]Poole*, *Kathleen[12]*, *George[11]Iaeger*, *Ada[10]Johnson*, *William[9]*, *Hiram[8]*, *Charles[7]*, *Ira[6]*, *Jonathan[5]*, *Nathaniel[4]*, *Nathaniel[3]*, *Humphrey[2]*, *John[1]*) was born on 16 Jan 1971 at Hillsboro, OR. She married Michael Burns on 29 Dec 1989 at Portland, Multnomah Co., OR. She and Michael Burns were divorced. She married Edward N. Long on 8 Apr 1994.

She lived in 1996 at Portland, Multnomah Co., OR.

Children of Jenny Kathleen[14] Poole and Michael Burns are:

    i.   CONNOR MICHAEL[15]; born 7 Jun 1991 at Portland, Multnomah Co., OR.

Children of Jenny Kathleen[14] Poole and Edward N. Long are as follows:

    i.   MICHAEL[15]; born 31 Aug 1988.

    ii. JENNA LEA; born 24 Apr 1986.

    iii. JEFFERY PATRICK; born 17 May 1995.

948. ELIZABETH JUNE[14] POOLE (*Patrick*[13]*Poole, Kathleen*[12],*George*[11]*Iaeger, Ada*[10]*Johnson, William*[9], *Hiram*[8], *Charles*[7], *Ira*[6], *Jonathan*[5], *Nathaniel*[4], *Nathaniel*[3], *Humphrey*[2], *John*[1]) was born on 19 Mar 1975 at Astoria, Clatsop Co., OR. She married Jeremy Glenn Holloway.

Children of Elizabeth June[14] Poole and Jeremy Glenn Holloway are as follows:

    i.   JACKSON WILLIAM[15]; born 20 Oct 1998.

    ii. MARGARET ANNABELLE; born 24 Feb 2000.

949. RICHARD DAVID[14] ANDERSON (*Marta*[13]*Poole, Kathleen*[12], *George*[11]*Iaeger, Ada*[10]*Johnson, William*[9], *Hiram*[8], *Charles*[7], *Ira*[6], *Jonathan*[5], *Nathaniel*[4], *Nathaniel*[3], *Humphrey*[2], *John*[1]) was born on 9 Nov 1972 at Bend, OR. He married (--?--) ?

Children of Richard David[14] Anderson and (--?--) ? are as follows:

    i.   JORDYN LYNN[15]; born 18 Sep 1996.

    ii. DAKODA; born circa Aug 2000.

950. ANDREA MICHELLE[14] ANDERSON (*Marta*[13]*Poole, Kathleen*[12], *George*[11]*Iaeger, Ada*[10]*Johnson, William*[9], *Hiram*[8], *Charles*[7], *Ira*[6], *Jonathan*[5], *Nathaniel*[4], *Nathaniel*[3], *Humphrey*[2], *John*[1]) was born on 19 Nov 1974 at Roseburg, Douglas Co., OR. She married Erich McShane Even, son of William Even and Bonita McShane, on 2 Jul 1999 at Portland, Multnomah Co., OR.

Children of Andrea Michelle[14] Anderson and Erich McShane Even both born at McKenzie Willamette Hospital, Springfield, OR, are as follows:

    i.   JUSTUS MCSHANE[15]; born 24 Jul 2000.

    ii. HUNTER MORGAN; born 4 Feb 2002.

951. CIAN MICHAEL[14] RUSSELL (*Christina*[13]*Carey, George*[12], *George*[11]*Iaeger, Ada*[10]*Johnson, William*[9], *Hiram*[8], *Charles*[7], *Ira*[6], *Jonathan*[5], *Nathaniel*[4], *Nathaniel*[3], *Humphrey*[2], *John*[1]) was born on 5 Nov 1976 at San Diego, San Diego Co., CA. He married Lissette Murro on 14 Aug 1999 at Escondido, CA.

Children of Cian Michael[14] Russell and Lissette Murro are as follows:

    i.   VICTORIA MERISE[15]; born 12 Mar 2000 at Biloxi, MS.

    ii.   IAIN JOSEPH; born 4 Jul 2002 at Camp Pendelton, CA.

952. CARY LYNN[14] DILLS (*Judy*[13]*Johnson, Orland*[12]*, James*[11]*, Lloyd*[10]*, William*[9]*, Hiram*[8]*, Charles*[7]*, Ira*[6]*, Jonathan*[5]*, Nathaniel*[4]*, Nathaniel*[3]*, Humphrey*[2]*, John*[1]) was born on 14 Apr 1965 at Tacoma, Pierce Co., WA. He married Danielle Kaasa on 2 Jul 1982 at Hoodsport, WA.

Children of Cary Lynn[14] Dills and Danielle Kaasa are:

    i.   DERRICK DOUGLAS LYNN[15]; born 30 Aug 1983 at Puyallup, Pierce Co., WA.

953. CHERYL[14] CRAIG (*Patty*[13]*Smith, Robert*[12]*, Francis*[11]*McHargue, Lulu*[10]*Johnson, William*[9]*, Hiram*[8]*, Charles*[7]*, Ira*[6]*, Jonathan*[5]*, Nathaniel*[4]*, Nathaniel*[3]*, Humphrey*[2]*, John*[1]) married Rick (--?--).

Children of Cheryl[14] Craig and Rick (--?--) are as follows:

    i.   (--?--)[15].

    ii.   ZACHARY TYLER.

954. KRISTINA MARIE[14] POFF (*Cynthia*[13]*Barnes, Bonnie*[12]*Boprey, Reatha*[11]*Hall, Leon*[10]*, Hiram*[9]*, Emmorancy*[8]*Johnson, Charles*[7]*, Ira*[6]*, Jonathan*[5]*, Nathaniel*[4]*, Nathaniel*[3]*, Humphrey*[2]*, John*[1]) was born on 2 Feb 1983. She married Cody Meachum in Apr 2002.

Children of Kristina Marie[14] Poff and Cody Meachum are:

    i.   HANNAH MARIE[15]; born 25 Oct 2001.

955. TAMIE[15] BROCK (*David*[14]*Brock, Lwrence*[13]*Gamey, Georgie*[12]*Iaeger, George*[11], *Ada*[10]*Johnson, William*[9], *Hiram*[8], *Charles*[7], *Ira*[6], *Jonathan*[5], *Nathaniel*[4], *Nathaniel*[3], *Humphrey*[2], *John*[1]) was born on 26 Sep 1965. She married Rodney Dufour on 16 Jun 1989 at New Orleans, LA.

Children of Tamie[15] Brock and Rodney Dufour are:

    i.   JARROD ANTHONY[16]; born 18 Mar 1991.

956. KIMBERLY[15] BROCK (*David*[14]Brock, *Lawrence*[13]*Gamey, Georgie*[12]*Iaeger, George*[11], *Ada*[10]*Johnson, William*[9], *Hiram*[8], *Charles*[7], *Ira*[6], *Jonathan*[5], *Nathaniel*[4], *Nathaniel*[3], *Humphrey*[2], *John*[1]) was born on 28 Oct 1966. She married Christopher Newton on 7 Feb 1997 at New Orleans, LA.

Children of Kimberly[15] Brock and Christopher Newton are:

    i.   MICHAEL JOSEPH[16]; born 18 Sep 1985.

957. ADAM THOMPSON[15] BROCK (*David*[14]Brock, *Lawrence*[13]*Gamey, Georgie*[12]*Iaeger, George*[11], *Ada*[10]*Johnson, William*[9], *Hiram*[8], *Charles*[7], *Ira*[6], *Jonathan*[5], *Nathaniel*[4], *Nathaniel*[3], *Humphrey*[2], *John*[1]) was born on 1 Aug 1971. He married Jane Marse on 23 Aug 1992 at Houston, TX.

Children of Adam Thompson[15] Brock and Jane Marse are as follows:

    i.   CANDACE NICHOLE[16]; born 3 Apr 1992.

    ii. DREW CURTIS; born 29 May 1993.

FAMILY PICTURES

Rachel Pratt (Viall) Johnson
Wife of Charles Alvah Johnson

George John Johnson
Son of Ira Johnson

Abel Pratt Johnson
Son of Charles Alvah and Rachel Pratt Johnson

William Warren Johnson of New York
Son of Charles Alvah and Rachel Pratt Johnson

Moriah Merrill Johnson
Wife of William Warren Johnson of New York

Charles Victor Johnson
Son of Charles Alvah and Rachel Pratt Johnson
And his wife, Emily Spann Johnson

Charles Victor Johnson
Son of Charles Alvah Johnson and Rachel Pratt Johnson

Emily Spann Johnson
Wife of Charles Victor Johnson

Hiram Alvah Johnson, Sr.
Son of Charles Alvah Johnson and Rachel Pratt Johnson

Hiram Alvah Johnson, Sr.
and Elizabeth Jane Whitley Johnson

Hiram Alvah and Elizabeth Jane Whitley Johnson

439

Nancy Johnson Brown
Daughter of Charles Alvah and Rachel Pratt Johnson

William H. Brown

440

Emmorancy Johnson Hall
Daughter of Charles Alvah and Rachel Pratt Johnson

Hiram Alvah Johnson, Sr.

Elizabeth Jane Whitley Johnson

Sophronia Johnson Dilmore
Daughter of Abel Pratt Johnson
And her husband, Richard Dilmore

Monroe and Emma Johnson Ransom
Emma Johnson, the daughter of Charles Victor and Emily Spann
Johnson of Illinois

Emma Johnson on left
Unknown person on right

Abel P. Johnson
Son of Charles Victor and Emily Spann Johnson

447

John Charles Johnson
Son of Hiram Alvah Johnson, Sr. and
Elizabeth Jane Whitley Johnson

Hiram Alvah Johnson, Sr. Family
Back Row: Francis, Rachel, Thurston, Hiram, Warren
Front Row: George Hiram, Sr., Elizabeth Jane, and John

John Charles and Violetta Gunsaules Johnson
and Lizzie

John Charles Johnson
Son of Hiram A. and Elizabeth Jane Whitley Johnson

Violetta Gunsaules Johnson
Wife of John Charles Johnson of Oregon

George Washington Johnson
Son of Hiram Alvah Johnson Sr.
and Elizabeth Jane Whitley Johnson

George Washington Johnson
Son of Hiram A. Johnson, Sr.
and Elizabeth Jane Whitley Johnson

Hiram Alvah Johnson, Jr. Family
Standing: Hiram III, Anna Grabenhorst Johnson, Myrtle, Ed
Seated: Claude, Amanda Jones Johnson, Marjorie, Hiram, Jr. and
Evelyn and Creta

Baby Robert Johnson, Hiram (known as Dick) Johnson III, William
Grabenhorst and Henry Grabenhorst

Myrtle Johnson
Daughter of Hiram A. Johnson, Jr.
and Amanda Jones Johnson

Herbert Johnson
Son of Francis (Frank) M. Johnson
and Emma Cosper Johnson

William Warren Johnson Family of Oregon
Back Row: Lulu, Charles, Eldon, Lloyd and Hester
Front Row: Leon, William Warren, Caroline Harris Johnson, and
Ada

Frank M. Johnson, Herbert T,
and Emma Cosper Johnson

Samuel Thurston Johnson
Son of Hiram Alvah Johnson
and Elizabeth Jane Whitley Johnson

Samuel Thurston Johnson

Rachel Johnson Earl Harritt

John, Chester, and Lizzie Johnson Daniel

Charles Virgil Johnson
Son of John Charles and Violetta Gunsaules Johnson

Maud Ethel Rundlett Johnson
Wife of Charles Virgil Johnson

Pearl Inez Johnson Shaw Stuart
Daughter of John Charles and Violetta Gunsaules Johnson

Etta Johnson Simpson
Daughter of John Charles and Violetta Gunsaules Johnson

William Warren Johnson of Oregon

John Charles Johnson Family
Standing: Pearl, Charles Virgil, and Etta
Seated: Archie James, Violetta, John Charles, and Lizzie

Linnie Young Johnson
Wife of Archie James Johnson

L to R: Ada May Johnson Mothershead, Hester Johnson Goodman,
and Lulu Johnson McHargue

Lulu, Leon, Toiley and George Iaeger, Sr.

473

Cleo Johnson Porter
Daughter of Archie James Johnson
And wife of Jack Porter

George Johnson Iaeger, Sr.
and Ada May Mothershead

John Charles and Violetta Gunsaules Johnson Family
On ground L-R: Doris Shaw, Wanda Johnson, Orlo Johnson, and
Charles Garth Johnson
Seated L-R: Pearl Johnson Shaw, Etta Johnson Simpson, A.J.
Johnson, Violetta Gunsaules Johnson, John Charles Johnson, and,
Lizzie Johnson
Back Row, L-R: Bert Shaw, Ruth Simpson Wagner, Elmo Johnson,
Linnie Young Johnson, Jack Porter, Zeta Johnson, Cleo Johnson
Porter, Chester Daniel, Lizzetta Tim Daniel, John Daniel, Darrell
Johnson, and Maud Rundlett Johnson

Doris Shaw Parsons

Zelma Simpson and Ruth Simpson
Daughters of Etta Johnson Simpson

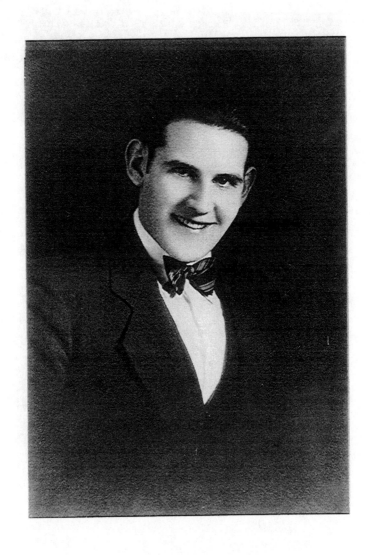

Charles Garth Johnson
Son of Charles Virgil and Maud Rundlett Johnson

Violette Marie Brewer Johnson
Daughter of Edgar J. and Grace M. Wilson Brewer
and Wife of Charles Garth Johnson

Archie James and Linnie Young Johnson
Left to right: children: Elmo, Zeta, and Cleo

Linnie Young Johnson
Wife of Archie James Johnson

Archie James Johnson, Sr.
Son of John Charles and Violetta Gunsaules Johnson

Acle Francis Johnson, Sr. and his wife,
Josephine Louisa Sanders Johnson

Acle Francis Johnson, Sr.

Children of Acle Francis Johnson, Jr. and Ann Agnes Cody Johnson
Left to Right: Michael S. Johnson, Kathleen Ann Johnson Paine,
Stephen Francis Johnson, Keith Thomas Johnson, Laura L. Johnson
Rossignol, and Shelly Marie Johnson Traumuller

Seven grandchildren of Acle F. Johnson, Jr. and Ann Agnes Cody
Johnson
Left to Right: Jason Johnson, Jennifer Johnson, Leah Traumuller,
Elyse Rossignol, Travis Paine,
Evan Traumuller, and Michael J. Johnson, Jr.
(not pictured: Kevin G. Johnson, and Seth Al Paine)

Acle Francis Johnson, Jr. and Ann Cody Johnson

Clarence Brown and wife, Carrie Cleland Brown

Clarence Brown

C. Donald Brown

Helen Brown Adams and Connie Brown McElwain

Carson and Martha Clark Buck
(Martha, daughter of Mabel E. Brown Clark)

Four Brown Generations
Front: Left, Emily McElwain Gorton and Jack,
and Helen Brown Adams
Back row: Connie Brown McElwain holding Kelly Gorton

Four Generations of William H. Brown Family
Seated Left: William H. Brown
Front: Charles Hiram Brown, son of Wm.
Right: Clarence Brown, son of Charles Hiram.
Center back: C. Donald Brown, son of Clarence Brown

Lloyd Leroy Johnson and Bertha Clark
Son of William Warren Johnson of Oregon

Richard Brown, Edwards, NY

Nancy Anne Ticknor
and Gerald Garth Johnson

LeAnne M. Johnson
and Michael A. Shaw

Lisa Marie Johnson
and Robert H. Ford

Aaron Johnson Shaw

Ryan Michael Shaw

James R. Ford
and Blake H. Ford

Geoffrey Garth Johnson

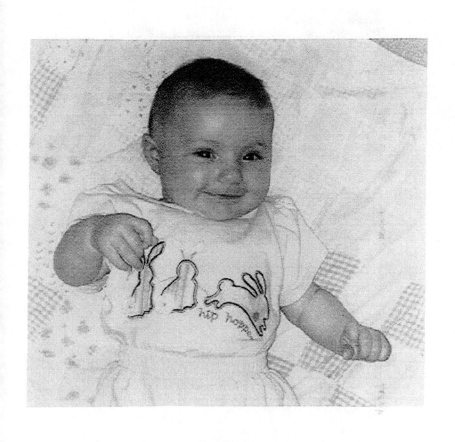

Samantha Jane Ford
Daughter of Lisa Johnson Ford and Robert H. Ford

Richard D. Brown and Barbara Fulton Brown

Back row, left to right: Rose Waits and Justin Waits
Front row, left to right: Cian Waits and Jamie Waits

Left to Right:
Chris Waits, Kathy Buck Waits, Dean Waits, Sarah Waits

Alvah Percival Brown

Charles Hiram Brown

Anne Therese, Daniel Joseph, Nina Louise, Joseph Anthony, and
Mary Elizabeth Buck Spadaro

Left to Right: Mark Christopher Mattus, Michael C., Anne Therese
Spadaro Mattus holding Mary Louise, and
Anthony P. Mattus

Left to Right: Rev. Timothy and Pamela Raven, Amee M. Raven
Spadaro, Daniel J. Spadaro, Mary Buck Spadaro, and Joseph A.
Spadaro

Robert Scott Walters, Nina Louise Spadaro Walters
Children: Left, Rebecca M., middle, Claire T. and, right, Joseph M.
Walters

Sarah Grant and Alvah P. Brown

Mabel Brown, daughter of
Charles Hiram Brown and Martha Noble Brown

Charles Clark

L to R: Charles Clark, Richard Connors, Harriet Clark, and
Gertrude Miner

Robert Boprey

Deborah, Courtney, David and Joshua Boprey

Shannon, Josiah, and Daniel Colbert

Kellie Boprey and Jack Reakes

Keith Barnes

Christopher and Anthony Boprey

Brandon and Corinna Phelix

Back: Gervaise, Lawrence and Olney Boulet
Front: Gerald, Louise, Arthur, Bernard, Lottie Boulet

Connor, David, Kim, Brandon, and Taylor McNeil

Cynthia Barnes Poff

Cody Satkowski

Marcia and Alex Satkowski

Corey Spencer

Keith and Bonnie Barnes

Brianne and Andy Cobb

Alexander Satkowski V

Arielle Satkowski

Thomas Spencer

Edwin Boprey

Reatha Hall Boprey

Jackie and George Spencer

Front: Clifford, Ellison, Reatha and Glenn Hall
Back: Leon and Mayme Hall

Mayme Clary Hall

Leon Hall

Harriet Clark

Left to Right
Eliza Cameron, Miles Cameron, Dort Cameron, Kirtley Horton
Cameron, Seth Cameron, Betsy Cameron, and Sarah Cameron

Richard and Gwen Connors

Back Row, L to R: Debby Connors, Amy Klima, Tom Connors
Front Row, L to R: Laura Klima Richards, Kelley Richards, and
Raymond Richards

FAMILY LETTERS

1847 – 1908

Letter from Hiram Alvah Johnson, Sr. to his mother and father, Charles Alvah Johnson and Rachel Pratt Viall Johnson and to his brothers and sisters in NY prior to going to Oregon from Illinois:

Pittsfield [Illinois]
Feb 16, 1847

Dear father and Mother: I improve this opportunity of writing a few lines to let you know that we are all well. I received your letter of the 24 Jan. this morning and was glad to hear from you all once more. I received Abel's [brother of Hiram] letter the 23 of Jan. and was very glad to hear from him. There is now a letter in the office for Charles [brother of Hiram] that came today from Edwards [NY]. Charles's family is well. He will write to you soon. We have been very healthy this winter. I now weigh 200 pounds. I am fixing to move to Oregon in the spring and I do not anticipate any danger from the Indians. You must not think I am going out of the world so that you cannot hear from me anymore for I expect there will be a mail route from here to Oregon in a short time and I expect there will be a railroad in a few years. Mother do not be uneasy about me. You shall hear from me often an[d] if I have good luck I will come and see you again in four or five years. I remain your son.

E. J. [Elizabeth Jane Whitley] Johnson and
H.A. Johnson

to: [*meaning "letter sent to"*] Charles and Rachel Johnson

I will now write a few lines to William and Nancy [Brown] and Alfred and Emmy [Hall]. Dear brothers and sisters: I will occupy a portion of this sheet in writing to you. You all feel very near to me and I should be very glad to see you all and I still expect as I told Nancy when I left her to see you all again if we live a few years.

If Oregon is the Country it is represented I shall expect to see you all come to the [this] Country. I think Charles [brother] will go there in a year or two. [he didn't] I will give you a general description of the Country as I can when I get there. I have not much news to write at

534

present. Elizabeth is making some bags to put flour in. Charles and George is playing about the house. It is a rainy day and very disagreeable. Give my respects to Brother Wesley and Sister Harriet [Harmon] and Sister Phila and James [Foster] and Charles, Brother Elihu and Sister Lovina [Phelps] and children. Tell them all I will write to them before I leave the States. I received a letter from Chauncy M. Philps [Phelps] this winter. He was well and getting along well. Write to every chance you can get. I must draw to a close by ascribing ourselves.

Yours,
E. J. Johnson / H.A. Johnson

Dear Brother Warren [William Warren Johnson of NY] and Sister Moriah [William Warren's wife]:

I just received your letter and I hasten to comply with your request. I am glad your [you are] are married for I know you both wanted to be very bad and I think Warren done first rate and Moriah too. And I am glad I had the opportunity of forming an acquaintance with her although it was short. I am happy to acknowledge her as a sister. You appear to express a great desire to accompany me to Oregon. I would like to have you along but I think you are joking about it. I have got me a new wagon done and everything ready as fast as I can. I expect to start about the middle of March. I will write to you again when I get to St. Joseph, Missouri that is the last settlement on the road. I will then write to you every time I meet anyone coming to the States.

We have had a very open winter here. There has been very little snow but considerable cold weather. I want you to write to me when you receive this. Direct your letter to St. Joseph, Missouri as I shall not leave there till the first of May.

H. A. Johnson

[to]: William W. Johnson/Moriah Johnson

535

Brother Abel [brother of Hiram] and Sister Lucy [Abel's wife]:

I will say a few words to you. I have not much more to write anyhow and I believe I will not write it. I am like the fellow that went hunting. He said he did not expect to kill anything anyhow and sure enough he did not.

H. A. Johnson

Letter from Hiram A. Johnson, Sr. to his parents, Charles and Rachel Johnson in Edwards, NY

Camp two miles from St. Joseph [Missouri]
April 28, 1847

Dear Father and Mother: I improve this opportunity in writing a few lines to let you know that we are all well and getting along well. We left Pittsfield [IL] the 5th of April and arrived at this place the 25th the distance about three hundred miles. I expect to have found a letter at this place from you but I have been disappointed. I expect we will leave this tomorrow or next day and cross the Missouri river and take into the wilderness where no white persons live but plenty of savages, we are all in good spirits and anxious to be on our journey. There is about three hundred wagons here and eight or ten hundred individuals. I expect there will be about 6 or 8 thousand souls go through to Oregon this summer. I will write to you again when we all get started and let you know how many there is. Elizabeth is not very stout. [she was pregnant with William Warren Johnson who we distinguish as from Oregon so as not confuse with William Warren Johnson of NY, brother of Hiram]. She will be confined in a few days but she as anxious to start as we should not have started this Spring and so we will trust to Providence and do the best we can. My cattle all looks well and stand it first rate. We have had no bad luck yet. The weather has been fine. I am in a great hurry and not much time to write. The prairie is green and covered with cattle and

536

everything looks fine. You will hear from me often. So no more at present but remain your affectionate son.

Hiram A. Johnson

[to] Charles and Rachel Johnson

If you can hear of any chance to send a letter to Oregon I want you to do it. Direct it to Polk County, Oregon Territory.

Letter to Charles V. Johnson [Pittsfield, IL] from Hiram A. Johnson, Sr. on First Day at End of the Oregon Trail

Oregon City
Sep 17, 1847

Dear Brother and Sister: I improve the present opportunity of writing a few lines to you to let you know we have all arrived safe in Oregon and are all well and have been well ever since I last wrote to you. We got along well without the loss of property although we got tired of traveling and our cattle got very much worn down. We have gone into a house three miles from Oregon City but I expect to leave here in a few days and go up the valley fifty or sixty miles [to near now what is known as Jefferson, Oregon] to settle myself. I have not had a chance to look around yet and therefore I cannot give you any satisfaction about this country. Oregon City is a very prosperous looking place and bound to be a place of great business. There is the greatest water power at this place I ever saw in my life but the Country around is heavy timbered and quite rough but all agree that the upper part of the valley is a beautiful prairie country. Crops is quite light here this season owing to the hard winter. I've not much news to write at present but I will write to you the first opportunity in the Spring. I believe this to be one of the healthiest Country in the world but I would not advise you to start to this Country till you hear from me again. Be sure and write to me in the Spring. Give my respects to all my friends. Send my best wishes to fathers folks.

537

So no more at present but remain yours.

Affectionate brother,
Hiram A. Johnson

Letter to William and Nancy Johnson Brown from Hiram and Elizabeth Johnson.

Santiam City [Oregon]
Dec 20, 1852

Dear Brother and Sister: Yours of Sept 21st came to hand by the last mail and I improve this opportunity of answering it. We was very glad to hear from you and glad to see you are punctual in answering my letters. And I will try and not be behind you in writing to you. We are all well with the exception of bad colds. It is a general time of health in this Country except some cases of mountain fever with the new emigrants. We are enjoying a cold spell of winter at present there has been four or five inches of snow on the ground for nearly a week but I think it will not last long.

I wrote a letter to Mother little over a month ago and informed her of the increase in our family and you will see by that letter that you spoke to[o] late in regard to the name. In regard to what I said when I went home about you girls I have forgotten I wish some information on that subject. Nancy when you write I want you to give me more particulars about the connections and old acquaintances. What has become of cousin Julia and Jan and Ann Laidlaw and Sally Allen. [?] And what has become of Aunt Lydia Harmon and James Harmon and everything that you can think of that would be interesting to me. Let me know what Warren's children's names is. Tell Warren he will have to do better than this or he will never have any boys to help him hoe that corn. And you must say it will never do to give up so Mr. Brown [William Brown, husband] for you must have someone to help you wash them dishes.

Tell Abel I can't wait much longer for him to come and build my barn. I intend to build it next Spring. It will be 36 x 48 feet with 15 foot posts. It will cost about 500 dollars. Pink had a calf last night. Old White face and Cherry had theirs last week. Nothing more of importance. Give our love to Mother and all the friends and connections.

Yours Respectfully
Hiram A. Johnson
E. J. Johnson

Letter to Mother [Rachel Pratt Viall Johnson] from Hiram A. Johnson, Sr., and Elizabeth J. Johnson

Santiam City [Oregon]
Oct 23, 1853

Dear Mother, Today is Sunday. There is no meetings news that I know of. We thought of going to Mr. Wells to see their sick child and I started out in the prairie to get a mare for Elizabeth to ride but the mare that I saw turned out to be a cow and so I turned back and as I cannot think of anything that will be more profitable I will talk to you a little while. We are all well except some of the children have a diarrhea. There is a good many children that have this complaint at present and some have died with it. I got a letter from Emmy [sister Emmorancy Johnson Hall] the last of last month and answered it the first of this month. The weather is still warm and dry. We had the first frost last night to kill anything in the garden. We have had considerable rain in the forepart of the Fall so that the grass looks fine and stock is doing well.

But the leaves of the trees seem to know that fall is here and frost or no frost they turn yellow and fall to the ground and there is no season of the year that reminds us so much of home and childhood days as the fall of the year when the nights begin to get long and we begin to sit up around the brisk fire and see the children scampering around the house. Then our mind naturally goes back to our own native

539

home when we to[o] was a child and our own dear Mother used to sit and knit or sew and talk to us of her childhood days and our dear Father could divert our young minds by his early adventures in that then new country. But those days is past. Since that time we have taken the parting hand with our friends started out on the voyage [voyage] of life to transact business for ourselves traveled in what we then called a distant land. Again returned to the land of our father's, renewed those bonds of love and friendship with those we held most dear, again said farewell. Since that time a dear father has been laid in the cold grave and we have traveled in a far distant land yes we are on the opposite side of the continent of north America from you. We are on the waters that flow into the Pacific while you are on those that flow into the Atlantic and the question naturally arises, shall we ever see each others faces again. Shall we ever again have the privilege of extending the hand of friendship and greeting a dear Mother and brothers and sisters and telling to each other our adventures, our joys and sorrows that has befell us since last we parted. I hope we may but I fear that pleasure is not in store for us. When I read Emmy's last letter and hear her say that Mother has so many poor spells that she is afraid she is not long for this world it gives me great pain to think that my dear Mother must pass off the stage of action and I cannot have the pleasure of seeing her again and help to smooth the bed of death for her as she passes from this stage of existence to fairer worlds above. But such is life. Today we are surrounded with parents and children and soon they are gone. Some to try the realities of the unknown world and some in distant lands where we can see them no more. But why indulge in thought of this kind. We all have our part to act and our destiny assigned us and we must not repine the Lord does all things well therefore let us hope for the best. I have not much news that would interest you. The emigrants continue to arrive though think they are nearly all in. There was two or three hundred wagons took a new route according to report and it is feared that they are in a suffering condition. The emigrants has had good health this season but have lost a good deal of stock on the plains. The country is settling up very thick and good claims is getting scarce. Give our respect to all the children. Tell them to write often. I shall expect a letter from you as [soon] as possible as you receive this. I am very anxious to get your likeness

540

[photo]. I understand from some of the children that you had one taken but it did not suit you exactly but if you have not a chance to get another taken send it along.

Yours respectfully
Hiram A. Johnson
Elizabeth J. Johnson

[to]: Rachel [Pratt Viall] Johnson

Letter to Rachel [Pratt Viall] Johnson from her son, Hiram A. Johnson, Sr.

May 15, 1854

Dear Mother: Again I write you a few lines to let you know that we are still well though Rachel has been quite unwell for a few days past but she is better now. I hope this will find you all well. I will continue to write once a month knowing how anxious you are to hear from us. I wrote those verses on the opposite page because I saw them in the Record [Christian Record, a newspaper] and fancied them. I hope others will not be verified in our call especially the first three verses.

I see [saw] a man the other day that lives near here that was formerly from St. Lawrence [St. Lawrence County, NY]. He tells me he is going back there on a visit this fall and says he will go and see you. I know it would be some satisfaction to you to see a man from this country. His name is Magone his people live in Ogdensburg [NY]. Crops look fine this Spring. The boys is going to school. They are very anxious to go to school and are learning fast. The fact is my children is all rather uncommon smart. Try and get the boys and girls to write often. Give our respects to all inquiring.

Yours as ever
Hiram A. Johnson

Here follows [are] the verses afore mentioned:
"We meet on earth no more" from the Christian Record,
May 15, 1854

1. We are scattered, we are scattered
    And upon the ocean wide
    On mountains high and in the glens
    And by the green hillside.
    Wherever we wander on the earth
    The voices of yore
    Are speaking in all sounds we hear
    We meet on earth no more.

2. We are scattered from the haunts of youth
    Of merriment and play
    And from the old brown homestead
    We have wandered far away.
    And thro the wide, wide world we roam
    And on the sea or shore
    The voice comes to us again
    We meet on earth no more.

3. We meet no more, we meet no more
    how sadly tolls the bell
    how mournfully the cadences
    upon the soft winds swell
    a sadness falls upon the heart
    we never felt before
    as a small voice ever says
    we meet on earth no more.

4. Hope beams upon the lonely heart
    The word of God is given
    To win us from the paths of sin
    And turn our steps to Heaven
    Where we shall meet the loved and lost
    Upon the golden shore
    Where tears and sighing never comes

Where parting is no more.

*Letter to Rachel Pratt Viall Johnson from John Charles Johnson,
her grandson*

Santiam City [OR]*
Nov 26, 1854
[*called Jefferson, OR
after this date]

Dear Grandma, Although I have never seen you yet I have heard my father talk so much about you. I thought I would write you a few lines to let you see how well I can write and to let you know that I would like to see you first rate. I am now twelve years old yet I cannot write very well this being a new country. I have not had a very good chance to go to school but I am determined to improve every opportunity and get the best education I can. Father tells me that if I live till I am grown he will fix me out and met me go the States and see all my relations though it seems to me now that I should not like to leave my folks so long but perhaps by that time I shall be glad to get the chance to go and see you all. I will now come to a close. Give my love to all my uncles, aunts, and cousins. Tell them all to write to me. So goodby[e].

John Charles Johnson

*Letter to William Warren Johnson [Edwards, NY] from Hiram A.
Johnson, Jefferson, Oregon*

Jefferson, Oregon
August 1, 1858

Dear Brother:

Received your letter some four weeks since. We was very glad to hear from you all once more. The reason that I did not answer it immediately I had just written to Nancy [Brown] and had used up all the news I had on hand. We are all well and hope this will find all my friends in your country well. It is very healthy here this summer, in fact I do not know of a sick person in this Country. We have had a beautiful summer. Plenty of rain, not very hot but very comfortable. We are through harvesting our hay and winter crops but there is considerable Spring grain yet to cut. Crops is as good as usual. Corn and vegetables will be better than before. Grass has been god and stock is getting very fat. Harvest hands got from three to four dollars per day. I do not have to hire any. I do most of the cradling and the boys do all the binding and the most of the mowing. They can cradle very well but I rather [like to] cradle than to bind. Charles and George make full hands at most kinds of work. Warren [son, William Warren Johnson] can mow very well but his crippled arm prevents him from doing most kinds of work. I intend to keep in school the most of the time. There is a great excitement in the Country and California in regard to new gold mines that have been found on Frazier and Thompson Rivers [Canada] These mines are mostly in the British possessions and extend into Washington territory. They are some four or five hundred miles northeast of here [Jefferson, Oregon]. They are represented to be very rich and extensive. I have not yet seen anyone that has been there. There has been a tremendous rush from California. I suppose there has some twenty or thirty thousand persons already gone to the mines. Some days there is three hundred pack animals pass by here from California going to the mines.

The report is that the water has been to[o] high to work the mines to advantage. But I suppose the water is down now so they can be fairly tested and we will soon know whether they are good or not. The rush of men through our Country caused provisions to take a great raise. Two weeks ago flour was up to 25-30 dollars per barrel. Bacon 50-100 cuts per pound but four or five steamships loaded with flour from San Francisco to Portland brought it down to about 15-18 dollars per barrel. But as I have sent you a paper and shall continue to send to you or Abel occasionally you will have a chance to see or hear of the progress of these mines and of the price of produce merchandise.

For my own part I think thousands are bound to be badly fooled with these new mines. But if they do prove good it will be the making of Oregon and I expect then you will be induced to leave your patch of hoop poles and come to this country. By the way what has become of Abel? I have not heard from him for a long time. Did he get lost up among the Spruce and Hemlock or was down in the swamp towards Hermon [NY] where old man Glaspy used to live? Tell him if he is alive I would like to hear him holler. I had a letter from Charles [Hiram's brother Charles Victor Johnson in Illinois] a short time since. They had another baby and he had to let me know about it. Maybe that's what Abel's waiting for. We have had a vacation in our school for four weeks but it commences again soon. I send six [children] most of the time which makes my school bill extremely high. My bill for the last six months was fifty-three dollars but I am determined to give my children a full education if I have nothing else to give them. But I must come to a close. Give my love to mother. Tell her I think of her often and would like to see her very much but cannot yet see my way clear to come and see you all but I still hope she lives a few years longer. I shall be able to come and see her. I want you all to write often. It gives me great pleasure to hear from my friends. Give my respects to your family and all the brothers, sisters, and friends.

Yours in the Bond of love,
H. A. Johnson

Letter from Abel P. Johnson, son of Charles Victor Johnson and Emily (Spann) Johnson in Illinois, to his parents

St. Louis, Missouri
Sept 1, 1862

Dear Father and Mother

I seat myself again this morning to answer your kind letter and to let you know that I am well and hope when these few lines come to hand

545

they may find you all enjoying the same blessing and I do count it a great blessing for I assure you there is not much comfort here for a sick soldier. [Abel was in the Civil War and was fighting in or near St. Louis, Missouri] There are 8 or 10 sick soldiers in our company. Some of them have been pretty sick. Louis Colvin is very sick at present. The doctor thinks he will die before a great while. They have been trying to get a furlough or leave of absence for him but it is impossible to get one [and] they will not give anyone sick leave, they have to go to the hospital and stay there 10 days unless they get able to join their regiment sooner and at the end of that time if they are still sick, they can go home. But Louis will never live that long if he has to go to the hospital. My health has been very good since I left home. I have had a light spell of the bowel complaint, but that is nothing here in camp. All the boys in the company has had that or nearly all of them. I am well of that though at present. Will and Mode are a little under the weather at this time and William has been rather unwell since he came here. Some of the time [portion not legible] sick though he is better at present and I think he will be all right in a few days.

We are still in Benton Barracks, but I guess we will leave here in a day or so certain. We are drawing our guns at present, but they are very common ones, old muskets worked over, but the Colonel has received them and we have to put up with them. They rather played off on us in the money line. Instead of 40 dollars, they payed [paid] us only $13 dollars. The State of Illinois had to pay it. I do not know whether we will ever get it or not, the Colonel says we will get it in a few days, but he don't know much more about that than I do. Whenever we get it I will send some of it home. I haven't enough worth sending now and I will need the most of it if not all of it. We have had a good many visitors in the last week [portion not legible] Roush has been here several days and Hanner Walkes and old Mrs. Mitchel [l] and Hash, Broody's wife and one or two others are here at present and a good many more are coming down to see their friends before they leave. I would like to see all of you before I get further off but I guess there is no chance at present. I don't want any of you to be uneasy about me, for I intend to take as good care of myself as possible and if I get sick, I have friends all around me that will take as good care of me as possible.

I got my likeness [picture] taken yesterday and I will send it home tomorrow. It is not a very good one but the best I could get at present. They were so crowded that it was almost impossible to get one at all. Tell Mary I will send her one before long whenever I have a good chance to get one.

You can draw some idea of the locality of Benton Barracks by looking at the engraving at the head of his letter. I have just now got my gun and time I got it. Word came from Colonel Baily that I would not have to pack it for he says he is going to keep us in the [portion not legible] as we are at present and as soon as he possibly can he is going to ship us in a brigade band. That is Will and me and Ford Spring, John Pever, Henry Coonrod and some other musicians that are here.

We have also received orders to be ready to march at half past 5 o'clock in the morning to Rolla. They may be countermanded before night.

I believe I have written all I know of at present. My love to the family and friends in general. So no more at present but remain your affectionate son.

A. P. Johnson

To: C.V. Johnson and E. Johnson and family
Still direct our letters as before. Excuse my scribbling for l am in a mighty hurry.

Letter from Abel P. Johnson to his parents, Charles Victor Johnson and Emily (Spann) Johnson

Salem, Missouri
Sept 24, 1862

Dear Father and Mother:

I seat myself again this beautiful morning to write to you a few lines to let you know that I am well at present. I received your letter Pa, dated the 10th and word also came to be by Mr. Barker that you and Mother were quite unwell and also two of the children but I hope that when this comes to hand it will find you all well.

You want to know in the first place how we are and what we do about washing. Well I will tell you just exactly how we manage. As far as the cooking is concerned we manage just as we did in [portion not legible] last winter. We hire it done and pay 50 cents a week and live as well as we would at home or nearly at least. Now about the washing. Well what washing we have done since we left the barracks we done ourselves.

We could get it done by paying 5 cents a shirt which is about as cheap as any one could ask but there was a creek close by and we had to [go] there to bathe so we thought we might just as well take our dirty clothes along and wash them ourselves as to pay for getting it done. Well enough on that subject.

You want to know also whether I have to drill or stand guard. I have to drill every other day and have been on guard duty twice since I left home. We have not got our band yet and I don't know when we will get it, but I am afraid we will not get it at all unless there is different regulations. The Colonel still says that he is bound to have a band, but it will make mighty little difference with me whether he does or not, for I would about as soon be a private as anything else as far as work is concerned the private has the easiest of any but enough on that subject.

We have to keep a sharp lookout here. There has been a good many bush whackers around here but they keep their distances pretty well. I suppose you heard awful news by what has been written back here, that we got into a fight and were all cut to pieces and that I was wounded. Well if we have had a fight I don't know anything about it and if I never get a worse wound than that I will get along first rate.

We are still here at Salem Port [portion not legible] on the [portion not legible] of the Ozark mountains. Our long looked for bounty has come at last and we will draw it tomorrow and also our overcoats all of which will be very acceptable, but I am done for this time. I want you to be sure and answer this letter.

Yours until death,
A. P. Johnson

[Note: Abel P. Johnson was killed May 5, 1863 in the Civil War]

Letter to Charles Victor Johnson and Emily (Spann) Johnson from Hiram A. Johnson

Jefferson, Oregon
Jan 4, 1863

Dear Brother and Sister,

I again take my pen to address you a few lines. We are all well and hope this will find you and yours well. We received a letter from you a short time since the first one for about two years. We was very glad to hear from you once more. We have had a dry fall and winter up to about a week since. We had a little flurry of snow night before last but it was all gone before morning. The weather is warm and pleasant. I have killed my hogs (45) and got the meat hung in the smoker house ready to smoke. I have most of my wheat in the mill ready to be floured. I have sold about six hundred bushels of oats at 50 cts per bushel and have considerable more for sale. Bacon is worth about 15 cents per pound, flour 7.00 dollars per barrel. Dry goods and groceries is high. For instance Sugar 12 to 15 cts coffee 28-30 Syrup 80 to 1.00 dollar per gal, salt 2 ½ factory 28 calico 18 to 20 [portion not legible] 3 to six shoes 1 to 2 Salem factory cloth (all wool) 1 to 2 [dollars per] yard.

I think times is somewhat better than they have been for several years money is more plenty, a good many is getting some money on their war debt (I got 800 dollars of mine) and there is considerable money coming in from the mines [in California]. The most however that come from the times is for supplys [supplies]. The mines in places are very rich and there has been great many men there yet I think that not one in ten has paid their expenses while probably one in twenty has got rich. Those mines however will be a great advantage to this country for making a market for our produce.

I presume the war does not affect us here as it does you in the States. Yet I deeply sympathize with our friends in the States and are very anxious as to the results of this rebellion. This State has already contributed some 19 thousand dollars to the Sanitary fund and are still engaged in the good work.

We have got the poles set for a telegraph from Portland [Oregon] to connect the telegraph from the States at Yreka [California] and expect to have the wire up early in the Spring. It now takes some six to eight days to get news from the Sect of War. We heard of the defeat of Burnside at Fredericksburg nearly two weeks since. We are satisfied someone was greatly to blame for that defeat, but it is hard to tell who. The people in this State are generally in favor of putting down this rebellion at all costs and hazards and are wiling to stand by the administration in all lawful endeavors to [portion not legible] the war yet we do think that with the money and men that have been at the disposal of the President he has not made that progress that might have been made. But we will hope for the best.

I was glad to hear that Abel [son of Charles Victor Johnson] was in the service of his country. That was much better than coming to the mines. I am satisfied that lots of men came to Oregon this season to get out of enlisting in the service. When the war closes we will be glad to see Abel in this country. We stayed all night a short time since with George Cook's folks. They live in Salem [Oregon]. They are well and getting along very well. The friends family Jansen your country [portion not legible] are generally well. Father Whitley [Elizabeth Jane Johnson's father, Samuel Whitley] is failing quite

550

fast. He cannot live many years longer. Him and the old woman [Catherine McNary Whitley] was over to see us a short time since. The old man send his best respects to you. He wants you to tell old Uncle James Burbridge [in Illinois] that he expects to soon leave this world and expects meet him in a better land. The old lady is very healthy.

Julia Ann writes her family [John Shore] lives with the old folks [Whitleys]. She has two boys. Eliza Ann is not very healthy; she has one boy and one girl. Ameline Mandrille has not very good health. She has I believe four children.

I think I have written to you that Catherine died six years ago last June. Her only child died also. Our boys (six) are all going to school this winter. Charles and George are getting to be very good scholars. Charley went to the mines last Spring got home sick and soon came back. He will be 21 next Spring. I believe I am about through. Write soon tell me all the news you can think of. I have forgot how many children you have and their names except Rachel and Abel. Give my best respects to all inquiring friends.

Perhaps you have forgotten the names of our children. Well here they are with their ages. Charles 21 in May, next George 19 in July, next Warren 16 in May, next Alvah [Hiram Alvah Jr.] 14 in March, next Thurston [Samuel Thurston] 12 in March, next Rachel 10 last November, Francis Marion 7 in December last.

Now I will close.

Respectfully yours,

H.A. Johnson
E. J. Johnson

Letter from Charles Victor Johnson, Pittsfield, IL to his brother, William Warren Johnson in Hermon, NY

Dear Brother, I received your kind letter a day or two ago and was so glad to hear from you again. I was still aiming to answer your first letter then I got your last. But I would have wrote again for it affords me the greatest pleasure to hear from you and the rest of my Brothers and Sisters although a quarter of a century has past since we parted probably for the last time. Yet it has not lessened my love and affections for you all although it seems like just days since I gave you the parting hand under the roof of our kind father and mother. Little did I think then it would be the last time but when I take a second thought and consider for a moment that father and mother has gone and at the same time when I look closer at home I see grandchildren a growing up round me, it reminds me that old time has rolled on tolerably rapped but so it is. We will soon have to give way to another generation.

Hope this will find you all well. We are not very well at this time. We have just heard from Abel in the army. He is sick again. He had a spell of fever some weeks ago and got about but has taken a relapse by exposure but I hope he will be well when we hear from him again. The small pox has been tolerable plenty not far from here so I noculated [inoculated] the children, and it has made Rebecca my oldest very sick but she is some better. Her health has been poor for the last eight months.

By what you say about crops in your country, I think we have not much reason to complain. You ought not to complain for you have no business to stay there when you could so easy come to this country where we never fail to raise everything we want to live on. I was never so attached to any place yet but what I would leave it when I know by doing so I could better myself and family. I have no doubt but what you could sell your place for enough to get a good place here. Kansas will be a good country to settle in when this war is over. A man can get 160 acres there just by settling on it and it is the handsomest country ever a man traveled over. I have been through it three different times, it is rich and healthy and mostly prairie.

I raised about 300 bushel of wheat this season. We had about 30 acres of corn. I don't know how much it made I fed a good deal of it to my hogs. I fattened 45 head of hogs I had 50 head of stock of hogs but the cholera has killed 25 of them. I have 30 acres of what on the ground and it looks fine. We have had the warmest winter here so far that I have ever seen in this country. I have ten head of horses. Five of them is over six years old, two of them 3 next Spring, and two colts last spring. I have sold all of my oxen. I sold a fine young mare last Spring.

The regiment my son is in had a fight the other day. Our boys got two killed and wounded 50 of the rebels. Our boys had artillery. The fought at Hartsville, Missouri.

Charles

Letter from Charles Victor Johnson to his sister, Nancy Johnson Brown

Sep 24, 1863
Pittsfield [IL]

Dear Sister Nancy, it has been a lonely time since I have heard from any of you although I wrote last. But I thought I would write again and see if I can get to hear from you. We are all in tolerable good health at present and hope this will find all alive and well, this Cursed rebellion that has been raging for the last two years has robbed me of my only son. He died in a six month campaign in May in 1861. He got home in March 6 and in August after volunteered for three years and on the first day of last May in the Battle of Port Gibson in the State of Mississippi while charge the rebel Batteryne was wounded in the thy [thigh]. His wound was thought to be slight but it proved to be fatal. It throwed him into the lock jaw and he died on the 5th of the same month. But he died a brave soldier his whole soul was devoted to his countries cause in putting down this ungodly rebellion brought on my slaveholders of the south and traitors of the

553

North. But Nancy it is a hard stroke on me. I tried to keep him at home when the war broke out but he said his Country needed him and he must go and so he went and I am robbed of one of the best and bravest of sons he was a noble young man and loved by everybody that knew him but he died a brave soldier and a devoted Christian. Nancy I want you to write to me as soon as you get this and let me know how you are all getting along. Let me know who of our friends have gone into the War if any. Tell what your prospects are concerning the crops in that Country. Crops are tolerable good in this part of the State. In some parts the early frost has done great damage. We had a severe drought the forepart of the season. Had no rain of any amount from March until the latter part of July. But for all that, are [our] wheat crop was splendid and the crop has come out beyond all expectations. There will be lots of crops to sell in this country. Tell me what there has been any drafting in your country yet. Tell Abel [his brother, Abel Pratt Johnson] I want him to write and let me know all what is going on. Tell me whether or not any of our connections is Copperhead. If they are just send them to me with a robe around their neck. I would like to go to your State and help hang that Copperhead Governor you have got there to rule over you. Well Nancy I have got two of the finest grandchildren you ever saw. A boy and a girl. The boy is going on three years old, his name is Charly. Their mother is larger than I am. So no more at present. Give our love to all friends.

C.V. Johnson

Letter to Sisters Nancy Johnson Brown and Emmorancy Johnson Hall from Hiram Alvah Johnson, Sr.

Jefferson, Oregon
Nov. 12, 1871

Dear Sisters Nancy and Emmy

I have concluded after so long a time to write you again. It has been a lone time since I have heard from any of my friends in the East.

554

But probably it is as much my fault as any body for as I get older I find it is quite a job for me to write a letter. We are all well and have enjoyed fair health since you last heard from us. George our second son, and Alvah [Hiram Alvah, Jr.] our fourth son went East of the mountains [Cascade Mountains in Oregon] last Spring with about 125 head of cattle. They are located in Wasco County about 200 miles from here. They were both down to see us this Fall and Alvah was married while he was here to a Miss Savannah Jones. Enclosed you will find Alvah's likeness [picture]. We have had a dry summer and fall. Crops was very good but not quite as good as usual. But the price is enough to make up for quantity. Wheat 1.15 to 1.30 per bushel; oats 75 to 1.00; potatoes 1.00; barley 1.00; butter 40 cts per pound; cheese 20 cts; corn 30-40. Last Spring calves 12, pork 6 ½ cts per pound.

This country is improving and settling up very fast. Land is raising in value and all kinds of property find a ready sale. The railroad is now completed on this East side of the Willamette [River] nearly 150 miles and graded some 40 miles further. It passes about one mile from our house and we hear the locomotive whistle at most all hours of the day. This makes times lively.

We can hear the trains for ten miles each way. The rainy season is now setting in and we expect a long dreary winter but yet we do not expect to freeze our fingers in feeding our stock but we will set in the house and see it rain and our stock will feed [on] the green crass and go in the fir groves and keep warm when it rains hard. I have rented out my farm to a family that lives in my old buildings. I furnish team and hack also our cows about 25 he has commenced plowing and sowing. He intends to put in 200 acres of grain. I get one half the year's hay and butter. So you see that we do not have much to do. We have only two children at home with us now, Rachel and Frank. Rachel is nineteen years old. Today I want her likeness to send to you but she has but one and won't met me have it. Frank is sixteen next month. He is going to school. He is getting a pretty good education. Thurston will be 21 next Spring and is working in a hosiery factory in Jefferson [Oregon].

I was talking all Summer of going East this fall but when it came to the pinch my wife cannot spare me. I have put it off till next fall and can't make any rash promises that I will go then. I think that some of you might come out and see us. I should think that some of your boys would leave that old place and come out to this new country and see their uncle. Tell Alvah [Brown] to leave the East and travel the West awhile and see if he can't find more light down towards sundown. You can make the trip in about ten or twelve days from your home to this place at a cost of about 150 dollars. I believe I have nothing more that would interest you. I want you to write often. There is a man working in the flouring mill at this place name of Erwin from Potsdam [NY]. He is going back for his family next Spring. Tell me all the particulars about all the brothers and sisters and their families. Give my best respects to all the connections and friends.

Very respectfully
H.A. Johnson

Letter to Nancy [Johnson] and her husband, William Brown from Charles Victor Johnson of Illinois

Time [Illinois...near Pittsfield]
Jan 2, 1880

Dear Sister and Brother

After waiting a long time I will try to write to you a few more lines to let you know that we are still alive and in tolerable good health for two old people like us. Emily [Spann, his wife] had a bad spell of asthma again this fall but has got over it again. I am crippled up with [problems with my] hip most of the time but still able to do my chores and cut my firewood. And I tended ten acres of corn this last season and made good corn.

Emma and Roe is living by themselves on the other part of the farm. He keeps some stock and he wanted to be where he could tend to them and be hand to his work. They are with us nearly every day. He helps get my wood and other hard jobs that I can't do handy. My children and grandchildren are all well.

I hope this will find you and your family and all of our friends well and enjoying yourselves. We had a very dry season here but we had a little rain in July, enough to save the corn crop. The wheat made itself without any rain and a fine crop we had. Then in the Fall some rain again enough to save the present crop that is now in the ground. We have got fifty acres sowed on our farm. And it covers the ground. We had the hottest weather in October I ever saw. The mercury was up to 75 and we in the shade. November was a beautiful month. December was tolerable cool. Some of the time only one snow that showed any on the ground. We have had two heavy sleets in the past ten days but it is now warm and is nearly all melted off. We all took diner at Phila's [daughter] yesterday devoured a big turkey and enjoyed ourselves very much.

Nancy ain't it hard that we are so far apart that we can never spend a happy Christmas together. But that seemed to be our lot.

How glad I would be if I could come your town and spend one winter. But I don't suppose I could stand it there through one of them long, dreary winters that you have there. What time I was there liked to have used me up. I was worse off with lungs than I thought I was at the time. I have had to be very careful ever since.

Now Nancy I want you to write to me as soon as you get this. Let me know if you have got out of that prison yet. Tell Warren [their brother William Warren] I would like to know why he never answered my last letter I wrote to him. Well I want you to write some to let me know how you are getting along and how Edwards [NY] is flourishing generally. Let me know how you like Upper Canada. I suppose you have been there since I saw you. I was through where your Brother lives when I came home. I think it is a very good country in there. It is not a great distance from where I used to live with I lived in that country. Tell me how the boys is making it. Well I will quit for this time. Nancy give me James

Harmon's address if you can.   Tell Emma [sister Emmorancy Johnson Hall] and Alfred to write.   Tell Nelly I want her to write me a letter.   We all join in sending our love and best wishes to you and children and all friends.

C.V. Johnson

Letter to Nancy [Johnson] Brown from Hiram A. Johnson

Salem [Oregon]
[After March,] 1881

[It appears that the beginning of the letter may be missing.]

Well we did not sleep quite as well as usual.   You can guess the reason.   But we are all right this morning.   Our election in this state passed off all right and peaceful.   We got away with it for our friend Garfield in good style.   [President Garfield was elected March 4, 1881 and was shot to death in September, 1881]   I was glad to see that old St. Lawrence [St. Lawrence County, NY] gave her usual Republican majority.   New York did splendid.   I am still running the Justice of the Peace office and the County Treasurers office.   I have a nice office in the Court House.   Wood, lights, and stationery are all furnished free.   I have received and disbursed about twenty thousand dollars since the first of July.   Now my dear sister I want you to write me a long letter.   Tell me all the news.   What are you all doing.   Is Wm. Martin still living?   What is the boys up to?   Does William [Nancy Johnson Brown's husband] work any now?   Tell about Warren's folks [Warren is William Warren Johnson, the brother of Hiram, Nancy, et al]   Tell him to write to me.   Wesley Harmon and Harriet still living?   How is Phila [Viall Harmon] and her folks?   Ask Emmy what the reason she never writes me a word.   Tell me all about her and Alfred [Hall] and the children.   Then there is Cornelia Rushton.   I used to think back then that she was a pretty nice kind of girl but perhaps I was mistaken as she won't speak to me since I was there.   Is James and Susan [Viall] Foster still living?   Well you see what I want. I want you to tell about the whole family and tell them all to write to me. Love to all.

Yours truly
H A Johnson

Letter to Nancy [Johnson] and William Brown from her brother, Charles Victor Johnson

Independence [Il]
March 25, 1883

Dear Sister and Brother

I got your kind letter yesterday and was glad to hear from you once all once more, but I am so sorry to hear of your poor health and Phil [Viall Harmon] it looks like she will never enjoy anymore good health. I was the most surprised to hear of Warren's [William Warren Johnson] affliction. I thought if there was a stout healthy one in our family it was Brother Warren. He was the very picture of health when I was there. I'm so sorry I did not know it last summer [1882]. We have a lady here that cures cancer in the first stage. Her left the secret with her when he died. I have known her father to cure a good many. He never used any medicine.

My family are all in tolerable good health. My wife does not have the asthma as bad as she used to. I am not very stout. I am used up generally. Well I am old and my work is about done. I can do chores round some. I am not able to work on the farm any more. Emma and Roe owns part of the old farm and we all live together. He works the back place. They got only one child little Warren [Ransom]. He will soon be six years old. I have three little grandsons about the same age. We have them here all together every two or three weeks then they make it lively.

Mary my oldest still lives in Missouri. [Mary Johnson married John Nicholson]   Five of their children is grown. Their oldest girl is

559

married. Charley their boy is of age. Mary's man has very poor health. He came to see me last summer.

It seems that you have had an old fashioned winter back there. I pity you. We had about six weeks very cold and the balance has been nice. One month good sleighing which was a great treat. We had a sleet that fell four inches solid ice. It was grand. It all went off in February. March has been beautiful so far. Feed is plenty. Thousands of shucks of corn fodder will have to be burnt to get it out of the way. We raised fine crops here last season. We have sold some of our stock. We only have eight cows now. We don't mile all of them, let the calves run with them, we have seven head of horses, stocks of all kinds is very high here, corn 50 cents, wheat one dollar. Potatoes one dollar. We raised a plenty to do us last season. Last year we had to pay 150 cents a bushel for all we used and have used

Susan [Viall] and James Foster has moved to the North part of this State some 250 miles from where I live. I have promised them that I will go and see them. I aim to go next month if I am well enough to make the trip. I would like so well to go down and see you all once more if I could. I have given up ever seeing any of your again unless I go there. I don't know that will ever be.

Now Nancy I want you to write again when you get this. Tell all about Warren's trouble, how it commenced and all about it. [he had cancer] William [Brown] I want you to tell me about Westminster and London [Canada]. London was a new place when I was there. I am taking a paper published in London. Give our love to all. I will quit for this time.

To: Nancy and William

From C. V. Johnson
And Emily Johnson

Letter to Nancy [Johnson] Brown from John Charles Johnson, son of Hiram Alvah Johnson, Sr.

Scio [Oregon]
Dec 7th 1885

Dear Aunt Nancy

I have not received any answer from the last letter I wrote you. We are all well. I have sent you the picture of Father's and Mother's family. We had them taken about 2 weeks ago. There is 7 children and we all got together the lst time for 18 years. I will send you a paper giving account of the meeting. I and George are setting by the side of father and mother and the next oldest stands to the right as you look at the picture it is Warren. Next Alvah next Thurston next Rachel next Francis. I sent a picture with yours to cousin Charles Johnson. Father is going to send the other folks a picture when Charly Johnson explains to him the position of the children. I never have regretted the trip I made to see you all and I never shall forget you. Tell all the relatives that I have not forgotten them. Tell Charly and Alvah to write to me. My business is as good as usual. We have had a mild winter so far. I hope some of the folks will come out some time. I sent on picture to Uncle Charles [Charles Victor Johnson in IL]. When you see the pictures you will see just how we all look for it is all natural. Write to me and give me all the news.

So good bye, Yours
J.C. Johnson

Letter to Nancy [Johnson] Brown from John Charles Johnson, son of Hiram Alvah Johnson, Sr.

Scio [Oregon]
April 24th 1886

Dear Aunt Nancy

I have been intending to write to you for some time. Our folks are all well. Our winter is over and everything looks green and nice. It

561

would like very much to see all you folks once more and I hope to make the trip sometime again. I will send you a picture of my oldest boy that he had taken a few days ago. You can see he had his overcoat on. I have sold out of the dry goods business. I sold to my brother Alvah [Hiram Alvah Johnson, Jr.] and my old partner Shelton. My boy Archie [Archie James Johnson] is working for them. He has hired to them for one year. He gets $60.00 per month. He went to business college this winter in Portland. [Oregon]. He got a diploma. He is a fine salesman and stock keeper. I am on our county ticket for office this year. I don't know whether I will make it or not. The democrats are about 300 majority in this county but I will get a good many democrats. Here at home my friends say I will be elected. George has a daughter [Rose E. Johnson] about 16 years old that is very bad off. She had the diphtheria and came very near dying. After she got over that she became paralyzed. She cannot talk nor swallow. She appears to have no use of herself. She is improving a little and we hope she will get better but she is very bad. I visited at Salem over Sunday and came home Monday. Show my letter to all the folks and tell them I very often get to thinking about all of them and be very glad to see them all again. We have a revival meeting here this month by the Baptist Church and Christian Church after the Baptist closed. They were both as fine meetings as we ever had here. I met with Bro. Rugg at Salem. [Bro. Rugg is likely George Ruggles Johnson son of William Warren Johnson of NY, and a grandson of Charles Alvah Johnson of Edwards, NY.] I told him about all you folks. He was glad to know someone that had been there. They had a revival in Salem [Oregon]. Over 200 persons confessed religion. Write to me a long letter.

J.C. Johnson

Letter to Nancy [Johnson] and William Brown from Charles Victor Johnson, Nancy Brown's brother

Independence [IL]
May 10, 1886

Dear Sisters and Brothers

I received your kind and long looked for letter a week or two ago. I was so glad to hear from you all once more. To hear that you will still in the land of the living and well and doing well. It is a great satisfaction to me to hear from you even if I can't have the pleasure of seeing you. Nancy I know you or Will [iam] might come and see me. I know you are amply able to come. We can't take any money or property with us when we are called on to leave the shores of time. We ought to see all the pleasure we can what little time we have to stay here. I am glad to say to you that we are as well as usual. My wife is hardly ever clear of the Phthic but her health other ways is very good. My health is better than it was two years ago. I am taking the world as easy as I can. I want to say here with family and friends as long as I can, but when the Master calls I am ready to go to meet those dear ones that have gone on before. I often think of that happy meeting it will be there to meet our dear children and Father and Mother and Brothers and Sisters that are waiting for the rest of us on the other shore. I am sure we will all know each other in the spirit land. We have had a fine spring here. The forest has been green for three weeks or more. Meadows and Pastures nearly big enough to mow. Stock getting fat on the grass. The prospects for wheat is much better than last year. We are selling cream to the creamery again this Spring. It pays very well. They come after it themselves. We have twelve cows but we are only milking half of them yet but they are good ones that we milk.

I was out to see my children in Missouri last fall. While I was there my grandson and granddaughter and great grandson came home from California. I had a good visit with them. Charley Johnson [John Charles Johnson of Oregon] was with me. I tell you he had a good time. I hated to part with Charley. He is a noble man. In a letter from him and Hiram the other day they were all well except one of George's [George Washington Johnson of Oregon] girls. She had diphtheria and was partially paralyzed. He has sold out his store. He says he is now going to take world easy. He is not a candidate for State Senator. My granddaughter and her oldest sister has gone back to California and her Father went with them to see the country.

Our children that is here come to see us generally every two weeks. I have a grandson here nearly as large as I am. I have three more that is about nine years old. They make things lively when they get together. I have to granddaughters here that is grown. Well as I have no news to write that would interest you I will quit for the present. I want you to write often. Tell Emmy to write. I want Phila to write to me. We all join in sending our love and best wishes to you and family and all inquiring friends. So good bye to all.

C. V. Johnson

Tomorrow I will be seventy one years old. My wife is seventy one past.

Letter to Sister Nancy [Johnson] Brown from Hiram A. Johnson

Salem, Oregon
July 29, 1888

Dear Sister Nancy

I have not heard from any of you for a long time. Have forgotten who wrote last. But perhaps if I write you will answer. We have not had as good health this last Spring as usual be. We are very well now. The last I heard from Phila [Viall Harmon] her was bad. I am anxious to hear from her and all the rest of you. The children and their families all very well except Rachel's husband. [John W. Harritt, second husband] He has not been well for years. They are in California now for his health. We have had a fine season here.

Crops of all kinds are abundant. Fruit is very fine. We have had a few warm days but this is a fine climate. There is a great many strangers coming to this country and it is filling up fast. There is many passing through from California where they have been attending the U.S. Teachers Celebration. They are well pleased with the Country. We had a great surprise party at our house the other night of which I will send you an account of in a slip from our City paper. When I look back over this 47 years and think of what has happened in that time, I am truly surprised. Our father, mother, brother, and our sister have gone down to the grave with some of our children and many of our friends and our lives are still spared. We hope for some good purpose. But our stay here is but of short duration. But I am persuaded and satisfied that if we live right a little while longer we will meet again in those "mansions" that our savior has gone to prepare for his children. Write and tell me all about the friends and connection. Love to all. Remember me to William and the boys and all the brothers and sisters.

Yours as ever
H.A. Johnson

Letter to Nancy [Johnson] Brown from Emma [Johnson] Ransom

Pittsfield [IL]
August 21, 1889

Dear Aunt

I will now send you your pictures as I promised. I have only just got the one home that we used. I had my pictures made as you advised. Just head and shoulders. This leaves us all tolerable well. Mother has had tolerable fair health this summer. I hope this will find you all well. We would like to hear from you all soon. Aunt I have forgotten who you said had the picture of Pa with me by him. Now I would so like to have it and if the one who has it will give it to me I will give them in return one of the new pictures I got of Pa's. Now don't forget to get it for me. Aunt Nancy I will send you my boys' picture that is his little dog laying by him. I would like to have your picture and Uncles to go in my Cabinet Album. I will try and write more next time. I will have to quit this time as I have a chance to send it to the Office. I thought the pieces of your dresses was so nice. The silk is beautiful. I always wanted one but have never got

565

able to afford it yet. Now please don't forget about that picture. And write soon. From your loving niece.

Emma Ransom

P.S. I will send you one of mine and my husband's pictures. They are tolerable dark but I guess they are like us.

Letter to Nancy [Johnson] Brown from Hiram A. Johnson

Salem, Oregon
April 18, 1890

Dear Sister Nancy: After so long a time I will try and answer your last letter. I had depended on Charley or Rachel to write you as I have been so nervous since I was sick. That it was with difficulty that I could write my name but I think they have not done so yet. I was much surprised and very sorry to hear of the death of our dear sister Emma [Emmorancy Johnson Hall]. It appears that she took sick the same day that I did the 19th of December last. I had a very severe attack of brain and lung fever that lasted nearly two months. For several days my life was despaired of and the doctors thought I must die and I cam to that conclusion myself but I felt that I was as ready as I ever would be and expressed myself as willing to go but our kind Heavenly Father desired otherwise and so I am still here but of course cannot expect to remain very long. I would like to have some more of the particulars of Emma's death. Express my sympathy and sorrow to Alfred and the dear children. I now have to announce to you the death of our son-in-law John Earl. Rachel takes it very hard. They never had any children. She will still make her home with us. I enclose you a slip from our local paper in regard to his death. I am regaining my health again but am not as well as formerly.

I have fell off about 40 pounds in weight. Charley and Alvah have both moved to Salem. Al is in business as you see by the heading of this. George is still in business here and doing quite well. Charley has accumulated considerable property in speculating land and city property here and in Seattle, Wash. We are having a wet [and] cold backward Spring. I take a great of satisfaction with my children and grandchildren. I keep a horse and buggy and do considerable riding around. Our folks are all quite well. Please write me again. Tell us more about all the connection. Give our love to all the friends and connections.

Very truly your brother
H A Johnson

Letter to Nancy [Johnson] Brown from her niece, Emma [Johnson] Ransom, daughter of Charles Victor Johnson

Apr 20, 1893

Dear Aunt: We received your letter and was so sorry to hear of Aunt Phila's [Viall Harmon] death. But we all have to go when we are called and there is few that live to the good old age. She did. Where is her son James [Harmon]? You know I have seen him. He was here when he was on his way back from Missouri to New York. How does he get along with his wife now? I thought it seemed so strange for him to go back and marry her again after they divorced. But there is lots of strange things happening now days. This leaves us all well except colds. I hope that it will find you all well. Mother is well but she can't see well enough to write. She send her love to all of you. Have you heard anymore from Uncle Hiram? Please write and tell me all about Elva. I mean Uncle Warren's [William Warren Johnson of NY] daughter. How is getting along and how many children she has. When we was young we wrote to each other so much. But I have not heard from her for several years. I think I told you that sister Becca's [Rebecca Emily Johnson Miller, daughter of Charles Victor Johnson] other girl was married last July. She married her sister's step son. They all live in Scott County. Becca just has one boy with her now. He is 16 years old. Charles, her oldest son, is working for his brother-in-law over in Scott County. So you see we are left without much family now. Just my boy and

567

her one boy. When her children was all at home they was with us as much as they was with her. You don't know how I miss them and I miss the girls help so much. I have had so much work to do this winter. I have sold over two hundred lbs. of butter since the first of January.

Well I must tell you what nice weather we are having. It has rained for two days and today is trying to snow. We have had some nice weather this Spring. We have planted potatoes and made garden. My garden stuff is all up large enough to hoe. I have 75 little chickens but this cold rain is hard on them. Our peach trees are all in bloom but there's no prospect for apples. Well it is time to get dinner and I will have to quit. Sister Phila [Johnson] has not been very well this winter. She has dizziness in her head and her feet pains her so she can hardly walk. Sister Mary and family was all well the last we heard. Well I must quite for this time. Hoping to hear from you soon. I remain your loving niece.

Emma Ransom

Letter to Nancy [Johnson] Brown from Hiram A. Johnson, Sr.

Salem, Oregon
March 4, 1895

Dear Sister Nancy Brown

I received a paper from you today and that puts me in mind that I have not written you for a long time. My health has been bad for a long time but am some better now. I have heart trouble which the Dr. says is liable to take me off at any time but I am not worrying about this. Wife's health is not very good but is able to be about all the time. Children's health quite good. Rachel and her family are living in one of our houses within twenty feet of the one we live in. She has undertaken to take care of us the rest of our lives. She comes over every morning and gets breakfast and does all the work for us so we have nothing to do unless we wish to. They also furnish all the provisions. We have our own rooms. We are to give her a certain portion of our property after we are done with it. I see by the paper you sent that cousin Henry Pratt's wife is dead. I have forgotten who his wife was. I was much surprised last summer to have an old Edwards [NY] man call on us it was Alex Noble. I remember him as a boy or young man. Said his wife was dead think he said she was a Laidlaw. Which of the Laidlaw girls was she? I have not heard from Abel for a long time. I think he did not like it because I did not let Ed [probably Elgin Johnson son of Abel Pratt Johnson] have money to go home. I did not have it at the time and thought was just as well for him to borrow money as for me to do so. Tell Abel that him and me are too near the end of our lives to fall out about such things and write me again as I am anxious to hear from him once more.

We have had a very fine winter no snow to amount to anything and not the usual amount of rain. The weather through February has been mostly sunshine and warm. This is a fine climate. Times are considered hard and money scarce but provisions of all kinds are plenty and cheap. Legislature has been in session for forty days here in Salem and things have been lively. Now Nancy write me a long letter and tell me all about the connections and their family.

I must tell you about one of our second cousins that I have found here. He is a grandson of Uncle Warren [this Warren must be a brother of Charles Alvah Johnson] his father's name was Ira [Ira Johnson, married to Abigail Furbush and father of Charles Alvah Johnson as well] and he is dead. This man's name is Elder and it was an accident that I found him. He came here two years ago and a letter that came for him was left at our house as I sometimes get letters addressed Elder Johnson but soon found out that it was not for me and went to work and hunted him up and found a cousin. He is a fine young man and had a fine wife and one little girl but his wife died two weeks ago and leaves him with his little girl in a desolate condition. He came from
Iowa here. Well I believe this is all. Love to your family and all the friends. Be sure and write. I was 76 the 18th of Feb.

H. A. Johnson

Letter from John Charles Johnson to Nancy [Johnson] Brown

Salem, Oregon
Feb 24, 1896

Dear Aunt Nancy,

I suppose no doubt ere this you have got the paper that gives the death of our Father and Beloved Brother [Hiram]. I calculated to write you but have not till now. The cause of his death was enlargement of the heart that had been working on him for over 2 years. For about 8 months he could not lay down more than ½ the night. He would have to set up in his chair sometimes all night. Poor man he suffered a great deal. So he got bad 6 weeks before his death. He suffered awful he could not get his breath. He suffered so that he wanted to die long before he did. Of course we all hated to give him up but we could see he never could get well and could see that it was better for him to go than to suffer so much. My mother and family is standing it very well. My sister Rachel has been living with Pa and Ma for over a year. So they have had the best of care. He died fully satisfied that there was a reward layed up for him in Heaven. Aunt Nancy I think of you a great many times. I think of how you rewarded me when I came to see you. I could not hardly make you believe I was your Brother's boy. Father had a great many questions to ask me about all the folks when I came back. We have had pretty hard times here. All of us have had our monies in Real Estate. Lost money as it has come down half within the last 2 years. I have been appointed receiver in a large Nursery Company. I will have a year's worth to settle it up. I get pretty good wages. I get $150 per month.

The folks here are all well. Show this letter to all the folks and tell them I often think of them. Tell them I am always glad to get letters from them and I want you to write to me. Show this letter to cousin Charly Johnson [son of William Warren Johnson of NY]. Tell him to write to me. When I get more time I need to write you a long letter. Give my respects to all the folks. Good bye for this time.

Yours,
J.C. Johnson

Letter to Nancy [Johnson] Brown from Rachel C. [Johnson, Earl] Harritt of Salem, Oregon

My dear Aunt,

It is with a sorrowful heart I write to you today to tell you my Dear Mother [Elizabeth Jane Whitley Johnson] passed away last Friday morning. I will send you the Obituary notice that was in our paper. She was ready and willing to go and be with Pa [Hiram Alvah Johnson, Sr.] She missed him oh so much and while our hearts are sad we know there was a happy reunion last Friday morning on the other shore. The last afternoon of her life she called for Pa's picture. We hung it on the wall at the foot of her bed. She died like a child going to sleep. Her suffering through her last sickness was, she said, only a feeling of weakness. We are so thankful for that.

I want to live the remainder of my days so that I may be permitted to meet my dear parents on that heavenly shore. Please excuse this short letter. I will write more next time.

Did you receive my last letter and photo? I sent it some months ago. I will be glad to hear from you. How I wish you lived where we might see you.

Yours in sadness
307 Church Street NE
Salem, Oregon

Letter to Nancy [Johnson] Brown from Rachel C. Harritt
Salem, Oregon

571

...who is very old I think about 80 and after visiting in Canada. Mrs. Sellwood has relations in New York. She expects to visit. They live in Gloversville [NY]. I see by the map that her route would seem to go near Edwards and if it does I am going to ask her to stop off a day and see you. It would do me so much good to have her come to me from you. You will find her a very pleasant lady. She was intimately acquainted with Pa and Ma for many years. Miss Sellwood is a maiden lady about 50 years of age. Her relatives are in Illinois. But she expects to make the trip to Canada with my sister-in-law. Now if you answer this letter before they start and let us know in regard to the route from Haltey, Canada to Gloversville, I will know whether she can stop at Edwards or not. If I do not get your letter before they start I can write to her in Canada.

Uncle Abel's [Abel Pratt Johnson) daughter Mrs. Stevens and family lived in Portland, Oregon over a year. They visited us once while they lived there and we enjoyed them so much. It was during our State Fair. They seemed to be delighted with Salem. My brother George [George Washington Johnson] and wife [Mary Parthena Jones] visited them in Portland and just before they left Portland for Boise City, Idaho I had planned to go visit them. I wrote the day before and found they was all packed and ready to move to their new home and as their train left before I could get there, I didn't get to see them. I was very much disappointed. She wrote me they was making the change on account of their little girl's health and that she would write me as soon as they got settled but I have not had a letter yet. I am going to write to her soon. We liked them very much.

My husband is quite well and still in the store. We are living alone now. Both of his daughters are married. We have had a delightful winter. We did not have any snow and but very little freezing weather. The grass is green as it can be and the buds are putting out and flowers are blooming in the yard. We may have blustery weather in March but I do not look for it. Now I am going to ask you again for yours and Uncle William's picture. The picture we have was taken so many years ago. I would like to see you now in your declining years and as we cannot hope to meet you on this earth we could have the pleasure of knowing just how you look. Do you have a picture of Grandpa [Charles Alvah Johnson] Johnson? We have Grandma's [Rachel Pratt Viall Johnson] picture enlarged and I also have the tin type that the enlarged picture was taken from if you do not have one I will send it to you. I would like so much to have Grandpa's picture. I have my dear parents picture enlarged in one frame and they look like they ought to speak to me. Oh how I miss them. My brothers are all well. Charley lives on his farm, George is still in the clothing store, Warren lives East of the mountains [Burns, Oregon] Alvah is in the insurance business, Thurston is telegraph operator in the same office for thirty years, Frank lives in Moscow, Idaho. Now I have written you a long letter and I am going to look for an answer soon. I hope this will find you and Uncle William in good health. I think the next time I write I will send you a picture of myself and husband. Goodbye for this time from your affectionate niece.

Rachel C. Harritt
307 Church St. NE
Salem, Oregon

Letter to Nancy [Johnson] Brown from Abel Pratt Johnson

Pine Valley [NY]
Oct 6th 1898

Dear Sister Nancy,

I guess its about time I write you again. I have forgotten when you wrote. I have been quite busy this summer. Worked nearly three months on the old house that I bought when we first came here. We have made it look somewhat better. Well Nancy we are all well and that is about all there is of us. The times are so close that we can sell nothing for more than ½ what we used to get. If I had $5.00 I would move to Edwards [NY] once more. I have plenty of hay to sell and oats but they won't pay but $5.00 for a ton and 65 cents for wheat and I won't let it go for that. So we will have to stay at home and eat it up. Deal is keeping house for me with her family mostly here the two oldest boys works out through the summer and stay at home through the winter. Dode [perhaps Dora A. Johnson] is in Elmira [NY]. Her man is a contractor but work is scarce. This summer Stella's [Stella Johnson] man [Charles Ward] is in Binghamton [NY]. They are doing fine. He gets $125 per month as a conductor. They had a vacation in September and went up where Homer Earls folks live and he went still further to Colorado. Their girl went with them. All free passage. They had a good time with Celia and Arn's folks. Jeff is in New York yet and has not been home this fall. Joe's folks is well and doing as well as can be expected. Susie is lame and Joe is old. Don't make so good a team. She fell down on the level floor and hurt her knee quite bad so she has to use her crutch again.

My boys I don't know what they are doing or hardly where they are as I have heard from them this summer. John [John C. Johnson] went boating as usual and Elgin [Elgin Johnson] went to Schenectady working for the Edison Company in the Electric Company. His folks are here at their home. He sends them money. Their older girl [Saphronia Johnson] married Arty Dilmore. He's a creamery man and lives in PA. She is here now on a visit. Has a baby boy [Sayre Albert Dilmore]. Deal's girl you know was married long ago. They have a boy two years old and they have parted and she works and he runs a creamery here. The only reason they parted is she don't like him or the baby. That's all we know. Well now you tell us as much as I have and leave out the bad if there is any. But I have told you all I know. Susie's man is off boating. Write soon. We should like to see you all this way if able.

> Your affectionate Bro. A.P. Johnson

Letter to Nancy [Johnson] Brown from Rachel C. Harritt

> Salem, Oregon
> April 2, 1901

My Dear Aunt

It has been a long time since I have heard from you. I did not get an answer from my last letter so I suppose it went astray. Since I have most my Father and Mother, I at times get so lonely I can hardly stand it. All of my aunts on my mother's side [Whitley] have passed away and you are the only one of my Father's sisters living. You can't imagine how glad I would be to see you and Uncle William. In the last letter I wrote I urged you to have a picture taken. I want to see how you look now. I have the picture of Grandma [Rachel Pratt Viall] Johnson that Pa had enlarged. I am very proud of it. I think she has such a sweet face. Did Grandpa [Charles Alvah Johnson] ever have a picture taken?

I have just lately heard that one of Uncle Abel's daughters is in Portland, Oregon. Her husband [Malvin Stevens] write to the Salem Postmaster and found out where we all lived. And he wrote to my brother George [George Washington Johnson]. He wrote and promised to come visit us which they promised to do. Do you know what he occupation is? I am so anxious to meet them.

Is Aunt Emily [Emily Spann Johnson] Uncle Charley's wife still living? My husband is still in the store. His two daughters are both married. The oldest one married a commercial traveler. His route is throughout Oregon and over the California line. The youngest one lives in Portland. Her husband is a machinist and works in the Willamette Iron Works. So there is only one son, 19 years old living at home.

We had a very mild winter. No snow to play on. Prospects for crops and fruit are good.

My brother Charles [John Charles Johnson] is out on his farm most of the time at work. It is about fifteen miles out [Jefferson, Oregon]. He has been working quite hard the last two years. His oldest, son, A.J., has bought a large farm lately. I think he gave about twenty thousand for it. It is large enough for three families. Brother George is still here in the clothing business. Warren is in Harney County.

Alvah lives in Salem. He has been Justice of the Peace for several years. Thurston is in the same telegraph office for over twenty years. Frank is in Idaho. His wife feel heir to a large estate lately. I believe now I have written everything of interest and will anxiously look for a good long letter from you. If it is hard for you to write, get someone to write for you. Though I would much prefer one from your dear hand.

My husband joins me in sending love to you and Uncle William and all our cousins. And please do not forget the pictures.

From your affectionate niece
Mrs. R. C. Harritt

Letter to Nancy [Johnson] Brown and William Brown from Rachel C. Harritt

Salem, Oregon
November 7, 1903

My Dear Aunt and Uncle

I received your good letter about two weeks ago and have waited for Mrs. Sellwood to return home and how that she has come, I write to you today. She arrived last Wednesday night on the late ten train. Her husband went to Portland on Monday. She arrived there Tuesday and they stayed there overnight and visited their three children who live there. Her oldest son Frank is a very successful Dentist. Her second son Willie owns a grocery store and Ethel's husband also owns an interest in the store and they all live there. They have one son and daughter living at home – Harold and Lillian. They have raised a nice family of children and you wouldn't wonder at it after knowing Mrs. Sellwood. Her brother, my first husband, was very much hike her in looks and disposition. Anything they would tell you could always be depended on. The Sellwoods were a very upright people. Mr. Sellwood's father and uncle was Episcopal ministers. He only has one brother living now and one sister who

576

visited at your house. And now I will tell you as I suppose you have already found out. She is a very peculiar old maid. It proved as we all predicted she spoiled Mrs. Sellwood's visit to a great extent. I do not know whether she is loosing her mind as she grows older or what the cause is. She tells things to strangers about her own folks that there isn't a word of truth in and seems to take a delight in doing it and yet she seems to think that she is a perfect Christian. Of course, we all know her here and do not pay any attention. But Mrs. Sellwood tells me that she annoyed her almost to death on their trip. Well Mrs. Sellwood was completely surprised on her return to find a new house in place of the old she left. No one had told her of it and when they came down from the train the children had the house all lighted up and she could hardly believe her eyes. It isn't quite a new house but just the same as it is all worked over and enlarged it hurried the carpenters to get it finished.

When she got home I was sick with a cold and not able to go out. So she came up and you may depend I was an interested listener when she told me all about her visit at your place.

Oh how I wish you was in that group picture. I have the picture that Pa had of you taken I should think about the same time the one you sent me. But I want to see you as you look now as I see a great change in Uncle William. Tell him I think he grows better looking as he grows older. Now can't you have someone take a Kodak out and you and Uncle stand out in the yard just as that group stood? Most all young folks here have Kodaks.

Mrs. S. told us all about the little boy. She thought he was very cute and she likes your grandson and his wife so very much. And she just can't get done telling me how nice you all treated them. She said you seemed now like her own relation. I was very sorry to hear of your sickness. Shingles is considered a dangerous disease here if it should reach around the body. I think they paint with iodine to keep it from spreading. Tell Uncle I think he was pretty brave to take such a long trip alone. It wouldn't have taken him much longer to have come out to see us. But remember my dear old Auntie must come along. Well I hope we may meet yet in this world. I think more about it now as

577

so many of my dear ones have gone on. Out of so many aunts that I once had, you are the only one left. My brothers are quite well. Frank, my youngest brother who lives in Idaho, has just been down settling his wife's father's estate. There is two heirs besides my sister-in-law. They will get about fifteen thousand a piece. I get letters occasionally from Mrs. Stevens, Uncle Abel's daughter. They live in Boise, Idaho.

The last letter I received from her she said her little girl's health was much improved. They liked Portland but was advised to go to Idaho on account of Marjorie's health. She wrote they had bought two properties there and one would bring them in good rent and he gets steady work at good wages.

My brother George and his wife have just got home from a trip to Southern California. They say they had a nice time and had fresh strawberries and her nephew was making a garden while they was there. We have had a lovely fall. Crops of all kinds was good. The rains are just starting in. My husband is very bush in the store. I am trying to persuade him to sell out and on onto something easier. He joins me in sending love to you all. I hope to hear from you soon. Goodbye from you loving niece.   Mrs. J. W. Harritt

Letter from Mrs. J. A. Sellwood to Mrs. William [Nancy Johnson] Brown

Salem, Oregon
September 13, 1908

Mrs. Wm. Brown
My dear friend,

I guess you will be very much surprised to hear from me as I have been silent so long but it is not because I have forgotten you or yours and not because I do not think of you often. I have had so much care and worry the last 2 or 3 years, yes and work, all together I have sadly neglected my letter writing. I suppose Rachel told you that I went back to Harley P.Q. Canada last Nov. to take care of my poor father who was then past 85 years old. I found him failing quite fast. He was not able to take a step unassisted after I got there. He lived about two months after my arrival. He was so rejoiced to have me with him to care for him and make his last days more pleasant. I remained after his death until things were settled up then visited my only aunt by blood relation stopping with her nearly 2 weeks as she would not consent to a shorter stay. We then came directly home. I wanted to visit, or should like to have visited you and my cousins in Springfield, Mass. and Gloversville, NY but I was too anxious to get home. My husband had been very sick and was gaining so slowly that I felt I could not stay and enjoy a visit with anyone. He is quite well again now and I feel very thankful to our kind and Heavenly Father for His many blessings. I hope you and yours are well. There has been many changes in your family since I visited you. I will never forget that visit. I shall always remember it as one of the most pleasant visits we enjoyed while on that trip. I wonder if Mr. Brown has forgotten the trip to the talc mines. The colts were a little nervous around the mines but all together we had a very nice time even though it did rain.

I have relics I got at those mines yet. Kind regards to all the family and may God bless and keep you all and if we never meet again here may we meet on that other shore where there will be peace and happiness forevermore.

Lovingly your friend,
Mrs. J.A. Sellwood

PS Rachel and John are well as usual I believe.

[Note: Mrs. J.A. Sellwood was a sister of John Earl, Rachel C. Johnson's first husband. The John in the "PS" refers to John Harritt, Rachel's second husband. Mrs. J.A. Sellwood was Laura A. Earl prior to her marriage Oct. 11, 1871 to Joseph A. Sellwood.]

582

Chistopher Paul, 319
Jon Brian, 319
Lee Alan, 319
Leo Everett, 211, 318-19
Matthew, 406
Murray Glenn, 319
Roger Joe, 319, 406
Suzanne Kay, 319, 406
Travis, 406

AVILA
Alberta Margarita, 186, 282

AYERS
W. D., 40

AXTELL
Heather, 342
Jacqueline Marie, 342
Jennifer Lew, 342
Larry LuRue, 243, 342
Patrick, 342

BABECKOS
Jennifer Lynn, 272
Kassandra Marie, 366
Marcella Dorene, 272, 366
Stephanie Ann, 366
William, 183, 272
William Brecht, 272, 366

BACKUS
Amy Lynn, 315, 402
Craig Patrick, 315
Gertrude, 117, 144
Thomas William, 315
William G., 208, 315

BAER
Kay, 162

BAILY
Colonel, 547

BAGBY

Martha, 128, 173

BAKER
Alice M., 135
Amilia, 106, 123
Brian Michael, 359
Frank Albert, 111, 135
Kevin Randall, 359
Margaret, 76-78
Michael, 260, 359
Thomas, 77, 78

BALDWIN
Pearl Theresa, 118, 145

BALLARD
Ann Denise, 259, 358

BALTZOR
Michael, 288, 389
Michelle, 389
Shari, 389

BARBER
A. C., Captain, 37

BARHYDT
Elsie G., 142

BARKER
Michael, 249
Mr., 548
Yongsoon, 275, 368

BARKLEY
Lou, 268

BARNES
Bonnie Kay (Boprey), 524
Cynthia Leigh, 316, 403
Ellison Louisa, 105, 118
Homer, 316
Horace, 118
Keith Francis, 209, 316,
    520, 524
Keith Joseph, 316
Kimberly Ann, 316, 403

BRENDS
  (--?--), 222
BRESETTE
  Dean, 209, 317
  Leonard H., 317
  Jeremiah W., 406
  Jill Marie, 317
  Michael Dean, 317
  Rick Jay, 317, 405
BREUSER
  Virginia, 185, 276-277
BREWER
  Edgar Joseph, 182, 480
  Grace M. (Wilson), 480
  Hannah, 87, 91
  Violette Marie, 133, 182
BRICE
  Cynthia, 201, 305
  Debbie A., 285, 383
BRIGGS
  Mitch, 287, 388
  Pauline, 155, 220
BRISTOL
  Gloria, 240, 339
BRITAIN
  Sarah Emma, 106, 126
BRITTEN
  (--?--), 72
BROADY. See JOHNSON,
  William Warren
BROCK
  Adam Thompson, 418, 428
  April Suzanne, 418
  Calli Joanne, 304
  David Guy, 367, 418
  Deana (--?--), 368, 418
  Kimberly, 418, 428
  Marlys Ann, 169, 245

Scott Raymond, 368, 418
Tamie, 418, 428
Tammy Lynn, 368
Vicki (--?--), 368, 418
Wayne, 200, 304
BRODIE
  Mr., 12
BROGDEN
  Michele Lynn, 370, 421-
    422
BROTHERS
  Natalie Nicole, 383
BROTHERTON
  Clark, 152
  Horace Alfred, 120, 152
  Mariah, 152
  Melvin, 153
  Merton, 152
  Milton, 152
  Myrtle, 152
BROWN
  Alexandra Kate, 399
  Alvah Percival, 13, 59-61,
    104, 117, 509, 515, 556,
    561
  Austin Lee, 398
  Barbara Ruth (Fulton), 492,
    506
  Betty Jean (Goodman), 187,
    283
  Carol Lebrun, 330
  Carrie Pearl (Cleland), 118,
    145, 489
  Charles Hiram, 12-13, 59-
    60, 104, 118, 495, 510,
    516, 561
  Charles Maclyn, 146
  Chris Edward, 283

588

Clara E., 13, 59, 104
Clara Pearl, 118
Clarence Charles, 118, 145, 489-90, 495
Clarence Donald, 145, 204, 491, 495
Constance Lucille, 204, 309
Delma Alene, 139, 191
Donald C., 204
Douglas Lee, 309, 398
Eliza, 15
Elizabeth, 337
Gregory Richard, 309
Harold Elmer, 117
Helen Martha, 145
Ian David, 399
J. C., 18
J. M., 25
Janet Ellen, 169, 244
John, 14
Joy Elaine, 169, 244, 245
Julie Renee, 245
Katherine (--?--), 146
Lauren Emily, 399
Lisa Marie, 309
Marian Manie (Cleland), 60, 104, 117
Manie Elnora, 117, 144
Marianne Lynette, 246
Mark Christian, 283
Mark Frederick, 310, 399
Martha Eliza (Noble), 13, 60, 104, 118, 516
Mary Ann, 169, 246
Mary Jean, 149, 212
Nancy A. (Johnson), 12, 13, 14, 59, 97, 104, 440, 534, 538, 544, 553-554, 556-

61, 563-8, 570-1, 573, 575-6, 578
Nicholas Mark, 399
Oswald Bower, 118, 145
Paul C., 187, 283
Percival H., 60
Richard Donald, 13, 204, 309, 492, 497, 506
Robert, 60
Sarah J. (Grant), 60-1, 104, 117, 515
Seth Douglas, 398
Sherman William, 14, 60, 117, 144
Sidney, 60
Wallace, 221, 330
Wesley Adam, 344
William Benton, 169, 245
William Crist, 127, 169
William David, 245, 344
William Harry (H.), 12-14, 59-60, 97, 104, 440, 495, 534, 538, 556, 558-60, 563, 565, 575-7, 579
William Ryan, 344
BROWNING
Raymond, 171
BROYLES
Nettie E., 114
BRUNNER
Jennie, 266, 363
BRYAN
William Jennings, 39
BRYANT
Shirley Ann, 172, 254
BUCK
Martha Elizabeth (Clark), 12, 493

BUCK cont.
Carson Perry, 12, 146, 204, 493
Frederick John, 205, 311
Heather Anne, 312
Heidi Jean, 311
William John Paul, 205, 312
William John Paul Jr., 312
BUCKINGER
John, 190, 289
BUCKINGHAM
Linda Kay, 256, 356
BUIST
Darryl John Jr., 303
Darryl John Sr., 198, 303
David Anthony, 303
BULLOCK
Becky, 319
BURANOSKY
James, 248, 348
Jane Renee, 348
BURBRIDGE
Charles Eugene, 221, 329
Donna, 221, 330
Emil Wayne, 330
Floyd, 155, 221
Floyd Jr., 221, 330
Floyd Roger, 330
Irvin Leroy), 221
James, 551
Karen Dian, 330
Lana Marie, 330
Lloyd, 221
Lyndle, 221
Nola Estella, 155, 220
Opal, 155, 221
Philip Paul, 330
Rela Jean, 330

Ross, 155, 221
Steven Kent, 330
Thomas, 122, 155
Thomas Eugene, 330
Thuman Paul, 221, 330
BURGE
Elizabeth, 278
BURGESS
Joyce Ina, 196, 298
BURKE
Dian Otela, 338
Holly Lynn, 338
Marsha Ann (, 338, 416
Thomas M., 239, 338
Thomas P., 338
BURNETT
Sherry, 216, 323
BURNS
Connor Michael, 425
Michael, 376, 425
BURNSIDE
Ambrose, General, 550
BURT
Hugh, 69, 83, 86
BURTON
Sandra, 195, 296
BUTCHER
Donald, 174
BUTLER
Gary, 203, 308
BYE
Effie Deloris, 373
BYERS
Joan, 282, 381
Lyall, 186, 282
Sandra, 282, 381
BYRNE
(--?--), 130, 178

591

592

Charles Rollin II, 207, 314
Charles Rollin III, 314
Charles Rollin Sr, 146, 207
Daisy, 176
David Brown, 207
Harriet Isabel, 146, 205
James Milton, 207, 313
John Evert, 207
Kevin Jan, 314
Mabel E. (Brown), 14, 118,
  146, 493, 516
Martha Elizabeth, 146, 204
Michael David, 245
Mildred, 122
Nona Jean, 142, 196, 197
Robert Arlynn, 344
Stephen Arlyn, 245
William, 105, 122
William Kyle, 344
William Kyle Wendell, 245,
  344
Wilma Fern (Brown), 169,
  245
CLARY
  James, 147
  Mayme Gertrude, 119, 147
CLAUSEN
  Darren, 271
CLAUSER
  David, 108
CLEEK
  Enid, 133, 182
CLELAND
  Jane (Kerr), 60, 117
  William, 60, 117
CLENDENNY
  Ricky, 415
  Robyn, 415

Ronnie, 337, 414-15
CLIFTON
  Ella, 152
CLOUGH
  Evelyn Frances, 159, 228
COBB
  Andrew Charles, 403, 525
  Brianne Janette (Satkowski),
    525
COCKAYNE
  Hilda, 150, 214-15
CODY
  Ann Agnes, 193, 292
COE
  Charles Adam, 419
  Thomas, 94
COFFEY
  Dana, 307
COLBERT
  Allen M., 405
  Daniel Malcolm, 405, 518
  Josiah Patrick, 405, 518
  Patrick Josiah, 316, 405
  Shannon Rose, 405, 518
COLBURN
  Hannah, 63, 94
COLBY
  Pearl Naoma, 124, 163
COLE
  Anna, 149
  Doris Ruth, 214, 320
  Durward Eugene, 150, 214
  Helen Louise, 214
  Sarah, 93
COLEMAN
  Ebenezer, 6, 8
  John, Deacon, 6, 66, 85, 87
  Mary (Ely), 6

COLEMAN cont.
　Mehitable (Johnson)
　　Hinsdale Root, 5-8, 66,
　　85, 87
　Nathaniel, 6, 8
　Ruth (Niles), 6
COLGAN
　Elizabeth, 117
COLLEY
　Betty, 210, 318
COLONEY
　Mayfred L., 120
COLVIN
　Anthoney Ben, 124, 163
　Audrey Mae, 163, 237
　Beulah Audry, 124, 162-163
　David Allen, 237
　Doris Ellen, 163
　Gladys, 124, 163-4
　Louis, 546
　Michael Albert, 237
　Minnerva Alice, 124, 162
　Nancy Ruth, 236
　Patrica Ann, 237
　Richard Orville, 163, 236
　Richard Stanley, 237
　Robert Lee, 236
　Sara Jo, 236
　Sharon Kay, 236
　Sidney Orville, 124, 163
　Sidney Robert, 163, 236
　Theodore, 106, 124
　Thomas B, 163, 237
　Thomas Engle, 237
　William Anthony, 237
　Winfred A., 163, 237
CONGLETON
　Carsie, 161, 234

CONNELLY
　Charles Michael, 204, 310
　Charles Patrick, 310
　Harriet Gertrude (Buck),
　　204, 310
　Mary Margaret, 310
CONNORS
　(--?--), 208
　Charles Richard, 205
　Deborah Jean (Cravens),
　　532
　Gwendolyn A. (Russell),
　　206
　Harriet Isabelle (Clark),
　　517, 530
　Richard H., 146, 205-6,
　　517, 532
　Thomas, 205, 313, 532
　William Richard, 205
CONWAY
　Amanda Alice, 375
　Clayton Scott, 375
　Earl, 279, 375
COOK
　Cathryn Alice, 281
　Dane Sue, 241
　David, 241
　George, 550
　Janice Kay, 241
　Joe, 167, 241
　Joe Ellen, 241, 340
COOLIDGE
　Calvin, President, 39
COONROD
　Henry, 547
COOPER
　Janis, 293
　Sarah A., 106, 126-7

CORBINE
  Wayne, 319, 406
COSPER
  Emma, 101, 114-15
  William, 114
COSTELLO
  Gloria, 177, 264
COULTAS
  Sue Ann, 175, 261
COWAN
  E. Antoinette, 183, 273- 4
COX
  (--?--), 340
  Easter Ann, 110
  Karl, 241, 340
  Mary Mae, 172, 253
  Peggy Ann, 279, 374
CRAIG
  Cheryl, 384, 427
  Verl, 285, 384
CRAIN
  Jason Eugene, 354
  Tony Eugene, 253, 354
CRANDALL
  Amy Louise, 296
  Clay Matthew, 295
  Theodore, 194, 295
CRANE
  Cynthia, 419
  Deborah Leann, 419
CRAVEN
  Amy Michelle, 395
  Emily Lauren, 396
  Jennifer Lynn, 395
  Jeremy Wayne, 396
  Kenneth Wayne, 298, 395
CRAVENS
  Deborah Jean, 205, 313

CRAWFORD
  J.W., 40
CREIGHTON
  Carrie Elizabeth, 119, 150
  James, 150
CREWS
  Alice A., 227
  All, 159, 227
CROCKER
  Louisa Bell, 196
CROSS
  Helen, 163, 236
CROUTER
  Maud, 115
CROWDER
  Angela Lynn, 415
  Curtis Dale, 415
  Phillip Dean, 338, 415
CRUM
  Clarence Rozie, 169, 243
  Gary Eugene, 244
  Gregory, 244
  Vickie Diane, 244
CULBERTSON
  James, 160, 230
  James Ernest, 230
CULP
  Alice Marie, 260, 358
CUNNINGHAM
  Wilbur, 120, 152-3
CURFRASS
  Lieselotte, 183, 273
CURR
  Shirley, 216, 325
CURRIER
  Mary, 216, 325
CURRY
  Dee Ann, 414

DODGE
(--?--), 130, 178
DODSON
Dr., 22
DOLHUN
Tamara, 206
DOLLOFF
James, 358, 418
Lindsey Jean, 418
DONNELLY
Billie, 271, 364
DOOLEY
Arthur, 208
DORAN
(--?--), 375, 424
Karynn Nicole, 424
DORMAN
Garnie E., 131, 179
DORPINGHAUS
Amy Christine, 299
Cleo A., 197, 299
Douglas James, 299
Theresa, 299
DOTTRAM
Jenifer Lynn, 281, 380
DOUGLAS
Donna Jean, 251, 352
DOVE
Melody Lynn, 198, 301
Roy, 301
DOWD
Mary Ellen, 276
DOYLE
Coy, 123, 160, 166, 229
DRAGER
Jack Leroy, 193
Vern Loren, 140, 192-3
Vern Loren Jr., 193

DREYER
Kelly Ann, 366
Patricia Ann, 366
Wesley, 272, 366
DRISCOLL
Helen, 161, 235
DUFOUR
Jarrod Anthony, 428
Rodney, 418, 428
DULACK
Arthur, 117
Joseph, 117
DUMONT
Armand, 154, 218
Donna, 218, 326
Joanna, 218
Paul, 218
DUNCAN
Betty E., 174, 259
Douglas Darrell, 233
Ronald Roy, 232
Roy, 161, 232
DUNHAM
Larry Joe, 262, 360
Lisa Diane, 360
Lori June, 360
DUNLAP
Garth, 243, 341
Kevin Joseph, 341
Kyle Allen, 341
DUNN
Carrie Lynn, 417
Ellison Eldora, 118
John Joseph II, 340, 417
John Joseph III, 417
Kellie Elizabeth, 417
DURBIN
Barbara, 178

Donald, 178
Leslie, 130, 178
Sandra, 178
DURELL
Linnie, 132, 180
DUTTON
Elizabeth, 125
DYGERT
Adelia, 153
Stanley, 146

EARL
Bryce Andrew, 364
Erin, 364
Homer, 574
James Frederick, 267
John, 101, 566, 576
Thomas Robert, 267, 364
Zee Floyd, 180, 267
EBERLY
Gerald, 249, 349
Michael Edward, 349
EDWARDS
Athol Glynn, 144, 202
Jaqueline Kay, 202, 307
Jean Marie, 202, 306-7
Joan Ann, 202
Mary A., 113, 139
Terry Lynn, 202, 307
Toni Lea, 202, 307-8
EGAN, 22
EISENBARTH
Maria, 197
ELKINS
Robert Edward, 333
Sharron LaVonne, 333
Thad Andrew, 333
Thadeus, 227, 333

ELLEDGE
Wilma Alberta, 416
ELLIOTT
Mary Jane Mollie, 101, 113
ELLIS
Holly, 350
Stephanie, 350
Thomas, 250, 350
Thomas (Jr.?), 350
ELMENDORF
Florence, 347
ELMER. *See* JOHNSON,
John Elmer
ELSTON
David George, 242, 341
Frank Brown, 168, 242
Frank William, 341
Jane Frances, 242
Jeanene Allison, 341
Nancy Elizabeth, 341
EMLER
Charles Richard, 218, 326
Charles Richard (Jr.?), 326
David Alan, 326
Stephen Matthew, 326
ENGLE
Edmore, 163, 237
ENGLEMAN
Herman, 164, 237
ENNIST
Mary Lucille, 205, 313
ERICKSON
Christopher Lloyd, 379
Constance Marie, 379
Kenneth, 260, 358
Tristan Carl, 379
William Howard, 281, 379

603

604

Joan Elizabeth, 314
Lorraine Jaquelyn, 402
Sharon Jane, 314, 402
Suzanne Marie, 314
GRASSFIELD
Nita Evelyn, 167, 240
GRATZER
Thelma Kathrine, 301
GRAVELINE
(--?--), 324, 412
Annette, 412
Brett, 412
GREEN
(--?--), 113, 139, 140
Billy, 140
Creta J. (Johnson) Stubbs
Stege, 455
Jerusha, 63-4, 91, 94-5
Nicole, 287
GREENE
Julie, 271, 365
GREENWOOD
Linda Mae, 191, 291
GREGORY
Bradley John, 344
Breana Jolene, 344
Jennifer Lynn, 246, 344
John Alvin Jr., 169, 246
John Benton, 246, 344
Nicholas Ray, 246
Shaila Kay, 344
GRIFFEN
Steven Mark, 363
GRIFFIN
Beulah Geneive, 298
Mary, 109
GRIFFITH
Deborah Fannie, 370, 420

GRIGNON
Carolyn Louise, 191, 290
GRIMES
Ike James, 289
James William, 190, 289
GROOMER
Carrie, 267, 364
GUNSAULES
Manuel, 25, 30, 110
GUTH
Brenda Jeanne, 254
David Brian, 254
Duane Eldon, 172, 253
Karen Janet, 254
Kathleen Marie, 253
Ronald Duane, 254
GUTHRIE
Evelyn, 221, 330

HACK
Elizabeth, 106, 123, 166
HAFFEY
Norma, 161, 233
HAIGHT
Eva, 139
HAILE
Celia, 9
John, 9
HALDANE
Carolyn June, 262, 361
David, 176, 262
Linda Sue, 262, 361-2
Nancy, 262
HALE
Michelle, 322, 410
HALEY
Elvira, 177, 263

606

Myrtle J. (Johnson)
  Williams, 113, 138-9,
    455, 457
  Ronald Kanzler, 191, 291
  Terri Lyn, 291
  Tracy Alene, 291
HAMILTON
  Chadwich Earl, 356
  Daniel Joseph, 356
  Joe Glen, 257, 356
  Justin Paul, 356
  Leslie Farrell, 173, 257
  Leslie Steven, 257, 356
  Piper Sue, 277, 372
HANCOCK
  Everatt Edgar, 163
HANFORD
  John, 71
HANNANT
  Susan Marie, 338, 415
HANSON
  (--?--), 272
  Carroll, 134, 183
  Willis, 183, 272
HARDIN
  Allison Renee, 348
  James Dean, 248, 348
HARDING
  Blane, 202, 307
  Christopher Aaron, 307
  Kyle Alexander, 307
  Marie Theresa, 307
  Toni Elizabeth, 307
  Warren G., President, 39
HARDY
  Louis, 216, 325
  Myrtle, 325, 412
  Roy, 325

HARMON
  Adoniram J., 99
  Albert G., 115
  Altha, 108
  Ann Eliza, 108
  Charles Viall, 102, 115
  Ebenezer, 97, 102
  Edward P., 108
  Emma A., 102
  Eunice, 99, 107
  Gertie C., 115
  Harriet C. (Viall), 10, 97-8,
    535, 558
  Harriett Adaline, 107
  Hiram H., 102
  James, 102, 538, 558, 567
  Lilly M., 108
  Lydia, 538
  Paul Osgood, 99, 107
  Phila (Viall), 10, 97, 102,
    535, 558-9, 564, 567
  Robert, 145
  Sophronia M., 99
  Susan V., 99
  Wesley O., 107
  Wesley Porter, 97-8, 535,
    558
  Wesley Porter Jr., 99, 108
HARPER
  Mary, 106, 125, 160
  Sarah Kisire, 106, 126
HARPOLE
  Lillian, 229, 335
  Wayne, 160, 166, 229
HARRIMAN
  Lisa Marie, 309
  Ricki Lee, 309

607

HESS
Hattie, 127, 168
HESSEMAN
Edna, 124
HIBLER
Ross E., 25-6
HICKMAN
Marcia Marie, 294
Mardell Rae, 295
Margo Ann, 295
Michel Philip, 295
Philip Perry, 194, 294
HILL
(--?--), 203, 308
Amy Elizabeth, 421
Annette Kathleen, 370, 421
Charles Edwin , 185, 276
Charles Edwin II, 370
Christina Marie, 420
Coy Dale, 276
David, 168, 241
Derick Montgomery, 420
Elizabeth, 152
Genevieve Lynn, 422
James Dale, 276, 369-70
James Dale Jr, 370, 420
James S., 203, 308
Jeffery Charles Walter Sr.,
370, 421-2
Jeffrey Charles Walter Jr.,
422
Kathleen May, 276, 371
Martha Ann, 276, 370-1
Michael Ralph, 241
Robert, 144, 203
Sarah, 203, 308-9
Stacie Lynett, 422
Taylor Nicole, 370

Teresa May, 370, 419-20
Timothy David, 241
HILLS
Joseph, 6
Mehitable (Hinsdale)
Dickenson, 6, 87
HINDS
John Eugene, 249
HINE
Patricia, 188, 284
HINSDALE
Ann, 87
Ann (Woodward), 5
Barnabus, 5
John, 5-6
Mary, 87, 91
Mary (Rider), 6
Mehitable. *See* COLEMAN,
Mehitable (Johnson)
Hinsdale Root
Mehuman, 6, 87
Robert, Deacon, 5
Samuel, 5-6, 66, 85, 87
Sarah, 87
Susannah (Rockwood), 6
HITCHINS
Hannah, 64, 66, 91
HITSMAN
(--?--), 204
Howard, 145, 203-4
HOAR
Cheryl, 197, 300
HOBART
Jael, 89
Judith, 89
HOBBS
Beverly Lynn, 335
Eldonna, 229

611

HUFFMAN cont.
James, 346
Lindsay, 346
HUGHES
Danny, 210
Ellen Marie, 317
Gary Lyle, 318
Gilbert, 119, 147-8
John Sr., 147
Kendra Lea, 317
Kenneth Gilbert, 210, 317
Lee Ethel, 148, 210
Lura Kay, 318
Lyle Gilbert, 148, 210
Patricia (--?--), 317
Patrick John, 317
Robert, 210
Sarah (--?--), 148, 210
HUGHS
Virdie May, 123, 159
HULICK
Joan Leach, 175, 260
HUMMEL
Will E., 103
HUMPHREY
Asa, 63, 95
Myrtle Irene, 346
HUNNEYCUTT
Allen, 181, 269
Dale A., 269
Diane, 269
Gary A., 269
Patricia, 269
HUNT
Billie Gay, 337
Caroline Sue, 337
Floriene, 238, 337
William, 165, 238

William Jr., 238, 336-7
HUNTER
Alma V., 123, 159
HURLEY
(--?--), 153
Amy Robin, 407
Carl, 153
Clara, 153
Erin Seanna, 407
Floyd, 153
Melvin Anthony, 214, 320
Phillip Anthony, 321, 407
Sheila Ann, 321, 407
Vera, 153
HYDE
May, 127, 168
HYNUM
Mary Dorothy, 344
HYSOM
Alva Lincoln, 163, 237
Jerry Lee, 237
Sandra, 237
Steven Larry, 237
Sue Ellen, 237

IAEGER
Ada May, 183
Charles Arrowood, 185, 276-7
Charles L., 136
Charles Schlenker, 112, 136
Dennis, 277, 372
George Johnson, 136, 184
George Johnson Jr., 185, 280
George Johnson, Sr., 473, 475
Georgie Catherine, 184, 275

Carl Emil, 158, 225
Carl Everett, 142, 196, 197
Carl Gregory, 197
Caroline E. (Harris), 20-1, 50, 57, 101, 111-12, 459
Carolyn Ann, 331
Carrie Ann, 415
Catherine (--?--), 141
Chad Philip, 270
Charles Alvah, 8, 10, 14, 96, 97, 430, 432, 433, 435, 436, 438, 440, 441, 534, 536, 573, 575
Charles Clair, 180, 268
Charles Garth, 36, 38, 133, 182, 476, 479, 480
Charles Lyndle, 239, 337
Charles Raymond, 222, 331
Charles Vance Jr., 201, 305
Charles Vance Sr., 143, 200-1
Charles Viall, 103, 116, 561, 570
Charles Victor, 8, 10, 11, 97, 99, 435-7, 445, 447, 534-5, 537, 545, 548-9, 553-4, 558, 560-1, 564-5
Charles Virgil, 26, 28, 30, 111, 133, 465-6, 470, 479
Charles W., 112, 136
Charles (son of Osca), 169
Christine Marion, 201, 305-6
Christopher James, 181, 270
Ciara Antoinette, 367
Clarence Elisha, 126
Clarence Elva, 111

Claude A., 113, 138, 455
Cleo, 132, 180
Clyde E., 111, 135
Courtney Rae, 393
Coy, 156, 222
Creta J., 113, 139-40
Dale Roy, 338
Dana Margaret, 167, 241
Daniel, 90
Daniel Elliott, 392
Daniel Mark, 198
Darcey Lynne, 295, 395
Darlene Carol, 183
Darrel Craig, 268
Darrel Glenn, 181
Darrell DeLos, 132, 180, 476
Daryl Lane, 295, 395
David (b. 1692), 90
David (b. 1719), 92
David (b. 1723), 92
David Edward, 8, 199
Deborah (bap. 1650), 66, 85
Deborah (b. 1682/83), 86
Deborah (b. 1703), 89
Deborah Ann, 201, 305
Deborah Kay, 327
Deborah Lynn, 267
Deborah (daughter of Donald Earl), 242
Deborah (daughter of Isaac), 90
Debra Lynn, 415
Delores Jean, 183, 274
Dennis James, 247
Dianna Eileen, 331
Dillion Ray, 349
Donald Alfred, 142, 196

JOHNSON cont.

Donald Earl (b. 1941), 331
Donald Earl (b. 1936), 168, 241
Donald Elton, 180, 267
Donald Macrae, 267
Donna Lee, 196, 298
Donna Marie, 338, 416
Doris, 149, 213, 214
Dorothy Alice, 183, 273
Dorothy Ethel, 36, 38, 133
Dorothy Jean, 145, 203-4
Douglas Leroy, 281
Earl, 168
Earl Ray, 222
Earle S., 117, 144
Edward Anthony, 199
Edward Lewis, 416
Edward Norton, 114
Edwin Claude, 138, 191
Edythe Madilla, 114, 141
Elder, 105
Eldon C. 23, 112, 459
Eleanor, 92
Eleanor Belle, 143, 201-2
Eleanor Louise, 196, 298
Elgin Abel, 102, 115, 569, 574
Elinor (Ellen) (Cheney), 5
Elisha (b. 1688), 65, 90, 92
Elisha (b. 1720), 92
Eliza Ann, 103, 116
Eliza B., 97
Elizabeth (--?--), 92
Elizabeth (b. 1637), 85, 87
Elizabeth (bap. 1619), 4, 68, 83

Elizabeth Anna Lizzie, 110, 131-2
Elizabeth Jane (Whitley), 15, 18-20, 28-9, 97, 101, 439, 443, 448-9, 451, 453, 461, 534-6, 539, 541, 551, 556, 561, 568, 570-71, 575
Elizabeth Kathryn, 290
Ella, 122, 156
Elmer Vernon, 126
Elmo Elton, 132, 180, 476, 481
Elnora M., 115
Eloise, 174
Emily (Spann), 10-11, 97, 99, 435, 437, 445, 447, 537, 545, 548-9, 556, 559-60, 563-5, 567, 575
Emma (Cosper), 458, 460, 576, 578
Emma A., 103
Eric Stafford, 225
Ethel Moriah, 116, 142
Etta Arzella, 110, 133
Eugene Dayle, 114
Eva, 126, 166, 248
Eva M., 125, 164-5
Evelyn M., 140, 192
Ferne Helen, 116, 143
Floy Benton, 126, 166
Frances Berneice, 114
Francis "Frank" Marion, 22, 101, 114, 115, 449, 458, 460, 551, 555, 561, 573, 576, 578
Frank R., 104
Frank. *See* Francis M.

JOHNSON cont.

621

Mark William, 261
JUNGWIRTH
Brett David, 379
Virgil John, 281, 379

KAASA
Danielle, 379, 427
KANADY
Dorothy, 158, 226
KANE
Cynthia Lee, 245
Hugh, Reverend, 14
Joy-Anne, 245, 343
Linda Kay, 245, 343
Melissa, 343
Michael, 343
Nancy Joy, 245
Rachel Sue, 245
Ralph Edward, 169, 244, 245
Ralph Edward Jr., 245, 343
KAUFFMAN
Alice, 148, 210
Madeline, 148
KAY
Thomas B., 41
KEELING
Howard, 135, 184
Melinda Mae, 184, 274
KEERD
Marjorie, 404
KEIL
Conrad, 246, 345
Duane Daniel, 345
Jill Denise, 345, 417
KEISTER
Howard Rucker III, 192, 291

Jeffrey William, 291
Leslie Ann, 291
KELLER
Sandra, 189, 285
KELLOGG
Martin, 87
KELLY
Amber Janice, 417
Amy Elizabeth, 417
Ashleigh Nicole, 417
Helen, 160, 230
Herbert Dwayne, 345, 417
June, 157, 224
Norman, 214
KENDERMAN
Teresa Jo, 261
KENDRICK
Anna, 95-6
Benjamin, 94-5
Caleb, 91, 94
KENNEBY
Pamela Jo, 244
KENNEDY
(--?--), 203-4
Michael, 145, 203
KENRICK
Deborah, 243, 341
KERLEY
Zena Lois, 396
KERN
Theresa Florine, 168, 241
KERR
Carolyn Kay, 259
Jane, 117
KESICKE
Claire Marie, 304
Eugene Thomas, 200, 304
Nicholas Paul, 304

KING PHILIP, 5, 7
KINGREY
Jake, 388
Samuel Perry, 287, 387-8
KINGSLEY
Eldad, 84
John, 68, 82, 84
Mary, 195, 296-7
KIRBY
Rod, 277, 372
KIRK
Annie L., 248
KIRKER
(--?--), 309
KLEIN
Donna Lee, 139, 191
KLENINE
Sadie, 155, 221
KLIMA
Amy Jean, 313, 532
Laurie Marie, 313, 401
KLOTZ
Daniel James, 300
Darcy Amanda, 300
Darren Jeffrey, 300
David Arthur, 197, 300
Dennis Joel, 300
KNAPP
Billie Kay, 170, 247
KNIGHT
Brenda, 197
Carolyn, 209
Selma Marlene, 244
KNOCKLE
Bret Allan, 245
KNUDSEN
Dirk Theodore, 295, 395
Konner Dirk, 395

Kord Tyler, 395
KNUTSEN
Gayanna, 371, 422
KOBLE
Daniel, 282
KOELER
Alfred, 156, 223
Barbara Josephine, 223
Robert Marion, 223
KOENIG
A. J., 124, 164
Marie, 164, 237
KOPSLAND
Barbara Lee, 141, 194
KORSCHUN
Susan Beth, 370, 420
KRAFT
Sunny, 368, 419
KRAUSE
Helen, 222, 331
KREIGEL
(--?--), 222
KUBESCH
Helen Margaret, 156, 223
KULMUS
Earl Edward, 163, 236
Edward C., 124, 162-3
Jane Audrie, 163
Linda Kay, 236
Steven Edward, 236
Virginia May, 163
KUNZEMAN
Eric, 414
Larry, 337, 414
Micah, 414
KUPFERSCHMID
Donald Ray, 254, 355
Scott Alan, 355

MAIN cont.
Stephanie, 230
Steve, 234
Susan Dorothy, 228
Susan Kay, 235
Susie Elizabeth, 159, 227
Sylvia Mable, 159, 226
Tade Marion, 123, 160
Theodore, 232
Thomas Fredrick, 164
Thomas Jefferson, 106, 125
Tracy L., 159, 228-9
Vaughn, 159, 227
Vernon G., 227
Virgil, 156
Virginia, 235
Walter, 125
Wendell, 125
Wilbert Richard, 161, 234-5
Wilbert Wallace, 235
William David, 235
William Edward, 225
William H., 106, 125
Wilma, 226
Zelma, 156
Zenna B., 160, 230
MALARA
Chase Domminic, 343
MALEE
Connie Sue, 235
Joseph A., 124, 162
Margaret Louise, 162, 236
Theodore, 162, 235-6
MALONE
Maureen Alice, 405
Patricia Jean, 331
Patrick, 222, 331
MALOY

John, 117
Joseph B., 117
Mary Rose (Brown) Dulack, 61, 117
MALTBY
Maryette, 102, 115
MANCHESTER
George, 259-60, 358
MANDRILLE
Ameline, 551
MANN
Alex Bradley, 423
Barbara Ann, 249
Bradley Charles), 371, 422
Charles, 370
Harley Charles, 276, 370-1
Howard, 171, 249
Kara Michelle, 371, 423
Katelyn Leeann, 423
Kyle Charles, 423
Mary Jean, 249
Taryn Laleen, 422
Zachery Blair, 422
MANNING
Jeffery Scott, 327
Jennifer, 327
Joanna, 328
Robert, 219, 327
MARBLE
Elizabeth, 63, 73-4, 96
Nathaniel, 73, 74
MARKWICK
Jane, 210
MARSE
Jane, 418, 428
MARSHALL
Alline, 221, 329
Caroline, 302

Mary L., 100
Sylvia, 100
PHILLIPS
Daniel Paul, 234
David Larry, 234
Larry Alvin, 231
Larry Oliver, 231
Marjorie Dorothy, 231
Oliver E., 160, 231
Richard L., 161, 234
Richard L. (b. 1951), 234
Richard Marshall, 231
Susan, 368, 419
PHILPS, Chauncy M.. *See*
PHELPS, Chauncy M.
PICKENS
Geraldine Lucille, 186, 282
Harold, 137, 186
John Lloyd, 186, 282-3
Sarah Lee, 381
Thomas James, 283, 381
PIERCE
Benjamin, 96
Benjamin Jr., 95, 96
Franklin, 96
Hester, 75-6, 78
John, 76, 78
Walter, Governor, 38, 40-1
PIKE
Adrienne Elizabeth, 327
Allen David, 218, 327
Daniel Allen, 327
PINE
Eileen, 238, 336
Elizabeth, 238, 336
Mardell, 238, 336
Walter M., 164, 237
PINKHAM

Donnie Ruth, 234
PIPER
Sherry Sue, 253, 354
PITCOCK
Brian D., 288, 389
Brianna Jae, 389
Morgan Caleb, 389
PLOMER
Margaret, 68, 84
PLYMPTON
Sabilla, 92
POE
Ora Belle, 275
POFF
Ashleigh, 404
Cynthia (Barnes), 522
Donald, 316, 403
Kristina Marie, 403, 427
Whitney, 404
Zachary Donald, 404
POLASKI
Jeffery Scott, 376, 424
Jerami, 425
Susan Marie, 279, 376
Taylor Campbell (, 425
POLICAR
David Victor, 297
James Marcus, 297
John Michael, 297
Marcus, 195, 297
POOLE
Albert Vernon, 279
Austin Patrick, 425
Eliza, 150-1
Elizabeth June, 376, 426
Esther Margaret, 376
Howard Gary Dean, 185,
279

William, 155, 219
PREECE
Carol Ann, 269
F. Robert, 180, 268
Robert Dwight, 268
PRESCOTT
A. W., 36
PRICE
Jerrod, 416
John, 338, 416
Mathew, 416
Tracy Ann, 316
PRONATH
Rosemary Katherine, 312, 401
PROSH
Hillery Jean, 370, 420
PUHLMAN
Caleb William, 387
Donald Robert, 286, 387
Rachel LeeAnn, 387
Zachary Kadin, 387
PURSLEY
Earl Wayne, 352, 417-18
Floyd Irvin, 251, 352
Gary Lee, 352
Jacob Wayne, 418
Patricia Elaine, 352

QUACKENBUSH
Richard William, 271
QUADROZZI
(--?--), 212
QUIMBY
Della, 126, 167
QUISENBERRY
Marcia, 193, 293

RABLE
Hester Catherine, 345
RADER
Carolyn Louise, 173, 257
Chisty, 258
Elizabeth (--?--), 173, 257
John William, 173, 257
Joyce, 257, 357
Karen, 258
Ralph Edward, 173, 257
Robert, 257
Steven, 257
Thomas, 257
William Paul, 128, 173
RAGAIN
Cameron Scott, 393
Mitchell Dale, 293, 393
Stevee Nycole, 393
RAINEY
Richard, 167
RAINS
Deanna, 352, 418
RAMPLE
Rose, 222
Shirley, 222, 332
RAMSEY
Mary, 86
RAND
Susanna, 84
RANSOM
Bernice, 131, 179
Emma Jeannette, 131
Emma Nancy (Johnson), 100, 110, 445-6, 556, 559-60, 566
Evelyn, 131
Faye, 129, 176

Mildred, 231, 335
Riley, 25, 35
SHEPPARD
Anne, 122, 156
SHERAR
Laurel Anne, 194, 294
SHERMAN
Benjamin, 84
Philip, 84
Thomas, 260
SHERROUSE
Carla Nicole, 271, 365
SHERWIN
Carolyn Sue, 259
Deborah, 129, 176
Gary Eugene, 259
Jessie Eugene, 174, 258-9
Jessie L., 129, 174
John Lawrence, 174, 258
John Neal, 258
Marilyn Kay, 258
Mary Elva, 174
Nancy Jean, 258
Ronald Lynn, 259
Wilma, 174
Winifred, 174
SHIELDS
Ann, 257, 356
Sandra Marie, 278, 373
SHINN
Brook, 248, 348
SHIVE
Alice Jeanette, 172, 253
Ami Annette, 354
Amy Elaine, 254
Bernice Betty, 172, 251
Brandy Renee, 354
Christy Nicole, 354

Connie Sue, 253, 354
Cynthia Jo, 255
Daniel Lee, 253
Darin Wayne, 254
Donald Eugene, 255
Dorothy Jane, 172, 254
Douglas Jay, 255
Henry Joseph, 172, 253
Jack Franklin, 172, 254-5
James William, 172, 252-3
James William Jr., 253, 353
Jason, 353
Jeffery Alan, 252
Jeremy, 353
Jeremy Joseph, 354
Jerry Lee, 253, 354
Joan, 253, 353-4
John C., 172, 254
John Charles, 254
Karla Joann, 255
Larry Richard, 252
Louis Richard, 172, 252
Mabel Leona, 172, 252
Mary Frances, 172, 251
Michael Allen, 253
Nancy Elaine, 253, 354
Norma Jean, 172, 255
Panela Sue, 252
Robert A., 128, 171-2
Ruth Ann, 255
Sally Ann, 255
Steve William, 253, 354
Steven Gene, 253
Teresa Sue, 254
Thomas Lee, 172, 255
Thomas Paul, 255
Vera Orlena, 172, 250
SHORE